Dreams, Where Have You Gone?
Clues for Unity and Hope

William G. McAtee

To: Tom Jones,

Here it is. Hope it brings
back fond memories of
our Glory days. Was
great fun to write —
Best wishes & peace,
Bill McAtee

Witherspoon
PRESS
Louisville, Kentucky

Credit: The front cover photograph was taken at Shakertown, Pleasant Hill, Kentucky, site of many "rocking chair gatherings" where Union Presbytery dreams were dreamed. Provided by H. William Peterson.

Cover design by Jeanne Williams
Book interior by Rachael Sinclair

First edition

Published by Witherspoon Press
Louisville, Kentucky

Web site address: www.pcusa.org/witherspoonpress

PRINTED IN THE UNITED STATES OF AMERICA

06 07 08 09 10 11 12 13 14 15 — 10 9 8 7 6 5 4 3 2 1

Library of Congress Cataloging-in-Publication Data

McAtee, William G.
  Dreams, where have you gone? : clues for unity and hope / William
G. McAtee. -- 1st ed.
    p. cm.
  Includes bibliographical references and index.
  ISBN 1-57153-065-7 (pbk. : alk. paper)
  1. Presbyterian Church--History. 2. Presbyterian Church (U.S.A.)
--History.   I. Gilliss, Martha S. II. Title.
BX8931.3.M33 2006
285'.109--dc22

                                                                    2006009017

To Buddy and Tina

Contents

Foreword

To comprehend a history, there is no substitute for reading primary sources and listening to the insights of people who experienced the events recounted. In 1884, when Alfred Nevin prefaced his massive *Presbyterian Encyclopedia*, an exposition of the beginnings of Presbyterianism and its incarnations in the late nineteenth century, a Presbyterianism in which Nevin had profound influence, he made grateful acknowledgment to a score of luminaries and pastors who had assisted him in the effort. He also asserted that he "availed himself freely of all appropriate material, without feeling it to be necessary to give specific credit . . ." Much of "all appropriate material" was from his own memory. The result was a major work, which both captured the names, biographies, movements, and institutions of the day and gave a severely personal view of Presbyterian history that had preceded. Mostly, though, it provided both primary and secondary data not available from any other source.

A number of other Presbyterian histories—the lengthy and informative *The Presbyterian Churches and the Federal Union, 1861–1869*, by Lewis G. Vander Velde, for example, or the three-volume *Presbyterians in the South*, by Ernest Trice Thompson—offer such insider views. Both histories were written by men deeply involved as participants and leaders in many of the events they record. Most histories of Presbyterian missionary enterprises and almost all congregational histories have been written by people who belonged to and usually helped lead the efforts and institutions.

Now the number has grown to include this work of William McAtee, who was deeply committed to the idea of "union presbyteries," helped in myriad ways to bring them into being, and provided direct guidance to one of the pivotal presbyteries through the extent of its existence. Most of those interviewed for the project likewise had responsibility for decisions and leadership that made the presbyteries possible and made them among the most creative and constructive governing bodies in the history of the Reformed in North America.

This work is important because it details the various and distinct histories of the presbyteries and the thoughts and theologies of many involved. It gives an honest and relatively modest account of the direct line from union presbyteries to the formation of the Presbyterian Church (U.S.A.).

William McAtee experienced the history as a white Southern man, one from the Deep South, to be more specific, who supported the creation of union presbyteries. He naturally turned to those around him, though some differed in background and conviction about the nature of union presbyteries. One can imagine a very different history drawn from the memory and research of someone African American, Northern, a female leader from any perspective, or even a white Southern man who did not bear actively a Scotch-Irish heritage.

Moreover, this story is told as a narrative, perfectly comprehensible from such a source. Narratives make the most readable histories, and I honestly think they tell the truest tale of the past.

In light of the argument of the book, I feel compelled to add a personal word: In 1970, as Union Presbyteries were first being authorized, I began teaching at Louisville Theological Seminary in Kentucky. I had been a stated supply, though ordained for graduate study in the Presbyterian Church in the United States (PCUS, or "Southern Presbyterian Church"). When, in 1971, I transferred to Louisville Presbytery, which had just become a union presbytery, from Memphis Presbytery (which certainly was not one), I quickly came to admire the ways a union presbytery operated. I found that if neither the so-called Northern Church (actually a national body comprising presbyteries and synods throughout the country) nor the Southern Church forbade it denominationally, something might indeed be possible to do in a union presbytery.

The "Union Presbytery Movement," as McAtee asserts it was, actually provided a constructive and permissive environment for people to forge new ministries and for congregations to engage in new mission. Moreover, since Louisville Presbytery formed part of a synod in the PCUS that also encompassed Tennessee, Alabama, and Mississippi to the south, and part of a synod in the UPCUSA stretching north to Ohio and Michigan, and both synods included all of Kentucky, it meant we "belonged" through the whole middle of American Presbyterianism.

The time of union presbyteries always seemed to me a "golden moment" in Presbyterian government. Though the presbyteries operated in very different ways North and South, I sensed a willingness of almost everyone to cut slack for others who operated in different styles.

McAtee quotes Maurice Telleen concerning movements, which he says are inhabited by "true believers." True believers who lead a movement are "convinced of both their inevitability and their superiority. The latter confers an aura of both practicality and pragmatism on them. Movements leave little room for meaningful dissent. They regard themselves as destiny. Movements are big on tunnel vision. Their tunnel. Their vision."

Dreams, Where Have You Gone?

That insight characterizes perfectly the perspective from which this creative and insightful book emerged. Their tunnel, their vision was a good and healthy one—full of resources and less weighted toward regulation than subsequent Presbyterianism. This is a long book about a brief time in American Presbyterianism. Radio commentator Dizzy Dean, who commented on baseball after having played the game, would doubtless call it in his inimitable way, "A long run for a short slide." But the course of Presbyterianism changed dramatically in the score of years of the union presbyteries.

Good reading in the work.

Louis B. Weeks
Union Theological Seminary
and Presbyterian School of Christian Education
Richmond, Virginia, and Charlotte, North Carolina

Preface

Historians have noted that too often they do not have firsthand accounts of historic events, therefore they must reconstruct those events forensically. What a difference our understanding of the great battles of antiquity would be if someone had conducted in their aftermath timely interviews of the participants. It is not merely those events of long ago that deserve our interest, but some of more recent vintage from which our understanding would benefit.

In The *Re-Forming Tradition*, one of the series of books titled The Presbyterian Presence: The Twentieth-Century Experience, only two sentences are devoted to something known as union presbyteries. "In the late 1960s, the PCUS[1] and the UPCUSA formed a number of union presbyteries. . . . Through union presbyteries and conservative defection, the balance of power in the PCUS turned toward reunion."[2]

Embedded in these two sentences, which seem to be a mere footnote to history, is a story that has not been fully told. Much has been written about the conservative defection, but little or nothing about union presbyteries. If union presbyteries played such an important role in shifting the balance of power in the PCUS toward reunion, should not the details of this also be known?

Unlike events in antiquity where eye witnesses did not have opportunity to leave oral accounts of their participation, the case of union presbyteries is another matter. At the close of the twentieth century, two decades after union presbyteries went out of existence, many key aging participants were alive to tell their stories.

In order that such an important opportunity not be lost, it was decided that an oral history research project would be in order to record the first-hand experiences and perceptions of what took place in the phenomenon known as the Union Presbytery Movement.

The research approach taken by the Project was basically that of a "perception study," which by nature is subjective. It followed an oral culture inductive "story" format rather than a tightly structured deductive method. It was more of an art than a strict science, verified and validated by multiple perception sources. Some minor factual details related to dates and events may differ from perception to perception based on each source's memory.

The Project had three major phases: The first phase was to tape unrehearsed interviews with a representative group of persons involved in or related to the Movement. (See Appendix C: Demographic Data, for summary description of the group.) The second phase was to proof, index, and print the interviews for placement in the archives of the Presbyterian Church (U.S.A.), in the Department of History at Montreat,

North Carolina, and other archives and libraries approved by the Department. The third phase was to write a book and/or articles growing out of the data gathered in the research.

Three periods of time were identified as the framework for the interviews. The first was the period before the 1969 PCUS Mobile, Alabama Assembly; the next period was when the union presbyteries were in existence; and the third period was after denominational reunion in 1983. The interviews were designed in part to determine who the person was and the role each person played and where; what were the motivations; barriers to be overcome; successes/failures; impact on denomination; role of the Consultation on Union Presbyteries (COUP); and learnings for the future.

A majority of leaders, who were responsible for making the Union Presbytery Movement possible, had either been born and/or served in the Border States or the Deep South. They included key people who were involved in changing the Constitutions to permit union presbyteries; those from all the union presbyteries who made them work; those who helped bring about reunion of the denominations; and those whose work gave insight into the context of the times.

From this group ninety-eight unrehearsed interviews were conducted. William G. McAtee, an active participant in the Movement and Researcher/Director of the Project, conducted ninety-four of the interviews. William L. Marshall, oral history advisor to the Project, conducted four interviews of the Researcher/Director. Marshall is the Director of Special Collections and Archives of the University of Kentucky.

The ninety-eight persons interviewed were a representative sample from all the union presbyteries and governing body systems in which these presbyteries were located. A few of these initially had reservations about, or opposed, union presbyteries and denominational reunion, but eventually led a segment of the church to "change its mind." Many other persons were significantly involved in making the Movement become what it was, but time and energy did not permit their inclusion.

People who lived in the non-overlapping areas of both denominations or those who opposed reunion were not significantly reflected in the Project. Some left the denomination and found homes in other denominations such as the Presbyterian Church in America (PCA), the Evangelical Presbyterian Church (EPC), and others. Some remained in the denomination but of late have struggled with the question whether or not there is a home for them in the PC(USA).

It is recognized that there are other experiences and different perceptions about this phenomenon than those reflected in the interviews; therefore, it would be erroneous to conclude that the

Dreams, Where Have You Gone?

interviews and findings of this Project are the final word on the subject. It is left to future researchers to follow the leads offered in these interviews and subsequent books or articles growing out of them to fill in the gaps.

The Silent Generation of "Young Turks," who entered "midlife" in the 1960s and initiated the Union Presbytery Movement, was now entering "elderhood" at the close of the twentieth century.[3] There was a sense of urgency in collecting the interviews since the overwhelming majority of the people had retired or were approaching retirement.

One of the poignant things about the Project was that sixteen[4] of the people interviewed died by the end of this third phase of the Project. Mr. E. D. McLean[5] of The McLean Foundation made it seventeen. It was known from the beginning that this might be the case, but it did not sink in that closest friends would be in the number.

The audiotapes have been transcribed, proofed, and indexed, creating over 2,500 pages of written text and are collected in the *Union Presbytery Movement Oral History Project,* © 2004 Department of History. The original transcribed interviews were placed along with the tapes and other research material[6] in its archives. In order to make the Project interview material available to more students and researchers, nine volume print sets have been placed in the libraries of Louisville, Austin, Union-PSCE, Columbia, Lexington, and McCormick Seminaries, Centre College Library, and the Office of the General Assembly Library. These transcripts may be accessed by researchers at the Presbyterian Historical Society's Web site: www.history.pcusa.org/.[7]

Now that the first two phases of the Project are complete, the time has come to write this book, relying heavily on the above-mentioned interviews of the Project, other primary and secondary sources, and the personal experience of the author. Two types of referencing are used in this book to cite sources of information. Regular endnotes are marked with a one-number designation running consecutively in each chapter. Special references to a particular research interview listed in Appendix B are marked by a two-number designation (e.g., 21-36) and are embedded only in the text, at the point of reference. The first number of this designation indicates the *Interview number.* The second number indicates the *Interview page number* on which the reference begins. This special reference application was employed as an economical measure to avoid unnecessary utilization of space in the endnotes.

Throughout the conception of the Project, conducting the interviews, and preparing them for the archives, the Researcher/Director was motivated by a strong sense of being on a mission to write an analytical and reflective account of the Movement in a larger historical context. Being an active participant in it created an extraordinary access to key persons, most of which were close colleagues through the years. With their voices still fresh in memory, the compelling reasons for writing this book were to do the following things:

- Show a debt of gratitude to those interviewed for their life and work
- Express a deep appreciation for their credible memories and perceptions shown for that dream they lived
- Record in the annals of history this important and significant story—*The Union Presbytery Movement*
- Provide from the participants' experience, for the current leadership of the PC(USA) and serious researchers, insights that will give clues for understanding the PC(USA) today and new directions that will be needed for it to take as a church in the future. And most importantly,
- Articulate learnings from its modern ecclesial heritage that will be essential in making the PC(USA) relevant to a postmodern world

Notes

1. Throughout this book abbreviations will be used as a shorthand way to denote specific Presbyterian denominations. The most frequently used are the following.

   PCUSA—The Presbyterian Church in the United States of America. The original mainline Presbyterian Church; for a period of time divided into Old and New School, North and South (then most of these groups reunited with the PCUSA); first to be called "The Northern Presbyterian Church" around the time of the Civil War; existed until 1958. Sometimes referred to as "U.S.A. Church."

   UPCNA or UPNA—United Presbyterian Church in North America. Formed in 1858 from three Seceder "Associate" or "Reformed" denominations; existed until 1958. The ones that did not join in the new denomination remained in the Associate Reformed Presbyterian Church (ARP).

   UPCUSA—The United Presbyterian Church in the United States of America. Referred to as "the Northern Presbyterian Church" or "the UP Church"; formed in a merger of the PCUSA and UPCNA; existed 1958–1983.

   PCCSA—The Presbyterian Church in the Confederate States of America. Closely identified with the Old School South; existed 1861–1865.

   PCUS—The Presbyterian Church in the United States. Referred to as "the Southern Presbyterian Church" or "the U.S. Church"; existed 1865–1983.

   PC(USA)—The Presbyterian Church (U.S.A.). The PCUS and the UPCUSA reunited to form it; sometimes referred to as "the Reunited Presbyterian Church"; has existed 1983–present.

CPC—The Cumberland Presbyterian Church, 1810–1906. Most of the CPC reunited with the PCUSA in 1906. Those that did not commit to that reunion remain as the CPC; 1906–present.

RCA—The Reformed Church in America. One of the larger Reformed churches created from other Reformed bodies; had a distinct Eastern branch and Western branch; exists to present.

RPCC—The Reformed-Presbyterian Church in Cuba. [IPRC—*Iglesia Presbiteriana-Reformada en Cuba.*] Created in 1967 from the Presbytery of Cuba, Synod of New Jersey, UPCUSA.

OPC—The Orthodox Presbyterian Church. Formed by those who withdrew from Princeton under Machen's influence; later some left it to form the Bible Presbyterian Church (BPC); has existed 1926–present.

PCA—The Presbyterian Church in America (originally National Presbyterian Church; name changed in 1974). Formed by ministers and congregations that withdrew from the PCUS; has existed 1973–present.

EPC—The Evangelical Presbyterian Church. Another conservative church formed in the 1970s, similar to the PCA; extended beyond the geographic bounds of the Old Confederacy; has existed 1970s–present.

2. Milton J. Coalter, John M. Mulder, and Louis B. Weeks, eds., *The Re-Forming Tradition: Presbyterians and Mainstream Protestantism* (Louisville, KY: Westminster/John Knox Press, 1992), p. 180.

3. William Strauss and Neil Howe, *Generations: The History of America's Future, 1584–2069* (New York: William Morrow & Co., 1991), pp. 288–289.

4. T. Morton McMillan, Jr., J. Allen Oakley, Dorothy G. Barnard, W. Richard Huey, Robert F. Stevenson, Albert H. Freundt, Jr., James D. Baskin, John W. Frazer, William S. McLean, J. Randolph Taylor, David L. Stitt, Lacy R. Harwell, Kenneth G. McCullough, Howard L. Bost, Thomas A. Spragens, James E. Andrews.

5. E. D. "Buddy" McLean was a deacon in the Columbia Presbyterian Church, Columbia, Mississippi. McLean and his wife, Justina "Tina" Walker McLean, were supportive of the author in this research project from the beginning through the McLean Foundation, a family foundation. The author was their pastor from 1964 to 1966. During that time McLean was the mayor of Columbia. It was a time of great societal and racial unrest. McLean, as mayor, was committed to exhibiting constructive leadership through these difficult times in a way that would create a more equitable and just community "because it was the right thing to do." During the election campaign, McLean went to every house in town, talking with the residents about the issues facing the community and saying in effect, "I want to be your mayor and resolve these issues together with you." Three black ministers and two white ministers, including the author, became one of his informal communication networks to the community. Under his leadership, a biracial committee was set up to address creating better communication within the community, securing open hiring of blacks as store clerks and on the police force, integrating of public facilities and schools, and improving

the voter registration process. These were achieved with a relative degree of calm, compared to neighboring towns of McComb, Hattiesburg, and Bogalusa, which were going up in flames and civil disorder.

6. A complete set of agendas of the nine COUP meetings, the minutes of the Joint Committee/Task Force on Union Presbyteries, and other union presbytery–related material is archived in the PC(USA) Department of History's Records of the Presbyterian Church U.S. Office of the General Assembly, Joint Committee on Union Presbyteries.

7. Researchers, in using this material, understand and agree to the following standard requirements: *Oral history* is a method of collecting historical information through recorded interviews between a narrator with firsthand knowledge of historically significant events and a well-informed interviewer, with the goal of preserving substantive additions to the historical record. Because it is primary material, oral history is not intended to present the final, verified, or complete narrative of events. It is a spoken account. It reflects personal opinion offered by the interviewee in response to questioning, and as such it is partisan, deeply involved, and irreplaceable. All literary rights in these transcripts, including the right to publish, are reserved to Presbyterian Church (U.S.A.) Department of History. No part of these transcripts may be quoted for publication without the written permission of the director of the Presbyterian Church (U.S.A) Department of History. Requests for permission to quote for publication should be addressed to the Presbyterian Church (U.S.A.) Department of History, 425 Lombard Street, Philadelphia, PA 19147, and should include identification of the specific passages to be quoted, anticipated use of the passages, and identification of the user.

Acknowledgments

When I decided to take early retirement, elder Ray Kramer, from Western Kentucky Presbytery, said, "Don't retire from something, retire to something." So with that advice I decided to see if there was anything unique worth telling in my almost forty years of service in the Presbyterian Church. Thanks, Ray, your advice was on target.

I was interested in doing some sort of "living research" in the form of collecting oral histories. As the Union Presbytery Movement was rapidly fading into the distant past and no one seemed interested in recapturing its significance, I chose this subject for my research project. The majority of my ministry was related to the Movement and its aftermath, providing me extensive firsthand knowledge of the subject. It was felt that being an active participant in the Movement provided me with connections to key persons who could provide credible perceptions of that phenomenon through the interviews. My being part of the story did not tend to inhibit those being interviewed, but seemed to enhance their participation.

Words cannot adequately convey my deepest appreciation to E. D. (Buddy) and Justina (Tina) McLean, whose encouragement and support made this project and book become a reality. The McLeans were members of the Columbia Presbyterian Church, Columbia, Mississippi. Mr. McLean was city mayor during the turbulent 1960s and made an outstanding contribution to working constructively for change during the civil rights movement of the day. I was very active as Mr. McLean's pastor in those efforts. The McLean Foundation awarded a major grant to me to direct the research project and write this book.

Thanks to Lexington Theological Seminary, which graciously permitted me to include this research project and lodge the grant with it as part of my Presbyterian Studies teaching commitment there. Glenn Ballard, Business Manager; Janis Redmon, Director of Accounting; and Robin Varner, Administrative Assistant, all at Lexington Theological Seminary, efficiently administered the grant.

A "great cloud of witnesses" in both Northern and Southern branches of the Presbyterian Church, with whom I had worked from the strategic position of a union presbytery, provided for this project a rich collection of perceptions and experiences related to the Movement through the 98 oral histories conducted in it. The book is my reflection on the findings of this study.

The interviewees formed the bedrock of the project. Without them, it would not have existed. The interview sessions formed the capstone of the edifice called "the Union Presbytery Movement" celebrating what we built together over many years. The personal interrelatedness among interviewees is evident as one reads through the transcripts of the interviews. There were very few interviewees with whom I had not worked closely through the years. Thanks to you.

Key persons among the interviewees deserve special appreciation. Flynn V. Long, Jr., who so early dreamed the dream, eloquently spun out "The Great Speckled Bird" and other tales reminding us of our contextual heritage, where we came from, and who we are. Charles M. Hanna, H. William Peterson, and Lewis L. Wilkins, as vocational colleagues with me, traveled many ecclesiastical trade-route miles creating the Movement story and drawing meaning from it. Robert C. Worley, through the McCormick Seminary Doctor of Ministry Presbytery Executive Track Program, helped me conceptualize and affirm what I was learning experientially.

It took the interest and work of a long list of folk to be able to capture and preserve this primary source information in the form of oral histories. I now acknowledge my deep appreciation for their time and energy in making this a reality to three audio-tape transcribers for their tedious labor; the staffs of the Department of History (Montreat), the Office of the General Assembly (Louisville), and the Louisville Seminary Library who guided me in this project.

Special thanks go to William L. Marshall, Director of Special Collections and Archives of the University of Kentucky, who gave me valuable advice regarding recording equipment and format for conducting the interviews. Being an experienced oral history interviewer, he could not resist volunteering to interview me at the end of my interviewing journey! From what he heard throughout the process, he was convinced that I was in a unique position to write a significant book on the subject. He continued to give gentle nudges in that direction until it was done.

Thanks to Wilma Lange, a retired copyeditor of the University Press of Kentucky, who applied her excellent proofreading skills to the various drafts of the book during the year the manuscript was being written; Frank A. Brooks, John W. Kuykendall, Marcia C. Myers, H. William Peterson, John M. Reagan, and Lewis L. Wilkins, who read parts of the manuscript, giving encouragement and critical advice that made it a better document; Clifton Kirkpatrick, who gave an enthusiastic endorsement for the book, and Louis B. Weeks, who readily volunteered to write the Foreword.

The enthusiasm for the project of the publishing team from Witherspoon Press could not have made this first publishing venture for me more enjoyable. A very special word of appreciation goes to this team made up of Sandra Albritton Moak, publisher; Martha S. Gilliss, project editor; Carl Helmich, copy editor; Jennifer Stewart, manager for production; Scott A. Dowd, coordinator for marketing; Jeanne Williams, art director, and others in the shop for the competent way in which they performed their jobs.

Finally, but not least, thanks to my wife, Millye, who has patiently endured my long hours upstairs squinting at the computer in the surrounding clutter of material generated by the project. Most importantly, she was extremely supportive before, during, and after the decade years of the Union Presbytery Movement itself while I rambled through them.

Part I: Birthing Dreams
Chapter 1
Introduction—The Dream

I would call it [the Union Presbytery Movement] a transitional success, that what it did was turn two whole denominations into a collection of union presbyteries. That's hard to reject, deny, or ignore. It was not the only factor that made reunion possible, but it was certainly a key one because it gave voice to people who said we've tried it, it'll work, we can get together and that has its greatest validity.
— James E. Andrews, former Stated Clerk, PC(USA) (02-17)

The dawn of June 10, 1983, broke beautiful and bright over Atlanta, Georgia, a fitting invocation to "the Day" for Presbyterians. By noontime the city was blanketed under the sweltering Georgia sun, a very different heat from the heat that rose from the Sherman-torched fires in the city over a hundred years before. This was the long-dreamed-of day when the more than ecclesiastical rupture created by the Civil War was finally to be healed with the reuniting of the Presbyterian Church in the United States (PCUS), commonly called "the Southern Church," and the United Presbyterian Church in the United States of America (UPCUSA), "the Northern Church."

The Dream hoped for in Reunion was a dream of strengthening and creating a new Presbyterian identity based on the churches' shared heritage, shared theology and shared vision of relationships to the community and the world. The Dream also was that, as the Presbyterian identity was strengthened in this marriage, we might address the legacy of racism by becoming more inclusive and diverse as a new church.

Could the Day be more than the cathartic ecclesial healing, though certainly that was important? Could it be that the significance of the Day reached far beyond the bounds of the Presbyterian Church to the nation at large? Was the Day one of those historic events that helped bring closure to one of the ravages of the Civil War and an antioxidant to the still-venomous residue of racism stemming from the institution of slavery? Was the Day the beginning of a new way for Presbyterians to *be church*? That was the Dream.

The General Assembly of the Presbyterian Church in the United States of America (PCUSA) met in Philadelphia, Pennsylvania, a little over a month after Union forces fired on Fort Sumter in 1861, and adopted the Gardner Springs Resolution, which endorsed the federal government. The commissioners from the Confederate States that had already seceded promptly returned home to form the Presbyterian Church in the Confederate States of America, predecessor of the Southern Presbyterian Church.[1] But the Day, June 10, 1983, in Atlanta, Georgia, was a new day, in a new South, forming a new church, all intricately entwined.

The General Assemblies of the two Presbyterian denominations were convened in two different parts of the World Congress Center in Atlanta. Each had separate business sessions to take care of last-minute items related to dissolving these predecessor denominations before disappearing into the history books, making way for the new Presbyterian Church.

One of the items of business of the Southern Assembly that morning was to act on the Report of the Committee on Assembly Operations (CAO) made by its chairperson.[2] The Assembly approved a two-million-dollar CAO budget without question, but got hung up on a $20,000 item to print the final edition of the *Ministerial Directory*, which it finally approved. The rest of the business went smoothly and quickly. The chairperson of the CAO presented John F. Anderson, the Moderator, with a walnut gavel crafted by Tom Vincell, a minister member of Transylvania (Union) Presbytery and a Louisville Seminary graduate, to be used to adjourn the last meeting of the PCUS General Assembly. The Moderator in accepting it said that Kentucky had the first union presbytery. A note from Missouri Union Presbytery soon reached his hand. The note pointed out that the Missouri presbytery was the first, but conceded it was easier to "use Kentucky walnut rather than a Missouri mule" for a gavel![3]

After the lunch break, the hall began to fill up with great anticipation. The final report of the Polity Committee was made, including a motion by Joyce Bauer, chairperson, that the reunion vote be taken. Before the vote was taken, the chairperson asked that committee assistant James D. Baskin, elder from First Presbyterian, San Antonio, Texas, be granted the privilege of the floor to offer a prayer, which was granted without objection. Baskin offered a prayer that turned out to be the last prayer of the PCUS Assembly.[4] The final reunion vote was taken and it passed by a unanimous vote. The body stood and sang two verses of "O God Our Help in Ages Past."[5]

Dr. Frank H. Caldwell, former Moderator, was asked to make the final motion to adjourn *sine die*. The Northern Assembly in the adjacent hall was running twenty minutes late on its agenda, so Dr. Caldwell and others used the time to reminisce and tell stories. Finally, word came that it was time to adjourn and Dr. Caldwell made the motion.[6] Moderator Anderson took the vote, declared the Assembly adjourned, then asked the Assembly to stand and sing the Doxology (26-9).

Flynn Long, Associate Stated Clerk, piped the Southern Presbyterians out of the hall as Moderator Anderson and Stated Clerk Andrews led the way up the escalator outside, where the Stillman College band greeted them with the jaunty beat of "When the Saints Go Marching In." The column from the Southern Assembly reached Techwood

Avenue, where they were to meet up with the Northern Assembly. They could hear a bagpipe band escorting the Northern Presbyterians from their meeting place to the somber strains of "Amazing Grace." The two columns mingled together and marched in pure exhilaration over this moment in history, surely a dream come true.[7]

Presbyterians from all corners of both denominations and honored guests, a rainbow of young and old, filled the fifteen or so blocks between the World Congress Center and City Hall. They marched shoulder to shoulder, a dozen or more across, five to six thousand strong. They sang. They waved banners. They wore buttons. Some proudly wore the words: "I'm from a Union Presbytery." Small children rode on their daddies' shoulders. Boys and girls ran and skipped. One young girl was seen roller-skating along with the crowd. Young people walked arm in arm. It was a festive mood. The front line reached the steps of City Hall just as the last group was leaving the World Congress Center. It was as if some great cosmic centripetal force was pulling this Assembly–City Hall multitude together by one common cause, although there were exceptions. Carl McIntire had a busload of folks picketing the event.[8]

There was momentary confusion at the steps of City Hall as the throng waited for Mayor Andrew Young to address them. No public address system was set up, but a bullhorn was quickly procured and Young eloquently spoke through it. During the proceeding, one of the marchers fainted from the heat and was moved inside City Hall. An announcement called for a doctor. Elder Noralie McCoy, a school nurse from Westminster Presbyterian Church in Piqua, Ohio, responded to the call. As she entered City Hall, whom should she find sitting on a chair between the double doors but Martin Luther King, Sr.[9] Daddy King was waiting patiently for the Presbyterians to come.

Daddy King knew them by their presence, those who had stood with his son, Dr. Martin Luther King, Jr., seeking justice through the civil rights movement. He knew they took considerable heat for their actions. Malcolm P. Calhoun, Church and Society staff person with the Board of Christian Education (PCUS), had stood with Dr. King on the platform of the Christian Action Conference, at Montreat, North Carolina, in August 1965, when Dr. King urged Presbyterians "to move beyond social reform to help create changes in the hearts and minds of people so they could accept individuals without prejudice."[10]

Lawrence W. Bottoms, staff person with the Board of National Ministries (PCUS), stood with the Memphis sanitation workers in their request for emergency assistance and got immediate approval by John Anderson, executive secretary of the Board, for an emergency grant of $5,000.[11] Richard M. Moon, Presbyterian minister to students in

Memphis, stood on the platform in Mason Temple with Dr. King on April 3, 1968, when he delivered his last speech, "I've Been to the Mountain."[12] Bottoms was with Dr. King at the Lorraine Motel in the waning hours of April 4, 1968 (85-4).

Daddy King's presence on the Day was almost as if he were granting patriarchal blessings of biblical proportions and an expression of thanksgiving on this historic occasion. Was it that he wanted to witness a partial fulfillment of a dream his son, Martin, had foretold on the steps of the Lincoln Memorial in Washington, DC, twenty long hot summers before? "I have a dream that one day on the red hills of Georgia the sons of former slaves and the sons of former slaveholders will be able to sit down at a table of brotherhood. I have a dream that one day, even the state of Mississippi . . . will be transformed into an oasis of freedom and justice."[13] There was a stirring in the heart of the author as he marched that day hoping this just might be the case. He was a fourth-generation Mississippian,[14] who yearned for a healing of the breach in his beloved church and the brokenness of the Deep South culture that had been so formative in shaping his life.

The crowds dispersed and that night gathered for the big worship service and Communion celebration. A banner, bread, and chalice preceded each presbytery set of commissioners, who took more than thirty-five minutes to assemble. The two Moderators read the declaration of formation. The highlight of the service came when 14,000 people sang the Hallelujah Chorus. Somewhere in the midst of this service it struck the author that "this thing is going to work!"—not because of all the jockeying for position by the principal leaders, but because of the movement of the Spirit among the people, the congregation of the faithful.[15]

The following day, June 11, the new Assembly convened. A whole new area of the World Congress Center, different from the areas where the two former Assemblies had met, was set up for the new Assembly. The entire downstairs was as big as twelve football fields. The first order of business was the election of a moderator. After about an hour, J. Randolph Taylor was elected by 75 percent of the vote on the first ballot. Before he was installed, one of the most moving times of the Assembly took place. On the stage, a jeweler forged the two Moderators' Celtic crosses, PCUS and UPCUSA, into one to symbolize the reunion of the denominations and our Scottish Presbyterian heritage. Actually the cross from the UPCUSA contained two Celtic crosses that had been forged together when the United Presbyterian Church of North America (UPCNA) and the Presbyterian Church in the United States of America (PCUSA) were merged in 1958.[16]

As the new Assembly settled in to do its work, confusion was evident, but it managed to stumble into the future. It was coming down off the mountain height into the light of reality. Lots of patience would be called for.[17] Now there was a taste of the beginnings of division before the new Assembly was barely up and walking.

The unity of spirit was tested during the final session of the Assembly when the motion to add four advisory members from the evangelical wing of the church to the General Assembly Council (GAC) was cut off without debate. Political win-lose raised its hoary head. The division was not along former denominational lines. Some in both the former Northern and Southern churches were furious. They felt that *The Plan for Reunion* had been approved and now this was an attempt to alter it before it could be tried.[18]

Some former UPCUSA members of the newly nominated GAC stormed off the floor issuing dire threats. At one point the author walked up to a group in heated debate out in a backstage area. It was a bad scene. Two of the former UPCUSA's more progressive members were assaulting a former PCUS member of evangelical persuasion so much that another PCUS member had to physically separate the combatants. The author found himself in the unusual position of being pastor to battered evangelicals. One was quoted as saying, "We may have cussed the opposition to their backs, but never to their face!" The group that left the floor cooled off and came back. This may have been the incident that galvanized the new GAC. It may have been nothing more than a harbinger of things to come, a little glimpse of earthly centrifugal force tearing at the Dream.[19]

And yet "the Day" was a new day in a new South forming a new church, all intricately entwined. How these three were so intricately entwined by cause and effect or merely by affinity is difficult to say—a consideration that must be looked at before this work is completed. But to understand the culmination of the Day requires a much more extensive look at the past to see what forces and events were at play leading up to it. Then, and only then, can a determination specifically be made about what role the reuniting of the two largest North American Presbyterian denominations played in bringing some modicum of closure to the American Civil War and the devastating effects of slavery.

One thing is certain. The Day would not have happened in the last two decades of the twentieth century had it not been for the unusual phenomenon known as the Union Presbytery Movement and its union presbyteries.

What Is a Union Presbytery?
Several years ago H. William "Bill" Peterson, former executive presbyter in Western Kentucky (Union) Presbytery, told the story of talking with a young Presbyterian pastor of a congregation in Kentucky who had

served there for nine years. The church was one of those churches that became a union church in the 1920s or 1930s. The pastor said something about union churches. Bill started talking about the Union Presbytery Movement and the pastor said, "Well, I know just a little bit about that, but I didn't realize it was so recent" (36-28). It was as if he had asked, "What is a union presbytery?" Others have had similar experiences.

Murray Travis recalled moving to another presbytery in 1981 after nine years as a member of the original Palo Duro (Union) Presbytery. Several years later he returned to Palo Duro, and upon his return he was approached by a lay member of the nominating committee, recruiting him to serve on a commission. He said, "Murray, we've got to have someone that still knows the story" (21-36).

Some do not know the story; others have forgotten. Persons who birthed and lived this dream of union presbyteries said over and over again that this was the most important and exciting time in their ministry.[20] But that was a long time ago and the world has changed in the intervening thirty years or more. What could something that seemed so significant in some remote memory mean for the PC(USA) in the twenty-first century?

The Union Presbytery Movement is one of the most unique stories in the history of North American Presbyterianism. Union presbyteries, presbyteries that were full members of both the United Presbyterian Church U.S.A. (UPCUSA) and the Presbyterian Church U.S.(PCUS), came into being and existed between 1970 and 1983. In the beginning, in 1970, nine union presbyteries were formed and became operational. The reunion of the denominations would not happen until almost a decade and a half later in 1983, at which time seventeen union presbyteries existed and an eighteenth was in the making.

By then they were no longer geographically confined to the Border States. In the act of reunion, all other presbyteries became union presbyteries whether they recognized it or were prepared for this fact. Many at the time were not aware that without union presbyteries, denominational reunion might not have happened in that generation.

This factual recitation of what took place in the Movement over three decades ago, though appearing unique on the surface, does not begin to suggest its true significance. The true uniqueness of the Union Presbytery Movement lies in the reality that it functioned in a countercultural manner in relation to the dominant ecclesiastical organizational culture of the times, which had a chronically dysfunctional flaw—a propensity for a win-lose mentality. The Union Presbytery Movement was birthed in a general dominant culture of the times that was counter to its own spirit and nature. Describing North American Presbyterianism as dominant is not to discount the lasting contribution it has made from its distinctive perspective of Christian faithfulness to the world of religion or to the civil society in which it was found. The countercultural manner of the Movement merely focused on shortcomings of the dominant culture that often do not find reflective light.

In the waning decades of the twentieth century, something emerged—a win-lose mentality—in the very dominant Presbyterian culture as church that added impetus to its serious decline. And now in the twenty-first century, left unattended, it may even threaten Presbyterian existence, as it has been known historically.

Historical Context

What was the origin of this dysfunctional flaw of the dominant win-lose Presbyterian culture in which the Union Presbytery Movement found itself for a brief moment in time as a functional counterculture, though at times itself imperfect? The answer depends on how far back one wants to go. Could it be said that it began in the wasteland of separation and rejection "East of Eden"? Could it be argued that seeds of frustration and defeat were planted at the Battles of Stamford Bridge and Hastings in 1066, those watershed battles that changed the course of English and Western history for centuries to come?

Could seeds of stubborn resolve and tenacity have been cultivated in the rocky strife that surrounded the Westminster Assembly in the 1640s and the adoption of the Westminster Standards by the Scottish General Assembly in 1647? Could seeds of anguish and despair have been watered by the sense of loss some experienced when the kingdom of Scotland ceased to exist with the passage of the Act of Union between Scotland and England in 1707? Could the seeds of bitterness and dejection have been nurtured that April morning in 1746 on Drummossie Moor, when Bonnie Prince Charlie's Highlanders were crushed in the last battle between a modern battle force and a premodern one on European soil, and then continued in the civil and ecclesiastical battles on the new continent?[21]

Could these seeds of fierce independence and contentiousness have been swept ashore as Puritans came to New England and Scotch-Irish Presbyterians landed in Middle Atlantic States during the eighteenth century? With psyches badly bruised from remnants of Lost Causes at home, could they have found new seasons in which to yield dark fruit in a new place?

More recently, the context of the North American experience provided ample enough incubation for dysfunction in the Presbyterian family. The institution of slavery and the American Civil War created a hemorrhage that has hounded civil and ecclesiastical societies for attention and healing in all succeeding generations. To some, the Lost Cause still was fought as recently as 1962 at Ole Miss in an American insurrection.[22]

On the heels of World War II, in the midst of the Eisenhower Era in 1954, two very significant events took place. The Supreme Court issued its landmark decision in *Brown v. Board of Education*. Reunion between the UPCUSA and the PCUS was defeated, another Lost Cause. These two events set the agenda for a new generation of ministers and lay leaders who were beginning to graduate from colleges and seminaries in both denominations.

Ecclesial Context

William Strauss and Neil Howe, in their book *Generations*, define this new generation as the Silent Generation who at this time was entering "rising adulthood."[23] The Silent Generation of Presbyterian clergy and lay leaders had been mentored by their predecessor G.I. Generation at home, in youth conferences, in colleges and in seminaries. From these mentors they received theological and sociological inspiration to seek a larger vision of what church and society might become. It was this larger vision that gave to those who founded the Union Presbytery Movement inspiration for a more promising way of being church that was counter to the separateness of the two dominant cultures of North American Presbyterianism at the time.

What specifically was the source of the driving forces and energy that gave birth to what is known as the Union Presbytery Movement? The motivation for the emergence of the Movement was basically twofold. It was based on theological conviction and practical necessity. It was felt that the Unity of the Church had been ripped asunder by denominational divisions over race and the vestiges of the Civil War. Worldwide witness to the Unity of the Church rang hollow and could not explain the existence of separate major Presbyterian bodies in the United States. The competition and duplication of missional effort in those Border States where there was significant overlap between the two major Presbyterian denominations grew to be ludicrous and "just plain stupid."

In one sense the Union Presbytery Movement was largely a Southern phenomenon or experience, since this was where deep-seated attitudes had to be changed. The majority of leaders who were responsible for making the Movement possible had either been born in or had served in the Border States or the Deep South. Others joined their ranks by adoption. They were predominantly men but also included a goodly number of "steel magnolia" women. They understood the meaning of Lost Causes but were not satisfied with that understanding. The dominant relational nature of the PCUS was the catalyst that brought the Movement into existence and the glue that held it together.

As this "Young Turk" Silent Generation of leaders entered midlife in the 1960s, they found themselves in one of the most turbulent decades the twentieth century had experienced—the Vietnam War, the civil rights movement, the assassinations, the women's movement, the environmental movement, Watergate, loss of respect for institutions, rise in crime, breakup of the family, and on and on. Many found themselves simultaneously deeply involved in the struggle for justice in many of these issues in a wide range of settings while working in the Union Presbytery Movement.

Constitutional Changes

It was in the midst of the "unfreezing" of social order in this decade that the Union Presbytery Movement took shape. It was not constitutionally possible for union presbyteries to exist in either denomination. There were constitutional provisions in both Books of Order that permitted union or federated churches. In the 1920s and 1930s some congregations in Border States simply became union churches and later steps were quietly taken by their respective General Assemblies to regularize what was already in practice.

A conscious decision was made not to use this method to create union presbyteries, but rather it was deemed wise to amend both Constitutions to make this possible. During the middle 1960s, steps were undertaken to amend the Constitutions. This was finally achieved in the 1967 UPCUSA Assembly in Portland, Oregon. Its passage was almost overshadowed by the vote to create the Confession of 1967. The final vote in the PCUS was achieved at the 1969 Assembly in Mobile, Alabama, which became a watershed in the life of that denomination. This was made possible by a simple majority vote of its presbyteries as an amendment to the Constitution and not one of organic union requiring a three-fourths majority. Some opponents claimed that this vote was unconstitutional or was achieved by "dirty pool" tactics.

Presbyteries along the Border States were poised to vote to become union presbyteries once "the way be clear." They plunged into the joyous task of making the omelet tasty once the eggs had been scrambled. The time during which union presbyteries existed was an exhilarating, sometimes frustrating, experience. For it was a challenge to live in two worlds where oftentimes there were conflicting constitutional provisions governing their life, and where a myriad of programmatic conflicts arose.

Consultation of Union Presbyteries

To deal with these issues and challenges, the Consultation of Union Presbyteries (COUP) came into being at the initiative of the union presbyteries themselves.[24] Earlier consultations called by General Assembly Councils had met with limited success. COUP was an informal gathering of representatives from the union presbyteries and their synods to meet and discuss common joys and concerns. It was a horizontal grassroots gathering of those who were experiencing something in common, though their specific situations differed. Ownership and energy were high. It was not satisfied with the dysfunctional flaw of the win-lose mentality.

COUP was official in that representatives were appointed by their respective governing bodies to be a problem-solving gathering for the good of the whole. It was unofficial in that the only actions it took were to make referrals to governing bodies for consideration and action. An open, reflective, flexible and inclusive stance characterized COUP. Its meetings became *the* place to be. Cooperating presbyteries, synods, and General Assembly agencies were invited to send representatives to enter the conversations.

There were nine consultations held from 1975 to 1983. One outgrowth was that a task force was formed to assist cooperating presbyteries that were considering forming union presbyteries. By 1982 there was a long list of cooperative efforts, which had been brought about at the General Assembly program and constitutional levels. These efforts were monitored by the Joint Committee/ Task Force on Union Presbyteries, created at the request of COUP, and assisted by the Task Force on Constitutional Problems.

Denominational Reunion

It is important to recognize that the existence of union presbyteries and COUP is a separate and distinct phenomenon from denominational reunion yet inextricably related to it. Changes permitting union presbyteries and approving the denominational reunion in both Constitutions were governed by the "old" polity of majority rule with minorities having rights. That has an inherent win-lose quality. A "new" polity governed COUP, decisions by consensus, that is inherently win-win. Each polity has distinct gains and losses.

Union presbyteries could have continued to exist had reunion failed. New union presbyteries might have continued to be formed and in time created a third General Assembly. However, this would not have furthered the cause of the Unity of the Church. Reunion made such a strategy unnecessary. There is a widely held opinion that reunion of the denominations would not have happened in 1983 without the existence and experience of the union presbyteries as catalyst. Some believe that it might have taken another decade or even a generation at least.

Following denominational reunion, union presbyteries, although they had already experienced reunion on a regional level, lost their unique sense of identity. The creative tension of living in two worlds and the energy this generated were gone. The horizontal experience presbyteries shared in COUP soon returned to an isolated vertical governance existence where there was little opportunity for them to gather.

For a while those who had lived the union presbytery dream brought a significant perspective to the formation of the reunited denomination at the General Assembly level. But this too was soon forgotten. Many of the dreams they held for what the new denomination might become soon faded. There was no way for them to exert leverage to that end the way they had done while being union presbyteries. Not only did the union presbyteries lose their identity, both former denominations lost theirs as well. The new denomination began a search for a new identity that is still elusive.

New Context

At reunion in 1983, hopes for the Dream were high. That day Presbyterians marched in the streets of Atlanta and an overwhelming sense of closeness—inclusion—gripped the crowd. It was a place where everyone, though very diverse, felt welcome, having come of their own accord; where their differences were seen as a plus for the whole; where everyone was at ease and accepted; where mutual trust engendered intimacy and relations grew; where there was a feeling of appreciation for all the stories that came together around the campfire of reunion. It was certainly a dream come true, a Pentecost, a partial fulfillment of Jesus' prayer "that the church might be one."

The dreamers hoped that including the diverse would be a crucial constructive factor in the healing process. The conviction that all this mattered would greatly shape how decisions would confidently be made in the future. This true sense of inclusion was the stuff out of which a new identity could be forged. The PCUSA, in the intervening years in its search for a new identity, became a more diverse church. Much to its credit, that part of the Dream was fulfilled. But diversity could become subtly destructive to the "peace, purity, and unity of the church" if the diverse were not included into one body. This destructive dynamic began to seep into the life of the reunited church. Some stories and voices of the past were included and others were not. How could the mistakes of the past be acknowledged without relegating the legacy of the past to a shameful dark corner, be it the legacy of ecclesial heritage or the legacy of exclusion?

In the last two decades of the postmodern twentieth century and the first decade of the twenty-first century, the new church, like the rest of society, experienced the fault-line shift in emphasis from corporate to individual values. Value for the common good shifted dramatically to special interest or single-issue values. Hard-achieved rights turned into entitlement on demand and the culture wars were on. Ecclesiastical family dysfunction once again raised its hoary head in extreme polarization, bringing ecclesial identity into question. The reunited church was living with the results of a negotiated hardnosed merger rather than the fruits of a consummated relational courtship, the likes of which had caused union presbyteries to flourish.

As the Dream of inclusiveness and diversity became institutionalized in the reunited church, the dysfunctional flaw of win-lose began to take on more significance. The constructive contributions of diversity were threatened by the failure to realize fully how essential true inclusion was in fulfilling the hope that "all be made one." This could be seen as the dynamics began to shift away from building relationships to debating issues. Tension began to grow in the reunited church between issue-related groups that had little true relational connections among them. Though there were many examples, two key issues were pitted in stark contrast against each other in the arena of forging a new identity of the new church.

One extreme held that the true identity of the new church would be found in maintaining a recognizable connection to its Presbyterian heritage. Critics felt that this did not necessarily espouse diversity, but was characterized by "the way we have always done it" mentality. The other extreme view maintained that "diversity rules" and the past be hanged. Critics felt this in itself was exclusive. No doubt deep in the recesses of this conflict, the failure to face and resolve the true relational dimension of inclusion had been forfeited to special interests.

Somewhere along the way in chasing the Dream, there was a failure to understand that effective inclusion of newcomers is not a process mutually exclusive to building on the strengths of the past together in creating a new way of being church. Could this failure in understanding have contributed to the Dream's being only partially fulfilled? Could it be that in the press for diversity and inclusiveness, identity was sacrificed?

Ecumenism, that Presbyterian-championed hallmark, was involved in the growing struggle for identity. In the classic sense of ecumenism, denominations maintained their identity but pooled their resources to do cooperative ministry. But given the lack of resources to do things denominationally, much less ecumenically, the post-denominational era began to flourish when the identity of church was all watered down and became murky. Everyone was becoming Metho-Bapti-terians and nobody really remembered the difference. Presbyterian identity was diluted and it was not clear what forces existed that were going to reconstitute its strength as distinctly "Presbyterian," assuming that was even desirable.

The new identity of the reunited church remains to be found. Hope abounds, not in rekindling a remnant Dream geared to overcoming the struggles emanating from the 1960s or 1980s, but in igniting passion for a new Dream keenly tuned to the realities of the twenty-first century.

Primary Questions

The primary questions now are: What was achieved by the Union Presbytery Movement, and what learnings might be gleaned from it that would inform the reunited PC(USA) as it searches for a new identity and faces the challenges of the twenty-first century? What dreams were unrealized that yet may be realized? What role did the Movement and the reunion of the denominations play in the healing of the scars created by the Civil War and racism, the residual effect of slavery? What was their place in American history? What impact did they have on society in general, or society on them, and did they make any contribution to the development of the new realities of North and South? But most significantly of all, what is the harvest from those ancient emotional and theological seeds sown so long ago in our spiritual and denominational heritage? What can be learned from the Movement's successes and failures that may shape the new postmodern identity of the PC(USA)? What can be learned that will inform future cooperative efforts, the creation of new union presbyteries, and even new ecumenical unions? And finally, what can be learned from its modern ecclesial heritage that will be essential in creating new dreams that will make the PC(USA) relevant to a postmodern world?

To seek answers to these and other questions, the book is organized in three parts.

Part I: Birthing Dreams

Part I is divided into six chapters. It provides the broad historical context of the Movement and describes how each segment of this context provided a formative prelude to the Union Presbytery Movement in the twentieth century and the Presbyterian Church (U.S.A.) in the twenty-first century.

Chapter 1, "Introduction—The Dream," shares the Dream and sets the stage in broad terms for all that is to follow.

Chapter 2, "Long Time Coming," explores the cultural and ecclesiastical origins of North American Presbyterianism from the old island kingdoms of Scotland and England with special attention to the traits of that heritage that were pertinent to the creation of union presbyteries and the eventual reunion of the denominations in 1983.

Chapter 3, "Arriving Immigrants," follows the migrations of the dominant British immigrants—English, Scottish, and Ulster Scots—to North America and enumerates the lasting traits of their legacy.

Chapter 4, "Presbyterians in North America," highlights how the history of Presbyterians in North America—with its irony of cultures, its wildfire revivals, its challenges of western frontiers, its devastating trauma over political polarities and human injustices, its organizational ruptures, its confessional collisions—was a formative prelude to the Union Presbytery Movement in the twentieth century and the Presbyterian Church (U.S.A.) in the twenty-first century.

Chapter 5, " Twentieth-Century Unions, Reunions, and Splits," focuses on how Presbyterians in North America through a series of turbulent events—well-intentioned mission endeavors, segregated judicatories and institutions, polarizing ecumenical movements, "separate but equal" stances, failed and disparate reunions, opportunist takeovers, rejected unions, and the irreconcilable trauma manifest among former relations, friends, congregations and families—set the final stage on which the Union Presbytery Movement in the twentieth century, and the Presbyterian Church (U.S.A.) in the twenty-first century, acted out their ecclesial dramas.

Chapter 6, "The Movement," addresses the genesis and broad cultural context of the motivational dreams emerging from the Presbyterian familial subcultures and networks that gave it purpose and direction. It tells about the relational origins of the Movement.

Part II: Living Dreams

Part II is divided into six chapters. It chronicles the life and times of union presbyteries. It shows the constitutional changes required and how they were formed; what their relations were to their synods; what role COUP played; and what it was like to live between "two worlds."

Chapter 7, "Prelude to Change," traces the political steps that had to be taken by isolated clusters of believers in the Movement's dream across the Border States and Deep South states in order to bring about the necessary changes in the two denominational structures so that union presbyteries could come into existence. Encouraged by a long courtship of cooperation, people in areas where the denominations overlapped sensed that the time for formal consummation was at hand. This prelude set the stage for a whole new era in the life of the two major Presbyterian denominations.

Chapter 8, "The Constitutional Divide," reveals the details of how a dramatic and historic turn of events culminated in the final crossing of a constitutional and political watershed at the 1969 meeting of the General Assembly (PCUS). The actions of that Assembly not only made it possible for union presbyteries to become a legal reality, but they changed the leadership and direction the PCUS would take over the next decade and a half, now making denominational reunion a live possibility.

Chapter 9, "Denominational Restructure," outlines how the sweeping actions of the Southern and Northern General Assemblies in 1969 set in motion plans that would create union presbyteries, but also would restructure boards and agencies as well as establish regional synods in both denominations on parallel tracks. The failure to pass the union synod amendment in the Southern Church was something of a relief, although some presbytery boundary alignments were needed in the new regional synods. It is difficult to appreciate fully the enormity of the organizational upheaval brought on in such a limited period of time by these restructuring efforts and the impact this had on the creation of union presbyteries.

Chapter 10, "First-Wave Union Presbyteries (1970–1972)," recounts the significance for these first-wave union presbyteries of the question, "What is a presbytery?" Their dream was that presbytery was one of the new ways of being church. Though the factors that brought about their organization were similar, this chapter tells how all union presbyteries were not alike, nor was the route by which they got there the same.

Chapter 11, "And Then There Were More (1979–1983)," shows how the Movement came to fruition in advocating and working for the continual development of union presbyteries, both in areas where both denominations had a presence and in areas where only one of them was currently at work. It shares the story of how the excitement and imagination of union presbyteries became contagious. It also indicates how the forming of regional synods from state-line synods in the reorganization of both denominations radically changed the meaning of "middle governing bodies" and gave union presbyteries a special place in the new order.

Chapter 12, "Between Two Worlds," looks at the origins of the "Consultation on Union Presbyteries," known as COUP. It tells of some pre-consultation gatherings that took place in the early days of union presbyteries, but with little impact. The need for consultations did not become clear for all the union presbyteries until two or three years into their existence. It became obvious that forces beyond the control of individual union presbyteries influenced many issues they all faced. COUP became the forum for sharing common concerns and finding mutual strategies to address them.

Part III: Recouping Dreams

Part III is divided into four chapters. It lays out the fact that dreams have ways of waxing and waning, and from time to time must be renewed in order to have lasting significance. With the coming of denominational reunion, union presbyteries in their two-world manifestation ceased to exist. Their dreams for themselves had been fulfilled in part, but their dreams for new ways of being church, though not always fulfilled, had value beyond their existence for the reunited denomination.

Chapter 13, "All Presbyteries, Union Presbyteries," examines the threshold of reunion that would make all presbyteries *de facto* union presbyteries, including the lingering interest in forming union presbyteries unilaterally in non-overlapping areas. It reviews the broader motivations and hopes for denominational reunion along with attendant threats, fears, reservations, and opposition. It reveals some of the critical concessions made in *The Plan for Reunion* to make it acceptable to those who had reservations about reunion. It describes the development of how some individuals came to change from con to pro and how this affected the final vote. Finally, it gives an emotional snapshot of the final actions that brought about reunion.

Chapter 14, "Place in American History," builds the case that union presbyteries and denominational reunion contributed, in part, to healing institutional breaches caused by the Civil War and racism, the residual effect of slavery. The juxtaposition of the industrialization of the South with the trauma of its desegregation via the efforts of the civil rights movement and the destructiveness of the Vietnam War set the context in which Presbyterians played a key role in the healing process, both corporately and individually. Powerful residues of racism still disturbingly linger on the ecclesial and civic landscape of the twenty-first century in spite of the new social, political, and economic developments that have occurred.

Chapter 15, "Threats to the Dream," asserts that, for all the positive contributions of the Union Presbytery Movement to North American Presbyterianism, several dynamics cohabited with it (and still persist in a more virulent manner in the twenty-first century) that threatened to negate much of what was achieved. These dynamics threatened the Dream and set in motion patterns of behavior that transferred from the time of the Movement over into reunion that landed the church on a path to polarization. This chapter takes a closer look at these threatening dynamics, which warrant special attention to see how they can be put in check, based on the experience of the Union Presbytery Movement.

Chapter 16, "Dreams, Where Have You Gone?" summarizes some of the realized and unrealized dreams of reunion as seen in light of the dreams of COUP. It tells of how some dreamed of shaping the new reunited church, only to watch as old patterns infected new structures and the church slid into the nightmare of polarization. It concludes with learnings and timely lessons from the Union Presbytery Movement that can be useful in recouping dreams, overcoming the divisions of today, and bringing unity and hope for tomorrow, if . . .

Where *did* the dreams go? The counter-cultured dreams of the Movement were all but dead, though a rich legacy remained. Is it possible that this legacy will be reclaimed? It is possible that the inheritance can be reclaimed. In the long run, recouping the Dream is basically a serious theological matter, a reality that was at the heart of the Union Presbytery Movement and how it impacted denominational reunion. What can be learned from the accomplishments and shortcomings of the Movement is of critical importance to the Presbyterian Church (U.S.A.) in its present-day search for "the peace, unity, and purity of the church."

It is absolutely imperative that these learnings be taken into account in the exploration and creation of any future unions with other denominations or ecumenical bodies. It is also absolutely imperative that these learnings be taken seriously if the PC(USA) is to regain any credibility and relevance in the postmodern world of the twenty-first century. Humankind and creation are spinning wildly out of control. All creation groans . . .

Epilogue

If the young are to dream new dreams and a few old ones are to have visions in a postmodern world, there must be a firm belief in the promise, "Behold, I make *all* things *new*." That includes relationships as well as organizations, *all* relationships and *all* organizations. A *new* language must be loudly spoken, piercing the culture of silence and separation, inviting *all* to experience the true freedom of welcome. And then, "People will come from east and west, from north and south, and sit down at table . . ."

What now? What was a union presbytery? What was the significance and dreams of the Union Presbytery Movement? Some do not know the story; others have forgotten; those who lived it are passing on. Someone who remembers the story must tell it. "So, Once upon a time . . ."

Notes

1. Lefferts A. Loetscher, *A Brief History of the Presbyterians*, 4th ed. (Philadelphia: Westminster Press, 1978, 1983), pp. 105–106.

2. William G. McAtee, the author, was chairperson of the Committee on Assembly Operations (CAO). In addition to his official duties with committees and on the platform, he had a front row seat for all the events of the final PCUS Assembly and the Reuniting Assembly. He marched in the second row of the throng to City Hall.

3. Living Devotional Letter from William G. McAtee to Ruth Settle, Transylvania staff, dated June 11, 1983, in personal collection of William G. McAtee. [Note: Each day of the sixteen-plus years that he served Transylvania Presbytery as executive, McAtee wrote someone in the Presbyterian system a letter reflecting on what he was engaged in that day, what was going on in the larger context of the church and the world, and a brief reflection on a scriptural passage. There are 6,000 of these letters. Also note: All documents hereafter identified as "Living Devotional Letter" are copies "in personal collection of William G. McAtee." All references in this book to items indicated as being in McAtee's personal collection will be archived at the Presbyterian Historical Society.

4. James D. Baskin, interview by author, November 18, 1997, Interview 26, page 9.

5. Living Devotional Letter from William G. McAtee to Ruth Settle, Transylvania staff, dated June 11, 1983.

6. Ibid.

7. Living Devotional Letter from William G. McAtee to Ruth Settle, Transylvania staff, dated June 11, 1983.

8. Ibid. Carl McIntire was an ultraconservative radio evangelist whose biblical fundamentalist, anticommunist, hawkish patriot message was frequently aimed at the Presbyterian Church. He was a perpetual protester at the annual meetings of both General Assemblies.

9. E-mail from John M. Salmon to William G. McAtee, dated 10/18/04, in personal collection of William G. McAtee. Salmon was elder McCoy's pastor and a firsthand witness to what took place at City Hall.

10. Joel L. Alvis, Jr., *Religion and Race: Southern Presbyterians, 1946–1983* (Tuscaloosa: University of Alabama Press, 1994), pp. 115–116.

11. Ibid., p. 125.

12. Unrecorded conversations between William G. McAtee and Richard M. Moon, when Moon was pastor at Faith Presbyterian Church (Transylvania), Morehead, Kentucky.

13. Jim Haskins, *I Have a Dream: The Life and Words of Martin Luther King, Jr.* (Brookfield, CN: Millbrook Press, 1992), p. 76. King delivered his "I Have a Dream" speech on the steps at the Lincoln Memorial in Washington, DC, on August 28, 1963.

14. The author's paternal great-grandfather, William McAtee, the first of six William McAtees in a row, was born in Kentucky in 1801. He traveled the Ohio and Mississippi Rivers as a "Kaintuck," floating produce to New Orleans and returning on foot via the Natchez Trace to Kentucky. Around 1840 he stayed in Mississippi and took possession of several hundred acres that became available when Andrew Jackson relocated the Choctaw Indians to the Arkansas and Oklahoma territories under the Treaty of Dancing Rabbit Creek. He turned the wilderness into a cotton plantation. He married Sarah Meek, the daughter of the Methodist Bishop of Alabama-Mississippi, who had come there as missionary to the Choctaw Indians. The author's maternal great-grandfather, Wm. G. Fatheree, served in the 1st Mississippi Light Artillery, Company D, Wofford's Battery. His unit was the first to engage and turn back General Sherman's forces in the Battle of Chickasaw Bayou, December 27–29, 1862. Five months later Sherman began his final siege of Vicksburg on May 20, 1863. Fatheree was killed during the second or third day of the siege when Sherman's forces overran Wofford's Battery.

15. Living Devotional Letter from William G. McAtee to Ruth Settle, Transylvania staff, dated June 11, 1983.

16. Living Devotional Letter from William G. McAtee to Peggy Collins, Transylvania staff, dated June 12, 1983.

17. Living Devotional Letter from William G. McAtee to Anne Stipp, Transylvania staff, dated June 13, 1983.

18. Living Devotional Letter from William G. McAtee to H. William Peterson, executive presbyter, Western Kentucky (Union), dated June 15, 1983.

19. Ibid.

20. See *Union Presbytery Movement Oral History Project*, © 2004 by Presbyterian Church (U.S.A.), Department of History, Volume 9, Master Subject Index, "Union Presbyteries: Feelings about Union Presbytery Movement."

21. Arthur Herman, *How the Scots Invented the Modern World* (New York: Crown Publishers, 2001; Three Rivers Press, 2001), p. 152.

22. William Doyle, *An American Insurrection: The Battle of Oxford, Mississippi, 1962* (New York: Doubleday, 2001).

23. Strauss and Howe, *Generations*, pp. 288–289.

24. The name of COUP initially was "Consultation *of* Union Presbyteries" because they and their respective synods were the main participants. After several years the scope of the consultation expanded. The *of* in the name was changed to *on* to reflect the new role of advocating the formation of new union presbyteries. Cooperating presbyteries and potential candidates were invited to participate.

Chapter 2
Long Time Coming

It all started in 1066 at the Battle of Hastings.
—T. Morton McMillan, Jr.[1]

Mort McMillan, one of the key strategists in the preliminary stages of the Movement, often said with a twinkle in his eye that what happened at the Battle of Hastings was that the English clans were destroyed and the Scottish clans remained intact. He said many of those dispersed English clans migrated to America and ended up in the North building textile mills. The Scottish clans that were not destroyed moved intact into South Carolina and Alabama, raising the cotton on Southern plantations that provided raw materials for those Northern factories (32-22).

Whether this is strictly historical caricature or simply myth, historians have been trying to sort out the achievements and conflicts of Presbyterians ever since, both North and South. North and South in this instance could refer to locations in the old island kingdoms of Scotland and England or the geographic areas of New World America. The positive contributions achieved by Presbyterians in both geographical locations may have been romanticized in myth to the point of diminishing their worth unrealistically. By the same token, some of the flaws of those realities may have been ignored, adding to the lessons lost from those experiences, caricatured or not.

War and conflict were recurring themes acted out in this part of history, either in the realms of religion or the machinations of government and the migration patterns of people resulting from both. As much as some would love to purge war from human experience, as they purge our hymnals of "Onward Christian Soldiers," war is still very much an ever-present reality overshadowing our lives. We define ourselves by the latest slogans—"Make Peace, Not War" or "Support Our Troops." All peace efforts are symbiotically tied to war—dreams of the absence of war—holding out hope against its inevitability. Wars have a way of providing watershed events in the drama of human existence. War embeds in our human psyche a lasting duet of win-lose, creating a sense that this is the way disputes were destined to be settled. Somebody has to win, and somebody has to lose.

But such a narrow view of resolution leaves the conqueror with a false sense of achievement and the vanquished with a devastating sense of "what if." Such resolution is too often a Pyrrhic victory. The combatants, some filled with overconfidence and others consumed with a desire for revenge, return to fight another day, in another place, in another way. It happens, not only in the brutal conflagration of war in the physical sense but also in the heated exchanges erupting in the emotional and verbal conflicts of uncivil discourse. This is especially true when polarization is extreme and the votes are close.

A cameo[2] look at pivotal events in medieval, premodern, and modern English and Scottish history, along with the dynamics and traits growing out of them, may help in understanding the origins of the contributions and the flaws from this heritage in the North American Presbyterian experience, especially with regard to union presbyteries and denominational reunion, as well as the Presbyterian Church (U.S.A.). To shed more light on these dynamics and traits, the following watershed events were selected for this study: the Battles of Stamford Bridge and Hastings (1066), the Westminster Assembly (1643–1649), the Act of Union (1707), and the Battle of Culloden (1746).

Battles of Stamford Bridge and Hastings (1066)

Did it begin with the Battle of Hastings? Or did it really begin at the Battle of Stamford Bridge a few days earlier? It was at Stamford Bridge that King Harold defeated the invading Norwegians in what has been described as "the last battle fought in England in which cavalry was not used. . . . The fighters hacking and slashing at each other this September [25th] afternoon could not know it, but this was to be the last time that the traditional infantryman battle would be fought in England."[3]

Tostig, a losing contender in a long running battle with King Harold, recruited the Scottish militia to join forces with the Norwegian invader, Hardrada.[4] Harold defeated this mixed military force at the Battle of Stamford Bridge, leading to speculation that the surviving Scottish combatants, being losers there, may not have been part of the Battle of Hastings. Probably they had retired to Scotland after the "lost cause" of Stamford Bridge to resume their wild and woolly lives building up their reputation as fierce warriors over the decades. This may shed some light on the myth about how the Scottish clans were left intact, while the English clans were dispersed at the Battle of Hastings.

Harold thought he had won a great victory, but it was not only his next-to-last battle—he would be mortally wounded in a few short days—it was the last battle depicted as medieval. He had to force-march his troops to the south of England to meet a greater challenge in the invading forces of William the Conqueror.

On October 14, 1066, King Harold was mortally wounded in the Battle of Hastings, in what could be termed the first premodern battle. "William's strategy was revolutionary. Archers, infantry and cavalry had been used before in continental warfare, of course, but probably never before had a commander planned to use them together with such precision. . . . William did not know . . . the influence which his tactics at Hastings were to have upon military history."[5] The archers were the prototype of the modern Scud missiles, used to "soften up the enemy"; the mailed knights on horseback were the prototype of modern "shock" armored divisions; and the infantry was simply the age-old foot soldiers doing "mop-up" operations.[6]

The fall of 1066 was a watershed in English and Western history. The medieval world was giving way to a world that would in time be known as modern. "The overwhelming fact about William's conquest is that out of the plotting and machinations . . . , the savageries, and a single battle on the sloping meadow of Senlac [on the peninsula of Hastings], there emerged a kingdom which was to grow in strength and influence for 900 years [to c. 1966]; until, that is, its Empire crumbled and it found itself searching for a new role to play."[7] Two distinct cultures of civil order began to develop in the aftermath of Hastings.

William added a highly structured, Norman feudalism to the Anglo-Saxon culture of England through a "military caste system coldly imposed from above as a sort of tax." This broader treetop structure of civil order became the basis of a nationalism that grew over the centuries. The Scottish culture, for many reasons of geography and Celtic temperament remained a more concentrated grass roots, "no-less-warlike tribal system." Personal loyalties, emerging from "an individual's honor in belonging to the tribe," created a "more democratic and compelling" way of ordering life.[8]

The reality was that the victory by William the Conqueror at the Battle of Hastings, while initiating a new era of national sensibility to conquered England, may also have contributed to the strengthening in subsequent years of the Scottish Highland clans that were a holdover from Scotland's feudal, not tribal, past. What held them together was the land, and holding it. The French-speaking Normans were as much their ancestors as the ancient Celts. The true prototypes of the Highland warriors, who fought for Prince Charles at Culloden, found their identity, not in the ancient Picts or Britons, but among those who fought alongside William the Conqueror.[9]

The two distinctions in civil order that began to develop in the aftermath of Hastings, though seemingly obscure and subtle, would have enormous future implications for the island kingdoms and the new world beyond. The lengthening medieval shadows of a gloomy September afternoon soon gave way to the dawning light of a premodern world. However, the flaws of war were perpetuated once more. In that singular defining instant there were winners and losers. The full consequence of the contributions and flaws of win-lose would be a long time coming.

Westminster Assembly (1643–1649)

It is important to note that every creed, every confession, every catechism, every declaration in the *Book of Confessions* of the PC(USA) came into being in the midst of a contemporary political and social upheaval, not simply an ecclesiastical one. The Westminster Assembly was not a quiet deliberative gathering of theological colleagues off in some ivy tower where the fine points of doctrine were quietly debated in a reflective manner. The decades leading up to the Westminster Assembly were turbulent with dissent. Church and state were not separate. Monarchs reigned by divine right. A struggle for ecclesiastical and temporal power between the crown and Parliament heated up to intense degrees through the reigns of James I and Charles I.

The coming of James I to the throne was a watershed in what was known at the time as the British Isles. The fact of his reign brought into being a pseudo-union of the kingdoms in those Isles under one monarchy. Simply decreeing a single monarchy does not a union make. "To put it bluntly: there was a union of crowns but no union of kingdoms and much of the violence throughout England, Ireland, and Scotland in the century that followed was the result."[10]

The Protestant Puritans initially were thrilled with James's ascent to the throne, thinking he would assure the return of a Presbyterian form of church government and a more Reformed theology. This was not to be the case. James was highly dissatisfied with the Kirk, "with its alarming notions about the rights of congregations to organize themselves, worship in their own ways, and settle their own church order. . . . If people could decide for themselves about religion, they might also decide for themselves about politics. . . . [T]he Church of England would remain Episcopal in its government."[11]

Relations deteriorated further under the reign of Charles I. Divorce and marriage had been an issue with monarchs in times past. It was no different with Charles. His marriage to a French Catholic for political reasons cast a pall over Protestants. Charles collided with Parliament over the levy of taxes. Parliament demanded that Charles sign a Petition of Rights when he imprisoned seventy people for refusing to pay "forced loans." The Petition was an admission "that his 'arbitrary taxation and imprisonment' violated the 'fundamental liberties of the kingdom.' "[12] Charles disbanded Parliament and ruled for eleven years by divine right alone.

Charles got no peace from the Scots Presbyterians. He finally tried to force the Anglican Book of Common Prayer on them. On Sunday, July 23, 1637, it was introduced in worship at St. Giles in Edinburgh. Pandemonium broke loose and what spread across Scotland like wildfire by the following April was the signing of the National

Covenant. Under the banner of religion, this covenant directly challenged the king's prerogative to make law without the consent of the Scottish people and approved by a free General Assembly and Parliament. It was almost certain that, through what might be described as Presbyterian democracy in action, Scottish people would oppose any proposal not to their liking.[13]

What ensued were the two Bishop's wars initiated by the Scots General Assembly in November of 1637 that, in effect, would be the end of the line for the Stuarts' monarchy. Civil war broke out in England, ending with the execution of Charles and ushering in the rule of Oliver Cromwell. The absolute rule of monarchy was dead. With the English Civil War, a new political concept came into being which declared that the governed must give consent to those who govern, taking its original cue from the Scottish Covenanters.[14]

Its own Civil War took its toll on the English Parliament. Facing defeat, it called on the Scottish Covenanters for help. Negotiations produced a document, an agreement known as the Solemn League and Covenant, signed by representatives of the Scottish Covenanters and what was left of the English Parliament. The English met their part of the deal by calling the Westminster Assembly into session.[15] It was to sort out the theological and civil issues generated by these struggles. The Solemn League and Covenant specified that "the Scottish Covenanters attack the Royalist forces from the north—in return for the sum of 30,000 pounds a month and an undertaking that there would be 'a reformation of religion in the Kingdoms of England and Ireland in doctrine, worship, discipline and government, according to the Word of God and the examples of the best reformed churches, and that popery and prelacy should be extirpated.' "[16]

This was the context in which the Westminster Assembly came into being and hammered out the Westminster Standards. The majority of the body was made up of members of Parliament. The five Scottish clergymen included could enter the debate but could not vote. Representatives from Reformed churches from other countries including the American colonies were invited, but did not attend. It was a long and drawn-out affair, with 1,163 sessions, running from 1643 to 1649.[17]

Power was the supreme polity issue—who should rule the church, who should rule the state—with theology forming its foundation. There were three parties at play here. The Anglican party said that the royal sovereign should rule both state and church. The Presbyterian party maintained that the elected representatives of the people should govern both in Parliament and in church presbyteries. Cromwell's party insisted on local autonomy for churches and limited powers for both king and Parliament.[18]

More fighting between everyone involved took place outside the Assembly while the debate raged on inside it. The Scots had initially held that their reason for signing the Solemn League and Covenant was an evangelism strategy. They wanted to convert England to Presbyterianism. It became clear that this was not going to happen. In actuality they were not committed to taking sides between the king and Parliament. However, they saw another opportunity to exchange pounds for flesh. They delivered the king to the Parliamentary Commissioners for 400,000 pounds. Having second thoughts about the delivery of Charles, they went through a series of secret negotiations trying to agree on a trial offer of getting England to be Presbyterian for three years. Things went from bad to worse. King Charles was executed. And the deal was off.[19]

Dissension reigned and the Westminster Assembly ended when Cromwell began to inflict his will on the proceedings. Presbyterian members were forcibly excluded in 1648, far from a win-win situation. This hardly seemed to matter, for the Scottish representatives had withdrawn to Scotland in 1647 and persuaded "the Scottish General Assembly to adopt the Westminster Standards for use in the kirk, replacing the Scots Confession of 1560 and the Heidelberg Catechism."[20]

The Reformed theological benchmark of order that would impact Presbyterians and other reformers for generations was set. Yet English Puritans split into "Presbyterians" who protested the execution of the King and "Independents" who supported it. The "Covenanters" would still be heard from. Though this gave subsequent generations the theological benchmark that is the Westminster Confession, the flaws of war and theological conflict were perpetuated once more. In that protracted and defining Westminster Assembly there were winners and losers. Again, the full consequence of the contributions and flaws of win-lose would be a long time coming.

The Act of Union (1707)

The second half of the seventeenth century was anything but calm and peaceful. Cromwell's great achievement was uniting England and Scotland under one regime, and later Ireland after he bludgeoned that island into submission in 1652. In achieving this remarkable feat, Cromwell earned undying enmity in all three nations. Oliver Cromwell, as a historical figure, was one whom Irishmen, Englishmen, and Scotsmen could agree to hate for centuries.[21]

Scotland during this period experienced a series of military occupations by the English military and cruel abuses to subdue the populace into submission. "The Killing Time taught Scottish Calvinists

Dreams, Where Have You Gone?

to hate governance from London, the Episcopal Church, and Englishmen in general—and Highlanders as well, since Lauderdale [the Secretary who ruled Scotland for Charles II] liked to deploy regiments drawn from the pro-Stuart Highland clans . . . for his military forays into the Covenant-ing southwest Lowlands."[22]

The Covenanters, the zealots of the religious right of that day, hated Satan more than they loved democracy. Anyone who opposed them ran the risk of being destroyed—whether king, bishop, or neighbor. They had no use for freely expressing one's own ideas, thoughts or opinions, values prevalent in modern democratic societies. Tolerance and rational restraint was not part of their makeup.[23]

When faced with brutal clashes with Lauderdale's troops sent to collect fines for attending unauthorized religious services, it was said that "the Covenanters . . . , as good Calvinists, knew that they were predestined to grace and so were more eager to die for their faith. In spite of the savage punishments inflicted upon them, their resistance continued unabated and as often as not they gave the Government forces as good as they got."[24]

The Glorious Revolution in 1688 brought about regime change in London that granted some relief from the constant political and religious strife, both in England and in Scotland. The kirk in Scotland gained more autonomy. Some of the Highland clans were troubled by the war King William II was engaged in on the Continent. In actuality, not much had changed. "The two kingdoms were still ruled by a single crown, with separate capitals and separate parliaments. But the balance between the two kingdoms had shifted. Economics, rather than religion, was becoming the new issue of contention. England had acquired an empire, reaching across the Atlantic to the New World, and extending south and east to Asia."[25]

Toward the end of the seventeenth century and into the early part of the eighteenth century, a group known as the Seceders, ancestors of the United Presbyterian Church of North America (UPCNA or UPNA), made their mark. They were not as fierce as the Covenanters, for they had not held firm to the Covenant of 1643. They were more similar in their strong Calvinist theology to the Low Church puritan Anglicans. However, because of their brand of Reformed theological belief, they fought a protracted fight with the Scots' General Assembly over most of the period the reestablished Scots Church existed, from 1690 until 1733. Theological, educational, practical, and polity concerns, rarely faced and never resolved, eventually led to schism.[26]

It was a battle between what some "saw as a definite slide away from essential Calvinistic theology in the Scots' kirk . . . that sounded like a defense of Arminian and Antinomian theology."[27] During this time, schism created the Associate Presbytery and Synod. Conflict continued when the Burgess Oath of loyalty was exacted in 1745 by the Synod, thus leading to another division with the formation of the Burgher and Anti-Burgher Synods.

In 1696 Scotland's Parliament passed the Act of Setting Schools, "establishing a school in every parish in Scotland not already equipped with one. . . . The result was that within a generation nearly every parish in Scotland had some sort of school and a regular teacher. The education must have been fairly rudimentary in some places: the fundamentals of reading and grammar and nothing more. But it was available, and it was, at least in theory if not always in practice, free."[28] This educational initiative laid the groundwork for the great advances of the Scottish Enlightenment of the eighteenth century.

Scotland's economy was still dependent on the feudal arrangements between landowner and tenant to feed its people. With the first of a series of failed harvests after 1695, there was not enough food for its one million people to eat. Scotland could not survive alone, so a simple decision was made to compete with England by doing what it had done by legislating a new economy.[29] This economic initiative capitalized on the imagination and inventiveness of the Scottish people. It would pay great dividends over succeeding generations, though not immediately.

A series of events in the period from 1696 through 1704 showed that the enmity between the two kingdoms had reached the breaking point. One of these events was a failed colonial venture in Panama led by the Darien Company, an attempt to economically rival the English merchants. One of its leaders, Andrew Fletcher, became a radical leader of the opposition to the Act of Union, those who could not abide any authority at all, particularly the Stuarts.[30] The freedom he espoused was for himself and his kind. In his scheme of things, this did not translate into freedom for all Scots. His solution for the economic depression Scotland faced was in "effect turning the Scottish peasantry into slaves, dividing up the indigent poor among the local landlords (such as himself), and giving the latter the power of life and death over their human herds."[31]

What counted for Fletcher was land that provided work for those employed on it and wealth for the owners.[32] He attempted, through his part in the Darien Scheme, to live out this belief, but it was a disaster. "Two thousand Scottish lives and three hundred thousand Scottish pounds had been lost . . . , hatred for England had reached new heights and . . . a number of other deplorable incidents still further exacerbated relations between the two countries."[33]

Another event was the Alien Act, passed by parliament in 1704— soon to be repealed in 1706—that stated that Scottish nationals living in

England would be considered aliens, thereby making it impossible for their heirs to inherit their English property. This in essence was a display of how much those in the southern kingdom detested Scottish nationals.[34]

The political, social, economic, and religious impasse was a nightmare. A solution had to be reached that both England and Scotland would find palatable. "Union" seemed to be the answer most considered. The English were pleased with the possibility, but the Scots had reservations. It was known in the southern kingdom as the Act of Union, while in the northern kingdom, as the Treaty of Union. No matter what it was called, the union of the two kingdoms in 1707 that created Great Britain as a constitutional body "was more of a shotgun marriage than the consummation of a long-standing love affair."[35]

The price paid "for representing 'North Britain,' as it was officially to be called, in the British parliament made the union a particularly bitter pill for the Scots to swallow."[36] They were in the classic position of being the smaller of the two entities considering merger. That position was characterized, with good reason, by the fear of being swallowed up by the larger entity. The larger body in a merger tends to pick up the best assets the smaller body has to offer, and cast off the rest. The Scottish reservations were to be proved warranted.

What the Scots had hoped union would mean was "a federation of two kingdoms . . . that would have allowed two 'Distinct, Free, and Independent Kingdoms [to] unite their separate interests into one common interest, for the mutual benefit of both.' "[37] What came into being with the Union of 1707 was the new Great Britain, ruled by one monarch and one parliament. The Scottish Privy Council ended up with no power. London was to be the capital and had "control over everything that affected both nations, including taxes, customs and excise duties, and military and foreign affairs."[38]

What began as a disadvantage in the loss of autonomy and pride, of being swallowed up by their southern cousins, in the long run turned into an overwhelming advantage to the Scots. The carrot held out to the Scottish Commission and the Edinburgh parliament to sign the treaty was "Scotland's admission into the English economy on advantageous terms. Thus Scots had full access to England's markets, including the colonies, while some Scottish industries, notably coal and salt, were protected from English competition."[39]

In the creation of Great Britain, the flaws of domestic strife and political conflict were perpetuated once more. In the negotiated merger of the two kingdoms, under the guise of "union," there were winners and losers. The larger body had the numbers. The smaller body was swallowed up. The full consequence of the contributions and flaws of win-lose would be a long time coming.

The Battle of Culloden (1746)

The more immediate consequence of the Act of Union came in 1708 when the English Parliament dissolved the Scottish Privy Council, taking away from the Scots "the one remaining intermediary body between them and the government in London. From that moment, the notion of a separate Scottish political interest had ceased to exist."[40] In short order, in 1709, another insult was added to injury by "the introduction of the English liturgy in Anglican church services in Edinburgh. The very use of the word liturgy conjured up visions of Catholic Mass, Popery, and the Scarlet Woman of Rome for devout Scots. . . . Anglicanism was now here to stay."[41]

The worst fears of the Scots were realized. It was evident that those Scots who had worked for the Union treaty thought it was a good idea at the time. But upon more measured reflection it became evident to them that the Treaty did not produce a union of equals but a merger of unequals. The Scots, the minority that thought it had rights, tried to reconsider what had been done. "When in 1713 a motion to repeal the Union was submitted to the House of Lords by Seafield and Argyll, who had both played such an important part in bringing it about, it was defeated by four votes."[42]

There were Scottish uprisings for decades. Wars were threatened and executed all across Europe. In some quarters the conflicts were less physical and more political. In the midst of all this, the son of an Ulster Scots Presbyterian preacher came to the fore and fomented a watershed in the world of ideas. His influence helped usher in the Scottish Enlightenment that was to impact Scotland, Great Britain, and Western civilization for decades.

Francis Hutcheson's writings in 1725 stirred severe negative reactions in the kirk, which saw in them the epitome of the "new light" tradition that held to a "natural" morality. This belief discounted the significance of the Ten Commandments and predestination.[43] But Hutcheson gained support from a curious source. Archibald Campbell, later the fourth Duke of Argyll, was a man of "large intellectual and scientific interests." He had strong connections in the Lowlands and in the Highlands where he was the head of the Campbell clan. His grandfather had fought on the losing side in the Battle of Sedgemoor in 1685 alongside his friend Andrew Fletcher. Campbell was a patron to Scotland's universities, especially the University of Glasgow. When a teaching opening came there, Campbell acted on behalf of Hutcheson. This was a key intervention in making Glasgow a key player in the Scottish Enlightenment.[44]

What Hutcheson really wanted to accomplish over most anything else was "to change the face of theology in Scotland." He felt the dogmatic teachings of John Knox were too intransigent and urged fellow clergymen to respond to moral questions parishioners struggle with on a daily basis. His agitating to make Presbyterian faith more humane caused controversy.[45]

In 1737 Adam Smith was one of Hutcheson's students. Smith heard Hutcheson teach that "Human beings are born free and equal. The desire to be free survives, even in the face of the demands for cooperation with others in society. . . . a natural right . . . [that] applies to all human beings everywhere, regardless of origin or status."[46] Hutcheson contended that this natural right went far beyond freedom of speech or freedom of religion; it challenged all forms of oppression. His writings "were 'an attack on all forms of slavery as well as denial of any right to govern solely on superior abilities or riches.' They would inspire antislavery abolitionists, not only in Scotland but from London to Philadelphia."[47]

Back to the political wars among the nations of the continent. Sentiment was rising on several fronts to overcome what to many had been a "lost cause," the restoring of the Stuarts to the throne of the now united kingdoms of England and Scotland. At times it was difficult to determine what the motivations were of the Jacobite factions in various locations. "Jacobites" was the long-held name of this restore-Stuarts-to-the-throne movement. The Act of Union brought anything but social stability to Scotland. For some of rural background, it was a matter of longing for the good old days when the Stuarts last ruled and everybody knew their station in life. In the Highlands, life as in the good old days was a present reality. There the clan chieftains' rule was nearly absolute, faithful in spirit to the only real kings they had ever known—the Stuarts.[48]

James, the last Stuart king, lived in exile in Rome. With age the fight had gone out of him, but his oldest son, Prince Charles Edward, as rightful heir appeared to be the most likely leader to restore this Jacobite dream. In early 1744, Charles left his father in Rome and went to France, where French forces had plans to invade England.[49] After several setbacks and with some monetary support from France, Charles landed on Scottish soil the following year with a small band of followers. He was not received with great enthusiasm. Lack of support from the mainland Jacobites did not deter his steadfast determination for his cause. He was bound to raise his standard and claim his right to be king. He set out for Edinburgh, gaining strength of forces as he went. In September of 1745, escorted by some kilted Highlanders, he made a triumphal entry to the strains of bagpipes.[50]

There were battles in Scotland that raged between Scots, a civil war known simply as the Forty-five. The division that split the Scots was

---

more than the usual divisions between class or religion, Highlanders or Lowlanders. Competing to identify a vision of what Scotland should become, and what direction it should take, created a deep cleft in Scottish culture itself.[51] Charles's supporters had a static vision for Scotland, attempting to hang on to dreams of what rural feudal Scotland once was. The Whigs, the government in power, thought the well-being of Scotland lay in a progressive future. Both were willing to fight and die for their cause.

For a while it looked as if Prince Charles would win the day. Though he had taken Edinburgh with relative ease, it was not clear what his real objective was. Was the objective to set Scotland free from the tyranny bargained away by the Union treaty and restore the old-world ways, or was its purpose to reinstall Charles as heir to the throne for all of Britain?

In the fall of 1745 Charles called a decisive council at Holyroodhouse, the home of his Stuart ancestors, where he was holding court. The upshot of the debate was that Charles prevailed by one vote. Turning his back on Scotland for the moment, he sent his army south in search of the larger prize. Finding no overwhelming opposition they did prevail against England, which was in chaos. Finally, some sentiment for "patriotic resistance and Scottophobia" began to emerge.[52]

Two Whig politicians exerted strong leadership that eventually tipped the scales in favor of the government. Archibald Campbell, the one who made it possible for Frances Hutcheson to be at Glasgow, threw the support of the powerful Campbell clan of the western Highlands to the side of the government. Duncan Forbes of Culloden, by the sheer force of his personality, persuaded the northern clans to remain faithful to the government forces of the Duke of Cumberland.[53]

On April 16, 1746, Prince Charles's dream would end at Culloden House, overlooking Drummossie Moor—the home of Duncan Forbes. His resources were depleted, his army ill fed and weak. Yet filled with honor, though knowing the error of their actions, they lined up for one final battle against the overwhelming forces of the Duke of Cumberland's redcoats, which were escorted to the squeal of the Campbell pipes, with drums rolling and battle flags flying.[54]

Not only did the Stuart dream die that day, this battle that pitted clansman against clansman was another last-of-its-kind battle between a premodern armed force and a modern one on European soil.[55] It was the beginning of the end for the clans themselves. Forbes reclaimed his shattered house at Culloden, but never received the recognition he justly deserved for staving off a general rebellion of the Highlands. The London government, not caring to sort out the good from the bad Highlanders, passed legislation that "abolished the ancient, hereditary jurisdictions of chieftains over their clansmen, including the so-called regalian rights, which made them virtual kings in their territories." The net effect of this was that a Highlander was free as an individual to enter into new agreements to work his own land and keep what he earned for himself. Through no fault of Forbes, it did turn out this way. "[T]he Highland clearances were still a long way off, and something no one could have foreseen in 1748."[56]

Social customs die hard even in the face of the overwhelming changes brought on by the impact of legislation and war. Some clan chieftains who were not totally destroyed at Culloden hung on to the old ways for a while, but their role as leaders was badly shattered. Their identity had been defined in terms of relationship to property. The economic engines of the time were beginning to crank out dramatic changes that further reinforced the loss of identity and self-respect. These "surviving chiefs, whether Jacobite or Whig, [turned] into mere landed proprietors, some, though by no means all of whom no longer felt the same sense of responsibility for their clansmen and dependents as formerly, but, in difficult times, were more concerned with making their estates pay."[57]

For the next century or more the development of the textile and other industries in growing urban areas demanded to be fed with a human work force, as well as natural raw material. The Highlands became a ready source for both, especially wool fiber. The most efficient use of the land was to turn ancient fiefdoms into large blocks for sheep farming. To do that, dependent tenants had to be removed. Those who were slow to leave were forcibly "dispossessed and evicted, those responsible sometimes expediting matters by burning the houses, . . . culminating in the notorious Sutherland clearances which continued well into the reign of Queen Victoria."[58]

There was a dramatic rural-to-urban shift in population. The population decreased in the Highlands and increased in the industrial areas. Thousands of Highlanders were "ready to accept any standard of living and any wage that would feed them. Low wages and long working hours were the rule. The expanding industries could absorb any amount of cheap labour. . . . The result of this sudden growth was fearful overcrowding and appalling living conditions with disastrous consequences for the health and general well-being of the population."[59]

In the Battle of Culloden and its aftermath, when the dreams of Stuarts and clan chieftains died and the demands of urban living escalated, the flaws of social strife and political conflict were perpetuated once more. Clearly there were winners and losers on the battlefield, on the farms, and in the cramped cities. The full consequence of the contributions and flaws of win-lose would be a long time coming.

Dynamics of an Inheritance

The foundation of an inheritance for future generations was laid in the dynamics of these pivotal events in medieval, premodern, and modern English and Scottish history with far-reaching and monumental impact.

Early on, the struggle between national and regional distribution of authority, with power the supreme polity issue, came to the fore. This was played out in both church and state as relationships between them developed and boundaries were established, emulating government by the consent of the governed. Some exercised power through elected representatives, some through local autonomy.

Creedal statements were formed as theological benchmarks in the midst of political and social upheaval. Universal application of hard, inflexible dogmas were later challenged by more humane, comforting efforts in facing moral questions of daily life.

Free exchange and expression of ideas, exhibition of tolerance, and rational restraint became the essential basis for universal educational opportunities.

Populations traumatically shifted from rural to urban settings. Agrarian economies gave way to urban and global economies, with their monetary engines fueled at the expense of workers. Low standards of living, low wages, and long hours produced disastrous consequences in the health and general well-being of the populace. Workers experienced pain inflicted through cruel abuses to subdue them into submission, which flew in the face of the belief that humans were born free and equal. Some people began vehemently to challenge all forms of oppression.

The emotional scars of "lost causes" triumphed, and lost dreams were crushed in win-lose games, whether on the field of battle or in chambers of uncivil discourse. Revengeful despair arose from Pyrrhic victories, and demonic polarization evolved when votes were close.

An overwhelming sense of poignancy prevailed through the pitting of family against family, yet fortitude was found to regroup and renew engagement on another day, in another place, and in another way.

Union and cooperation seemed to be a perfect solution to political, social, and religious divisions, yet loss of autonomy and pride sometimes came when larger and smaller entities merged or coalitions overshadowed special interests.

The dynamics of this social history over a long period of time shaped the origins of an identifiable culture that, in a later time and place, would emerge as "Scotch-Irish." This long dynamic process formed beliefs, attitudes, customs, and loyalties that found their way from Scotland, through the Ulster Plantation in Northern Ireland, to the distant shores of North America and into the culture of North American

Presbyterianism. As migrants moved on in search of a better way of life, these radically different environments recycled the culturally formative process and produced new winners and losers in new contexts. The full consequences of the contributions and flaws of win-lose would be a long time coming.

Notes

1. Statement made in several unrecorded conversations with the author over the years. Biographical sketch in T. Morton McMillan, Jr., interview by author, September 29, 1997, Interview 05, transcript, p. 1.

2. See James G. Leyburn, *The Scotch-Irish: A Social History* (Chapel Hill: University of North Carolina Press, 1962), Appendix II, "Important Events in Scottish History." For a more extensive chronology, see pp. 335–337.

3. Edwin Tetlow, *The Enigma of Hastings* (New York: St. Martin's Press, 1974), p. 128.

4. Ibid., p. 105.

5. Ibid., p. 184.

6. Ibid., pp. 184–185.

7. Ibid., p. 199.

8. James Webb, *Born Fighting: How the Scots-Irish Shaped America* (New York: Broadway Books, 2004), p. 32.

9. Herman, *How the Scots Invented the Modern World*, p. 122.

10. John Morrill, ed., *The Oxford Illustrated History of Tudor and Stuart Britain*, chap. 4, "Three Stuart Kingdoms," by John Morrill (New York: Oxford University Press, 1996), p. 74.

11. Jack Rogers, *Presbyterian Creeds: A Guide to The Book of Confessions* (Louisville, KY: Westminster/ John Knox Press, 1985, 1991), pp. 148–149.

12. Ibid., p. 149.

13. Herman, *How the Scots Invented the Modern World*, pp. 19–20.

14. Ibid., p. 21.

15. Fitzroy MacLean, *Scotland: A Concise History* (New York: Thames & Hudson, 1983; rev. ed., 1993), p. 122.

16. Ibid.

17. *The Constitution of the Presbyterian Church (U.S.A.)*, Part I, *Book of Confessions* (Louisville, KY: The Office of the General Assembly, 1999), p. 118.

18. Ibid.

19. MacLean, *Scotland: A Concise History*, pp. 125–129.

20. *Book of Confessions*, p. 118.

21. Herman, *How the Scots Invented the Modern World*, p. 29.

22. Ibid., p. 30.

23. Ibid., p. 21.

24. MacLean, *Scotland: A Concise History*, p. 136.

25. Herman, *How the Scots Invented the Modern World*, pp. 30–31.

26. Albert R. Stuart, *Diminishing Distinctives: A Study of the Ingestion of the United Presbyterian Church of North America by the Presbyterian Church* in the United States of America (Rock Stream, NY: privately printed, 2000), p. 3.

27. Ibid., p. 4.

28. Herman, *How the Scots Invented the Modern World*, pp. 22–23.

29. Ibid., p. 32.

30. Ibid., p. 40.

31. Ibid., pp. 41–42.

32. Ibid., p. 42.

33. MacLean, *Scotland: A Concise History*, p. 150.

34. Herman, *How the Scots Invented the Modern World*, p. 35.

35. W. A. Speck, *A Concise History of Britain, 1707–1975* (Cambridge: Cambridge University Press, 1993), p. 18.

36. Ibid., p. 21.

37. Herman, *How the Scots Invented the Modern World*, p. 39.

38. Ibid.

39. Speck, *A Concise History of Britain*, p. 20.

40. Herman, *How the Scots Invented the Modern World*, p. 55.

41. Ibid.

42. MacLean, *Scotland: A Concise History*, p. 157.

43. Herman, *How the Scots Invented the Modern World*, p. 78.

44. Ibid., p. 79.

45. Ibid., p. 81.

46. Ibid., p. 82.

47. Ibid., p. 83.

48. Ibid., p. 136.

49. MacLean, *Scotland: A Concise History*, p. 169.

50. Ibid., p. 171.

51. Herman, *How the Scots Invented the Modern World*, p. 148.

52. Simon Schama, *A History of Britain, vol. 2, The Wars of the British, 1603–1776* (New York: Talk Miramax Books, Hyperion, 2001), pp. 378–380.

53. Herman, *How the Scots Invented the Modern World*, p. 149.

54. Ibid., pp. 150–151.

55. Ibid., p. 162.

56. Ibid., p. 157.

57. MacLean, *Scotland: A Concise History*, p. 193.

58. Ibid.

59. Ibid., p. 194.

Chapter 3
Arriving Immigrants

By 1720, . . . an estimated 90 percent of the free colonists had English, Scottish, or Ulster Scot ancestors. . . . By 1820, . . . this figure was still a round 80 percent; and of the remainder, roughly half consisted of German or Dutch stock—peoples whose history had been intertwined with that of England. As late as the 1830s, the free population of the United States was almost entirely Northern European and Protestant.
—William Strauss and Neil Howe[1]

The diversity of the ethnic population in the United States in the early twenty-first century is a relatively recent historical phenomenon, with the exception of Native Americans, who had populated the land for millennia. It is a fact that British immigrants dominated the development of North America for two centuries after Plymouth and Jamestown. It would be a disservice to the facts to consider "British immigrants" to be one homogeneous entity, for there were at least three major subsets with many variations within each—English, Scottish, and Ulster Scot. Each brought their unique cultural identity and made distinct contributions.

The business of the dominant culture in the colonies and the fledgling nation, both secular and religious, was conducted in an almost singular British vanilla flavor. It must be noted, however, that "African Americans—living side by side with colonists in substantial numbers and amounting to nearly a fifth of the population by 1776— were undoubtedly a greater defining influence on American society [than Native Americans at that time]. But the vast majority lived in four southern colonies where that influence was strictly controlled by the institution of slavery."[2] The reality of this institution set the North American agenda for more than two centuries to come.

To understand the context of the Union Presbytery Movement in the twentieth century and the dynamics of the Presbyterian Church (U.S.A.) in the twenty-first century, it is crucial to be able to trace and understand particularly the historical meandering migrations of the Scottish immigrants, in the context of other cultural migrations, for by their migrations they greatly contributed to the development of the dominant culture in North America.

Migrations

Civil upheaval and ecclesial conflict rooted in Scottish heritage shrouded the migration of Presbyterians to Northern Ireland and the New World. There was some correlation between the violent upheavals and the mass migrations of both winners and losers in the aftermath. These Scottish

---

migrations do not tell the whole story of immigration to North America from other parts of Europe and the rest of the world, but they certainly played a dominant role. Their influence shaped every aspect of life in the New World, whether political, social, economic, or religious.

Their cultural dynamics and traits followed the Scottish immigrants through the Revolutionary and antebellum periods, the tragedy of Civil War, the World Wars and the Great Depression, and through postwar boom to the brink of the turbulent 1960s and 1970s. How "Presbyterian" became manifest in various geographical areas is a story fraught with caricatures and stereotypes, theological and denominational differences, cultural and sociological contradictions. The effects are still residual in the twenty-first century. But first, what about migrating Scots in general?

It was not the simple moving of a set of people from one geographical location to another that was significant, although this was no small undertaking, considering the modes of transportation of the times. The significant thing was that, along with whatever meager possessions they could gather and carry with their tired and hungry bodies, they brought along their prejudices and limited worldviews, their wounded psyches shaken by political, social, economic, or religious losses they had suffered. They brought their culture and their ways, and some part of "home" to comfort and sustain them in their new place. They often sought out new places that reminded them of home. Some found such places; others did not.

Mort McMillan, after his visit to the MacMillan ancestral Kirk and Castle in Scotland, told of sharing photographs taken in Scotland with his father back home in Alabama. He asked his dad, "Where were these pictures taken?" Without having been told where, his father replied without hesitation, "At Old Scotland outside Monroeville [Alabama], around the church where we grew up." The McMillans and other Scots before them had found a place that even looked like home and settled there. Here they continued their heritage—hunting and fishing, making a living, raising their families and yes, glorifying God.[3]

From the beginning of their life in the New World, these newcomers of Scots descent were motivated by many dreams, some seeking ways to extract wealth from the New World's vast natural resources, some breathing the fresh air of freedom from oppression, some seeking simply to carve out their own individual destiny. These dreams took many forms.

The Scots—Lowlanders and Highlanders

Many people living in North America in the twenty-first century, who claim to be descendants of Scottish ancestors, do not know their direct lineage. They may simply refer to those ancestors as "Scots," giving the notion that they stem from one clearly defined "national stock." Some even hold to the belief that Scots were racially and ethnically identifiable in a biological sense. It is reasonable to believe that certain unique attitudes, customs, and moral standards do develop through the daily life of those living in a particular geographic location over long stretches of time, and that they form what might be described as "national character."[4] Such common human behaviors can be passed on from generation to generation, not through biological inheritance or as inherent racial attributes, but through experiential acculturation.[5]

Whatever the designation, it is true that the Scots ancestry that moderns dream about was anything but homogeneous. This can be illustrated best by examining the origins of two distinct groups of Scots—Lowlanders and Highlanders. The Lowlands were comprised of low lands in the south and east of Scotland. There were few imposing natural boundaries separating this region from England to the south, save for the River Tweed, or prohibiting relatively easy movement within. The Highlands were the craggy mountainous areas west and north of the Lowlands.

The Lowlanders were descendants of a biological mixture of many strains that occupied those Lowlands over a long period of time, and not in any sense a single, pure race. James G. Leyburn, writing in his classic social history of the Scotch-Irish, numbered the ancestry from many sources. The earliest three were the aborigines of the Stone Ages; the Gaels, a Celtic people; and the Britons, another Celtic group, who came from the south. After a lengthy period came the Romans, then the Teutonic Angles and Saxons. Ironically, another Celtic tribe, the Scots, invaded from Ireland. There was a sprinkling of Norse pirates who occasionally made it their home. The Normans came up from the south after William had conquered England; Flemish traders sometimes remained in the eastern Lowlands; and then came the Englishmen, a grand biological mixture in their own right, more predisposed to Teutonic than Celtic strains.[6]

Early signs of civilization, though progress was slow, began to develop in the Lowlands around the twelfth century. The clan system was in decline and was replaced by feudalism. Though the clans had all but vanished by the 1600s, certain vestiges of the clans remained in the form of fierce loyalty to one's overlord, and were demonstrated "in violent feuds, raids, and other acts of lawlessness."[7]

James Leyburn described the outward forces that shaped the character of the Lowlanders: "the comparative isolation from the great world, the backward agricultural methods, the centuries of conflict with the English, the particularism of a feudal system that undermined any

---

tendency toward constitutional institutions, the niggardly soil, the meager life of the mind." Still their hardy nature did not allow them to yield to these forces. The Scots Lowlander "early learned to fight back, to give blow for blow, and then, when he had done his best, to endure."[8]

A streak of stubbornness ran deep in the Scots "that made Calvinism, already congenial to the national spirit, even more rock-ribbed than its Genevan counterpart." Because violence prevailed and there was little rule of law, the meting out of justice was taken into one's own hands and was seen as an expression of common sense of a somewhat ruthless variety.[9]

The ancestral heritage of the Gaelic Highlanders was less complicated, deriving overwhelmingly from Celtic ancestry.[10] The Highlands was "the home of the clan and its kilts and tartans." It was perceived, for good reason, as "the home of wild tribesmen who kept the country in turmoil" until the Battle of Culloden changed all that in 1746. Religious life was filled with primitive superstition until the Presbyterian Church became the Kirk of Scotland. The kilt of that day was little more than a breechcloth, "a mark of bitter poverty and wildness," not the rarely used chieftain's classy regalia of "kilt, brooch, sporran, dirk, and bonnet"[11] so often proudly paraded to bagpipes in modern-day Presbyterian festivities.

Scotland would shake off being one of the poorest and most backward countries in Europe, progressing "from something near barbarism in 1600 to civilization." It would shed its primitive ways of the Middle Ages, swinging "from ignorance to a passion for education, from backwardness in most fields to daring achievement, from static traditionalism to dynamic individualism—and all of this in the space of two centuries."[12] At the same time, wave upon wave of ambitious emigrant Scots left their homeland in search of a better life, thereby depleting, though giving to others, its most precious human resource.

Ulster Plantation and the Scotch-Irish

Who were these emigrant Scots that so boldly pulled up stakes and moved out? Society in Scotland at this time was still feudal in nature, divided into classes into which a person entered by birth. Upward mobility from bottom to top was almost an unknown event. The peasants made up the bottom of the heap. To be labeled as a peasant did not imply being dull or stupid. In reality, many exhibited great thrift or ambition. The term "peasant" was simply a description of one's station in life and what one did. As a tiller of the rocky soil, the peasant did not have the privileges or carry the responsibilities of the nobility. These positive attributes gave many of them the "get up and go" necessary to leave their misery behind and strike out on a new and exciting venture, since they were not able to rise above their own class.[13]

Migrations tended from the beginning to take place in waves. Possibly the earliest account of the uprooting of the Scots from their homeland, mainly peasants and not the nobility, was the migration that began when James I decided in 1610 to designate thousands of acres of land in six counties of Northern Ireland for resettlement purposes, known as the Plantation of Ulster.

This migration consisted mainly of Lowlanders from Scotland and English from London. James's design for Ulster Plantation was "to civilize Ireland by settlers with British ways, not to confirm Irishmen in their intransigence."[14] These peasant settlers of Ulster Plantation were commonly referred to as Ulster Scots. Their descendants became known decades later in America as "Scots-Irish" or "Scotch-Irish," a term rarely used in Scotland or Ireland.[15] Some modern Americans of Scotch-Irish descent, who claim to be the progeny of Scots nobility, may be clinging to a fabricated mythic lineage that, if the truth be known, would produce a rude awakening.

James I felt that Highlanders did not exemplify "British ways," and therefore they were deliberately excluded. The effect of this exclusion was not total, since some Highlanders on their own crossed the short watery distance separating the Western Isles and part of Argyll from the coast of Ulster. They seemed to be more welcomed than the Lowland by the native Irish because they spoke Gaelic and sometimes were followers of Catholicism. Highlanders in their small numbers, however, did not play a significant role as progenitors of the Scotch-Irish.[16]

James I saw this migration of Lowlanders and English to Ulster as the solution to the Catholic problem of the day in Ireland. These waves of emigrants had to pledge their loyalty to James in the Oath of Supremacy. The Lowland Scots were the majority influence that shaped Protestant Ulster. These Ulster Scots were zealous spiritual keepers of the fundamentalist religious heritage bequeathed to them by John Knox. They were egalitarian to the core and championed the cause of education, especially for their clergy.[17]

For more than a century these Ulster Scots lived out their lives in Ulster. These were hard years and this new environment no doubt reshaped to a degree the Scottish character traits they brought with them. Heated debates have arisen over whether they intermarried with the native Irish or adopted their Catholic religion. A full exploration of this question is beyond the scope of the present work.[18]

What is significant is that those who emigrated from Scotland to Ulster Plantation, though they came with the intention of permanently settling with their families there, found that the conditions were little better than at home in Scotland. Some descendants of the original settlers, when the opportunity arose, moved on to America to better themselves with the same sense of adventure as their ancestors. This was even more risky than coming to Ulster in the first place. In Ulster they had proved very adaptable, a dominant trait of the Ulster Scots. It was matched by another trait—there were simply "points on which they would not compromise."[19] Both traits would not go unnoticed in the New World.

The New World

James I also sent other emigrant waves directly from Scotland across the Atlantic to the New World. Some navigated into Chesapeake Bay and settled the James River region. The Virginia Company that founded Jamestown in 1607 was within a few years exporting tobacco. It sent out a party to Plymouth in 1620 to establish another settlement there. The motivation for emigration to the Americas at this time was the result of private, not governmental, efforts and was fueled by "religious dissent and anti-Hispanism, the quest for profit, and the agricultural depression at home."[20]

Others went farther north to found the desolate rocky colony of Nova Scotia. This venture was to fail. But Scottish merchants were persistent. In 1684 Glasgow, entrepreneurs advertised for volunteers to go to "Province of New-east-Jersey in America" to enjoy the fruits of an abundant life. But because the English merchants controlled the colonies and closed them to open competition, the Scots resorted to smuggling.[21] The Killing Time and military occupation in the Lowlands by the British between 1667 and 1680 engendered great animosity in Lowland Scots. Although they harbored this great hatred for London, the English would not outdo them. Fueled by this conflict and drawn by the economic rewards of the New World, Lowland Scots began to make their presence felt as early as the 1680s in all areas of colonial life, especially following the Glorious Revolution in 1688. This strong influence in the areas of commerce, government, education, and religious life continued to grow, well into the eighteenth century.[22]

At the close of the seventeenth century, some of the attempts to establish Scottish colonies in the New World to compete with the powerful London merchants failed in a relatively short time. However, this did not stymie the Scots' spirit in the long term. The stakes were too high. Though initially they were not able to establish a legal foothold in the New World, they eventually persevered and survived. Finally, smuggling gave way to more honorable trades and their legal presence was assured.

The Act of Union in 1707 created serious discontent among the Lowlanders who had opposed it. It reached a boiling point in 1713, when the motion to repeal the Union was defeated by four votes. It is not insignificant that in that same year, Ulster Scots came to Worcester, Massachusetts, to serve as Indian fighters. They created a fiercely guarded boundary between the English settlers and the "savage wilderness" beyond. Many had come as indentured servants, but, not being inclined to obedience to any authority, did not remain servants for long.[23]

The Great Scotch-Irish Migrations

Natural disaster struck at home in 1717 when the harvest failed. This triggered the first of five great waves of Scotch-Irish emigrants between 1717 and 1775 with fewer numbers in between.[24] Leyburn contends that after the American Revolution, "the Scotch-Irish were no longer a separate national stock, but were Americans." The farther they had moved into the frontier, the less they considered themselves anything but Americans. After the United States was established, little attention was paid to those immigrants, as a group, from Ulster.[25] But in 1717 it was a different story.

People were starving and emigration seemed to be the only way out. It was a treacherous trip. Many perished in the harsh conditions of the sailing ships. This first wave of Ulster Scots arrived in Philadelphia to the great shock of resident Quakers. This was the beginning of the great hordes of Scotch-Irish who streamed through the middle colonies and found their way "deep into the three great river valleys and mountain ridges: up the Delaware Valley into southeastern Pennsylvania; south across the Potomac into the Shenandoah Valley, and then even farther south, beyond the Piedmont into the Carolinas."[26]

The emigrants brought with them vestiges of their particular Presbyterian heritage. The Westminster Standards, adopted almost a century before for use in the Scottish kirk, "came to New England with the Puritans (Independents) and to the Middle Atlantic states with the Scotch-Irish Presbyterians. In 1729, the standards were adopted as the confessional position of the newly organized Presbyterian Synod in the colonies."[27] Covenanters brought to the North American continent their own sentiments about the tumultuous events that produced the Westminster Standards. All was not permanently resolved by the mere adoption of these Standards, either originally in 1648 or in 1729. They would prove to be the focus of great heated theological battles throughout the nineteenth and the twentieth, and even into the twenty-first century.

Lowlanders came to America. Scotch-Irish came to America. And finally Highlanders were the last to come. The Highlanders were fleeing the aftermath of the defeat at Culloden in 1746. Many found their way to Cape Fear River in North Carolina. The topography was nothing like the Highlands of home. It consisted of "flat, low-lying, humid marshes, red clay soil with scrub-pine forests; but the land was cheap and available, and the Highlanders carved out farms for themselves and their families."[28]

West and South

The eastern seaboard could not for long contain the waves of emigrants that landed on its shores. Emigrants who came directly from Scotland and England tended to stay settled along the Tidewater and seaboard, fulfilling the role of plantation master and merchant chiefs. The restlessness of the Scotch-Irish propelled them west and south toward new frontiers, deep into Central Appalachia. They sought new land as a stage on which to parade their rugged individualism. Some displayed the disdain for Episcopalians and their colonial taxes for the established Anglican Church. Many Scotch-Irish showed no qualms about commandeering cultivable land from Catholics, a practice they had learned in the colonization of Ireland. Native Americans were no barriers to them either. They thrived on a good fight, a precursor of what they thought it took to win the American West.[29]

They portaged the Alleghenies, followed the rivers through Western Pennsylvania and traveled down the Ohio, joined those coming from the New and Kanawha Rivers, to the wide Missouri, and proceeding on down the Mississippi to New Orleans. Eventually they found their way to the Northwest, following Lewis and Clark. They floated the Clinch and Tennessee Rivers into Tennessee and the mid-South. Some cut through the Cumberland Gap on buffalo trails into Kentucky to meet up with those who had floated the Ohio. Many settled along these byways, while others pressed on.

They traveled inland from the East Coast, up the Santee and Catawba Rivers into North Carolina. They moved into the interior of South Carolina along the Congeree. By the end of the eighteenth century they had established themselves farther down in Georgia along the Savannah River. These became the jumping-off places to travel across land on Native American trails into Alabama and Mississippi into the Old Southwest.

Life on the frontier was not all that free from conflict. Guns and knives were required accessories, and young boys were trained to use them to defend the honor of self and family. Feuds that started in the Highlands of Scotland often were continued here. The legendary battles between the Hatfields and McCoys in the hills of Kentucky and West Virginia were reminiscent of the clashes between the Campbells and MacDonalds in the Highlands in Scotland.[30] Justice in this raw culture was many times meted out by vigilantes and Regulators, much in the style used in the Scots Borders at home. One such vigilante, Captain William Lynch, lent his name to a harsh form of frontier justice known as "lynching."[31]

Lynching would be employed a century later by night riders in hooded sheets claiming a twisted legacy of clan. Six young Confederate veterans founded a social club after the Civil War ended. These well-educated, relatively affluent officers chose a Greek word, *kuklos,* meaning "circle," for the name of their club. All being of Scotch-Irish decent, they added the familiar reality of "clan" to the name, changing the first letter to match letters in the Greek word.[32] What had started out as a club for their own amusement turned ugly over time as the original intent was lost and a more violent strand of Scotch-Irish comrades and others appropriated the name.

Revolution

But before all this was complete, there was a different kind of migration. Once again the call to arms came in the name of independence in the mid-1770s. It created a dilemma for Scots Highlanders, Lowlanders, and Scotch-Irish alike. They were again faced with a decision about loyalty or disloyalty to the Crown. Revolution was in the air and Scots thrived on it, regardless of loyalties.

Highlanders that had recently arrived tended to follow the Crown in the American Revolution. Two veterans from opposing sides at the battle of Culloden rallied Highland immigrants from the Mohawk Valley of New York to the British cause.[33] The wail of bagpipes, played by kilted Highlanders, escorted the Redcoats into battle against the frontiersmen in buckskins. The Scotch-Irish, who had proved themselves in fights from "the Indian trouble" were "rough, ingenious, adaptable, ready to endure hardship" when time came for many to join the War for Independence on the American side.[34]

Two and a half decades after the War of Independence was fought and won, one more wave of Highlanders came to America. The Clearances changed the face of the Highlands forever. In the areas where the land could not sustain the population, there were no good choices for those who wanted to stay. The choices were emigration or starvation. "In the first three years of the nineteenth century, more than ten thousand people left for Nova Scotia and Canada; by the 1820s it was twenty thousand a year, most from the Western Highlands."[35]

Other Migrants

The migrations of Scots, be it from rural to urban Scotland, through Ulster, or across the great Atlantic Ocean to the New World, were not the only migrations during the seventeenth through nineteenth centuries that impacted Protestantism in North America. Some were voluntary migrations while others were involuntary. Migrants of other Reformed traditions from the continent became part of the religious mixing pot—emigrants from the Netherlands, France, Italy, Germany, Switzerland, and other countries in eastern Europe. They were Dutch Reformed, Mennonites, Huguenots, Waldensians, Brethren, Moravians, Hutterites, and others.

Other migrations in North America, though not originally of Christian persuasion, were involuntary. They had a profound effect on Protestantism and Presbyterianism in North America. Sometimes the involuntary immigrants were ignored or discounted as if they did not exist or were invisible at best. Yet the presence of these involuntary immigrants was a factor that profoundly shaped the civil and ecclesial fabric of life on this continent throughout all ensuing centuries.

The first of a long stream of Africans were brought in 1619 to the Tidewater plantations in Virginia to work the manual economic engines of the day. "[T]hey were doubtless sold by the Dutch captain as slaves, but were probably bought by the Virginians as indentured laborers, since it was to be more than forty years before slavery would be defined in Virginia."[36] Fellow Africans sold these Africans into slavery for years to foreign slave traders. Their migration did not end with their coming to this country, but continued involuntarily on the trading blocks. In time they migrated voluntarily along the dangerous underground railroads of the nineteenth century and along the above-ground railroads of the twentieth century to the industrial cities of the North.

The other involuntary migrations were not of a people that had emigrated from another land. Those who were not initially slaughtered were uprooted and relocated from their homeland along many a "trail of tears." These were Native Americans, seen as impediments to the progressive expansion of the dreams of new frontiers in the hearts of European immigrants. Their once proud and advanced civilizations were violently treated and almost totally annihilated, with the remnant of their people being constricted to humiliating and debilitating reservations lasting into the twenty-first century.

The heritage of these involuntary migrants, who were once discounted and deemed invisible, could no longer be ignored. New immigrants arriving in the late twentieth and early twenty-first centuries challenged the agendas of these involuntary migrants. The hard-won opportunities of the 1960s civil rights movement for native-born black African Americans held little emotional currency for these new immigrants from Sudan, Kenya, Ethiopia, Latin America, and the Caribbean who share the same skin color. Add the immigrants from Asia, the Indian subcontinent, the Middle East, and Eastern Europe, along with Hispanic immigrants over many years, and the results of refugee relocation as a justice concern. Attempting to understand the impact of migrations to North America then takes on a whole new dimension in the twenty-first century.

This new dimension is critically important to explore and must not be ignored. But this is another story yet to be told. It is beyond the scope of this study, which focuses on tracing how the meandering migration of Scots brought a heritage to North America that is foundational in understanding the dynamics of the Presbyterian Church (U.S.A.) in the twenty-first century. Clearly there were winners and losers in all the migrations. The full consequence of these migrations is still to come.

The Legacy

Social customs and dynamics of all kinds die hard even in the face of legislation or wars to change them to the contrary. Migrations of people—triggered by ecclesiastical schisms, shifts in political and economic structures, or natural disasters—become carriers of customs and worldviews forward to future generations as if they were some form of social DNA. Issues that once were resolved in seemingly decisive watershed moments were not truly resolved, but came back in conflicted exchange once more in another time and place.

This cameo recitation of examples of the defining moments in British and Scottish history begins to make evident, not a linear progression of history, but a circular pattern. What goes around comes around. What then was the legacy of this rich and tumultuous Scottish heritage brought to North America by these meandering Scots migrants? What were some of the dynamics and traits of this legacy?

The first trait of this legacy was the foundational role theology played in the Scottish heritage, though sometimes it got lost in the heat of battle. Theology and religious beliefs were often cast in terms of absolute certainty or flexibility. For some, the free exchange of ideas, the freedom to express one's opinions, meant nothing. Austere religious dogma, with static visions of faith and culture, sometimes known as Old Light, was the order of the day for them. The Westminster Confession was their cornerstone. For others, flexibility, tolerance, and rational restraint were everything. They basked in the progressive vision of practical New Light applications of faith to daily life guided by continual revelations of the Holy Spirit. Old Light/New Light debates accompanied the migrants to the New World. These perspectives were institutionalized and perpetuated. Later versions of these debates were manifest in the great theological controversies of the nineteenth, twentieth, and emerging twenty-first centuries.

The second trait of this legacy was a deep commitment to providing education for everyone. The small parish schools ignited the broad-based impetus for the Scottish Enlightenment. The intellectual centers of Aberdeen, Edinburgh, and Glasgow provided the theoretical and practical knowledge base that capitalized on the native Scottish inventiveness and imagination. The enlightenment propelled this feudal nation into a prominent place of leadership among the nations of the world in all walks of life.

The influence of enlightened Scottish emigrants to the New World determined the direction taken there in the realms of commerce, industry, the military, law, government, education, and religion. New centers of learning were formed in colleges and secondary schools. Presbyterians established schools to educate their clergy.

The development of education fell behind for a while as the frontier of the New World was pushed westward across the Alleghenies. A significant number of Scotch-Irish had an aversion to formal education. Their thought processes were more concrete than abstract. Their customs and values were handed down by word of mouth, not in the written forms of the academy. Presbyterians brought mission schools to remote areas of the country where this oral culture prevailed, in order to prepare the populace to embrace its form of religion.

The ability to provide enough educated clergy to administer the sacraments in proper Presbyterian order was one spark in the Old School/New School controversy. Attempts to meet this clergy shortage sprang up in the sacramental-harvest festivals like those at the Cane Ridge. Church divisions ensued and new frontier churches were formed over the fault lines of these debates. In later decades the evolution of Cumberland Presbyterian churches was a further example of this development. In the latter part of the twentieth century, the emergence of commissioned lay pastors was an outgrowth of the same long-term issues. Yet, in all of this, education was a dominant trait brought by these Scottish immigrants to the New World.

The third trait of this legacy was the competing or overlapping of the roles of church and state. The political and social context of the times often informed the ecclesial directions of the church as well as theology. In those times the people went to great lengths to define who would rule the state, who would rule the church, and how the two would relate. At times the state was the church and the church was the state, with no boundaries between the two.

When separate lines between church and state seemed to become clear, and the role of each was defined, fractures reoccurred in each and the lines blurred once more. Divisions in the church over how its polity would be ordered resulted in not one, but three forms— episcopal, representative, and congregational. In the state, when the divine right of kings was all but dead, short-lived resurgent efforts were advanced for its restoration. The upshot was the creation of a delicate balance between the monarchy and Parliament. For both church and state, government by the consent of the governed became the rule. Boundaries between church and state were constitutionally set in the founding of the new nation across the Atlantic, eliciting continual heated debate over the exact interpretation and role of religion in civil affairs.

The fourth trait of this legacy was the divergent views on how a body of people could best be arranged for social, economic, political, and religious structures of corporate life. For some the most favorable expression was through the family or clan, with its clear feudal structure that was closely bonded to the land. As the shift from rural to urban settings took place, a wider overarching framework, ordering life to fit new economic realities, was required. The growth of corporate industries beyond the scope of family cottage industries brought on the development of newer complex structures to manage them. Power shifted from the clan chieftains' hands to emerging regional and national centers of power.

Though the power shifted, the fiercely independent, stubborn nature of the Scots was preserved in the migration across the Atlantic. For some it was expressed in how they organized their grand entrepreneurial industrial ventures in budding urban areas. Their view of how things got accomplished was reflected in how they best saw their civil and religious government structured. This germinated from the embryonic seeds of nationalism sown after Hastings.

For others, family and place were deeply ingrained in their spirits. No matter how often they followed their restlessness, family and place were paramount in their minds. Property was a source of identity. Their strong antiauthoritarian streak and a sense of local autonomy governed their patterns of migration—where they went and how they structured all aspects of their lives. Those of this persuasion tended to gravitate toward isolated rural areas where land was cheap and plentiful.

The fifth trait of this legacy was the role that the concept of union played throughout certain periods of this Scottish history in attempts to pull together groups of people in various religious or civil configurations. How union was perceived, and the consequences of that perception—both were critical to the success or failure of attempted configurations. This was particularly true of the Union of 1707. The problems between Scotland and England were at the breaking point and union seemed to be the solution. This was not the result of a long healthy courtship between equals, even though it was characterized this way. It was a classic example of what happens in a so-called "union" when one entity is much larger than the other.

The reality was that the smaller body felt that it was being swallowed up by the larger body. Whether or not this was true, it was an emotional reality. This seemed to be more descriptive of what happens in a "merger," when the larger body picks the smaller body clean of its good parts and discards the rest on a figurative dump heap. Dreams for union were rarely fulfilled when it was approached as a merger of this sort. Some could care less about union because they saw this as a form of aristocratic control that they despised. Migrants, winners and losers alike, brought their scars of understanding union-merger in this way to the New World and experienced its consequences on occasion. The flaws of union as a solution nonetheless became institutionalized and perpetuated.

The sixth trait of this legacy was the presence of the win-lose phenomenon. There were winners and losers in all aspects of life in those defining moments in Scottish history, whether secular or sacred. Winners, in their overconfidence, developed myopic visions of what now might be, making their victories Pyrrhic. The prize won was, upon further reflection, not what it seemed to be. Losers, no matter how noble they were in defeat, often had a sour taste in their mouths. Losing by close votes especially fostered dreams of what might have been and engendered smoldering feelings of revenge. And before long, combatants regrouped to fight once more. What was started at home in Scotland was continued by subsequent generations on North American soil, a virtual repeat run at lost causes. Original intent often was forgotten, but the flaws of win-lose nonetheless became institutionalized and perpetuated. Winning and losing were never completely fulfilling in themselves.

The seventh trait of this legacy was a burning desire for freedom—freedom of religion, freedom of speech, freedom to live one's life according to the dictates of one's conscience, freedom to choose who would govern. The litany goes on and on. The harsh conditions under which the Scots lived engendered a fiercely independent spirit that often erupted in violence. Even so, the combination of this burning desire for freedom with this fiercely independent spirit translated into a belief that all forms of human oppression must be challenged.

Thus a strong antislavery sentiment was generated. But not all Scottish emigrants brought these sentiments to the New World. Some who had advocated making Scottish peasants slaves at home, or engaged in transporting indentured servants to the New World, no doubt had little qualms in promoting the slave trade as a reliable source of cheap labor for the new, burgeoning plantations. Freedom was "for me and my kind."

As the force of these two views of freedom competed for attention in the New World, the stage was set for the most devastating war ever fought on this continent. The Civil War ripped the political and social fabric of the Republic asunder. It robbed the nation of an entire generation of the flower of its youth. The wounds inflicted on its people and society by this Civil War were still very much evident well beyond the national crises of the Great Depression and World War II. Some residual effects from the Civil War linger, almost lost in the growing global crises of the twenty-first century.

In summary, the legacy that emerged from the Scots, English, and Scots-Irish migrations did not produce a singular definition for each identified trait, but rather the traits in their extremes were characterized by contrary dichotomies. *Theology* was characterized either by static dogma or flexible evolving revelations. *Education* was championed either by the erudite abstractions of academia or through the concrete, everyday common sense of oral tradition. *Church and state* were seen as either having coterminous boundaries or as totally separate in their spheres of influence. *Social, economic, political, and religious structures* were arranged either from treetop national views or from grassroots, local autonomy perspectives. *Union*, as a resolution to secular or sacred structural problems, was approached through the eyes of either unionists or seceders. *Win-lose* was the decision-making mode of choice in verbal conflicts and violent wars, often with little attention paid to the long-term unresolved consequences or what happened to the participants in the process. *Freedom* for everyone was forged in the epic crucible of the Civil War that pitted abolitionist against slaveholder.

The traits of this legacy have left their fingerprints all over the Union Presbytery Movement in the twentieth century and the Presbyterian Church (U.S.A.) in the twenty-first century. Clearly there were winners and losers in this legacy. Again, the full consequences of the contributions and flaws of this legacy would be a long time coming.

Notes

1. William Strauss and Neil Howe, *The Fourth Turning: An American Prophecy* (New York: Broadway Books, 1997), p. 94.

2. Ibid.

3. From an unrecorded personal conversation with the author. Also, McMillan's Presbyterian and Scottish heritage was confirmed in a postcard from this same visit to the old castle and church of the MacMillans that he sent the author in July of 1976; He described a Celtic cross with a hunting scene on one side in the graveyard. Mort was an avid turkey hunter. He also mentioned seeing some "Great Trains!" in the personal collection of William G. McAtee.

4. Leyburn, *The Scotch-Irish: A Social History*, p. 67.

5. Ibid., p. 65.

6. Ibid., pp. 65–66.

7. Ibid., p. xvi.

8. Ibid., p. 67.

9. Ibid., p. 68.

10. Ibid., p. 65.

11. Ibid., pp. xvi–xvii.

12. Ibid., p. xv.

13. Ibid., p. xiv.

14. Ibid., p. xvii.

15. Ibid., p. xi.

16. Ibid., p. xvii.

17. Herman, *How the Scots Invented the Modern World*, p. 65.

18. See Leyburn, *The Scotch-Irish: A Social History*, part II, "The Scots in Ireland," for further discussion.

19. Ibid., p. 153.

20. John Morrill, ed., *The Oxford Illustrated History of Tudor and Stuart Britain*, "Britain and the World under the Stuarts," by John Reeve, p. 418.

21. Herman, *How the Scots Invented the Modern World*, p. 67.

22. Ibid., p. 231.

23. Ibid.

24. See Leyburn, *The Scotch-Irish: A Social History*, pp. 179–183, for estimates on the number of emigrants during these years.

25. Ibid., p. vi.

26. Herman, *How the Scots Invented the Modern World*, p. 233.

27. *The Constitution of the Presbyterian Church (U.S.A.)*, Part I, *The Book of Confessions*, p. 118.

28. Herman, *How the Scots Invented the Modern World*, p. 231.

29. Ibid., p. 233.

30. Ibid., pp. 236–237.

31. Ibid., p. 237.

32. Michael and Judy Ann Newton, *Ku Klux Klan: An Encyclopedia* (New York: Garland Publishing, 1991), p. vii.

33. Herman, *How the Scots Invented the Modern World*, p. 249.

34. Leyburn, *The Scotch-Irish: A Social History*, p. 230.

35. Herman, *How the Scots Invented the Modern World*, p. 304.

36. James McBride Dabbs, *Haunted by God* (Richmond, VA: John Knox Press, 1972), p. 41.

Chapter 4
Presbyterians in North America

[T]hat first law of ecology: We can never do just one thing. Action, or inaction, has consequences: both benign and terrible, trivial and important, intended and unintended. We are born into a web of life that both precedes and follows us. Some of it is understood and much of it isn't. But we are each simultaneously part of the picture and one of the painters. Neutrality is not an option. Mindlessness is, but neutrality isn't.
—Maurice Telleen[1]

The Rev. Jin S. Kim, president of the evangelical group Presbyterians for Renewal, in a sermon during a worship service at the 216th General Assembly in June of 2004, reminded the body that "the Korean Presbyterian Church [a relative latecomer in Korea] is sometimes seen by U.S. Presbyterians as 'a youthful upstart.' " Meanwhile, he said, 'Scotland is seen as the fount of pure Presbyterianism.' " He went on to chide "U.S. and European Christians for their tendency to regard Asian and African churches as 'less worthy' because they are products of Western missionary efforts."[2] Such a critique is well founded.

In future studies, attention must be paid to those recent heritages that have sprung up as a result of the missionary efforts around the world by the Western Presbyterian cultures, primarily from Scotland and North America. However, this study is limited to the Presbyterian heritage that was brought to the New World by the dominant British migration. The profound impact that Scottish heritage has had cannot be lightly overlooked, because it is foundational for understanding Presbyterianism everywhere, dominant or missional.

It is not enough to note that the British migration landed on the shores of North America, crossed the mountain ranges, floated the rivers, traced the buffalo trails to an ever-expanding frontier, transmitting the traits of the English and Scottish heritage. Though this is the case, a discussion of where and how this worked out specifically for Presbyterians in the general context of New World life is necessary for understanding the scope and significance of the Union Presbytery Movement. The particular geographic location where Presbyterians settled, and its historical and sociological setting, along with the traits of their immigrant legacy, gave definition to who these people became.

It was the assumption of this study that the Union Presbytery Movement was basically a Southern phenomenon in origin, though it certainly did not preclude Northern involvement as well. The use of this description may have been immediately objectionable and limiting to some. The difference between Southern and Northern involvement may have been evident only in scope and sense of urgency. The difference may be much deeper than this.

There was something inherently different in the way persons from different regions of the country behaved and how they viewed the political structures and fashioned the social organizations in which they lived. Evidence for this was borne out when close attention was given to the background of the key participants in the Movement.

Once these assumptions were recognized as having validity, it was clear that there was no way to avoid the dominance that the institution of slavery and the Civil War had on this definition of Presbyterians. The Civil War was the catastrophic test of the Republic that determined whether it would survive in this New World. The South was the largest geographic region in the country that experienced, for good or ill, the lost cause of war. Volumes have been written about the history of slavery and the Civil War. It is not in the purview of this study to recount lengthy details of this history, but it is important to focus on some aspects of it, along with the immigrant legacy, in order to outline the broad "web of life" in which the Union Presbytery Movement was birthed.

The Irony of Cultures

Presbyterians followed the earliest and subsequent migration patterns of the British immigrants. Over the decades a significant Presbyterian presence was felt from Philadelphia to the Tidewater of Virginia. They came down the Shenandoah Valley in Virginia into the Piedmont in Mecklenburg County, North Carolina. They filled the Susquehanna Valley and the three rivers area at Pittsburgh. They inhabited the coastal plains and sand hills of the Carolinas and Georgia. The frontier called and they went down the Ohio and crossed the Cumberland Gap to "Kaintuck" and beyond to Missouri. Overland they left the Mid-Atlantic east coast to travel the piney woods and the black belt of Alabama and Mississippi. They crossed Tennessee into the Louisiana Purchase and on to the Mexican territories of the Southwest. In time the rivers and buffalo traces gave way to railroads that maintained their connection from one place to another.

At first glance, a casual observer might be tempted to assume that Presbyterians were all-alike-Presbyterian no matter where they were across the wide landscape of the New World. But this was not the case. One need only remember the contrary dichotomies of the traits that characterized the legacy of their Scottish heritage to realize that this could not possibly be so. Couple this with the variously difficult demands of the diverse physical environments where they landed, and it is no wonder that great differences became evident.

James McBride Dabbs, in *Haunted by God*, made the case that there is basically one American culture derived originally from

European antecedents. He also held that in the South there was distinct variance to this dominant culture. His contention was that this distinction emerged as early as 1607 with the founding of the Virginia settlement in Jamestown. This was very distinct from "the landings at Plymouth in 1620, and the more important landing at Massachusetts Bay in 1630." Dabbs, in his analysis, went on to point out that "from the beginning, the two groups, north and south, under the influence of religious ideas, of land and weather, and of the slow effect of time, became increasingly different for some three centuries."[3]

Though some Puritans settled in the South, the dominant culture in early New England was Puritan, and the dominant culture in the South was non-Puritan. This distinction was there, according to Dabbs, long before the Scotch-Irish came in droves to the South in the eighteenth century.[4]

Sometimes the groups exhibited the legacy traits from their Scottish and British heritage in similar ways. More often they were vastly different in behavior. One thing they both cherished was the call of the wide-open spaces of the New World that was such a contrast to the social, political, and religious confinements of the Old World.

People of the Southern non-Puritan culture tended to hold on to the past, though they clamored for individual freedom from Old World constraints. They sought out isolated settlements and were not concerned with improving the social order or planning for the future. They believed that if individuals were given the opportunity to express their freedom, social arrangements would emerge. Their strong affinity for place found expression in their plantations, which in a way became new versions of the Old World landed gentry estates. Family and those to whom one was related were paramount in their lives. Their religious temperament made them one with the world about them.[5]

The Northern Puritan culture tended to want to forget the past. They named their place "new" England. They wanted to move away from the Old World constrictions on abstract ideas and find ways to express those ideas concretely in the New World. Their religious convictions made them greatly suspicious of the world about them and they were forever skeptical of what it did to them. They withdrew into towns and carved urban centers out of the wilderness. They ordered their lives on the foundations of common consent for the common good.[6]

The irony of these valid cultural descriptions was that they were contradictory in reality in many ways. The Puritan towns (those that later became urban centers) of the North started out to be communities of faith that were supposed to conquer and convert the wicked wilderness into outposts of God's kingdom on earth. But in doing so, because of the great natural resources available and their industrious ingenuity, the conquerors became enormously wealthy over the centuries. "[T]he saints became Yankees; the individualism of their religion found expression in the individualism of their economic life. The structures built originally to keep men in the service of God became structures chiefly occupied with bringing wealth to the few who controlled them."[7]

By the same token the more subtle irony was that an extraordinary sense of community grew out of the isolated, selfish "places" of the South. Dabbs contends that this was a result of the fact that individuals experienced their relationships, not simply through bloodlines, but through institutions. "Of these [institutions], the plantation was probably the most important; the strength of the family and the importance of race rested mainly upon the plantation." He goes on to say that "perhaps this is the basic paradox of the South: that an institution created mainly for exploitation should have become, by the grace of God, we would say, one of the key institutions in creating a culture with a considerable degree of humanity."[8]

Understanding this paradox is almost impossible from the faraway perspective of the twenty-first century, as it was too in the 1960s. Dabbs observed, "To admit that the plantation was probably the most important institution in the South is for many people today to admit that nothing worthwhile was created in the South."[9]

Yet, to understand the Union Presbytery Movement and the Presbyterian Church (U.S.A.), it must be acknowledged that no greater factor accentuated the differences between Northern and Southern cultures than the institution of slavery. Animosity and ambiguity over this institution, and subsequent racism, has divided and reshaped Presbyterians from revolutionary colonial times until well into the twenty-first century.[10]

The Great Awakening

To characterize Presbyterianism as being monolithic in nature during the more than three centuries that it has been in North America is certainly inaccurate and misleading. It would also be a mistake to think that the reunion of the denominations in 1983 was the act of putting two Presbyterian bodies back together that had been divided at the time of the Civil War. The truth of the matter is that, at any one given point in time, there have been more than two denominations at play in the great dividing or healing moments of Presbyterian history, though two may have appeared to be dominant.

In the early 1700s the religious piety that marked former decades was in decline. By the 1730s the Great Awakening jump-started a renewed religious fervor. The austere religious practices of the elite were supplanted with the demonstrative emotional revivalism of the masses. The Great Awakening "stimulated moral earnestness, missionary zeal, philanthropy, cooperation across denominational lines, and the founding of educational institutions. It gave new value and confidence to the average man and so contributed to the development of democracy in America. It strengthened the nonestablished churches more than the established, and so helped to prepare for religious freedom."[11]

Tension began to grow between the contrary religious, educational, and social traits that were inherited from the Scottish legacy. Nowhere was this better seen than in the split the church experienced in 1741 in the aftermath of the Great Awakening. At stake was the clash between the Old Light theological positions of the Synod of Philadelphia, with its demands for an educated clergy in the strict Calvinistic mode and the more revivalistic fervor of the New Light Synod of New York. This did not last long, for a reunion was forged in 1758 on the basis of the Westminster Standards. Following lengthy conversations a meeting of the minds was reached "by reuniting on a platform of mutual concessions, [which] tacitly acknowledged the futility and unwisdom of having divided."[12]

In 1753 both the Burgher Synod and the Anti-Burgher Synod in Scotland sent missionaries to the New World. They settled among the Scots-Irish immigrants in the Susquehanna Valley in Pennsylvania. For some reason they did not continue the theological battles from home with the same intensity.[13]

Over the next century various "Associate" and "Reformed" Seceder denominations came into being, merged, and changed among these settlers. The two most prominent were the Associate Presbyterian (AP) and the Associate Reformed Presbyterian (ARP) denominations. One of the earliest mergers of such groups came on the home mission fields in Oregon. Both communions in this area were geographically and ideologically remote from other Seceders in the eastern states. Their numbers and resources were scant. The debates over testimonial issues back East were irrelevant to their work among the Native Americans. This was especially true of old Scots controversies that were totally invalid in the American context. In the 1840s the United Presbyterian Church of Oregon was created from the Associate and Associate Reformed synods.[14]

Beginning in 1842, a long series of conversations began among the three main Seceder denominations. Representatives from the Reformed Presbyterian Church of North America (RPCNA), not being able to agree on the "nature, meaning and full extent of public covenanting," withdrew from the discussions. By 1858, most Seceder denominations were united to form the United Presbyterian Church of North America (UPCNA or UPNA). All were a part of this union except one New England Presbytery and the Synod of South Carolina that had withdrawn from the main body in the mid-1830s.[15]

This new denomination was built on the foundation of Scripture, the Westminster Standards, and the "Articles of Testimony." The "Articles" contained strict clauses against slaveholding, joining secret societies, observing open communion with those not agreeing to the "Articles," and singing songs in worship except those inspired by the book of Psalms. Strict adherence to this foundation was exacted from members in good standing by the signing of a public covenant.[16]

Crossing New Frontiers

The new PCUSA Synod of New York and Philadelphia took up the challenge of continuing the missionary work begun by the New Light Presbytery of Hanover in the south and the west. It established new mission points and presbyteries in and across the Alleghenies with a few ordained clergy. The general context in which this took place was punctuated with the presence of slavery and the displacement of Native Americans.

In 1775 a group of Presbyterian elders by the name of McAfee from Virginia, came up the Salt River in central Kentucky looking for land. They surveyed six-hundred-acre plats and returned to Virginia to get their families. Their return to Kentucky was interrupted because they stayed home to fight in the American Revolution. Upon their return they established New Providence Presbyterian Church in 1784, naming it after their home church in Virginia. Later, Robert Livingston McAfee would lead another contingent of Presbyterians to Missouri and found yet another New Providence Presbyterian Church there (11-14).

Even though the Declaration of Independence declared that it was self-evident "that all men are created equal," it was obvious that African slaves were not included. Native Americans were rarely considered other than as objects of evangelism. A few Presbyterian ministers, such as David Rice, opposed slavery in no uncertain terms. He publicly denounced slavery as a sin, and for this was forced to leave Virginia for the new frontier in Kentucky.[17] He would not be the last pastor to have to leave a congregation because of conviction of the wrongness of slavery and racism.

David Rice arrived in Kentucky in the early 1780s and became known as the father of Presbyterianism in Kentucky. Hanover Presbytery in Virginia, a member of the Synod of New York and Philadelphia, worked with Rice, and with New Providence, Danville, Mt. Zion (later First, Lexington), and Old Paint Lick Presbyterian

Churches, to found the Presbytery of Transylvania on October 17, 1786. This was the first presbytery "across the woods" west of the Allegheny Mountains.[18]

Along with all the trials of the new frontier life, including attacks from Native American tribes from across the Ohio River reaching into what had been their hunting grounds in Kentucky, Rice faced many challenges of establishing new churches and training pastors to serve them. The controversy over slavery, which initiated Rice's departure from Virginia, followed him to Kentucky. In eleven short years the Presbytery of Transylvania was embroiled with the question of whether slavery was a moral evil. They responded to that in the affirmative. But they left unanswered the question of whether a slaveholder was guilty of moral evil. Their answer of record was, "[R]esolved that the question now before presbytery is of so much importance that the consideration of it be put off till a future day."[19] Whether that question was ever taken from the table, may not be as significant as the fact that the struggle to answer that question, and the overarching question of slavery, raged for decades across the Border States and every geographic location where Presbyterians lived.

The Coming Storm

During the period from 1780 to the mid-1830s several things happened to tip the balance in the antislavery/slavery debate. Several Northern states passed legislation abolishing slavery while Southern states increased their anti-abolitionist opposition. Ineffective legal efforts were made to stop the slave trade, and some proposed creating colonies in Africa for freed African Americans. As the move toward freedom for slaves gained momentum, slave rebellions increased, triggering more abusive treatment of slaves in slaveholding states. "The most famous of all the insurrections was that of Nat Turner in Virginia, in 1831."[20]

The Presbyterian Church during this same period was also faced with great evangelistic challenges from the frontier's westward movement. It was by far the strongest denomination on the continent. The Presbyterian Church had a common heritage with many of the other Christian groups, either denominations or voluntary societies. It was an early time of ecumenical cooperation in many areas. Out of these cooperative efforts came the Plan of Union in 1801.

The Plan made it possible for congregations to be a part of both Congregational and Presbyterian denominations at the same time. They could choose available pastors from either. Pastors and members could serve in either or both structures. Disputes could be settled in either discipline. Both denominations became involved in foreign and home mission work. Although this seemed to work for a while, the differences between them were too great in critical areas and difficulties became insurmountable.[21]

John Witherspoon, president of the College of New Jersey (which later became Princeton University), had immigrated to this country in 1768 and brought with him a full array of thought from the Scottish Enlightenment. His educational style of free inquiry and of "Scottish commonsense realism" spread throughout the colonies in the hearts and minds of his students. The conviction of his thought had a profound effect, not only on the development of the Presbyterian Church, but also on the shaping of the country as he helped develop and sign the Declaration of Independence.[22]

His openness to divergent points of view opened the way for more traditional orthodoxy. In 1820 Charles Hodge joined the Princeton faculty, and over the next fifty-eight years he developed his systematic theology. Later it was referred to as "the Princeton Theology." Even though it was given this name, there were others not associated with Princeton who warmed to the direction it took and made valuable contributions to it. It became a hallmark "in the writings of antebellum Southern Presbyterians such as Robert J. Breckinridge of Kentucky, Robert Lewis Dabney of Virginia, and especially James Henley Thornwell of South Carolina."[23]

Crossing the mountains into the frontier created a serious problem for those with a strong bias for having educated clergy to defend the faith and tend the flock. The distances were great and the ranks of clergy were thin. The revivals in the early nineteenth century spread across the frontier like wildfire and exacerbated this clergy shortage. Transylvania Presbytery and Cumberland Presbytery, which was an outgrowth of Transylvania, had taken up the practice of ordaining ministers "whose education was said to be unsatisfactory, and who rejected part of the Westminster Confession of Faith as teaching 'fatalism.' "[24] This was not acceptable to the General Assembly. Most of the Cumberland Presbytery left the PCUSA in 1810 and created an entirely separate denomination, later known as the Cumberland Presbyterian Church. It would not be until 1906 that a large part of it would be reunited with the PCUSA in an organic merger. Those who did not participate in the merger continued to carry the name, Cumberland Presbyterian Church.

Old School/New School

The "platform of mutual concessions" on which the Presbyterian Church had been reunited in 1758, and the ecumenical spirit of the Plan of Union (1801), were becoming tested and tread worn. The divergence in theology and practice was too great. The Cumberlands were gone and left the door open. The center gave way to the polarization of the extremes and in 1837 the PCUSA was split asunder into what were called the Old School and the New School.[25]

The Princeton Theology at that point in its development provided a strange wedding between classic Calvinism based on the Westminster Confession and Arminianism's highly individualistic conversion decision for Christ. Each party to the spilt could find in the Princeton Theology something to support its position. The Old School held close to Westminster's basic tenets while the New School energized by the frontier revivals went in a more socially aggressive direction, challenging the predestinarian part of Westminster that questioned the individual being the initiator in conversion.[26]

The Old School maintained that the missionary effort should be done through denominational agencies, while the New School leaned toward voluntary associations. The split was not on sectional lines based on the underlying issue of slavery, but rather was based on theological issues and differences over how the church would govern itself.[27] Though the New School remained silent on slavery for a while, it became an issue in 1857, leading to the withdrawal of its constituency living in the slaveholding states to form a separate denomination known as the United Synod of the Presbyterian Church in the U.S.A.[28]

Initially, the Old School addressed the slavery issue somewhat differently, in a seemingly indirect fashion. Over the decade between 1848 and 1859 there were great debates within the Old School between Thornwell and Hodge over the nature of the church. Thornwell maintained that the Christian church was basically a "spiritual body," not to be connected with secular bodies or social issues, although it was acceptable for individuals to express their faith perspectives in these matters. Confrontation of the evils of slavery head-on by the church was avoided. Hodge held that it was imperative to speak out in the face of violations by the government, or society, of Scriptural moral injunctions. This was similar to the New Light's insistence that the church had the moral obligation to address social issues.[29] The catch phrases of these two positions—"the spirituality of the church" vs. "the social gospel"—framed the debate of the nature of the church and its moral responsibilities for decades.

This indelicate balance could not be maintained as the clouds of secession and Civil War darkened. The Northern branch of the Old School leaned heavily toward a national view of government for both church and state. The Southern branch was committed to the sovereignty of the states. The tide shifted dramatically in this standoff shortly after Fort Sumter was fired upon. The Old School Assembly in 1861, hoping to avoid a division along regional lines, debated what was known as the Gardner Springs Resolution. Its intent was to get from Southern Commissioners an indication of support for the Union of states. When it passed, the Southern commissioners withdrew and became the Old School South. On December 4, 1861, this remnant formed The Presbyterian Church in the Confederate States of America (PCCSA).[30]

Not all Presbyterians in the South or Border States were in the PCCSA at the beginning of its existence. The Southern branch of the New Light denomination, which had become known as the United Synod of the South when the Civil War started, was finally absorbed by the PCCSA, thereupon making the New School nonexistent in the South.[31]

Presbyterian churches in Maryland, Kentucky, and Missouri, though torn internally, remained in the PCUSA during the Civil War. The General Assembly in 1865 drew up a Loyalty Oath that greatly offended these Border State Presbyterians. The oath required that it be signed by all commissioners who desired to be seated at the next Assembly in 1866. The Kentucky Synod, divided over what response to make, formed two Synods. Robert J. Breckinridge led one group that met the requirements of the Assembly. Another group formed an independent synod, renouncing the jurisdiction of the Assembly. It later joined the Presbyterian Church in the U.S. (formerly PCCSA) in 1869. So Presbyterians in Kentucky were divided, not by the Civil War *per se*, but by having their loyalty severely questioned.[32]

Also in 1869 another denominational realignment took place when the PCUSA (New School) and the PCUSA (Old School) reunited to form simply the PCUSA. The old theological fight over "rigorous interpretation of predestination" had gone out of them. They were more interested in facing the challenges of how to live out "God's love for humanity" in the wake of the utter destruction of the Civil War. Efforts to revise the Westminster Confession would last all the way from the failure to do so in 1892 until 1967, including the conciliatory amendments of 1903.[33]

Other efforts were made following the cessation of the hostilities of the Civil War to begin conversations leading toward the reuniting of Northern and Southern Presbyterians. By 1886, both Assemblies agreed to meet in Baltimore. At this time a motion was made, in effect, to take the initiative toward bringing about this reunion, but no affirmative action was taken. Two grandfathers of William B. Kennedy were commissioners to the Southern Assembly in Baltimore in 1886. One of his grandfathers, "who wrote *The History of the Synod of South Carolina* later, made sure that there was a footnote that said he voted for immediate return to relationships, whatever the form of the motion was" (53-2). The matter was not dropped, but through the years other attempts were made to bind the wounds of separation.

Confessional Collisions

For several decades, the focus was on the theological differences that raged within both denominations, North and South. The heated evolutionist-creationist controversy, which was generated in 1859 with the publication of Darwin's *Origin of the Species*, had been somewhat sidetracked by the Civil War. But now it was back on track, proceeding at full steam in the midst of radical social change. The rise of modernism, which included the use of the "higher criticism" in the field of biblical studies, added fuel to the firebox.

The issues were focused in the highly publicized Briggs controversy. Although Charles A. Briggs, professor at Union Seminary in New York, believed the Bible was a sufficient record of God's revelation to humankind, especially through God's Son, Jesus Christ, Briggs was nonetheless censured in 1893 and suspended from the Presbyterian ministry for his application of this "higher criticism" to the Scriptures. A majority of Presbyterians at this time held a more strict and literal view of Scripture.[34]

Presbyterians turned to their doctrinal foundation, the Westminster Confession, to steer them through these turbulent doctrinal waters. Some found that Westminster was not explicit enough to give direction to the doctrinal understanding of the work of the Holy Spirit, especially as it related to the inspiration of the Holy Scriptures. Also there was concern over the relation between the gospel of God's love and grace to the whole world and the church's mission to the world. The mood was not to produce a new confessional replacement to Westminster. So two new chapters (XXXIV and XXXV) and the Declaratory Statement, an authoritative declaration about election and saving grace for those dying in infancy, were added to the Westminster Confession through the amending process of the Presbyterian Church U.S.A. in 1903. This, however, did not completely resolve the confessional collisions in the minds of some.

The theological clash between modernism and the biblical authority of classic Calvinism escalated into a full-fledged battle centered at Princeton Seminary in the mid-1920s. The heirs of Charles Hodge—his grandson, A. A. Hodge, together with Benjamin Warfield and J. Gresham Machen—led the way in the defense of "the fundamentals" of the faith, still in the process of being defined. At the heart of the controversy was the determination of the confessional foundation

---

of the denomination, and, above all, of who would make that determination. Machen led the fundamentalist side of the fight in the 1926 and 1927 PCUSA General Assemblies and lost. Though he would not consider his liberal opponents as being not Christian, he would not accept their liberalism as being Christian. He withdrew from Princeton and the PCUSA and formed the Orthodox Presbyterian Church (OPC). This was the first major split among Presbyterians in the twentieth century.[35]

The departure of the fundamentalists from Princeton did not bring an end to the theological and confessional debates. They showed up at the time in the UPCNA and the PCUS, but with not exactly the same rancor as in the PCUSA. The UPCNA adopted a new Confession in 1925 (revised in 1945) that found the right balance of words regarding the authority of Scripture that made it acceptable to both "inerrantists and noninerrantists." There was some "noise of conflict" in the PCUS when Kenneth J. Foreman (later to teach at Louisville Seminary) took issue with the plenary inspiration of Scripture, and when Ernest Trice Thompson (of Union Seminary in Richmond) supported the use of the higher criticism in interpreting the Bible.[36]

The major development, however, was the rise of neo-orthodoxy, which was not a systematic exposition of a "unified school of thought" but a movement. It had many names and took many forms. It was the theological umbrella under which many professors in Presbyterian seminaries stood. This stance was over against the extremes of liberalism by "asserting the centrality of scripture," on the one hand, and the rigidity of fundamentalism by "arguing for the validity of biblical criticism," on the other. It tried to pull together in one place the human sinful character, both of individuals and of social organizations. It was for its adherents a theology that "was a human and historical construct."[37]

The PCUS had its own version of wrestling with the same confessional issues the PCUSA had faced in amending the Westminster Confession in 1903. In 1942, the PCUS General Assembly amended the Confession of Faith by adding Chapter IX, "Of the Holy Spirit," and Chapter X, "Of the Gospel." These chapters did not represent new or major theological revisions, but simply pulled together in one place what was expressed implicitly in existing chapters of the Confession.[38]

One of the outcomes of the union of the UPCNA and the PCUSA in 1958 was the formation of the Special Committee on a Brief Contemporary Statement of Faith. It later made a recommendation to the UPCUSA General Assembly in 1965 calling for the development of The *Book of Confessions*.[39] Edward A. Dowey, Jr., of Princeton Seminary chaired the committee that brought the "Confession of 1967" and The

Book of Confessions to the 1966 UPCUSA General Assembly, where they were adopted and sent to the presbyteries for approval. Eighty-eight percent of the 188 presbyteries voted in the affirmative, far exceeding the two-thirds majority needed.[40] This represented the high-water mark of neo-orthodoxy in American Presbyterianism. Understanding of God's reconciliation through the life and work of Jesus Christ was expanded to include a social ethic to be exemplified in the social witness and ministry of the church. The contemporary creedal statement, known popularly as C-67, and the *Book of Confessions*, within which it was placed, were finally adopted by the UPCUSA General Assembly in Portland, Oregon, in 1967.[41] Both went far beyond the scope of Westminster.

The PCUS in 1962, being still committed to Westminster, felt that there was a need to have a contemporary educational interpretation of it. To that end the General Assembly that year approved "A Brief Statement of Belief" but did not send it through the confessional amendment process to the presbyteries. The matter did not end here. In 1969, at the PCUS General Assembly in Mobile, Alabama, a committee was named to develop a confessional statement couched in contemporary language that would speak to the current generation in the life of the PCUS. Al Winn chaired this committee and produced what Harry Hassall referred to as the "Al Winn Poem . . . a poetic way of doing serious theology." Hassall was involved in the fight that defeated it as a confessional standard, thinking that "if we defeated it, we'd go back to our roots and have Westminster" (65-21).

"A Declaration of Faith," the proper name of "Al's poem," and its companion *Book of Confessions*, with their neo-orthodox tone, passed the 1976 PCUS General Assembly, but failed to gain the requisite majority vote in the presbyteries. The irony of this failure was that "A Declaration of Faith" became more widely used liturgically, in both the Southern and Northern Presbyterian Churches, than the "official" Confession of 1967.[42]

The final confessional collision came at the time leading up to 1983 when the *Plan for Reunion* between the PCUS and the UPCUSA was being negotiated by the Joint Committee on Reunion. There were those, like Dr. McDowell Richards and Doug Harper, who felt that we "should not simply have a mechanical union, but a clear theological union." They felt that there should be at least "A Brief Statement of Faith," but preferably a *Book of Confessions*, as part of the union package. When several people including Doug Harper, Tom Gillespie, Bill Phillippe, and others got together to look at a document that Gillespie had prepared, it was obvious that there was not time to produce a satisfactory work.

What ultimately the group did produce over that long weekend turned out to be what became Chapter 2 of the Form of Government in the *Book of Order*, "The Church and Its Confessions." The theological point was made in this way. They also pushed for and got an Article of Agreement included in *The Plan* specifying the committee that finally produced the existing "A Brief Statement of Faith," an assignment that took over seven years, not a weekend (57-14).

The history of Presbyterians in North America—with its irony of cultures, its wildfire revivals, its challenges of western frontiers, its devastating trauma over political polarities and human injustices, its organizational ruptures, its confessional collisions—was a formative prelude to the Union Presbytery Movement in the twentieth century and the Presbyterian Church (U.S.A.) in the twenty-first century. Clearly there were winners and losers in this history. Once again, the full consequences of the contributions and flaws of this history would be a long time coming.

Notes

1. Maurice Telleen, "The Mind-Set of Agrarianism . . . New and Old," in *The Essential Agrarian Reader*, ed. Norman Virzba (Lexington: University Press of Kentucky, 2003), p. 53.

2. *General Assembly News* (Richmond, VA), June 30, 2004.

3. Dabbs, *Haunted by God*, pp. 18–19.

4. Ibid., p. 19.

5. Ibid., pp. 19–22.

6. Ibid.

7. Ibid., p. 23.

8. Ibid., pp. 24–25.

9. Ibid., p. 24.

10. Special Committee of the 201st General Assembly (1989), *All-Black Governing Bodies: The History and Contributions of All-Black Governing Bodies* (Louisville, KY: Office of the General Assembly, 1996). This volume is a history of the many contributions to the Presbyterian-Reformed story in North America made by African Americans from early colonial times into the twenty-first century. It makes an outstanding case for how the African American presence has been a key role in shaping the identity, the policies made, and the direction mission has taken by the PC(USA) and its predecessor denominations.

11. Lefferts A. Loetscher, *A Brief History of the Presbyterians*, 4th ed., pp. 68–69.

12. Ibid., pp. 69–70.

13. Stuart, *Diminishing Distinctives*, p. 5.

14. Ibid., p. 7.

15. Ibid., p. 6.

16. Ibid., pp. 8–9.

17. Special Committee of the 201st General Assembly (1989), *All-Black Governing Bodies*, p. 11. From Winthrop D. Jordan, *White over Black: American Attitudes toward the Negro*, 1550–1812 (Chapel Hill, NC: University of North Carolina Press, 1968), p. 300f.

18. *Guidelines of the Presbytery of Transylvania* (Union), Preface, April 1971, p. 1.

19. Special Committee of the 201st General Assembly (1989), *All-Black Governing Bodies*, p. 14. Extracts from the *Minutes of Transylvania Presbytery*, October 5, 1797, quoted in Andrew E. Murray, *Presbyterians and the Negro—A History* (Philadelphia: Presbyterian Historical Society, 1966), p. 11.

20. Special Committee of the 201st General Assembly (1989), *All-Black Governing Bodies*, p. 13.

21. Loetscher, *A Brief History of the Presbyterians*, pp. 85–87.

22. Joel L. Alvis, Jr., *Religion and Race: Southern Presbyterians*, 1946–1983, p. 4.

23. Ibid.

24. Loetscher, *A Brief History of the Presbyterians*, p. 80.

25. See Lewis G. Vander Velde, *The Presbyterian Church and the Federal Union, 1861–1869*, for a detailed account of the prominent role Presbyterians played facing the national crises presented by slavery, the Cival War, and Reconstruction. Vander Velde gives an in-depth analysis of the 1837 Old School/New School split over differences in theology and emerging styles in church governance; of how the Old School struggled with the issues of these national crises; of the impact of Congregationalist influences, growing out of the 1801 Plan of Union, on the New School positions concerning church goverance and views on slavery; of the sharp provocation and revolt over denominational loyalty in the Border States, especially in Kentucky and Missouri; the division of the Old School, North and South; and the subsequent reunion of the Old School (North) and New School (North). Vander Velde's classic work provides a critical understanding of the historical context for the extremely daunting challenges faced by the Union Presbytery Movement in achieving its goals and fulfilling the Dream of the reunion of the denominations in 1983.

26. Coalter, Mulder, and Weeks, eds., *The Re-Forming Tradition*, p. 121.

27. Loetscher, *A Brief History of the Presbyterians*, pp. 96–97.

28. Ibid., p. 99.

29. Ibid., p. 109.

30. Ibid., p. 106.

31. Ibid., p. 110.

32. *Guidelines of the Presbytery of Transylvania* (Union), p. 2.

33. Coalter, Mulder, and Weeks, eds., *The Re-Forming Tradition*, p. 122.

34. Loetscher, *A Brief History of the Presbyterians*, pp. 129–130.

35. Coalter, Mulder, and Weeks, eds., *The Re-Forming Tradition*, pp. 123–124.

36. Ibid., p. 126.

37. Ibid., p. 127.

38. James Benjamin Green, *A Harmony of the Westminster Presbyterian Standards* (Richmond, VA: John Knox Press, 1951), p. 71.

39. Edward A. Dowey, Jr., *A Commentary on the Confession of 1967 and An Introduction to the Book of Confessions* (Philadelphia: Westminster Press, 1968), p. 11.

40. Loetscher, *A Brief History of the Presbyterians*, p. 162.

41. Coalter, Mulder, and Weeks, eds.., *The Re-Forming Tradition*, pp. 131–132.

42. Ibid., pp. 133–134.

Chapter 5
Twentieth-Century Unions, Reunions, and Splits

You know, part of my career has been teaching Presbyterian history. . . . I would not at all be surprised within a decade to see another major division. Every century in America has seen at least one major Presbyterian denominational division. And it looks to me things are building up the way they did in the 1820s and '30s, you know, they produced the New School/Old School division. It's a sad thing of course, but it looks to me like the symptoms of such a thing are coming up. Whereas, I'd like to see all the split peas of Presbyterianism come together.
—*Albert H. Freundt, Jr. (17-25)*

The ecclesial wars of the twentieth century oscillated between confessional collisions and the temptation to either split or reunite denominations. During the twilight decades of the nineteenth century and the dawning decades of the twentieth century, a sharper delineation emerged in the definitions of the purpose of the church. There was a concerted effort to establish strong biblical and theological underpinning for whatever definition was espoused. The aftermath of the Civil War and the rapid growth of modern industrialism had produced new social and economic pressures on society at large. A segment of the church was satisfied with the saving-the-souls-of-individuals purpose, while another segment felt that the church had a moral responsibility to corporate society.[1]

Christian Unity

During this time various evangelism efforts were undertaken and various programs were established through neighborhood houses in urban areas, as well as in rural parishes, to meet all sorts of human conditions. New learnings from the field of sociology formed the basis for many of these efforts. In these evangelical and socially focused efforts, both at home and abroad, denominations discovered the need to work together under the banner of "Christian Unity." The time was ripe for "non-denominational cooperation of Christian individuals, church federations, and church mergers."[2]

Presbyterians in North America joined other Presbyterians and Reformed bodies around the world in 1876 to form what later became known as the World Alliance of Reformed Churches. The countries of the world were coming closer together and becoming more interdependent. The Federal Council of the Churches of Christ in America came into being in 1908 when thirty or so churches, including the Northern Presbyterians, felt the need to have a visible manifestation of the "Unity of the Church."[3] The Southern Presbyterians were not part of the original Federal Council but joined it early on and later became a member of the National and World Councils of Churches.[4]

However, as a precaution against the loss of its autonomy as a denomination, the PCUS was willing to form "federations" with other denominations as a way of expressing "fraternal relations." As a further safeguard against taking precipitous actions leading to organic union with other bodies, the Southern Church amended its Constitution in 1914 to require ratifying action by three-fourths of its presbyteries in cases effecting church union.[5]

One cannot wax too eloquently about the "Unity of the Church" or tout its reality during this time because in this case a very significant segment of the Presbyterian Church in North America basically was just that, segmented spiritually, emotionally, and physically from the main bodies of Presbyterianism. Following the Emancipation Proclamation, until well into the twentieth century, Presbyterians both North and South faced their moral and missional responsibilities toward the newly freed slaves and their descendants in many different and ambiguous ways.

Sometimes theology and doctrine became veiled rationalizations for more deeply held racial prejudice and used in this way to justify a plethora of denominational decisions. It was not possible to identify precisely whether theology or racism was the singular basis for any particular decision. Sometimes it seemed as if decisions were motivated out of a deep sense of "white" guilt to "make it right" for past sins, an emotion that in later generations became the hook on which, for some, the drive for reparations would be hung. At other times it seemed as if a deep concern for humanity was the driving force in their actions. Sometimes it seemed that they were almost oblivious to the fact that their well-intentioned mission initiatives were creating second-class citizens in the kingdom, an obvious oxymoron.

What was certain, however, was that racism, which filled the emotional and prejudicial gap created by the abolition of slavery, became combined with highly charged theological differences and dominated the agendas of all considerations of unions, reunions, splits, and other denominational mission efforts and structures.

Freedmen, All-Black Judicatories, and Institutions

Immediately at the close of the Civil War, the PCUSA was concerned with the plight of the recently emancipated slaves with regard to their education and religious instruction. The General Assembly appointed a committee on the Religious Education of the Freedmen that became a departmental committee along with the Committee of Home Missions.

Eventually by 1923 it came under the Board of Domestic Mission (later National Missions). One of the strengths of the work of this committee was that educational institutions, from parochial elementary schools to colleges, seminaries, and medical schools, were established all across the Southeast. This was part of the legacy given to them by Scotch-Irish Presbyterians in the geographical areas. These educational institutions became a primary channel for evangelism among African Americans.[6]

The pattern adopted by these home or national mission agencies was to link a clinic and a school with a congregation to form these cohesive ministries. This was the mission strategy used with African Americans, with Native Americans in the Southwest and Northwest, with poor whites in Appalachia, and later even in Cuba. It proved to be an effective feeder system for gaining communicants and steering young people into post-secondary schools and seminaries, where they were trained as leaders in various fields to serve their constituents. These African American institutions remained a key component in black Presbyterian ministry well into the mid-twentieth century but faced a new source of competition when public education became desegregated.

These new educational opportunities and growing financial requirements put enormous stress on those institutions and raised survival questions. Were it not for the strong loyalty and pride of those who had received their education from them, and the substantial Presbyterian denominational subsidies, these educational institutions might not have lasted as long as they did. Those that have survived into the twenty-first century face a bleak future, especially with the shrinking of denominational resources to prop them up and because of questionable accreditation.

Black Presbyterians who were brought into the PCUSA through these evangelism efforts following the Civil War and during Reconstruction were at times faced with a great dilemma. First, they were isolated from their brothers and sisters in the North by time and distance. Second, they were surrounded by a paternalistic and less than cordial attitude from Southern Presbyterians in their area. Third, they were highly dependent upon the financial resources of the Freedmen's Committee in order to survive. Though they wanted no part in a paternalistic church system they so detested, they nonetheless at times drifted into that flaw anyway.[7] Part of it may have been a matter of control from "up North." Part may have been a matter of control from "amongst us."

Following the end of the Civil War there was a growing desire by black Presbyterians to be free from the control of white Presbyterian governing bodies. New all-black presbyteries were established. In 1868 the Synod of the Atlantic (PCUSA) was formed with Catawba, Atlantic, and Knox presbyteries. In 1870 plans were made to add Fairfield, Yadkin, and East Florida presbyteries to the Synod. The mission work in these presbyteries enabled new congregations to be established over a wide area of Virginia and North Carolina. By 1887, the original Synod of the Atlantic was divided and Catawba Synod was created out of Catawba, Cape Fear, and Yadkin presbyteries.[8]

A year later in 1888, the Presbytery of Southern Virginia was established and joined Catawba Synod. Catawba Synod (UPCUSA) continued until 1972, when it was merged with Baltimore and New Castle presbyteries to form the Synod of the Piedmont. Because of the strong racial-ethnic identity that had been built up over the years in the Catawba Synod, those four presbyteries became "part of the Catawba Inter-presbytery Program Agency (informally called the 'unit') that provided a unifying structure until reunion in 1983." This was a way that national agencies dealt with these presbyteries in a corporate way. The Catawba Unit was dissolved with the realignment of presbytery and synod boundaries in 1988.[9]

Throughout the decades that these all-black institutions and governing bodies existed, the original dilemma—time and distance, hostile surroundings, dependence on outside funding, the desire to be free of the paternalistic flaw, patterns of outside control—still haunted black Presbyterians. They were not spared the reality of this dilemma or the temptation for some of them to succumb to its spell.

An example of this paternalistic flaw could be seen years later as the money flowed from the national church to regional areas. It was the perception of one former presbytery executive, commenting on this situation in the Synod of the Piedmont (UPCUSA), "that there had been this real unofficial thing in the old Catawba Unit. . . . [E]very year the New York office would send him [the executive of that unit] three or four hundred thousand dollars. . . . And he would dispense that money to all these pastors that were aided and he really had the power of a pope in these areas. And there was a love-hate relationship between him and all his pastors because they hated their dependence on him but they also saw him as their lifeline economically. And so it was quite a dynamic" (86-21).

The long experience of all-black institutions and governing bodies created proud traditions that formed them as members of the PCUSA. It shaped their identity where the strengths outweighed the weaknesses incurred in being separated from the mainstream of Northern Presbyterianism. There are, however, residual consequences of the experience that play a critical role in shaping the identity of the PC(USA) in the twenty-first century.

The Southern Presbyterian Church took a different approach. Prior to the Civil War there was an effort to evangelize slaves, and many African Americans became members of white Presbyterian congregations, relegated to the balconies of their buildings. For many Southern Presbyterians following the Civil War it was unthinkable to allow the blacks to participate in the government of the church or to establish anything like structures in which to govern their own religious activities. As a result there was a mass exodus of blacks to other denominations.[10]

For whatever reasons, Southern Presbyterians held fast to their belief in an educated ministry and their commitment to evangelizing the freedmen. To that end Stillman Institute, a two-year school, was formed in 1874 for the purpose of training "colored ministers." At one point its format was extended to include a four-year curriculum, but it went back to being a two-year institution before long. With the growing number of black ministers being trained, the next logical step was to find a way to organize the churches they served into governing bodies. This created an awkward situation for the white Presbyterians who did not want to include them in their own governing body system.[11]

As a result, so-called "independent" all-black presbyteries were formed for their congregations and ministers, but were not related to any higher church court. These presbyteries sprang up in North and South Carolina, Alabama, Mississippi, Louisiana, and Texas. Most of the ministers in these presbyteries received financial support from the Executive Committee on Home Missions of the PCUS. There was growing interest in finding a way to connect these governing bodies. In 1898, the Afro-American Presbyterian Church was formed and was funded largely by the PCUS General Assembly. Two of the strongest presbyteries, Central Alabama and Ethel in Mississippi, remained connected to the PCUS and did not join the new denomination. This segregated denomination, not being able to sustain itself financially, was doomed to fail.[12]

By 1916, being interested in maintaining some form of governing body structure to which all-Black presbyteries could relate, an Ad Interim Committee of the PCUS General Assembly recommended that an Afro-American synod be formed that would be a part of the PCUS. Out of this the Snedecor Memorial Synod came into being in 1917. It was named after the former superintendent of the Committee of Colored Evangelism who had once served as principal of Stillman Institute. The Synod would exist until 1952. The existence of this segregated synod "committed the denomination, perhaps unwittingly, to maintaining a black constituency within the limits of Presbyterian polity."[13]

Forming segregated governing bodies in the 1890s was not limited to African Americans. The Synod of Texas, in 1892, organized a Mexican-American presbytery in the Southwest to "foster contacts among Spanish-speaking congregations, allowing benevolence money to be spent on other projects."[14] No doubt this was well intended, but nonetheless it was an interesting use of segregation as a rationale for good stewardship.

CPC/PCUSA Reunion (1906)

The Cumberland Presbyterian Church existed for a little over one hundred years, although the circumstances for which it left the PCUSA had changed. It had taken issue with the mother church over "the alleged 'fatalism' of the Westminster Confession and the denomination's insistence on an adequately trained clergy." These were not the same hot-button issues in the early twentieth century as they had been when the frontier was being opened. The CPC approached the PCUSA seeking to negotiate a reunion.[15]

There was, however, a very important condition the CPC insisted on when it came to an agreement with the PCUSA. Since the bulk of the CPC was in the Border States and in the South, it "insisted upon racially segregated governing bodies as a condition for entering the union." Commissioners from Catawba and other black presbyteries vigorously opposed the recommendation to no avail. It was adopted by the General Assembly and "approved by presbyteries a vote of 188 to 45 with eight abstentions."[16] The boundaries of presbyteries and synods were then redrawn to ensure racial segregation.

Two synods, made up predominantly of black constituents, were formed: Tennessee (later Blue Ridge) and Canadian. They were located in Alabama, Mississippi, Tennessee, Arkansas, Kentucky, and parts of Texas and Oklahoma. These two synods were sufficiently geographically distant from those African American Synods in Virginia, the Carolinas, and Georgia that had been created as a result of the Northern Church's earlier missionary efforts.[17]

In 1907 the Synod of Canadian was established with three black presbyteries—Kiamichi and Randle in Oklahoma, and White River in Arkansas. There were two Choctaw Indian congregations within Kiamichi. One was later dissolved and the other was returned to the Presbytery of Choctaw. A quarter century earlier, African blacks were adopted as members of the Choctaw tribes that had owned them as slaves. One final note was about all-black governing bodies formed in the merger of the CPC and PCUSA. Lincoln Presbytery was created in the Synod of Kentucky as an African American geographical presbytery.[18]

Dreams, Where Have You Gone?

The opportunity to address the possibility of integrating the judicatories in the bounds of the CPC was forfeited in favor of drawing "separate but equal" presbyteries and synods in overlapping areas. This was predicated on the Supreme Court's 1896 "separate but equal" doctrine and indicated that there was little difference among most Presbyterians, North or South, in attitudes regarding race.[19]

It was not surprising that such a stipulation succeeded in passing, for little more than a generation had passed since the Emancipation Proclamation. This action remained in force until the provision was abolished in 1967, some sixty-one years later. Some had looked upon the CPC/PCUSA Reunion (1906) as effectively changing the character of the PCUSA from being merely "the Northern Church," a regional church, back to being the national church it was before the Civil War.[20]

But the perception that the PCUSA, and subsequently the UPCUSA, was a national church was not universally accepted for a long time. Even after the formation of the PC(USA) in 1983, some sentiment existed that the Northern Church had been something less than a national church. Jill M. Hudson said, "Even though the former UP Church . . . presented itself as a national church, it had a regional feel, and the region was the East Coast. . . . That was the predominant, I think, style and feel, even though it had churches in the South. Most of them were racial/ethnic congregations except for a sprinkle here and there" (90-21). Almost twenty years after the 1983 reunion, this East Coast regional feel was the dominant memory in this observer's perception. Even more significantly, the incorporation from the South of former CPC churches (1906) and a few UPCNA churches (1958) along with all the mission fields in the Southwest and in Alaska, still did not give it a national church feel in this person's view. She was not alone in this perception.

PCUS/PCUSA Reunion (1955)

By mid-century, the country had survived two World Wars sandwiched around the Great Depression. Now society was emotionally electrified by the Supreme Court desegregation decision of *Brown v. Board of Education*, a radical departure from how schools had been segregated by race. In this volatile context Presbyterian reunion discussions began to heat up.

Nowhere was there a more poignant example of the ecclesial hemorrhage caused by the collision of polarities over theology, race, and reunion than in the Synod of Mississippi (PCUS) in the mid-1950s. This was but one vivid illustration of what was taking place in many different forms in the PCUS all across the South.

In the 1930s, the Synod of Mississippi had been embroiled in a theological controversy, in which a party led by William H. McIntosh, pastor of the First Presbyterian Church, Hattiesburg, Mississippi, and others filed charges against Charles E. Diehl, president of Southwestern at Memphis because of the liberal views he held regarding the Westminster Confession and the Catechism. Dr. Diehl was exonerated of the charges. The synod elected McIntosh to the board of trustees of the college, but Southwestern never seated him, which led to a legal case (17-9).

Also, in the early 1930s, before Westminster Seminary's split with the Northern Presbyterians, the Synod's Education Committee conferences at Belhaven College had a professor from Westminster as one of the platform speakers each year for three consecutive years. There seems to have been an innate kind of classic Calvinism or conventional Presbyterianism connecting the Synod of Mississippi and Westminster Seminary. When the split with the Northern Presbyterian Church came in 1936, with the founding of the Orthodox Presbyterian Church, Westminster professors were no longer invited to the platform at Belhaven College (17-7).

Belhaven College in the 1950s continued to be a magnet drawing more conservative ministers from denominations other than the PCUS into the Synod of Mississippi. There was some speculation by those native to the area that this was a concerted effort by these "ecclesiastical carpetbaggers" to take over the College and the Synod for their purposes. One such person was John Reed Miller, who in 1951 came as an instructor at Belhaven, then received a call to First Presbyterian Church in Jackson, Mississippi. Miller was originally ordained as a minister of the UPCNA before transferring his membership to the PCUS. He served in the late 1940s as president of Knoxville College, the college established by the UPCNA as part of its mission to the freed African Americans following the Civil War.[21]

Race, often under the guise of theology, was a key issue in the 1954–55 attempt to reunite the UPCNA, PCUS, and PCUSA. The UPCNA dropped out of the reunion effort before it came to a vote. In 1954 the PCUS General Assembly voted 283 to 169 to send the plan of organic union of the remaining two denominations to their respective presbyteries for ratification. The PCUS presbyteries voted and reported to the General Assembly in 1955, 42 in favor and 43 opposed, thus failing to get the three-fourths majority for ratification required in organic unions.[22]

The session of the First Presbyterian Church of Brookhaven, Mississippi, the home church where William H. McAtee, the author's father, was pastor, had opposed the Plan of Reunion. This congregation was but a microcosm of the pain and distress experienced by the PCUS at this juncture over the collision of theology, race, and reunion. With the reunion question settled for the time being, the Session was deeply distressed over the PCUS Council of Christian Relations' authority to make "deliverances concerning social, political, and economic questions." In a public resolution of record it declared its objections based on the Westminster Confession of Faith's statements regarding the church's mission, separation of church and state, and the right to private judgment in all secular matters. It strongly affirmed that the church's mission was the "divinely appointed task of preaching the gospel [of individual salvation] through faith in the shed blood of Jesus Christ." Furthermore, it went "on record [as] disapproving the belief that segregation is unchristian and further as disapproving [the belief] that segregation is discriminating." The vote by the session on the resolution was unanimous.[23]

By contrast, other presbytery votes in 1955 were not always unanimous one way or the other; some were ambiguous. Leonard E. Woodward, being pastor of a union congregation at the United Presbyterian Church, Harrodsburg, Kentucky, was able to vote in both the Northern and Southern presbyteries when the reunion votes took place. He was originally from Alabama and was more traditionally a PCUS minister. When he went to the UPCUSA (Northern) presbytery meeting he voted for it. When he went to the PCUS (Southern) presbytery meeting he voted against it. Later James W. Gunn, pastor of the Lebanon United Presbyterian Church, another union congregation, asked why he voted the way he did, Woodward replied "that he did not mind the Northern Church coming to us, but he didn't want to go join them" (37-7).

Following the 1955 defeat of reunion between the PCUSA and PCUS, many of those who had worked in that losing cause did not give up on relating to each other. They channeled their energies into cooperative efforts, especially in areas of mutual interest and geographic proximity. Sometimes they thought up preposterous ideas to bridge the gap between the denominations. El Paso Presbytery had four churches in New Mexico. Someone got the bright idea that the solution to the failed reunion was to expand El Paso Presbytery to include southern California, because there was no western boundary, strictly speaking, to the PCUS at that time (23-5).

On a more realistic note, all of the Southern churches in West Texas were sprinkled in with Northern Presbyterian churches and there was very little contact between them. It was very difficult to explain to people that when they moved from one location to another and joined the Presbyterian Church, in many cases they had changed denominations. And consequently, all the ministers that they had known all their life were no longer members of their church, and they did not have any contact with what was going on in their former denomination (23-5). This was but an inkling of the issues that would be faced in the decades ahead.

Orthodox Presbyterian Church Presence

In the aftermath of the failed vote to reunite the PCUS and the PCUSA in 1955, the opportunity seemed ripe by some to consolidate the conservative position gained in the winning effort by capitalizing on the racial tensions of the time. The impetus for such an effort came from an increasing number of graduates and students coming to the Synod of Mississippi from Westminster Seminary. Albert H. Freundt, Jr., a newly ordained minister in the Synod and later an instructor at Belhaven College and professor at Reformed Theological Seminary, spoke of some of the heroes of his youth as being graduates of Westminster, but they had become disillusioned with the Orthodox Presbyterian Church for one reason or another (17-7).

Freundt did not believe there was, as some believed, a concerted strategy by the Orthodox Presbyterian Church to capitalize on the racial situation and political turmoil in the Synod at the time in order to "take it over." Though Freundt did not really believe that there was any grand plan to take over Mississippi Presbyterianism, he did know that there was some openness to this in Mississippi. He based his opinion on his observations that wherever William J. Stanway went as pastor (Stanway was an influential Westminster graduate), more and more conservative ministers appeared in those presbyteries. Stanway went in the early 1950s to serve the First Presbyterian Church, Hattiesburg, Mississippi. This was a congregation William H. McIntosh had served for many years. It was more of a network thing, rather than some big plan or conspiracy. If one controlled the call system, one invited and called whom one knew (17-9).

Another minister, who came to Mississippi to teach at Belhaven College in 1954, and who later taught at Reformed Theological Seminary, was Morton H. Smith. Although he was a 1952 graduate of Columbia Seminary, he had studied for a year at Westminster Seminary. In response to the PCUS General Assembly report "The Church and Segregation," Smith "claimed that there was no biblical condemnation of segregation, a case that sounded strangely like Thornwell's answer to the question on the sinfulness of slavery."[24] Smith was known to criticize the policies and programs of the PCUS and was an outspoken advocate of the racial status quo.[25]

In 1956 P. B. Burleigh, a native-born Scotsman, was received into membership of Mississippi Presbytery to serve a brief pastorate in

Meadville. His ministerial journey had taken him on a circuitous route through the Methodist Episcopal Church, the PCUSA, the OPC to the PCUS. On March 13, 1957, he sent William H. McAtee, the author's father, a letter warning that "The Synod better get wise to the purposes of the OPC, etc or they will someday be very sorry."[26]

Enclosed in Burleigh's letter to McAtee were two letters he had received from John P. Galbraith, general secretary of the Committee on Home Missions and Church Extension of the Orthodox Presbyterian Church in Philadelphia. In the first letter dated November 10, 1955, Galbraith wrote to Burleigh about the prospects of a call to ministry in a Home Mission field in the Presbytery of Ohio (OPC) and the difficulties they were facing there. He encouraged Burleigh to "continue to minister the Word to whatever people will come in the interim." He reiterated how slow things work in changing pastorates. Although Galbraith hated to suggest that Burleigh leave the OPC, he asked if he might consider a pastorate in the Southern Presbyterian Church. Then Galbraith wrote: "But a number of our men who are in full sympathy with the Orthodox Presbyterian Church have entered the Southern Presbyterian Church with an ultimate view of coming into the OPC with their congregations if the time arises in the Southern Church when it unites with the Northern Church, *if the Liberalism becomes uncontrollable there*" [italics added].[27]

Galbraith gets very specific about the location of such a prospect. "There is one particularly bright spot in the Southern Church and that is the Synod of Mississippi. A Westminster Seminary graduate [actually Morton Smith only attended Westminster for one year before graduating from Columbia Seminary] is in that Synod and teaches at Belhaven College, which is under the control of the Synod." Galbraith went on to write, "He and some others in the Synod are very anxious that the Synod be filled with ministers of the *right caliber* [italics added]. I should judge that there would be fine fellowship in such a synod, and you really would not be out of the atmosphere of the Orthodox Presbyterian Church."[28]

Evidently Burleigh, in a return letter, responded positively to Galbraith's suggestion about the Synod of Mississippi. Galbraith responded: "I think it would be advisable to start making contacts in the Southern Church right away. Yes, it was to Morton Smith whom I wrote concerning you. It is interesting that he was suggested to you also, from another source [handwritten note in the margin says: 'Dr. Bell & Dendy—P. B. B.']. I have not heard from him in reply to my letter, but I shall write to others to make contact. But I do think that the Synod of Mississippi, *under the present conditions* [italics added], would be a very good place to try to locate since it would help the whole movement for the Reformed Faith more than in any other spot that I can think of outside the OPC."[29]

The combination of *"uncontrollable liberalism"* and the *"present conditions,"* i.e., desegregation, provided a fertile ground for *"right caliber"* ministers of Machen's fundamentalist persuasion to flourish, particularly in the Synod of Mississippi. The author's father would not live to see the full import the warnings of these letters, for he died a year after receiving them on March 18, 1958, while attending a Board of Trustees meeting at Southwestern at Memphis. The pulpit he served for fifteen years as a loyal member of the PCUS was filled after his death by Robert J. Ostenson, a Fuller Seminary graduate.

Burleigh would surface once more in 1971, soon after the author became Associate Executive of the Presbytery of Transylvania (Union) in Kentucky. He was seeking to relocate once again and remembered the familiar name of McAtee as a possible connection for such a ministerial relocation. He presumed he would be forgotten "after the passage of so many years." It had not gone according to the original intent of who had suggested he go to Mississippi.

He used the occasion of a letter to the author to reflect on what was taking place in the PCUS as a result of OPC-type involvement. "I remember so well your father who defended me against some of those fire eaters in that presbytery. Your father was one among so few who tried so hard to keep the peace and with so little success. They are worse now than in those days. They and their fellow conspirators who so solemnly declare that their purpose is to preserve the Presbyterian Church, U.S., rather than preserving it are doing their utmost to assassinate it."[30] Whether it was an organized conspiracy, a concerted strategy, or simply through a network of like-minded associates, the influence of Westminster Seminary and the OPC presence were felt in the Synod of Mississippi in significant ways at a very vulnerable time in its life. Many ministers of this persuasion were instrumental in the denominational split that was to follow in the 1970s.[31]

UPCNA/PCUSA Union (1958)

In the mid-1950s, when it was clear that there would be no reunion between the PCUSA and the PCUS, talks immediately began to achieve a union between the PCUSA and the UPCNA to form the UPCUSA. There were several factors at work in the dynamic of this union effort. One factor had to do with the northern geographic location of most of the UPCNA congregations by this juncture in history. The early strong antislavery stance of the UPCNA put many communicants living in the South in an unpopular position, thus leading many to migrate to the North. A few congregations remained across the Border States along with the educational and mission work among African Americans in the South.[32] This union, then, was not shaped so much by regional and racial divisiveness caused by the Civil War as by other factors.

One reality at play in this union was the disparity in size between the two denominations, in which the smaller body (UPCNA) felt swallowed up by the larger body (PCUSA) when the UPCUSA was formed. This was at once both an emotional phenomenon as well as the reality of how the corporate life of the new united church was affected. The author, in the early 1970s, met a woman who many years before had come as a Christian educator to one of the UPCNA mission churches in Kentucky. She was lamenting the loss of "her church." This was shortly after Transylvania had become a union presbytery. She was not talking about this union presbytery effort, but was referring to the 1958 UPCNA-PCUSA union that had taken place a decade and a half earlier. Old traditions and customs die hard, remaining strong in the sentient recesses of the heart.

Several distinctive practices and beliefs of the UPCNA became extinct in a relatively brief span of time following the union with the PCUSA. The UPCNA experienced a loss of corporate identity as the ministerial and denominational leaders of the UPCNA came to be outnumbered by those of the PCUSA. In sorting out the two radically different approaches to how theology was studied and practiced, the methodology of the PCUSA dominated theological debates. The ten seminaries of the PCUSA greatly overshadowed the influence of the one former UPCNA seminary in educating ministers. The UPCNA perspective and identity were further diluted when its seminary, Pittsburgh-Xenia, merged with Western Seminary (PCUSA) to form Pittsburgh Seminary (UPCUSA). One person from the former UPCNA tradition summed up his conclusion about loss of identity: "The full dissipation of the seceder identity took about 10–15 years to accomplish, but by 1975 it was pretty much a *fait accompli*."[33]

However, the deep commitment by former members of the UPCNA to the Westminster Standards became very evident in the debate of the Confession of 1967 in the UPCUSA. In 1965 many former UPCNA lay leaders were heavily involved in the original formation of the Lay Committee that opposed C-67. The Lay Committee's purpose was to defend the primacy of Westminster as the creedal basis of Presbyterian doctrine and polity. They were concerned that the new social agenda of C-67 was a serious departure from what they perceived to be the teachings of Scripture and the Reformed heritage.[34] One wonders how much the UPCNA seceder practice of signing public covenants influenced the call for signing the declarations of the Confessing Church movement in the PCUSA at the turn of the twenty-first century, since that movement tended to be a strong presence in former UPCNA geographical regions.

RCA/PCUS Union Attempt (1968)

In the early 1960s serious union discussions took place between the RCA and the PCUS. The Joint Committee of 24 was formed as the official committee to develop the union proposal. Many in the PCUS were still grieving as losers in the PCUS-PCUSA reunion attempt (1955), so their interest was stymied for any further reunion discussions with the PCUSA at this moment.

According to Flynn Long there were "people like Warner Hall and Sherrod Rice and Aubrey Brown and Marshall Dendy and hundreds of others who were the senior ministers of the church at the time," who were very interested in seeing this RCA-PCUS union take place. Long felt "that they were for RCA union because they would take anything in a pinch than just have to stay PCUS forever. And they didn't think union with the USA church would ever take place. I mean, if it would take another hundred years, so they said, 'We'll settle for half a loaf and join with somebody' " (23-20). John B. Evans observed that these "central leaders, of which I wasn't one at that time . . . at all . . . wanted to take some step to overcome the very regionalism of PCUS" (56-5).

The presbyteries of the PCUS in the Border States were beginning to discuss finding ways to become more engaged with the UPCUSA than merely through cooperative ministries. They were concerned that an RCA-PCUS union might jeopardize a more formal union at the presbytery level with the UPCUSA presbyteries in these overlapping geographical areas. The RCA had very few congregations within the bounds of the PCUS, a few in Kentucky and a few in Florida. Some perceived this union as being "for most of the PCUS, a union with somebody that would never bother us. And it would not solve the problem of the continued friction between the PCUS and . . . the United Presbyterian Church [UPCUSA]" (23-15).

By 1966 there were isolated pockets of folks exploring what it would take to create union presbyteries, since many union congregations had existed for several decades. Some interested parties in Central Texas Presbytery began to draft some overtures proposing amendments to the *Book of Church Order* (PCUS) and the *Book of Order* (UPCUSA) that would permit the creation of union presbyteries and union synods. Long affirmed "that one of the things we needed to do was to be sure that the RCA proposal, and the union presbytery proposal as well, had within it language which would not sever the tie in the border Synods between the USA and the PCUS" (23-15). The pro-RCA union leaders perceived the presbyteries in the Border States as maybe voting against this union on these grounds. In reality people from the Border presbyteries were astute enough politically to realize that union presbytery and synod chapters would not pass without the support of the pro-RCA union folk.

The people who were supporting RCA union weren't sure whether pro-union presbytery people in the border synods would support the RCA union. In a caucus between the two groups it was decided "that if they would accept the changes in the union presbytery proposal, to allow it to take place even if union with the RCA took place, that we would buy RCA union" (23-19). Long went on to say, "And we also tried to make sure that they understood that the quid pro quo involved in that, without ever saying it, was that if we'd support RCA, they'd support union presbyteries. . . . You know, we were not against them and we didn't want them to be against us because we felt like that basically, in terms of issues before the church, . . . [they] were not our enemy. . . . But they were on a different tack than we were" (23-20).

As it turned out, the PCUS approved the union with the RCA, but the RCA rejected it. It may have been another case of the smaller body feeling like the larger body would swallow it up. It may have been the case that there were not enough geographical overlaps between the two denominations to have generated a sense of familiarity. There may have been some theological differences, especially in the Western wing of the RCA, which appeared to be much more theologically conservative than its Eastern wing, with whom many in the PCUS had worked in joint educational ventures.

For whatever reason, it was the observation of John Evans that "there wasn't any overwhelming sadness that we got turned down that I could see" (56-5). Evans did say, however, "that the real plus of the RCA vote was the fact that the required majority of PCUS voted for it. And I think that is a really good plus, that aids union presbyteries and aids Presbyterian reunion. I don't have any doubt in my mind about that. That . . . we could then say, you know, 'We've already addressed that we don't want to be a regional Church' " (56-6).

Evans also commented that "there were people in the Eastern part of the Reformed Church that felt like . . . we would have made some improvement, from their standpoint, if they joined with us. . . . [T]hey had work in California. So there was a whole sense that even though that church was a third the size of PCUS, it did represent a kind of a national presence" (56-6).

PCA Split (1973)

By the 1960s, pressure had been building from many sources that tested whether the theological and ecclesial center of the PCUS would hold off the divisive tendencies of the extremes. One extreme tended to rally around unadulterated devotion to the Westminster Confession and fundamentalist-leaning theology, around racial issues to maintain ecclesiastical control, and around anti-union sentiments to ward off anything that hinted of ecumenism. The other extreme gravitated toward a theological view more akin to a liberal interpretation of Scripture, openness to integration of the races and other social justice matters, pro-union leanings, and support of cooperative ecumenical alliances. The author experienced firsthand the ecclesial and secular turmoil of the 1950s and 1960s while being a candidate for the ministry and serving two PCUS pastorates in Mississippi. It was a great time for a fourth- generation Mississippian to be at home.

Again the Synod of Mississippi (PCUS) afforded a window through which to view how these conflicts in extremes were acted out, though similar dramas were staged all across the South. Various political maneuvers were executed with the appearance of military precision. The agendas of middle and higher church courts became the battleground for these engagements. Sometimes it was a test over which side would prevail in electing the moderator for the day's session. On another occasion it would be as intricate as gerrymandering presbytery boundaries to gain the advantage. In 1961, the five presbyteries in the Synod of Mississippi were reduced to three by a fourteen-vote margin to contain the influence of the conservative extreme.

By the early 1970s, other similar evidence of gerrymandering was seen in the formation of the new regional synod that encompassed Mississippi, Alabama, Tennessee, and Kentucky. Initially, two synods were proposed, Mississippi-Alabama forming one and Tennessee-Kentucky forming the other. The ultra-conservatives' forces dominated the organizing convention of the proposed Mississippi-Alabama Synod, giving the impression to some that the new synod in this configuration might become a prime candidate for withdrawal from the PCUS. Under review, the General Assembly Boundaries Committee would not approve the proposal and sent it back to the negotiating table. The final result was the formation of the Synod of the Mid-South, which included presbyteries from all four states, thus shifting the balance of political power in the new synod to those loyal to the PCUS. This was a factor that played a part in the PCA split in 1973.

Sometimes the struggle was over examination for reception of ministers into membership of presbytery. The most notorious case was the "Mac Hart Case" in Central Mississippi Presbytery, which dragged out in the church courts—the presbytery, synod, and General Assembly—for three years in the early 1960s. During this time Hart served a congregation in Meridian, Mississippi, on a temporary basis and was never installed before he received another call to a church in Arkansas. It was a test of a certain brand of theological orthodoxy, though some felt it was a litmus test over race.

Dreams, Where Have You Gone?

One bright spot in the standoff between the extremes was when a group of younger ministers from both sides had gotten their fill of this ridiculous situation. It had almost gotten to the point where they could not even be seen talking with "the opposition" by members of their respective parties. In an attempt to heal the breach, it was decided to hold a conference, not in the context of a church court at which votes were taken, but in a setting where persons from both sides could present papers on various social and ethical topics of the day for discussion.[35]

The Christian Ethics Conference was held at Belhaven College, Jackson, Mississippi, May 30–June 1, 1966. It was a liberating experience for the conferees. They soon discovered they shared many similar views on the subjects discussed. Where they differed, there was no fear of recrimination for doing so. Relationships were formed at this conference that would abide for a lifetime. A style of working together was established that would see the conferees productively through many subsequent ecclesial debates. Some vowed never again to get into a standoff like the one that had separated them before the conference.

As the decade of the 1960s was winding down, the 1969 meeting of the General Assembly in Mobile, Alabama, became the watershed event of the mid-twentieth century in the PCUS. This Assembly enacted many "liberal" agenda items, including passing the union presbytery chapter. This—along with establishing the Joint Committee on Reunion with the UPCUSA, the Committee on the Consultation on Church Union (COCU), the Declaration of Faith Committee, and others—proved too much for the more "conservative" wing of the Church to take.

The move to withdraw was begun. It would become a reality by December 4, 1972, when the National Presbyterian Church was formed. This happened within months after the original union presbyteries became operational and 112 years to the day after the formation of the Presbyterian Church in the Confederate States of America. This new denomination was later known as the Presbyterian Church in America (PCA). The first General Assembly of the PCA convened at the Briarwood Presbyterian Church, Birmingham, Alabama, in 1973. It was composed of ministers and elders who were no longer willing to be members of the PCUS. The reason given, in part, was that the "PCUS had abandoned the Bible and the historic Reformed creeds and based its authority on human reason and not divine will."[36] Morton Smith was elected as stated clerk of the PCA General Assembly at its first meeting.[37]

At the outset the split took some 260 churches with nearly 41,000 communicants from the PCUS, mostly from Mississippi, Alabama, and South Carolina. There were 171 of the 260 churches and 108 of the 191 ministers from these three states that joined the PCA. This did not mean that all the conservatives left the PCUS.[38] Those who stayed struggled with the issues that caused the others to leave. For various reasons, some gradually changed their positions enough to find a place in the PCUS, while others wondered why had they stayed and contemplated when the next opportunity might come along to leave. A number of ministers decided to stay because they did not want to give up their vested pension plan.

There were mixed emotions about the departure of those who formed the PCA. Al Freundt, who remained a member of the PCUS and PCUSA while being a professor at Reformed Seminary until his retirement, felt that "both sides in the case of division are worse off than they were before." He went on to say, "I know a lot of my liberal friends didn't think that, and they were glad to see the PCA go, but the PCA, and I think the PCUS, both lost something, a balancing element . . . when that division took place. And I think they've become more and more unlike each other than they were before" (17-25).

The PCA split and the race issue created an almost irreconcilable trauma that was painful for friends, congregations, and families to experience. Freundt talked about how he tried to keep up with former friends who had moved over to the PCA. He said it was like living in two worlds. Some people cut him off because he did not go with them. Others cut him off over his stand on the race issue, as was the case with John Reed Miller. Freundt did say he discovered that Miller had mellowed by the time he visited Miller in a nursing home (17-25).

The session of the author's home church in Brookhaven, Mississippi, led the congregation in a decision to withdraw from the PCUS and become a congregation in the PCA. The decision of the higher courts of the church stipulated that they could leave, but their property and other assets would go to the less than twenty members who favored remaining in the PCUS. The session decided not to contest this decision in the secular courts, on the basis of the scriptural injunction to settle disputes without taking them to court.

Those of the congregation who left felt the wrenching experience of leaving the place where for decades their marriages had been performed, their babies had been baptized, their professions of faith had been made, their Christmas pageants had played, and loved ones had been memorialized in death. Those few who remained faced the daunting challenge of maintaining a viable ministry in that place. This whole painful relational hemorrhage played itself out on the open stage of the local community. The author asked his beloved high school English teacher, who had stretched his horizons through literature and introduced him to a world less provincial than the one in which he had grown up, "why did you vote to leave?" She replied, "Because the elders said it was the thing to do."

The author had cousins in other Presbyterian congregations who had withdrawn and heavily supported financially the establishment of the Reformed Presbyterian Seminary, the focal point in the development of the PCA in Mississippi and a place for preparation of ministers for service in the PCA.

The author's aunt, Doris McAtee Rice, who had gone to California in the 1940s, returned to retire in nearby Hazlehurst, Mississippi. While in California she became an elder in the La Rambla Presbyterian Church in San Pedro and served with distinction in higher judicatories of the PCUSA. When she moved back to Mississippi, the First Presbyterian Church in Hazlehurst did not recognize her ordination. The pastor was Adrian E. DeYoung, a Westminster Seminary graduate. When the congregation withdrew to the PCA, she became a "radio member" of Central Presbyterian Church (PCUS) in Jackson, Mississippi, a ministry to individuals left stranded in surrounding towns by the PCA split. She received the sacrament of Holy Communion quarterly from elders of that congregation who traveled a distance to visit her. Her funeral service, however, was held in the local PCA sanctuary in Hazlehurst.

These are but a few illustrations of the countless fractures of relationships all across the PCUS caused among friends, congregations, and families by withdrawal to the PCA. No doubt there were people who went to their graves never speaking to former relations on "the other side" or even reentering their sacred places of earlier days. This was especially poignant in a region where relations and place were the bedrock of its culture. Over time, some rejoiced that they were able to resolve their differences to a point where they got a second chance to relate to one another.

The stage was now finally set for the last major reunion of the twentieth century. Bill Peterson, reflecting on the Union Presbytery Movement, was concerned that its significance with regard to the PCUS-UPCUSA Reunion (1983) had become lost at the close of the twentieth century. For him, its significance was seen in an analogy of a train he used regarding that reunion: "the Committee on Reunion was the engine of that train, but the union presbyteries fueled it. And, I think without that, you know, that train would have stopped dead in its tracks" (36-27).

The twentieth-century unions, reunions, and splits of Presbyterians in North America—with the well-intentioned mission initiatives among recently emancipated slaves, the contorted and ambivalent creations of all-black judicatories and institutions, the polarization of the PCUS by the ecumenical movements of the twentieth century, the "separate but equal" stance taken in the CPC-PCUSA Reunion (1906), the failed PCUS-PCUSA Reunion (1955), the opportunist presence of the OPC, the gross disparity in the UPCNA-PCUSA Union (1958), the rejection of the union proposal (1968) between the RCA and the PCUS, and the irreconcilable trauma manifest among former relations, friends, congregations and families by the PCA split (1973)—were a formative prelude to the Union Presbytery Movement in the twentieth century and the Presbyterian Church (U.S.A.) in the twenty-first century. Clearly there were winners and losers in these twentieth-century unions, reunions, and splits. The full consequences of the contributions and flaws of those experiences would be a long time coming.

But the time has come to look in depth at the Union Presbytery Movement and tell the stories of the relations, realities, and roles of union presbyteries in the larger saga of North American Presbyterianism in which the dreams were lived.

Notes

1. Loetscher, *A Brief History of the Presbyterians*, 4th ed., p. 133.

2. Ibid., pp. 134–135.

3. Ibid., p. 135.

4. Ibid., p. 125.

5. Ibid., p. 124.

6. Special Committee of the 201st General Assembly (1989), *All-Black Governing Bodies*, pp. 42–43.

7. Ibid., p. 45.

8. Ibid., pp. 48–49.

9. Ibid., p. 49.

10. Alvis, *Religion and Race: Southern Presbyterians*, p. 13.

11. Ibid., p. 14.

12. Special Committee of the 201st General Assembly (1989), *All-Black Governing Bodies*, pp. 56–57.

13. Alvis, *Religion & Race: Southern Presbyterians*, pp. 14–15.

14. Ibid., p. 15.

15. Special Committee of the 201st General Assembly (1989), *All-Black Governing Bodies*, p. 51.

16. Ibid.

17. Ibid., p. 40.

18. Ibid., p. 50.

19. Ibid., p. 52.

20. Loetscher, *A Brief History of the Presbyterians*, p. 135.

21. E. C. Scott, Stated Clerk, *Ministerial Directory of the Presbyterian Church, U.S., 1861–1941, Revised and Supplemented 1942–1950*, p. 477; James A. Millard, Jr., Stated Clerk, *Ministerial Directory of the Presbyterian Church, U.S., 1861–1967*, p. 383. [Note: These will be referred to as Min. Dir. 51, or Min. Dir. 67, or by whatever year other volumes were published.]

22. Loetscher, *A Brief History of the Presbyterians*, p. 125.

23. "Brookhaven Presbyterians Record Sentiment on Segregation Issue," *Lincoln County Advertiser*, November 28, 1957.

24. Alvis, *Religion and Race: Southern Presbyterians*, p. 136.

25. Ibid., p. 143.

26. Letter from P. B. Burleigh to William H. McAtee, dated March 13, 1957, in personal collection of William G. McAtee. This letter and the two enclosed letters from John P. Galbraith to P. B. Burleigh, offer information and insight into some of the inner workings and difficulties faced in the OPC at the time, other than the information about intentions related to prospects in the Synod of Mississippi.

27. Letter from John P. Galbraith, General Secretary, The Committee on Home Missions and Church Extension, The Orthodox Presbyterian Church, to P. B. Burleigh, dated November 10, 1955, in personal collection of William G. McAtee.

28. Ibid.

29. Letter from John P. Galbraith, General Secretary, The Committee on Home Missions and Church Extension, The Orthodox Presbyterian Church, to P. B. Burleigh, dated November 18, 1955, in personal collection of William G. McAtee.

30. Letter from P. B. Burleigh to William G. McAtee, dated March 4, 1971, in personal collection of William G. McAtee.

31. The following biographical data illustrate the connection between Westminster Seminary, OPC and/or other "outside" influences in the Synod of Mississippi and the PCA split. Traces of networking are seen here. The data are taken from *Min. Dir. 67* and *Min. Dir. 75*. (*Directory years and pages are indicated in parentheses.*) Abbreviations, punctuations, and entries are replicated as they were printed in the directories:

    —William J. Stanway, Westminster Seminary, 43; p, Macon & Center Point chs, Macon, Miss & Shuqulak, 45–51; asso p. 1st ch, Hattiesburg, 51–, p. 1954–; Mod, Syn Miss, 65. (*67– p. 529*). Prof, RefTSJ, 73–; dism to NPC [PCA], Ap 18, 1974. (*75–p. 607*).

    —Peter De Ruiter, Westminster Seminary, '31; recd, 50, CMiss Pby; p, Macon & Center Point chs, Macon, Miss & Shuqulak, 50–56; Edwards, Miss, 56–60. (*67–p. 143*). p Petal [Hattiesburg suburb], Miss, 66–69; dism to Grace Pby [PCA], Oc 16, 1973. (*75–p. 161*).

—Morton H. Smith, Westminster Seminary, 51; prof, BelhC, 54–63; guest lect. WestmTS, 63–4; prof, RefTSJ. 64–73. (*67–p. 517*). dism to MissVal Pby [PCA], Jl 19, 73. (*75–p. 592*).

—Adrian E. DeYoung, Westminster Seminary, 39; recd Jl 22, 58, Miss Pby; p. 1st ch, Hazlehurst, Miss, 58–67. (*67–p. 143*). dism to Evan Pby, Nv 8, 1973. (*75–p. 162*).

—Robert J. Ostenson, Fuller Seminary, 53; Ord Oc 25, 53, Miss Pby; p. Brookhaven, Miss 58–65. (*67–p. 423*). erased fr roll BCO 111–3 [renounce jurisdiction], Dc 18, 1973, Ever Pby. (*75–p. 483*).

—Jack S. Ross, BelhC, 61, BA; Ord JL, 64, CMiss Pby; p. 1st ch, Philadelphia, Miss, 64–68. (*67–p. 483*). p, 1st ch, Hazlehurst, Miss, 68–71; p, 1st ch, Brookhaven, 71–3; dism to Grace Pby [PCA], Oc 16, 1973. (*75–p. 551*).

32. Special Committee of the 201st General Assembly (1989), *All-Black Governing Bodies*, p. 52.

33. Stuart, *Diminishing Distinctives*, pp. 2–3.

34. *The History of the Presbyterian Lay Committee*, p. 1, available online [http://www.laymen.org/].

35. Unpublished *Manuscripts [papers] Presented at Christian Ethics Conference*, Belhaven College, Jackson, Mississippi, May 30–June 1, 1966, in personal collection of William G. McAtee; Papers and Presenters: "Christian Responsibility in Changing Social Patterns"—Park H. Moore, Jr.; "Some Observations Regarding the Biblical and Theological Principal and Responsibility of the Church in a Changing Social Order with Special Reference to the Issue of Race"—Julius J. Scott, Jr.; "The Southern Presbyterian Church and Race Relations (Synopsis)"—Albert H. Freundt, Jr.; "Church and State Relationship in Its Present Aspects"—William G. McAtee; "Current Systems of Christian Ethics"—Stuart B. Babbage; "The New Morality—A Critical Evaluation"—Norman E. Harper; "The Ethical Implications of the 'God is Dead' Theology"—Walter E. Elwell; "Changing Views and Responsibility of Marriage and Home"—Sefton B. Strickland, Jr.

36. Alvis, *Religion and Race: Southern Presbyterians*, p. 133.

37. Ibid., p. 143.

38. Ibid., pp. 136–137.

Chapter 6
The Movement

And the truth is that most of us come to our theological or ecclesiastical positions because of the way we were raised, and where we were raised, and who we knew as we grew up and where we went to school, and what our life experiences have been. And, if we can be exposed to other people's life experiences, we can sometimes come to a whole new understanding of what's really going on around us. That's what the Great Speckled Bird's really about.

—Flynn V. Long, Jr. (24-3)

How was it that this long and complicated effort of creating union presbyteries—the Union Presbytery Movement—became labeled as a "movement"? What qualities did it possess that warranted this designation? What activities did this designation describe? Why was it not named something else? When did it become a movement? It was almost impossible to name that point in time when the term "movement" entered the nomenclature surrounding this phenomenal development in American Presbyterianism.

H. William Peterson, in writing a commentary on the Union Presbytery Movement in 1979, referred to the beginning of the "movement." For Peterson, it may have been inaccurate to call the creation of the initial group of nine or ten union presbyteries, between 1970 and 1972, a "movement." He felt: "We were too much involved in trying to find out who we were and what we were doing to be labeled a movement."[1]

He went on to qualify his observation by saying: "In spite of what some persons might have accused us [of doing], we were not in the process of trying to bring into existence new union presbyteries."[2] Peterson, however, pinpointed 1979 as the moment "that the union presbytery movement really became a movement."[3] He based this on the fact that the Presbytery of Mackinac (UPCUSA) in Michigan began exploring the possibility of becoming a union presbytery. Also, in that same year the Presbytery of Grace (Union) was established. So creating new union presbyteries was one way of defining what constituted the origin and definition of the Union Presbytery Movement.

Maurice Telleen, writing in the article "The Mind-Set of Agrarianism . . . New and Old," made reference to an understanding of movements. "Movements are the natural habitat of true believers. . . . Movements come and go. . . . Movements, almost by definition, are compelled to be certain or 'right.' So it is not surprising that they tend to be self-righteous." Furthermore, these true believers, having strong convictions

---

of being right, were "convinced of both their inevitability and their superiority. The latter confers an aura of both practicality and pragmatism on them. Movements leave little room for meaningful dissent. They regard themselves as destiny. Movements are big on tunnel vision. Their tunnel. Their vision."[4] Whether this definition and assessment of true believers was totally applicable to those in the Union Presbytery Movement warrants further exploration. However, there is no doubt that there were true believers in the Movement who had strong convictions and were filled with a sense of destiny, although there was ample room within it for meaningful dissent.

One definition of "movement" in *Webster's Collegiate Dictionary* is: "A series of acts or events tending toward some definite end; as the prohibition *movement; pl.* activities of a person or a group of persons."[5] The opening quote of this chapter by Flynn Long suggests that there are formative experiences that shape how persons or groups of persons act later in life in movements of their choice. This is particularly true in understanding the persons involved in the Union Presbytery Movement. (On Flynn Long's "Great Speckled Bird" lecture, see chapter 15.)

Kin and Place

One of the most significant defining activities in Southern culture is the introductory ritual of playing "Who do you know?" or "Who are you related to?" It is more than a simple social convention or pleasantry. The answers may have several meanings. Implicit in the questions is an attempt to establish a frame of reference, a genuine effort to determine what "relation" might exist between the parties involved that will inform the present situation. It gives a significant clue as to what was the relational context of the experiences that shaped the persons in the past and who they are in the present and future.

Webster's Dictionary defines "relation," as used here, as "a person connected by consanguinity or affinity; a relative."[6] Webster's defines "consanguinity" as "1. Blood relationship; kinship. 2. Any close relation or connection; affinity."[7] So a "relation" might be someone to whom one is kin by blood, by the accident of birth; or to whom one is related by affinity, by a volitional choice. Sometimes it matters to make this distinction; sometimes it does not.

This sense of extended family powerfully resonated with the ancient "Celtic tie of kinship" transmitted to America by Scottish and Scots-Irish immigrants. In a highly individualistic society characterized by such ties of kinship, one understands that what constitutes being "one of the kin," was a matter of honor to give loyalties in service to the leader who exhibited certain values and mores. Ethnicity was no barrier to such ties, though if threatened, one might oppose a common enemy "on racial or national grounds."[8]

Originally, although loyalties were depicted in a military context where one's obligation of service was to the tribal warrior-chieftain, the tie was not limited to that context. The kinship cohesiveness of Scots was founded, not so much on previous origins, as by facing challenges or adversity collectively in the tribes or clans that absorbed them. James Webb cites the eminent Scottish historian T. C. Smout as contending that the Normans attempted to destroy this kind of kinship by espousing "impersonal, territorial loyalties that pyramided their way up to the English king, a system that encouraged the more nationalistic form of racism."[9] These two senses of loyalties followed immigrants to America.

The second most important defining activity question in Southern culture after "Who are you related to?" is "Where are you from?" Place is more than a street address or coordinates on a map. Place, though it has certain geographic qualities, is an occasion for meaning. Here is where something meaningful happened. It may be simply an ordinary occurrence or a seminal, life-changing experience. Regardless of which one it was, it all fits into a hierarchy of meaning for the persons involved.

If one is to understand fully the Union Presbytery Movement, one must first understand the concept of "being related" and then, the importance of "place" in that phenomenon. It is reasonable to assume, based on what Flynn Long said about how our theological or ecclesiastical positions are formed, that years before the Movement existed, "being related" was elemental in that formation. It was the vehicle that shaped what someday our experiences would be in the Movement.

"Being related" was all about people: how they were connected; how their connections were created and maintained; how they were motivated and how they overcame barriers to fulfill their dreams and aspirations. It is instructive to take a closer look at how people involved in the Movement were shaped by "being related" and where those meaningful connections took "place."

Relations and Connections

For generations in the PCUS, sons followed fathers and sometimes grandfathers into the ministry in local pastorates or the mission fields. In earlier years daughters became directors of religious education (DREs, later DCEs) or they married ministers and became "helpmates" in ministry. Sometimes women also were commissioned to the foreign mission fields where their service was more readily accepted and appreciated. After Rachel Henderlite was the first woman ordained by Hanover Presbytery (PCUS) on May 13, 1965, the door was open for other daughters and sisters to enter the ministry.

The most obvious and basic relation was the family—nuclear or extended. Though not totally unique to the PCUS, its family systems were about as prolific as a good stand of kudzu, a plant imported to the United States from Japan in 1876 for the Centennial Exposition in Philadelphia, Pennsylvania. It was initially brought as an ornamental houseplant and livestock feed, but later used to control soil erosion in the Southeast. It had deep, enormous taproots and grew uncontrollably all over everywhere.[10] A careful study of the *Ministerial Directory of the Presbyterian Church, U.S.* would be like trying to untangle a system of kudzu vines engulfing the old home place to see where they led and what were the connections. It would clearly illustrate how many family names were repeated generation after generation and intertwined with other family names by blood, by marriage, or by affinity.[11]

To get a better glimpse at how this worked, for example, take the "relation vine" labeled with one John M. Reagan's name and begin to pull on it. Reagan grew up in the little town of Hartford, Alabama. His maternal grandfather, a graduate of Columbia Seminary, had been pastor of the Presbyterian Church there. When Reagan was growing up, Robert H. "Bob" Walkup, a student at Louisville Seminary, served the church, alternating with the Presbyterian Church in Ozark, Alabama. Reagan had "a real good experience during that time with the Presbyterian Church."[12]

Reagan's mother wanted him to attend Southwestern at Memphis when the time came for him to go off to college. He was not interested in a liberal arts school, but wanted to study in the School of Chemistry at Alabama Polytechnic Institute (later Auburn University), thinking he might go to medical school. While at Auburn, Reagan got very involved in Westminster Fellowship at First Presbyterian Church where John H. Leith was the pastor. Leith later left to become professor at Union Seminary in Richmond, Virginia. Under the influence of Westminster Fellowship and mentored by Leith, Reagan sensed a call to the ministry (76-2).

Since Reagan was preparing to go to seminary at Columbia, his mother suggested that it might be a good thing for him to work for the summer at Montreat. His brother Joe was already working there as a bus driver and busboy. Reagan heard that the best job at Montreat was gate boy, but word was that Davidson boys had a monopoly on the gate boy jobs. But he applied anyway. Reagan was told later that Roy Jones, a member of the Hartford Presbyterian Church, put in a good word for Reagan with Jones's brother-in-law, James G. Patton. Patton was the executive secretary of the General Council of the General Assembly at the time. Though not certain of the efficacy of this reference, Reagan got the job along with Will Kennedy and Randy Taylor. Kennedy, who had two Presbyterian minister grandfathers, was from Wofford College. Taylor, who had grown up in the North China Kiangsu Mission (PCUS), was from Davidson. Taylor would become the first moderator of the PC(USA), the reunited church, in 1983. And now Reagan, who was from a small town in Alabama, was from Auburn. The monopoly was broken (76-2).

The three college boys lived in the gatehouse, a strategic place to observe all the comings and goings around Montreat and expand their connections with the PCUS. Reagan remembered being on the gate one day when a Mrs. P. P. McCain came through with her daughter Todd in the back seat along with their dog. He claimed he didn't even notice Todd and had no particular relation with her during that summer. He was dating another girl. Todd McCain later became Reagan's wife. Mrs. McCain was the first woman vice-chair of the Democratic Party in North Carolina and was said to have made the motion on the governing board of the University of North Carolina to admit blacks to that institution (76-4).

After that summer, Reagan chose Columbia Seminary because it was the closest seminary to home and the one the Synod of Alabama supported. He said it never occurred to him to go anywhere else. "I just sort of automatically went to Columbia" (76-4).

At that time the president of Agnes Scott was James Ross McCain, who was Todd McCain's uncle, with whom she lived. Reagan courted Todd in "Uncle James Ross's living room" (76-7). Reagan had other entrees to persons in high places. Felix B. Gear was Reagan's favorite professor at Columbia Seminary. It did not hurt that Todd McCain's good friend was Felix Gear's daughter, Muriel. Muriel would later marry A. M. "Mac" Hart, Reagan's roommate at Columbia. Reagan spent time at the Gear home helping with yard chores and having theological conversations with Dr. Gear (76-5).

Out of these conversations and studying with Dr. Gear, Reagan was encouraged to do graduate study at the University of Edinburgh "to get the liberal arts education I should have gotten before I went to Seminary" and according to Gear, to get a view of the gospel in another cultural context. Gear had studied there and had done his thesis while living in the United States. Reagan immersed himself in his studies at the University, but did not complete a paper on the religious philosophy of James McCosh, president of the College of New Jersey, which became Princeton University in 1890. The paper was not submitted before he returned home. He worked on it before he went to the mission field in Japan. He resubmitted it, but it was not accepted. James Ross McCain, former Moderator of the PCUS, on the Moderator's stationery wrote John Baillie, Reagan's faculty advisor and principal of the Divinity School, asking what it would take to make it acceptable. The answer was it would need extensive revision. Reagan, embarrassed by this high level attention, chose not to redo the paper since he got what he felt was needed for his intellectual development. He never finished his degree (76-6).

As for pursuing the Gear connecting "relation branch," Gear had served as pastor of the Columbia Presbyterian Church in Columbia, Mississippi, in the 1930s. In the late 1940s it had been served by Marsh M. Calloway, who was instrumental in guiding the author's call into ministry at presbytery church camps and conferences. The Columbia church was the author's last pastorate in Mississippi in the 1960s. Gear left Columbia, Mississippi, to become a professor at Southwestern at Memphis from the mid-1930s to mid-1940s. Later he served the Second Presbyterian Church in Memphis as pastor until he went to teach at Columbia Seminary. In 1964, as Moderator of the PCUS General Assembly, Gear on his own authority moved the meeting of the General Assembly from Second Presbyterian Church in Memphis to Montreat, because Second Church would not seat black commissioners.

The "relation vine" goes in many other directions and intertwines in interesting ways if one pulls on the Walkup, Taylor, and Kennedy branches. The Walkup "relation branch" had strong connections between Louisville Seminary, Alabama, and Mississippi. Walkup graduated from Louisville Seminary, the seminary he had chosen because it was truly a union seminary, supported by both the Northern and Southern Presbyterian Churches. He was greatly influenced there by Frank H. Caldwell, a fellow Mississippian. He was ordained by North Mississippi in his home church at Senatobia, where William H. McAtee was his pastor. Frank Caldwell and McAtee were in Louisville Seminary together with C. Morton Hanna. Hanna would later teach at Louisville Seminary and the author would serve with his son, Charles M. Hanna, Jr., on the executive staff of Transylvania Presbytery.

W. H. McAtee left Senatobia to serve as pastor at Brookhaven, where Bob's father Robert Lee "Jake" Walkup had been pastor before Bob and his twin brother John were born. Jake had followed William E. Phifer at Brookhaven; afterward he ended up in Senatobia as stated supply serving Bob's grandparents. Phifer's two sons, William, Jr., and Ken, became Presbyterian ministers. Ken served on the faculty at Louisville Seminary.

Bob Walkup, after being ordained, went to Alabama and served his first pastorate in Ozark and later became Home Missions Secretary for Mobile Presbytery. There he served on the candidates committee and gave oversight to Mort McMillan in his candidacy process. Bob left Alabama and became pastor of the First Presbyterian Church, Starkville, Mississippi, where he had a great influence with students through the Westminster Fellowship at Mississippi State.

Frank A. Brooks, Charles L. Stanford, Smiley E. Johnson, and Albert Sidney "Shep" Crigler all found their way into the ministry and to Louisville Seminary under Bob's guidance at Mississippi State. A. D.

Hildebrand, a graduate of Louisville Seminary, served as campus minister at State during this time. Bob would be mentor in coming years for Brooks, Stanford, and the author, when they later became pastors in the Synod of Mississippi.

Along the Taylor "relation branch," bonds were formed with other missionary children in the PCUS China Mission—Randy's brothers Alf and David, Lewis H. Lancaster, Jr., Robert P. "Bob" Richardson, Jr., Robert G. "Bob" Patterson, Jr., and others with last names of Farrior, Montgomery, Currie, Junkin, and Bell. Many of these attended the Shanghai American School together and some were students at Union Seminary in Richmond.[13] Bob Patterson roomed with Lewis Lancaster at Shanghai School and David Taylor at Union Seminary. While at Union, Patterson met the author's sister, Emma Jane McAtee, who was attending the Assembly's Training School (ATS).

Bob Richardson was the son of Robert P. "Pete" Richardson, a classmate of W. H. McAtee at Southwestern Presbyterian University at Clarksville, Tennessee. Pete Richardson was later vice-president of Southwestern at Memphis. During this time the author attended Southwestern, and Pete's son Bob Richardson served as pastor at First PC, Hazlehurst, Mississippi.

Jane McAtee did her summer fieldwork at Camp Choyeh, a presbytery camp in Livingston, Texas, along with Mary V. Atkinson, Margie Crowe, John M. Coffin, and Adrienne I. Thompson. Thompson later married Dean A. Bailey, a Louisville Seminary graduate, who would serve First Presbyterian Church, Grenada, Mississippi. After graduating from ATS, Jane McAtee taught kindergarten at First Presbyterian Church, Midland, Texas, where R. Matthew Lynn was pastor and Flynn V. Long, Jr., was assistant pastor. Lynn would be elected Moderator at the 1969 Mobile General Assembly and Long would become associate stated clerk of the General Assembly. McAtee then moved to Memphis to be a kindergarten teacher at Idlewild Presbyterian Church, where Paul Tudor Jones, a Louisville Seminary graduate, was pastor. It is here where she reconnected with Bob Patterson from Union-ATS days and later they were married.

Pulling on the Kennedy "relation branch" leads in strong ecumenical and educational directions. It has already been noted that Will Kennedy had two grandfathers who were minister commissioners to the 1886 PCUS General Assembly in Baltimore that met jointly with the PCUSA General Assembly to discuss the possibility of reuniting the two. Will was steeped in history, as associate professor at Union Seminary in Richmond, and he was devoted to preparing "teaching elders" to be knowledgeable and effective Christian educators.

One of Kennedy's greatest contributions was putting together the staff of the Board of Christian Education (BCE) in the mid-1960s that built on the newly launched Covenant Life Curriculum. John Reagan served on the staff of the Board of Christian Education as "missionary-in-residence" at the invitation of Kennedy, the very first of this type of program utilizing missionaries during a home assignment. This network of relations, brought together in the staff of the BCE, would become one of the more formidable networks in the cause of the Union Presbytery Movement and denominational reunion, the details of which will be chronicled later. It pulled together people from other networks across the PCUS where strong relations and connections in other settings had already been formed. Kennedy left the BCE and made worldwide connections as staff at the World Council of Churches in Geneva, but as far as the Movement was concerned he had made his greatest contribution. On one of his early visits to the WCC's member churches, Kennedy helped the National Christian Councils of Japan, where Reagan served as Associate General Secretary of Education, become involved in encouraging Japanese churches to be concerned about general education in Japan.

The story of John Reagan's relations and these other extended connections may seem a bit excessive as they are pursued two or three or more degrees of separation from Reagan. But it illustrates how people in the PCUS lived and thought. It shows how people understood "church" and how one made decisions. It is a story about how relations and connections were made and how influential mentors shaped young lives. It suggests the importance of where one went to school, how informal networks impacted formal structures and how place was a significant ingredient in that process. The names of many persons involved in the Union Presbytery Movement appeared in the Reagan story. It is but one small example of an understanding of "family" and "being related" and "place" that was replicated all across the PCUS.

"Family" is but one "place" where relations and connections are made. The community of faith is not limited to one place or simply a collection of individual places, though the local congregation appears to give it the most permanent lodging. In the Presbyterian relational or connectional system, there are temporary or limited-term expressions of community that are equally valuable and formative. A closer look at those is instructive in understanding the role these temporary communities of faith played in the Movement, which itself was one.

Camps and Conferences

One of the extensions of the local community of faith has been through youth camps and conferences. Countless young Presbyterians have in their spiritual memory banks images of campfires or small-group study circles, mountain top experiences or inspiring presentations that touched and changed their lives. These images usually were identified by a single word, the name of the place where the meaningful experience occurred—Belhaven, Hopewell, Ferncliff, Cedar Ridge, Bluestone, Burnamwood, Massanetta, Mo-Ranch, Montreat, Triennium. Many knew the date as if they were labeling these image memories for a scrapbook. No doubt many remembered some counselor or speaker asking: "Have you ever thought about entering the ministry or 'full-time' Christian service?" Many lay leaders, elders, and clergy in the church today have had this experience and are where they are today because of that question.

One of these that holds a special place in the hearts of Presbyterians of the former PCUS is Montreat—The Mountain Retreat Association Conference Center in western North Carolina. Over the years it has been an emotional and spiritual anchor for many different constituents. There are those who are part of the college, those who come for specific short-term conferences or events, those who own cottages, and those who work there in the summer. Boards and agencies of the PCUS each year held their own conferences to bring their troops in from the field for rest and inspiration. Montreat was *the* place where the Southern Presbyterian family gathered for decades to sit on its porches to tell stories of great exploits in the church, share the pain of failure, plot new ecclesiastical strategies, and find new energy to go back "out" into the world. It was a place where great meetings of the General Assembly were held and landmark decisions that shaped the direction of the PCUS were made.

To understand the culture of the PCUS, one must understand the culture of Montreat. The Presbyterian Historical Foundation [now the Presbyterian Historical Society], the depository of sacred artifacts and records of the PCUS located on the grounds of Montreat for decades, gives a classic illustration of its culture. Individuals came to the Foundation to read local histories and piece together their spiritual roots. University and seminary researchers came to delve seriously in this treasure trove of Southern Presbyterian history to discover new meaning in its existence.

In 2004 a proposal was made by a task force, appointed by the Committee on the Office of the General Assembly (COGA), to consolidate the Historical Society office in Montreat with the office in Philadelphia because of budgetary considerations. The task force did not seem to understand fully the culture of Montreat and the PCUS. Friends of the Historical Foundation at Montreat, Inc., was formed to explore alternatives to consolidation. In a letter to interested parties, recipients were reminded that the Historical Foundation was an integral part of Montreat. "Truly it is a treasure house of precious records that informs us of God's gracious providence which has brought us to this time and enables us to discern His intentions for the church in the future."[14] A plea was made not to move these religious symbols from their proper historical archival repository. As of this writing, the outcome was yet to be determined.

Camps, conferences, and conference centers have played a significant role in shaping the lives of members and leaders as well as the corporate expressions of the community of faith.

Church Colleges and Campus Ministries

In the PCUS, church colleges and campus ministries on state university campuses were but an extension of the leadership recruitment system for the denomination, be it for the ordained ministry or for lay leadership in local congregations and higher courts of the church. The role of Westminster Fellowship was illustrated in the John Reagan story. Westminster Fellowship was a doorway into ecumenical relations as well as a recruitment system for church leadership.

Both of these features were seen in a story told by Wayne P. Todd, who was a member of Westminster Fellowship while attending Southwestern at Memphis. He said that at one time he was elected president of the Assembly Youth Council of the PCUS. His younger brother, Newton, was a member of a PCUSA church in Miami and was almost elected as moderator of the Assembly Youth Council of the PCUSA, but ended up as vice-moderator. They attended meetings together as fraternal delegates from their respective denominations (82-2). Wayne also said that when he was moderator of the Synod of Tennessee Westminster Fellowship (WF), he met Flynn Long for the first time. Flynn was doing public relations for Austin Seminary and came to a Synod WF retreat to talk with students about coming to Austin (82-3).

Not only were colleges part of the feeder system into seminaries, they provided a great opportunity to build relationships that would last a lifetime. During the late 1940s and into the 1950s, there was a continuous line of six members of the Alpha Tau Omega fraternity at Southwestern that would play significant roles in the Union Presbytery Movement. Although they were not all there at the same time, they learned their politics in similar fraternity and campus elections. They made divergent choices of seminaries to attend, but their paths crossed later at strategic points in the Movement. They were Graham Gordon, '49; Robert P. Richardson, '51; Wayne P. Todd, '52; T. Morton McMillan, Jr., '53; William G. McAtee, '56; and Lewis L. Wilkins, '58. Gordon, McMillan, and McAtee went to Louisville Seminary; Richardson and

Todd, to Union Seminary in Richmond; and Wilkins to Austin Seminary. Stories like these were repeated in PCUS church-related colleges and campus ministries all across the South.

Seminaries

The formation of the leaders of the community of faith continued to flow from families to institutions of higher education to yet another place: the seminaries. All four PCUS seminaries were considered to be institutions serving the regions where they were located: Union—upper East Coast; Columbia—lower East Coast and Deep South; Louisville—Mid-West and Mid-South; Austin—Southwest. Historically, seminaries in the PCUS were under the control of the synods. In the PCUSA they were controlled by the General Assembly.

Though there seemed to be a general connection between certain colleges and particular seminaries in the PCUS, it was not always followed. It was sometimes unclear why these connections were made, but a case can be made that it had something to do with where the railroads ran. Just as the rivers had provided effective transportation for the great population migrations of an earlier century, so it was that the migration of church leaders as they progressed from college to seminary was greatly enhanced by railroad's ribbons of steel in the twentieth century, creating new relations in new places. Passenger trains continued to make some contribution to the movement of pastors and church leaders as they moved about on their clergy permits, passes that afforded them inexpensive transportation, well into the 1960s.[15]

Davidson was seen as a feeder for Union Seminary in Richmond; Southwestern, for Louisville Seminary; Presbyterian College, for Columbia Seminary; and Austin College, for Austin Seminary. Students from other colleges and state universities generally went to seminaries supported by their synods or to the seminaries closest to them. Some PCUS students went to non-PCUS seminaries "up east," where different sets of connections were made. Once students graduated, the seminaries functioned ordinarily as a placement service for their region and their graduates.

Originally, there was an attempt in 1806 to get a theological library and school at Hampden-Sidney College, since there was a shortage of pastors in Virginia. The PCUSA General Assembly canvassed the presbyteries to see "which of three possibilities they preferred: (1) one strong seminary in a central location; (2) one seminary for the North and one seminary for the South; (3) one seminary in each synod." The presbyteries leaned toward the first and the Assembly established one centrally located seminary for the denomination at Princeton in 1812.[16]

This still did not provide pastors for the South. Union Seminary (Richmond), the oldest of the four PCUS seminaries, was established in 1823 to fill the need for pastors in the Mid-Atlantic states that Princeton did not meet. By the middle of the twentieth century, Union was generally seen as a progressive seminary open to the trends of neo-orthodoxy. Students were deeply influenced by professors Ernest Trice Thompson, John B. Bright, Jr., and others in their views on theology, biblical interpretation, and church history. Thompson was a strong advocate for the reunion of the denominations. Students of Thompson frequently referred to him as being the chief motivator for their being involved in the Union Presbytery Movement and the denominational reunion effort.

Columbia Seminary in Columbia, South Carolina, was formed in 1828 to offset the shortage of clergy to serve congregations farther south, in South Carolina and Georgia. Subsequently it was moved to Decatur, Georgia, to be more centrally located to serve the South-Atlantic and Deep South States. It was generally perceived to be a more conservative seminary, reflecting the culture in which it was located.

By the mid-1950s it was more evenly divided between classic Calvinistic and neo-orthodox theology. The theological spectrum was covered by professors like Manford G. Gutzke, Felix B. Gear, and J. McDowell Richards. Richards had baptized an infant named T. Morton McMillan, Jr., in the early 1930s while pastor at Thomasville, Georgia (05-27). Gear and Richards were very much involved in the reunion of the denominations. Columbia Seminary, not being in a Border State, was less involved in the Union Presbytery Movement. However, the connection to the Movement was through individual students. John Reagan noted that students who became the leadership of the PCA were in his class at Columbia. He said, "we had the most divided class I think that's ever gone through Columbia. And I was not one of the extreme right wing" (76-8).

Louisville Seminary (LPTS) was unique in that its roots were in both the Northern and Southern Presbyterian Churches. To cope with the rapid expansion of Presbyterianism beyond the Alleghenies and the need for ordained clergy there, several seminaries came into existence. Presbyterians in Indiana, feeling that Princeton was too far away to meet their needs, established Hanover Seminary in 1827. In Kentucky, Father Rice informally tutored aspiring candidates in the early days of Transylvania Presbytery. Training of ministers began more formally at Transylvania Seminary (College) and later in a theological department at Centre College in 1828.[17]

The Old School–New School split of the PCUSA in 1837 complicated the seminary education picture. Hanover Seminary, the only unofficial Old School seminary west of the mountains to serve the Ohio and Mississippi River valleys, moved to New Albany, Indiana, in 1840 and changed its name to New Albany Seminary. The Synod of Kentucky was a supporting synod of this seminary, among other synods in the geographical area. By the mid-1800s, the Old School General Assembly wanted officially to have a seminary it controlled in the "West." There was a strong bid by Kentuckians, led by Robert J. Breckenridge, to have Danville chosen as the site. Its bid was chosen by the Assembly, and on October 13, 1853, Danville Theological Seminary (DTS) was formally established. It was supported by synods bordering the Ohio and Mississippi rivers from Ohio to Mississippi. The creation of this seminary was a crippling blow to New Albany Seminary.[18]

Within a decade Danville Seminary found itself caught in the Border State slavery and antislavery conflicts generated by the Civil War and its aftermath. Following the meeting of the General Assembly in 1866, many Kentucky Presbyterians left the PCUSA over the "loyalty oath issue" and aligned themselves with the newly formed PCUS. Danville Seminary decided to remain with the Old School Assembly (North). This, along with the reunion of the Old School General Assembly (North) and the New School General Assembly (North) by 1870, created further problems for Danville Seminary. In the 1880s there was a failed attempt at "joint occupancy" or control of the seminary by the PCUS and the PCUSA.[19]

This reunion left the PCUS without a seminary in this geographical area. The Synod of Kentucky (PCUS) decided to create an institution of theological education in conjunction with its Central University in Richmond, Kentucky. The PCUS General Assembly was also interested in establishing a seminary to serve its churches in the "Southwest" or Ohio and Mississippi River valleys. After protracted negotiations regarding location, "The Theological Seminary of the Southwest," later named Louisville Presbyterian Theological Seminary, was located in Louisville, Kentucky, and began operation on October 2, 1893.[20]

The final decade of the nineteenth century was filled with financial difficulties for both Danville and Louisville seminaries. Once again solutions to these and other problems were sought in merger of the weakening institutions. Fears and perceptions of each other's doctrinal stances fueled opposition to the plan. However, practical necessity swayed the decision. In 1901 the Synods (PCUS) of Kentucky and Missouri together with the General Assembly (PCUSA) embarked on a most unusual "union" venture in the two largest Presbyterian denominations. Combining the legacies of Danville Seminary (PCUSA) and the remnants of the theological department at Central University along with Louisville Seminary (PCUS) and the remnants of the theological department at Southwestern Presbyterian University at Clarksville, Tennessee, they formed the new Louisville Presbyterian Theological Seminary (LPTS).[21]

Old School Calvinism dominated the theological stance of the seminary for more than a quarter of a century, until the older faculty who were present from its beginning came to retirement. They were replaced with faculty that tended to have a more neo-orthodox bent. By middle of the twentieth century, Louisville, as a union seminary, became bastion of support for efforts in bringing about reunion of its two parent denominations. Frank H. Caldwell and William A. Benfield, Jr., were often referred to as persons who were greatly influential in enlisting students and others in that cause. The experience of students attending the seminary was such that it was hard to determine the denominational membership of the faculty or other students. Fieldwork assignments provided exposure to "the other denomination," often with the discovery that there seemed to be very little difference between the two.

In 1902, Austin Seminary was the last of the four PCUS seminaries to be organized. It was definitely the seminary of the Southwest, located in a region of the country that was both "Southern" and "Western" because Texas was essentially divided into East Texas and West Texas. East Texas was "about as close to Mississippi as you can get. And West Texas was totally different" (66-3). Austin tended to be considered West Texas in outlook. West Texan memory was dominated by wars with Mexico, rather than the Civil War.

Certain secular politicians of the time would not think of themselves as "liberals," but would label themselves as "Western progressives." Lyndon Johnson, Sam Rayburn, and Jim Wright all belonged to the Western Progressive Democratic Party. They were not initially "for civil rights *per se*, but when push comes to shove, they stood for it." The society was extremely segregated. There were "cultural racists" who accepted the world about them and did not see any need to do anything about it. But at a personal level, some thought of themselves as accepting everyone as equals (66-3).

In the ecclesial world there were those who considered themselves "progressives." Some felt that the "Unity of the Church" must be acted out in some tangible way. This was vividly illustrated during the vote in 1955 to reunite the PCUS and PCUSA. El Paso Presbytery (PCUS) was the only presbytery in the PCUS that voted unanimously for this reunion (23-5).

The progressive spirit found in the political and ecclesial world of West Texas was reflected at Austin Seminary in its theological bent and its political worldview. Many on the faculty at mid-twentieth century were considered to be pro-union and would play important roles in the denomination and reunion efforts. In 1945 David L. Stitt came to Austin Seminary from Missouri to be president. In the decade prior to that he had served as a member of the Committee on Cooperation and Union in the General Assembly (PCUS) (52-2). In the 1950s, Austin Seminary faculty contributing to its progressive climate were: C. Ellis Nelson, later president of Louisville Seminary and deeply involved in Christian Education curriculum development in both the PCUS and the UPCUSA; T. Watson Street, later executive of the Board of Foreign Missions (PCUS); and James A. Millard, later Stated Clerk of the PCUS.

Early on in the 1950s there was a movement to develop joint sponsorship of Austin Seminary with the Presbyterian Church U.S.A. David Stitt recalled one meeting between representatives of the two denominations in Austin Seminary's new library, where "we voted unanimously to go ahead with it. But, they [PCUSA] couldn't raise the necessary money. We [PCUS] offered half interest for one-half of the wealth of Austin Seminary at that time; if they could raise half of what we were worth, we'd sell them half interest. But they couldn't do it, and so the deal fell apart" (52-3).

Ellis Nelson told a different version of what happened in the union seminary discussions. Nelson, though not present at the meeting, had heard an interesting story told about this effort, that he said was "hitherto proven to be true . . . but it's probably been enriched, Texas-style." The story went that the Seminary was represented by Toddy Lee Winn, who was a very important person in those days in Texas. He gave a chapel at Austin College. He and David Stitt got along well. He helped support the Seminary. He was a lawyer, a banker, an oil person, and head of the Texas Presbyterian Foundation. The meeting was held somewhere in East Texas, according to this story, Tyler or somewhere, with representatives from the Presbyterian Church U.S.A. At that time the synod executive in Texas for the Presbyterian Church U.S.A. was Hoytt Boles (29-4).

They discussed the possibility of having a joint sponsorship of Austin Seminary. But in the discussion, it soon became evident that the Presbyterian Church U.S.A. was not prepared to give any financial support, or very little, to this enterprise. Thereupon, the story goes, Toddy Lee Winn had no reason to stay at the meeting any longer and walked out. At the higher level of Board members, in some sort of an official meeting, the Southern Presbyterian Church was not about to have joint ownership and control of the Seminary if there wasn't to be joint financing (29-4).

Regardless of which part or parts of these versions of the story describe the actual way the decision was made, the fact remains that the decision was made by colorful characters not to make Austin a union seminary. When David Stitt was asked years later if he had any regrets that Austin was not able to pull off making it a union seminary, he replied: "No, I think that's probably for the best. . . . It would have created problems which we didn't have . . . [among] personalities" (52-16).

McCormick Seminary played an important role in the Movement and reunion of the denominations. Though not a PCUS seminary, its roots were in the Ohio River Valley, adjacent to Kentucky geographically, and it was definitely Old School in its theological perspective. After a few years of competition with Danville Seminary for the allegiance of Old School Presbyterians in the region, New Albany Seminary moved to Chicago, Illinois, in 1859. It would "eventually become McCormick Theological Seminary and pass into denominational control" as the Presbyterian seminary for the Northwest.[22] By the middle of the twentieth century it was fully responsive to the urban context in which it was located. However, later it did have influence beyond its geographical region in an area overlapping with that of the PCUS.

Clearly there was a connection between McCormick Seminary and the PCUSA churches in West Texas, probably thanks to good passenger train connections. Ken McCall said that "it was very clear in Texas when I grew up that there was only one Seminary. That was McCormick and you went there to prepare yourself to come back to Texas and become a part of the local Mafia, or the 'real group' or whatever. So we once in a while had some strange duck who went to Princeton, but that was discouraged, and of course one could not go to Austin Theological Seminary" (66-2).

Trinity College [later University], where McCall attended, was the PCUSA feeder college in Texas for McCormick Seminary. Hoytt Boles, Sr., as executive of the PCUSA Synod of Texas, functioned as that denomination's unofficial "placement officer" for McCormick Seminary. Boles had been his pastor when he was growing up, so, McCall said, it was pretty much decided where he would go to seminary (66-4). Boles was known by some as "Bishop Boles" for the way he ran the synod and worked the placement-relocation system (58-8).

It was clear that the Southern Church and the Northern Church in that area were at odds with each other. At one point the Southern Church was developing Mo-Ranch as a conference center and offered the Northern Church a chance to be part of it as a joint ministry. McCall remembered "Hoytt Boles being very vociferous about the fact that we had rejected it" (66-1). There was a whole generation of "Boles' Boys" loyal to him for many years in West Texas Presbyterian politics (75-8).

One contribution by McCormick Seminary to the Union Presbytery Movement and the reunion of the denominations was the impact of the Doctor of Ministry Presbytery Executive Track. Robert C. "Bob" Worley, its director, in the 1970s served as organizational consultant to various governing bodies and agencies in the PCUS (75-1). He revealed how interrelated the McCormick program and the PCUS really were.

John F. Anderson, executive of the Board of National Ministries (PCUS), in a conversation with Worley said, "I don't want to leave this Church as a Southern Church. When I die, I want to die in a new, united Church. . . . Bob, what could I do to help that? . . . What are the points of entry into the Church where you can make a difference?" And Bob said, "I think if you could get a different breed of Presbyter Executive, that would help greatly." And Anderson said, "What would that look like?" So Bob described a program. Anderson said, "How much would it cost?" And Bob suggested an amount. Anderson replied, "Well, I'll provide the money, you put the program together." And that's exactly how the whole Doctor of Ministry Presbytery Executive Track at McCormick originated (75-8).

This produced a different generation of executives for the church that had a very different agenda for the church. As Worley became more familiar with the PCUS, especially as he worked with Palo Duro (Union) Presbytery, his assumptions proved correct. He said, "I'd met some of the old-timers in the Deep South who were Stated Clerks and General Presbyters combined, and had everything controlled, and you know, nothing was going to happen while they were there. I mean, they were like Hoyt Boles, only in the Deep South" (75-8).

Each of these seminaries—Union, Columbia, Louisville, Austin, and McCormick—were temporary or limited-term expressions of communities of faith that were valuable and formative in shaping the leadership of the church and the direction the denominations would take. At mid-twentieth century these seminaries were still dominant forces in the Presbyterian relational or connectional system. They were places where lasting relations and connections were made that helped define Presbyterian identity. This had a profound effect on the Movement and denominational reunion. By the 1970s and 1980s they were no longer able "to forge a distinctive Reformed theology or ecclesiastical identity." Though most of the faculty were Presbyterian, the emphasis on ecumenism, diversity, and pluralism led the curriculum to focus increasingly on "cross-cultural exploration of the nature of Christian faith and witness" and not on scholastic Calvinism or even neo-orthodoxy.[23] By 2005 one-third of the candidates under care of the PC(USA) attended seminaries not affiliated with it, thus further eroding a distinctive denominationally trained leadership identity.[24]

Fields of Service

Persons left these temporary educational havens in the mid-twentieth century to enter a larger world of service where old relations and connections were renewed and new ones were made. It was not simply a matter of getting a call as pastor to a local congregation through the seminary placement system and other informal relational networks. These informal relations had developed in families, in camps and conferences, at colleges and campus ministries, and at seminary. They often got intertwined and rearranged as persons moved about from one call to another. A detailed study of these informal pastors' networks throughout the twentieth century in key places such as Kentucky, Missouri, and Texas would be highly instructive as to how old relations and connections were renewed and new ones were made. This was illustrated earlier in the John M. Reagan story and will be seen below in connection with the effort to change the Constitution and to implement the Union Presbyteries chapter.

To understand fully how and where these connections were made and remade, one has to understand the division of responsibilities in the PCUS. The courts of the PCUS, in addition to their ecclesiastical functions, were like a set of concentric family circles radiating out from the core family—the congregation—to the session, the presbytery, the synod, and the General Assembly. The family gathered from time to time at stated meetings, committee meetings, and various conferences. Here the church families interconnected and lived out their identity as Presbyterians. They knew what the Presbyterian Church was about and gave it spirited support.

The broader church's programmatic responsibilities were assigned to strong boards and agencies, each with strong executives by which they were immediately and intimately identified. When someone in the PCUS said: "Watson Street," people thought, Board of Foreign Missions; "Marshall Dendy," Board of Christian Education; "John Anderson," Board of Church Extension (later National Ministries); "Larry Stell," General Council; "Evelyn Green," Board of Women's Work, and so forth.

These boards and agencies were assigned primarily to particular courts for implementation of program. Foreign Missions and General Council were primarily General Assembly assignments; Christian Education, synod assignment; Church Extension or National Ministries, presbytery assignments; Women's Work, synodical and presbyterial assignments. Sessions and local congregations knew exactly where to turn when specific promotional information or program material was needed for local programs.

Two of the boards supported offices and personnel in the field. Church Extension, formerly known as Home Missions, had Church

Extension secretaries in presbyteries to do new church development and other mission activities that were an extension of local congregational mission in that area. Christian Education had synod regional directors with oversight of ministries in colleges and other programs in higher education, such as campus ministries. They also were responsible for conferences and synod schools. They introduced new curriculum as it was produced and provided leadership training events in presbyteries and local congregations.

The Board of Christian Education with its system of regional directors played a unique role in the Union Presbytery Movement and ultimately in denominational reunion. Along the Border States these regional directors worked most closely with their regional director counterparts in the UPCUSA. In some instances, one person filled both positions.

Other boards were places where previous networks intermingled, but not to the same extent as in the Board of Christian Education. The Southern Church had a tradition of having persons go from the pastorate to national or regional boards and agencies in staff positions and then return, after they had served in various positions across the church. From the mid-1960s until the Board of Christian Education (BCE) was consolidated with other General Assembly boards and agencies to form the General Executive Board (GEB) in Atlanta in 1973, there were some twenty-two staff persons working for the BCE from previous networks that were involved at some point in the Movement and the denominational reunion effort. Some were from more than one network. Of these twenty-two, there were six Synod Regional Directors of Christian Education,[25] with the rest considered national staff. Two served on both regional and national staffs at different times.[26]

There were five that had served pastorates in Mississippi;[27] six graduates of Southwestern at Memphis during the one decade mentioned earlier;[28] and eight graduates of Louisville Seminary.[29] Six had served pastorates in Kentucky;[30] two had spent some of their childhood on the foreign mission field.[31] When they left the employ of the BCE, at one time or another, eight were in presbytery staff positions;[32] five were in synod staff positions;[33] four were with the General Executive Board;[34] five were in teaching positions;[35] three were in ecumenical staff positions;[36] eight were back in pastorates;[37] one returned to the mission field;[38] one was executive director of Montreat;[39] and one retired immediately.[40]

Through a wide array of ecumenical commitments made by the Board of Christian Education, relations and connections were made with other church leaders in numerous denominations and settings. The Covenant Life Curriculum, the use of which in some quarters became the litmus test for loyalty to the denomination, was co-produced with the Cumberland PC and the Reformed Church in America. There were other cooperative program efforts in many areas between the PCUS and UPCUSA Boards of Christian Education. Another area of cooperation was the Joint Education Development Committee (JED), an ecumenical group from several denominational units concerned with educational issues.

On a wider scale was the national United Ministries in Higher Education (UMHE), which was concerned with all sorts of college and campus ministry issues. The Council on Theological Education was concerned with Presbyterian seminaries. The Cooperative College Registry, a pool of 500 church colleges that cut across all denominational lines, focused on trying to recruit faculty and other issues held in common. It was made up of representatives from Presbyterians, both Northern and Southern, United Church of Christ (UCC), Methodists, American Lutheran Church (ALC), Lutheran Church in America (LCA), United Brethren, and others. The Southern Association of Presbyterian [PCUS] Colleges met to figure out how to work and do things together. They always invited counterparts from other Presbyterian denominations, both black and white, to participate. Out of this a most interesting project was developed for church colleges and state universities in Appalachia (56-2).

In addition there were many examples of ecumenical and cooperative work done in other program areas of the church on national, regional, and local levels. The Coalition of Religion in Appalachia (CORA), a broad-based ecumenical group, and the Commission on Appalachian Ministries (CAM), the Presbyterian version, were involved in a myriad of justice and empowerment concerns in Appalachia. Presbyterians were involved in state and local councils of churches and other ecumenical alliances and cooperative efforts dealing with human need, too numerous to name here. New personal relations and connections were made that served the mission of the church well, living out Presbyterians' strong commitment to ecumenism.

One of the most important and influential parts of the relational and connectional system of the PCUS was the Women of the Church organization, WOC, as it came to be known. Long before women were admitted to ordination as ministers and elders, they were a not always silent or invisible force to be reckoned with. Originally, they were known as "women's auxiliaries with circles" and were anything but un-directional or ancillary to the life of the church. Their Bible studies strengthened and molded their faith and spirits. They taught Sunday school classes and cared for many of the social and pastoral concerns of the church. Their benevolence giving was legendary. They brought about real change in the church as a result of their Birthday Offering and other activities.

Their organization was clearly defined and highly functional, though they did not have regional staff, but were guided by elected volunteer presbyterial, synodical, and assembly councils. There were strong national staff to give guidance and maintenance to all aspects of "women's work." The WOC had a distinctive Southern style and strength, that would later be problematic for some as it moved to reconcile itself with the United Presbyterian Women (UPW) of the UPCUSA in forming the reunited church and thereafter. Nonetheless, the contribution the WOC made to union presbyteries and the reunion process was enormous.

Radical changes to the PCUS, brought on by actions of the 1969 PCUS General Assembly (Mobile), would prove to be a defining watershed moment in the history of the denomination, the details of which will be explored later. What is important at this point is that some of its actions brought about major disruptions in the relational dynamics and connectional structure of the PCUS that characterized its unique nature. The full significance of these major disruptions was overshadowed by the euphoria of other progressive accomplishments achieved at the time.

Who would have even dared to ask the question: "Dreams, where have you gone?" To do so would have been tantamount to giving tacit support to the belief that dreams might not come true. This was not the operative question of the day, because dreams existed that were believed and were transforming—*a new way of being church, and creating union presbyteries was the way.* The most pressing question then was, "*How* could we bring about constitutional changes to permit their existence, not *Could* it be done?"

The formative relations and connections—within nuclear and extended families; through camps and conferences and conference centers; at church colleges and campus ministries; in seminaries and later in fields of service—shaped the leaders of the Union Presbytery Movement in the twentieth century and, maybe to a lesser degree, shaped the new generation of leaders of the Presbyterian Church (U.S.A.) in the twenty-first century. But the orderly pre-1960 world, in which these relations and connections were made and seemed secure, was rapidly disintegrating and flying apart. Clearly there were winners and losers in these relations and connections. The full consequences of the contributions and flaws of those formative experiences would be a long time coming, for ghosts of Stamford Bridge and Hastings *et al.* were lurking in the shadows undetected.

Notes

1. H. William Peterson, *And Then There Were ~~Ten, Eleven~~, Twelve! Anymore?— A Study of the Union Presbytery Movement—1970–1980*, unpublished, 1979, in personal collection of William G. McAtee, p. 13.

2. Ibid.

3. Ibid., p. 17.

4. Maurice Telleen, *The Mind-Set of Agrarianism . . . New and Old, in The Essential Agrarian Reader*, ed. Norman Virzba, pp. 52–53.

5. *Webster's Collegiate Dictionary* (1948), s.v. "movement."

6. Ibid., s.v. "relation."

7. Ibid., s.v. "consanguinity."

8. Webb, *Born Fighting: How the Scots-Irish Shaped America*, p. 38.

9. Ibid.

10. "The Amazing Story of Kudzu," available online [http://www.cptr.ua.edu/kudzu/].

11. Many of the biographical details in this section were gleaned from the *Ministerial Directory of the Presbyterian Church, U.S.* (all editions) or from the author's memory.

12. John M. Reagan, interview by author, September 2, 2000, Interview 76, pp. 2–3. Additional information for this and the following Reagan endnotes were obtained from an untranscribed phone conversation with Reagan on December 28, 2004.

13. From an unrecorded conversation by author with Robert G. Patterson November 1, 2004.

14. Letter from James A. Cogswell, chairperson, Friends of the Historical Foundation at Montreat, Inc., to "Friends," September 24, 2004.

15. See William G. McAtee, "Rivers, Railroads and Relations" [A Tribute to Bob Walkup Before He Left Us], for a fuller account of these concepts, unpublished, in personal collection of William G. McAtee.

16. Loetscher, *A Brief History of the Presbyterians*, pp. 90–91.

17. Rick Nutt, *Many Lamps, One Light* (Grand Rapids: William B. Eerdmans Publishing Co., 2002), pp. 2–3.

18. Ibid., pp. 3–5.

19. Ibid., pp. 17–23.

20. Ibid., pp. 24–26.

21. Ibid., pp. 47–49.

22. Ibid., p. 2.

23. Coalter, Mulder, and Weeks, eds., *The Re-Forming Tradition*, p. 214.

24. Statistic provided by the PC(USA) National Ministries Division, Leadership and Vocation Office, August 9, 2005. The one-third of PC(USA) candidates attending non-PC(USA) seminaries compares to: 40% in the Reformed Church in America; 60% in the United Church of Christ; and 10% in the Evangelical Lutheran Church, which funds its seminaries significantly and has other controls on candidates.

25. Synod Regional Directors of Christian Education: J. F. Austin (Oklahoma), James A. Nisbet (Mississippi), J. Allen Oakley (Missouri), J. Harold Jackson (Arkansas), Theodore A. Jaeger (Missouri), Graham Gordon (Kentucky).

26. Served on both regional and national staff: James A. Nisbet and Graham Gordon.

27. Mississippi pastorates: James A. Nisbet, Robert P. Richardson, Jr., J. Moody McDill, Frank A. Brooks, Jr., William G. McAtee.

28. Southwestern at Memphis graduates: Graham Gordon, George A. Chauncey, Robert P. Richardson, Jr., T. Morton McMillan, Jr., William G. McAtee, Lewis L. Wilkins.

29. Louisville Seminary graduates: Graham Gordon, Ernest Stricklin, J. Allen Oakley, John A. Kirstein, T. Morton McMillan, Jr., James W. Gunn, William G. McAtee, H. William Peterson.

30. Kentucky pastorates: Ernest Stricklin, Graham Gordon, T. Morton McMillan, Jr., H. William Peterson, James W. Gunn, George A. Chauncey.

31. Childhood on mission field: Hugh F. Halverstadt (Africa) and Robert P. Richardson, Jr. (China).

32. In presbytery staff positions: J. F. Austin (Bethel), J. Allen Oakley (St. Louis, Elijah Parish/Lovejoy and Giddings Lovejoy), H. William Peterson (Western Kentucky), William G. McAtee (Transylvania), J. Harold Jackson (North Alabama), Lewis L. Wilkins (Palo Duro), John B. Evans (New Harmony), H. Davis Yeuell (interim in John Calvin).

33. In synod staff positions: J. Harold Jackson (Mid-South and Living Waters), John A. Kirstein (Mid-South), Lewis L. Wilkins (Mid-South and Lincoln Trails), H. Davis Yeuell (Virginias, interims in Covenant and Northeast), James A. Nisbet (Southeast).

34. With General Executive Board: Mary V. Atkinson, George A. Chauncey, John B. Evans, Robert P. Richardson, Jr.

35. In teaching positions: Ernest Stricklin (Ohio University), J. Moody McDill (University of Richmond), Graham Gordon (Hampshire College), Hugh F. Halverstadt (McCormick Seminary), William G. McAtee (adjunct at McCormick, Lexington, and Louisville Seminaries).

36. In ecumenical staff positions: William B. Kennedy (WCC), James W. Gunn (NCC), Lewis L. Wilkins (Louisiana Council of Churches).

37. Back in pastorates: John B. Evans, J. F. Austin, Frank A. Brooks, Jr., John A. Kirstein, Robert P. Richardson, Jr., T. Morton McMillan, Jr., Theodore A. Jaeger, Lewis L. Wilkins, stated supply.

38. Returned to mission field: John M. Reagan (Japan).

39. Served as executive director of Montreat: H. William Peterson.

40. Retired immediately: Malcolm P. Calhoun.

Part II: Living Dreams
Chapter 7
Prelude to Change

Whereas, the proposal hereinafter advanced will neither subtract from the denominational strength nor eradicate the loyal and faithful relationships and obligations toward their respective higher judicatories and denominations which the Presbytery of Central Texas (U.S.) and the Presbytery of Brazos (U.P.U.S.A.) acknowledge and intend to maintain, but will rather enhance them by enlarging the relationship, responsibilities, and ministry of both courts in this area of their jurisdiction, providing a single, mature, and vital Presbyterian program of oversight to our churches and a strongly supported Presbyterian program of nurture and mission to the glory of our Lord and to the credit of the Reformed tradition; Now, therefore, The Presbytery of Central Texas, respectfully overtures the General Assembly to amend the Constitution of the Presbyterian Church in the United States . . .

—From the Presbytery of Central Texas Overture regarding Union Presbyteries[1]

Practical necessity has always generated the spark of imagination and ingenuity in the human spirit that has led to creative solutions to almost insurmountable problems. For years, elements of the Southern and Northern Presbyterian Churches lived in geographic proximity in certain areas of the country, notably in or near the Border States. They related to each other basically in three ways: they competed with each other, they cooperated with each other, or they summarily ignored each other. Sometimes the competition was fierce, for instance, in the area of new church development. Comity agreements about geographical separation were reached, in some cases only to be ignored. Creative joint mission initiatives were undertaken but were encumbered by the necessity of obtaining un-amended, fast-track authorization by both parties, each having very different funding systems. On occasion, one denomination had almost no awareness that the "other" denomination even existed, and could care less.

There were, however, persons who felt that all of these were unacceptable behaviors for Presbyterians to exhibit, and they began to tinker with ways to change the situation. They had been cooperating across denominational lines for years and had overcome all kinds of obstacles created by having two separate systems. They came to the conclusion over time that it would be much better and make more sense to have one system rather than two. The idea of creating a "union" presbytery began to emerge.

But the issue was, how to make that happen. They could simply put two presbyteries together in a "union" presbytery, as congregations had done years before, and ask the higher courts to regularize it after the fact. Or they could, in effect, ask permission of the higher courts first and then unite two presbyteries. This would require some change or addition to the Constitution. The time to do nothing had passed.

Two Routes to Take

Sometime around 1964 or 1965, an informal and unofficial discussion about which route to take to make union presbyteries a reality took place at Grace First Presbyterian Church in Wetherford, Texas. Flynn Long, William M. Gould, John W. Cunningham, and others were there from the PCUS. J. Hoytt Boles, Fred A. Ryle, Jr., and others were there from the UPCUSA. Ryle would later become pastor at Grace First PC. This was an interesting congregation.

The first route explored was based on their long experience with union churches or congregations: simply have two presbyteries take action to unite. There had been two Presbyterian churches in Wetherford. Grace PC had been PCUSA, and First PC had been PCUS. They decided to "come together" but not "unite." For thirty years it had been their practice to ask their respective presbyteries to appoint a stated supply pastor who happened to be the same person. The pastor was not technically the pastor, and in this way the churches got around the necessity of actually uniting (23-7).

Central Texas Presbytery (PCUS) had a long history of cooperative work with Brazos Presbytery (UPCUSA) and other predecessor presbyteries. They had a history of creating union or federated congregations. First PC Church of Fort Worth was one of the oldest and largest federated churches in both denominations, dating from early in the twentieth century. The mission committee of these two presbyteries decided that any new churches established would be union churches (23-6).

It was in this context that this idea about union presbyteries began to germinate as a way of helping Grace First deal with its presbyterial connections. It was clear to those present that they could make a case for the two presbyteries simply to take action to unite. This was based on the theory that presbytery is the basic court, judicatory, or governing body of the Presbyterian Church. "If you don't have presbyteries, you don't have Presbyterianism. . . . General Assemblies do not create the Presbyterian Church; presbyteries create the Presbyterian Church. In fact, they authorize the membership of the General Assembly" (23-8).

Furthermore, the theory maintained, "the basic apostolicity and the basic catholicity of the church in the Presbyterian system [are] carried out through a presbytery. And if you don't have presbyteries, you're no longer catholic in the Reform[ed] sense, because presbyteries ordain people for ministry, and organize churches" (23-8).

The second route explored was the one requiring a constitutional amendment. Chapter 31 of the *Book of Church Order*, titled "*Federated*" or "*Union*" *Particular Churches*, had been added earlier to accommodate an existing reality. The group felt that it was time to draft a sample chapter for union presbyteries based on Chapter 31 as precedent. Flynn Long drafted a handwritten document, which he said is still in his file, as a prototype for what would become Chapter 32 of the *Book of Church Order* (PCUS) and Chapter 37 of the *Book of Order* (UPCUSA). The group gave its approval of the draft and suggested it be tested out with constitutional and political experts at the General Assembly level (23-8).

Sometime in mid-1965 Flynn Long and John Cunningham flew to Atlanta to consult with James A. Millard, Stated Clerk of the General Assembly, and others like John F. Anderson. With Millard, Long said they had a very cool reception. And in the course of the conversation, Millard made a comment to Cunningham and Long, the basic thrust of which was, "Why don't you kids go back home until you're dry behind the ears, and quit trying to mess around with the work of the General Assembly? We're involved in union with the RCA Church, and important things are happening, and this is just not important, and you don't know what you're talking about. And, just go . . . why don't you just . . . withdraw that thing? You're as crazy as those people in Kentucky and Missouri" (23-9).

On the plane going home, Long and Cunningham wondered what Millard meant by that last statement. They concluded that there must be some "people in Kentucky and Missouri that are as crazy as we are . . . working with the U.S.A. Church, and we need to get up there and see them." So when they got back to Texas they talked about what they discovered with Richard W. "Bill" Jablonowski and Leroy B. "Roy" Horn, who were very interested (23-9).

Someone provided the four of them with a private plane and they flew up as soon as they could and met with Richard "Dick" Huey and others from Missouri, and T. Morton "Mort" McMillan, Jr., and others from Kentucky.[2] They shared the draft of the overture containing the Union Presbytery chapter that Central Texas Presbytery (PCUS) planned to send to its General Assembly and Brazos Presbytery (UPCUSA) planned to send to its General Assembly. They all went away from this meeting very enthusiastic about the prospects for their plans and committed to continue meeting to work on strategies for getting the overtures passed (23-9). Later somebody commented to Cunningham, "What in the world did you people do to Morton McMillan in St. Louis? . . . because he came back . . . just ready to take on the world" (23-10).

The Synod of Kentucky (PCUS) voted in its stated meeting on June 16, 1965, to ask the Synod of Kentucky (UPCUSA) to join it in establishing a joint committee of five from each synod, "to bring before these two bodies a plan looking forward to a reunion of the two Synods of Kentucky, which would not be contrary to the laws of our Church."[3] This action by both Synods of Kentucky was what got the subject of union synods on the table for both denominations. The joint committee met on September 22, 1965, discussed the issues involved, and made plans to invite the Stated Clerks of the two General Assemblies, James A. Millard (PCUS) and Eugene Carson Blake (UPCUSA) to the next meeting in October to ask for their suggestions, comments, and reactions.[4]

On October 29, 1965, at a meeting of the Kentucky Joint Committee, a discussion was held about the constitutional changes necessary to allow the two Synods to unite, and it was "concluded by common consent that 'a union Synod presupposes union Presbyteries.' "[5] Since it seemed almost like a footnote to the primary focus and overtures about union synods, the question of union presbyteries was added to the agenda of the Kentucky Joint Committee. The General Assembly Stated Clerks were unable to attend this meeting.

A letter of November 1, from Gordon L. Corbett, executive, Synod of Kentucky (UPCUSA) to fellow UPCUSA executives, indicated that "Dr. Millard responded [to the initial invitation] in a manner that gave us the impression that he would not be interested in meeting at any time. Dr. Blake indicated a keen interest in meeting when our schedules could be mutually worked out."[6]

Blake met with the Kentucky Joint Committee on December 4, 1965. He had already met, on November 11, with the Joint Strategy Committee of the presbyteries of Central Texas (PCUS) and Brazos (UPCUSA). Phil Bembower attended the Texas meeting, and in his report of November 15 to the Kentucky Joint Committee he told about Blake's recitation of the background on how the union church chapters got into the respective Constitutions. Blake said "They [the chapters] came into being early in the 1940s, when several Kentucky presbyteries 'jumped the gun' and formed union churches before there was such a thing." Blake went on to say that "the original committee which wrote the existing union church chapter was given a mandate to legalize an accomplished fact, and was 'rigged' in favor of union churches." Dr. Blake said he "wrote the original wording 'reluctantly,' recognizing the fact that the basic church structure makes such a thing 'not possible.' The chapter was written also with the hope that no 'contingencies' would develop requiring the use of the mechanisms of recourse."[7]

Blake said that "at the time the chapter was written, only about 25 churches were involved, so possibilities [for 'contingencies'] were few."

He did raise a concern that "the possibility of legal situations arising at presbytery or synod level is much greater." His final comment was: "If the chapter on union churches is good, then the current proposals are in order." But according to Bembower, this basic premise was, in Blake's mind, still questionable.[8] It was obvious by now, no doubt due to Blake's comments about the legal risks at the presbytery and synod levels, that it would be politically wise to forego the route of having two presbyteries unite, announce what had been done and wait to see what the General Assemblies would do about it. The union church chapters in the Constitutions provided the precedent but not the model for achieving union presbyteries and synods.

Millard met with the Kentucky Joint Committee on January 24, 1966, at which time he made comments about how the Assembly process would handle the union presbyteries and union synods overtures. He also "warned of the danger that some in the U.S. church might see this effort as an attempt to becloud or hinder the [PC]US-RCA merger, and he sought to interpret to the committee why some elements in the General Assembly might oppose such amendments."[9] One of the outcomes of this warning was that, just in case the PCUS-RCA merger passed, the wording in the drafts of the chapters on union presbyteries and union synods was changed "so that it included the word 'classis' and 'consistory' and all the language that was necessary to make it possible for that to work" (23-16).

The route of amending the Constitution by introducing new chapters on union presbyteries and union synods was the consensus route by advocates in Kentucky, Missouri, and Texas. The groups in these synods had carefully coordinated their efforts by exchanging working drafts of overtures and proposed chapters on union presbyteries and synods to ensure that they would be identical. The minutes of meetings of the official strategy committees in the three synods almost always included representatives from the other committees.

As a result, Central Texas (PCUS) and Brazos (UPCUSA) and other presbyteries overtured their respective General Assemblies regarding an amendment to the Constitution to permit the establishment of union presbyteries. Central Texas Presbytery (PCUS), at a meeting in Grapevine, unanimously adopted the overture. It seemed fantastic to someone in Atlanta that a presbytery would adopt something that extreme without a dissenting vote. Flynn Long's response was, "But, Central Texas Presbytery was interesting in that respect; we had a presbytery that would go for broke" (23-11). Other presbyteries and synods followed suit in crafting overtures with regard to union presbyteries and synods. The formal process was finally launched and the proposals would eventually find their way before both General Assemblies.

1966 UPCUSA General Assembly (Boston)

There were two significant amendments to the Constitution considered at the 1966 UPCUSA General Assembly (Boston). One was the proposal regarding the *Book of Confessions*, and the other was the proposal to permit union presbyteries and synods. John H. Swan, who attended the Assembly, recalled that one of the laypeople in the congregation he served was a member of the national committee that was working on the first one. "So I did get caught up in the *Book of Confessions* and thought that was a wonderful, wonderful step forward in the life of the Church. . . . To me, it was the great step . . . the Confession of '67 and the *Book of Confessions*." When asked about the proposal to permit union presbyteries and synods, Swan's reply was, "Yeah, if it was there [*chuckling*], I wasn't aware of it" (81-3). It appeared that the union presbyteries overture was treated respectfully as a routine matter, with only commissioners from the Border States having a real clue as to what it was all about.

The Assembly received six overtures relating to union churches, presbyteries, and synods. They came from the presbyteries of Brazos, St. Louis, Transylvania, Sedalia, Western Kentucky, and Washington City. In making its case, the Brazos Overture #44 cited the fact that Central Texas Presbytery (PCUS) covered the same geographical area and was approximately the same size as Brazos Presbytery (UPCUSA). Having competing parishes in most locales was "frequently confusing to our people and the general public, often detrimental to good order, likely to divide the Reformed witness, and certainly conducive to competitive and wasteful administrative, plenary, and financial effort." It cited the existence of union or federated congregations as the constitutional precedent for its request. It mentioned numerous areas where cooperation in mission and ministry already existed between the two presbyteries. Finally, it argued that passage of the amendment "will neither subtract from the denominational strength nor eradicate the loyal and faithful relationships and obligations toward their respective higher judicatories."[10]

The Assembly voted to send down the overture from the Presbytery of Brazos (UPCUSA) as it related to churches and presbyteries. It referred the rest of the overtures dealing with union presbyteries and synods to the Commission on Ecumenical Mission and Relations (COEMAR) for consideration and asked that it report its findings to the next Assembly.

There was one glitch, however, before the overture was finally passed. James H. Rucker, Sr., told how he had spent an afternoon in the committee, listening to the debate considering the overtures on the union presbyteries and union synods chapters. The committee voted and were coming to the floor of the Assembly with a recommendation to permit union synods and union presbyteries, but had taken out the part that would include "classes" of the Reformed Church of America, their term for presbyteries.

That night at the Stated Clerk's dinner, Rucker ended up seated next to Gene Blake. In conversation Rucker told Blake about the committee's recommendation, "at which point he had a conniption fit and . . . ran out to find one of his lieutenants to find out what had really happened." Blake proceeded to "call the committee back into session, which was typical Gene Blake. . . . He did not know until I told him just in casual conversation at dinner that that's what had happened, that I was kind of surprised" (39-5). This is how the RCA provision ended up as part of the final recommendation regarding those chapters in the *Book of Order* (UPCUSA).

There were two other significant actions taken at the 1966 UPCUSA Assembly (Boston) that had ecumenical ramifications. William P. Thompson, an elder who had been practicing law for about twenty years in Wichita, Kansas, had served as Moderator of the UPCUSA General Assembly in 1965. Eugene Carson Blake was coming to the end of his term as Stated Clerk and leaving to become Secretary General of the World Council of Churches. Thompson was elected to succeed him as Stated Clerk in 1966 (01-1) This represented a very significant change in leadership at this position in the UPCUSA.

The other significant action came in response to Overture #41 from the Presbytery of Cuba, a member of the Synod of New Jersey. This Presbyterian witness in Cuba had been developed by the Board of National Missions in response to an initial request from Christians already in Cuba. The current overture called for the release of the Presbytery of Cuba from membership in the UPCUSA in order to become independently the Reformed-Presbyterian Church in Cuba (RPCC). An Administrative Commission was established to implement this request.[11] It reported to the next Assembly that on January 22, 1967, the RPCC was duly organized in a meeting at First Presbyterian Church, Havana, with William P. Thompson, Stated Clerk (UPCUSA), in attendance.[12] Ecumenical partnerships between the RPCC and the PC(USA) were established in the last decade of the twentieth century, with one of the partnerships being between Villa Clara-Sancti Spiritus and Transylvania. The author served as an International Volunteer in Mission as a Cuba specialist for six years after his retirement as executive presbyter of Transylvania Presbytery.

1966 PCUS General Assembly (Montreat)

Aubrey Brown, editor of *The Presbyterian Outlook*, wrote several people who were going to be commissioners to the 1966 PCUS General

Assembly (Montreat), asking them what they thought was the most crucial action the Assembly could take. When George B. Telford, Jr., got Brown's letter, Telford wrote him saying "the most important thing the Presbyterian Church can do would be to move from the status of observer to participant in COCU [the Consultation on Church Union]," which at that Assembly it did. Telford went on to say, "That's not obviously directly relevant to the Union Presbytery Movement, but it is to say that the Union Presbytery Movement did not sit in a vacuum. It was surrounded by and fed, in my judgment, all those other ecumenical initiatives that were going on in the Church" (45-3).

There were three things of note about this General Assembly: The way the voting went, the general mood of the Assembly and the issues it had to face playing off the dis-ease of the times, and the reception the union presbytery and synod overtures received. This Assembly elected Frank Caldwell as Moderator of the General Assembly by a vote of something like 198 to 125. Caldwell was president of Louisville Seminary and a very good liberal leading light of the church at the time. Everybody knew Dr. Frank. And the General Assembly elected him Moderator.

This was the year that the Poor People's March was taking place, during the time of the General Assembly in the spring. Martin Luther King, Jr., was marching with the poor people on Washington, DC, living in tent cities and camping out on the mall. They had moved through North Carolina, and the churches in North Carolina were just really upset. It was a re-creation of the whole segregation problem and there was a lot of emotion involved. The Assembly spent almost a whole afternoon debating whether or not to adopt a resolution supporting or opposing the march. Finally, the Assembly came up with "a compromise that basically was opposed to it, but didn't say so in ugly language" (23-16).

It was also the General Assembly where there were issues having to do with capital punishment, issues about the church's involvement in Vietnam, and the possibility of union with the Reformed Church in America. The Assembly was very negative about all these things, and it passed resolutions voting down the support of any liberal-sounding political or social issue. The people in charge of Christian relations, social issues, and ecumenical relations were very despondent, and it looked like a really bad Assembly (23-16).

This Assembly received a Commissioners' Resolution about the continuing complaints originating from "the evident disorder in the life of the Synod of Mississippi." It cited the fact that the A. M. "Mac" Hart case in the Presbytery of Central Mississippi "had not been adjudicated after four years." It also mentioned "the creation of an unauthorized seminary [Reformed Theological] in the bounds of the Synod of Mississippi by teaching and ruling elders." Finally, it listed "the unwillingness thus far of the presbyteries of the Synod of Mississippi to receive into their membership the Negro churches of the Presbyterian Church U.S. within their bounds as requested by the General Assembly of 1965" as further evidence of its disorder. The Assembly authorized the appointment of an *ad interim* committee "On Mississippi Visitation."[13]

Flynn Long said he came to this Assembly as an observer and for the sole purpose of helping get the Central Texas union presbyteries overture passed. He had been a commissioner to the 1959 PCUS Assembly, but went home and told his presbytery that "as far as I was concerned, I didn't care if they never sent me back to the General Assembly. I thought it was an absolute, idiotic waste of time, that that was not where the church was, and that it was peripheral to what my ministry was about." Long said they had about four votes they could count on, three ministers and "an elder from the First Presbyterian Church at Hamilton, Texas, who told us that he didn't know what this was all about, but he was a good Democrat and he would vote the party line" (23-16).

Several items of business came before this Assembly that were pertinent to relations between the PCUS and the UPCUSA. Over the past few years communications were exchanged between them concerning reunion possibilities. Requests from the UPCUSA General Assembly for dialogue were repeatedly answered in the negative by several PCUS General Assemblies. At this Assembly the Standing Committee on Inter-Church Relations had before it overtures from seven presbyteries and three synods requesting some action to initiate that dialogue. One presbytery overture stated its concern this way: "We believe that these communications are but the most recent of the repeated pleas of a parent for her child; and we believe it unseemly for a child continually to ignore the cries of her parent for reconciliation."[14]

There were ten other overtures before the Inter-Church Relations Standing Committee that reflected another perspective of the times. In one form or another there were requests that the General Assembly either review its stance regarding the National Council of Churches or simply withdraw outright the PCUS membership from the NCC. This was a reaction to the social action stance of the NCC, where for example it attempted "to influence particular legislation where there is no clearly defined moral issue at stake," or where the NCC appeared to speak "for the churches" and not "to the churches" on social issues. Other overtures requested that the PCUS affiliate itself with more conservative national or international associations as an alternative to membership in the NCC.[15]

These two sets of overtures reflected the fissure that was growing over the divergent perspectives on ecumenism in the denomination. But these did not match the divisiveness that would eventually be generated by the four overtures related to union presbyteries and synods from the Presbyteries of Central Texas, Louisville, St. Louis, and Northwest Missouri. The one from Central Texas was the most extensive since it proposed in detail a new Chapter 32 on Union Presbyteries (Classes) and a revision of Chapter 31–2 on Union Churches.[16] Also there was an overture from the Presbytery of Everglades that called for an alternative to union presbyteries. Its request was for a study that would create a program that would allow for "free interchange and reciprocity which will permit and encourage any church, presbytery, or synod which would like so to do, to move freely and without prejudice, with its respective property assets, from the membership and the jurisdiction of the one church to the other."[17] This was the forerunner to the "escape clause" included eventually in the 1983 *Plan for Reunion*. The Everglades overture was answered in the negative the following year.[18]

When these five overtures were received by the Stated Clerk, they were referred to the Permanent Judicial Commission under rules that required its advice on "interpretation of the Book of Church Order" and "questions on amending the Constitution" before the overture came to the Assembly for consideration. Evidently they had also not been received before the deadline specified by the Standing Rules of the Assembly. This meant that these overtures could not be considered substantively by the 1966 Assembly.[19] Flynn Long allowed as though "it was a rule I'd never heard of, and seemed to us to be pure bureaucratic nonsense." When they came to the floor of the Assembly as a procedural matter, three Texans—Robert E. Adcock, William M. Gould, and Long—made "kamikaze speeches, which was kind of like getting up and running your head right into a brick wall, just BAM! . . . and the people of the General Assembly were nice enough to not say anything ugly, and we sat down and they voted to send it to the Judicial Commission. . . . [W]e figured, we lost it" (23-11).

But the loss was not permanent, because the Judicial Commission was going to bring it back to another Assembly and maybe another one and another one. Dr. E. T. Thompson later gave Long some sage political advice. "Flynn," he said, "any unique or changed proposal that comes to the General Assembly in the PCUS requires at least three General Assemblies before it's given any kind of hearing" (23-13).

On the last day of the Assembly, a proposal came for the PCUS to cease being just an observer at the Consultation on Church Union, and to become a full participant. Before the Assembly, on the drive from

Richmond to Montreat, George Chauncey and Will Kennedy had gone by Charlottesville and picked up George Telford. Telford said, "We need to get a resolution to go into COCU." Chauncey and Kennedy thought that would be a good idea, wondered if there was a chance to get it passed. Telford did not know much about COCU but he had an Episcopal priest friend who given him the material about it. The Episcopalians were already in COCU at this point. They read the material on the way down and talked about it (53-25).

After they got to Montreat in their pre-Assembly caucus period, they gathered a dozen people together at Dave Holt's house up on Oklahoma Terrace to discuss the issues coming before the Assembly. As they sat around the table, Telford said, "I want to put this COCU thing together." So they talked about it and someone said, "We need a commissioner to sign the resolution and some other commissioners to support it." They looked over the commissioner list and chose Ruth Eagleton Terry Hopper (Mrs. W. H. Hopper, Sr.) from Louisville Presbytery for the reason that "she's ecumenical and that she'll do it" (53-26). She was the first woman elder commissioner to the PCUS General Assembly, though she was erroneously listed in the Roll of Commissioners simply as "W. H. Hopper."[20]

So Telford and Kennedy went down to the Assembly Inn lobby and talked with Mrs. Hopper. And George explained what it was, showed her the draft of the resolution to go into COCU, and she said something like, "Mr. Kennedy, you wrote that book on *Into Covenant Life*, do you think this is a good thing?" And Kennedy said, "Mrs. Hopper, it's dead on to what our Church ought to believe and basically does believe and it's a good thing." And she said, "I'll sign it." And she signed it and was listed correctly as "Mrs. W. H. Hopper, Sr.," along with five other signers.[21] The resolution came up to the floor. In the middle of the debate, Kennedy recalled that a young missionary stood up and said, "My name is Larry Richards and I'm a missionary of the Southern Presbyterian Church in Iran and Persia, and I've been working there for eight years. There's not been any result in terms of conversion or making much difference. But one thing I have learned, that in a mission world there is no way we can mend our fences *seriatim*." And much to everybody's surprise, the resolution passed. According to Kennedy, "there were a lot of things in the air that set up a kind of positive risk-taking stance that was unusual" (53-46). (Note: Dictionaries commonly define seriatim as "serially, one after another.")

After that proposal passed, the Assembly adjourned. Flynn Long looked at the vote and said, "That's really interesting." The vote was almost exactly the same as the vote for the election for the Moderator on the first day. And he thought, "That's really weird" (23-13).

On the way home Long got to thinking about what he had observed in that vote and the people he had met. He made a lot of new friends like George Telford and Will Kennedy. He made connections with a lot of people there from Kentucky and northern Virginia and West Virginia and Missouri and Arkansas and Oklahoma, who thought union presbyteries were not a bad idea. And so he became aware that there was a segment of the upper PCUS [Border States] that was, for the most part, in favor of union presbyteries (23-13).

A broader political base to get the union presbytery and synod chapters passed was beginning to take shape. Will Kennedy later commented on the significance of the COCU vote: "I think it was tremendously significant. We would not be reunited if it hadn't been for that maneuvering and for the vigorous leadership of those [who were for] Union presbyteries and the folks from them and [COCU folks who] connected with them . . . and the fact [that] what happened after that vote . . . there were enough of you who moved into key presbytery and synod positions to build on the reality that was already there and keep it working and to try to help the rest of the Church come along" (53-26).

When Long got home, he did further analysis of the two votes that caught his eye. Long took the *Minutes* of the General Assembly that had a list of the commissioners in it, which he had not looked at before. He discovered that because of his "purely providential" background he could probably name those in that General Assembly who voted for Frank Caldwell and those who didn't; and who voted for the Consultation on Church Union and who didn't. He was amazed! "I suddenly discovered that I knew just one heck of a lot of people. A lot of them had gone to college with me; a lot of them from Louisiana; I'd grown up with them in Texas; there were friends of my father's; there were people in the Union Seminary, people from Davidson College, people that are kin to my mother, who were kin to my father, it just went on and on and on." And, he decided then "that if it was that predictable, no commissioner from Central Texas Presbytery was ever going to go to a General Assembly again without knowing to the nearest degree possible, how many votes he had on that floor. . . . And that's the background of why I went to the General Assembly [PCUS] in 1967, as an observer (23-13).

1967 UPCUSA General Assembly (Portland)

The 1967 UPCUSA Assembly (Portland, Oregon) was an historic Assembly. The long-awaited final action to approve the Confession of 1967 and the new *Book of Confessions* was slated to take place at this Assembly. The Confession of 1967 was prepared by the Special

Committee on a Brief Contemporary Statement of Faith. This committee was first appointed in 1958 as part of the process that brought about the union of the UPCNA and the PCUSA. The complete proposal for the creation of the *Book of Confessions* was submitted in the report of the committee to the 1965 General Assembly.[22] This report was widely studied by the denomination as part of its deliberative constitutional amending process. Edward A. Dowey, Jr., underscored the importance of the new Confession of 1967 because it was "meant to be the living edge of the church's confession and has been very much on the mind of the whole church throughout the procedures of writing, revision, and adoption."[23]

A new Special Committee of Fifteen took all the input from the study of the original proposal and drafted a revised text to be presented to the General Assembly in 1966. It was approved and sent to the presbyteries, where more than the requisite two-thirds of them voted in favor of changing the confessional stance of the church. The 178th General Assembly (Portland) voted the final approval of the *Book of Confessions* and the Confession of 1967.[24]

This action on the *Book of Confessions* was the most prominent thing on the minds of the commissioners at the Assembly, overshadowing the union presbyteries and union synods amendments. The union presbyteries amendments had gone to the presbyteries for ratification under the Form of Government provision (*Book of Order* 64.032) that required only a simple majority affirmative vote of the presbyteries. This was easily achieved. The results of the actions of the presbyteries indicated that the overtures on union churches and presbyteries were ratified by a vote of 175 to 5 in the presbyteries. Those presbyteries opposing it were: Cayuga-Syracuse, Matton, Peoria, Sioux Falls, and Yadkin.[25]

The affirmative vote by the presbyteries on the chapters on union churches and presbyteries were treated respectfully as a routine matter by the Assembly and were declared adopted. They went into effect immediately and were placed in the Form of Government.

The union synods overture (#45) from the Presbytery of Transylvania, which had been referred to this Assembly from the previous Assembly, was taken up by the Commission on Ecumenical Mission and Relations (COEMAR). This overture, as rationale for its request, noted that both the PCUS and UPCUSA synods had a common background that was in the "latter part of the second century of continual existence, witnessing to this common origin." Even through "more than one hundred years of separation a common Reformed doctrine has [been] maintained with theology and constitution, Book of Common Worship and Discipline congruent." It pointed out the ease with which ministers and members have been transferred from one branch of the Presbyterian Church to the other. Sometimes, however, it was "confusing to our constituencies and detrimental to our full ministry in Kentucky, a stumbling block and a sin against the Church of our Lord Jesus Christ."[26]

On recommendation of the Commission on Ecumenical Mission and Relations (COEMAR), the union synods overture (#45) from the Presbytery of Transylvania was sent down to the presbyteries for ratification by a simple majority vote.[27] The results reported at the following Assembly in 1968 indicated that all the presbyteries but Southern Virginia had ratified the union synods overture.[28] The amendment was declared adopted and went into effect immediately in the Form of Government.

COEMAR was the department where there was the greatest support for these amendments and for denominational reunion, according to William P. Thompson. When asked if the Commission considered union presbyteries as stepping-stones to denominational reunion, Thompson replied, "I never discussed that with any of them, so I really can't tell you what their views were" (01-3).

James E. Andrews, who attended the Portland Assembly as first-year editor of the tabloid newspaper *General Assembly Daily News*, did not remember being intensely involved in the union presbytery and union synod process. Andrews said, "I would most likely [have] been involved in something ecumenical at that point" (02-4). Evidently, Andrews did not see a family reunion as an ecumenical endeavor.

1967 PCUS General Assembly (Bristol)

Kentucky strategists had talked among themselves about going to the 1966 Assembly (Montreat) with overtures containing proposed union chapters, but they did not get their act together in time for that. With the experience of the Central Texas, Louisville, St. Louis, and Northwest Missouri overtures, it was decided to target the 1967 Assembly meeting in Bristol, Tennessee, for the big push. It had been felt all along that the key battle would be in the PCUS Assembly. It also was felt that, if Gene Blake urged it, the UPCUSA Assembly would probably pass these overtures without much opposition, which did indeed happen in Boston in 1966.

A crucial meeting was held in St. Louis in the spring of 1967 with people from Missouri, Texas, and Kentucky, the majority being from Kentucky. Here the strategy was laid out for getting the overtures through the Bristol Assembly. Part of the strategy was that, in addition to the four overtures carried forward from 1966, new overtures were to be sent from the Synods of Kentucky, Missouri, and Oklahoma; and from the Presbyteries of Muhlenberg, Missouri, Potosi, and Potomac.[29] One serendipitous accomplishment of the St. Louis meeting was that the relations formed in this group through its discussions formed the basis of R. Matthew Lynn's running for Moderator two years later (05-4).

Wording of the chapters on union presbyteries and union synods was revised. The synod overtures contained chapters on union synods that were identical to the text in the Synod of Kentucky overture. The presbytery overtures contained chapters on union presbyteries that were identical to the text in the Presbytery of Central Texas overture.[30] Also, the union church chapter was revised in places. Part of the strategy was for elder Thomas A. Spragens and Mort McMillan, both commissioners to the Assembly from Transylvania, to get support from a group that was mostly in the eastern part of the PCUS, that is, Virginia and North Carolina basically (05-5).

Randy Taylor and Welford Hobbie were key leaders in what's called a Fellowship of Concern that was organized in the basement of Westminster Presbyterian Church, Charlottesville, Virginia, where George Telford was pastor (45-3). This "voluntary association" had to do with furthering racial justice issues and supporting ministers in the Deep South who had gotten in trouble over the racial issue. But that group, which at the previous Assembly had supported the COCU resolution, was also, by this time, very actively opposed to the Vietnam War. They were a social issue–oriented group whose members were seen as allies of the Movement and in favor of denominational reunion (05-5).

By the time the advocates got to the Assembly in Bristol, there was one thing that had not been anticipated, but it became the crucial issue in the eventual passage of these chapters. The Permanent Judicial Commission recommended to the Assembly a three-fourths-vote format for sending it down to the presbyteries. It had been assumed all along by the union chapter advocates that, in being sent to presbyteries for advice and consent, these chapters would be considered as simple amendments to the *Book of Church Order*, which took a majority vote in the presbyteries, not as organic union and consolidation with other ecclesiastical bodies, which took a three-fourths vote in the presbyteries.

The Standing Committee on Inter-Church Relations, based on the recommendation of the Permanent Judicial Commission, brought in a report recommending that the Assembly approve amending the *Book of Church Order* to permit union presbyteries and synods. But it recommended that the matter be sent down to presbyteries under the three-fourths rule of Section 30-3 (BCO), since in their judgment, this was tantamount to organic reunion. Several commissioners had their votes recorded in the negative regarding the Section 30–3 (BCO) recommendation.[31]

Mort McMillan said, "I remember a sense of panic that swept over several of us. I was sitting right in front of L. B. Horn, Jr., who was a Commissioner from John Knox Presbytery in Texas. . . . [W]e knew we couldn't get three-fourths of the presbyteries to do it. We figured if we could ever get a simple majority, one or two votes edge would probably be what it would take." Horn leaned up and said to McMillan, "Talk. Delay this vote." And McMillan said, "Why?" And Horn said, "I've got to think of something."[32]

Marshall C. Dendy, executive secretary of the Board of Christian Education, was Moderator. Dendy afterward asked McMillan, who would soon become a member of the staff of the BCE, what in the world he was doing. He knew something was going on but he couldn't figure out what. McMillan recalled, "I had got up and started asking dumb questions about the implications of this and got in this harangue with the Moderator. Dendy . . . as moderator should have just ruled all of my junk out of order, but he allowed me a little slack while I was talking. And right in the middle of it, Horn tapped me on the shoulder and said, 'Okay sit down, I got it' " (05-6).

It seemed almost certain that the motion to send down the amendments to presbyteries on the three-fourths rule would pass in this Assembly. If it ever got sent down on that basis and failed, it would be ten years or more before an effort to create union presbyteries could be mounted again. It was suggested that a motion be made to refer this to an *ad interim* committee of three, appointed by the Moderator, to review, with representatives of the UPCUSA and RCA, the related union presbytery/synod overtures and bring back to the next year's Assembly a recommendation for "a uniform procedure to the highest judicatories of the three Churches" [PCUS, UPCUSA, RCA] as how to accomplish the constitutional amendments. So the year's delay by referring it to a special committee was the "least worst" thing that could happen. The referral passed and the union presbytery strategy group worked between the 1967 and 1968 Assemblies with that special committee (05-6).

This had been an intense political struggle. McMillan characterized it this way: "I think once we got into it, there was kind of a young Turk attitude. Because some people didn't want us to do it, we were going to show 'em." McMillan went on to allow that after that vote in Bristol to defer the decision, Flynn Long was driving in the car back to the hotel up the street that is the Virginia and Tennessee state line. "We were talkin' about how bad we felt and right in the middle of it, Flynn just stopped the car and leaned out and vomited in the street. Right there on the state line of Tennessee [and Virginia]. That was how intense it was" (05-14).

The group in opposition to union presbyteries and synods was not idle at this Assembly. A Commissioners' Resolution was submitted that called for the elimination of Chapter 31 (BCO), the chapter on federated or union churches. The rationale for this resolution was that up to this point in history both the Northern and Southern Churches were governed by the "same faith and order" on which these federated or union congregations depended "for their harmonious existence."

However, for the signers of the resolution, with the adoption of the new *Book of Confessions* earlier in the year, the UPCUSA had not only a different confession of faith, but it had "discarded altogether one of the three Westminster Standards, namely the Larger Catechism." Furthermore, in the newly altered ordination vows, ministers and elders had to "no longer pledge their acceptance of any specific creed, even the new confession."33

This was in reference to two ordination vows in the *Book of Order* (UPCUSA). One asked the ordinand to vow to perform the duties of a minister "under the authority of the Scriptures, and *under the continuing instruction and guidance of the confessions of this Church* [italics added]." The other one asked the ordinand to "promise to be zealous and faithful in studying the Scriptures, the *Book of Confessions* [italics added], and the *Book of Order* . . . and in furthering the peace, unity, and purity of the Church."34

From the PCUS perspective, the background about the significance of ordination vows goes all the way back to the corrective action of the PCUS General Assembly in 1924. It was during the height of the fundamentalist controversy, when there was an effort to enforce strict adherence to a set list of "fundamentals," that one of the ordination vows was amended. Ordination question number two prior to 1924 had simply asked the ordinand to vow to "sincerely receive and adopt the Confession of Faith and the Catechism of this Church, as containing the system of doctrine taught in the Holy Scriptures." This is how it was printed in the report to the Assembly in 1924.35

There were several overtures to the 1924 Assembly wanting to add a number of points to be specifically affirmed. One of the overtures, from Ouachita Presbytery, asked the General Assembly "to make a declaration concerning certain doctrines of the Christian Church." The Assembly answered the overture by declaring: "Because of the clarity and fullness of the presentation of Christian truth in our Confession of Faith and Catechisms, and in the absence of any disposition to question the fundamental truths as set forth in these symbols of our faith, the General Assembly reaffirms its faith in the great fundamentals of our Church as set forth in our Confession of Faith and Catechisms, and declines to make additional declarations of doctrine."36

However, it is interesting to note that in the thoroughgoing revision that was enacted into law by the PCUS General Assembly in 1925, ordination question number two was amended on the floor by the addition: "and do you further promise that if at any time you find yourself out of accord with any of the fundamentals of this system of doctrine, you will on your own initiative, make known to your Presbytery the change which has taken place in your views since the assumption of this ordination vow?"[37] This question was expected to establish and monitor the orthodoxy of candidates. No doubt it was included in the face of not getting a set list of "fundamentals" added to the ordination vows. This issue would resurface during the early years when union presbyteries were in existence and even into the twenty-first century.

The resolution at the 1967 General Assembly that called for the elimination of Chapter 31 (BCO) was referred to the Permanent Judicial Commission for consideration. The Commission was to report its findings to the 1968 General Assembly.[38]

The votes in 1967 General Assembly had been close, as Flynn Long knew they would be. Long showed up at a pre-Assembly caucus interested in social causes, hosted by Randy Taylor, Aubrey Brown, Will Kennedy, and others, carrying the little black bag that would become legendary. For Long, those causes were never high on his agenda, but he discovered that the people most likely to be ecumenical were also involved in this caucus. After working through a list of issues, someone turned to Long and asked, "What do you think ought to be our prime issue?" And Long said, "I don't know what your prime issue is, but you don't have but 225 votes out there on that floor and that ain't enough for a majority." Long thought Aubrey Brown was going to faint, but Brown managed to ask, "How do you know that?" Long replied, "I just do. I'll just tell you that that's it" (23-17).

John B. Evans and William B. Kennedy had served as campaign managers for Marshall Dendy's moderatorial election. This was very tricky since Evans and Kennedy were working for the Board of Christian Education where Dendy was executive secretary. Kennedy said, "But they were doing the same thing in Atlanta." When time came for the vote, Evans and Kennedy were sitting behind Dendy up close to the front of the auditorium. When they were voting, Evans said to Dendy, "Now Marshall, this is not a campaign for president of the first grade class. This is serious business for the future of the Church and you deserve it and we've worked our tails off to try to get you in. Don't you dare vote for P. D. Miller." Dendy won by one vote. Kennedy said later, "And, of course, you never knew, but it was indicative of how close that one was and that made a difference" (53-17).

The vote for Moderator took two ballots. The total votes cast in the first ballot was 452, more than the number of officially enrolled commissioners.[39] The floor was cleared of all but commissioners, 451 in number. On the second ballot Marshall C. Dendy was elected Moderator by a vote of 226 to 225 over P. D. Miller.[40] This was one more than the number of votes Long had told them they had on the floor that wasn't a majority. At that point Long said, "I guess my stock in trade moved up a notch that they thought maybe I knew something that they didn't know." What he had in the black bag was simply the list of commissioners and where they were from. He could come close in telling the votes by whom he knew, to whom he was related, or to whom he was kin (23-14).

When the last report was completed, P. D. Miller exercised his personal privilege and gained the floor. He made the following statement: "Because of the warm personal relations running back over many years and in addition to the resolution of thanks already adopted, I move that the Commissioners stand in appreciation of Dr. Dendy for the magnificent and gracious manner in which he has presided over the sessions of the 107th General Assembly."[41] It was adopted by a rising vote of appreciation.

Cynics of a much later generation might consider this as simply political posturing that launched next year's moderatorial campaign. But even though Miller lost this year's election by one vote, this was a genuine gesture of civility of a bygone era, truly an expression of the fundamental role relations played in the life of the PCUS. It was also a shining testament to the old polity of majority rule.

The prelude to change—choosing which of two routes to take to make preliminary steps toward union between denominations, launching and passing a new *Book of Confessions* in the UPCUSA, struggling with more or less ecumenical involvement in the PCUS, avoiding a premature end to union chapters in the PCUS by delaying a decision through referral, experiencing a one-vote-majority election of the General Assembly Moderator—set the stage for a whole new era in the life of both denominations. Clearly there were winners and losers in this prelude to change. The full consequences of the contributions and flaws of this time of preparation would be a long time coming, but ghosts of Stamford Bridge and Hastings *et al.* were beginning to emerge from the shadows.

Notes

1. *Minutes* of the One-Hundred-Sixth General Assembly (PCUS), Montreat, NC, April 21–26, 1966, p. 44.

2. Key people in Texas: R. Matthew Lynn, Flynn V. Long, Jr., William M. Gould, John W. Cunningham, Roy B. Horn, R. W. Jablonowski, J. Hoytt Boles, Fred A. Ryle, Jr. Key people in Missouri: W. Richard Huey, Joseph B. Ledford, Robert J. Rodisch, Thomas C. Cannon, Kenneth R. Locke, Cecil G. Culverhouse, Thomas H. Cavicchia, J. Allen Oakley, Theodore A. Jaeger. Key people from Kentucky (other than committee listed below): Charles M. Hanna, Jr., Ralph Hawley. Key person from Nashville Presbytery who participated in some meetings: Mac Freeman.

3. Wm. Philip Bembower, chair of Joint Committee of Kentucky to the two General Assembly Stated Clerks, identical letters of invitation; copy of Millard's letter dated October 4, 1965, in the file of T. Morton McMillan, secretary of Joint Committee; copy of McMillan file in personal collection of William G. McAtee.

4. Ibid. Minister members of the Kentucky Committee: Wm. Philip Bembower, chair; T. Morton McMillan, Jr., secretary; Olof Anderson, Gordon L. Corbett, Graham Gordon, Julian P. Love, and James H. Rucker, Sr. Elder members: R. G. Matheson, J. T. Orendorf, and Thomas A. Spragens.

5. *Minutes* of the Reunion Committee [Kentucky], October 29, 1965; copy of minutes in the file of T. Morton McMillan, secretary of Joint Committee; copy of McMillan file in personal collection of William G. McAtee.

6. Letter from Gordon L. Corbett to J. Hoytt Boles, Dawson W. Tunnell, Robert J. Rodisch, James E. Spivey, Eugene Carson Blake; copy of Corbett's letter in the file of T. Morton McMillan, secretary of Joint Committee; copy of McMillan file in personal collection of William G. McAtee.

7. Memo from Philip Bembower, chairman, to Kentucky Reunion Committee, November 15, 1965; copy of memo in the file of T. Morton McMillan, secretary of Joint Committee; copy of McMillan file in personal collection of William G. McAtee.

8. Ibid.

9. *Minutes* of the Reunion Committee [Kentucky], January 24, 1966; copy of minutes in the file of T. Morton McMillan, secretary of Joint Committee; copy of McMillan file in personal collection of William G. McAtee.

10. *Minutes* of the One-Hundred-Seventy-Eighth General Assembly (UPCUSA), Boston, MA, May 18–25, 1966, pp. 47–48. The other overtures mentioned are found on the following pages of this set of *Minutes*: St. Louis Overture #43, p. 47; Transylvania Overture #45, p. 54; Sedalia Overture #53, p. 61; Western Kentucky Overture #63, p. 65; Washington City Overture #72, p. 72.

11. Ibid., pp. 43–44.

12. *Minutes* of the One-Hundred-Seventy-Ninth General Assembly (UPCUSA), Portland, OR, May 18–24, 1967, p. 546.

13. *Minutes* of the One-Hundred-Sixth General Assembly (PCUS), Montreat, NC, April 21–26, 1966, pp. 105, 117. The committee appointed by the Moderator was: Rev. Charles L. King, chairman, Rev. Marion Boggs, Rev. W. John Millard, T. M. Barnhardt, and Dr. Edward D. Grant.

14. Ibid., p. 35.

15. Ibid., p. 37.

16. Ibid., pp. 43–50.

17. Ibid., p. 48.

18. *Minutes* of the One-Hundred-Seventh General Assembly (PCUS), Bristol, TN, June 8–14, 1967, p. 234.

19. Rules applied here were from "Form of Government," Section 20-6 on interpretations of the *Book of Church Order*, Section 20-7 on questions of amending the Constitution; and Assembly's Standing 7.3 regarding the timing of when overtures are to be delivered to the Stated Clerk.

20. *Minutes* of the One-Hundred-Sixth General Assembly (PCUS), 1966, p. 19.

21. Ibid., p. 95. The commissioners who signed the COCU Resolution were: Rev. George Telford, Lexington Presbytery; Rev. Wm. Richard Huey, St. Louis Presbytery; Rev. Fred R. Stair, Jr., Atlanta Presbytery; Rev. William B. Kennedy, Hanover Presbytery; Mrs. W. H. Hopper, Sr. [elder], Louisville Presbytery; and Ed. S. Hughes [elder], Central Texas Presbytery. This demonstrates the close connection between the COCU advocates and the union presbytery advocates.

22. Dowey, *A Commentary on The Confession of 1967*, p. 7.

23. Ibid., p. 11.

24. Ibid.

25. *Minutes* of the One-Hundred-Seventy-Ninth General Assembly (UPCUSA), 1967, p. 79.

26. *Minutes* of the One-Hundred-Seventy-Eighth General Assembly (UPCUSA), 1966, p. 54.

27. Ibid., pp. 516, 533.

28. *Minutes* of the One-Hundred-Eightieth General Assembly (UPCUSA), Minneapolis, May 16–22, 1968, p. 89.

29. *Minutes* of the One-Hundred-Seventh General Assembly (PCUS), 1967, pp. 233–234.

30. Ibid., p. 57.

31. Ibid., p. 88. The commissioners who recorded their negative votes were: Wm. V. Barnett, T. M. McMillan, Jr., Wm. Richard Huey, Warren L. Moody, Jr., James H. Elder, Jr., James B. White, A. M. Hart, Charles C. Moody, L. B. Horn, Jr., John B. Danhof, W. S. Blanton, Jr., T. Hartley Hall IV, J. L. Davis II, Stephen B. Rybolt, John H. McEwen, Jr., Rex E. Brown, Michael F. Murray.

32. McMillan, Interview 05, p. 6. McMillan in the interview erroneously identified the commissioner seated behind him as John W. Cunningham. Upon later verification Roy B. Horn, Jr., had to be the commissioner. McMillan in his interview also said they were frantically passing hand signals to Flynn Long in the balcony, trying to figure out what to do. Long later said John Cunningham and Bill Jablonowski and others were involved in that. Long said, "No, I wasn't in the balcony at this one. I was out in the foyer holding a black briefcase" (23-16). This was one of the earliest sightings of the notorious black briefcase!

33. *Minutes* of the One-Hundred-Seventh General Assembly (PCUS), 1967, p. 60. The commissioners who signed this resolution were: W. Jack Williamson, East Alabama; (Rev.) J. Wayte Fulton, Everglades; (Rev.) Albert H. Freundt, Jr., Central Mississippi; (Rev.) Robert Strong, East Alabama; (Rev.) J. W. Everett, Bethel; L. S. Weir, Bethel; (Rev.) G. Aiken Taylor, Asheville; (Rev.) George Dameron, Everglades; (Rev.) Robert W. Cousar, Jr., Westminster; (Rev.) Angae R. Shaw III, Abingdon; (Rev.) Mike L. Andrews, Westminster. This gives an idea of who the opposition was and where they were from.

34. *The Constitution of the United Presbyterian Church in the United States of America*, Part II, *Book of Order* (Philadelphia: Office of the General Assembly, 1967), paragraphs 49.043 and 49.047.

35. *Minutes* of the Sixty-Fourth General Assembly (PCUSA), San Antonio, TX. May 15–22, 1924, p. 126.

36. Ibid., p. 63.

37. *The Book of Church Order of The Presbyterian Church in the United States*, Revised Edition (Richmond, VA: Presbyterian Committee of Publication, 1925), pp. iii, 69.

38. *Minutes* of the One-Hundred-Seventh General Assembly (PCUS), 1967, p. 60.

39. Ibid., p. 57.

40. Ibid., p. 61.

41. Ibid., p. 136.

Chapter 8
The Constitutional Divide

Amendments to the Book of Church Order may be made only in the following manner:
> *(1) The approval of the proposed amendment by the General Assembly and its recommendation to the Presbyteries.*
> *(2) The advice and consent of a MAJORITY [caps added] of the Presbyteries.*
> *(3) The approval and enactment by a subsequent meeting of the General Assembly.*
> — *Book of Church Order 30-1 (1961)*

Full organic union and consolidation of the Presbyterian Church in the United States with any other ecclesiastical body can be effected only in the following manner:
> *(1) The approval of the proposed union by the General Assembly and its recommendation to the Presbyteries.*
> *(2) The advice and consent of THREE-FOURTHS [caps added] of the Presbyteries.*
> *(3) The approval and consummation by a subsequent meeting of the General Assembly.*
> — *Book of Church Order 30-3 (1961)*

A Presbytery may permit one of its constituent churches to enter into "federated" or "union" relationship with a particular church of another Reformed body under the specific terms of an agreement entered into by the highest court of each denomination.
> — *Book of Church Order 31-1 (1961)*

The Presbyterian Church in the United States in 1968 showed signs that it was coming to a situation very similar to that of water falling on a narrow ridge of geological high ground, when there is a moment's hesitation before it decides which direction the runoff will take. It is a place like the Continental Divide; some water goes in one direction and the rest goes in a diametrically opposite direction.

It was a church struggling with the same issues that faced the social order of the country at large. Authority in all quarters was being challenged. Institutional upheaval was besetting the country. Sides were being taken on every issue imaginable. This could be seen in the issues brought in the overtures to the General Assembly in 1968 regarding union efforts and requesting withdrawal from the National Council of Churches and COCU.

As was mentioned earlier, the Southern Church amended its Constitution in 1914, requiring ratifying action by three-fourths of its presbyteries in cases effecting church union. From a 1968 perspective the three-fourths rule seemed fairly stringent. But it must be remembered that at the time this was a progressive move, since prior to 1914 the *Book of Church Order* had no provision in it for organic union with any other ecclesiastical body.[1] The three-fourths rule was a serious obstacle to anyone proposing anything that could be construed as leading to full organic union with other bodies. It was clear to the advocates of union presbyteries and union synods that the only way their proposals would pass was if they were considered amendments to the *Book of Church Order.* This would require only the advice and consent of a *majority* of the presbyteries. The opposition was equally clear in their minds that these proposals were, in effect, an attempt at organic union, thus requiring the advice and consent of *three-fourths* of the presbyteries.

1968 PCUS General Assembly (Montreat)

P. D. Miller was elected Moderator of the 108th General Assembly (PCUS). Two of the major issues before this Assembly were the RCA-PCUS union proposal and the union presbytery and union synod overtures.

With reference to the first major issue, the Assembly heard the recommendation of the Joint Committee of Twenty-Four that had developed the Plan of Union between the PCUS and the RCA. Both the PCUS General Assembly and the RCA Synod "affirmed their confidence in the Providence of God and their serious enthusiastic purpose to proceed as rapidly as possible looking forward toward the union of our two churches." A very thorough process had been followed in its creation. The committee enlisted scores of members of both denominations in exploring ways of "expressing our unity in Christ and witnessing more effectively to the Gospel." They received well over 2,000 suggestions and comments about the Plan and incorporated many into the final draft. After a deliberate strategy of three readings of the Plan, the PCUS Assembly in 1968 adopted the report of the committee as a whole by a vote of 406–36. The Plan would be sent to the presbyteries for advice and consent under the three-fourths rule.[2] This action was almost overshadowed by the other major issues before the Assembly.

The second major issue was more complex. The moderator of the Bristol Assembly had appointed the *ad interim* committee whose purpose was to bring a recommendation to the next Assembly regarding the union presbytery and union synod chapters. The chair of the special committee was Paul Tudor Jones, pastor of Idlewild Church in Memphis. The *ad interim* committee came back to the 1968

Assembly with a recommendation that the constitutions of the three churches regarding union churches needed to be revised and new additions to the constitutions needed to be made to cover union presbyteries and synods. The committee made no official recommendation regarding how to send down the amendments to presbyteries for advice and consent. But the Permanent Judicial Commission, which always looked at constitutional changes, made a strange kind of recommendation to the Assembly, "that in order to be unquestionably constitutional, it would be best if we sent it out under the three-fourths rule" (05-7). So the battle between the three-fourths majority rule and the simple majority rule had yet to be fought.

Flynn Long, a commissioner to the Assembly from Central Texas Presbytery, studied the list of commissioners and presbyteries in preparation for the Assembly. It became apparent that not only were there presbyteries that were predictably opposed to reunion, but they were also extremely regional in their geographical situation. One major block of opposition consisted of a number of people who were identified as being "Concerned Presbyterians." This "voluntary association" was led by Kenneth Keyes in Florida and a number of other people in Mississippi and Alabama. They were adamantly opposed to the possibility of union presbyteries because their basic opinion was that the United Presbyterian Church (UPCUSA) was probably, in their words, "an apostate church." In checking their background, Long discovered that a great number of them were born in the North and had graduated from Westminster Theological Seminary. A number of them had become pastors in Florida, Mississippi, Alabama, and places in Georgia. According to Long, they had "become professional Southerners or at least professional Southern Presbyterians in the process" (23-17).

It was Long's general opinion that they did not reflect the grassroots feeling of what the Southern Presbyterian Church was really all about. Their basic source of information about what was going on in the church was what they read in the *Southern [Presbyterian] Journal.* Since it was largely negative, they were led to believe whatever they had heard without ever hearing the two sides of the issue. It was reasonably easy to identify the presbyteries with commissioners following the perspective of the Concerned Presbyterians and know they would be opposed to union presbyteries (23-18).

The union presbytery advocates knew and were related to people in presbyteries in the Border States of Texas, Missouri, Arkansas, Oklahoma, Kentucky, northern Virginia, and West Virginia. They were able to assure themselves before the 1968 Assembly that the commissioners from those areas would very definitely support the union presbyteries proposal and would know each other. They would be ready to take whatever action was necessary to keep the overtures alive and to get them sent down to the presbyteries with a simple majority vote (23-18).

Long also discovered connections between people in Mississippi and people in Kentucky, and a number of friendships and alliances in support of Louisville Seminary that existed in places like Alabama and Mississippi. Some in Georgia had a different, positive feeling about the church. They were extremely gracious and not nearly as negative about the world in general or church politics in particular as they were made to seem by some of the people that headed up the Concerned Presbyterians (23-17).

The area where the vote would be won or lost would be among the people outside of the Border States, who did not really care one way or the other about the issue. Convincing these people to support union presbyteries was made more difficult because the official waters had been muddied by the Permanent Judicial Commission's recommendation of the three-fourths majority rule.

To counter this, the union presbytery advocates had caucuses to make very clear to everybody the difference between organic union with the three-fourths rule and amending the constitution to permit union presbyteries and synods by majority rule. It was not enough for the advocates to know these differences; they felt that it was crucial for every commissioner also to know them. By the time the Assembly convened, the votes were analyzed and the advocates knew every commissioner by name. Roy Horn and Flynn Long had practically gotten this down to a science. Long later said, "We'd go through everything and talk to people all over the country, and we had a magnificent telephone bill but we knew everybody in that Assembly and where they were likely to be [on this issue]." The list was divided up and personal contact was made to conduct a mini-polity course on the differences between majority and three-fourths rules (23-22).

A person who was very helpful in this was Dr. E. T. Thompson, who by this time was retired and living in Richmond. Mort McMillan remembered Dr. E. T. at the Assembly, "crippled you know, hobblin' around, walkin', limpin' around with a *Book of Church Order* stuck in his hip pocket and button hole'n commissioners, pulling it out and flipping to that [Chapter] 30-1, 30-3 . . . carefully explaining . . . what's at issue" (05-7). The involvement of Dr. E. T. in this way gave authority and credibility to the simple majority rule among commissioners who were in doubt.

The advocates were still concerned about the impact of the Permanent Judicial Commission's ruling. The mind-set in Assemblies back then was that authority figures were enormously important. The Permanent Judicial Commission then had a kind of special aura about it, so when it spoke, it spoke with authority. James Millard, Stated Clerk of the General Assembly, used to speak of the PJC "as the finest legal minds in our denomination." The advocates were not sure what the Stated Clerk might say about the PJC's ruling on the floor of the Assembly, so they figured they needed an authority figure to speak on behalf of their position (05-7).

The advocates decided that Dr. Frank Caldwell was the authority figure they needed. He was the retiring Moderator and as such had privileges of the floor. Graham Gordon and Mort McMillan were the two chosen to go and talk to Dr. Frank and get him committed to speak. Dr. Caldwell in his own wordy style said, "I am excessively loath to exercise that privilege, exceedingly loath to exercise that privilege," to which Gordon and McMillan "played dirty pool" with him in a sense. They said to him, "Well, we are who we are because of you. It was your leadership when we were in seminary." McMillan had been in seminary in 1955 when the PCUS-PCUSA reunion vote failed. Gordon had been a pastor then in Kentucky, having graduated earlier from Louisville Seminary. Dr. Caldwell was co-chairman of the reunion committee on the PCUS side along with Harrison Ray Anderson on the PCUSA side. After some more theatrics where Gordon even reportedly shed a few tears in talking about this, Dr. Caldwell finally said, "Well, if we just felt it was essential, he would be willing to do it." But still he said, "I just, I'm not sure it would be wise for me to do it." He was not sure about how he would get the floor. It was decided that one of the advocates' commissioners would get the floor and defer to Dr. Caldwell for his opinion (05-8).

The Moderator of the General Assembly, who had been the loser by one vote at the Bristol Assembly the previous year, was Dr. P. D. Miller. Flynn Long had known Dr. Miller for a number of years and Miller was a friend of Long's father. Dr. Miller's daughter, Belle Miller McMaster, would later become one of the division directors of the General Assembly Council of the PC(USA) in 1983. His son, P. D. Miller, Jr., was an associate professor at Union Seminary (Richmond) at the time.

Throughout the General Assembly, Long wore a bright green suit. He later said, "[I]f you wore that suit nowadays, you would probably be shot. . . . But in those days, it was the time when colored shirts were in and weird-colored suits. And this was a bright green checkered suit, kind of kelly green . . . and I had a tie that went with it that matched it. And it was really sharp looking. But the good thing about it was that you could spot me a mile away and know who it was." Dr. Miller was losing his eyesight and his hearing, so Long said he sat on the front row to make sure that the Moderator recognized who he was. Long said, "[I]t became apparent that I could get the floor anytime I wanted. And if I couldn't, I could get it for somebody else" (23-22).

The opposition to the union presbyteries proposal was led by commissioners Robert Strong, pastor of Trinity Presbyterian Church in Montgomery, Alabama, and Elder W. Jack Williamson, a lawyer from Greenville, Alabama. These two were perennial commissioners from East Alabama Presbytery. Some of their opponents had at one time considered in jest presenting them with 20-year attendance pins. Williamson would later become the first Moderator of the PCA Church when it was organized (05-9). Bob Strong never withdrew into the PCA, but stayed in the PCUS in retirement.

Jack Williamson approached every speech at the General Assembly as though he were addressing the bar. At one time it was said he even called the Moderator "your honor." There was another lawyer, from Kansas City Presbytery, who was on the side of the union presbytery advocates. He was recruited by the organizers and told that "your job at this General Assembly is whatever Jack Williamson says, you just rattle him." According to the report, this guy was about 6 foot 8, a great big fellow, and could not be missed. In Anderson Auditorium at Montreat everyone was seated in those circular pews so that "it was kind of General Assembly-in-the-round, no tables or anything like that. You had to keep it all in your head" (23-21).

When the time came for the debate, Strong and Williamson were seated on one end of the front row and Long and the lawyer from Kansas City were on the other end, evidently so they could keep an eye on each other. The advocates unleashed their "roll out the border strategy."

People were designated to stand up from every presbytery in the whole border of the PCUS and speak in favor of the union chapters. Their instructions were: "The first thing you get up and say is where your Presbytery is and . . . that you're from Kentucky or Missouri or West Virginia or northern Virginia or Texas or Oklahoma, so that people understand that they're talking about people in the whole northern segment of the PCUS." This was a significant area of the church because, for one thing, it contained three of the four seminaries of the denomination. The key to the strategy was that when Flynn Long stood up and spoke for something, that green suit was a signal for them to get the floor and make their pitch. So when the union chapter issue came to the floor, the debate went like clockwork. All the college and seminary connections and relations of the advocates were on the floor as planned (23-23).

The most important part of the "border strategy" was to have their authority figure speak in favor of the union presbytery chapters, because the Permanent Judicial Commission had recommended it needed a three-fourths vote. The speeches of the opposition were punctured with the "We can't oppose the Permanent Judicial Commission" argument. Right at the pivotal moment in the debate, Flynn Long stood to be recognized. Dr. Miller, the Moderator, said, "Flynn, do you wish to speak to this?" And Long said, "Yes, sir. I would like to speak to this" (23-24).

Long got up and said, "I am for union presbyteries. . . . I am in favor of the proposal for union presbyteries being sent down for a simple majority vote, simply because it's simply not organic union. I think my position has been pretty well stated." Long went on to say that he would like to yield the floor to somebody that has something to say to you about this. He then proceeded to introduce to the General Assembly Dr. Frank A. Caldwell, who was the past president of the Louisville Theological Seminary and past Moderator of the General Assembly in 1966. Long described Dr. Caldwell as "one of the distinguished statesmen and judicial authorities within this denomination." In case there was someone that didn't know who the president of the Louisville Seminary was, or the past Moderator, there was no question now (23-24).

Dr. Caldwell made a powerful statement about the need for sending the union presbytery proposal to the presbyteries under the simple majority rule. He told of his experiences in Kentucky and having served an institution that belonged to both denominations. He also countered the Permanent Judicial Commission's recommendation to send the proposal to presbyteries under the three-fourths rule just to make sure it is unquestionably constitutional. He said, "[I]t's either constitutional or it's not constitutional," and indicated that "This is a political statement. . . . [They are] trying to please everyone and we can never please everyone" (05-8).

Mort McMillan told of "one of those strangely dramatic moments in meeting in Anderson Auditorium." During this debate, when Jack Williamson, the perennial elder commissioner from East Alabama Presbytery, was speaking against the motion, a thunderstorm began to brew. When the thunderstorm broke, and the lightning was popping all around, the power went out and left Anderson Auditorium in the dark. Afterward McMillan jokingly told Williamson that "God was goin' to get him, [God was] angry with him." Then the vote was taken and the motion passed to send the chapters down under the simple majority rule (05-8). It passed the General Assembly by a fairly narrow vote, not an overwhelming vote, but it was significant enough; there was a very clear majority to send it down under the majority rule (23-25).

McMillan quoted Jack Williamson and Bob Strong as having said, "[Y]ou boys are gonna pass this thing, and when you do that, that means you're gonna get reunion of the denominations, and we are not going with it." McMillan said he really thought it was in this moment that the PCA Church began, at least in the minds of the opposition, though it was several years before the PCA was organized. The action of the 1968 Assembly on union presbyteries and union synods, according to McMillan, "put us in a presbytery by presbytery fight" (05-9).

PCUS Presbyteries' Advice and Consent

On the heels of the 1968 Assembly (Montreat), a major political campaign in the presbyteries was joined between the proponents of the union chapter amendments led by the border synods coalition and the opposition, who coalesced around the Concerned Presbyterians. Both sides were well organized and connected. Presbyteries began their deliberations and voting on three major constitutional union proposals—merger with the RCA and amendments of the BCO to provide for union synods and union presbyteries—in the late fall of 1968 and early winter of 1969.

When the votes were reported to the Stated Clerk of the General Assembly by the spring of 1969, the results of the union presbyteries vote showed that all the presbyteries in the Synods of Kentucky (4), Missouri (5), Oklahoma (3), and West Virginia (3) had voted for it. A majority of presbyteries in the Synods of Arkansas (2 of 3), North Carolina (5 of 9), Tennessee (2 of 3), Texas (5 of 6), and Virginia (5 of 7) had also voted in favor of it. Additional presbytery votes were picked up in the Synods of Florida (2 of 5), Georgia (1 of 6), and Louisiana (1 of 3). Thirty-eight of the seventy-seven presbyteries had voted in favor of the union presbyteries amendment.[3]

All the presbyteries in the Synods of Alabama (5), Appalachia (5), Mississippi (3), and South Carolina (8) voted against the amendment. A majority of the presbyteries in the Synods of Florida (3 of 5), Georgia (5 of 6), and Louisiana (2 of 3) voted nay. Additional nay presbytery votes were picked up in the Synods of Arkansas (1 of 3), North Carolina (4 of 9), and Virginia (2 of 7).[4] The nay vote came to a total of thirty-nine. On this vote the union presbytery amendment was defeated 39–38. It failed to gain a simple majority by one vote in the presbyteries. The geographical distribution, as could be expected, was such that the nay votes tended to be cast in the Deep South and the yea votes tended to be cast in the Border States. Had the maps of the voting by presbyteries been colored in those days, they might have been colored gray and blue.

In an overwhelming number of the presbyteries, regardless of whether their vote was yea or nay, it was very clear what their intent was in the matter by the decisive margins of their votes. Only five presbyteries that recorded numerical totals had votes with margins of five or less. Suwannee Presbytery voted 43–40 in favor of the amendment and Fayetteville Presbytery voted 36–35 in favor of it. Those voting the amendment down were: Mobile Presbytery by a vote of 20–19; North Alabama Presbytery by 31–26; and Winchester Presbytery by 33–31.[5] The Plan of Union with the RCA received the requisite three-fourths majority by a slim margin. The union synods amendment was defeated by a vote of 40–37. The union presbyteries amendment was defeated by a vote of 39–38.[6]

The *Concerned Presbyterian*, a newsletter "Dedicated to Returning the Presbyterian Church U.S. to its Primary Mission," headlined its bulletin no. 12 (April, 1969) in bold letters: **"Majority of Presbyteries Vote "No"—Union Amendments Defeated."** Its page-one lead paragraph stated that "In the opinion of many members of the Presbyterian U.S. constituency, Tuesday, February 17th, will go down in history as one of the most important days in the history of our beloved Church. That was the day when the presbyteries of Nashville and Southwest Georgia cast the deciding votes which defeated the Union Synods and Presbyteries amendments *by a majority vote*."[7]

The editorial went on to express gratitude to God "that so many presbyteries realized the inherent dangers in this attempt of the liberals to fragmentize the Church." It further stated: "Many believe that this vote could well mark the turning point in our struggle to return the leadership of the Church to men who believe that its primary mission is to win the unsaved to Christ." Finally a debt of gratitude was expressed to those "who worked long and hard to encourage informed ruling elders to stand up and be counted at their presbytery meetings . . . [and to] both ministers and ruling elders who . . . voted their conscientious constitutional convictions and helped win this significant victory for the Faith and Order of the Church."[8] Harry S. Hassall, a graduate of Louisville Seminary who strongly opposed union at this time, summarized the initial vote on the union presbytery amendment this way: "We beat it by one. Fair and square" (65–11).

Votes to Reconsider

Eighteen persons who had led the effort to pass the now-defeated union presbyteries and synods overtures met in early spring in Louisville, Kentucky, to see what could be done to "increase cooperation with the UPCUSA in border areas." At the close of the meeting, John W. Cunningham spoke for the group through a press release. The release summed up the feelings of the group by quoting an unidentified participant: "The border can't wait for the Southern Presbyterian Church. The Mission of the Church is suffering, held back by the inaction of the Presbyterian Church in the United States, which heeds the voices of reaction and ignores the anguished cries of the border presbyteries and synods." The release also pointed out that "expressions of like concern were received from UPCUSA sources," although there was no indication that they were "officially represented" at the meeting. The release stated: "A small task force was named to draw up specific proposals to be presented to a subsequent meeting of representatives from both Churches."[9]

Richard K. Johnson, executive secretary of the Presbytery of Northwest Missouri, wrote a letter on March 13, 1969, to numerous individual acquaintances in presbyteries across the Southern Church that had voted against union presbyteries and synods urging them to reconsider their votes. Included in the mailing were other executive secretaries of presbyteries. This was perceived by some as being "official communication" from one presbytery to another, and thus reported the letter to their respective court as such. Others deemed the letters personal and did not forward them to the court. The issue raised in the letter reached the floor of Albemarle Presbytery (North Carolina) but did not receive the two-thirds majority necessary for reconsideration. It never reached the floor of Nashville Presbytery.[10] Later Johnson in a letter to Wayne Todd said, "The letter which I wrote to over forty individuals was certainly not by any stretch of the imagination, a circulation of one court by another."[11]

Harry Hassall, then an opponent of union, recalled the proponents' effort in this way: "[P]ro-union forces enabled or sought to get 21 Southern presbyteries to reconsider [their vote]. . . . They were successful in three, one of which was in Dallas." He went on to say, "[T]he reason they were successful was that, from our point of view, a rump-call[ed] meeting of that Presbytery, I believe it was Northeast Texas at the time . . . was called for when Bill Elliott was known to be already planning to be out of town. And, [I believe] that the vote switched by about three votes." His observation was that "From our perspective, you just don't take another vote on a Constitutional issue. You go back to the next Assembly and if they want to try it again, that's fair. We felt that union presbyteries came into existence in an unfair and unconstitutional way. It doesn't mean we were right, [but] that's how we felt" (65-11).

Mobile Presbytery Vote

The other two presbyteries that were successful in their reconsideration efforts and changed their previously narrow-margin, negative votes on the union presbyteries amendment were Mobile Presbytery and North Alabama Presbytery. Mobile Presbytery seemed to be the logical place to target the effort for reconsideration, since support for the amendment had failed by one vote at its Winter Stated Meeting on January 21, 1969. Its vote on the union presbyteries amendment was 38 for and 39 against. Interestingly enough it passed the union synods amendment by a vote of 22–18.[12]

Duncan Naylor was the Home Mission superintendent of Mobile Presbytery. Naylor was basically for the union chapter amendments, but sometimes got things confused. In the winter meeting Naylor voted against union presbyteries and for union synods. And his reasoning, he said afterwards, was it would be just better to do it at the synod level. The reality was that there could be no union synods unless there were union presbyteries. Proponents of these amendments always thought that the union synod chapter was a throwaway in any case. The synod chapter could be voted down and if all the presbyteries in a synod were union presbyteries, the synod would be a *de facto* union synod. But, because of Naylor's swing vote, Mobile Presbytery voted against the union presbyteries chapter by one vote (05-9).

Sometime in late February or early March, Flynn Long was up in Richmond meeting with Mort McMillan, Will Kennedy, and others facing the fact that the union presbyteries amendment was losing by one or two votes in the presbyteries. McMillan by this time was on the staff of the BCE in Church and Society. Kennedy said to McMillan, "You are the one who's got all the ties 'cause Mobile is your own presbytery. Maybe you could get them to reconsider." So, McMillan started shooting for reconsideration by Mobile Presbytery (05-10).

McMillan made several contacts to see what the possibilities might be. A call was made to James H. Gailey, Jr., professor at Columbia Seminary, who was a member of Mobile Presbytery. He had not been at the Winter Meeting of Presbytery but agreed to come to the Spring Meeting and support the reconsideration effort. McMillan contacted the moderator and stated clerk of the Presbytery to alert them to what was coming. "They were both in favor of making a try" (05-10).

McMillan contacted his dad, T. Morton McMillan, Sr., an elder in Monroeville, Alabama. His dad had not been at the Presbytery meeting in January and really was not for reunion of the denominations, but he was a states' righter. And his attitude was, "If you people in Kentucky want to do that and those people in Texas want to do that, I'd let 'em do it. We're not gonna ever do it in Alabama," he said, "but I'd vote for that." So, he agreed to get his Session to send him to the next Presbytery meeting as elder commissioner and he would make a states' rights speech on behalf of the union presbyteries amendment (05-10).

John Reagan, missionary-in-residence at the BCE, was at a continuing education event at Columbia Seminary where "Dr. Gear's boys" were invited back to study and renew old acquaintances. John was studying labor union history. Word had reached there that the union presbyteries amendment had failed and Mobile Presbytery had voted against it by one vote. Will Kennedy called Reagan and said, "John, why don't you go down there and get Mobile Presbytery to change its vote?" Reagan replied, "I'm working on something that's important to me, something to the effect [where] 'the rubber meets the road.' " Whatever Kennedy said was enough to let Reagan know that he wanted to go (76-15).

Reagan went to Mobile and stayed with David H. Edington, Jr., who was the stated clerk of the Presbytery. Reagan said to Edington, "Dave, you know, I would like for us to reconsider our action on voting against union presbyteries." And Edington said, "Well, John, I think we did the right thing to vote against it. But I'll help you do it." Reagan characterized Edington as "a real Presbyterian in that he wanted good debate and he would help make it possible even if it was not something that he supported." As stated clerk, Edington advised that someone who had voted in the negative majority needed to ask for reconsideration (76-15). Mobile Presbytery met in its Stated Meeting on April 15, 1969, at Government Street Presbyterian Church, Mobile, Alabama, only nine days prior to the One-Hundred-Ninth meeting of the PCUS General Assembly in the same location. Duncan Naylor, who had voted in the negative majority on the union presbytery amendment in January, made the motion to reconsider. McMillan recalled that Naylor got up and said in effect, "I was confused with what I did last time and I voted against this and I really should have voted for it because that's where my conviction is. I'm gonna ask you to reconsider it" (05-11).

The motion was ruled in order, though there was opposition to it. It was expected that the opposition would say it is not legal under *Robert's Rules*. They held that reconsideration was possible only during the same meeting the original motion was made, not the next meeting. The Moderator, upon advice of the Stated Clerk based on a commonly held opinion at the time, ruled that the reconsideration was legal if requested no later than the next meeting of the court. The motion to reconsider was passed by the requisite margin, speeches were made pro and con, including the states' rights one promised by Elder McMillan, Sr., and Mobile Presbytery by an 8 or 10 vote margin changed from "against" to "for" the union presbyteries amendment (05-11).

John Reagan remembered Mort McMillan saying, "You know, that was a history-making event. And if it hadn't happened, union presbyteries wouldn't have happened, and if union presbyteries wouldn't have happened, the union with the Northern Church would not have taken place." Assuming McMillan's assessment to be correct, Reagan described his role in that effort, "in terms of the overall strategy and so forth, very minute, minuscule. But in terms of importance, extremely important" (76-15).

North Alabama Vote

And after Mobile Presbytery changed its vote, Wayne Todd in North Alabama Presbytery, which had initially voted against the amendment by a narrow margin of 31–26, got the Presbytery to reconsider and they changed their vote from "against" to "for" it (05-11).

Complaints to the Synod of Alabama were brought in both Mobile and North Alabama Presbyteries. The Mobile complaint was submitted by minister commissioners John Eddie Hill[13] and W. H. Harville.[14] Elder commissioners were Thomas A. Crocket, Jr., and R. L. McAlister. The North Alabama complaint was submitted by minister commissioner James M. Baird[15] and elder commissioner Nall Leach.

These complaints were very similar in nature. Complainants in both Presbyteries claimed they were aggrieved by the irregularity of the proceedings of Presbytery, the impairment of procedural rights of the parties, the improper vote on the amendments, the manifestation of bias and prejudice in the way the amendments were brought before Presbytery.[16]

The Mobile complaint added that failing to give notice before the luncheon that the matter would be brought to the floor, and making official statements that "nothing of any importance would be considered after noon," seemed to encourage many commissioners to leave the meeting during the noon recess. It further indicated that there seemed to be "an ecclesiastical political conspiracy to hide the proposed reconsideration until the final minutes and unfairly catch the opponents unaware and unprepared and absent because of no previous notice of warning about such an important matter, and further by refusing an effort to be fair by voting down a motion to call a special meeting of Presbytery or continue . . . in adjourned session with proper notice to reconsider the matter."[17] This specification in the Mobile complaint seemed not to have as much to do with "ecclesiastical political conspiracy" as that the opposition simply got procedurally outmaneuvered. The Synod of Alabama voted "that the complaint as a whole be not sustained," in effect allowing the vote in favor of the union presbyteries amendment by Mobile Presbytery at its Stated Spring Meeting to be its official "advice and consent" in the matter.[18]

In addition to the grievances common to the Mobile complaint, the North Alabama version added that the motion to reconsider was "improper and out of order." It also took issue, stating that "the Bills and Overtures Committee report was in error in stating that a 'simple majority either way will carry the motion.' "[19] The Synod sustained all

---

but one of the specifications in the complaint—the one regarding bias and prejudice in how the matter was brought before Presbytery—and sustained the complaint as a whole. This seemed ironic and strange for the Synod to do since it did not sustain the same specifications in the Mobile complaint. Nonetheless, this in effect reinstated the vote against the union presbyteries amendment by North Alabama Presbytery at its Stated Winter Meeting, which remained its official "advice and consent" in the matter.[20]

Wayne Todd filed a complaint with the General Assembly against the Synod of Alabama, but the judicial process meant that it would not come to the General Assembly until its meeting in Memphis, Tennessee, in 1970, a year later.[21] Todd said, "he never really got a hearing before the Assembly's Judicial Commission. They upheld the Synod in telling North Alabama Presbytery how it had to vote on that issue. But, by the time they were acting on it, it really was a moot point anyway because it [the union presbyteries amendment] had carried Assembly-wide" (82-8).

What had been an advice and consent defeat for the union presbyteries amendment in the winter of 1969 in the presbyteries by a vote of 38 for and 39 against was now in mid-April a victory for it by a vote of 40–38. Even if Northeast Texas Presbytery had not reversed its original negative vote, and even though North Alabama Presbytery's effort at reconsideration was not upheld, the Mobile Presbytery's final affirmative vote would have created a one-vote favorable margin.

Word did not spread very widely across the church of this dramatic and historic turn of events after the Mobile Presbytery vote. Most people did not know until they got to the 1969 General Assembly in Mobile that the union presbyteries amendment had in fact passed.

1969 PCUS General Assembly (Mobile)
The big agenda for the 1969 Assembly (Mobile), as planned by the leaders meeting on April 24–29, 1969, was to have been the consummation of the RCA union with the PCUS. But that spring the PCUS had voted for it and the RCA's had turned it down by failing to pass it in their classes [presbyteries]. There was a sense that the old guard leadership of the PCUS Church had their last gasp effort with the RCA union attempt because it was the only way they saw to get the PCUS out of the box it was in. They did not see creating union presbyteries as a real option in the larger union discussion. They were not opposed to it, but they did have some fears about it. The new guard kept telling them that the RCA would not pass the vote. And when that RCA union vote failed, the old guard really didn't have anything. It was sort of the end of an era of old guard leadership, and

into that vacuum the new guard came in the 1969 Assembly. Mort McMillan remembered how, late in the 1969 Assembly, George Chauncey, fellow staff in Church and Society (BCE), looked around and said, "My god, we're the fathers of the Church" (05-14).

In the days leading up to the opening session of the 1969 Assembly, Flynn Long made a significant discovery. He said he knew then how it would come out. He was aware of the fact that some presbyteries, who suddenly saw some possibilities and who were very upset about the death of RCA union, elected specific commissioners to the Mobile General Assembly. Long recalled that when he first saw the list of who the commissioners were, "I was aghast." Long shared this with John Cunningham: "John, do you realize we're going to an Assembly where we've probably got seventy-five percent of this Assembly on our side?" Cunningham replied: "How do you know that?" Long: "I've gone over the list, and that's who it is" (23-25). The implications of that became evident very early in the meeting.

On the first night of the Assembly, even before the election of the Moderator, a motion was made by somebody representing the Concerned Presbyterians, Inc., perspective with respect to a routine referral of an item of business to an Assembly Committee. The Committee on Assembly Operations had made a proper referral, but the Concerned Presbyterians, Inc., people wanted to change it to another committee where they thought they had a better chance with it. John Cunningham and William J. Fogleman were both commissioners to the Assembly.[22] Cunningham asked Long's advice about what to do concerning the referral. Long suggested "the thing to do is just to stall them as long as you can, and let Fogleman come up with the proper motion" which Cunningham did. Fogleman then made some alternative motion and the General Assembly voted down the Concerned Presbyterians' resolution (23-26).

According to Long, at this point "nobody knew what the votes were, except a few of us." Later Long said to Fogleman, "How about that?" In response Fogleman asked, "You want kill on every one of them, don't you?" Long said, "At this point I do, because I think the way the Southern Church is going, if we don't carry everything we possibly can, we'll never change the nature of the church." They now concluded that the direction for the Mobile Assembly was set and it was not necessary to do any further organization to control the vote (23-26).

This conclusion was soon confirmed by the election of the Moderator, which it was crucial to win because of the Moderator's extensive powers of appointment. In those days *ad interim* committee members were not elected by the Assembly but were appointed by the

Moderator. Kenneth Hobbs, elder commissioner from the Presbytery of the Southwest, nominated R. Matthew Lynn, minister commissioner from the same presbytery, as Moderator. Hobbs stumbled as he went up the stage and almost fell down, and then made this "rip-roaring machine gun speech." Later some friends accused him of stumbling on purpose to gain sympathy, an old lawyers' trick (23-25).

Many of the supporters of Lynn were seated in the balcony when the Assembly was electing the Moderator. David Stitt turned to Flynn Long who was sitting next to him, and asked, "How is this going to turn out?" Stitt suggested: "Why don't you write what you think it will be on a piece of paper, and I'll write what I think it [the vote] will be on a piece of paper." So they did. Stitt was not sure Lynn would win because he already had lost one Moderator's election. Stitt, who thought he knew the church, shared his numbers after the vote. He missed it by about fifty votes or so. Long missed it by two votes. Stitt said, "My God, that's scary! How did you know that?" To which Long replied, "Oh, it's just one of those things. Sheer luck" (23-25).

After Matthew Lynn got elected Moderator, a group of people caucused in the Holiday Inn in Mobile to see what they wanted this Assembly to accomplish, feeling now that they could "do anything within reason." The major accomplishments were to establish Ad Interim committees on New Confession of Faith Together with Book of Confessions, on Union with the United Presbyterian Church in the U.S.A., and on Restructuring Boards and Agencies of the General Assembly.[23] The work of the Ad Interim Committee on Restructuring Synods and Presbyteries was continued[24] and the work of the Ad Interim Committee on the Consultation on Church Union was reaffirmed when the Assembly received its report.[25]

A resolution was passed warning that the programs and activities of Concerned Presbyterians, Inc., "do not promote the peace, unity, edification and purity of Christ's Church."[26] A special committee was appointed "to study the relationship of the Reformed Theological Seminary of Jackson, Mississippi, to the peace, purity, and unity of the Presbyterian Church in the United States."[27] The work of the Ad Interim Committee on Mississippi visitation was continued in order to "concentrate on matters relating to the life and work of Central Mississippi Presbytery . . . and make a special effort to establish a working arrangement among those of differing opinions."[28]

Flynn Long's recollection was that after about the fourth day of the Assembly, James Millard, the Stated Clerk, walked out of the Government Street Church in Mobile, and Mort McMillan said, "Jim, we're about to introduce a resolution to change the Lord's Day to Monday," . . . and Millard said, "If you propose it, it'll pass" (23-27). Bill

Fogleman said the only thing that failed to pass at that Assembly was a proposal to change the place of the 1971 Assembly, which was set for Massanetta Springs, Virginia (05-11).

Albert H. Freundt, Jr., who was in attendance at that Assembly, said, "[T]here were four or five big issues or measures . . . which really changed, I think, much of the direction of the PCUS" (17-10). One of those was the final vote on the union presbyteries chapter. Dorothy G. Barnard, who later became moderator of the 1981 Assembly (Houston), remembered the Mobile Assembly as her first Assembly, as a member of the Board of Women's Work, and everything was brand new. She said she would never forget Bill Fogleman "sitting on that front row . . . looking back with his hand up on the pew . . . at the group as they took their vote . . . and I think he was countin' all those votes he knew he had and you all had worked so hard to get. But it was a high moment, and we knew it. We knew that was a watershed moment" (09-2).

Bill Peterson's recollection of the Mobile Assembly was that it was his first contact with some of the political forces, in the Southern Church particularly, and he was a part of all the caucusing that went on. As a commissioner from Louisville Presbytery, he was on the committee that had to deal with things like reunion and union presbyteries. After the union presbyteries amendment was approved, Peterson remembered having this long discussion in the caucus where he said, "No, you really ought not to do a Committee on Reunion. You know, we've gotten so much now, let's let it sit." And, he added, "I lost that discussion." Somebody then wrote the Commissioners' Resolution that got the Committee on Reunion formed (36-4). Thomas L. Jones could vividly still picture that Holiday Inn where the caucus met after the evening sessions to "decide some preposterous thing to go for the next day." Jones felt that "[with] someone like Matthew [Lynn] sitting in the [Moderator's] chair . . . everything just kind of came together. We got too heavy really probably but . . . we got the Assembly to vote for the Hunger Program and somebody moved that they cancel the dinner on the USS Alabama, nobody wanted to do that [hold the dinner]" (85-6).

As the days of the Assembly unfolded, Peterson remembered the great elation over the whole thing. Toward the end of the Assembly he said, "you could almost hear the 'yea' votes for the more progressive things start in the back of the room, and by the time they'd reach the front of it, it was like a steam engine, it would just roll through the whole place." He also remembered some of the folk, particularly those aligned with the Southern [Presbyterian] Journal, being totally devastated. "I think in the long haul, [because] there were some other things that happened, . . . this was also the Assembly where the big-steeple preachers lost their power in the Southern Presbyterian Church. And, there were some who were pretty wiped out with that." He said one that stuck out particularly was Bill Elliott of Highland Park Church in Dallas. Highland Park Church was a very different church after that Assembly. This was another example of the change of generations as well as a political watershed (36-5).

Harold Jackson, a commissioner from Washburn Presbytery, had been watching the "growing sentiment of reaction to what was happening in the civil rights movement." What he began to see was a deeper and stronger entrenchment of the conservative, right wing of the church, reaction against what they perceived happening in the society, and the increasing pressures on the church around the issue of integration and civil rights. The Assemblies had begun more and more to reflect the right/left kind of dynamic. It was a growing struggle between those "who were obviously interested in trying to conserve or preserve a past and a heritage, and those who were aware of the need for continual change and reformation" (40-3).

Watershed Moments

The 1969 Assembly, from Jackson's perspective as a commissioner, was a turning point "because the moderate to liberal forces in that Assembly, among the Commissioners there, had gained a very strong, dominant role in that Assembly, and in its Standing Committees. As the committees began to bring reports, the moderate to liberal side of the Church, represented in these Commissioners, was a predominant voice in that Assembly" (40-5).

One of the major debates was around religion and science, "not really different from the current debate [twenty-first century] in many areas of the country about creationism" (40-5). According to Will Kennedy, who was looking on from the balcony, there were a bunch of young Strong guys, followers of Robert Strong, who got off on evolution. They made these speeches on evolution that made people wonder what in the world is this all about? Where is this coming from? This was two generations after Scopes and so it was hard to believe that these people were seriously arguing against evolution. "And so those guys got identified as Strong's troops." Later while Kennedy was leaving the church, he approached Strong, whom he had gotten to know over the years and said: "Dr. Strong, you can take care of your enemies, but the Lord protects you from your friends." And Strong just shook his head because he knew he was dead in the water (53-18).

Harold Jackson remembered very clearly that there was discussion and debate around curriculum content in Christian Education, about some of the moves and changes in curriculum. The support by the Assembly, in the religion/science debates, for what the BCE was doing with the Covenant Life Curriculum affirmed a broader, "more liberal" interpretation of Scripture. Some of the growing public interest in and response to higher criticism (e.g., historical-critical study of the Bible), which had been a part of theological education for a number of years, began to emerge in these Assembly debates. There was almost no major area of debate or issue or concern where this liberal/conservative dynamic was not apparent (40-03).

One night in the after-session caucus at the Holiday Inn, the subject of committee appointments came up. Will Kennedy said, "We need to do something to influence the Moderator about who should be appointed to all these committees." Flynn Long asked him, "Well, do you have a list of who you'd like?" Kennedy paused, then said: "Well, I really haven't given it much thought but we sure would like to talk to him." Long replied, "Well, he's going to be over here in about fifteen minutes." And sure enough, in a few minutes Matthew Lynn, the Moderator, walked in. Silence overcame all these people sitting around the room who had been caucusing in secret all the time, but had never talked to a Moderator as part of their strategy. Lynn sat down and said, "Well, I've got all these committees to appoint; who would you boys like for me to appoint?" (23-28).

It was free-range Texas Mafia style meets eastern liberal establishment, something entirely new to most of the people present. Earlier someone had pinned the label "Presbytery Mafia" on a work group in old Central Texas Presbytery that had been assigned to create a new purpose and design for the Presbytery.[29] That moniker evolved into "Texas Mafia" and got mythically attached to a politically active group in Texas that coalesced around a progressive agenda. Flynn Long recalled that, "the myth had circulated that there was a Texas Mafia, and if there was anybody who was the head of it, it was probably me. And no manner of denials or anything would help [dispel the myth], and Mort [McMillan] and several others were not much help either" (23-30).

Wayne Todd recalled that Lynn "appointed really sharp, good people to almost every committee. Just wall-to-wall good people. They didn't always have the same viewpoint, but they were all good people." In Todd's view, they were not only "the right kind of people," they were very "competent people." Todd went on to lament that after reunion in 1983, he was involved in trying to get the folks who were going to be the leadership in the reunited church to do the same thing. "But, they started playing a game, I think, of trying to put together the noisiest opponents on any issue on a committee, so that they became political committees instead of competent committees" (82-13).

There were several major voices from the conservative side. One was an elder from New Orleans named Edwin W. Stock, Sr., whose son was a Presbyterian minister. Stock spoke frequently, arguing whatever the issue was from a hard conservative position, until some felt that there were diminishing returns from his contribution (40-5).

Jack Williamson, from East Alabama Presbytery, was probably one of the strongest of the conservative commissioners there. He talked about the preservation of the values in the Presbyterian Church U.S. and of its historical confessional standards and stances. Williamson was one of the leaders in the growing sentiment by many across the southern part of the Southern Church for establishing a denomination that would be truer to those historical perspectives and its confessional standards (40-5).

One very poignant moment came for Will Kennedy as he watched how Walter Johnson and Jack Williamson related. Johnson, known by family and friends as "Bubba," was the brother of Arline Taylor, Randy Taylor's wife. Johnson and Williamson were the two floor managers of sorts for the opposing "liberal" and "conservative" forces respectively and Johnson had won all the big ones. On one of the last times when they spoke on an issue, they passed each other in the aisle, "and ole Walter hugged Jack and they hugged each other." Johnson already had cancer and would be dead in less than a year, but for Kennedy "it was another one of these signals of the oddity of family Church on these huge issues" (53-18).

Harold Jackson's personal recollection was that, when a group was leaving the Government Street Church in Mobile, where the Assembly was meeting, he overheard Williamson talking to a colleague, a good friend, about how very distressed and angry he was at the Assembly since he and his side had really lost every vote on every major issue. Jackson heard him say, "publicly, though not for publication, I'm sure, that this was the last time he intended to be beaten in a General Assembly." And within a matter of months he was really working with other strong leadership to form the Presbyterian Church in America, which did begin to build momentum within a year or two afterward (40-5).

Mort McMillan looked back on the 1969 Assembly (Mobile) and concluded, "[B]ecause of the union presbytery vote and that surprising reversal, that, in a sense, opened a door, and most of what happened for the next 20 years in the denomination, really moved from there." To underscore this, McMillan remembered Lewis Wilkins, the year after reunion in '83, at the 1984 Assembly, one evening saying, "This is the last night of the 1969 General Assembly." McMillan was careful to say that "none of us, who started this movement in Kentucky, Missouri and Texas, had any notion of what all we were doin'. We were all working on what, for us, really [was] local, small area products. But it had implications beyond that. I know when the time came, that we did finally get a plan of union to vote on for the denominations . . . we had enough union presbyteries established . . . we were getting it *de facto* anyway" (05-12).

One of the last pieces of business acted on at the Mobile Assembly was to ask the Moderator, Matthew Lynn, to serve as a Fraternal Delegate to the Meeting of the General Assembly of the UPCUSA, which would be held May 14–21, 1969, in San Antonio, Texas.[30] Randy Taylor was already named as a Fraternal Delegate. The sending of such delegates was a long-held practice in both denominations. Lynn wanted to go to that Assembly in San Antonio to bring a message from the Southern Church "that we want to seek reunion." This meant a lot to Lynn "because he had spent his ministry in Texas, struggling with United Presbyterians where the lines get all mixed up and don't have any particular rhyme or reason." According to Taylor, Lynn "did a splendid job of bringing his enthusiasm for this cause. And United Presbyterians were ready. They had been hoping this would happen, well, ever since the previous vote in 1954." Upon returning home after spending a week with Taylor in San Antonio, Lynn called Taylor and asked him if he would chair the PCUS portion of the Joint Reunion Committee. Taylor was happy to accept because of his experience as pastor of Church of the Pilgrims in Washington and Central Presbyterian Church in Atlanta, which showed him "clearly that we were wasting our time by duplicating effort" (54-3).

With the adjournment of the 109th General Assembly in Mobile, Alabama, on April 29, 1969, the constitutional and political divide in the PCUS had been crossed. The first phase of the Union Presbytery Movement story was completed. Union presbyteries could now become a legal reality. Clearly there were winners and losers scattered across this constitutional divide. The full consequences of the contributions and flaws of this watershed moment would be a long time coming, but ghosts of Stamford Bridge and Hastings *et al.* were distinctly more visible and noisy in a full spectrum of boldness and bitterness.

Notes

1. *The Book of Church Order of The Presbyterian Church in the United States* (Richmond, VA: Whittet & Shepperson, Printers, 1908), p. 60.

2. *Minutes* of the One-Hundred-Eighth General Assembly (PCUS), Montreat, NC, June 6–11, 1968, p. 94.

3. "Presbytery Voting on 3 Major Union Proposals," *The Southern [Presbyterian] Journal*, April 9, 1969, p. 8. Contains the tally of presbytery voting on three major constitutional union proposals—merger with the RCA and amendments of the BCO to provide for union synods and union presbyteries.

4. Ibid.

5. Ibid.

6. Ibid.

7. "Majority of Presbyteries Vote 'No'—Union Amendments Defeated," *The Concerned Presbyterian*, bulletin no. 12 (April 1969), p. 1.

8. Ibid.

9. *The Southern [Presbyterian] Journal*, April 9, 1969, p. 6.

10. Ibid., April 30, 1969, p. 5.

11. Letter from Richard K. Johnson to Wayne P. Todd, July 14, 1969, in Wayne P. Todd File, Presbyterian Historical Society

12. *The Southern [Presbyterian] Journal*, April 9, 1969, p. 8.

13. *Ministerial Directory of the Presbyterian Church*, U.S., 1983 edition, p. 316. John Eddie Hill was dismissed to the ARP on December 13, 1982, before the 1983 Reunion. He was pastor at Columbia, Mississippi, from 1973–79. [The Columbia Presbyterian Church, where Gear, Calloway, and McAtee had served, eventually went into the PCA.]

14. *Ministerial Directory of the Presbyterian Church*, U.S., 1975 edition, p. 264. W. H. Harville was divested of office under BCO 111-3, July 18, 1972, by South Mississippi Presbytery.

15. Ibid., p. 28. James M. Baird was removed from the roll of Augusta-Macon Presbytery on July 26, 1973.

16. *Minutes of the Synod of Alabama*, 1969, pp. 31–40.

17. Ibid., p. 34.

18. Ibid., p. 36.

19. Ibid., p. 39.

20. Ibid., p. 40.

21. Letter, with Complaint enclosed, from Wayne P. Todd to James A. Millard, Jr., Stated Clerk, June 8, 1970, in Wayne P. Todd File, Presbyterian Historical Society

22. Key Movement leaders (presbyteries) who were commissioners: Robert R. Collins (Missouri), John W. Cunningham (Central Texas), William J. Fogleman (Brazos), James W. Gunn (Brazos), John R. Hendrick (Brazos), J. Harold Jackson (Washburn), Cecil M. Jividen (Potomac), W. Walter Johnson (Northeast Texas), William S. McLean (Washburn), H. William Peterson (Louisville), John M. Reagan (Mobile).

23. *Minutes* of the One-Hundred-Ninth General Assembly (PCUS), Mobile, AL, April 24–29, 1969, p. 128.

24. Ibid., p. 201.

25. Ibid., p. 86.

26. Ibid., p. 98.

27. Ibid., p. 110.

28. Ibid., p. 56.

29. Long, Interview 23, p. 4. Long reported that his then wife said about the Presbytery work group, " 'I think that you all are secretly plotting, and . . . this is probably Presbytery Mafia.' This later became the origin, as far as I'm concerned, of the name, 'Texas Mafia' . . . which existed, if it ever existed, only in this particular instance that I'm talking about."

30. *Minutes* of the One-Hundred-Ninth General Assembly (PCUS), 1969, p. 128.

Chapter 9
Denominational Restructure

While all the courts have the same great commission and serve the same ultimate purpose, their mechanics and methods of operation may, of practical necessity, be somewhat different. There is no best plan of structure (organization). However, where possible, structures at all court levels should be similar enough to correlate so that program can be implemented. Local problems, conflicts and misunderstandings are best handled by the lowest possible court of jurisdiction. However, the higher courts are in a better position to arrive at the most advisable church-wide policy, methods of procedure, opportunities for broad parallel activity and witness to the wholeness and the unity of the Church.
—Minutes of the One-Hundred-Eighth General Assembly (PCUS)[1]

Ferment for change permeated both Southern and Northern Presbyterian Churches in the late 1960s. Sweeping actions of the Southern and Northern General Assemblies in 1969 set in motion plans that would create union presbyteries, but that also would restructure boards and agencies as well as establish regional synods in both denominations on parallel tracks. It is difficult to appreciate fully the enormity of the organizational upheaval brought on in such a limited period of time by these restructure efforts and the impact this had on the creation of union presbyteries. A mixed blessing was granted by the failure to pass union synods as part of the deal; eventually there were two sets of regional synods to accommodate in lieu of one less structure to negotiate.

Church and societal growth in the 1950s following World War II began to disturb the sleepy and comfortable arrangements by which both denominations had ordered their lives over the previous decades. The social trauma that challenged the authority, and at times the very existence, of institutions of the 1960s did not spare the ecclesial world. New learnings from the fields of sociology and behavioral science introduced new understandings about how groups and organizations function. New technologies were being created on how to change groups and organizations in order to enhance more effectively their performance. The pace of change itself was beginning to accelerate.

Up to this time both denominations had functioned with their differing views of strong boards and agencies at the national levels. It was assumed, though not always actually the case, that the roles of synods, presbyteries, and local sessions were commonly understood in their respective spheres. Some very distinct differences did exist in the definition of these roles in each of the denominations, though they were gradually growing to be more alike than previously was assumed. A sense began to grow that the way the denominations were ordered was not adequate to administer the mission of the church in these changing times. But it was more than simply adjusting governing body boundaries or rearranging the boxes on an organizational chart. It went much deeper than that, for it had to do with power and freedom, two signs of the times.

Structural Glue

It does not make much sense to talk about the Unity of the Church in only theoretical terms. For the concept to have validity it must be visualized in some tangible form. Throughout history of the church there have been various images employed to characterize this concept. One graphic illustration would be to use the image of the "glue that holds the church together." Two very critical ingredients that must be utilized in stirring up this pot of ecclesial glue are power and freedom. What will be the recipe for folding them into the mix?

Lefferts A. Loetscher, in his book *The Broadening Church*, ably struggled with these two ingredients as they were operative in the Old School/New School reunion of 1869. He was trying to understand the Unity of the Church as the driving force at work in that reunion and in the decades afterward through the turn of the century in the PCUSA. He contended that the "forces that were really decisive in the discussion were not theological, but ecclesiastical; not ideological, but sociological and physical." He noted that the chief glory of American Christianity was: "Amazing activity in Christian service at home and abroad . . . and to this activity the Presbyterian Church has contributed its full share."[2]

This flurry of activity created new promotional and administrative challenges. The church's response was that it had to develop the necessary and steadily increasing centralized power to administer these rapidly expanding programs. More aggressive leadership directed the existing official boards and agencies, and new executive agencies were created to meet the expanding needs. Loetscher noted that: "These developments in the Church exactly paralleled the increasing activity and centralization of the federal government during these years."[3]

As the administrative power expanded, the Unity of the Church was threatened. The theological clash between modernism and the biblical authority of classic Calvinism posed a theological fracture that threatened the centralized missionary zeal and activity of the church. Freedom and power collided at the heart of this debate. Loetscher pointed out that "the Presbyterian Church was forced, in order to preserve its unity, to decentralize control over the theological beliefs of its ministers and candidates for ministry." He observed that the solution to the problem of freedom and power was solved for that moment "by simultaneously increasing administrative centralization and decreasing theological centralization; increasing physical power while at the same time anxiously seeking to prevent its trespassing on the realm of the spirit. This also was a concession to the pluralistic character of modern culture."[4]

The General Assembly (PCUSA), by adoption of the report of the "Special Commission of 1925," clearly described the legislative and executive powers of the General Assembly as being "specific, delegated, and limited, having been conferred upon it by the Presbyteries; whereas the powers of Presbyteries are general and inherent."[5] It stated that the Assembly could issue declaratory deliverances to witness to the church's corporate faith, cautioning that such action "may be misconstrued as a virtual amending of our organic law by another method than that prescribed the Constitution." The report also noted that executive or legislative deliverances are subject to modification or repeal at any time by a majority vote of the Assembly.[6]

The distinction between "delegated" and "inherent" powers was clearly illustrated in how the Special Commission defined them in the section on "Essential and Necessary Articles." This section established a watershed moment in the theological history of the church since the reunion of 1869. The divisive theological debate of the day was between the positions on the right taken by Dr. J. Gresham Machen in *Christianity and Liberalism*, and the Auburn Affirmation on the left. Though the Commission never directly addressed either, it tended delicately to counter the Machen position. What was rendered especially critical by its action was the question of how articles of faith were to be determined as "essential and necessary."[7]

The Commission held that the Adopting Act of 1729 "conferred no authority upon any judicatory to state in categorical terms what doctrines were 'essential and necessary' to all candidates." The Commission held that the Presbytery exercises "inherent authority" when determining adherence of candidates for licensure and ordination to "essential and necessary articles of faith." It further specified that the General Assembly could not determine in general what is "essential and necessary," but that only in adjudicating a specific case did it have "a right to decide questions of this kind . . . [but it must] quote the exact language of the article as it appears in the Confession of Faith." In essence, by taking this stance the Commission denied that the General Assembly had "the right to define authoritatively the 'essentials' of the Church's faith." It thereby "eliminated the 'five points' [of fundamentalism] as a source of controversy and gave the Church greatly desired peace."[8]

Throughout the ensuing years the sphere and power of "administrative centralization" expanded throughout the structures of the PCUSA. Growing out of the understanding of the Presbyterian Church as a "connectional" system of church government was the perception that some uniform administrative policy for the whole church would exemplify the best practice consistent with the theory of the Unity of the Church. The "glue of connectionalism" became the mandate to control funds and personnel from a central position. Some perceived this to be a "we know best what you need" approach, and the whole system was caricatured as "ecclesiastical imperialism." Connectional terminology was brought into the bureaucratic vocabulary in an effort to support this approach. The caution rendered in 1925 about issuing "declaratory deliverances" seemed to be cast to the wind when applied to "administrative centralization." The PCUSA did have a theological understanding of church governance that was explicitly corporate in nature and structure and included the power to speak on behalf of the church.

Power and freedom were issues with which the PCUS struggled from its inception and which on occasion threatened its unity and its very existence. The PCUS was not spared the theological clash between modernism and the biblical authority of classic Calvinism of the 1920s. It too was caught up in the zeal for foreign missions, and there was a need for an orderly way to coordinate these activities. Some contended that being so absorbed in foreign missions was simply a form of avoidance of domestic issues closer to home. Growing out of the understanding of the Presbyterian Church as a "relational" system of church government was the perception that some familial administrative policy for the whole church would exemplify the best practice consistent with the theory of the Unity of the Church. The glue that bound the Southern Church together was the power of relations and "friendly persuasion."

Some have characterized the PCUS form of governance as one big family sitting out on someone's front porch (session) making decisions and then going into the county seat town (presbytery) and "getting it done officially." Sometimes somebody had to be sent "way off up there" (synod or General Assembly) to take care of business beyond the county line. This characterization was deceptive and only partly true. The PCUS, though shaped by the ideological beliefs rampant in society at the time of its birth, did have a theological understanding of church governance that was basically relational in nature and corporate by implication.

In both denominations there was a genuine attempt to proclaim that there was more to the church than a local gathering of the faithful. Presbyterians attempted to distinguish themselves from congregationalists by saying "we are 'linked up' (hence 'connected') or 'related' (hence 'kin') to others across the land (or part of it) in a special way. This makes us all part of something that is greater than any of its parts or even the sum of its parts."[9]

This distinction was more than a matter of differentiating terms in an interdenominational spat. It has been a crucial distinction in legal court cases involving church property. A judge on the Kentucky Court of Appeals in a case contesting local or presbyterial ownership of property asked what type of church government was used in the Presbyterian Church, "hierarchical or congregational?" The response was "hierarchical," the operable term used to describe the existence of a series of courts of jurisdiction that make up the Presbyterian system of government.[10] He ruled in favor of the presbytery.

Both the Northern Church (UPCUSA) and the Southern Church (PCUS) sought "structural glue" that would bind the broader body together with theological and organizational integrity. The UPCUSA ordinarily operated under a "centralized administrative" model and the PCUS under a "decentralized administrative" model. These tendencies can be seen in the restructure of boards and agencies and the creation of regional synods in both denominations in the early 1970s.

Restructure of Boards and Agencies (PCUSA-UPCUSA)

Whereas the Southern Church early on took its dominant cue for organizing itself from the theological doctrine of the "spirituality of the church," the organizational cue for the Northern Church came, to a considerable degree, from corporate America. This is not to imply that the Northern Church was bereft of theological underpinnings or that the Southern Church was oblivious to corporate methodologies. The development of "complex, hierarchical enterprises in business, government, and other areas of American life" in the late-nineteenth and twentieth centuries, which many Presbyterians had participated in, seemed to be very influential in shaping the Presbyterian Church. All three major Presbyterian branches were affected differently by time and degree by this development.[11]

During the decades leading up to 1920 a variety of quasi-official boards and agencies had sprung up across the PCUSA in response to a plethora of causes—schools and colleges, foreign missions, Sabbath Day observance, and the like. Membership on their governing bodies came from the geographic areas where they were located. Competition was intense for financial support from local congregations. Little coordination was achieved between the competitors, resulting in duplication of effort and confusion in responsibilities.[12]

A Special Committee on the Reorganization and Consolidation of Boards and Agencies (SCRCBA) was appointed by the PCUSA General Assembly in 1920 to bring some order out of the organizational chaos. John Timothy Stone, former Moderator of the General Assembly and pastor of Fourth Presbyterian Church in Chicago, was named to chair the committee. It was not long before the influence and expertise of Robert E. Speer, secretary of the Board of Foreign Missions, became evident in the committee through his friendship with Stone. Speer proposed that a central council be formed "to provide continuity, respond to new concerns, advise the Moderator, and promote efficiency." In addition he "proposed consolidating the entire work into four boards—a Board of Foreign Missions, a Board of Home Missions, a Board of Education, and a Board of Relief and Sustentation." This became the concept that the committee reported to the 1921 General Assembly, where it "received a thunderous ovation."[13] The plan took on a corporate character through its central headquarters (the General Assembly), whose general council coordinated the work of several operating divisions. Strong control was centralized at the top, although the work was, in a sense, internally "decentralized" in the headquarters.[14] Each division was responsible for one piece of the overall work, including producing, funding, and promoting goods and services that were delivered to its regional offices (synods). These regional offices in turn passed these goods and services on to local retailers (sometimes presbyteries, but mostly local sessions) for consumption there. In reverse this system was used to mobilize and coordinate support for its corporate national and international projects through specific apportionments and benevolence ratios. The primary administrative officer was the Stated Clerk. Divisions had directors or managers who administered the enterprise with businesslike methods and efficiency.[15]

Following the enthusiastic receipt of its report, the membership of SCRCBA was expanded and its work continued until it brought the detailed proposal to the 1922 General Assembly. The proposal was formulated with strong opposition from the previously semi-autonomous agencies that had considerable vested interest in the past. Representatives of the Board of Missions for Freedmen argued that concerns of black Americans would be greatly diffused even to the point of loss of identity. The same was true of the Women's Board of Home Missions, which feared a loss of women's benevolent giving should it be commingled with the general mission funds of the General Assembly. These and other objections notwithstanding, the Assembly, after a five-hour debate, adopted the plan for restructure.[16]

Some of those "other objections" had come from a vocal minority who, somewhat reflecting the theological tension of the 1920s, had opposed the plan on the grounds that the centralized power was contrary to the church's polity and that employing "experts" to run the business would increase bureaucratic trends, thus moving the denomination away from the sphere of local congregations.

The new structure managed to shape the direction of the PCUSA for forty years, with some changes. William P. Thompson, who was Stated Clerk in the twilight years of this organizational configuration, commented that "somehow the church placed in those positions persons with real leadership skills." Their individual identity personified the work of the strong boards and agencies they represented and created a more intimate contact with the church at large (01-10).

When the PCUSA-UPCNA union took place in 1958 forming the UPCUSA, the Committee on Ecumenical Mission and Relations (COEMAR) was created to function in place of two foreign mission boards and three committees responsible for interchurch relations. The thrust of its mission emphasis was no longer that of sending missionaries, but of developing partnerships with independent Christian communities around the world.[17] COEMAR, which had a department concerned with ecumenical relations, was, according to Thompson, "the place where the support was greatest" for denominational reunion as well as the union presbytery concept (01-2).

With the dawn of the 1960s several mainline denominations began to undergo major structural reorganizations as well as revision of the church's theological and liturgical standards. In 1963 the UPCUSA General Assembly set up a Special Committee on Regional Synods and Church Administration (SCRSCA) to propose new structures that reflected the cultural and ecclesial challenges of the times. The committee struggled with the realities of cynicism toward the government, the trends toward localism, the corrosive results of the Vietnam War, the more obvious recognition of racial injustice, and the mushrooming urban sprawl with its attendant white flight to the suburbs. The committee brought a report to the 1966 General Assembly that indicated there was no clear consensus on restructuring the church to be more effective in doing its mission, although there was strong sentiment reflecting a growing regionalism and the desirability of some form of regional synods.[18]

The committee, keenly aware of the theological controversy surrounding the adoption of the Confession of 1967, in 1968 presented to the General Assembly a carefully thought-through "Design for Mission" that had a strong preference for regional synods. It also contained strong provisions for clearly defined responsibilities at each governing body level, and for mutual accountability between them that would capitalize on the growing energy of localism for the larger good.

After a year of debate and some changes, the "Design for Mission" passed by a three-to-one majority vote at the General Assembly in 1969.[19] This action went far beyond approving a simple organizational restructure. Richard W. Reifsnyder stated that "the church committed itself to revamping the General Assembly boards and agencies to fit into a participatory, decentralized scheme of planning and facilitating the support of a unified mission . . . at a national and global level."[20]

The General Assembly took several implementing actions, sending down to presbyteries the necessary amendments to the *Book of Order*, under the title of Overture H, which was based on many of the key principles of the "Design for Mission." It outlined the roles of sessions, presbyteries, synods, and the General Assembly with regard to the priorities of the whole denomination; defined the broad powers and policies of the General Council and other General Assembly agencies, including how elected members would reflect broad representation from across the church; specified how election, review, and evaluation of churchwide administrative executive staff were to be conducted; and created a churchwide interlocking system for program planning, budgeting, and evaluation, known as PPBE.[21]

The "Design for Mission" required "a division of responsibilities that provides both flexibility and distribution of authority for decision-making within a framework of interdependence and unity of mission." It made clear that such division required "assignment of the task or function to the unit of the Church best able to perform it."[22] One of its goals was "to locate the administration of mission so that it is performed by the lowest judicatory that can most efficiently and effectively accomplish it."[23] The final proposal that was adopted made significant shifts of responsibility from synods to presbyteries and sessions,[24] although it "ensured the role of synods as the major link in expediting denominational priorities throughout the church."[25] The presbyteries overwhelmingly ratified Overture H.

The 1969 Assembly (Portland) established the Special Committee on General Assembly Agencies, which was chaired by Orley B. Mason, a businessman from Ohio. Over a two-year period the committee produced a plan that called for the creation of a General Assembly Mission Council with the authority to supervise the other agencies. In addition it established several new entities. The Program Agency gathered in one place the functions of the former Boards of National Missions and Education, as well as COEMAR. The Vocation Agency focused on developing, guiding, and assisting ministers and laypeople working in professional service to the church. The Support Agency was concerned with stewardship development and program interpretation. And the Council on Administrative Services (CAS) had sweeping responsibilities with regard to synod and presbytery administration and staffing.[26] CAS was one guardian vestige of the "glue of connectionalism" as it oversaw the funding and concurrence in executive staff selection across the church-wide system.[27]

Serious concerns and reservations were heatedly raised along the way by the leadership of the former boards and agencies as the plan was developed. There was no consensus about how the new organization should be structured, though there was a feeling that restructure was necessary. Some felt that the "Design for Mission" set the broad parameters for a new direction, but that the details were to be left up to the former General Council. As the power struggle grew among these strong leaders to no resolve, they were surprised when William P. Thompson, the Stated Clerk, stepped in and "ruled [that] the General Assembly had authorized wholesale restructuring," in essence affirming the direction of the Special Committee.[28]

The final proposal was presented at the 1971 meeting of the General Assembly in Rochester. The sweeping restructure of the boards and agencies of the UPCUSA was approved with little dissent. It was overshadowed by the controversy over the grant to the Angela Davis legal defense fund.[29] In the wake of all this turmoil, it took two years to implement the plan. The new restructure put to rest the decades-long era of strong UPCUSA boards and agencies.

Years later, upon reflection, Thompson did admit, "I have some feelings of nostalgia about the strong agencies in both denominations [UPCUSA and PCUS]. It seems to me sometimes that they were able to accomplish things that we find difficult today because, rather than having agencies with particular orientations, we have a single programmatic entity, namely the General Assembly Council with sub-departments that do these particulars" (01-10).

Restructure of Boards and Agencies (PCUS)

It must be remembered that from the beginning the fundamental difference between the PCUS and the PCUSA with regard to how the church was to be organized, especially its boards and agencies, was basically a theological matter. The overriding theological concern in the origins of the PCUS, the one that shaped its mission and structure into the early decades of the twentieth century, was the doctrine of the "spirituality of the church." The foremost proponent of this doctrine and the leading light in the formation of the PCUS was James Henley Thornwell. His position was that if it was not in Scripture, it was not within the jurisdiction of the church; and that "mission boards were unscriptural." He was unequivocal in his view that "the church's mission was solely to promote the glory of God and human salvation and had nothing to do with voluntary associations for civil and social purposes."[30] The fulfillment of these purposes was left to the freedom of the individual conscience.

What sprang up was a proliferation of executive committees at various levels of the Presbyterian system of governing bodies, or "courts," as they were known. The executive committees were related in loose fashion to these courts, but were not necessarily "of them" in the same jurisdictional sense as the boards and agencies of the PCUSA were. To avoid any hint of centralized power, they were dispersed geographically across the church. The court that initiated an executive committee to conduct some benevolent activity had the freedom to elect people of its choice to serve on it and was given considerable freedom to pursue its work with some, but not too much, direction. This continued for a half century until 1927, when the PCUS established, for efficiency and economy, a forty-four-member umbrella Committee on the Assembly's Work, with all the former executive committees as subcommittees of it. This lasted only a few years because it was "perceived as centralizing too much power and contributing to declining receipts."[31] After its collapse, the number of executive committees continued to expand.

By 1949 it became evident that there were too many of these executive committees and they were too spread out to meet the missional needs of the PCUS. A plan of restructure was adopted by the General Assembly that created five boards—World Missions, Church Extension (later National Ministries), Christian Education, Annuities and Relief, and Women's Work. Their respective boards elected executive secretaries. In addition, there was an Office of the General Assembly and a General Council responsible for various financial and program-coordinating activities.

Still there was considerable fear of "centralization" in the church, but strong executive leaders brought familiarity and respect to the autonomous work of each board or agency. The location of these boards and agencies in several geographical locations added to the sense of "decentralization." Years later, an evaluative comment on the genius of that design was that it was difficult to locate a specific target when one wanted to attack "the General Assembly."

The 1949 plan of restructure in time proved to have its deficiencies. The General Council was originally intended to have a stronger coordinating role to go along with the built-in "self-modification function" among the specific boards and agencies. According to a later evaluation of the system: "There has been much modification *within* a number of Boards and Agencies, but little *between* them." The system did not have within it the will or the strength to change its structure or find the necessary cooperation to adjust its overall priorities. The chief executives did not always come to "one mind" when they had joint decision-making meetings. This often led to a duplication of functions. Each cause developed strong loyal followers across the church, and at times this detracted from the "unity" of the church. One report to the General Assembly stated that "The feeling of alienation, indifference, and 'no confidence' about much of the Assembly's work is caused by the increasingly dysfunctional structures within which and by which that work must be done."[32]

William J. Fogleman chaired the Ad Interim Committee on Restructuring Boards and Agencies appointed by R. Matthew Lynn, Moderator of the 1969 PCUS Assembly (Mobile). Lynn was careful to see that the committee was geographically and theologically diverse with no member having any current relationship with one of the boards. James E. Millard, Stated Clerk of the General Assembly, in contrast to the practice of the UPCUSA, was not involved in the work of this committee. Robert C. Worley, a specialist in church organizations from McCormick Seminary, was hired to consult with the committee and provide organizational models for its consideration. This committee kept in contact with the restructure committee of the UPCUSA and on occasion held joint meetings with them.[33]

The restructure committee brought its proposed plan for adoption to the 1972 meeting of the PCUS General Assembly in Montreat. It must be remembered that this plan was not constructed in isolation from other significant developments in the denomination. It was not just union presbyteries that were coming into existence during this time, but there was a power shift taking place among the synods, presbyteries, and local congregations. They were becoming more deeply engaged in all sorts of mission enterprises with "increasing sophistication and usefulness," to a large degree because the General Assembly agentry had "led the way in these developments." This was not lost on the restructure committee as it developed its plan. It asserted "that a 'new regionalism' is a fact of life within the church and that it cannot be stifled by ignoring it." Some, fearful of fragmentation of the church, concluded "that the new plan represents a radical capitulation to the spirit of regionalism." But the committee felt it made "positive use of this trend to tie the system together."[34]

Some of the key organizational principles underlying this plan were as follows: "To have an effective central coordinating/integrating body. To shift the locus of activity to the lowest level where optimally effective. To coordinate all communications through one central agency. To have less autonomy in boards or board-type units. To have one central office with functional satellite offices."[35]

In summary, the proposed restructure had at its core the General Executive Board (GEB), accountable directly to the General Assembly, with three subsystems that were to work together to carry out their programs in light of each other's functions. First, there was the priority-building system that would shift decision-making power away from separate units to the Assembly itself. Second, there was a program system that would carry out the priorities and goals set by the General Assembly. The GEB was divided into five working divisions: National Mission, International Mission, Corporate and Social Mission, Professional Development, and Central Support Services. Third, there was a communication system, with staff having joint calls by the GEB and a particular synod; this was to be the two-way channel of communication between the constituents and the agentry of the church. Finally, there was a separate and independent Office of Review and Evaluation that was to monitor these systems and make suggestions about how to make improvements in performance and structure.[36]

This restructure was an undertaking exceeding anything that had been attempted in the denomination before. It called for the giving up of powerful self-interests to make room for a more diverse, inclusive, and representative body of persons to fill the structure. The PCUS had a long tradition of limited terms for those serving as staff in its executive board and agencies. This was continued by ordinarily, but not necessarily, having a limit of two four-year terms for those serving on the GEB.[37]

The plan was adopted by the General Assembly. The dream of the restructure committee was to introduce a new era in open governance of the PCUS. Richard W. Reifsnyder, in commenting on this action, said: "Hopes were high that the processes of inclusiveness and accountability would help overcome potential divisions and that management procedures would enable the church to develop unity in mission." But this dream was tainted from the beginning. When time came to fill the elected member positions on the GEB before the Assembly adjourned, the nominating committee struggled long to come up with a representative slate. No doubt its decisions were influenced by the theological turmoil that was punctuated with the threat of withdrawal of a significant segment of the church to form the PCA. Also the 1972 Assembly (Montreat) was moderated by L. Nelson Bell, who was known for his conservative theological and ecclesial positions. According to Reifsnyder, "the restructuring began with people selected for the GEB on the basis of political considerations, rather than beginning with the intended training period."[38]

Robert J. Rea, Jr., was one of the first associate staff persons hired. He served on a mission strategy team that worked with presbyteries and synods. One staff assignment was to work with the union presbytery task force when it came into being. Rea compared the General Executive Board with the UPCUSA General Assembly agencies before their restructure. The GEB had a sophisticated structure in which everyone knew each other at 341 Ponce de Leon Ave. (Atlanta), the PCUS headquarters building. It was less bureaucratic than the agentry at 475 Riverside Drive, (New York), the UPCUSA headquarters with its separate boards and agencies, which Rea described as a "highly bureaucratic [organization] which had its own efficiencies and there was a clear order, hierarchy, lots of rules and regulations." He added that when he went there on business, a sense of anonymity was pervasive. There were "literally times that I introduced New York staff on the third floor to New York staff on the fifth floor because I knew them [from] working with them in different committees" (47-6). Reflecting on those early years at GEB, Rea said there was "so much going on with this new organization, so much transition. We were never able to hire the staff that the structure had originally envisioned, so most of us had two or three jobs" (47-4).

The GEB got off to a rocky start. The creation of a new management style that shifted from an "assertive executive authority" to a "general staff directing the facilitation of the process" resulted in great tension between those accustomed to one style or the other. The selection of a woman and an African American as division heads injected another new dynamic. There were other problems. The priority system did not work, in part because of residual agendas from previous agencies. It was difficult to get reliable information on which to base decisions. The communication system did not function completely as envisioned because the regional communicators were not fully trusted in some synods. In 1975 a major review was set in motion that resulted in major revisions. The corporate leadership model was replaced with the older executive officer arrangement. To get away from negative "executive" connotations, the name was changed from the General Executive Board (GEB), to the General Assembly Mission Board (GAMB). Patricia McClurg became administrative director in 1977 and brought a combination of strong leadership and a collegial style to the organization that was greatly expected.[39]

Regional Synods (UPCUSA)

In the minds of those who in 1968 reported to the UPCUSA General Assembly in the "Design for Mission," as previously mentioned, was a deep commitment "to a participatory, decentralized scheme of planning and facilitating the support of a unified mission." They envisioned the synod as being the primary connection between the national and local levels of the church. This called for a very different system from the one under which the Board of National Missions and other agencies had operated for years with regard to the lower judicatories.

Kenneth L. McCall, describing the old system, said presbyteries that were not major urban centers looked to their synods as the go-between for financial support for their work from the Board of National Missions. The large urban presbyteries—Chicago, Detroit, Philadelphia and New York, St. Louis, and others—were called "Special Administrative Units" of the Board of National Missions. They dealt directly with the Board of National Missions, not through the synod, for their support (66-8). There were sixteen Special Administrative Units involving seventeen presbyteries that negotiated directly with General Assembly agencies, with nothing more than general review by their respective synods. This meant that there were 35 synods and 16 special administrative units negotiating with General Assembly agencies.[40]

As these metropolitan areas began to sprawl, a core city remained but burgeoning suburbs that together were considered as "a single economic and sociological unit" surrounded it. From a church perspective, in most instances existing presbyteries did not include all the congregations in a given metropolitan area. The Special Committee on Regional Synods and Church Administration, formed by the Assembly in 1963, considered creating metropolitan-wide judicatories that would facilitate mission between the inner and outer city. The problem for the church was that urban centers often crossed one or more state lines and presbyteries existed in state-line synods. So the concept for regional synods came into being in an attempt to meet this specific challenge.[41]

Robert F. Stevenson, who as Associate Stated Clerk was involved in the regional synod development, remembered that "it was never intended that there would be a presbytery realignment except maybe in the metropolitan areas" (16-8). Kenneth Neigh, executive for the Board of National Missions, wrote the original proposal for regional synods. He had come to the Board from Detroit, where he "had made the Synod and the Presbyteries identical as far as staff. So, the staff of the Synod was the staff of all the Presbyteries in Michigan" (66-6).

At the time the proposal was evolving, the country was going through a period where the political rhetoric was "Power to the People." This rhetoric of "power at the lowest possible level . . . get everything nearer to the local level," according to Ken McCall's perception, "got incorporated [in the Neigh proposal] as a rationale for doing what nobody had any reason for doing. . . . And the only purpose of the original proposal was to take three or four places in the country . . . where the boundaries did not make any sense anymore . . . and alter those boundaries, to take into account how a metro area worked. That's the only reason for this thing. The rest of the people in the country didn't need it" (66-24).

The Assembly's Committee struggled for a number of years with these considerations and finally came to understand that most of the land mass of the United States was not in metropolitan areas. The Committee abandoned the idea of establishing only metropolitan regional synods. As McCall said, it "became a proposal to reorganize the whole country" (66-24).

The Presbytery of St. Louis sent an overture to the 1967 Assembly containing a section "On the Study of the Possibility of Approximately 50 Regional Synods." The Assembly took no action on the overture and referred it to the Special Committee.[42] During 1972, the organizational planning for the proposed regional synods approved by the General Assembly was completed. Fifteen regional synods, uneven in size and number of churches and communicant members, were operational by the beginning of 1973. Some covered huge geographical areas with few communicant members. There were four synods with population over 200,000 that were given one additional representative on three major General Assembly agencies.[43]

One of the highly held values in the plan was that of widespread participation in developing a comprehensive strategy for the whole church "in light of," all of the mission strategies of the different judicatory levels of the church. There was no universal understanding of the meaning of "in light of," although an almost unlimited number of inter-judicatory, time-consuming consultations took place, diligently attempting to fulfill the expectation of trying to make the plan work. The PPBE (program planning, budgeting, and evaluation) church-wide system was unwieldy and eventually collapsed of its own weight after a few years.[44]

One thing that proved effective, for the most part, was the inclusion in the *Book of Order* of a provision for executive staff service at the presbytery level. This was a new and innovative concept, especially in locations where most of the staff services had been provided at the synod level. At the beginning, CAS, the Council on Administrative Services, was heavily involved in funding and concurrence of staff at the synod and presbytery level, but in time this responsibility was relinquished to the synod, and in some cases to the presbyteries themselves. Wide arrays of programs were created in presbyteries, supported by new schemes of "resource redistribution," but in time a pinch was felt from declining funds. At the heart of all this activity was a significant shift in power with a sense of increasing freedom from earlier forms of organizational restraints.

There were some unintended consequences from the formation of the regional synods. David B. Lowry, who had served as Stated Clerk and assistant executive of the Presbytery of Detroit, thought about the years when the regional synods were beginning to live out the purposes for which they were established. He remembered, "the reality was that the decentralizing train was moving right past the synods [*chuckling*]. It had initially been, with Kenny Neigh and others in our administration, the great revolution, [that] was 'devolution' from the Board of National Missions to synod; synod-level clout and control of money and so forth." Lowry concluded, "I don't know whether Kenny [Neigh] even anticipated that the train wasn't going to stop there [*chuckling*]. . . . It just went right on past, just blew its whistle on by [*laughter*]" through the presbyteries to the local congregations (35-14).

Ken McCall pointed out that it was quite an adjustment for presbyteries like Detroit. "[W]hen the Synod became that administrative unit for all presbyteries, it was quite a change . . . you just can't look to Detroit as the special place. We've got all these others we haven't taken in account. So, I'm not sure the Synod ever made that adjustment, personally. I don't know whether it ever managed it" (66-8).

This massive restructure of the UPCUSA—of boards and agencies and regional synods—had taken ten years to create and only had a shelf life of ten more years. The overall effectiveness of this approach may not have been systematically ascertained before denominational reunion created a new round of reorganization.

Regional Synods (PCUS)

The Conference on Restructuring Synods and Presbyteries, held at Montreat, North Carolina, April 23–25, 1968, produced comprehensive findings that guided the General Assembly in developing its strategy for restructuring the PCUS synods and presbyteries. The report recognized that "while all the courts have the same great commission and serve the same ultimate purpose, their mechanics and methods of operation may, of practical necessity, be somewhat different." It further stated that there "is no best plan of structure (organization). However, where possible, structures at all court levels should be similar enough to correlate so that program can be implemented."[45]

The conference recognized that "local problems, conflicts, and misunderstandings are best handled by the lowest possible court of jurisdiction." It also pointed out as important that "the higher courts are in a better position to arrive at the most advisable church-wide policy, methods of procedure, opportunities for broad parallel activity and witness to the wholeness and the unity of the Church." To these ends, it concluded that all courts should be structured for mission, review, and pastoral oversight, giving careful attention to the responsibilities of "exclusive original jurisdiction" assigned each court by the *Book of Church Order*.[46]

P. D. Miller, Moderator of the 1968 PCUS Assembly (Montreat), appointed the Ad Interim Committee on Restructuring Synods and Presbyteries. Harvard A. Anderson, executive secretary of the Synod of Florida, was named as chair to guide the committee, which was made up of one representative from each synod.[47]

The committee was instructed to devise a plan based on the recommendations found in the report of the Montreat Conference on Restructuring and report it to the 1969 PCUS Assembly (Mobile). The committee was to take into account the following factors: mission responsibilities of the church in the area; number and distribution of churches to provide sufficient members and resources to fulfill its mission; cultural, sociological, and economic factors; boundaries between political subdivisions; past commonality of interests and identity; and jurisdictional lines of other denominations. The courts were to be structured in "regular gradation between the General Assembly and presbyteries." They also were to take seriously the need to realign presbytery boundaries, considering the above factors and using the principles adopted by the Conference on Restructuring, before making recommendations on realigning the synods.[48]

The committee began its work in earnest but soon discovered the enormity of the task. In its report to the 1969 PCUS Assembly (Mobile), Harvard submitted that the committee "found a surprisingly large openness—even eagerness—for restructuring widespread in the General Assembly and a number of regional plans already either vaguely or specifically incubating." However, the recommendation was to extend the work of the committee for another year and report findings and recommendations to the 1970 Assembly (Memphis).[49] Though this was granted, the extension did not prove sufficient and eventually the report was rescheduled to be presented at the 1971 Assembly (Massanetta Springs).

The Ad Interim Committee on Restructuring Synods and Presbyteries brought in a comprehensive recommendation to the 1971 Assembly. It detailed the purpose, today's problems, and considerations for developing new presbyteries. It concluded with the implications of these findings for new synods and recommended that seven regional synods be formed out of the existing fifteen synods. They would be: Synod A—Virginia, West Virginia, Maryland and District of Columbia and a few counties in North Carolina; Synod B—North Carolina; Synod C—Kentucky, Tennessee and a few counties in Virginia, Georgia, Arkansas and Missouri; Synod D—Arkansas, Missouri, and Oklahoma; Synod E—Louisiana, Texas and a few counties in New Mexico; Synod F—Mississippi, Alabama and a few counties in Florida; and Synod G—South Carolina, Georgia, and Florida.[50]

It was ordered that those making up the membership of these proposed synods were "to meet in convention for the purpose of organization not later than the Spring of 1972 . . . and that July 1, 1973, be the effective legal date for the establishment of the proposed new synods and the presbyteries which they create." The Assembly appointed conveners and clerks *pro tem* for each of the proposed synods and instructed them to give notice of the time and place of the meetings.[51]

One interesting caveat in the report was the provision "that if the 1972 General Assembly votes a plan of union with the UPCUSA Church and three-fourths of the presbyteries approve union by January 31, 1973, then the conventions will not meet and the files of the convention committees will become part of the consideration of the proper planning committees of the new united Church."[52] The vote on a plan of union was never proposed.

The recommendation also called for the appointment of a commission made up of one teaching elder (minister) and one ruling elder from each existing synod "empowered to readjust a particular boundary line of a proposed synod when requested by an existing synod. The commission was to begin its work July 1, 1971, and cease to function December 31, 1975. John S. Brown, pastor of Ginter Park Presbyterian Church, Richmond, Virginia, was named chair of the commission.[53]

Over the course of a year, requests did come from existing synods for what amounted to more than "readjustment of boundaries." Florida and North Carolina became separate synods by those names; South Carolina and Georgia became the Synod of the Southeast; Virginia, West Virginia, Maryland and District of Columbia became the Synod of the Virginias; Arkansas, Oklahoma, Louisiana, Texas and a few counties in New Mexico became the Synod of Red River; Missouri became the Synod of Mid-America; and Kentucky, Tennessee, Alabama and Mississippi became the Synod of the Mid-South.[54]

The creation of this final synod came out of a very traumatic situation in which the proposed Synod F's convention was taken over by ultraconservative and anti-union forces in Alabama and Mississippi. There were fears that they might try to take this synod out of the PCUS. The Commission on New Synod Boundaries found the situation untenable and ordered proposed Synods C and F to convene in convention and organize a regional synod out of the existing synods of Alabama, Mississippi, Tennessee, and Kentucky. This was accomplished and the synod was named the Synod of the Mid-South. This was the final blow for the opposition forces. Congregations and ministers, mainly in Alabama and Mississippi, began the exodus to the PCA in 1973.

These new regional synods had a profound degenerative impact on the unique relational nature of the PCUS, though this was rarely acknowledged. State-line synods had been undelegated, which meant that every session had the same minister-elder representation at synod as it did at presbytery. This created a sense of ownership and awareness of the purpose of synods. Synod meetings were almost like annual campground meetings or family reunions. When the regional synods came into being as delegated, which meant that only a few elders and ministers were elected each year, the relational sense of closeness and meaning was lost. Synod became as remote to most sessions as the General Assembly. Some of the larger presbyteries took on the feel of the former state-line synods. There was a tendency toward becoming more corporate than family at the synod level.

No Union Synods

Setting in motion the restructure of boards and agencies and the creation of regional synods was part of the larger ecclesial context of the far-reaching actions taken by the 1969 PCUS General Assembly (Mobile), in which union presbyteries were constitutionally authorized. At the time it was difficult to fathom the dramatic change that all these actions unleashed on the PCUS. The union synods amendment that had been defeated in presbyteries in the PCUS in 1969 by a vote of 40–37, was not to be taken lightly in comparison to all the other changes wrought in Mobile. It was symptomatic of deeper fissures in the PCUS. A postmortem on that vote yielded a variety of perceptions about why it turned out that way. Harry S. Hassall, a leading opponent of the union presbyteries and synods amendments, recalled that, "much to our chagrin the union presbyteries amendment passed on a reversal of the original vote." However, mustering some measure of satisfaction, he commented, [W]e had a great deal of energy and we were able to find enough money to defeat . . . union synods. We beat that fair and square." He did concede: "But you didn't have to have that to get what you wanted" (65-11).

William P. Thompson, Stated Clerk of the General Assembly (UPCUSA), in later years stated that he was "very positive about union presbyteries. I was familiar with a number of union churches and was aware of the contribution that they were making to the hoped for union of the two denominations, and I felt that to introduce union presbyteries as the next step would advance that process in a material way. I felt that the formation of union synods was somewhat more remote." (01–2)

Mort McMillan, a proponent of these union measures, surmised that "there were people in North Carolina, Virginia who were not directly involved, but who were willing for others to have a union presbytery, but thought maybe doing a union synod is going too far. Keep it localized" (05-16). McMillan went on to say he had heard secondhand that some had argued "if you voted in a union synod, you could force some people in a presbytery to be in a union they didn't want to be in, so let's just keep it at the presbytery level." This seemed to reflect "that the PCUS always was, and the remnant of that that we still have, is, much more presbytery oriented than synod oriented" (05-17).

James D. Baskin, a ruling elder from First Presbyterian Church, San Antonio, Texas, believed that it was "blocked politically because there were those that felt that organic reunion of the denomination was happening through the backdoor. . . . I do believe that [was] the reason the push for union synods failed" (26-7). The hue and cry of "backdoor reunion" would be heard as a discounting argument for a long time. The "backdoor" argument was rebutted by persons in the border synods who viewed union presbyteries as "the 'front door' constitutional approach to increase cooperation between the two denominations."[55]

No matter what the reason, the problems facing those who anticipated creating union presbyteries were made more complicated by the failure to pass the union synods amendment in the PCUS. The creation of union presbyteries, after the final enabling action in 1969, could not be postponed because of this failure. Other adjustments would have to be found. Originally, the concept was that there would be a single union synod made up of several union presbyteries. But now the situation required union presbyteries to relate to two separate synods, one PCUS and the other UPCUSA.

Historically, the boundaries of almost all of the synods along the Border States coincided with the boundaries of the states where they were located. This was true of the Synods of Texas, Missouri, and Kentucky. Occasionally one would have a congregation or so in a neighboring state. By the late 1960s it was a different situation in Arkansas and Oklahoma. The PCUS synod extended to both states. The two synods covering Washington, DC, displayed the clearest non–completely overlapping configuration of any along the Border States. The Synod of Virginia (PCUS) was mainly in Virginia, but extended to Washington, DC, with a few congregations in the Baltimore, Maryland, area. The Synod of Chesapeake (UPCUSA) included congregations in Baltimore, Maryland; Wilmington, Delaware; and Washington, DC.

Being related to two synods was not as great a problem in state-line synods as in non-state-line synods; it would become more problematic later, in two or three years, when more regional synods that crossed state lines came into being. The boundary problem in pairs of the synods that were anticipating having union presbyteries was that the boundaries of existing presbyteries within them were not always coterminous. The creation of union presbyteries, after the final enabling action in 1969, could not be postponed because of these boundary problems or the failure to have union synods. Other adjustments would have to be found. Steps were underway for a long time to minimize this situation where there was an inclination to realign presbytery boundaries.

Realigning Presbytery Boundaries

The Synod of Texas (PCUS) met shortly after the 1969 Mobile Assembly to consider re-doing its presbyteries to make them conform to the UPCUSA presbyteries in Texas. Also, the other issue was that there were too many presbyteries in Texas. The PCUS Synod voted to reconstitute its boundaries by changing its rules at the 1970 synod meeting (23-29). Fewer presbyteries were created in both synods, in configurations that facilitated the creation of union presbyteries. Flynn Long said that "this was kind of an avant-garde thing that Fogleman [William J.] was involved in, I'm sure, and Bob Bass [Robert W.] and a number of others, with respect to trying to make it possible for better relationships with the UP's to be established and to make the boundaries coordinated" (23-28).

Both PCUS and UPCUSA Synods of Missouri were well along the way to requesting the formation of the Union Synod of Missouri. The two Synods of Missouri, at concurrent Special Meetings held on February 6, 1969, in anticipation of being constituted as a Union Synod, adopted a four-presbytery plan as the basis for realignment of coterminous presbytery boundaries.[56] But their overture, which had passed the UPCUSA General Assembly, was thwarted by the action of the PCUS presbyteries.[57] There had been years of cooperation between the two synods in many program areas, making the plan highly desirable.

The first proposal for realignment had only three presbyteries in each synod: one anchored by St. Louis in the east, another around Kansas City, and the other one sort of an hourglass in between. This was later revised to create four presbyteries that fell roughly in the northeast, southeast, northwest, and southwest quadrants of the state. This plan was adopted unanimously after much political wrangling and debate and became a satisfactory solution to not having a Union Synod (08-10). In time, though, the Synod of Missouri and its successor, the Synod of Mid-America, would function as a *de facto* union synod.

The PCUS and UPCUSA Synods of Kentucky had a long history of cooperative work in a full range of programs, Christian Education being the centerpiece. The presence of union congregations from the 1920s and 1930s fostered the building of bridges that continued to underscore the unreasonableness of separation. The fact that the undelegated meetings of the Synods usually met concurrently at Centre College and other locations created a sense of an annual "family reunion" for the elders and ministers from congregations all across the commonwealth. One synod would sit on the left side of the aisle, one would sit on the right side, and the union churches would sit in the middle. Many times common votes were taken, but separate records kept.

Through the years numerous presbyteries in both denominations seemed to be restructured with regularity. With the prospects of having union presbyteries, a plan was developed to have three union presbyteries, with eastern, central, and western locations. One unique factor was that the former Regional Director of Christian Education, a single position shared by both synods, was dissolved and three associate presbytery executive positions were created to carry out educational functions for the presbyteries and the synods. The same person, David E. Rule, served as the last moderator of both Kentucky synods.

The Synod of Arkansas/Oklahoma "set the pace for the future" in that this was the first non-state-line synod in the PCUS within which a union presbytery would be formed. It had been created on January 1, 1969, by the merger of the PCUS Synods of Arkansas and Oklahoma.[58] The creation of this new synod was intended to make it more geographically compatible with the UPCUSA synod should a union synod become possible. Its name was reversed to reduce confusion that had existed prior to that time with its UPCUSA counterpart, the Synod of Oklahoma/Arkansas, with which it had had cooperative work in Christian education and church extension for years.

The final area where two synods would form a union presbytery in the first wave was the Washington, DC, area. The unique thing about this situation was that neither of the two synods involved, Chesapeake (UPCUSA) and Virginia (PCUS), had coterminous boundaries nor were they state-line synods. This was another first, but it would be a common occurrence in the future.

In restructure, both denominations were struggling with a balance between power and freedom in the search to find the "structural glue" that binds the broader body together with theological and organizational integrity. Both were striving to exercise control over funds and personnel through administrative centralization (UPCUSA), attempting to maintain relations and friendly persuasion through administrative decentralization (PCUS), shifting responsibility for mission closer to the lowest level where optimally effective, and creating new synod and presbytery configurations that would take into account the current contextual realities. Both were realigning presbyteries that were anticipating becoming union presbyteries, in order to minimize the rate of failure to create union synods. All this restructuring more than frayed the edges of the status quo; it rent the fabric of "how we have always done it" from top to bottom.

Clearly there were winners and losers in this time of denominational restructure. The full consequences of the contributions and flaws of this time of reordering of ecclesial life are still a long time coming, but ghosts of Stamford Bridge and Hastings *et al.* began to romp a bit more freely across the organizational terrain. Let the union presbyteries begin.

Notes

1. *Minutes* of the One-Hundred-Eighth General Assembly (PCUS), 1968, "Findings of the Conference on Restructuring Synods and Presbyteries," p. 251.

2. Lefferts A. Loetscher, *The Broadening Church* (Philadelphia: University of Pennsylvania Press, 1954), p. 92.

3. Ibid., p. 93.

4. Ibid.

5. Ibid., p. 133.

6. Ibid., p. 134.

7. Ibid., pp. 134–135.

8. Ibid.

9. William G. McAtee, "*Circulating Funds in the Re-United Church? A Contribution to the Informal Discussion Concerning What the New Church Is to Become . . .* ," unpublished paper, winter 1983, in personal collection of William G. McAtee.

10. Ibid.

11. Coalter, Mulder, and Weeks, eds., *The Re-Forming Tradition*, pp. 100–101.

12. Milton J. Coalter, John M. Mulder, and Louis B. Weeks, eds., *The Organizational Revolution: Presbyterians and American Denominationalism* (Louisville, KY: Westminster/John Knox Press), 1992, p. 56.

13. Ibid., pp. 58–59.

14. Ibid., p. 61.

15. Coalter, Mulder, and Weeks, eds., *The Re-Forming Tradition*, p. 101.

16. Coalter, Mulder, and Weeks, eds., *The Organizational Revolution*, pp. 59–60.

17. Ibid., p. 63.

18. Loetscher, A Brief History of the Presbyterians, pp. 173–175.

19. Coalter, Mulder, and Weeks, eds., The Organizational Revolution, pp. 67–68.

20. Ibid., p. 70.

21. *Report on Regional Synods and Church Administration: Design for Mission*, (Philadelphia: Office of the General Assembly, UPCUSA, 1969).

22. Ibid., p. 13.

23. Ibid., p. 14.

24. Ibid., pp. 8–9.

25. Loetscher, *A Brief History of the Presbyterians*, p. 176.

26. Ibid., p. 179.

27. McAtee, "*Circulating Funds in the Re-United Church?*" p. 3.

28. Coalter, Mulder, and Weeks, eds., *The Organizational Revolution*, p. 71.

29. Ibid., p. 73.

30. Ibid., p. 63.

31. Ibid., p. 64.

32. *Minutes* of the One-Hundred-Twelfth General Assembly (PCUS), "Report of Ad Interim Committee on Restructuring Boards and Agencies as Amended," Montreat, North Carolina, June 11–16, 1972, p. 87.

33. Coalter, Mulder, and Weeks, eds., *The Organizational Revolution*, p. 76.

34. *Minutes* of the One-Hundred-Twelfth General Assembly (PCUS), 1972, p. 88.

35. Ibid., p. 86.

36. Ibid., pp. 92–100.

37. Ibid., p. 94.

38. Coalter, Mulder, and Weeks, eds., *The Organizational Revolution*, p. 78.

39. Ibid., pp. 82–83.

40. *Minutes* of the 180th General Assembly (UPCUSA), 1968, "Design for Mission—A Preliminary Proposal, p. 258.

41. Loetscher, *A Brief History of the Presbyterians*, p. 174.

42. *Minutes* of the 180th General Assembly (UPCUSA), 1968, p. 248.

43. Loetscher, *A Brief History of the Presbyterians*, p. 177.

44. Coalter, Mulder, and Weeks, eds., *The Organizational Revolution*, p. 79.

45. *Minutes* of the One-Hundred-Eighth General Assembly (PCUS), 1968, p. 251.

46. Ibid.

47. Ibid., p. 136.

48. Ibid., p. 129.

49. *Minutes* of the One-Hundred-Ninth General Assembly (PCUS), 1969, p. 201.

50. *Minutes* of the One-Hundred-Eleventh General Assembly (PCUS), Massanetta Springs, VA, June 13–18, 1971, pp. 282–290.

51. Ibid., p. 131.

52. Ibid.

53. Ibid.

54. *Minutes* of the One-Hundred-Fourteenth General Assembly of the Presbyterian Church in the United States, Louisville, KY, June 16–22, 1974, p. 276.

55. Peterson, *And Then There Were ~~Ten, Eleven~~, Twelve! Anymore?* p. 12.

56. *Minutes* of the 137th Stated Meeting of the Synod of Missouri (PCUS), June 9, 1969, p. 21.

57. Peterson, And Then There Were . . . Twelve! Anymore? p. 12.

58. *Minutes* of the 117th Annual Session of the Synod of Arkansas (PCUS), May 21–22, 1968, p. 16.

Chapter 10
First-Wave Union Presbyteries (1970–1972)

The purpose of the union shall be the furtherance of a united witness and mission, the administration of a single program of nurture, sustenance, and growth of the Church within the union Presbytery (Classis), and the oversight of all churches within its bounds by a union Presbytery (Classis), which will hold title to the properties of the uniting judicatories and provide the functions and fulfill the duties of a Presbytery (Classis), as specified in the Constitution of each Church.
—Book of Church Order 32-2 (2) (1970)

Those who proposed the overture that brought it into being did not construct this new paragraph from the *Book of Church Order*, which described the purpose of a union presbytery, off the top of the head. It was the product of a long, evolving process of reflection on the questions: "What is a Presbytery? What shall it be? How will its life be ordered? How does it relate to the other parts of the body of Christ?" This was not simply a cerebral exercise by a select group of cloistered intellectuals, but it was incubated through long years of experience. Graham Gordon, Regional Director of Christian Education for the Synods of Kentucky, noted that union presbyteries came "not just simply out of necessity, . . . it was also conviction" (74-2). And the conviction was that being together made a stronger witness to the unity of the church than being separated. It was a matter of theology as well as practical necessity. That conviction was not totally realized, because some of the dream regarding union synods had not crossed the constitutional divide.

The first wave of union presbyteries came into being in a three-and-a-half-year period following the 1969 Mobile Assembly. It was during this period that what became known as the "original nine" union presbyteries were established. One started and was dissolved in order to make room for others in its synod. Another was started but reconstituted to incorporate other presbyteries. During this time, attempts were made at succeeding General Assemblies to overturn the 1969 decision, to no avail. The reality of union presbyteries provided for those upset with the PCUS one convenient reason for withdrawing into the PCA.[1]

Following the Mobile Assembly, it took six to nine months before the first pair of presbyteries could vote to adopt a plan for union. The others followed at a pace dictated by their particular circumstances. Each new union presbytery was unique, depending on its own historical setting. However, some similarities and commonalities did exist among them.

Missouri (Union)

On March 12, 1970, the Union Presbytery of Northeast Missouri, the first union presbytery, was formed out of the Presbyteries of Missouri (PCUS) and Kirk (UPCUSA). These presbyteries were, respectively, members of the Synods of Missouri (PCUS) and (UPCUSA). Cecil G. Culverhouse, pastor of First Presbyterian Church, Fulton, Missouri, said in the congregation he served he never heard anybody not being in favor of the union presbytery. As far as the presbyteries were concerned, the vote to become a union presbytery was "either unanimous or very nearly. There may have been one or two [opposed], but it was overwhelming. We were ready." There was a sense that it was long overdue. . . . [It] just doesn't make any sense [not to do it]. . . . It was important, but it wasn't such a big deal. It was like [the] family had been living together, [the] man and wife had been living together awhile and they decide to get married" (12-7).

Soon after the organizing meeting, Kenneth R. Locke was elected executive presbyter. Locke had served as field representative for the Board of National Missions (UPCUSA) and adjunct staff for the Synod of Missouri (UPCUSA). He focused on men's work and church planning in the northwest section of Missouri. Locke said he "was told to concentrate on the cause yelling the loudest" (11-5).

Before the union presbytery was formed, Locke had been assigned to Kirk and Missouri Presbyteries, though men's work was dropped. When Locke became executive of the Missouri Union, he occupied the same office he had before the synod moved out. The work continued to be very much like it had been (11-6). According to Locke, no noticeable changes in the outlook of the congregations were very evident after the union presbytery came into being. The same problems existed, but any changes in attitude were positive because of the larger fellowship and stronger presbyteries.

When laypeople got together it was difficult to tell in which presbytery they had been. With the ministers, it was a different story. Some of them had their roots grounded heavily in the politics of their former denomination. Some got swept away and some of them got "dethroned." There were no people on the nominating committees with an ax to grind as far as who did what in the presbytery, "and it was great." Occasionally somebody would say, "We have to have somebody from either side always on the committee," and the laypeople would say, "Forget it, the reason we became a union presbytery was to get away from that. We want an open operation" (11-7).

One of the changes that came was due to the size of the new presbytery. If it hadn't been for the union presbytery, Culverhouse was not sure that the old PCUS presbytery would ever have had a staff. "We were small and we really didn't need one. Everybody knew everybody and helped everybody. . . . About 35 churches are all we had" (12-7). The new presbytery had 84 churches, one-third PCUS and two-thirds UPCUSA.[2] Culverhouse also felt that the large geographical size of the presbytery made it difficult for the presbytery to be what it ought to be, that is, "in essence, the bishop, the overseer of the individual ministries and congregations. . . . We hardly knew each other. . . . We've tried to split up into districts, but since those districts have no power, no real reason for being, except to get to know each other, they never work." He did point out that while the districts did not work, it was more because of size than because it was a union presbytery (12-9).

The spirit of cooperation was good, and not just at the church. The attitude in Missouri was a very open and positive one. Robert R. Collins, then pastor of First Presbyterian Church, Mexico, Missouri, said, "I grew up in the South, went to school at the University of North Carolina, and in many ways I am a Southerner, but I became a Midwesterner. I liked their honesty, their willingness to accept people who didn't agree with them. I just felt like there was very little façade about them" (52-4).

Dorothy G. Barnard's perception was that rural Missouri, "which we call out state, and that would be anything that's not in St. Louis or Kansas City," was pretty open to some things. "They are not conservative in the same way. They would probably vote conservatively, but they are probably more open to . . . ecumenical work. . . . Maybe because they were smaller, churches were smaller there and they work better together." Barnard felt that this was very different from St. Louis, where "the thing that influenced us the most, and you always hate to attribute it to one source, but Central Presbyterian Church was our biggest church here in this Presbytery. And it was really the tail that wagged the dog" (09-3).

On January 23, 1973, the Presbytery of Northeast Missouri (Union), meeting at First Presbyterian Church, Columbia, Missouri, was reorganized as Missouri (Union) Presbytery. Additional churches were added to bring the total number of churches to 91.[3] With reunion of the denominations, the union presbyteries were voted out of existence in effect. Because there was a lot of pride in their union presbytery heritage and their groundbreaking participation in it, Missouri (Union) was the only presbytery that kept "union" in its name. When it came time to decide to take it out, "the presbytery just took the parentheses off of it" (46-16).

John Calvin (Union)

The Union Presbytery of John Calvin (Union), the second union presbytery, was formed out of the Presbyteries of John Calvin (PCUS) and Carthage-Ozark (UPCUSA), effective March 12, 1970. They were respective members of the Synods of Missouri (PCUS) and (UPCUSA). The original plan that realigned the Synods of Missouri presbyteries had designated both John Calvin and Carthage presbyteries each as "Southwest Presbytery" in preparation for becoming a union presbytery by that name. Before the effective date they overtured their respective synods requesting that the name be changed to John Calvin (Union) Presbytery, which was granted. The organizing meeting of John Calvin (Union) Presbytery was held on April 11, 1970, at Woodland Heights Presbyterian Church in Springfield, Missouri.[4]

There had been a succession of smaller presbyteries in several denominations that would eventually become the basis for this new Presbytery. One predecessor presbytery to John Calvin (PCUS) was part of what had been Lafayette Presbytery, which had covered all of Western Missouri from the Arkansas border to the Iowa line. The eight churches in Southwest Missouri had pulled away from that sometime in the late 1950s or early 1960s and formed John Calvin Presbytery (15-5).

When the union presbytery was formed, there were 48 churches in the UPCUSA presbytery and 8 in the PCUS. A close look at the cornerstones of five or six UPCUSA churches along old US 60 going down through southwest Missouri indicated they were originally Cumberland Presbyterian churches. There were a few former UPCNA churches just over the state line in southeast Kansas (98-32).

The PCUS churches were a little concerned about being swallowed up, but it did not turn out to be much of a problem. To a degree this was avoided by the way the committee drew up the standing rules. The eight churches and ministers all felt that they had a say and were a part of it after their initial reluctance; they felt included in everything (15-5).

Thomas H. Cavicchia was elected executive presbyter and took office in October of 1971. He said, "the only dissension, if you can call it that, . . . [was] when it came to the vote to elect me as Executive Presbyter. There were three negative votes. After the vote, John R. Tranbarger, who was pastor of Hill Crest Church, that was a PCUS Church, came up to Tom and said, "Tom, I was one of those three negative votes." Tom assumed his elder was another one and was not sure who the third one was. Tranbarger said, "I wasn't voting against you. I was voting against the idea of an Executive Presbyter" (15-6).

That was reflective of the style of those former presbyteries. Ecclesiastical authority resided in the stated clerk. The two presbyteries had been somewhat similar. In spite of their size, they both had a very strong Christian Education program at the presbytery level (15-7). The UPCUSA had a Field Administrator for the Board of National Missions. Harold J. Person served in this capacity. He had served as Sunday School

Missionary in Southern Missouri and the Old Iron Mountain Presbyteries for years and years. And when that position was abolished, Person was hired half-time on the synod staff with some responsibilities and half-time with John Calvin Presbytery to work with small churches (15-6).

Western Kentucky (Union)

The Presbytery of Western Kentucky (Union), the third union presbytery, was formed out of the Presbyteries of Muhlenberg (PCUS) and Western Kentucky (UPCUSA), effective July 1, 1970. They were respective members of the Synods of Kentucky (PCUS) and (UPCUSA). On that day the two presbyteries convened in the City Park of Henderson, Kentucky, located across the street from the new Presbyterian church. Planners of the event were keenly aware of the power of symbols.

The Presbytery of Western Kentucky (UPCUSA) gathered on the north side of the park. The Presbytery of Muhlenberg (PCUS) gathered on the south side. Minister and elder commissioners from the four union churches gathered in the middle. On a given signal, the two presbyteries converged from the north and the south on the middle ground. There the Presbytery of Western Kentucky (Union) was formed. The great significance of this for Kentucky Presbyterianism was that, more than a hundred years earlier, in 1866, the Synod of Kentucky split here in Henderson over the loyalty oaths that the General Assembly of the Presbyterian Church U.S.A. had exacted from all commissioners. And now the split was in part healed.[5]

The Synods of Kentucky Reunion Committee had made a report to the 1969 Synods meeting outlining a specific plan to reunite the synods and their presbyteries. There was great disappointment "to most members of the committee" when they learned that union synods were not yet permissible. "It is our hope that this endeavor will not have been in vain but that the papers produced, including the specific plan, will be of use to others as they make preparation for union." There being nothing more for the committee to do, it was discharged with thanks.[6]

The hope of the committee came to almost immediate fruition, for before the 1969 Synods meetings were adjourned, they approved the plan for union for the Presbytery of Western Kentucky (Union) with only one dissenting vote, which was followed by spontaneous applause.[7] This paved the way for the historic event just described, held in Henderson, Kentucky, on July 1, 1970.

The formation of this union presbytery was made easier because the two presbyteries were very similar in size, both in numbers of churches and geographic displacement. Muhlenberg Presbytery (PCUS) had 25 churches and 23 ministers; Western Kentucky (UPCUSA) had 26 churches and 27 ministers; and there were four union churches between them. Moreover, there were five towns that had some of both denominations.[8]

John Robert Booker was called to be the executive presbyter of the new presbytery. Booker, who had served as Regional Director of Christian Education for both synods, was instrumental in building on the plans called for by the Kentucky Reunion Committee. Part of the plan was that the three Kentucky union presbyteries would call associate executives in Christian Education to fulfill many of the functions the Regional Director had performed, but with a focus on the presbyteries. Part of the job was to staff TREPCE, the "Tri-Presbytery Christian Education Cabinet," which was responsible for the Synods' Christian Education programs. In October of 1970, H. William Peterson was called as associate executive for Western Kentucky (Union).

The mission of the new presbytery was simple and clear. The founders "were convinced that God had led them to be the united witness of being a union presbytery." Their mission was to unite and work out the details later. This was what the focus of the work was during the first three years.[9]

Years later, Bill Peterson described it this way: "Western Kentucky's sense was, 'Let's get married and work out the details.'. . . And the spirit in Western Kentucky . . . was that we are going to work out all those details, and . . . there was a kind of driving force to make that happen. . . . Bob Booker was really a major player in that process. . . . And there was just a good, good spirit" (36-7).

Jill M. Hudson remembered those early years under the leadership of Booker and Peterson. They were instrumental in helping her discern her call to ministry. Hudson had moved to Paducah, Kentucky, in 1969 and become involved in Youth Ministry in the presbytery and beyond. Peterson and others in Christian Education affirmed her gifts and supported her growing experience of call to ministry. One Sunday, Booker preached a sermon "about the future of the Church and his own personal sense of excitement about where the new denomination was going." She said she had this real sense that she wanted to be a part of that. She went on to say that because of that sermon it "became absolutely crystal clear that I was supposed to go to Seminary. . . . It was just amazing. It's the only time in my life I've ever had that kind of clarity, but it was just crystal clear" (90-4). Hudson, shaped by the spirit and leadership of Western Kentucky (Union) Presbytery, had many effective years in ministry and became an executive presbyter herself.

Ozarks (Union)

The Presbytery of Ozarks (Union), the fourth union presbytery, was formed out of the Presbyteries of Washburn (PCUS) and Arkansas (UPCUSA), on November 24, 1970, meeting at the First Presbyterian Church, Clarksville, Arkansas. They were respective members of the Synod of Arkansas/Oklahoma (PCUS) and the Synod of Oklahoma/Arkansas (UPCUSA). Ozarks (Union) would be dissolved in 1974 as one of the parties to form the Presbytery of Arkansas (Union).

The sixty-five or so congregations of Arkansas Presbytery (UPCUSA) were located primarily in the northwest quadrant of the state of Arkansas. Most of these congregations had belonged to the Cumberland Presbyterian Church before it reunited with the Presbyterian Church U.S.A. in 1906. There were strong churches in Fort Smith, Fayetteville, Bentonville, and the Rogers area. Helen Walton, a member of First Presbyterian Church, Bentonville, was a very active leader in the presbytery and would later be the first presbytery representative to the Consultation on Union Presbyteries (51-10).

The congregations of Washburn Presbytery (PCUS) were located in the south central part of the State. William S. McLean, pastor of the Pulaski Heights Presbyterian Church, Little Rock, prior to the time of the union, said: "We were really not too much aware of their [UPCUSA] existence down in the south [of] Arkansas. . . . [I]t was very strange to live together and still not be very much aware of one another" (51-10). The leaders in the presbyteries began to have some exploratory meetings, and a very real possibility of creating a union presbytery began to emerge. McLean said: "Once the ball started rolling, I felt a very positive reaction on the part of all the people in the old Washburn Presbytery" (51-3).

These two presbyteries exemplified their two respective denominational styles. It was clearly seen in how each approached the matter of funding or presbytery staff. These two presbyteries, plus the other two PCUS presbyteries—East Arkansas and Ouachita—that did not elect to join the union presbytery, had no more than 7,000 or so communicant members and did not have the financial or numerical strength to have any full-time executive staff. Their ecclesiastical governance functioned under what was known as the Stated Clerk Model with a moderator, a stated clerk, a treasurer and a presbytery council. The stated clerk and treasurer were part-time employees if not volunteers (51-4).

The funding approach for the PCUS was presbytery oriented; it was raised there and, other than benevolence contributions, it stayed there to cover its operating expenses. The UPCUSA approach was that money was sent up to the Synod and General Assembly, and then it came back down to presbytery in various ways. Initially, there was some tension or discomfort with this in the new presbytery (51-5). There was some concern over how to distribute the General Mission (UPCUSA term) or General Benevolence (PCUS term) contributions that would reflect past experience. This was resolved after the first year by instituting a plan that by the end of nine years they would divide this, giving 50–50 between the denominations.[10]

As far as setting up a presbytery structure, there was interest in getting it operational immediately and "also to assure parity between the two presbyteries and between Teaching and Ruling Elders." However, it was also expressed that "after the first year of operation as a Union Presbytery, there will be no necessity [for] and no consideration given to parity between the 'old' presbyteries."[11]

The issue of staffing was addressed in the second year of its existence by declaring "that the Presbytery, in the interim and until Presbytery makes decisions in regard to permanent staff, consider the present Synod-level staff persons of both Synods resource persons to all churches." It was carefully noted that "Presbytery is to be supplied in a mailing the names, addresses, and Synod staff position of each such person involved."[12]

In the interim the formation of the regional synods put these permanent-staffing decisions on hold. At the same time serious conversations began about expanding the Union Presbytery to include all of East Arkansas Presbytery and two-thirds of Ouachita Presbytery with the remaining one-third going to Pines Presbytery to the south in Louisiana. This reorganization would involve most of the state of Arkansas except the little southern third of Old Ouachita. As McLean exclaimed: "And that was a new ball game" (51-4). Before this could be worked out, the Synods of Red River (PCUS) and Sun (UPCUSA) had come into being. These synods included the presbyteries in Arkansas, Louisiana, Oklahoma, and Texas.

Central Texas (Union)

On January 1, 1971, Central Texas (Union), the first union presbytery in Texas and the fifth overall, was formed out of the Presbyteries of Central Texas (PCUS) and Brazos (UPCUSA). They were respectively members of the Synods of Texas (PCUS) and (UPCUSA). By the mid-1970s another realignment of the presbyteries in the Synods of Texas was imminent. The organizers had to face the issue, "Do we make a union presbytery out of Central Texas Presbytery, or do we just wait and work on the new presbyteries?" Flynn Long reported: "Our decision was that we had better scramble the eggs while we got the chance" (23-29). Because of the realignment of presbyteries in both Synods, this presbytery was dissolved in less than a year, to clear the way for more union presbyteries to be formed over the next few years.

The significance of the brief life of Central Texas (Union) was found in the preparation for its birthing that took place in the old Central Texas Presbytery (PCUS). In the late 1950s the presbyteries in Texas underwent a major reorganization with new boundary lines. One of those presbyteries became the old Central Texas Presbytery. One little irony was that Central Texas Presbytery did not really include Central Texas; it was really in North Texas. As it often happens in these kinds of new alignments, the new presbytery took a while to get itself going. There was a lot of controversy. The presbytery had no single mind or direction. A group got together and decided that what was needed was to create some sort of theological or ideological basis for how a presbytery ought to be organized and put together. What ought its basic purpose and function to be? It was thought that if the presbytery would agree to that philosophically, then it could devise a plan for developing a workable presbytery (23-5).

Flynn Long recalled that the group was known as "The Society for the Reformation of Presbyteries." It was a voluntary association that met on numerous occasions, without any official sanction whatsoever. The group, according to Long, studied papers on Calvin and Knox, the Reformed Church, liturgy, worship, and church politics. A paper was written called "The Basic Function and Purpose of Presbytery," which the presbytery adopted. It then appointed a committee of seven persons, four laymen and three ministers, to develop a plan for organizing and restructuring the presbytery (23-5). This was the committee referred to earlier as the "Presbytery Mafia."

The theory underlying the organizational plan they devised was that the presbytery had two functions. The first was to order its ministry—all matters related to calling and caring for ministers. The second was to order its churches—all matters related to oversight and support of congregations. The theological and ecclesial basis for this was that the presbytery, as the basic court of the Presbyterian denomination, had the authority to ordain people for ministry and organize churches. The presbytery, made up of several congregations, was the smallest unit in the Presbyterian system that was fully the church. The basic apostolicity and the basic catholicity of the church in the Reformed sense were carried out through a presbytery (23-8).

Everything else of a programmatic nature was to be left up to an *ad hoc* task-force type of arrangement with all the aspects of a sunset law, rather than being structured into the life of the Presbytery. It also had all the aspects of moving the direction of the church closer to the local congregation. The underlying concern was: "How did the local church do its mission, get its work done, deal with its people, that made sense? How does the Presbytery support the local church in fulfilling this mission?" (23-8).

The Presbytery also had to be aware of the presence of the other Presbyterian denomination while addressing the differences between denominations and the geographical disparity of churches in Texas. All these factors were oftentimes an impediment to helping people understand the church as a whole (23-8).

In the course of organizing the new PCUS presbytery, one of the concerns was that, although Central Texas Presbytery covered a geographical area similar to the area covered by Brazos Presbytery (UPCUSA), there was a major difference in ecclesiastical focus. The problem was that most of the mission and work of the PCUSA church were centered in the synod and not in the presbyteries, which was the distinction between the two denominations. J. Hoytt Boles was the synod executive for the PCUSA synod at that time. The presence of the federated and union churches in the area provided the impetus to work together in order to bridge these differences through what was called the Joint Mission Committee (23-6).

As they began to work together, they became very much aware that doing joint mission and providing joint financing for mission projects between two presbyteries was an extremely complicated situation because there were two financial structures going all the way to the General Assembly. Particularly in the PCUSA case there was a different attitude from the PCUS as to how things were paid for. In the PCUSA the funding patterns were more top down, hierarchically, than the local or regional funding patterns of the PCUS. Any resolution that the Joint Mission Committee devised had to have an "un-amended, fast-track authorization from both presbyteries" (23-7). At times this became difficult to accomplish, causing some problems.

Finally, the question came up: "Why don't we just unite these two presbyteries . . . just put them together . . . just vote to join each other?" This had been done in creating union congregations. But as has been noted, this route was rejected and the constitutional amendment route, though more complex and time-consuming, was chosen as the more prudent option. This was the incubation process in which the "union presbyteries and synods" overtures to both General Assemblies originated that amended the Constitutions (23-7). This was the experience that the Central Texas Presbytery group brought to the constitutional strategy sessions with folk from Missouri and Kentucky in the mid-1960s.

Kansas City (Union)

The Presbytery of Kansas City (Union), the sixth union presbytery, was formed out of the Presbyteries of Lafayette (PCUS) and Kansas City (UPCUSA), effective January 1, 1971. They were respective members of the Synods of Missouri (PCUS) and (UPCUSA). The original plan that realigned the presbyteries in the Synods of Missouri had designated Lafayette and Kansas City Presbyteries each as "Northwest Presbytery."

Kansas City (Union), based on its former presbyteries, was predominantly a Northern presbytery. About 85 to 90 percent of its churches were from the former UPNA and USA denominations, with the remaining 10 percent from the former PCUS (47-7). And yet there was something about it that had a Southern flavor. Ronald L. Patton remembered that when arguments on the floor of Presbytery started to fractionalize, Richard K. Johnson, the executive presbyter, would invariably be up, and in a style with "a little bit of southern accent" guide the discussion in a more wholesome direction (14-30).

Again, Christian Education was a common denominator among the predecessor presbyteries. Because the presbyteries along the boundaries between Missouri and Kansas overlapped state lines, Regional Directors of Christian Education from both PCUS and UPCUSA denominations in Missouri and Kansas worked together across the area. Fred S. Malott, UPCUSA Regional Director in Kansas and the UPCUSA Regional Director in Kansas City, Missouri, joined forces with J. Allen Oakley, PCUS Regional Director in Missouri, to lead joint Christian Events. Malott remembered that the synod schools were "where it made a difference, the biggest difference. And I remember that Oakley worked with us on Sunday Schools and then we worked on the Missouri Synod Schools." Malott, with reference to forming the new union presbytery, said all that planning and working together "surely prepared us for 1972" (42-12).

Henry C. Barnett, who had been recording secretary of Solomon Presbytery (UPCUSA) in Kansas for years, came to Kansas City Presbytery (UPCUSA) in 1941 and within a year was elected stated clerk of that presbytery. Barnett pointed out that when he came, along the borderline between Kansas and Missouri in the Kansas City area, one could not help but be aware of the presence of the United Presbyterian Church. It had started the Village Presbyterian Church, which was the largest in the country (35-3).

However, in the years leading up to the formation of the union presbytery, "we did things together, and as a society, as a community." One example was that the ministers of Kansas City, not only from one denomination but from all the denominations there, met every Tuesday and would take turns presenting a paper to the group. The pastor of the Village Presbyterian Church was a leader in that. The heritage of the former UPCNA, UPCUSA, and PCUS denominations was very much present in the new union presbytery (35-3). Barnett was later elected stated clerk of the Presbytery of Northwest Missouri (Union) that later became Kansas City (Union). "I was privileged to be a part of that whole union business" (35-2).

Louisville (Union)

The Presbytery of Louisville (Union), the seventh union presbytery, was formed out of the Presbyteries of Louisville (PCUS) and Louisville [Transylvania] (UPCUSA), effective January 1, 1971. They were respective members of the Synods of Kentucky (PCUS) and (UPCUSA). It took these presbyteries longer, in contrast to how Western Kentucky (Union) did it, because they worked out a bunch of details and then got married (36-7). 'One member of the family took exception to the wedding.

Chester Hall, elder on the session of First Presbyterian Church, Louisville, filed a complaint stating "that we had acted illegally to form this union presbytery." The synod met at Caldwell Chapel on the campus of Louisville Seminary to hold a hearing on the matter. Charles L. Stanford argued the case for the union presbytery, which prevailed. One of the sticking points settled at the General Assembly level dealt with property issues (07-11).

In July of 1970, several of the Kentucky presbytery boundaries were changed to bring them into conformity with those in future mergers. Part of the Presbytery of Transylvania (UPCUSA) was joined with Ebenezer Presbytery (UPCUSA) in eastern Kentucky to form Ebenezer-Transylvania (UPCUSA). The remainder of it was renamed the Presbytery of Louisville (UPCUSA).[13] There was also a question about the financial situation of the Louisville Presbytery (UPCUSA). Somebody raised the question about absorbing some big debt but it turned out not to be so (07-11). When the time came, the two Louisville Presbyteries voted to merge and name the new presbytery the Presbytery of Louisville (Union). Representatives from the former presbyteries affirmed each other in their new union in a service of worship at the Louisville Seminary chapel very early in January 1971 after the effective date. Stanford remembered, "It was a celebratory time. Everybody was happy. Everybody that I knew was happy" (07-12).

Stanford recalled that one of the things that had to be worked out very early was who gets to go as commissioner to the General Assembly. A committee was appointed. Thomas L. Jones was on it. The committee brought back a report to the presbytery, that in order to qualify to be a commissioner to the Assembly, there were a number of criteria to be met. Stanford said they "were connected with the word 'and'; do this, this, this, 'and' this and you can qualify. And it just almost eliminated all of us, the way I looked at it. And so I fussed and fumed about that." Al Winn stood up and said, "Well, this is simple. We'll just change the word to 'or.' " Stanford said it was "changed to 'or' and then the embarrassing thing, I was the first Commissioner elected under the new rules" (07-13).

M. Ralph Weedon was elected presbytery executive and stated clerk, Charles A. Davis, Jr., associate executive in Christian Education, and John A. "Jack" McLaney, recording clerk. McLaney worked with Ralph Hawley, stated clerk of the former Presbytery of Louisville (UPCUSA) to structure presbytery meetings and what was going to be done about records internally. McLaney lamented that "it was not my favorite job to do, but, you know, it was something that needed to be done" (06-28).

Transylvania (Union)

The Presbytery of Transylvania (Union), the eighth union presbytery, was formed out of the Presbyteries of Guerrant-Transylvania (PCUS) and Ebenezer-Transylvania (UPCUSA), effective January 1, 1971. They were respective members of the Synods of Kentucky (PCUS) and (UPCUSA). The process leading up to this union had a series of "presbytery marriages" to contend with, which created a monumental organizational task. In 1960 there was a merger of the PCUS presbyteries of Lexington-Ebenezer and Transylvania to form the Presbytery of Transylvania (PCUS). In 1968 this presbytery and the mountain Presbytery of Guerrant merged to form the Presbytery of Guerrant-Transylvania.[14]

Charles M. Hanna, Jr., in a period from 1967 to 1971 before he was elected executive presbyter of Transylvania (Union), was executive of five predecessor presbyteries and never moved his office. David E. Rule was elected stated clerk; William G. McAtee, associate executive presbyter in Christian Education; and Jack E. Weller, associate executive in Mission for Transylvania (Union).

The name Transylvania, meaning "across the woods," was retained as a historical designation. The first presbytery by that name, taken from the Transylvania Land Company that first settled in the region, was formed on October 17, 1786. It was the first presbytery west of the Allegheny Mountains, and one of the original sixteen presbyteries when the General Assembly was formed in 1789.[15] Its boundaries extended from Chillicothe, Ohio, on the north; to Shelbyville, Tennessee, on the south; from the ridge of the Allegheny Mountains on the east; to the Pacific Ocean on the west.

The formal consummation of Transylvania (Union) occurred at a special meeting in the First Presbyterian Church, Lexington, Kentucky, on January 10, 1971. The theme for the occasion was "Celebrating Our Unity in Christ." Special guests were Moderator William A. Benfield, Jr., General Assembly (PCUS); Moderator William R. Laws, Jr., General Assembly (UPCUSA); moderator C. Eric Mount, Sr., Synod of Kentucky (PCUS); and moderator Irvin S. Moxley, Synod of Kentucky (UPCUSA).

The real challenge for Transylvania Presbytery (Union) lay not only in the melding of two ecclesiastical heritages, but in bringing together into a functional body the very different cultures of the "mountain" and the "bluegrass" regions. It had inherited the home mission fields of three former denominations—UPCNA, PCUSA, and PCUS—all with very different understandings and approaches to mission work in Appalachia. Two-thirds of the presbytery had been PCUS churches; one-third had been UPCUSA.

David Rule observed that "even though within the Synods of Kentucky, there was a lot of cooperative ministry going, there was some feeling that it was hampered by the separation of the two bodies and that when they became union presbyteries that much facilitated the working together." Rule went on to say that he thought the "so-called average Church member in Kentucky wasn't even that much aware of two different denominations" (04-9). He said his wife grew up around Morris Fork, a U.S.A. mission field, from which young people went to Highland, a PCUS mission school not too far away. They did not realize they were U.S.A. young people going to a PCUS school. They simply thought they were going to a Presbyterian school (04-10).

Another challenge was to keep the small-presbytery spirit and feeling in a huge presbytery that increased the PCUS presbytery by a third and was going to more than double the United Presbyterian presbytery (04-16). One way the small feeling in the large organization was kept was by creating regions of the presbytery that came together two times a year for fellowship, study, and sharing regional concerns. No business was transacted other than that which facilitated their regional life. This proved beneficial through the years.

John W. Frazer was elected the first moderator. He said, "I guess the decision was made that if we were going to go toward a union presbytery it would probably be wise to have an elder rather than a pastor for the first one." Upon reflection, Frazer admitted that "with really very little knowledge of what was happening, I was sort of plucked up, but I felt very strongly that we needed to do this, and simply got into it and we started muddying the waters . . . and in the good old British tradition, we muddled through. I'm not sure we knew that much about what we were doing, any of us. Council was genuinely concerned and they were folks who did care and I think we came through fairly well in that first year" (41-3). Frazer recalled going to a presbytery meeting in Hazard and "just the joy of seeing folk from different traditions come together, and break bread together, and enjoy one another, you know, it was wonderful" (41-6).

National Capital (Union)

The Presbytery of National Capital (Union), the ninth union presbytery, was formed out of the Presbyteries of Potomac (PCUS) and Washington City (UPCUSA), effective January 6, 1972. They were respective members of the Synods of Virginia (PCUS) and Chesapeake (UPCUSA). Washington, D.C., was a unique setting in which to form a union presbytery. Several factors contributed to the openness to this possibility.

When lay Presbyterians from all across the country, North and South, came to Washington to live and work, most of them did not pay any attention to the distinction between Northern and Southern churches, so they would join the nearest Presbyterian church where they moved. There were many Northern Presbyterians in Southern congregations and vice versa. A lot of the regionalism had already melted at the congregational level. Another factor was that a great many of the pastors were refugees from the Deep South who had parted company over the civil rights issue. They were liberally oriented and socially oriented (86-3). They had shed the regionalism that one might find in a presbytery of the Deep South or a presbytery way up North. There was a kind of cosmopolitan blending that had gone on that made the communication between the two presbyteries extremely easy (86-4).

Edward A. White served as an urban mission specialist in both Potomac and Washington City Presbyteries. This was at the peak of the civil rights movement, the Martin Luther King, Jr., assassination in 1968, and then the Poor People's Campaign that following summer. White was much involved both ecumenically and with the two presbyteries in response to those events.

He was the bridge person between the two presbyteries and "spent countless meetings" with James B. Ficklin, the Church Extension secretary of Potomac Presbytery (PCUS), and Graydon E. McClellan, the general presbyter of Washington City Presbytery (UPCUSA), in discussions preparing for the union presbytery vote (86-2). Later he worked with the joint committee of ten—five people from each presbytery who engineered the design for the union presbytery (86-5).

When it came time for the votes in the two presbyteries, the sentiment was overwhelmingly in favor of the union presbytery. Washington City Presbytery voted 174 to 0 in favor of the union, and Potomac Presbytery voted 85 to 9. The nine basically represented three or four churches that later left the denominations (86-5).

Several Potomac Presbytery (PCUS) churches in the Baltimore area were transferred to the Presbytery of Baltimore (UPCUSA). There were some who did not want to go who felt "it was going to be too conservative [chuckle] in the U.S.A. Church . . . and then vice-versa there were some who had some misgivings [that] the PCUS Church was probably as progressive, however, by no means liberal, but as progressive as . . . most of us had encountered in our [PCUS] denomination" (91-3). Several churches in the southern part of Washington City Presbytery (UPCUSA) in Virginia were transferred to the Presbytery of Southern Virginia (UPCUSA) in the Synod of Catawba.[16]

Most of the things the leaders worried about were practical and organizational things. The Presbytery Council was reduced to a size smaller than those of the predecessor presbyteries. A decision was made to start the presbytery with only the committees mandated by the two Constitutions, and then to let the rest of the structure emerge after it became a union presbytery, rather than having it all in place before union took place. According to White, this "was a wise decision. We started with that minimalist model" (85-6).

William R. Sengle, who was the pastor at the Old Meeting House Presbyterian Church, Alexandria, Virginia, was the first moderator of the union presbytery. Old Meeting House had a long history of pro-union activities related to its strategic location and dedicated leadership.[17] Sengle had grown up in the Deep South and "then done the unthinkable thing of going to Yale Divinity School," which, according to Ed White, "meant that greatly limited where he could be a minister in the PCUS after that" (85-3).

Cecil M. Jividen reflected on the process for calling an executive presbyter. Questions were asked like: "What kind of person do we want as our leader? Do we want someone who is more pastoral or someone who is more like an executive person who would administrate?" Some leaned toward pastoral skills, while others, like Jividen, felt a person with strong administrative skills was needed, "because everything was so up in the air and we needed somebody who had some experience" (91-6).

Edward White was elected the presbytery executive of the new union presbytery. He provided, according to Jividen, "an awful lot of the training regarding leadership in a whole new, different way, like much more [a] consensus thing" (91-5). White was a good administrator, and having worked with both presbyteries in his position previously, already had contacts and knew people in both presbyteries. He was very socially conscious. Jividen said White did not allow the union presbytery "to become a navel gazing kind of new institution" but one that continued "to be in ministry and not just worry about our structure" (91-6).

Jividen felt that the pastors were very encouraged by White taking on the role of "lightning rod" in his "barn busting sermons" on issues like Vietnam. He would go into churches for special times to preach and would say something like, "Well, if you're a pastor and your session is thinking about how best to serve not just yourselves but the nation and our particular area, [then] . . ." This was a poignant moment in a church whose membership might be made up of 80 percent government employees, including the military. "It made what most of the pastors were saying seemed rather anemic . . . but it kept the presbytery really humming and being effective both in ministry as well as doing committee work" (91-6).

Palo Duro (Union)

The Presbytery of Palo Duro (Union), the tenth union presbytery, was formed out of part of Central Texas (Union) and the Presbyteries of Southwest (PCUS) and Plains (UPCUSA), effective January 6, 1972. They were respective members of the Synods of Red River (PCUS) and Sun (UPCUSA).

Murray W. Travis told how he and other members of Plains Presbytery (UPCUSA) got together in the middle 1960s with representatives from Southwest Presbytery (PCUS) for fellowship and sharing of mutual concerns. Out of these informal conversations came a variety of cooperative efforts like that at Chimney Spring, the camp and conference center. They also reached "comity agreements" on where to start new church developments among the geographic "checkerboard pattern" of distribution of their congregations (21-3).

Carolyn Taylor, an elder in Westminster Presbyterian Church (PCUS), Lubbock, Texas, said in reflecting on those times: "I think behind it all was the feeling among all the laypersons that this split has been there long enough. We want to prove that Presbyterians can live together . . . and that, I think, was uppermost in most laypersons' minds at that time, . . . the driving force that caused them to want to get together (21-6).

There is another piece to the story that was critical in understanding the focus on defining "What Is a Presbytery." During the year-and-a-half period when all the Texas presbyteries were getting ready to vote the union presbytery questions, people like Clements E. Lamberth, Jr., in Lubbock were instrumental in obtaining Robert C. Worley of McCormick Seminary to consult with those churches that were soon going to have one union presbytery or two separate presbyteries. For a year and a half, with Bob Worley's assistance, the questions were put to the folks, not in terms so much as "Do you want to be a union presbytery?" The question was: "If you have to be a presbytery, what do you want it to stand for, to be like, to work on?" (20–10).

According to Paul D. Young, who would become the first general presbyter of the new union presbytery, it was very clear why the presbytery existed. He said the short way to say it was: "The presbytery existed for the sake of the congregations, so that the primary value was the congregations, their pastors and people. And the task of the presbytery was to enhance the life of the congregations and the pastors." Young emphasized that "there was no way that presbytery could be the enemy. It didn't exist for its own sake, or for some mission that it contrived, but the presbytery's identity and its mission were written by the sessions and the folks who met in numerous gatherings for a year and a half before the presbytery came to being."

When the vote was taken on becoming a union presbytery, there were only two negative votes. Through this process the goals of the presbytery became clear. They drew a road map for its life and clearly defined what everyone's task was, including the general presbyter's (20-11).

While there was not always agreement and there were negative votes on some issues, the presbytery, according to Young, was never divided during the sixteen years he was there and "it was always able to struggle with issues and come to conclusions that, I would say, everybody, or certainly almost everybody, could live with comfortably." Young summarized its uniqueness by saying: "I always describe that presbytery as a pro church presbytery, and, what I mean by that is that, it was not pro congregation, nor was it pro clergy, and I think the mistake often made is, a lot of presbyteries decide you either have to be pro congregation, or pro session or pro clergy. We were pro church, which meant both [all] those entities were included" (20-12).

Arkansas (Union)

On January 15, 1974, the Presbytery of Arkansas (Union), the eleventh union presbytery, was formed out of the Presbyteries of Ozarks (Union), part of Ouachita (PCUS), and East Arkansas (PCUS). They were respective members of the regional Synods of Red River (PCUS) and Sun (UPCUSA). This historic meeting was appropriately held at First Presbyterian Church, Little Rock, Arkansas, the first Presbyterian church organized in the territory.[18] William S. McLean concluded that, "when we finally went into Arkansas Union and disbanded East Arkansas and two-thirds of the Old Ouachita Presbytery, some of those folks had their question marks. But it still worked out very, very [well]" (51-3).

The search committee recruited McLean for the job of executive presbyter. William J. Fogleman, executive of the Synod of Red River, was most influential in McLean's decision to accept. Fogleman told him, "You know, if union presbyteries can work in an area like this with so disparate groups involved, it's going to be one of the primary things . . . that is going to lead to Church reunion." He said, "If union presbyteries fail, the chances for Church reunion are very, very remote." And finally, "You've been here twenty-two years, you're respected and trusted by everyone who knows you; if anybody can pull it off in terms of the leadership that would be asked of the Executives, you can" (51-3).

With a great deal of satisfaction McLean later said much was learned from this experience. "Because the people from the Southern Church were so presbytery-focused, they did not see some of the advantages of a broader mission orientation that comes from being serious about Synod-level activity . . . institutions and racial, ethnic concerns and other mission concerns. . . . [I]t was a learning process for both sides of the fence" (51-6).

Barbara Campbell Davis observed from her perspective on Synod staff that there were not too many PCUS African American churches in the Synod of the Red River. But a number of African American churches were picked up in Arkansas in that union presbytery; several of them were from UPCUSA backgrounds (89-5). McLean pointed out that in all the PCUS presbyteries prior to the union presbytery, there were only about three or four black churches. There were fourteen or fifteen in the UPCUSA (51-6).

When the funding process started changing, it really upset the black congregations because they were used to a pattern of having it come straight from New York with very little supervision. So when the new presbytery evaluation and funding began, it really scared them. They had seen themselves as black churches being supported by New York, and not related to the white congregations around them. But they found that being in the new presbytery gave them a better relationship to the white congregations in the area, without being dependent upon the General Assembly funding. They also found that they were treated very generously and very pastorally, and this gave them a better feeling about being in a presbytery as a congregation, working with other congregations, than they had before when they were getting the funding from New York (51-6).

Arkansas (Union) was the final union presbytery formed in the "first wave of the original of union presbyteries." Eleven presbyteries had been formed but two were dissolved and absorbed into successor union presbyteries. By 1974, there were nine "original" union presbyteries that remained operational until reunion in 1983.

Clearly the winners outnumbered the losers by a long shot in this first wave of union presbyteries. The full consequences of the contributions of these historic events would be a long time coming. The successes were more evident than the flaws, and ghosts of Stamford Bridge and Hastings et al. were shoved back into the shadows in these quarters for a decade or more to quietly bide their time.

Notes

1. Peterson, *And Then There Were ~~Ten~~, ~~Eleven~~, Twelve! Anymore?* p. 12.

2. Document from Kenneth R. Locke to H. William Peterson dated 4-20-78, in H. William Peterson Collection, Presbyterian Historical Society This was sent to Peterson as he was preparing to write *And Then There Were ~~Ten~~, ~~Eleven~~, Twelve! Anymore?—A Study of the Union Presbytery Movement—1970–1980.*

3. Ibid.

4. *Minutes* of the Twenty-Fifth Stated Meeting (Winter 1970) of John Calvin Presbytery (Southwest Presbytery), PCUS.

5. Peterson, *And Then There Were . . . Twelve! Anymore?* p. 6.

6. *Minutes* of the One Hundred-Sixty-Eighth Meeting of the Synod of Kentucky (PCUS), Louisville, KY, June 24–25, 1969, pp. 16–17.

7. Ibid., p. 22.

8. Ibid., pp. 65–67.

9. Peterson, *And Then There Were . . . Twelve! Anymore?* p. 6.

10. *Minutes* of the Initial Stated Meeting of Union Presbytery of the Ozarks, Clarksville, AR, November 24, 1970, p. 2.

11. Ibid., p. 6.

12. *Minutes* of the Stated Meeting of Union Presbytery of the Ozarks, Little Rock, Arkansas, January 26, 1971, p. 23.

13. *Guidelines of the Presbytery of Transylvania* (Union), p. 3.

14. Ibid., p. 3.

15. Ibid., p. 1.

16. *Minutes* of the Special Meeting of the Synod of the Chesapeake (UPCUSA), Catonsville, MD, May 1, 1971 (Meeting as a Delegated Synod), p. 12.

17. Donald C. Dahmann to William G. McAtee, e-mail, February 10, 2005. "The Meeting House in Alexandria, situated at the fertile verge between the rest of Virginia and points south AND Philadelphia and points north into New England, provides some interesting 'union' efforts—A union congregation that lasted from 1874–1880, created 'looking for a union of the whole Presbyterian family North and South' which it was hoped would come about within the six years the experiment was planned to run—pastor was J. J. Bullock, who served as Moderator of PCUS at 1888 centennial meetings. A union meeting of local presbyteries in 1952, which some expressed the hope would be an annual event; it occurred only one time—Ken Phifer was then pastor. Push to create National Capital Union Presbytery, [of] which Bill Sengle, pastor here 1960–86, was rewarded with election as first moderator."

18. *Minutes* of the Stated Meeting of the Presbytery of Arkansas (Union), Little Rock, AR, January 15, 1974, p. 18.

Chapter 11
And Then There Were More (1979–1983)

It is the intent of Union Presbyteries, through such instrumentalities as the Consultation on Union Presbyteries and the Joint Committee on Union Presbyteries to: . . .Encourage, assist, interpret, advocate and work for the continuing development of Union Presbyteries, both in areas where both denominations have a presence and in areas where only one of them is currently at work.

—Handbook of COUP (1980 Revision)[1]

With the advent of the 1970s, the first wave of union presbyteries experienced a honeymoon period in their new life. Long years of preparation accelerated the positive formation of underlying feeling usually attendant when new groups or organizations form. Getting to know each other and be known exemplified a genuine sense of welcome; openness to how decisions were to be made was clearly communicated; confidence in common goals grew through intentional widespread involvement; and mutual acceptance fostered growing trust.

The original union presbyteries, in the first few years of their life, were a haven of relative stability in the organizationally dislocated terrain of emerging boards and agencies as well as newly formed regional synods. As the boards, agencies, and regional synods in two denominations became organizationally defined and stabilized, the union presbyteries discovered they held in common not only celebrations but mutual concerns as well. This began to crystallize by 1975 as the union presbyteries found common cause in their annual consultations where they discovered everyone did not have to "reinvent the wheel" each time around. All the presbyteries along the Border States that were poised to become union presbyteries, when it was constitutionally possible to do so, had formed during the first wave years between 1970 and 1972.

One area that had been only partially effective in creating union presbyteries in the first wave, as had been hoped, was in Texas. The Synods of Texas, in order to facilitate the establishment of union presbyteries, realigned their presbytery boundaries in the early 1970s, creating five identical presbytery areas in both churches in anticipation that all of them would become union presbyteries (50-6).

As part of that process, five organizing conventions were called for, designated as Conventions A, B, C, D, and E (27-6). The only union presbytery to emerge immediately from this convention process was Palo Duro (Union), which was described earlier. At least two sets

---

of presbyteries in the Synods of Texas had voted to become union presbyteries, but the votes had failed by small margins; one had failed twice. Seven years would elapse after the last union presbytery in the first wave had been established before another one would be formed anywhere. The new regional Synods of Red River (PCUS) and Sun (UPCUSA) would be instrumental in the creation of six more union presbyteries.

Grace (Union)

The Presbytery of Grace (Union), the twelfth union presbytery, was formed out of the Presbyteries of Covenant (PCUS) and Trinity (UPCUSA), effective January 1, 1979. They were respective members of the Synods of Red River (PCUS) and Sun (UPCUSA). The Presbyteries of Covenant (PCUS) and Trinity (UPCUSA) had been designated as Convention C in the Synods of Texas' organizing conventions process of the early 1970s. There were approximately seventy churches in Covenant Presbytery (PCUS) that were formerly from a non-union PCUS presbytery and seventy churches that were union churches because they had belonged to the now defunct Central Texas (Union) Presbytery. Trinity Presbytery (UPCUSA) had seventy churches that were formerly from a non-union PCUS presbytery and the same seventy union churches shared with Covenant (PCUS) (50-4).

When the time came for the vote to become a union presbytery in the early 1970s, Trinity (UPCUSA) voted almost unanimously for it. Covenant (PCUS) missed the required two-thirds by two or so votes. A clear majority of the PCUS presbytery wanted to be a union presbytery but a sizeable minority dramatically opposed it, the opposition mainly coming from Highland Presbyterian Church in Dallas (50-7). Linda B. Team, a presbytery staff person, remembered "the disappointment and surprise that people came away with" from that vote (27-6).

The Presbytery of the Covenant (PCUS) called R. Matthew Lynn, the former Moderator of the PCUS General Assembly (1969), who was within a few years of retirement, as its general presbyter. Lynn began to encourage cooperative programming with Trinity Presbytery (UPCUSA), which in the eyes of the Highland Park resistance was a betrayal of the vote not to become a union presbytery. They took the vote to mean there should only be distinct and separate programs for the Presbytery of the Covenant (PCUS). Though Lynn felt he never betrayed anybody, the passions about him were that high (50-7).

A. M. "Mac" Hart was called as general presbyter of Covenant Presbytery (PCUS) in 1974. Although the tension with Highland Park still existed, Hart soon found common cause with John W. Cunningham, general presbyter of Trinity Presbytery (UPCUSA). They proceeded to lead the presbyteries in setting up almost identical committee structures except where there was a constitutional difference; for instance the Southern Church had a Commission on the Minister and His Work, and the Northern Church had a Ministerial Relations Committee (50-8).

Beth Wells, who started being involved in the PCUS Women of the Church (WOC) in 1972 at the presbytery level, became aware that there was a UPCUSA United Presbyterian Women (UPW) because John Cunningham and Mac Hart had encouraged the two groups to do things together (60-3).

According to Linda Team, life in Covenant Presbytery (PCUS) "administratively, was nightmarish, but it was fun, too, because in a sense, . . . we were administering three separate Presbyteries . . . the western part of the Presbytery that was Union, and the eastern part that was either PCUS or UPCUSA. . . . [We] had to cooperate for the sake of the union churches so that they didn't have duplicative administrative relationships." Team said the "cooperative structures . . . made some of the anti-reunion people pretty nervous from time to time. And we had to walk a pretty narrow line on some things" (27-6).

Hart recalled that there were "some things they had to do separately but otherwise, the divisions and committees met jointly and proceeded with a common program and did as much as they could jointly." He went on to say: "At first, when I arrived, the two presbyteries would meet on back-to-back days, and the representatives from the seventy union churches would stay overnight, and the next day they'd vote on much of the same stuff they voted on the day before [chuckle]." Finally the two presbyteries met jointly in one place with two moderators and in doing so, each developed ownership for what the other was doing. A system was set up where agenda items that pertained to one presbytery were voted by it, and vice versa, in each other's presence. Hart said that "for awhile, we emphasized doing everything twice and emphasized the inconvenience and the absurdity of it. And, that, I think was not lost on folks" (50-8).

Hart supposed that for about six months, the thinking at Highland Park was "give the new guy a little while and see if he is going to reverse the cooperative stuff. I suppose they decided it wasn't going to happen." In the spring of 1975, Highland Park Church pulled a quarter of a million dollars out of their benevolent giving through Covenant Presbytery (PCUS). Hart recalled: "They were giving . . . about three hundred and fifty thousand dollars a year to the benevolences of Presbytery, Synod and General Assembly; they cut that to one hundred thousand in the middle of the year. It felt to the rest of the system like . . . blackmail, and the system said 'we're not going to let that happen' " (50-8).

The presbytery was not in a mood to back down, so it asked the synod and General Assembly to take their cuts and was able to absorb the cut; the churches increased the giving and the work continued with no major losses to programs that needed to happen. Hart emphasized the feeling that Highland Park had "given it the best shot that didn't work. And after that point, the opposition from Highland Park was not something the rest of the system said 'we've got to be scared about, we've got to walk around' " (50-8).

It was fairly clear that Highland Park would not change its opinion and that the rest of the system clearly wanted to be union. In 1978 the leadership, the councils, and the two presbyteries decided it was time to look again at the issue of being a union presbytery and voted to become Grace (Union) Presbytery, effective January 1, 1979 (50-9).

In the spring of 1979 the Women of the Church (WOC) of Covenant Presbytery (PCUS) and the United Presbyterian Women (UPW) of Trinity Presbytery (UPCUSA) had their uniting meeting of Presbyterian Women in Grace (Union) Presbytery. Beth Wells was the last president of Covenant Presbyterian Women, and the first president of Presbyterian Women (60-3). Wells served on the General Assembly Joint Committee/Task Force on Union Presbyteries.

The constituting meeting of Grace Union Presbytery was very moving. William P. Lytle, Moderator of the UPCUSA General Assembly, preached the sermon; one of the liturgists was Rebecca Weaver, a professor of historical theology at Union Seminary (Richmond); another liturgist, who celebrated Communion, was John F. Anderson, the host pastor; Sara Bernice Mosley, Moderator of the PCUS General Assembly, a member of that presbytery, and an elder in one of its churches, gave the charge to the co-executive presbyters and the presbytery (50-19).

One issue that almost jeopardized the vote to become a union presbytery was what to do about the general presbyter. To have a single general presbyter meant making a choice between John Cunningham, the general presbyter of Trinity (UPCUSA), and Mac Hart, the general presbyter of Covenant (PCUS). Hart said, "to pick either one of us . . . and to not pick either one of us would [have] probably shot the thing down." The solution was to call both as co-executive presbyters even though there were some "people who said you can't do that, you have to be one—the buck stops here kind of person; this won't work." Because Cunningham and Hart were very good friends and had worked cooperatively for long enough, it did work. Hart recalled with great sadness that, not long after they were elected co-executives, Cunningham, a "beautiful, beautiful human being," was diagnosed with chronic leukemia and had that for three or four years before he died in 1983 (50-20).

Hart remembered an issue that came up later after denominational reunion in 1983. Because so many liked to be a union presbytery and had such an extremely good feeling about that experience, the question became whether to keep the "union" in the name, Grace (Union) Presbytery. The final decision was to drop "union" in celebration of the reunion of the denominations. Hart with wistful lament said, "we're ultimately glad we did but there was some pain to that" (50-13).

Indian Nations

The Presbytery of Indian Nations, the thirteenth union presbytery, was created out of churches from the former of the Presbyteries of Oklahoma (PCUS) and Washita (UPCUSA), effective January 16, 1980. They were respective members of the Synods of Red River (PCUS) and Sun (UPCUSA). This was the first presbytery not to include "union" in its official name.

The incentive to become a union presbytery was more than just the practical aspects. J. Richard Hershberger, a UPCUSA pastor in Oklahoma City, recognized that "for some of us there was a theological reason . . . the body ought to be one . . . and there's a practical side to the theology." He went on to elaborate: "Presbyterians ought to be united for the sake of the ministry in the area. Persons coming into the area from one place or another were really unable to distinguish whether a church or local congregation was a member of one denomination or another . . . and it just made sense to not bother them with that kind of a polity concern" (77-5).

Hershberger said some questions and doubts did exist. They were more logistical in nature, rather than substantive differences. Washita Presbytery (UPCUSA) had five or six meetings a year and the Oklahoma Presbytery (PCUS) had maybe two. The questions were, "Why do we need to meet that much?" or "Can we get along with fewer?" Hershberger said, "[W]e had to compromise on a lot of those things." He also felt "the general impression was overwhelmingly positive, and I think largely because we had been doing so much cooperatively already" (77-5).

Kenneth G. McCullough, Synod's Field Director of Christian Education for the PCUS and UPCUSA, said that long years of acquaintance in the Oklahoma City area with pastors and staff of the PCUS synod and presbyteries went a long way in making the union presbytery workable. He did recall later that there were questions about the union on the part of some pastors in some smaller churches because the PCUS churches and membership outnumbered those of the UPCUSA in Oklahoma. McCullough suspected that those who held positions of responsibility in their presbytery "wondered if they were going to be recognized as leadership potential in the larger one" (78-3).

McCullough said these concerns were soon put to rest to a large degree because of how the PCUS leaders in the union movement at that time reached out across the denominational lines. He cited two leaders in Oklahoma City as cases in point. One was Murdoch M. Calhoun, pastor at Central Church, Oklahoma City, the largest church of the PCUS presbytery. The other person was John Ed Withers, who was pastor of a smaller church in the presbytery, which itself was a union church with the United Church of Christ. According to Murdock, "John Ed, I suspect, was not afraid of unions" (78-3).

Another positive reality was the association among ministers in the Greater Oklahoma City area. There was a group of ministers from both denominations that got together called the Geneva Clerics. They met several times a year, and out of this came many suggestions about doing things together (77-2). Hershberger, co-moderator of the Joint Education Committee (Washita-Oklahoma Presbyteries), said, "[W]e did things like, all our teacher education, our vacation Church school training, other leadership education events for particular purposes; we did all that jointly for a number of years before we were a union, so it was sort of a grassroots kind of a thing" (77-4).

Eventually, instead of having to have co-chairs for committees that met together, it came to having one chair for various committees. Hershberger recalled: "Rather than concerning ourselves with having equal numbers on everything, we could just do the job and make the nominating committees' tasks easier." This was important in getting the camp or conference operations together. The camp that was within the bounds of Oklahoma Presbytery (PCUS) was eventually sold and all the efforts went into the Dwight Mission Camp, which was in Washita Presbytery (UPCUSA) (77-6).

One area of common opportunity in both denominations was the mission work among the Native Americans. In the years before the union presbytery, J. F. Austin served the Synod of Oklahoma (PCUS) as Field Representative for both Church Extension and Christian Education. During that time there was close cooperation with the UPCUSA because the synod offices were both in Oklahoma City (83-3).

Austin said "we were real good friends, so we worked together. But it was not a union Synod." Ken McCullough was the UPCUSA Christian Education staff person and Doug Majors was the Church Extension person. Austin stated, "we worked with the Indians, we worked with Church Extension, we worked with Education. Ken McCullough was Christian Education and worked with the Indians, and Doug Majors was Church Extension and primarily working with the Indians. And then there was another fellow that lived over at Sallisaw who also worked with me among the Indians. . . . We had a cooperative venture" (83-3). Austin went on to say, "I think that they were very glad that we were working together. . . . They [UPCUSA] were . . . a lot weaker than we [PCUS] were in Oklahoma, and I have a feeling that that's probably one of the reasons why we were able to cooperate together" (83-4).

Murdock M. Calhoun, the last moderator of Oklahoma Presbytery (PCUS) and first moderator of Indian Nations Presbytery, recalled that they worked out "a union where there would be fairness on both sides, and so far as I can remember it was a very cordial kind of a working arrangement. . . . I don't recall that there was a whole lot of opposition to it. . . . I found that the spirit was highly cooperative, and that was a great and happy surprise, that we did not have any difficulty. We were similar kinds of people in Oklahoma." Calhoun, in his colloquial way, added, "if anything, those who came from the denomination North of God were a little more conservative than those of the South" (80-3). Most importantly for him in thinking about the formation of the union presbytery, "[W]hat's to keep us from joining together? It seems as natural as a family living in one house" (80-4).

Indian Nations Presbytery was officially organized on January 16, 1980, meeting in the Calvin Presbyterian Church, Oklahoma City. Ruling elder Johnnie Diltz, retiring moderator of the former Presbytery of Washita (UPCUSA), presented Murdock M. Calhoun with the gavel and welcomed him to office. Among the honored guests who brought greetings on the occasion of its first meeting as a union presbytery were William J. Fogleman, general presbyter of the Synod of Red River; Raymond V. Kearns, interim executive of the Synod of the Sun; Howard L. Rice, Moderator of the General Assembly (UPCUSA); and James E. Andrews, Stated Clerk of the General Assembly (PCUS).[2]

Calhoun recalled some final thoughts about his experience as the first moderator of Indian Nations Presbytery. "The new Stated Clerk of the new union Presbytery, Ken McCullough, was a most cooperative and gentle man . . . whom I enjoyed working with greatly. . . . And that's what I remember most, the cordiality" (83-4). Calhoun went on to say, "and when the union [reunion of the denominations in 1983] came, we . . . at our level of work didn't see much change. . . . The change had already occurred. . . . You know, the truth is, we probably carried on at the practical, local level, in the old tradition" (83-5).

Tres Rios (Union)

The Presbytery of Tres Rios (Union), the fourteenth union presbytery, was formed out of part of Central Texas (Union) and the Presbyteries of Tres Rios (PCUS) and Tres Rios (UPCUSA), effective June 24, 1980. They were respective members of the Synods of Red River (PCUS) and Sun (UPCUSA).

No doubt existed that the organizing conventions of the two Synods of Texas in the early 1970s assumed that the Presbyteries of Tres Rios (PCUS) and Tres Rios (UPCUSA) would become a union presbytery. However, the efforts at creating a union presbytery between the two presbyteries named Tres Rios initially was anything but successful. They voted twice on the issue, in 1972 and 1973. The PCUS presbytery defeated the union presbytery concept both times by a very narrow margin.

According to Charles J. Hollingsworth, who came to be the general presbyter of Tres Rios (PCUS) on December 1, 1975: "There was a lot of bitterness left because the feeling was that retired ministers had been brought in on letters to vote against it." To understand some of the reasons why the vote failed in the PCUS presbytery, one has to understand the demographics and the dynamics at work in the two presbyteries. Hollingsworth said of the PCUS presbytery: "I think they'd rather be a big frog in a little pond than a little frog in a big pond" (22-3).

This was not because they were smaller or the weaker of the two, but according to Hollingsworth, "I think they saw themselves being swallowed up in a system that was far more massive than those in the PCUS were accustomed to, less personal." He went on to say he thought the feeling was that Tres Rios (UPCUSA) "was wanting to become union so they could get the money from the PCUS Presbytery. As it turned out it was the UP Presbytery that had all the money and didn't know it because the treasury had squirreled it away and never made a report [*chuckling*], . . . hundreds of thousands of dollars, virtually" (22-3).

Tres Rios (UPCUSA) consisted of only about sixteen churches; therefore, "everybody in the Presbytery who could breathe, had some job." There really was no "presbytery office" in Tres Rios (UPCUSA), only the stated clerk functioned as the officer of the presbytery. The PCUS presbytery, which did have an office and a general presbyter, had roughly twenty-eight or twenty-nine churches, and consequently, even though they had a large structure, they had a much smaller percentage of participation on the part of both lay people and ministers (22-3).

Both were folksy in their own way, but according to Hollingsworth, Tres Rios (UPCUSA) "tended to follow the strictures of the UP system much more closely in terms of things like weighting pastoral positions for salary. . . . And they would spend whole days in a consultation of people in the Presbytery, weighing those positions, ranking them, putting a dollar figure with the weighting that they came up with." That was far from the style in the PCUS presbytery. "The closest they had ever come to doing anything like that was when they brought Bob Worley [consultant from McCormick Seminary] in 1971–72 to do a goal-setting event. They came up with twenty-five priorities for the Presbytery, most of which became very unwieldy and unmanageable" (22-2).

Nothing much came of that, Hollingsworth recalled, except that "when I was interviewed I had to deal with those twenty-five priorities, and then after I was called, had to sort out what was realistic and do-able and what was unrealistic and do-able." He said in the executive search process, the committee could not agree on "what emphasis to put on pastoral care of pastors which was a result of the walking wounded from two failed votes on Union . . . and what to do with program. . . . And I hunch that was part of the reason I was hired, because I could win those two" (22-2).

In late 1976 Tres Rios (UPCUSA) invited Hollingsworth to serve as general presbyter. The two presbyteries began a process of setting up a joint office (22-2). Some considerable consternation was caused the UPCUSA hierarchy because they were not used to dealing with having an executive presbyter and a stated clerk who were not members of one of its presbyteries. Hollingsworth fondly remembered: "[Having] this unofficial name appearing on official documents in the UP system [*chuckling*] caused a little visible upset, too [*chuckling*]. It was fun" (22-7).

Hollingsworth allowed that when "we moved into the joint office of the Presbytery, we just simply had like committees meet together in joint and concurrent sessions. . . . It was not a structural problem, because the design for both Presbyteries had been almost identical. There were minor differences, but not major ones. So that transition was actually pretty easy" (22-4).

Still there was some residual bitterness left, primarily in the PCUS presbytery, over the previous lost votes on becoming a union presbytery; where one person who had voted for union presbytery would not cross the street to shake hands with that . . . [so-and-so] who had voted against it. Also this bitterness was very noticeable in the UPCUSA presbytery where persons would say: "Why should we go through this one more time, only to lose again?" Hollingsworth said what was critical, however, was that the more the committees worked together, the more the trust level developed and the more the question began to be asked, "Why shouldn't we be one, organically?" (22-5).

The two presbyteries of Tres Rios became much more serious about becoming a union presbytery because they had some union churches from old Central Texas (Union) Presbytery, and through their participation in the Consultation on Union Presbyteries (COUP) they were invited to attend the Consultation as cooperating presbyteries in an observer capacity in 1977 (22-2). Over the next two years the rough places became smooth so that the third time the vote was taken, becoming a union presbytery passed. Tres Rios (Union) Presbytery could be said to be, in part, a product of the COUP advocacy strategy for creating union presbyteries.

On June 24, 1980, the Constituting Meeting of the Union Presbytery of Tres Rios was held in the Trinity Presbyterian Church of Midland, Texas. The long ago dreams of R. Matthew Lynn and Flynn V. Long, Jr., both of whom had labored in this city and predecessor presbytery a quarter of a century before, had now come true at the presbytery level. The resolutions passed that day rejoiced "for the support and presence of the official visitors representing the judicatories or groups in our denomination, including the Moderators of the General Assemblies and the Moderators of the Synods of the Sun and Red River." It also celebrated the "witness and mission of our two presbyteries . . . and the unity and oneness we have felt and now feel together."3

In the years immediately prior to reunion in 1983, Hollingsworth served as chair of the Joint Committee/Task Force on Union Presbyteries. He served as general presbyter of Tres Rios Presbytery (PCUSA) until the 1990s ran out. When pointed out that Hollingsworth at his retirement was the last general presbyter with union presbytery experience, he responded by saying: "I'm not sure that I don't feel a little bit ambivalent about being labeled 'T. Rex.' [chuckling]" (22-12).

New Covenant (Union)

The Presbytery of New Covenant (Union), the fifteenth union presbytery, was formed out of the Presbyteries of Brazos (PCUS) and Gulf Coast (UPCUSA), effective July 1, 1980. They were respective members of the Synods of Red River (PCUS) and Sun (UPCUSA).

In the organizational convention plan of the Synods of Texas in the early 1970s, the Presbyteries of Brazos (PCUS) and Gulf Coast (UPCUSA) occupied about the same geographical area in Texas, excepting that Gulf Coast had a few churches all the way over in Louisiana to New Orleans. Gulf Coast (UPCUSA) was a fairly small presbytery, about thirty-five churches, including a half dozen or more from what was called the Southwest Bohemian Presbytery stemming from a Czech Brethren group going back to the 1890s. Brazos (PCUS) was quite large, about eighty-five, including a few predominantly African American, Native American, and Hispanic congregations (28-2).

Over the years these presbyteries had engaged in various cooperative mission and educational ministries responding to the growing urban needs of the greater Houston area. In the 1960s they were involved in an ecumenical ministry at the Port of Houston, campus ministry at local institutions, experimental ministries in deteriorating inner city, and sharing of educational resources and events. H. Richard Siciliano was urban mission associate in Gulf Coast; L. Robert Frere was mission associate in Brazos; and Florine "Killer" Miller was educational associate in Brazos.

Preparation for the vote on becoming a union presbytery in 1971 as part of the organizing convention plan was very simple. John R. "Pete" Hendrick, co-chair of the reunion committee, recalled that the committee announced: "Here it is . . . here's the rubric," and both sides said, "We're going to bring it to a vote." The presbyteries brought it to a vote; Brazos (PCUS) brought it to a vote and it was defeated "by three, four, five votes," according to Hendrick (28-3). It was difficult to get the required two-thirds majority for passage.

Hendrick went on to say that the person who swayed it was Dr. Charles L. King, the retired longtime pastor of First Presbyterian Church, Houston. Hendrick recounted that Dr. King was not opposed to reunion, but he did not want this "back door approach to reunion, and he made one of his marvelous *ex cathedra*, 'The King has spoken,' addresses on the floor of Presbytery, and whipped us." Playing on a term used in civil rights at that period, "maximum feasible integration," Hendrick said both presbyteries immediately passed a motion that called for "maximum feasible cooperation. . . . In other words, we're not going to be a Union Presbytery, but we're going to cooperate in every way" (28-3).

By 1972, William J. Fogleman had left Brazos (PCUS) as executive presbyter to be general presbyter for the Synod of Red River (PCUS). John Hendrick became executive presbyter of Brazos (PCUS) and H. Richard Siciliano, executive presbyter of Gulf Coast (UPCUSA). Cooperation between the two presbyteries increased in many ways.

In an effort to overcome "convenient adherence" (i.e., "failure to comply") to earlier comity agreements on location of new churches, Central Presbyterian Church (UPCUSA), which was in the same block of First Presbyterian Church (PCUS), decided to move out to a newly annexed suburb of Houston. An elder of the church bought the property and turned it into an ecumenical office complex and invited the two presbyteries to locate their offices there. This greatly enhanced cooperation by sharing space and staff, thus laying a piece of the foundation that supported the eventual union of the two presbyteries (31-7).

To overcome the bitter feelings over previous new church developments and comity agreements, the presbyteries decided that each new church that was developed would be a union church. Several were in fact established on a fifty-fifty basis. Gulf Coast brought its share in the form of low interest National Mission loans and grants for staff. Brazos contributed land (31-5). This, along with putting the Christian Education and National Missions Committees together, went a long way to create a good feeling about the possibility of creating a union presbytery in the future (31-2). Because of significant differences in approach in each system, the most difficult areas in which to cooperate for a long period of time related to: the presbytery councils, stewardship, and ministerial relations (28-4).

By the end of the 1970s, both presbyteries reached the conclusion that it was time to give creating a union presbytery a second chance. When Brazos (PCUS) formed its committee on union presbyteries, David L. Stitt, pastor of the Bellaire Presbyterian Church, was asked to be its chair. He told them he would serve "if they'd put M. Douglas Harper on the committee." Harper was, according to Stitt, "a very fine pastor of St. Andrew's Presbyterian Church in Houston and would be a very thorough man, although he opposed union" (52-3).

Harper consented and later said he felt personally challenged by the invitation since they had decided to "co-opt the opposition" and "by that time, I had been appointed to the Joint Committee on Union working on denominational union" (57-4). Harper went on to say it was not his intention to sabotage the plan by making it bad, but wanted it to be the best possible plan it could be, "so that if we had to live with it, we wouldn't have to live with a deliberately flawed document. And I think we drew up a very good plan" (57-5).

Harper and the elders from his church spoke against adopting the plan when it was presented to Brazos (PCUS). Harper said, "they [those in favor of the proposal] were folks whom I respected, but [who] I thought really hadn't thought through all the implications. . . . I've always been much interested in polity, and I felt we could be creating a polity mess" (57-3).

Stitt had the last rebuttal and said "there was nothing new in what they said, that we'd heard all of those before, but we still felt it was a good plan and we should go ahead with it." The presbytery voted overwhelmingly to become a union presbytery with Gulf Coast (UPCUSA) and adopted a new name for it, the Presbytery of New Covenant (Union) (52-3).

Harper remembered very vividly the presbytery meeting where it became clear that "we were going to be a union presbytery." He took the floor and invited the presbytery to hold the first meeting of the union presbytery at St. Andrew's Presbyterian Church in Houston, where he was pastor. He added: "I think you're wrong, but I'm going to do everything I can to make it work, because that's the way I understand that we live together in the Church. You make your point. When it's done, it's done, and then . . . whatever mistakes are made, you don't make them worse by what you're doing." Harper was very much a part of it and worked very hard to make it work. In retrospect he said, "[I]t worked pretty well, really. Many of my fears were not realized" (57-5).

David Stitt concluded, "you can work with a man like that, although you disagree with him. If he's willing to bow to the will of the majority of presbytery, it shows that he's a good Presbyterian" (52-3).

On June 28, 1980, a worship service celebrating the constituting of the Presbytery of New Covenant was held at St. Andrew's Presbyterian Church, Houston, Texas. Participating in the worship service was Charles A. Hammond, Moderator of the General Assembly (UPCUSA) and David L. Stitt, Moderator of the General Assembly (PCUS). The theme of the service was "We are a New Creation."[4] John R. Hendrick and H. Richard Siciliano were elected co-executive presbyters (31-3).

Mission (Union)

The Presbytery of Mission (Union), the sixteenth union presbytery, was formed out of the Presbyteries of Del Salvador (PCUS) and Alamo (UPCUSA), effective October 15, 1980. They were respective members of the Synods of Red River (PCUS) and Sun (UPCUSA). This was the last union presbytery to be formed in Texas.

The ordering of new presbyteries in both denominations as a result of the synods' organizing convention plan in 1971, upset some people in the PCUS, because it came externally to them "from above." Harry Hassall recalled that, "my friends in what became [first, Del Salvador (PCUS) then] Mission [Union] Presbytery were in South Texas Presbytery and John Knox Presbytery. They were not at all interested in losing their Presbytery identities. And Synod made them do it" (65-19).

This contingent's perspective produced a certain tension with those of a different persuasion who had come into Del Salvador (PCUS) from the dissolution of Central Texas (Union). Harsh competition had existed over the years between Trinity University (UPCUSA) in San Antonio and Austin College (PCUS) in Austin. According to E. L. Coon, associate general presbyter (AGP) of Del Salvador (PCUS), a certain amount of hostility was perceived as coming from professors and teachers at Trinity University. He said certain remarks were heard like, "Now, PCUS, you all are just a little, old, southern, regional denomination, and the UP church is a national church across the whole nation." Coon described it as "a kind of an elitist, condescending sort of an attitude, so . . . bad blood existed for a long time between the Alamo Presbytery and Del Salvador Presbytery" (30-6). Nothing was done in the way of a committee study about a union presbytery until many years later because folks weren't interested in it (30-8).

Alamo Presbytery was the smaller presbytery in number, outnumbered by the other presbytery on an order of seven-to-one (26-5). Any church in their presbytery could host a meeting of Presbytery. Their meetings were less formal, laid-back with lots of discussions. Rafael Sanchez, Jr., was the executive presbyter (30-7).

The meetings of Del Salvador were highly scheduled, more formal, more strictly and tightly organized, and moved along to action kinds of

---

things. It had stronger committees at work with more money available to do programming (30-7). The main office for Del Salvador was in Austin, with Robert W. Bass as general presbyter (GP) and E. L. Coon as associate general presbyter (AGP); R. Clement Dickey, AGP, was in the regional office in Corpus Christi; and Robert J. Sebesta, part-time AGP, was in Harlingen (30-5).

There was a feeling on the part of some of the Alamo Presbytery folks, according to Coon, "that Del Salvador, under the leadership of Robert W. Bass, was an aggressive presbytery that kind of ran roughshod over folks and made hasty and decisive kinds of decisions" (30-7). There were those in Alamo (UPCUSA) who had said "for a long time they wanted no part of a union presbytery if Bob Bass was going to be the Executive, or if he was going to have anything to do with it" (30-6).

Coon was quick to say, however, that everyone worked hard to overcome these hard feelings. He said Bass "tried real hard to dispel some of these anxieties, . . . to work cooperatively with the Exec from Alamo Presbytery, who at the time was Raf Sanchez." Coon described Sanchez as "a real neat guy and easy to get along with, [who] gave Bass a hard time, . . . in humorous and funny kinds of ways, in order to get along (30–6).

From a lay perspective, ruling elder James D. Baskin, moderator of Del Salvador (PCUS), said much was accomplished due "to the fact that the two Presbyteries, their councils and their Executives, had been cooperating." Joint structures began to emerge and joint meetings were held. Baskin concluded, "there was very little difference between them. . . . It was more a paper difference than there was an objective one" (26-3). The time had come to consider seriously becoming a union presbytery.

The two presbyteries convened at Westlake Hills Church in Austin in the early fall of 1980 to vote on the proposal to become a union presbytery. They voted separately and then Alamo Presbytery joined Del Salvador for a celebration. According to Moderator Baskin, "the spirit was good. . . . I didn't hear a single grumpy voice." He attributed this to the cooperative efforts already mentioned and how "Bill Fogleman had so drawn the lines [presbytery boundaries]" (26-3).

Bob Bass died of a heart attack in the summer of 1980 before the Presbytery vote on becoming a union presbytery. Bob had written on a piece of paper his prediction of the outcome of the vote in Del Salvador Presbytery, had put it in an envelope and given it to his secretary. And after the vote passed, the secretary made that note public. Bob had come within five votes of what the vote turned out to be. Del Salvador voted overwhelmingly to become a union presbytery. Alamo Presbytery's vote was unanimous, and the two presbyteries came together (30-6).

The new presbytery decided not to call an executive presbyter immediately, but to work with a "kind of a three-headed" associate executive setup—with Emerson I. Abendroth from Alamo Presbytery; and E. L. Coon and Angus W. McGregor from Del Salvador—to fulfill the executive role until a new executive could be called. The new executive, who was called in 1982, was L. Frere, former executive presbyter of Louisville (Union) (30-7).

The name, Mission, was chosen for two reasons: primarily, because mission was the business the presbytery was about; and the other was, that in San Antonio and farther down in the valley, there were quite a number of old Spanish missions that go back to years before the Anglos came (26-6).

In retrospect, Coon recalled how the two presbyteries came to the new beginning: "We moved into more amiable relationships, committees were appointed and studies were done to move us toward a union Presbytery. And then, with Bob Bass's death, that just sort of sealed it. And the Presbytery maybe is kind of a memorial for Bass, and all the good work that he had done. . . . Because his heart was with the Church. I don't know of anybody that I've ever worked with that loved the Church more than Bob Bass in his obstreperous ways [*chuckling*]" (30-8).

Southwest Florida (Union)

The Presbytery of Southwest Florida (Union), the seventeenth union presbytery, was formed out of the Presbyteries of Westminster (PCUS) and West Florida (UPCUSA), effective January 1, 1982. They were respective members of the Synods of Florida (PCUS) and South (UPCUSA).

Florida, as a geographical and sociological destination, was very diverse and complex. "Snowbirds" made it the location of choice, coming in search of sunny recreation and warm retirement. Presbyterians from up North and from the Midwest brought various experiences of what it meant to be Presbyterian, in most instances not caring or knowing any difference. Cuban and other Hispanic immigrants came into South and Central Florida introducing a very different culture from the so-called "natives" in the Panhandle, who were more akin to folk in Alabama and Georgia than those in tropical Florida.

The Presbytery of West Florida (UPCUSA) was a very large presbytery that stretched over the central part of the state, up the west coast north to the Georgia line and to the panhandle of Florida, a distance almost as far as from Pensacola to Chicago. It had thirty-five congregations or so, including an African American congregation in

Tallahassee that consisted largely of the faculty and administration of Florida A & M. Being so spread out created the reality of isolation, giving the perception that this presbytery "consists of a bunch of congregationalists," which was far from the truth. It only met four times a year and was "laid back" (71-6).

Lacy R. Harwell, campus minister at the University of Florida and later pastor at Maximo Presbyterian Church, St. Petersburg, said West Florida Presbytery "took care of its business in very short order and [would] linger over lunch, sing a lot of hymns and it was much more like a big house party" (71-7). Meetings of Westminster Presbytery, which was larger numerically and financially, were as "different as night and day" according to Harwell. He said there was a "fine point debate on every issue concerning the *Book of Church Order* and the *Book of Confessions*, and general theology." Commissioners from union congregations had to go to both presbytery meetings and "they just heap rather go to a West Florida meeting than to Westminster," in Harwell's opinion (71-7).

Thomas M. Johnston, who was the moderator of West Florida Presbytery at that time, declared that the primary strategy shared was "building bridges and establishing relationships from which other things could grow." His primary bridge-building activity was as co-chair of the Social Action Committee of the PCUS and UPCUSA Synods of Florida's Social Justice Committee, which dealt with "potentially troubling liberal-conservative kinds of issues you get into in social justice." Johnston said it was "the first place where we, in fact, made the marriage" and "the only place in the PCUS and UPCUSA Synods of that time where there was such a relationship" (79-3).

Robert E. Veley, a graduate of Louisville Seminary who chaired the Committee on Ecumenics, recalled, "[O]ne of the things that began to unite us was camp and conferences" (69-4). Other cooperative ministries existed between Westminster and West Florida in the areas of retirement housing, campus ministries, Hispanic ministries, and new church development.

During the 1960s and 1970s there was a strong denominational emphasis on developing youth ministry and new congregations. The majority of new congregations organized in the United Presbyterian Church, according to Harwell, were organized by West Florida Presbytery. He attributed that largely to the fact that they attracted people of all denominations coming into Florida. They also took advantage of the fact that nobody seemed to be applying for funds from the Board of National Mission's Central Capital Resources Agency, established for this purpose (71-13).

Some contention had existed over the years between the two presbyteries over new church development. There was a comity agreement about the location of new churches, but there was always the feeling, especially with some in the Westminster Presbytery (PCUS), that maybe West Florida (UPCUSA) was not living up to their comity (70-3). Also there was lingering anxiety on the part of some people in Westminster (PCUS) about the financial stability of West Florida (UPCUSA) caused by some mishandling of funds by one of its officers (68-7).

This soon dissipated when Robert L. Thompson, executive presbyter of West Florida, collaborated with John D. MacLeod, Jr., executive secretary of Westminster, to adopt a policy in their respective presbyteries that committed them to making all new church developments union congregations (68-10).

Lacy Harwell declared, "it was not the *Book of Order*, nor theological points that was driving [establishing a union presbytery], it was necessity." The dual reality of keeping two sets of books and attending two presbytery meetings in a growing number of union congregations soon "did not make any sense to anybody" (71-7).

Harwell recounted, "when it came time to organize Southwest Florida Presbytery, the driving force was so strong and the experience was so broad, and the expectations in the pew was, what took you so long [*chuckle*]" (71-11). He remembered with great glee: "I kept asking, if they do it in the Border States, why can't we do it down here. I mean we're on the southern border [*laughter*]" (71-18).

The Presbyteries of Westminster (PCUS) and West Florida (UPCUSA) met in a joint meeting on October 27, 1981, took action on all matters "relative to the formation of Southwest Florida Union Presbytery, including those regarding structures, staffing and staff personnel, election of Commission, Committee and Board memberships." A Constituting Meeting and Celebration was held on January 3, 1982, at the first Presbyterian Church, St. Petersburg, Florida. John H. LaMotte was the first moderator and was presented with a stole worn by the pastor of the first union church in the two presbyteries.[5]

In a subsequent year, Esther Rolston Jones, mother of Thomas L. Jones, became the first woman moderator of Southwest Florida (Union). She had served as the president of the Synodical of Florida and according to her son, Tom, "was a little ole stooped white haired woman" who was not reticent to give "fiery pro-feminist speeches" (85-16).

There was considerable energy spent on balancing the selection of the new executive presbyter between the two presbyteries. The original plan was to call Robert Thompson and John MacLeod as co-executives, which was not universally supported. The tension was relieved when MacLeod accepted a call as general secretary of the Synod of North

Carolina before action was taken to call them. Thompson was elected executive by a small majority vote and served the presbytery for a relatively brief period of time (70-6).

William M. Clark, a PCUS pastor from Tennessee, was called as associate executive, commonly referred to as "deputy executive." This had a salutary effect on some of the former PCUS constituents that made up a majority of the new presbytery. The southern part of the Southwest Florida (Union) was made up of a large contingent of the former PCUS presbytery and kept pushing for a division of the new one almost as soon as reunion took place. In a short time this southern part became Peace River Presbytery (PCUSA) and called Clark to organize it and serve as executive (70-6).

Eastern Oklahoma (Union)

The Presbytery of Eastern Oklahoma (Union), the eighteenth union presbytery, was created out of churches from the former of the Presbyteries of Oklahoma (PCUS), Eastern Oklahoma (UPCUSA) and part of the Presbytery of Washita (UPCUSA), effective July 13, 1982. Some of these churches had been members of Indian Nations (Union) for a brief time. They were, respectively, members of the Synods of Red River (PCUS) and Sun (UPCUSA) and the last union presbytery to be formed by them. The only two presbyteries in these synods that did not become union presbyteries were South Louisiana (PCUS) and Pines (PCUS) (89-5).

The Presbytery of Eastern Oklahoma (UPCUSA) went from the Kansas line to the Texas border, and covered about one-third of the eastern part of Oklahoma. Washita Presbytery (UPCUSA) had only fifteen of the churches involved. One-fifth or so of the congregations came from the former Presbytery of Oklahoma (PCUS), having some Indian Parishes and other churches in southeastern Oklahoma.

William G. Henning, Jr., who had served as executive presbyter of Arkansas (Union) and later became interim executive of East Oklahoma (PCUSA), emphasized that one of the key factors at play in 1981 and 1982 when East Oklahoma (Union) was being formed was the significant presence of Native American Missions in Oklahoma (61-10). There was work among the Choctaws, Creeks, Chickasaws, and other groups. Choctaw Parish was a UPCUSA mission and Indian Parish was PCUS, having Choctaw and Chickasaw churches (88-13).

These mission fields had drawn support from all across both denominations, but those support lines, Henning perceived, were damaged when the regional synods and Indian Nations (Union) were organized. He noted that a few churches in the southern part of eastern Oklahoma shouldered the burden of support for these Indian Missions and "it wasn't until Eastern Oklahoma [Union] got welded into a solid unit that those links of support came back" (61-10).

This was affirmed by J. Richard Hershberger, associate pastor of Westminster Presbyterian Church, Oklahoma City. He said his impression was that places like Goodland Home, in Hugo, Oklahoma, which was originally an Indian work but now is different, "is still supported by a lot of people in Indian Nations Presbytery even though it's outside the bounds of our Presbytery because of the historic connection" (77-7).

One point of connection in the formation of the new presbytery was in the area of women's programs. Marilee Story, who was presbyterial president of United Presbyterian Women (UPCUSA), in 1981 served as president of the Synodical of Sun (UPCUSA) and chair of the Coordinating Council. Both of these offices put her in contact with the Women of the Church (PCUS) where they began to get acquainted with each other. The two synods also began to share some staff (88-2).

Story said that, "as we became better acquainted we found out that most of what we were sort of at cross purposes about, were actually the same thing and they had different names." At their Executive Council meeting, Story recalled how she and Sylvia Washer, her counterpart in the PCUS who much later became Executive Presbyter of Mission Presbytery (PCUSA), were "the ones who kind of had the conflict [*chuckling*] at the first small group meeting . . . and after we'd worked together for a while, I think at one point she began to explain United Presbyterian Women, and I began to explain Women of the Church! [*laughing*] So, we had come together" (88-4). Story later became administrative assistant at the Eastern Oklahoma Presbytery office.

Continuing to relate to those of differing opinions was so critical. Estha F. Nowlin, elder at Saint Andrews Presbyterian Church (UPCUSA), Tulsa, Oklahoma, was very involved on the Union Presbytery Task Force. She had extensive experience working with Presbyterian women at presbytery and synod levels. One important part of that was to get to know some who were not in favor of union. One such person was this "absolutely delightful, wonderful woman by the name of Cherokee Rose Crocker." Crocker was "just almost adamant that the Church should not reunite. Southern Church was good enough for her. It had been all those years, and she didn't see any reason to change it." Through many meetings together at First Church in McAllister, Nowlin, and Crocker became wonderful friends. Nowlin said that over the years every time they met at a presbytery meeting in the church in McAllister, she would say to Crocker, "Now, you remember, this is where we met for union" (84-4).

Chapter 11   227

Nowlin fondly remembered working on the union presbytery task force, where she formed lasting relations with those from other presbyteries. Some reluctance existed on the part of the folk from old Washita Presbytery (UPCUSA), who felt feeling that their fifteen congregations might get swallowed up by this new larger presbytery (84-6).

Another fact was that the existing presbytery office was located in Muskogee, Oklahoma, and according to Nowlin, some felt, "Well, that's too far away, and there's going to be a movement to move the presbytery office to Tulsa, which of course did happen later." Nowlin said these fears, about being swallowed and the inconvenient distance from the presbytery office, did not materialize because "there's always been an effort to be very inclusive of the churches down South." The Presbytery Council meetings were moved around, and department/division meeting days were scheduled to meet around the presbytery. She observed that, "our relationship developed slowly, but developed well through the years." Sometimes she said she encountered the feeling: "Well, we used to do it when we were the Southern Church." Nowlin speculated: "I just think that's still there. I think in many ways we're still fighting the battle of the Confederacy [*chuckling*]" (84–6) In the final analysis, fears and discomforts notwithstanding, Nowlin concluded that the union presbytery "was a good thing for this Presbytery [Eastern Oklahoma (UPCUSA)], and I think certainly for Washita Presbytery" (84-4).

North Alabama (Union)

The Presbytery of North Alabama (Union), the nineteenth union presbytery, was formed out of the Presbyteries of North Alabama (PCUS) and Huntsville (UPCUSA), effective January 1, 1983. They were respective members of the Synods of Mid-South (PCUS) and South (UPCUSA).

North Alabama (PCUS), in 1971, had about four times as many members in twice as many congregations as Huntsville (UPCUSA). The boundaries were not exactly coterminous but were very close. There was a part of North Alabama Presbytery, south of Anniston, that was not a part of Huntsville Presbytery. North Alabama (PCUS) had an executive secretary, D. Doug Wilkinson, as staff, whereas Huntsville (UPCUSA) had only a stated clerk, Ed Dalstrom. When the Synod of the South (UPCUSA) came into being in 1972, Howard Walton was elected to serve as executive presbyter of Huntsville Presbytery as well as Mississippi and West Tennessee Presbyteries. J. Harold Jackson was called to serve as general presbyter of North Alabama (PCUS) on January 1, 1973.

In these years there was some cooperative work between the presbyteries in Christian Education. Wayne P. Todd, longtime pastor at First Presbyterian Church, Florence, chaired the North Alabama Christian Education Committee that built a camp at Camp Maranatha. Huntsville Presbytery joined them in some cooperative work there. Although Dalstrom and Todd ended up being the co-chairs of a cooperative committee, Todd said, "[W]e knew we could not get the votes for a true union presbytery at that time." He added, "it was because of the attitude and the feelings in the Northern Church. . . . [T]hey were so much smaller and they were fearful of getting all swallowed up if they went into a merger" (82-4).

Cooperative work continued during the years between 1973 and 1979. There were some shared committee meetings and concurrent meetings of the governing bodies. North Alabama (PCUS), being in the new PCUS Regional Synod of the Mid-South, was in close relation with the three union presbyteries in Kentucky that were in the UPCUSA Regional Synod of the Covenant. This opened the door to participate in joint Synod Schools. This, and other activities between the two regional synods with the bridge union presbyteries between them enhanced union presbytery possibilities in Alabama (40-4).

When John L. Williams was interviewed for the general presbyter position in 1980 with North Alabama (PCUS), he asked them what kind of ecumenical connections or work they envisioned. The answer came through very clearly that they were in serious discussion with Huntsville (UPCUSA) about forming a union presbytery and that it was not "just some side conversation." The first time Williams met with Presbytery Council after he accepted the call, there were people in the room from the Huntsville Presbytery Council participating in the meeting (13-4).

Although the two presbyteries had engaged in cooperative efforts, Williams felt that there was still a need to build stronger relations between them. Together with the leadership of Wayne Todd, they began conversations around questions like: "What do we have to do to bring about a union presbytery? What are the benefits for all of us? Will it, in fact, enhance the mission of the Presbyterian Church in this region or this part of the country?" Out of these discussions a whole series of joint presbytery meetings were set up where Huntsville Presbytery and North Alabama would meet in the same place; literally in the same building at the same time "rubbing shoulders with each other," sometimes together for certain things, sometimes apart for certain kinds of business. Their meals were together, all the fellowship times were together and all of their worship was together. They did joint planning (13-5). Even a new three-way union congregation was established that included congregants from the PCUS, UPCUSA, and the Cumberlands (13-9).

These events took place over a two-year period where people got acquainted with one another and began to talk seriously about forming a union presbytery. In late 1981, two critical votes were taken over the issues: "Do we proceed to form a union presbytery? Do we write covenants of agreement? What do we do now? Do we go ahead?" In both presbyteries, the answers were yes, declarations of intent. As Williams recalled, in Huntsville Presbytery it was by five-to-one margin; in North Alabama, it was a solid two- or three-to-one margin (13-6).

Some opposition cropped up in North Alabama voicing a familiar concern over being swallowed up, not by the smaller Huntsville Presbytery, but by the larger UPCUSA, that translated into "New York!" It was not simply about style, philosophical, or theological difference, but, according to Williams, though "never fully revealed, . . . it was really a throwback to the Civil War. . . . [I]t was usually out of congregations that still bore in their history some feelings about events after and during 1861; . . . you could go into those congregations and you would still hear stories, literally from the 1860s, about what those nasty Yankees did to us" (13-7).

A joint committee hammered out Articles of Agreement, according to Williams, the purpose being, "when we eventually voted to become a union presbytery, we weren't just voting to unite. We had a plan" (13-11). The two most significant articles in this long document dealt with how the per capita and general mission dollars were to flow and questions about property. An agreement was reached to make adjustments on the division of money over a three-year period, because the two presbyteries had that imbalance in membership. Williams said they wanted to move gradually "because there was a lot more [money] coming out of North Alabama than Huntsville . . . so we had to work out a way that was viewed as equitable, but didn't just do it all at once to shock the system" (13-12). The plan also dealt with structures and staff.

The two presbyteries met concurrently on February 16, 1982. Huntsville Presbytery passed it without any problem, but there was a fight in North Alabama. Speeches were made against it and for it. One commissioner speaking in favor of it said, "The entire PCUS is looking at us. And what we do is gonna affect what the whole denomination does in reunion." One pastor who had indicated he was for it, got up and opposed it. The moderator, according to Williams, initially made an "I think I'm for it" speech, somewhat waffling, "so he could go home" (13-14).

An initial voice vote was taken and a subsequent roll call vote affirmed it. The moderator cast the deciding vote that provided the exact number of yea votes for the required two-thirds passage. Williams recalled that those who prevailed did not use the occasion to celebrate in front of the folks who opposed it, and conciliatory things were said afterward (13-15). The Synods approved the presbyteries' actions calling for the creation of North Alabama (Union) on January 1, 1983. *The Plan for Reunion* of the denominations was being circulated at this time. Between February 16, 1982, and the official beginning date, a called meeting of North Alabama (PCUS) was held to hear concerns about property presented by some who had opposed the union presbytery vote. Their issues had arisen over a provision in *The Plan for Reunion* of the denominations. They were heard but their requests were denied. Some felt it was nothing more than one last attempt to sabotage the union presbytery (13-16).

A time of celebration was set at the constituting meeting in early January 1983, to kick off the new union presbytery. By this time, PCUS presbyteries were well into voting on denominational reunion. Williams reported later that people from outside the area told him that "when North Alabama voted to become a union presbytery, that in some ways was a turning point for some of the rest of us. . . . [I]f that can happen in the Deep South, then reunion is something we better take more seriously than [we] had been" (13-14).

St. Augustine

The Presbytery of St. Augustine was formed out of the Presbyteries of Suwannee (PCUS) and Northeast Florida (UPCUSA), effective January 1, 1983. They were respective members of the Synods of Florida (PCUS) and South (UPCUSA). Had denominational reunion not passed in 1983, it would have been the twentieth union presbytery, but in fact, a case might be made that it was the first new presbytery formed in the reunited PC(USA).

Northeast Florida (UPCUSA) was a very large presbytery that stretched just north of Miami, all the way up the east coast and over to Pensacola in the panhandle (44-5). Its presbytery office was in Cocoa Beach within the bounds of St. Johns Presbytery (PCUS). Suwannee (PCUS) was located in the northeast sector of Florida. Suwannee (PCUS) had 58 congregations and Northeast Florida (UPCUSA) had only 8 of its congregations within the bounds of Suwannee (PCUS). One was an African American congregation in Jacksonville (44-3).

Edwin W. Albright, Jr., pastor in Suwannee Presbytery upon graduation from Louisville Seminary in 1965, recalled that, as a youngster he visited the church his grandfather served in Weirsdale and never was aware that it was a Northern Church. Albright said in his early years as pastor, there was no cooperation between the denominations. He was amazed at "how little awareness and little caring there really were across the heavy, heavy line between United Presbyterians and PCUS in North Florida" (44-3).

Some were aware of each other and were more aggressive in maintaining the differences. Donald L. Harris was a UPCUSA new church development pastor in Jacksonville and said that the congregation he served "was started as salt in the Southern Church's wound" (72-5). By that he meant that it was located halfway between two Southern churches that were three miles apart. Northern Presbyterians were moving south into that area and wanted "a Yankee church." Harris said "that literally, people would drive by a Southern church to come to us. And conversely they'd drive by me to go to a Southern church, and that was very rigid. And only after my congregation grew dramatically did we get well beyond those old southern-northern days" (72–6).

In 1974, J. Robert Booker, the first executive presbyter of Western Kentucky (Union), became the EP for Northeast Florida (UPCUSA). Along with Ed Albright, who by this time was the associate executive of Suwannee (PCUS) and was completing his Doctor of Ministry degree in the McCormick Seminary Presbytery Executive Track, led the way in overcoming this divide between denominations. Albright told how Robert L. Thompson, executive of West Florida Presbytery, approached him regarding starting new congregations. Their first union congregation was in Gainesville in 1974. Albright added, together with Booker, "we did one new church every year. And they all were union churches, all through the 1970s, early 1980s. . . . I don't think that translated in anybody's mind to a union presbytery until the late 1970s when Jack Swan moved to Jacksonville and began to take a lot of initiative" (44-6).

John H. "Jack" Swan, pastor at The Palms Presbyterian Church (UPCUSA) at Jacksonville Beach, out of his own loneliness, took the initiative to form a support group of four ministers. Albright remembered those early days, "the reaching out didn't come from the majority, it came from the minority. You know, the UP Church." Swan was instrumental in working their support group into a much larger support group, and relationships were built primarily in the Jacksonville area (44-5).

As Booker's executive responsibilities took him around Florida, he began to have a vision about how to form four union presbyteries around Jacksonville, Tallahassee, Pensacola, and Orlando. Those four hubs were the glue that would make this all happen in each location. The four presbyteries Booker envisioned never constituted as union presbyteries, but became new presbyteries in the reunited church in 1983 (44-8).

By 1980, steps were taken to plan for the formation of a union presbytery under the leadership of Bob Booker and Ed Albright. They were joined by key pastors like Jack Swan and Cecil R. Albright II, pastor of the Henry Flagler Memorial Church (UPCUSA) of St. Augustine. Cecil Albright, a graduate of Louisville Seminary and no relation to Ed Albright, was one of the first persons ordained by Louisville (Union) in 1971.

A Provisional Council and Structures were created, approved and in place in May of 1982, before the 1982 PCUS Assembly (Columbus). Based on what had been learned by having four union churches in both presbyteries, equal representation was given to each presbytery on the Provisional Council (44-7). It soon became apparent that any differences between the presbyteries or any issues that were being dealt with, like property or ordination of women, "weren't what they were perceived to be." Harris attributes this "to Ed Albright and how we [UPCUSA] were received. . . . They could have easily just kind of played the old tune and said 'you all come if you like, but you know, we've got the driver seat, we got the vast majority,' " but they did not (72-7).

One issue to be resolved was that the office of Northeast Presbytery (UPCUSA) was located within the bounds of St. Johns (PCUS) (73-11). According to Dennis M. Salmon, a pastor in Northeast Presbytery, Bob Booker wanted the Cocoa Beach Office to remain, with one staff person to serve as pastor-to-pastors, to exercise care because of the "horrendous turnover of pastors in this area." Salmon said, "Bob realized that this is a hard place to minister, and that preachers get torn up all the time here." The idea to keep that office open did not prevail (73-12).

Everything was to become official on January 1, 1983. The Provisional Council and Structures were in place by May 1, 1982, "so, if reunion didn't pass, we wouldn't miss a beat; and if reunion did pass, we didn't miss a beat either because the Provisional Council took over." Ed Albright recalled, "instead of being called a union presbytery, it was just called [St. Augustine]. . . . [W]e went through a whole process of naming the new presbytery." The new union presbytery never came into being because reunion was voted in 1982–1983 (44-7).

The selection of the executive presbyter, one critical issue that was problematic in other presbyteries, did not develop here. Bob Booker, on his own, took himself completely out of the running very early on, thus giving him credibility to work for the best possible outcome. He was not interested in creating a volatile situation in a co-executive model. Ed Albright believed, "Bob Booker literally gave himself away—got some good theology—and created what today in Florida are four really strong presbyteries" (44-8).

Clearly again the winners outnumbered the losers by a long shot in this final wave of union presbyteries. The full consequences of the contributions of these historic events would be a long time coming. The contributions were more evident than the flaws, and ghosts of Stamford Bridge and Hastings *et al.* danced in the twilight in these quarters only to experience a temporary respite.

Notes

1. *Handbook of the Consultation on Union Presbyteries and the Joint Committee on Union Presbyteries* (1980 Revision), pp. 6–7.

2. *Minutes,* Initial Meeting of Indian Nations Presbytery, January 16–17, 1980, p. 3.

3. *Minutes,* Constituting Meeting of the Union Presbytery of Tres Rios, June 24, 1980, p. 24.

4. *Minutes,* Constituting Meeting of the Union Presbytery of New Covenant, June 28, 1980, pp. 63–70.

5. *Minutes,* Southwest Florida Union Presbytery, January 3, 1982, Constituting Meeting Celebration.

Chapter 12
Between Two Worlds

"Societies have to develop organized instruments to achieve their military, political, economic, social, religious, and intellectual objectives. The problem, according to Quigley, is that all instruments eventually become "institutionalized"—that is, vested interests more committed to preserving their own prerogatives than to meeting the needs for which they were created. Once this happens, change can come only through reform or circumvention of the institutions. If these fail, reaction and decline set in.

—Bill Clinton, recalling the words of Professor Carroll Quigley of Georgetown University[1]

The first wave of union presbyteries had been created with few or at best sketchy "organized instruments to achieve their objectives." Most spent those early years between 1970 and 1972 in the afterglow of celebration of their birthdays. They were not too aware of, or concerned about, the detailed consequences of their new creation and of living between two worlds. Days were absorbed with untangling a myriad of operational issues and sorting out divergent bank accounts. They knew there were larger problems to be solved, but their newfound life together gave them confidence that any obstacle could be overcome when necessary.

The rest of both denominations were preoccupied with restructuring national boards and agencies (UPCUSA–1971; PCUS–1972) and creating regional synods (UPCUSA–1972; PCUS–1973). Both Assemblies' General Councils, recognizing potential problems caused by the fledgling union presbyteries, called a consultation of representatives of the existing eight union presbyteries and those contemplating union. They met with representatives of boards and agencies in St. Louis on January 6, 1971, with M. Ralph Weedon, executive secretary of Louisville (Union) presiding. The Councils presented an agenda and other items were added.[2] The laundry list that day would be the recurring list over the coming years.

In true Presbyterian fashion, the consultation asked the General Assemblies' Stated Clerks and executives of the General Councils to convene a task force to study conflicts, concerns, and hang-ups concerning union presbyteries made up of General Assembly and presbytery representatives.[3] The significant thing about the consultation was, though the list of issues was on target, there is little evidence that much was done with the issues as a result of the meeting. One can

---

speculate that the timing of the issues and the ownership for doing anything about them by the presbyteries had not reached a critical point.

One known result of the work of the task force was that its subcommittee on Diversity and Inclusiveness convened a consultation of women in St. Louis on September 27–29, 1973, to react to the current draft of *A Plan for Reunion.* The consultation made major recommendations regarding language; provision for equal opportunity and compensation; provisions for equal representation; interim women's program strategies for the church; and suggested revisions to *A Plan for Reunion* based on the other recommendations.[4] One assumes, based on later drafts of the plan, that these recommendations were taken seriously.

In retrospect it has been difficult to determine the extent of the impact these early gatherings had on finding real solutions to the problems faced by this first wave of union presbyteries. It appears to be limited. Although the Joint Committee on Constitutional Problems of Union Presbyteries (JCCPUP) established by the General Assemblies did deal with some constitutional conflicts, it failed to meet the full scope of concerns posed by the union presbyteries themselves.

What became very clear was that the convergence of the demands growing out of all the new structures emerging in both denominations created substantial problems for union presbyteries, and a concerted effort had to be made to find solutions.

Origins of COUP

The response made to these complex demands by the union presbyteries was the formation of the Consultation of Union Presbyteries (COUP), a truly unique phenomenon in North American Presbyterianism.

When Transylvania (Union) came into being in 1971, a new executive staff was put in place under the staffing pattern approved as part of the plan of union by both Synods of Kentucky. As part of the formation of the UPCUSA regional synods in 1972, the union presbyteries in Kentucky were put in the provisional Synod KMO (Kentucky, Michigan, Ohio), later named the Synod of the Covenant.

The Council on Administrative Services (CAS), a part of the General Assembly (UPCUSA) restructure in 1972, took seriously its sweeping responsibilities with regard to synod and presbytery administration and staffing. CAS set a policy that all synod and presbytery staff positions were to be declared vacant and persons who had been in those positions were eligible to reapply. A process for reestablishing these synod and presbytery positions was put in place. The Councils of the three Kentucky union presbyteries appointed negotiating teams and prepared negotiating positions.[5]

The Presbytery of Transylvania (Union) met in the Log Cathedral at Buckhorn, on September 6, 1973. The meeting became known in folklore as the "Pitchfork Meeting" when the commissioners got riled up for the first time in the presbytery's young history. In the course of the Moderator's report on activities of the General Council, C. Richard Doyle, elder from First Presbyterian Church, Lexington (former PCUS), announced that the Council had sent a team to the Synod Negotiation to negotiate for "our presbytery staff." The entire body was stunned, thinking, "We'd just hired our staff, what do you mean? We decide who will be our staff," reflecting a former PCUS style (93-28).

Lon B. Rogers, elder from First Presbyterian Church, Pikeville (former UPCUSA), an elected member of the former Board of National Missions (UPCUSA), being deeply upset, got up and made a motion that the stated clerk be ordered to go to the telephone and "call our team back immediately." Then Albert "Shep" Crigler III and Emmett H. Barfield, Jr., both former Mississippi PCUS pastors who had migrated up to Kentucky, got up and made speeches urging caution, saying in effect, "Wait a minute. We came from a place where we [figuratively] shoot first and ask questions later. Let's wait and see what they have to report before we get into this." Ironically, they prevailed, which was an interesting reversal of positions taken by the commissioners speaking for and against the motion (93-29).

Riding back to Lexington from the meeting, the author, who was the associate executive, said to Charles M. Hanna, Jr., the executive, "Charlie, this is the third time in four years that I've lost a job, I'm getting kind of weary of this. We need to send a message to the folks in the Synod that we really are different." A letter was drafted that Hanna sent to Lawrence W. McMaster, the synod executive, who was a high-powered top-down UP-type manager [with a phone in his car long before cell phones!]. It said, "We need to sit down and have a consultation about what makes the union presbyteries different" (95-3).

As a result, an educational type of consultation was called where representatives from the three union presbyteries in Kentucky, representatives of the Synod of the Covenant and the Synod of the Mid-South, as well as observers from both General Assemblies met at Louisville Seminary on December 6–7, 1973. Each governing body was to pay the expenses for its representatives. A design team, made up of Tom M. Castlen, William G. McAtee, and Charles L. Stanford, led the consultation. The objectives, in addition to getting to know each other, were to share where each synod was in its reorganization, identify issues of mutual concern, determine alternative solutions for these issues or ways to discover solutions, and appoint a continuing planning group.[6] Time was spent discovering where the connections or nonconnections were between the two systems with the union presbyteries in the middle. A long list of concerns was generated. What stood out was the difference in style, terminology, and philosophy between the denominations and how this impacted personnel both in selection and deployment. The development of two new overlapping regional synods stretching from Mackinac to Mobile put an inordinate demand on elected representatives and staff that were deeply committed to connectionalism and participation in decision-making in both synods.[7]

The record shows that at the close of the consultation only two decisions were made and that was by consensus. It formed an ongoing group to plan further negotiations and decide in which direction consultations will move, and specified that it be made up of one representative from each union presbytery, three members of the original design team, and one representative from each synod. This consultation and its simple action set the tone and style for how future consultations were to be conducted.

Those named by each governing body as representatives to the continuing planning group were: Tom Castlen and William Whitledge (later replaced by Elaine Homrighouse), Synod of the Covenant; John A. Kirstein (Lewis L. Wilkins was added later), Synod of the Mid-South; Charles L. Stanford, Louisville (Union); Charles H. "Chuck" Moffett, Jr. (later replaced by H. William Peterson), Western Kentucky (Union); and William G. McAtee, Transylvania (Union). Tom Castlen was named convener and the group chose for its name "the Committee of Eight." No more than seven persons ever served at any given time, but no one ever noticed. It was still known as the Committee of Eight.

The secret of the consultation's success was in the design based on the relational style of operation demonstrated by the Kentucky union presbyteries. The relational model, rather than a highly structured corporate model, professes that getting to know each other first before tackling a decision agenda, is more productive than simply "getting down to business" right off the bat.

The relationships formed in this consultation, based on sharing of mutual joys and concerns, carried over into future consultations and would blossom through the years as non-union presbyteries from each synod paired up to engage in a variety of exchange programs that included council members, work groups, and youth delegations. The payoff for these bridge-building activities was a deeper understanding of each other's culture and the discovery that myths about each other were not necessarily true. Because of these partnerships, several presbyteries that had not been so inclined in the past, voted for reunion of the denominations when the time came.

The most significant positive learning that came out of the consultation was the real understanding that "we are different and we've got some things we've got to work on." Mac Freeman, executive of the Synod of the Mid-South, and Larry McMaster, executive of the Synod of the Covenant, were very much in support of that understanding.

The author, in a letter to McMaster about the consultation shortly after it was over, reiterated some of the union presbytery and synod concerns that were raised there, but declared, "I have the distinct feeling . . . in time we will look back on it as a milepost event for many reasons." An invitation was also extended to McMaster to come down to Kentucky for some "rocking chair time" to "reflect on what's happening to us."[8] McMaster responded, "I am sensitive to the fact that the problems reflected by Union Presbyteries in Kentucky have not received adequate or intensive consideration." He went on to say that he welcomed the "rocking chair" invitation and made a commitment to come down "shortly after the first of the year."[9]

The tragedy was, McMaster did not have a chance to make good on his commitment. He dropped dead of a heart attack within weeks after he had responded. Although he did not see the final results of the consultation, he had shared in laying the groundwork for a very positive future for the Kentucky union presbyteries and those synods (95-3).

Because of the overwhelming positive outcome of this consultation, rather than meet with just the same group, the Committee of Eight decided the following year to invite representatives from all the union presbyteries, as well as their synods and observers from the General Assembly, to come to Kentucky for another consultation. This 1973 Covenant (UPCUSA)/Mid-South (PCUS) Consultation became the prototype for the nine Union Presbytery Consultations to follow, "organized instruments to achieve their objectives."

Nine Union Presbytery Consultations

Classic Presbyterian polity formally organizes the church in a gradation of courts or judicatories—session, presbytery, synod, and general assembly—that creates a clearly defined vertical flow of power and authority between them. There is little opportunity for lateral or horizontal interchange, for example, over mutual concerns between sessions and sessions, presbyteries and presbyteries, or synods and synods in that organizational gradation. In the 1970s the "unclassical" polity concept of consultations was added to the lexicon of experience at all levels of the church.

The Consultation of Union Presbyteries was created as a grassroots venture and it took off, not because somebody called it together from the national level, but because its energy and authenticity were generated from the inherent powers of its presbyteries (94-18). COUP's viewpoint was not simply from the bottom up vertically through the system, but it added a strong horizontal dimension that made it truly multidirectional. Its power and authority were, not over and against that of the formal official structures, but informal and derived from the union presbyteries its membership represented.

Bill Peterson described COUP as "a major exercise in consensus decision-making, a major exercise in working toward common visions that weren't often stated. I don't think we ever sat down and did a vision statement for that Consultation on Union Presbyteries." Peterson went on to say that, as a gathering of presbyteries, it was "totally unofficial, except as a presbytery-based organization . . . the method of officialdom that was different. . . . It didn't have to have a General Assembly or a Synod say, 'You all need to get together and meet.' It just did it . . . that's part of the freedom of it" (36-24). It was a corporate version of Dabbs's comment mentioned earlier: "Give individuals the opportunity to express their freedom and social arrangements will emerge."

In essence it was a voluntary association, where representatives were selected and sent at the expense of the governing bodies that chose to participate. It was made up of representatives from the union presbyteries and their respective synods, as well as those from General Assembly levels. Over time, the invitation list expanded to include cooperating presbyteries, and "interlopers [who] suddenly kept showing up at the meetings . . . intrigued by what was going on in this group, people who wanted to become a part of it to see what they could learn for their own turf" (20-17).

COUP was basically a consensus building, problem-solving gathering based on mutual concerns for the union presbyteries and the common good of both denominations. All representatives thoroughly engaged freely in the explorations and were involved in shaping the potential solutions by injecting views from their perspectives. When COUP acted, it did so mainly by consensus in an advisory capacity. Its recommendations entered the formal official structure of both denominations at varying levels of gradation—to councils, agencies, governing bodies—by way of communications or recommendations. Each receiving entity would then take whatever official action it deemed wise by altering administrative policies and practices or sending overtures to other governing bodies requesting changes.

Continuity was maintained over the course of the nine consultations in the nature of the group itself, its energy and commitment. There was no problem getting people to come. The rosters and the attendance records indicate that almost without exception all union presbyteries had representatives present for all nine consultations. It was a high priority in the life of those presbyteries (95-15). COUP never got to Quigley's point where it was more committed to preserving its own prerogatives than to meeting the needs for which it was created.

The Committee of Eight provided leadership for the first consultation. Other people stepped up as it rotated around to different locations. Groups that volunteered to host the gathering generally provided the planning and event leadership. From the beginning, it was a shared leadership model based on getting the job done, not a "Sun god" model with one bright figure at the top (95-15). Many different styles of leadership were exhibited.

The format of the meetings included a variety of activities. Much time was spent in small work groups exploring topics the planning committee had established from previous consultations and new concerns from the various governing bodies. These work groups generated the basic recommendations that were presented to the plenary sessions for refinement and approval. Although some of the minutes of the consultation indicate that some motions were made and seconded, this usually simply reflected the recording style of the secretary. Rarely were decisions anything other than unanimous in approval. No action was taken on anything less than unanimous, making *Robert's Rules of Order* superfluous. Worship was central to the events.

Some felt that the Consultation (COUP) acted as a shadow organization for the whole church, in terms of looking at things that were happening denominationally and working on changing some of the things that were not liked in that process. Peterson recalled that "there were major fights about whether it was a small General Assembly or not. I can remember we kept saying it wasn't" (36-25).

There were others who questioned the constitutionality of the Consultation before the first one ever met. Charles L. Stanford, Jr., moderator of Louisville (Union) at the time, sent out letters of invitation to the First Annual Consultation to everyone on the list, including the Stated Clerks of the General Assemblies. Stanford said he got a letter from William P. Thompson, Stated Clerk of the UP General Assembly, saying, "You can't have that meeting. You don't have any right to invite presbyteries to come and talk." Stanford wrote him back and said something to the effect, "Well, we're going to have this meeting and if you want to come, you're welcome to come." The record shows that Thompson was represented by Robert F. Stevenson, associate stated clerk (07-17).

1975 Consultation—Louisville, Kentucky

The Consultation of Union Presbyteries, confidently labeled by the planning committee as "the first annual," gathered in Louisville, Kentucky, on May 5–7, 1975, at The Vineyard, a Roman Catholic retreat center. The three Kentucky union presbyteries and their two synods hosted the Consultation. The total number of participants attending this meeting (63) included 37 representatives of the nine union presbyteries and 18 from synods. Cooperating presbyteries had 2 representatives, and General Assembly resource persons accounted for 6.

Each union presbytery told "its story" and heard the stories described from the perspective of the General Assemblies and Synod. From these stories they were "to determine what commonality and differences exist among us" and "to sharpen the list of issues we are experiencing, both now and in the future." In this context, the Consultation proceeded "to develop jointly agreed upon strategies to resolve some of the issues facing us." The underlying theme was "to celebrate the fact of union presbyteries."[10]

It was a euphoric meeting. People who came from all over the country shared a common discovery. Charlie Stanford said he did not have any idea who they were, "but they came in there dealing with the same issues. . . . All of us were hurting with the same hurts." Being together in this setting unencumbered by "rules or regulations" was very cathartic. "We hardly did anything by vote anyway. Almost everything was consensual. . . . [I]t was just a great time" (07-17).

The design of the meeting allowed for issues and concerns to rise from within the gathering. Each judicatory team had been given an advance assignment to relate its positive experiences as a union presbytery and list the problems it faced in "living between two worlds." During the course of the meeting, participants would gather, sometimes in judicatory teams, sometimes in small mixed groups, and sometimes in plenary session. Data generated in one kind of group would be dealt with by the other two kinds of groupings, with the data continuously circulating until consensus was reached.[11]

Even though the Consultation was conducted in a laid-back atmosphere, the results were very detailed and specific. The record shows, for every issue that survived the circulating process, there were a concise statement of the problem; an objective for resolving it; a strategy for achieving the objective, with a time line and persons to implement and monitor the activity; targets of the strategy; and resources needed to carry it out.[12]

Advocacy for resolving the issues faced by union presbyteries was one major concern. The original Joint Committee on Constitutional Problems of Union Presbyteries (JCCPUP) was too narrowly defined and ineffective in getting at the complex issues. The Consultation recommended to the two General Assemblies that JCCPUP be terminated and a new committee/task force be formed with broader responsibilities for advocating for union presbyteries and increasing cooperation between the UPCUSA and PCUS, monitoring and routing issues and concerns, serving as an official channel of communication between the official structures and the Consultation, and making recommendations to the two General Assemblies' Judicial Commissions regarding constitutional and judicial problems.[13]

This recommendation was well received by both the General Assembly Mission Council (GAMC-UPCUSA) and the General Executive Board (GEB-PCUS) and created a critical link between the official structures and the Consultation throughout its life. One denomination set the unit up as a task force, the other one set it up as a committee. Ron Patton, from Kansas City (Union), became its first chairperson. He said when time came to give it a name, "we took both names. It's like we're not going to argue, let's do it." So it became known as the Joint Committee/Task Force on Union Presbyteries (JC/TF for short) (14-12). An Ad Interim Committee on Constitutional Problems of Union Presbyteries was retained to deal specifically with those types of issues.

Other issues that the strategies addressed included annual financial and membership statistical reports to the General Assemblies, which initially created almost useless data about union presbyteries; unclear definition of "equitable distribution" of mission funds; and confusing budget interpretation and generation of funds. There were discrepancies in personnel placement policies related to dossier distribution and methods of processing calls; differences in ordination philosophies, examination of ministers, and ordination vows. The strategies called for sharing the experience of union presbyteries that could inform the development of *The Plan for Reunion*, and for monitoring the results of the first consultation and its continuation.[14]

Communications and overtures growing out of these strategies were forwarded across the structures of both denominations. A special consultation was called for in October on "Interpreting One Mission." This fall Consultation was to deal with concerns of union presbyteries caused by the Major Mission Funding Campaign in the UPCUSA, issues related to dual mission interpretation training and promotional pieces, and special offerings.[15]

Ownership generated by and for the First Annual Consultation far exceeded the expectations of those who participated. The discovery that together they could find solutions to mutual problems renewed the participants' energy and creativity. A sense of joy from being a union presbytery along with others overrode the inconveniences and challenges of living between two worlds.

1976 Consultation—Louisville, Kentucky

The Second Annual Consultation also convened in Louisville, Kentucky. It was held March 1–3, 1976, at The Vineyard, hosted by Louisville Presbytery (Union). This time, however, the Synods of the Sun and Red River provided the planning committee. The Committee of Eight monitored the continuity between the consultations. The total number of participants attending this meeting (54) included 35 representatives of the nine union presbyteries and 12 from synods. Cooperating presbyteries had 1 representative and the General Assemblies had 6 resource persons.

If the first annual consultation were characterized in terms like "euphoric, harmonious, celebrative," then the terminology describing the second annual consultation would be more like "realistic, contentious, and celebrative." Some of the differences of style in the leadership and in the union presbyteries themselves began to be apparent. Participants coming to the Consultation for the first time brought new perspectives and approaches to the process. The interval between gatherings produced mixed results regarding assignments made, causing some minor discord.

According to the report made to the Committee of Eight by Charles Stanford of the first meeting of the Joint Committee/Task Force that met at The Vineyard in Louisville on November 17–18, 1975, the JC/TF got off to a shaky and uncertain start.[16] Bob Rea, on behalf of the GEB (PCUS), convened the meeting expecting a chairperson to be named by the group. Stanford said that "the meeting continued leaderless and directionless through its duration." However, he did report that Ron Patton from Kansas City (Union) was elected chairperson.[17]

The report indicated that the group "seemed to think that their purpose was to work for the passage of *The Plan for Reunion* and spent most of the time on that subject. No one seemed to know what their assignment was as spelled out in the 1975 COUP report. Only about half of the group had attended the Consultation, and there was some indication that they did not feel organically or psychically related to COUP. Stanford summarized his feeling about the start of JC/TF: "It's the Alka-Seltzer that accounts for the overall favorable tone of this report."[18]

As a result of this progress report made to the 1976 Consultation, the *Handbook for the Joint Consultation of Union Presbyteries and the Joint Committee/Task Force on Union Presbyteries* was produced. It clarified underlying assumptions that COUP was to describe "the role/functions/tasks" of the Joint Committee/Task Force and that the life of COUP was "permanent until rendered not needed by the systems." A covenant for three years was reached between "the nine [union] presbyteries, the cooperating presbyteries and synods and any non-union presbyteries within union congregations who care to unite in this agreement." The agreement specified that each judicatory send up to four persons including representatives to the JC/TF, with consideration to women and minorities, to the annual consultations. It also specified that COUP would utilize the JC/TF, which was created by the General Assemblies at COUP's request, as the vehicle for transmitting the concerns of the Consultation to the agencies of the churches.[19]

The rationale, composition, accountability/reporting, and functions of JC/TF were specified. It was made clear that JC/TF was accountable to the GAMC (UPCUSA), the GEB (PCUS) and all participants of COUP, through an annual report and distribution of its minutes. Composition of the planning committee for COUP and its administrative guidelines were also outlined.[20]

Some ambiguity about the official name of COUP existed at this point in that sometimes it was referred to initially as a Consultation *of* Union Presbyteries, at other times, as a Consultation *on* Union Presbyteries. This may have been incidental at this point, but it would be addressed officially when the *Handbook* came up for revision at a later meeting.

The Consultation recommitted itself to finding ways for a more equitable distribution of mission dollars; also for making the Major Mission Fund a joint effort of both denominations, providing clear promotional materials for joint special offerings, creating a common process for equipping candidates for ordination, developing one procedure for circulation and use of Minister and Church Information Forms, and coordinating overtures for General Assembly action. A resolution on COUP's commitment "to the accomplishment of church union at an early date" was prepared and plans were made to have caucuses of union presbytery commissioners to the General Assemblies as needed. Special attention was drawn to the work of the PCUS' Ad Interim Committee to Study the Role of Middle Governing Judicatories, urging that prior to any drastic action regarding synods, the PCUS share the data gathered by the UPCUSA.[21]

Consensus on the purpose for the existence of COUP remained absolutely strong. As specified in the new *Handbook*, Paul D. Young, convener for the 1977 Consultation to be held in Kansas City and Ron Patton, member of JC/TF from the host area, were named. To be named later were three members from the host area, one to serve as administrator. The Consultation was closed with readings from Isaiah and prayer led by R. Alan James, director of the UPCUSA/PCUS Joint Office of Worship.[22]

1977 Consultation—Kansas City, Kansas

The third annual meeting of COUP convened at the Breech Training Academy in Overland Park, Kansas, February 7–9, 1977. The routine of the Consultation settled into a pattern of worship, hearing reports of what had been accomplished since the last meeting of COUP, and processing new issues and concerns. Some progress had been made since last time in several areas but there was much to be ironed out in others. Common statistical reports were a perennial challenge.

The total number of participants attending this meeting (57) included 31 representatives of the nine union presbyteries and 8 from synods. Cooperating presbyteries had 3 representatives and General Assembly resource persons numbered 15.

In 1976 the PCUS experienced yet another restructure of its national agentry. The GEB arrangement with several executive heads did not function to meet the needs of the church, so a new structure was created known as the General Assembly Mission Board (GAMB) with a single director as its head. The internal disruption generated by this restructure extended to some of the cooperative attempts that originated with COUP. The response to the 1976 request that a common approach be developed between the denominations on funding the ongoing mission of the church had gotten no further than the "talking stage," but there appeared to be some openness on the GEB/GAMB and GAMC to continue the conversation.[23]

In response to General Assemblies' overtures growing out of last year's Consultation, the request for a joint office of vocations was referred to special study committees making this possibility three to four years away at this point. Other overtures related "to interchangeability for candidates" between both denominations were passed by the General Assemblies and sent down to presbyteries for ratification.[24]

Given the historical differences in the union presbyteries and their current relationships with their respective synods, it was concluded that no single definition of "equitable" could be reached. Each union presbytery was encouraged to arrive at its own definition of an "equitable distribution" of their per capita and mission dollars. This was not to be done as an exercise in isolation, but each union presbytery was asked "to arrive at its definition in concert with the synods and General Assemblies . . . and report this to the 1978 COUP."[25]

Progress was made in consolidating and reducing the number of special offerings union presbyteries were asked to receive. John M. Coffin, staff of the GAMB (PCUS), recalled, "[T]he union presbyteries said to us that we are going to take three offerings. Which one do you want us to drop?" (03-7). The selection process was more collegial than this suggested, so that eventually the Christmas/Joy Gift Offering and the One Great Hour of Sharing became the initial common special offerings.

If the Major Mission Fund Campaign was to work in union presbyteries, it was essential to include PCUS General Assembly and Synod projects in each presbytery's prospectus. The Consultation encouraged union presbyteries to negotiate with both General Assemblies and Synods for their prospectus to include projects in both denominations to create "a sense of wholeness" to their participation. Kansas City (Union) considered conducting "an experimental" union presbytery campaign in the 1977–78 Cycle, in preparation for other union presbyteries' participation in the 1978–1979 Cycle.[26]

New issues were identified and addressed. After a lengthy conversation with representatives of the Board of Pensions (UPCUSA) and the Board of Annuities and Relief (PCUS) about mobility between the Pension/Annuity plans, medical coverage, vacancy dues, the Consultation asked John Calvin (Union) to overture the General Assemblies "to request the Board of Annuities and Relief (PCUS) and the Board of Pensions (UPCUSA) . . . to bring their plans closer together with attention to: problems that prevent members moving back and forth, guaranteeing protection, and making sure the comity program works."[27]

The involvement of women in both denominations at all levels appeared on the agenda for the first time as a critical concern. It would remain as a major focus in subsequent consultations. Some issues identified at this Consultation needing attention were inventory of style of relationships of women's organizations to judicatories; joint work between United Presbyterian Women (UPW) and Women of the Church (WOC) in areas of Bible Study, Mission Year Book for Prayer, data banks, common statistical forms and funding; new models for women's task forces; duplicate but not parallel advocacy roles of the UPCUSA's Council on Women and the Church (COWAC) and the PCUS's Committee on Women's Concerns (COWC); monitoring of adherence to constitutional requirements for equal representation on decision-making bodies of the church. The planning committee was instructed to include Women's concerns on the agenda for 1978 COUP.[28]

In closing, COUP asked the planning committee also to recruit representatives from cooperating presbyteries for participation in COUP, to co-opt one of their number to serve on the planning committee, and to place their concerns on the agenda for 1978 COUP. An alert was sounded about the impact on denominational reunion in light of the trends in the vote on "A Declaration of Faith" and *The Book of Confessions*.[29] Another question for future consultations was: What shall union presbyteries do if the vote on reunion fails?

1978 Consultation—Washington, DC

The Fourth Annual Consultation convened in Washington, DC, on February 21–23, 1978, at the National 4-H Center, hosted by National Capital (Union), which provided the planning committee. Almost double the number of participants attended this meeting (101) as compared to each of the previous three meetings. The number of representatives of the union presbyteries (38) and synods (14) remained constant with past experience. The greatest increases came in cooperating presbyteries representatives (17) and General Assembly resource persons (32), both very significant shifts.[30]

One reason for these shifts was the growing recognition of the importance of the role played by COUP. As a result of a flurry of overtures "about how churches may work toward being reunited" sent from COUP last year, both General Assemblies in 1977 approved several recommendations whereby each Assembly urged its agencies to undertake cooperatively all work on a joint basis where constitutionally and legally possible; established a common site and date for Assembly meetings every other year, beginning in 1979; encouraged the formation of union presbyteries and union new church developments; encouraged joint meetings of synods, presbyteries, and councils in overlapping areas; and encouraged joint program events at all levels. COUP also had recommended that the PCUS GA reconsider recommendations for union synods.[31]

More specifically, the increases in the number of COUP participants came through invitations to persons related to the four major issues or concern areas called for on the agenda. Key recommendations emerged from the following concern areas.

In the area of representation, the councils of the nine union presbyteries were urged to conduct a two-year pilot project on that portion of *The Plan for Reunion* calling for a Committee on Representation and report its results.[32]

In the area of Women's Organizations, women in union presbyteries were asked to consider being called "Presbyterian Women." Other recommendations suggested use of common names of women's organizations at the national level be explored; creating joint Bible study programs, Mission Yearbooks, and interpretation pieces; dividing funds equitably by current presbytery formula; receiving three seasonal Special Offerings for both heritages; and advocating for women to answer God's call to serve in positions in the entire church.[33]

In the area of cooperation, COUP and JC/TF committed to being a resource to cooperating presbyteries considering union. Other recommendations included asking synod executives to convene a meeting and identify opportunities for cooperation and union; asking the GAMB and GAMC to consider doing joint churchwide planning and calling a joint national staff conference with union and cooperation as high priority agenda.[34]

In the area of social concerns, the GAMC and GAMB were asked to develop models that would assist middle courts and sessions to become more involved in social concerns and jointly publish public policy statements of the two Assemblies. Union presbyteries were urged to support the three-year Presbyterian IMPACT Food Policy Campaign.[35]

Progress reports regarding on-going projects indicated that several presbyteries agreed to do a pilot project to promote just two special offerings—Advent and Lenten; no agreement had been reached on definition of "equitable distribution" of funds; all union presbyteries were participating in the Major Mission Fund; a common statistical form, once declared as impossible to have, was now a reality; a parallel study of the two pension plans was available; the Joint Strategy Committee of the GAMC (UPCUSA) and GAMB (PCUS) had identified 132 areas of cooperative work underway with another 153 suggested for exploration; and there was no immediate prospect of combining the Vocation Agency (UPCUSA) and the Professional Development Office (PCUS).[36]

Bob Lamar and Randy Taylor, co-chairs of the Joint Committee on Union, reported that the third draft of *The Plan for Reunion* was ready for study. They also invited representatives of COUP to speak at the upcoming General Assemblies to tell the story of what the Union and Cooperating Presbyteries and Synods have achieved.[37]

Beth Wells commented years later that one of the things she remembered about the Washington Consultation she attended was "the incredible worship, which was dynamite. Joan Salmon-Campbell came to the Washington [Consultation] and did worship. And being from a Texas local church, that was impressive" (60-12). The theme was: "Towards Becoming One . . . that you may know what are the riches of His glorious inheritance."[38]

A letter of condolence was sent to Mrs. Joanne Thomas, widow of the Rev. Harold Thomas, who lost his life during the flood in Kansas City in September. Thomas was a participant and worship leader in the 1977 Consultation.[39]

1979 Consultation—Dallas, Texas

The Fifth Annual Consultation convened in Dallas, Texas, on February 20–22, 1979, at the Executive Inn, hosted by the Synods of Red River and Sun, which provided the planning committee. The number of participants who attended this meeting (112) was 11 more than the previous year, including 40 representatives of the union presbyteries and 20 from synods. Joining the union presbytery contingents were those from the less than two-month-old Grace (Union), the first of the second wave to be formed. The cooperating and other presbyteries had 37 representatives, an increase of 10. General Assembly resource persons had 15 in attendance, a decrease of 17.[40] Again these shifts reflected specific invitations extended.

One recommendation from the last consultation was that a representative from Louisville Seminary be invited to participate in this and subsequent consultations since it is "our only 'union' seminary." As a way of building bridges between the Seminary and COUP, Thomas L. Jones, vice-president of the Seminary, was invited to lead the worship throughout this Consultation and participate in its deliberations.[41]

A history of COUP and an inventory of its accomplishments were presented. The Joint Strategy Committee of the GAMC and GAMB, the in-house body for tracking referrals, reported that an extensive inventory of 239 areas of joint and cooperative work already existed. It cautioned that, since "the structures of the two denominations are not natural fits, consequently efforts at joint work are especially cumbersome." To create single structures would require major structural changes and "neither denomination seems to look kindly toward prospects called restructure." As an expression of its deepening partner relation with COUP, the committee called on COUP "to poke us if we're going too fast/slow. . . . Dream dreams with us beyond our immediate tasks."[42]

The nature of the Consultation, with new people coming to each consultation, underscored the necessity of adequate preparation and briefings in advance. Work groups topics, based on advanced data from the participants, were: staff roles in cooperation and union; moving and shaping the structures toward cooperation and union; creating and maintaining a political climate conducive to cooperation and union; opportunities for a new identity; and individual and institutional initiative to cooperation and union.[43]

COUP seemed to come of age and produced a prolific amount of work resulting in a ten-page report of its actions. Some of the new recommendations generated by this Consultation were: to provide time for the discussion of the role of staff in cooperating and union presbyteries at the winter 1979–1980 Joint National Staff Conference; to address the fears of minorities concerning reunion and to invite a representative of the Black Caucus to sit on the 1980 COUP planning committee; to address fears of employees who feel they may lose their positions due to reunion, not letting this possibility develop into overt opposition to reunion; and to foster relationships between presbyteries that are not overlapping as a witness of affirmation of union presbyteries.

COUP also went on record: to encourage synods to study the impact of new union presbyteries on institutional support; to urge the creation of joint offices of evangelism, church development and hunger programs; to brief GA moderatorial candidates concerning union presbyteries and invite Moderators to meetings of COUP; to enlist support of seminaries in articulating for their students the full reality of union presbyteries and prepare their graduates to labor in either denomination; and to revise the *Handbook*, including a change of the official name of COUP to "The Consultation on Union Presbyteries." A highlight of the event was a banquet celebrating life together as union presbyteries and honoring the Rev. Matthew Lynn for his work for the church and for union.[44]

Later a strategy was conceived to get a person from a union presbytery to run for General Assembly Moderator of both denominations in the same year "to symbolize a sense of unity to the society and the worldwide church of Jesus Christ pending such possible election." A draft resolution was prepared for presentation to both Assemblies asking "whether there are any legal reasons why one person could not moderate both General Assemblies the same year." This attempt was made to no avail (85-13). One summary comment made a penetrating observation about the success of COUP over its five-year life and "its growing influence on the life of American Presbyterianism." It also proclaimed, "for the sake both of our own faithfulness and our responsible participation in the PCUS and UPCUSA," the time had come for serious reflection in future consultations "on the role of COUP in the historical development of American Presbyterianism; on the theological definition of this kind of consultative/council process as a legitimate new feature in the working polity of our denominations, and on the future administrative and ecclesiastical relationships which will enable us to continue in responsibility toward this new thing into which God is leading us."[45] This challenge was never fully met in any thorough or systematic way.

1980 Consultation—Ft. Mitchell, Kentucky

The Sixth Annual Consultation met in Fort Mitchell, Kentucky (near Cincinnati), on March 5–7, 1980, at the Drawbridge Motor Inn, hosted by the Louisville Presbytery (Union) and a Kentucky-based planning committee. Harold Daniels, Marie Cross, and Bob Neal led worship for the Consultation, which included the sacrament of the Lord's Supper.[46]

The total number of participants attending this meeting (121) included 49 representatives of the union presbyteries and 18 from synods. The fledgling Indian Nations Presbytery became the next of the second wave of union presbyteries to send representatives to COUP.

Cooperating and other presbyteries had 36 representatives and General Assembly resource persons accounted for 18. The increase this year came from the ranks of union presbytery representatives.[47]

The usual round of "telling our stories" kicked off the opening plenary session that included a viewing of the new filmstrip, "I'm from a Union Presbytery." A banquet was held in the evening, at which time the two General Assembly Moderators, Dr. Albert Winn and Dr. Howard Rice, spoke informally about the hopes for, barriers to, and suggestions for advancing the cause of union. This was like preaching to the choir! A birthday cake was served in celebration of the 10th birthday of union presbyteries.[48]

Reports heard were on: JC/TF noting that its name was changed to Joint Committee on Union Presbyteries (JCUP); progress of a union presbytery stewardship event; the ever-present equitable funding issue; follow-up actions since the last COUP; two synods' experience in the union synod movement; and a survey on union related issues in the past and what that meant for projected union votes.[49]

Two work tracks were provided for participants. Track I was for representatives from cooperating or interested presbyteries to explore issues facing presbyteries contemplating becoming union. Out of this track came several recommendations: to provide people resources to assist these presbyteries; to develop a printed resource on how to strategize for and bring into being a Union Presbytery and all related issues; to include curriculum modules in the *Handbook* for this purpose.[50]

Participants from Track II, the regular track for raising and solving problems, created a long list of recommendations. Some of the more significant included appointing a strategy team to brainstorm detailed future scenarios for union presbyteries if union failed; affirming the recognition that both UPCUSA and PCUS are confessional churches, and that historically both churches have been equally stringent in requiring subscription to their confessional stances; and recognizing that the constitutions of both denominations have basically the same stance regarding ownership of church property.[51]

COUP also recommended support for an overture from the Synod of the Covenant to the UPCUSA General Assembly that asked the Joint Committee on Reunion "to observe a moratorium on writing reunion plans" in order to "allow time to develop and foster other forms of cooperation, partnership, relationship and communication." A similar proposal for a commissioner resolution to the PCUS Assembly was proposed.[52] Almost in contradiction to these recommendations, COUP sent the Joint Committee on Reunion another communication urging them to immediately enter into conversation with a "competent firm of relocations consultants" to guide the two denominations in selection of a common headquarters' site for either a reunited church or two separated ones engaged in common mission.[53]

COUP called for "a well designed program embodying practical approaches to racial reconciliation;" a staffing pattern that reflects a culturally pluralistic church; and well-defined affirmative action policies seeking persons who "understand theological concepts, good management principles and the willingness to implement the directives of these policy making boards."[54]

With each annual meeting of COUP, the issue list continued to proliferate, to the point that future design teams were instructed to set priorities, established by the *Handbook*, to guide decision-making proposals generated in the Consultation.[55] COUP asked JCUP to produce a printed piece that would "be of help in understanding union presbyteries and in guiding those who are interested in exploring this organizational option." The product of this assignment was the booklet *A Realization of Togetherness: An Introduction to Union Presbyteries.*[56]

1981 Consultation—Wichita, Kansas

The Seventh Annual Consultation met in Wichita, Kansas, on March 11–13, 1981 at the Holiday Inn Plaza, hosted by the Synods of Mid-America that provided the planning committee. It was noted that, in keeping with the action of the 1980 COUP requesting that all joint meetings be held in states that have ratified the Equal Rights Amendment, this meeting was being held in such a place.[57]

This consultation had the highest number of participants attending (144) of all the nine consultations held. The new Union Presbyteries of Tres Rios, New Covenant, and Mission swelled the ranks of representatives (51) from the fourteen union presbyteries. However, for the first and only time, the twenty[58] cooperating or interested non-union presbytery representatives (55) outnumbered the union presbyteries. This may have been due in part to the geographic proximity of the Northern and Southern Kansas presbyteries. Eight cooperating or interested synods had 13 representatives and there were 25 representatives from both General Assemblies' agencies and committees.[59] A newly instigated travel pool proved to be of great assistance in defraying costs.

Randy Taylor, co-chair of the Joint Committee on Reunion, reported the committee intention to present *The Plan for Reunion* to the 1982 Assemblies and asked COUP to provide major support for it. Bob Frere reported on the "to-be-established" group named "Friends for Reunion" that will develop a national network to coordinate reunion efforts. COUP endorsed this and urged its presbyteries and synods to become involved.[60]

Sam Lanham reported on the PCUS Permanent Judicial Commission's advisory opinion, in response to a Reference from the Synod of the Mid-South, that the Synod was without the constitutional authority to receive Mackinac Presbytery as a union presbytery unilaterally without benefit of an overlapping PCUS presbytery. Material was distributed regarding the Mackinac proposal presented by William G. McAtee (pro) and Albert H. Freundt, Jr. (con) at the PJC hearing on November 20, 1980.[61]

Charles Hollingsworth outlined a strategy to oppose the PJC's opinion at the upcoming PCUS Assembly. Charles Kriner noted that there were seven presbyteries presently considering becoming union presbyteries unilaterally in the category of "pairs without partners." COUP encouraged them to proceed with such plans. The Presbytery of Southern Kansas announced its plans to vote on the day following COUP, March 14, declaring its intent to become a union presbytery.[62]

The women's concerns workshop focused on the need of preparing guidelines for becoming a union presbyterial, and a handbook of operations once established.[63] The evaluation indicated some unhappiness with the fact that so much time was spent on the union presbyterial issue that not enough time was given to exploring solutions to problems of national cooperation.[64] This quandary would carry over to the next consultation.

Issues related to Higher Education were presented generating a series of recommendations. The Association of Presbyterian Colleges (PCUS) and the Presbyterian College Union (UPCUSA) were encouraged to begin cooperative projects to build relationships that would lead to a merger of the two organizations. Colleges in areas where the denominations overlapped that were related to only one denomination were encouraged to seek a covenant relationship with the other denomination in preparation for eventual reunion. Also early consultation with the UPCUSA was essential for any PCUS churchwide higher education and/or capital funds campaign contemplated for the late 1980s so that projects for union presbyteries could be provided.[65]

Worship again was a critical ingredient, this time in the form of a musical worship service presented by the "Angels" of the First Presbyterian Church of Wichita. At another point the consultation was "treated to a concert of rousing gospel songs sung by a mixed chorus led by the T. S. (Texan-Scot) Troubadour." The annual banquet was keynoted by an address from the Moderator of the UPCUSA General Assembly, Charles Hammond. PCUS Moderator David Stitt was invited, but was unable to attend because of a conflict in schedule.[66]

Ken Locke, retiring chair of JCUP, announced that Beth Wells was elected as the new chair.[67] The *Handbook* was revised one final time and a new cover heading was added titled "The Story of the Union Presbytery Movement."[68]

1982 Consultation—Washington, DC

The Eighth Annual Consultation returned to Washington, DC, on February 1–3, 1982, at the National 4-H Center, hosted by National Capital (Union), which provided the planning committee. This was the second largest gathering (128) in COUP's short history. Southwest Florida brought the total of union presbyteries to fifteen with 56 representatives present. Sixteen cooperating or interested non-union presbyteries had representatives (24) who joined the representatives (17) of nine cooperating or interested synods; the representatives (22) from both General Assemblies' agencies and committees; and other individuals (9), including four members of the church press, to round out the roster.[69]

Worship was the centerpiece of the Consultation led by the folk and dance choirs of the Oaklands United Presbyterian Church of Laurel, Maryland. Opening worship included the sacrament of the Lord's Supper. A creative puppet presentation interpreted the issues and concerns before COUP.[70]

The Joint Committee on Reunion was prepared to present *The Plan for Reunion* at the concurrent meetings of the General Assemblies in Houston, and send *The Plan* to the presbyteries for ratification during the fall of 1982 and spring of 1983. This made reunion reach a crescendo on the agenda for COUP. Bob Lamar, co-chair of the Joint Committee, and Jim Andrews, PCUS Stated Clerk (in the absence of Dottie Barnard, PCUS Moderator), presented in an after-dinner dialogue the State of the Mission of each denomination as the decisive votes in the presbyteries on reunion drew near.[71]

A spirited panel discussion of very divergent views on strategies for reunion consumed a morning session. The panelists were: Tom Jones (National Capital), Bill Fogleman (Red River/Sun Synod Executive), Doug Harper (Covenant Fellowship of Presbyterians, New Covenant), Bill McLean (Arkansas executive), Harry Hassall (editor, *Open Letter*), and Randy Taylor (co-chair, Joint Committee). Each led a small group on effective strategies and reported findings back to the plenary session. Bob Davidson, UPCUSA General Assembly Moderator, shared his perspective on issues and concerns, including reunion, over a lunch break.[72]

G. Daniel Little, executive director of the GAMC (UPCUSA), in response to allegations that the staff at 475 Riverside Drive represented "an organized center within the United Presbyterian Church of opposition to *The Plan for Reunion* and to the prospect of a reunited church," made a clear statement to the contrary to COUP. Little later

---

affirmed that the GAMC was providing "an open, orderly and responsible process . . . for examining the issues involved in preparing for reunion" as "a healthy entry into the new context which will be created by reunion."[73]

The most emotionally laden moment came during a panel presentation on the reunion concerns of women and blacks. The panel was seated in the round with COUP seated and standing in an outer ring. The panel consisted mainly of newcomers to COUP. It was moderated by Carroll Jenkins (Synod of the Piedmont executive) with Margee Adams (ordained clergy of National Capital and chair of UPCUSA's organization of Church Employed Women), Alice Smith (Synod of the Virginias and vice-chair of PCUS's Committee on Women's Concerns), Laura Kerns (Catawba Presbytery) and George Wilson (Southern Virginias Presbytery) participating.[74]

Women's concerns had been bubbling throughout several COUP meetings, but the differences and gulfs between UPW and WOC, between COWAC and COWC, were dramatically articulated in a new public way. These differences and gulfs would linger long after reunion.

COUP experienced the first concentrated pained black concerns about reunion. Highlighted concerns were: how to hold on to their power base in the new church; how to develop black leadership and more articulate spokespersons for minorities; what does fair representation mean when presbytery and synod boundaries are realigned; what will result in the shift from strong synod structures to strong presbytery structures; will large congregations control presbyteries through larger numbers of commissioners; how to get black and white congregations involved in effective ministry in emerging urban areas; and how to address cultural diversity.[75] This laundry list of ethnic minority concerns set a basic agenda that would last well into the twenty-first century.

The rest of the Consultation focused on various reunion issues related to structures, mission, and funding in the reunited church. Emphasis was placed on replicating in the reunited church, where possible, the "horizontal relationships—'rocking chair' decision making—consensus of values" that have been the hallmark of COUP.[76]

1983 Consultation—San Antonio, Texas

The Ninth and final Annual Consultation was held in San Antonio, Texas, on March 12–14, 1983, at the Menger Hotel, Alamo Plaza, hosted by the Texas Presbyteries, which provided the planning committee. Ninety-one representatives attended this historic event. Eastern Oklahoma (Union) and North Alabama (Union) brought the total of union presbyteries to seventeen with 55 representatives present.

Cooperating or interested non-union presbytery representatives (7) joined the representatives (16) of the cooperating or interested synods and the representatives (13) from both General Assemblies. Only representatives from St. Augustine Presbytery were absent.[77]

The spirit of the Consultation was festive. Reunion appeared to be a reality based on voting trends in the presbyteries. COUP early on recessed to watch a parade. The Minutes of the meeting said "that the City of San Antonio had staged such a celebration in honor of Presbyterian reunion, although the City claimed it was St. Patrick's Day."[78] Some wag wondered if there was any symbolism related to COUP's final meeting at the Menger Hotel, "across the alley from the Alamo," where Teddy Roosevelt had once used the hotel as a recruiting office for his trip to San Juan Hill!

Worship was sprinkled throughout the time together, with a bilingual flavor provided by singing some songs in Spanish. There was a feeling that something special was about to end and something special was about to begin. To make the most of this shift, a reflection paper was drafted for the Consultation to consider titled "Major Learnings from the Union Presbytery Experience Which May Be Applicable to Denominational Reunion." Considerable attention was given to areas of hurts caused by reunion with a critical list of suggestions for healing in the church.[79] A group created a special set of study questions to accompany the reflection paper that was circulated in advance to COUP and JCUP for responses. The results were presented to the Consultation under the title of "Administrative Implications of Reunion" ("A.I.R.") for discussion and later sent to the Joint Committee on Reunion.[80] The details of these and other learnings will be addressed in a later chapter.

COUP expressed itself regarding the new Special Synod and Presbytery Boundaries Committee, advising on how it should be set up and how pastorally to deal with issues it would face. It noted that *The Plan for Reunion* contained no job description for the new Stated Clerk. COUP expressed hope that the style and duties of that office would not follow the old patterns of both former denominations. It was asked that Kenneth R. Locke prepare a written history of union presbyteries and that it be sent with all records of COUP to the Historical Foundation in Montreat.[81]

Charles Hollingsworth, Chair of JCUP, recommended that any leftover COUP funds be given to Friends for Reunion for its advocacy work, and then if there were a balance, it be turned over to the Office of the General Assembly to assist in transition expenses. The report suggested that Union Presbyteries drop the use of the word "union" in their names as the new denomination comes into existence. JCUP finally recommended that this be its last meeting.[82]

The Union Presbytery Movement, in a few rare moments, flirted with institutionalizing COUP and its political successes as an "organized instrument." In its finest hour it resisted yielding to the old polity of win-lose and the vested interests that would do otherwise. It remained committed to the needs and objectives for which it was created and those were now met. Above all, it knew when to cease and desist, which is rare among established church organizations. The question was put to the Consultation: "Will there be issues in the future which are unique to the present 17 union presbyteries and which might require some continuation of COUP or a similar organization?"[83]

Though a few had second thoughts in later years, at this time the small groups roundly "expressed desires to celebrate the COUP experience and to recognize the ingenius [sic] contributions of COUP, especially the consensus style." COUP took no action to meet in 1984. "It is therefore to be assumed that COUP is disbanded with dignity, thanksgiving, and celebration at the close of this meeting." With a declaration by Mac Hart that COUP had finished its business, William K. Hedrick closed with prayer and led a hymn, and this extraordinary part of the life and times of union presbyteries was over.[84]

Life between two worlds, in the day-to-day experience of a union presbytery itself or the corporate existence within COUP, contained a myriad of challenges, but the rewards for finding a new way to be church far exceeded the thorny side of such a dichotomy. Winners almost completely overshadowed the losers in this life between two worlds. The full consequences of the contributions of these extraordinary events would be a long time coming. The contributions were more evident than the flaws, but ghosts of Stamford Bridge and Hastings *et al.* had not been completely exorcised.

Notes

1. William Jefferson Clinton, *My Life* (New York: Alfred A. Knopf, 2004), pp. 77–78.

2. *Notes*, Consultation on Union Presbyteries, St. Louis, MO, January 8, 1971, p. 1 (in personal collection of William G. McAtee).

3. Ibid., p. 10.

4. *A Summary*, The St. Louis Consultation, September 27–29, 1973 (in personal collection of William G. McAtee).

5. *Minutes* of Transylvania (Union), Report of the General Council, September 6, 1973.

6. *Report*, PCUS/UPCUSA CONSULTATION (Synod of the Covenant—Synod of the Mid-South), Louisville Theological Seminary, December 6–7, 1973, p. 1 (in personal collection of William G. McAtee).

7. Ibid., pp. 1–4.

8. Letter from William G. McAtee to Lawrence W. McMaster, December 9, 1973 (in personal collection of William G. McAtee).

9. Letter from Lawrence W. McMaster to William G. McAtee, December 26, 1973 (in personal collection of William G. McAtee).

10. *Report*, Consultation on Union Presbyteries, The Vineyard, Louisville, KY, May 5–7, 1975, p. 1 (in personal collection of William G. McAtee).

11. Ibid., p. 7.

12. Ibid., p. 10.

13. Ibid., pp. 11–12.

14. *Report*, Consultation on Union Presbyteries, May 5–7, 1975.

15. *Report*, Special Union Presbytery Consultation, "Interpreting One Mission," Thompson Center, St. Louis, MO, October 21–22, 1975 (in personal collection of William G. McAtee).

16. *Report* to the Committee of Eight, General Assemblies' Joint Special Committee/Task Force on Problems of Union Presbyteries, The Vineyard, Louisville, KY, November 17–18, 1975, in personal collection of William G. McAtee. First Members of JC/TF: Dr. Fitzhugh Spragins, Arkansas (Union); *Rev. Wayne Porter, John Calvin (Union); Rev. Ron Patton, Kansas City (Union); *Rev. Jack McLaney, Louisville (Union); *Rev. Ken Locke, Missouri Union; Rev. Ed White, National Capital (Union); Rev. Charles Kriner, Palo Duro (Union); *Rev. David Rule, Transylvania (Union); *Ellen Pierce, Western Kentucky (Union); Rev. David Lowry, UPCUSA General Assembly Office; Rev. Richard Thomas, UPCUSA GAMC; Rev. Jim Andrews, PCUS General Assembly Office; *Rev. Bob Rea, PCUS GEB. Others present: Rev. Flynn Long, PCUS General Assembly Office; *Rev. Charles Stanford, Committee of Eight; *Rev. Paul Long, convener of 1976 COUP; *Rev. Smiley Johnson—Paul Young's Pilot. (*Indicates participant attended 1975 COUP.)

17. Ibid.

18. Ibid.

19. *Handbook for the Joint Consultation of Union Presbyteries and the Joint Committee/Task Force on Union Presbyteries* (in personal collection of William G. McAtee).

20. Ibid.

21. *Minutes* of Joint Consultation of Union Presbyteries, The Vineyard, Louisville, KY, March 1–3, 1976, Attachment: "Commitments and Assignments Growing Out of the 1976 Joint Consultation on Union Presbyteries," pp. 1–5 (in personal collection of William G. McAtee).

22. *Minutes* of Joint Consultation of Union Presbyteries, March 1–3, 1976, p. 2.

23. *Report* of Consultation of Union Presbyteries, Breech Training Academy, Overland Park, KS, February 7–9, 1977, p. 1 (in personal collection of William G. McAtee).

24. Ibid.

25. Ibid., p. 7.

26. *Report* of Consultation of Union Presbyteries, February 7–9, 1977, p. 7.

27. Ibid., p. 4.

28. Ibid., p. 5.

29. Coalter, Mulder, and Weeks, eds., *The Re-Forming Tradition*, p. 134. The 1976 PCUS approved both "A Declaration of Faith" and the *Book of Confessions*, but both failed to gain the required two-thirds majority ratification by the presbyteries in the spring of 1977 after COUP had met.

30. *Report* of Consultation on Union Presbyteries, National 4-H Center, Washington, DC, February 21–23, 1978, in personal collection of William G. McAtee.

31. *Minutes* of the One-Hundred-Seventeenth General Assembly (PCUS), 1977, p. 173.

32. *Report* of Consultation on Union Presbyteries, February 21–23, 1978.

33. Ibid.

34. Ibid.

35. Ibid. IMPACT was "an interreligious grassroots political action network for which U.S. food policy is a special priority and whose members are expected to communicate with their congressional representatives at least 3 times a year." Encouragement for PCUS support of IMPACT was included in a policy paper, "An Appeal to the President and the Congress of the U.S. for a Morally Responsible U.S. Food Policy," adopted by the One-Hundred-Seventeenth General Assembly, Nashville, TN, June 18–24, 1977, see *Minutes*, p. 185.

36. Ibid.

37. Ibid.

38. *Report* of Consultation on Union Presbyteries, February 21–23, 1978.

39. Ibid.

40. *Report* of Consultation on Union Presbyteries, The Executive Inn, Dallas, TX, February 20–22, 1979, in personal collection of William G. McAtee.

41. Ibid.

42. Ibid., Attachment: Joint Strategy Committee Report.

43. Ibid., p. 1.

44. Ibid., pp. 1–10.

45. *Report* of Consultation on Union Presbyteries, February 20–22, 1979, Reports of Issue Groups, p. 11.

46. *Minutes* of Consultation on Union Presbyteries, Drawbridge Motor Inn, Ft. Mitchell, KY, March 5–7, 1980, in personal collection of William G. McAtee.

47. Ibid., Roster.

48. Ibid., p. 1.

49. Ibid.

50. Ibid. p. 2f.

51. Ibid., pp. 8–9.

52. Ibid., pp. 5–6.

53. Ibid., p. 10.

54. Ibid., pp. 12–13.

55.   Ibid., p. 17.

56. *A Realization of Togetherness: An Introduction to Union Presbyteries*, in personal collection of William G. McAtee. It was initially prepared in 1980 by David E. Rule, John A. McLaney, and Flynn V. Long, Jr., and provided a useful what-is and how-to-become manual for union presbyteries. It gave a brief history of union presbyteries; how they became a possibility; what were the advantages, disadvantages, and problems to be faced; how to proceed to form one; what is the constitutional pathway, and what can other presbyteries learn from Mackinac. It still is relevant to anyone contemplating becoming a union presbytery in the twenty-first century.

57. Kenneth R. Locke, Letter of Invitation, February 27, 1981, Attachment H, in personal collection of William G. McAtee.

58. *Minutes* of Consultation on Union Presbyteries, Holiday Inn Plaza, Wichita, KS, March 11–13, 1981, p. 1, and List of Registrants, in personal collection of William G. McAtee. Cooperating or interested presbyteries represented: Southeast Missouri, Elijah Parish Lovejoy, Northern Kansas, Southern Kansas, Greenbrier, Grafton and Parkersburg, Muskingum Valley, Cincinnati, Mackinac, North Alabama, Middle Tennessee, Eastern Oklahoma, South Louisiana, Western New York, Norfolk, Southern Florida, Florida, West Florida, Westminster, and Everglades.

59. Ibid., p. 1, and List of Registrants.

60. Ibid., pp. 2–3.

61. Ibid., p. 3.

62. Ibid.

63. Ibid., p. 4.

64. Ibid., Evaluation, p. 1.

65. Ibid., p. 5.

66. Ibid., pp. 1–2.

67. Ibid., p. 1.

68. Ibid., p. 6.

69. *Minutes* of Consultation on Union Presbyteries, National 4-H Center, Washington, DC, February 1–3, 1982, p. 1, and List of Registrants, in personal collection of William G. McAtee.

70. Ibid., p. 1.

71. Ibid.

72. Ibid.

73. Letter from G. Dan Little to synod and presbytery executives, to exempt staff at 475 Riverside Drive, and to a number of selected individuals, February 12, 1982, in personal collection of William G. McAtee.

74. *Minutes* of Consultation on Union Presbyteries, February 1–3, 1982, p. 1.

75. Ibid., pp. 4–5.

76. *Minutes* of Consultation on Union Presbyteries, Menger Hotel, Alamo Plaza, San Antonio, TX, March 12–14, p. 1, and List of Registrants, in personal collection of William G. McAtee.

77. Ibid., p. 1.

78. Ibid., notes from various discussion groups of COUP, "Hurts and Healing."

79. Ibid.

80. Ibid.

81. Ibid., JCUP Report to Consultation.

82. *Minutes* of Consultation on Union Presbyteries, March 12–14, p. 1.

83. Ibid.

84. Ibid.

Part III: Recouping Dreams
Chapter 13
All Presbyteries, Union Presbyteries

Well, maybe another way . . . of putting it, is that, in those days we still believed in a world that could be put right, and we're not so sure, this generation is not so sure of that, and maybe doesn't dare hope for that, just hopes it can get its issue straightened out. . . . I don't know what we thought Presbyterian Reunion was going to achieve but it was sort of like the kingdom would be here.

—A. M. "Mac" Hart (50-24)

With the dawn of the decade of the 1980s, the contagious excitement and imagination of union presbyteries and the extraordinary run of consultations helped bring the two dominant Presbyterian denominations to the threshold of reunion that would make all presbyteries *de facto* union presbyteries approximating the coming of the kingdom in the minds of some. The last wave of union presbyteries was established, although there was interest in forming union presbyteries unilaterally in non-overlapping areas. COUP accelerated its focus on restoring the Unity of the Church by advocating for denominational reunion, a close but by no means foregone conclusion. As in any case of radical change, threats, fears, reservations, and oppositions were a real presence. These were not completely insurmountable obstacles, but attention had to be given them if reunion was to become a reality. In some cases, persons who initially opposed reunion changed their position and ended up supporting it. Others opposed it to the end, but finally had no choice but live with it. The story of the Union Presbytery Movement would not be complete without a recitation of some of the more pertinent incidents related to these obstacles.

Unilateral Union Presbyteries

The Union Presbytery Movement, in its creative enthusiasm, was perceived by some as inadvertently posing potential threats to denominational reunion. These centered on strategies to create new union presbyteries in non-overlapping areas. The most famous example of such an attempt was by Mackinac Presbytery in the Upper Peninsula of Michigan. Being a member of the Synod of Covenant (UPCUSA) placed Mackinac in relationship to the Synod of the Mid-South (PCUS) through the three union presbyteries in Kentucky that were members of both Synods. On one occasion the two Synods held a concurrent meeting that involved pairing up a non-union presbytery from one Synod with a non-union counterpart in the other Synod.

Mackinac (UPCUSA) and Mobile (PCUS) found each other. They discovered they were more similar than different. They were similar in size and demographics; were geographically on the edge of their respective denominations and states; shared seasonal church members who wintered in the South and summered up North; and had pastors who in the past had served in the other presbytery.

Ken McCall, executive of Mackinac Presbytery, remembered that the phrase "Mackinac to Mobile" emerged in the conversation; it was not a plan, it was not even a slogan. It came up in the context of thinking, "what would happen someday if the Synod ended up being from Mackinac to Mobile kind of thing?" For McCall it was just a way of opening the door through which to walk and develop a relationship with Mobile Presbytery. McCall felt like the people in Mobile were extremely cautious about it at that point. No patterns existed for developing this kind of relationship between Northern and Southern presbyteries. What came out of it were joint work camps for young people and pastors' exchanges, both of which were successful in building relationships (66-11).

William H. "Billy" McLean, executive of Mobile Presbytery, recalled that the folk from Mackinac wanted to establish "sort of a partnership-sister presbytery" relationship. It was never anything like the partner relationship Mobile already had with the Yucatan Presbytery in Mexico. McLean said that they were closer to the Yucatan and it was probably cheaper to go there than it was to go to Mackinac. McLean appreciated the fact that Mackinac "was interested in reaching out to us" and was willing to participate (97-8).

From this conversation and these events arose the myth that Mackinac and Mobile were trying to form a union presbytery; that was far from the truth. The myth was perpetuated by union presbytery advocates far removed from either of these two presbyteries. According to McLean, Mobile was much more oriented along the Gulf Coast, toward Tallahassee or to New Orleans, than even north inland into Alabama, from which it was politically separated. When talking about new presbytery boundaries, it made more sense to form a coastal presbytery with West Florida and South Mississippi (97-9).

McCall said Mackinac was more interested in forming a union presbytery without a partner, or unilaterally, because it understood its constitutional definition as, "basically a union presbytery was simply the name of a presbytery that itself was part of two separate denominations." This interpretation was similar to a union congregation that belonged to two denominations. So it seemed simple enough that if Mackinac were allowed to become a part of the PCUS, it would be a union presbytery. Mackinac proceeded in that direction (66-12).

At the request of COUP in 1977, the UPCUSA General Assembly acted to "encourage the presbyteries to consider the formation of union presbyteries wherever possible."[1] The PCUS General Assembly took similar action.[2] In order to make this happen where Mackinac was concerned, a Commissioner's Resolution was presented in 1979 requesting the PCUS Assembly "to establish a new synod in the states of Michigan and Ohio, which synod's presbyteries would be union presbyteries of the Synod of the Covenant of the UPCUSA." The Commissioner explained that this was an effort to "test the desirability of cooperation and union." The rationale also was based on the "high mobility of increasing numbers of Presbyterian pastors and members between union and non-union presbyteries in both denominations and their desire to keep their former ties."[3] It was referred to the Ad Interim Committee on the Constitutional Problems of Union Presbyteries.

Two amendments of note to the *Book of Church Order* that had relevance to the union issues were passed by the 1979 PCUS Assembly and sent to the presbyteries for advice and consent. One was an amendment that would make the creation of union synods constitutionally possible. This amendment had been defeated in 1969–1970 when the union presbyteries amendment passed. By March 1980 it had failed a second time by not obtaining a simple majority.[4]

The other amendment had to do with "proportional value or weighted voting" when voting on constitutional changes, a method that determined the number of votes a presbytery got, based on its membership. The existing unit system was closer to the Senate model and weighted voting more closely resembled the House of Representatives model. The 1978 PCUS Assembly had sent it to the presbyteries for advice and consent, but it failed to receive a simple majority. The 1979 Assembly sent it back a second time to the presbyteries, this time requiring a three-fourths vote. Only 15 votes were needed to defeat it and by January of 1980 this amendment had already received 24 no votes. It is interesting to note that at the same time the presbyteries were defeating "weighted voting" they were passing the amendment admitting baptized children to the Lord's Table.[5]

In 1980 the Ad Interim Committee on Constitutional Problems of Union Presbyteries recommended that the PCUS Assembly decline to establish a "new Synod of Ohio and Michigan" but went on to say that it "does not perceive any Constitutional barriers to the organization of additional union Presbyteries." The Commission concurred with the arguments that "Union Presbyteries are a grassroots movement; such expression of the unity of Christ's Church produces positive results in the discipleship of persons and the mission of the court; interest in Union Presbyteries is growing." It encouraged the formation of union presbyteries so that when a sufficient number have been organized, "they may then request organization as a Synod."[6]

While waiting for this decision from the PCUS General Assembly on the proposed new synod in Michigan and Ohio, Mackinac Presbytery voted on December 7, 1979, to petition the Synod of the Covenant (UPCUSA) and the Synod of Mid-South (PCUS) to organize it as a union presbytery in conformity with the requirements of both Constitutions.[7] The Synod of the Covenant approved the Mackinac Plan of Union in June 1980.

The Synod of the Mid-South received the proposed plan as a communication in September 1980 from Mackinac, and by way of Reference to the General Assembly, sought a ruling on its constitutionality. Mid-South deferred action on the proposed plan pending the Assembly's answer to this Reference. The Synod's moderator appointed Albert H. Freundt, Jr., and William G. McAtee to represent the Synod in the hearing before the Permanent Judicial Commission on November 20, 1980, in Atlanta. Freundt filed an addendum to the Reference from Synod opposing the Mackinac Plan and McAtee filed an addendum and a supplemental brief in favor of the Plan. Being put in this formal adversarial position placed an inordinate amount of stress on the personal relationship between the two presenters. However, evidences of mutual respect at the time indicated that neither one hoped their relationship would be hurt over this controversial win-lose matter. Over subsequent years this hope was fulfilled.[8]

Also included in the material presented to the Commission was an overture to the General Assembly relative to the Mackinac Plan adopted by the Presbytery of Middle Tennessee, on July 15, 1980. It called for an amendment to the *Book of Church Order* that explicitly allowed a Union Presbytery to be created from a single Presbytery (Classis) of one Reformed body by its Synod, if the two or more Synods which would then have jurisdictional authority were to give their concurrence.[9]

Freundt, in his presentation before the Commission, did not question whether union presbyteries were constitutional; the desirability of Mackinac as a constituent presbytery of the Synod of the Mid-South; or the geographical consideration as primary. The primary question for Freundt was whether the PCUS Constitution has a provision for a new, unique, and unanticipated kind of union presbytery—one which belongs to another denomination and is without any desire or intention of uniting with an existing PCUS presbytery. He contended that no such provision existed in the Constitution, a contention that would eventually be sustained by the Permanent Judicial Commission. He preferred a constitutional amendment, such as the one suggested in the Middle Tennessee overture, to rectify this situation. Freundt also was deeply concerned that a new precedent might be set whereby a number of presbyteries would be established having no direct historic ties with the PCUS, but would use this only as an opportunity to vote for denominational organic union.[10]

McAtee maintained that the Mackinac Plan was constitutional, holding: there were no constitutional provisions that exclusively restricted the formation of union presbyteries in the manner suggested; no provision mandated that Synods be made up of at least three geographically contiguous presbyteries; the Plan was consistent in spirit with *BCO* 32 both in its constitutionality and missional purposiveness; a logical constitutional interpretation existed for allowing a synod to extend its jurisdiction to a presbytery belonging solely to the jurisdiction of another Presbyterian denomination; these constitutional propositions in no way as being construed to negate the Synod of the Mid-South's sole prerogative to determine the wisdom of approving or not approving the Mackinac Plan.[11]

Incidentally in his presentation before the Commission, McAtee countered the geographical concern about Mackinac not being contiguous to the other presbyteries in the Synod of the Mid-South, by pointing out in the original list of presbyteries constituting the First General Assembly in Augusta, Georgia, in 1861, included the Presbytery of Hanchow (Hangchow), China, that was attached to the Synod of Kentucky. It was later removed, not because of geography, but because the General Assembly did not have the power to establish presbyteries.[12]

The two opposing positions presented before the PJC were classic examples of the very different ways each of the two Presbyterian denominations interpreted the Constitution of the church. Freundt's constitutional position was in keeping with the PCUS tradition: if it is explicitly permitted, you can do it; if not, you cannot. That may have explained the outcome of the PJC's opinion. McAtee held to a position that was more akin to the traditional UPCUSA approach, if it is not explicitly prohibited, you can do it. These were two very different styles, both of which began to become operative in union presbyteries. This bifurcated style of interpretation may have given rise to the convenient adage of choice frequently heard circulating around union presbyteries, "It's easier to ask for forgiveness, than it is for permission."

The profound difference in these two views grew out of the history of the two churches in the context of the country's history during and following the Civil War, a war that took place in a time of great national expansion from which the South was isolated. While the war raged mainly in the South, the main part of the nation continued its expansionist activities—construction of transcontinental railroads, reception of immigrants and the like—not putting all its energies into the war, at one point almost losing it because of this. James E.

Andrews, reflecting on this expansionist history, pointed out how it dramatically affected the constitutional life of both denominations (02-6).

What ecclesiastically emerged in the Northern Church was what Andrews called the Lane-McCormick Seminary pragmatic view of the Constitution, an attitude that said, "[I]f we haven't tried it, let's do it." This was later developed into the Swearagin Commission Report of the 1920s, which said in effect "that all powers which are not specified in the Constitution devolve upon the presbytery and shall be exercised as presbytery wishes pending amendment by the Assembly or judicial definition." Andrews commented that it was "exactly what the U.S. Constitution says about all powers [devolving] upon the states if they are not specified someplace else" (02-6). Great debates occurred, both secularly and ecclesiastically, over the years as to what was specific and what was devolved.

Andrews went on to say that the PCUS had a much more theologically defined understanding that "[T]he powers of all governing bodies are the same as they are defined by the Constitution, which means that if you don't have constitutional authority to do something, you can't do it." These two very different styles lingered well into denominational reunion. Andrews observed, "the major impact was not seen until 1983 when we went into a reunion Constitution where the Southern view [PCUS] was expressed and the UPs [Northern] felt that they had been run over by a freight train . . . things that they had done naturally were suddenly unconstitutional. And it is only within the last couple of years [in the 1990s] that they've reversed that" (02-7).

Stringent opposition to and support for the Mackinac Plan existed well beyond the confines of the deliberation of the PJC. Harry S. Hassall, executive editor of *The Open Letter*, had written in its February 1980 edition that "the strange notion of having Michigan UP[CUSA] presbyteries declare themselves to be union presbyteries" was what he called "the divisive road" to union. He felt that this approach avoided "the long, slow process of the Joint Committee on Reunion and shortcuts and powers its way along toward union, piecemeal and in a *de facto* fashion." He said "they cannot wait for the slow, legal process of obtaining forthrightly the constitutional majorities of the whole church," a process he predicted would happen no sooner than the early 1990s.[13]

M. Douglas Harper, Jr., who would oppose the formation of his own Presbytery of New Covenant (Union), labeled the Mackinac Plan as "The Mackinac Maneuver" in the March 1980 edition of *The Open Letter*. He initially thought it was a "tongue-in-cheek" proposal, but came to maintain that it was clearly unconstitutional and was a disservice to Friends of Reunion. He did not deny that such an effort could "testify to the unity of Presbyterianism." It seemed more likely "to add to the *de facto* or backdoor unions, and to add a presbytery to the voting list of the PCUS presbyteries when the time comes to vote on denominational reunion." Harper felt that "The Mackinac Maneuver" would be seen "as one more piece of evidence that those who will pay any price for union are still at work in the PCUS."[14]

Harper recalled years later that he "at that point was certainly, if not controlled [by], heavily, heavily influenced by what I saw going on in denominational union." He felt that "anything that threw us off course, I thought was bad news. I wanted us to move on for that [reunion] vote. I thought we had the makings of something that would fly, and I wanted us to go on for it" (57-19).

Southern Kansas Presbytery (UPCUSA) voted on March 14, 1981, declaring its intention to become a union presbytery unilaterally.[15]

1981 PCUS General Assembly (Houston)

The opinion rendered by the Permanent Judicial Commission (PCUS) to the 1981 General Assembly regarding the Reference from the Synod of the Mid-South was that the "Synod should be advised that it is without constitutional authority to receive Mackinac in the manner proposed." There was no evidence of "authority for the reception of a union presbytery prior to the adoption of Chapter 32 [Of Union Presbyteries (Classes)] of the *Book of Church Order*." The opinion went on to declare, "[W]e find no express power from which we can reasonably imply such in a manner not set forth in Chapter 32." Finally, the Commission held that no device, based on an analogy to Chapter 31 [Of Union Churches], "could be contrived to accomplish the desired result justify a construction of the *Book of Church Order* in a manner so as to ignore its plain language."[16] The Commission also reported to the Assembly that it took no action on the Middle Tennessee Overture "because of a tie vote in the Commission."[17]

The report of the PJC would come before a Standing Committee of the Assembly so that the Committee could hold hearings and fashion a final recommendation to the Assembly.[18] The COUP forces were not satisfied to sit idly by and accept the PJC's opinion about the Mackinac Plan without a political skirmish in the General Assembly committee. Some COUP members were not sure if reunion would pass in the presbyteries and felt that Mackinac, Southern Kansas, and others deserved a clear answer at this Assembly instead of being put off two years, until after the possible defeat of the union vote. Randy Taylor, co-chair of the Joint Reunion Committee, felt there was a real chance for reunion to pass.[19]

Taylor remembered a debate in the Joint Committee on Reunion about the impact of a positive vote on the Mackinac Plan on the larger issue of the impending vote on denominational reunion, but the Committee "couldn't come to any conclusion as to what to do, and I finally made the decision that it was an easement . . . easing up of the access to union presbyteries." Taylor said, "funny you remember what you had to decide [*chuckling*]" (54-12).

What Taylor had to decide was: "Do I want to push this side door of union presbyteries wide open and thus offend the minority that I was working with to try to get them to vote? And I figured union presbyteries are going to prosper without this necessary extra step, and so I opposed it [Mackinac-Unilateral Union]." Taylor was a supporter of union presbyteries but wondered if it would not be wise to "table without prejudice" the Mackinac Reference and the Middle Tennessee Amendment. He said "there was about 48 hours there where the people thought I was crazy." For Taylor, it was "a political choice that somebody had to make, and I just happened to be in the hot spot. And, it was a gamble; it was a decision, we can go for reunion if we stay this course and not speed up the union presbytery process." He also added, "[W]hat I was trying to do, I was trying to nurse South Carolina along [for reunion]" (54-13). He knew that passing the reunion amendment would depend on picking up critical affirmative votes in the Deep South presbyteries.

Mac Hart later reported that immediately before Taylor was asked to speak on the Assembly floor, in the debate on the Middle Tennessee amendment, he asked if Hart did not think it wise to table the matter. Hart responded that he would think so only if the Assembly insisted on sending it down under the three-fourths rule. Taylor spoke to the Assembly and recommended the tabling, which prevailed.[20]

This felt to some like a breach in the pro-union ranks. Taylor's actions caught some participants in the Mackinac effort by surprise. Hart wrote them later saying this was not a sudden whim on Randy's part or his being used by those who are "agin" us. Hart felt that it was an expression of Taylor's integrity and his reading of what was best for the church at that moment. His objectives were to head off a pre-union vote rift in the pro-union forces and to allow a fallback possibility if the union vote failed. It amounted to putting it on hold, rather than letting it be killed. Hart personally would not let this episode stand in the way of working together with those who were afraid the Mackinac Plan would jeopardize the union vote.[21]

The time in 1981 in Houston was a time of building relationships since both General Assemblies were meeting in the same building. In gleeful flip-flop irony the Northern Assembly met in the southern part of the building and the Southern Assembly met in the northern part. There had been an attempt, through an overture to the PCUS Assembly from Transylvania (Union), to make the Moderator of the UPCUSA Assembly an honorary Moderator of the PCUS Assembly. The PJC's opinion was that this was a gesture of honor and respect not a matter of power and authority requiring an amendment to the *Book of Church Order*. Furthermore, the Assembly declined to act on the overture since it already had the power to grant such an honor through amending its Standing Rules, if it so desired.[22] Ordinarily, such honor and respect was by custom afforded the Moderators through exchange visits between Assemblies.

Dorothy G. "Dotty" Barnard, Moderator of the PCUS Assembly, recalled the most memorable time of the Houston Assembly from her point of view, was when time came for the Moderator's traditional visit to the other Assembly. Flynn Long was acting as the Stated Clerk at that time because Jim Andrews, Stated Clerk, was off the floor for some reason. Barnard asked Long, "When do I go?" And Long said, "Whenever you want to." Then Barnard asked, "Who can I take?" And he said, "Anyone you want." She said, "Well, let's take everybody" (09-17).

When Barnard approached the podium in the Northern Assembly by herself, it was announced that she was the PCUS Moderator and everyone stood up and applauded her. That was the cue for the all the PCUS commissioners to enter from the wings of the hall and pair up with a UPCUSA commissioner. The instructions were to take their name tags—one was horizontal and the other vertical—and make a cross out of these "individual little pieces of blue," then greet each other with a big hug. Barnard said the "UPs [UPCUSA commissioners] didn't know what in the world was going on . . . all these people coming in and going up and hugging them [*laughter*]" (09-18).

Barnard recalled that Robert M. "Bob" Davidson, UPCUSA Moderator, regained his composure and said, "I guess you realize that Dotty brought the whole assembly with her." He then said to her, "Let's sing 'Blest Be the Tie that Binds.' " And she remembered saying to him, "Don't push your luck. Let's sing 'Amazing Grace.' [*laughter*] And he laughed." Everybody stood up and sang "Amazing Grace" and held hands. Then the PCUS Assembly went back to its side of the hall (09-18).

One man later said to Barnard, "I thought that was a really corny idea and I wasn't going to go." He said, "I stood by the side and watched all these people file in, and finally I got caught up, why not? I joined the group." He concluded, "That was a very meaningful thing to me and I want you to know it changed my mind." Some days after the Assembly, people wrote her and said, "You know, I knew at that time it [reunion] would happen" (09-18).

Con to Pro

The Spirit still had its work to do, but there was evidence that there were shifts in "con" to "pro" feelings and positions. The hardcore opposition had been gone to the PCA for almost a decade, but there

---

were enough "undecideds" left to make the outcome hang in the balance. Some in the PCUS, who based their opposition to reunion on theological grounds, found kindred spirits in the UPCUSA. Gradually new perceptions of the possibilities arising from reunion began to emerge, if certain conditions were part of the deal.

Harry S. Hassall felt that many in what he called the "loyalist conservative camp" considered the whole issue of union, to mend the gap of the 1861 schism, was not framed around the right issue. Their perspective was that the key schism needing to be dealt with was 1837, the Old School/New School split and the subsequent reunion of the Old School North and New School North in 1869. These modern Southern conservatives holding to Hassall's perspective felt the 1869 reunion did not deal with the real issues; they believed it "was more emotional, the victors in the Civil War getting together." Those issues, in part, "had to do with property, they had to do with subscription, they had to do with how you look at the Biblical record, how do you do union?" (65-8).

The schism of 1837 for Hassall was basically "a correction of a failing of American Presbyterianism in 1801 when, without any Constitutional behavior, they simply declared that there would be a plan of union with the Congregational Church which made good sense if you were strictly looking at things from the structure point of view, as the whole Christian movement moved West." He strongly felt it "made very little sense if you looked at things from a theological point of view because the Congregationalists had no true boundaries for their ministers. And so from our point of view, we felt that the Congregationalists had overwhelmed particularly the Northern Presbyterians" (65-8).

The history of the Southern Church (PCUS) was 95 percent Old School, meaning it was conservative and Westminster-oriented. Hassall believed that in the proposed plan of reunion with the Northern Church in the 1980s, the Southern Church "was being sort of propagandized to join a church from which we had not split. We had split from the Old School North . . . not the Northern Church . . . [whose] structures were heavily dominated by the thinking of the New School that we thought had been corrected in 1837." Hassall went around the country talking to people: "Let's deal with the theological issues and many of the issues, Constitutional issues, that came up in 1837. And if we do that, then the 1861 issue should be resolved." In his mind this would help create a more conservative reunited Church in 1983, avoiding "a takeover from a liberal Church" (65-9). Hassall recognized that all this "was very complicated, but many of us felt that the arguments in the 1960s and 1970s for union were falsely based on the wrong union. . . . But of course, we changed our minds" (65-10).

Hassall also had opposed the "Declaration of Faith" in 1977, although he felt, "what I still call the 'Al Winn Poem,' . . . was a poetic way of doing serious theology . . . and from my perspective . . . I perceived, we had no operational theology." Ironically though, its defeat was one of his reasons later for changing from con to pro on the union issue. He became more willing "to look at a national reunion that would bring theology back to us," believing that "we'd go back to our roots and have Westminster" once again as the Confessional basis for the church (65-21).

With the successful defeat of the "Declaration of Faith," Hassall felt that "we had the troops, we had the people, we had the contacts; we knew we could defeat union indefinitely." But being deeply touched by what President Carter had achieved by getting the two antagonists from Egypt and Israel together to talk peace, Hassall began to believe "maybe there's hope in the Presbyterian Church. . . . After all, we are brothers and sisters." So Hassall came to the conclusion that "defeating union *per se* was not a worthy goal for my ministry." He also was realistic in believing that in the next twenty-five years enough new people would come into the PCUS who were not concerned about these issues and "we would probably lose because of the generation gap" (65-22).

Hassall admitted that he was disillusioned and doubted that his cohorts in the Covenant Fellowship of Presbyterians (CFP or COFOP)— what he called the moderate Zion of the South—would ever be able to forestall the inevitable denominational reunion. A major turning point came for him when William P. Thompson and James E. Andrews called a meeting in August 1978 at Louisville Seminary to talk over reunion prospects. It was a large group from both denominations representing pro and con on reunion; maybe forty or fifty on each side. This was the first time in Hassall's experience "that any serious effort had been made to get the people who were not going along with the program to come in any serious numbers." Powerful speeches were made, but one person, Edwin G. Townsend, a graduate of Columbia Seminary and now a UPCUSA pastor on Long Island, turned the tide. According to Hassall, Townsend was very angry. He "came up to Bill Elliott, Andy Jumper, Doug Harper, Harry Hassall, one or two others, and . . . shook his finger in our face and said, 'Harry Hassall, are you against union? Are you against union down to your soul, down to the toes of your feet? Or could there ever be a union you could vote for?' All of us thought and all of us said, 'Yes, there could be union we could support' " (65-22).

About ten days later there was a meeting of the Board of Covenant Fellowship in Montreat. Those who had been at the Louisville meeting were sitting around on the front porch of William Black Home talking about how Townsend had asked them, "Could we change our position?" Townsend had said one last thing to each person: "Well, if you think you could ever be for union, develop a laundry list and some of us will work to get it passed." So as the group sat and rocked on that front porch, Andy Jumper started writing on the back of an envelope the things the group called out that, if they could be put in a plan of union, "we might possibly be able to support it." The thirteen points that were generated represented "a very significant change in the Covenant Fellowship's position, from being clearly anti-union, perceived across the board, to possibly supportive of a certain kind of reunion" (65-23).

Hassall's job as executive secretary of COFOP was "to sell those [thirteen points], first to our constituency . . . and we lost a whole bunch of our constituency because we had betrayed them . . . and we lost a lot of our money." Then he had to convince both General Assemblies and the Joint Committee on Reunion that COFOP was serious in its intentions. Many pro-union advocates did not believe this was more than another devious COFOP strategy. The committees of both Assemblies meeting in Kansas City in 1979 listened to COFOP's presentations and were convinced that two persons, who represented the "loyal conservatives" from each denomination, should be added to the Joint Committee on Reunion (65-23).

Hassall said that one night during the Assembly he went out for ice cream across the street from the Mulbach Hotel and who should walk in but Al Winn, the PCUS Moderator. As they sat and talked, Winn said to Hassall, "I've got to appoint two people from the Southern Church, from the conservative side. You're a part of that. Who do you think I should appoint?" And Hassall said, "There are only two people who can carry the conservatives. And they're both white males. . . . Doug Harper and Andy Jumper. . . . I know that it goes against all the diversity statements, but if you appoint those two, and they ever agree to support a plan of union, it will pass." Winn later appointed them (65-23).

According to Hassall, the thirteen points of the Covenant Fellowship proposal were seriously considered by the Joint Committee on Reunion. Some of them were bought, some of them were modified, some of them were promised in the future. All were carefully considered, not all passed. The thirteen points were then published in *The Open Letter*, "never knowing the kind of ripple effect this would have on the whole union debate and the historic consequences of thereby making union eventually possible."[23] From then on the Covenant Fellowship began to support the possibility of union. Hassall traveled throughout the South in September–October 1982 visiting eighty communities, meeting with 1,600 people, talking to the hardest core conservatives and lobbying them for their support of *The Plan for Reunion*.

Hassall considered the 1981 final edition "Gold Plan" [the color of the cover of the second printing] to be the best plan "that would retain for Southern conservatives, a place at the table." Not all were convinced and in many places Hassall said he was "vilified as a traitor." The reunion amendment finally passed in the spring of 1983 by far more than the three-fourths required. Hassall did point out that, if a change of fifty individuals in thirteen presbyteries had changed their yes vote to a no vote, it would have been defeated. Hassall professed, "I really believe that my travels had a lot to do with getting those last votes on board for reunion. So I'd come a long way, individually. Never agreed to the constitutionality of your union presbyteries, but acknowledged its existence and I sought to make my peace with it and work with you guys wherever I could" (65-24).

Al Freundt said there were several turning points for him in his decision to shift from con to pro on the reunion issue. A colleague of his from Atlanta and Sam C. Patterson, president of Reformed Seminary and also a member of the PCUS, "convinced me that one should at least in theory always be for the Unity of the Church. And that if you were opposed to union at one time or another, it ought to be because there were faults in the particular plan." Freundt came to the conclusion "that I had to look more favorably on the possibility of union" (17-18).

Another turning point was participation on the Board of the Covenant Fellowship of Presbyterians and in the cataclysmic change of mind at the particular aforementioned meeting held at Nelson Bell's house at Montreat. The conclusion was, "if certain things were in the Plan of Union, that they would be willing to work for that union and I was part of that" (17-18).

The final turning point came during the development of Freundt's major project in the McCormick Seminary's Doctor of Ministry program. Two of his colleagues in the program—James N. "Jimmy" McGuire, pastor in Brandon, Mississippi, later pastor of an EPC Church in Michigan; and William O. "Bill" Lowrey, pastor of Christ's Community Church, Clinton, Mississippi, later with the Washington office of the PC(USA)—encouraged Freundt to undertake a new kind of process for approaching the reunion vote in Central Mississippi Presbytery "in an open and honest fashion." The Presbytery was greatly divided over this issue; McGuire was never for reunion and Lowrey seemed to be supportive of it (17-19).

Convinced that an attempt at open and honest political decision-making was desirable, several meetings and events were scheduled in the Presbytery, from small groups to large group presentations by different sides. The Delphi process, suggested in Norman Shawchuck's McCormick course, was employed that had as its motto, "Take the Middle Way," from Apollo's Oracle at Delphi, circa 900 B.C.[24]

The design required a series of rounds in which information was generated through anonymous questionnaires and the results rated in the group to the end that options were reduced until the group arrived at consensus. As participants shared the opinions through the questionnaires, those holding "extreme" views were allowed ample opportunity to justify them. The theory held that, as background information on the subject was accumulated, there was "a tendency for people to move closer towards the center of the distribution of opinion, because pressure to so move is directed not from individual to individual but rather generally from the group, there is still room for the dissenting individual to remain aloof without fear of repercussions or remonstrations."[25]

Freundt later acknowledged that "you get caught up in the process with everybody else and you . . . tend to accept the outcome." He, with some pride pointed out with tongue in cheek, boasting to David Snellgrove, executive presbyter of St. Andrews Presbytery, that Central Mississippi Presbytery "had a better percentage vote per union than the St. Andrews Presbytery." This was rightly so due to the leadership he gave in the Presbytery and in this effort (17-19).

The reunion issue for M. Douglas Harper, who had grown up in Mississippi, was subtle and, in many ways, complex. His problem with reunion was not entirely theological, other than "the multiple confessions [Confession of 1967] question." He did not fear that "our Southern Presbyterian Zion was going to be violated" by those folks coming in with reunion. He said "I'd learned very early on that there were at least as many people in the UP[CUSA] Church that thought the way I did, as in the PCUS, and I felt pretty good about that. So, those were not matters of great concern to me" (57-7).

The problem he had came from the way some were fighting reunion. This created in him a "revulsion against the kind of theological obscurantism . . . this fear of the different . . . which I saw kind of coming to a head in the PCA move, . . . people who could not distinguish between real friends and real enemies, if I can put it that way." This revulsion, for Harper, "probably made me realize that I'd better look at myself to see how much of that was in me, and begin to deal with it." He said that certainly was not what he had learned from W. H. McIntosh, his pastor in First Presbyterian Church, Hattiesburg, Mississippi, or from the author's father in summer synod youth conferences (57-7).

Harper did not see "how any Presbyterian certainly could ever be theologically opposed to the union of Christians." In later years he was asked by some folk whether he regretted being part of bringing about union. He said, "Absolutely not." They said, "Well, what about all the problems?" He said, "We had those." But Harper was deeply concerned over the way people drew up sides over "Are you for or against union?" Everything in the General Assembly revolved around the diverging opinions over this question. The practical reason to support reunion for Harper was that the church was "unable to move forward until we settled that question one way or another." Although he originally opposed it, being in a union presbytery gave Harper an additional incentive to push on for union. He had discovered how it simplified things (57-9).

Theologically crucial for Harper was "what does really constitute the heart of the faith, and what can we agree to disagree about?" This became referred to as the essential tenets in the ordination questions in the new *Book of Order*; what is important, and beyond that, what's not so important (57-8).

Other Opposition

Other opposition to reunion took many different subtle and not so subtle forms, by no means the predominant perspectives of both denominations. Nonetheless, it was a reality. Some stemmed from limited contact and a lack of understanding of each other's cultures. Other folk felt threatened by perceived differences about what it meant for Presbyterians to be church. A sense of foreboding hung over some out of a feared dilution of missional directions. Some felt outmaneuvered from lack of a certain type of political savvy. For some, suspicions arose simply from too closely held narrow organizational perspectives and turf protection. Some simply did not trust "Yankees" or, conversely, "Southerners."

M. Anderson Sale, former general presbyter of Missouri Union Presbytery and Presbytery of the Peaks, in reflecting on where there was opposition to reunion, remembered certain groups spreading "all that kind of stuff, which essentially was saying the Yankees are going to take over and they're going to lead us down the road to sin and degradation and social witness and all that kind of stuff . . . and that's bad" (46-5).

Jill M. Hudson, who had grown up in Western Kentucky (Union), was an associate pastor in Trinity Presbytery (UPCUSA) in Texas and participated in 1976 in the beginning union presbytery discussions that led to the formation of Grace (Union). She said she felt "at home" and "it was really exciting to be there at those merger points because we were part of a handful of people who knew both sides really well" (90-7). She was called in 1978 to be associate executive in the Synod of Lincoln Trails (UPCUSA) and experienced a very different "one denominational" climate. It soon became clear that her primary connection now, in what she called a "pure, one-stream mentality," was "to the UP[CUSA] system" where she said it was the first time "I had ever as a Presbyterian experienced that kind of division" (90-10).

Much of the political conversations was against reunion, with "lots of suspicion of what was called the Southern style; lots of concern about the demise of a programmatic synod, because the UP synods were very strong and very programmatic at that time . . . and the PCUS presbyteries were very strong; . . . a lot of concern about what was going to happen to synods." As things would leak out in terms of the plans, like the property issue, she heard a "lot of strong, staunch EPs [executive presbyters] who thought that the escape clause for the churches [PCUS] was just unconscionable." Hudson was most aware that "they just simply did not understand the difference in the culture, that reunion would have never happened had that escape clause not been in there." It was almost a self-righteous perspective that was not willing to do what it took to make reunion work by cutting each other some slack (90-11).

Howard L. Bost, a longtime elder from Second Presbyterian Church, Lexington, Kentucky, served for many years as an elected member on the Board of National Missions and the Program Agency of the UPCUSA. Bost was involved in the creation of the University of Kentucky Medical School; served on the National Missions liaison group that negotiated the transfer of the Appalachian Miners' Hospitals to Appalachian Regional Hospitals; and a member of the Jacob Javits congressional committee that created Medicare. From these perspectives of transition he developed a keen eye for the dynamics in organizational restructures. Reflecting on the reunion of the denominations that he supported, Bost observed that some staff persons "felt threatened . . . that merging with the Southern Church would be a depressant on a lot of the kind of aspirations and a lot of their dynamic approach[es]." He was not sure it "was ever really expressed by many but I would say that was kind of common and so it [reunion] was not approached with the kind of enthusiasm and the kind of optimism that would have been very important . . . that's normal" (99-31).

Bost was aware that some folk in the Northern Church did not perceive the Southern Church as being willing to undertake what the Board of National Missions did in Eastern Kentucky with the mine workers' hospitals, believing this was not something for the church to do. In a word, a lot of people had sort of forebodings that felt reunion would bring about a "dilution" or an "erosion" of the mission of the church. "It would move us in the opposite direction." Bost felt this perspective "didn't really take into account this whole situation. We were looking at it from a relatively narrow perspective" (99-32). He wondered whether, "if we had had some more exchange and some more integration in a way over a period . . . , kind of grew together, it might be a healthier and a little different outcome?" (99-33).

Robert F. Stevenson in retrospect thought "the UPCUSA Church was not prepared for reunion." He had had a view from his associate stated clerk's position inside the UPCUSA of the inner workings of both denominations. He knew the political capacity of his denomination and he said: "Very few knew what went on at Montreat . . . that a lot of the affairs of the Church [PCUS] for the next year were settled in Montreat, that certain period in the summer at the gathering . . . and the UPCUSA Church didn't know how to play that kind of politics" (16-13).

Carol E. Davies, an ordained elder in PCUS from Independence, Missouri who served as a member of the National Executive Committee of UPW (UPCUSA), had a unique vantage point to observe the internal struggle women in both denominations had with reunion. She recalled that in various workshops and meetings she attended, "PCUS people, not just the women" expressed the fear of losing their identity and place by being swallowed up in the new denomination. This "was as strong as the UP [women's fear] of losing their autonomy." She went on to explain that the hardest concept for many UP women to understand was "what it had taken for PCUS women to be part of the whole Church. . . . I don't know whether many ever did" (49-11).

Articles of Agreement

Doug Harper said he had no regrets about denominational reunion; "I just regret we wasted so much time doing other things before we finally got around to it. . . . Fascinating experience." The long drawn out process "was one of the most difficult experiences I ever had" (57-13). Harper had a unique perspective from which to make that observation. Not only did Harper serve on the Joint Committee on Reunion, he had the unique distinction of having been the only person to participate in the rewriting of both the *Book of Order* and the *Book of Confessions*, three historic strands in American Presbyterian history (57-15).

Years later Harper admitted it was very difficult to separate these three strands and the suspicion raised by Al Winn's naming Andy Jumper and himself to the Joint Committee on Reunion. Some felt they were there to sabotage the deal. They both had participated in Covenant Fellowship for Presbyterians, "at that time viewed as an anti-union group. . . . There were some folks who were, but officially we never were." The significance of these nominations for Harper came when he realized "that out of what appeared to many to be an opposition group, came finally the real possibility of getting something done." He remembered, when Jumper and he were put on that committee, Jumper said to him: "Now, these folks may have time to work another nine years. I don't. . . . Let's get this thing done and get out." Harper said, "We're going to get the best plan of union we can get, and I'm going to try [to talk] people into buying it, and that's my commitment." Harper felt they were faithful to that commitment and for many the suspicions were ameliorated (57-16).

Hammering out the Articles of Agreement was very difficult. Harper said, "my purpose was to do what it took to make it happen, and what I thought it took to make it happen was not the same thing as what some other folks thought it ought to take." The main problem was "the practical politics of getting it done" (57-14). There were certain things that became trust building trade-offs essential to mutual support for reunion. These dealmakers sometimes resulted in everyone not being happy.

Article 8, one of two key dealmakers, mandated the Committee on Representation and spelled out its makeup, a concrete manifestation that "implemented the Church's commitment to inclusiveness and participation which provides for the full expression of the rich diversity within its membership."[26] Some opposed this mandate, not because they were against having wide diverse representation in the structures of the Church at all levels, but because the provision for this particular committee was an unamendable Article of Agreement and cannot be removed from the *Book of Order*. Article 9 provided a mechanism through the Committees of Representation by which women, both of the majority race and of racial ethnic groups, would be assured fair representation in the decision-making of the Church.[27] There was a time-limited provision of six years by which the women's groups of the two denominations would develop joint programs and organizations.[28]

These articles sometimes had unexpected consequences. Robert E. Adcock, a member of the Joint Committee on Reunion and later a member of the Committee on Office of the General Assembly (PC(USA)), recalled that Bill Thompson, Stated Clerk, received a heated telephone call from a member of the Black Caucus Advisory Committee, exercised over how tough a deal it was for the "so called northern side" to meet the terms of Article 8. Some presbyteries "would not have any Black or ethnic minority representation to fulfill that mandate." He declared: "They wanted . . . to bring in people . . . bus them into the Presbyteries that didn't have any. That's how far out it got." This proposal never materialized (62-13).

In addition to Article 8 on representation, the other key dealmaker article was Article 13, a provision for congregations to leave under certain process with their property. "That went against the grain, especially for the UP[CUSA] folks . . . they had a whole different understanding of property than we [PCUS] did" (57-14). There was a time limit on this "escape clause" that stipulated: "Any petition for dismissal with property filed later than eight years from the consummation of union shall be handled under the appropriate provisions for such a request in the Form of Government."[29] Harper's perception on these key dealmaker articles was "we had to have Article 13 for the South. We had to have Committees on Representation [Article 8] for the UPs to trust us" (57-14).

A far more significant conviction for Harper was "that you should not simply have a mechanical union, but a clear, theological union." Harper felt, notably along with J. McDowell Richards, former president of Columbia Theological Seminary, and others, that a "Brief Statement of Faith" should be a part of the union package. There was a concerted effort undertaken to make that become a reality. William R. "Bill" Phillippe and Harper gathered a group that met for several days to have a go at writing such a draft that would be proposed. Thomas W. Gillespie was the writer for the group. It soon became evident that it was an impossible task for such a short time (57-14). However, the group proposed that a section be included in the Articles of Agreement calling for an appointment early on by the General Assembly of a committee "representing diversities of points of view and of groups within the reunited Church to prepare a Brief Statement of the Reformed Faith for possible inclusion in the Book of Confessions."[30] One by-product of the long weekend was a document Gillespie wrote that eventually became Chapter II of the Form of Government in the *Book of Order* "The Church and Its Confessions" filling the theological gap until "A Brief Statement of Faith" was produced a number of years later (57-14).

Randy Taylor, as first Moderator of the reunited Assembly, appointed twenty-one persons to serve on the special committee to prepare "A Brief Statement of Faith." One of those persons was Jack B. Rogers, who later developed a chart of the "Tenets of the Reformed Faith Expressed in the Confessions of Our Church." Ordinands are asked to "sincerely receive and adopt the essential tenets of the Reformed faith as expressed in the confessions of our church" by an affirmative response to this question number three of the ordination vows. Rogers referenced as the source of these "tenets" the *Book of Order*, chapter 2, G-2.0100–.0500 and the ordination vows in G-14.0405.[31] A growing debate has emerged in the early twenty-first century as to whether these two citations are synonymous or do the *Book of Order* and the *Book of Confessions* hold something else to be *the* essential tenets. Maybe the limitations placed on the General Assembly (U.S.A.) by the Special Committee's recommendation in 1925 restricting its authority to define the "essentials of the Church's faith" to be held by ordinands, lingered on into the twenty-first century.

Harper's final reflection on this challenging time in the church had to do with how these serious debates had to be conducted. He acknowledged that in the many debates over the years he finally figured out that "I had to assume that everybody was acting in good faith because I think it's death to dialogue when . . . you act on the assumption that somebody else is doing this in bad faith." He said that it was absolutely essential that one "must deal with issues . . . on the assumption that everybody is honest in what they're saying and from their point of view, have good reasons for it. You never can assume bad reasons, or you'll never get anywhere" (57-17).

1982 General Assemblies

Estha F. Nowlin, an elder in Saint Andrews Presbyterian Church (UPCUSA) in Tulsa, Oklahoma, was a commissioner to the 1982 UPCUSA General Assembly (Hartford). Nowlin was very active in the committees and councils of the Synod of the Sun (UPCUSA), including Presbyterian Women, and had served on the Union Presbytery Task Force of Washita (PCUS) and Eastern Oklahoma (UPCUSA) that planned and formed Eastern Oklahoma (Union) Presbytery. At the Hartford Assembly she lobbied to be on the Standing Committee dealing with denominational reunion because she felt she had something to offer. In chairing a subcommittee, she encountered a minister from Washington State. She remembered that, "every comment that I would make that would be favorable for reunion, he would counter it with something negative." Sometime after the reunion vote passed she recalled on Sunday morning having brunch with Helen Walton, and this gentleman walked by and patted her on the shoulder. He said, "I've got to tell you something." And she replied, "What's that?" He said, "Well, after listening to you and some of the other people who were so much in favor of reunion, I've got to tell you that I came here committed to vote against it. But I changed my vote" (84-7). The presbyteries of the UPCUSA over the following year would heartily concur by an overwhelming majority.

Linda B. Team, an Assembly committee resource person, recalled that the initial vote in the three-vote process on denominational reunion came at the 1982 PCUS General Assembly in Columbus, Georgia. In those days, organic union amendments to the *Book of Church Order* required an initial affirmative vote by the Assembly, the requisite three-fourths majority advice and consent vote by the presbyteries, and finally a second affirmative vote by the subsequent Assembly. Team said she believed "one of the finest moments in the

Presbyterian Church" was when Moderator John Anderson called for that initial vote at the Columbus Assembly (27-14).

In her memory it was extremely one-sided, 430 to 30, or an approximate ratio. There were only "a very small handful of people who opposed it, although there may have been others in the room who would have but they just didn't." Everyone stood in awe of what took place that day, "the culmination of so many years of work and striving and praying." She remembered the caring way in which Anderson "called on the body not to celebrate in a way that would be insensitive to the opponents of the vote. . . . The Doxology was sung, but there was no cheering and applause. It was a very, very emotional time for everyone, but it was handled with such sensitivity that there was no triumphalism on the part of the people who had finally accomplished their purpose" (27-14). Matthew Lynn was observed quietly standing off to the side watching his dream come true during this vote, one of the highest moments in the history of North American Presbyterianism.

The long wait for the results of sending the reunion amendments to the presbyteries for advice and consent was now begun. Doug Harper, years later in retrospect, remembered how Bill Phillippe, longtime minister member of the UPCUSA, and he became good friends in that process of working together on different aspects of denominational reunion. Phillippe called Harper from Atlanta the day when the vote in Augusta-Macon Presbytery put the count over the needed three-fourths majority. Harper could not but notice the irony of where this happened, "since Augusta was the place where the [PC]US, then the Presbyterian Church in the Confederate States of America, was started." Phillippe told Harper he "wanted to be the one to tell you that union is passed." Harper mused, "You know, it's a thing you remember with gratitude, that people who in many ways have different points of view, and Bill and I certainly do . . . But, we were colleagues and friends, and there are others, many others, are like that" (57-19).

New Synod and Presbytery Realignments

When reunion of the denominations became a reality, all presbyteries became *de facto* union presbyteries in a sense, whether they realized it or not. They were all new presbyteries in a newly reunited denomination, many without ever having that long, cooperative lead-up time with a presbytery of the other predecessor denomination. On the surface this seemed like a simple and straightforward fact. However, different ramifications were experienced in different locales in the church. It meant one thing for the existing union and cooperating presbyteries. For language-speaking and racial ethnic presbyteries it was an entirely different matter than it was for overlapping regions of the Southeast. A very different reality existed in the non-overlapping portions of both denominations. Fewer non-overlapping areas existed in the Southern Church than in the Northern Church.

In some ways, the farther away the non-overlapping regions of the Northern Church were from the Border States, the less immediate was the impact of reunion on those regions, or so it seemed. Lack of contact engendered many reactions. Some cared less about this "attractive nuisance" and quickly got on with business as usual with no real change in their immediate denominational perspectives. Others took an apparent attitude that it is about time those recalcitrant Southerners came back to the Mother Church. Still others seemed oblivious to the whole thing. In any case, these perspectives were devoid of the real excitement and renewing spirit generated by the newness of the reunited church, making them *de facto* union presbyteries in name only.

The situation faced in the overlapping, non-cooperating regions within the former boundaries of the PCUS was more complex. The same was true in language-speaking and racial ethnic presbyteries. They were not immediately "joined" with another presbytery to form a new presbytery. Article 7 of the Articles of Agreement created a Special Committee on Presbytery and Synod Boundaries to oversee the long and tedious process of negotiating boundary realignments of "governing bodies where Presbyteries and Synods of the existing Churches overlap and for other Presbyteries and Synods as necessary."[32] The expectation was that this "shall be accomplished no later than ten years following the uniting General Assembly."[33] However, in situations "involving Presbyteries based on racial ethnic or language considerations, or Presbyteries whose membership consists of predominantly racial ethnic persons," application could be made for an extension of time with the expectation that realignment would be accomplished "within fifteen years after the uniting General Assembly."[34]

The full account of this Boundary Committee process, though beyond the scope of this book, tells an intriguing story of how reunion was perceived and played out in these boundary negotiations—sometimes happily, sometimes unhappily. What happened in synods that had experienced union presbyteries is of particular interest to this study.

A series of consultations were held across the church at the direction of the Boundary Committee to determine the new configurations. The Synods of Red River/Sun (Texas, Oklahoma, Louisiana, Arkansas) and Mid-America (Missouri, Kansas) made the decision basically to maintain the presbytery boundaries they had shared during the union presbytery days when they had functioned as *de facto* union synods, though there were some perfunctory attempts by neighboring synods to explore other possibilities.

In other parts of the former PCUS it was a different story. A comprehensive study of population, membership, and financial figures was made in five synods covering nine states in preparation for a Five-Synod Boundaries Consultation [sometimes referred to as the Nine-Synod Consultation] held in Atlanta, Georgia, on December 12–14, 1983. Based on the data collected, seven potential synod models were constructed from the profiles of the five synods and nine states. Those synods and states were Covenant (Michigan, Ohio, Kentucky); Mid-South (Kentucky, Tennessee, Alabama, Mississippi); South (Tennessee, Alabama, Mississippi, South Carolina, Georgia, Florida); Southeast (South Carolina, Georgia, Florida), and Florida (Florida).[35]

The union presbyteries from Kentucky and North Alabama along with the rest of the presbyteries in Alabama, Mississippi, and Tennessee from the Synods of the Mid-South (PCUS) and South (UPCUSA) formed the Synod of the Living Waters (PC(USA)). Every effort was made to create a new entity, though it seemed presbyteries from the Synod of the South were, in effect, incorporated into an existing synod. However, the transition into this new synod was made easier by long years of cooperative work as well as sociological and theological similarities. The most traumatic part of this decision came when the three Kentucky presbyteries had to say good-bye to the Synod of the Covenant (UPCUSA), now made up of presbyteries in Michigan and Ohio.

Southwest Florida (Union) and St. Augustine (Union-to-be) and the other presbyteries in Florida, Georgia, and South Carolina from the Synods of the South (UPCUSA), Southeast (PCUS), and Florida (PCUS) formed the Synod of South Atlantic (PC(USA)). The challenge for this synod was geographical, theological, and sociological distance. It is a long way from Miami to Rock Hill, SC, on all three counts. In this mix were former PCUS presbyteries in South Carolina and Georgia that had not only voted against this reunion, but also had overwhelmingly voted against reunion in 1955. It also contained remnants of former UPCUSA all-black presbyteries that over time had witnessed the erosion of their power bases through various realignments.

John B. Evans, as a newly ordained minister in Charleston Presbytery (PCUS), remembered the 3,000 or so United Presbyterians centered around Charleston in some vigorous African American churches "that didn't want anything to do with us [PCUS] in 1954 and 1955 because they didn't trust white Southern people for very good reasons" (56-8). One of the greatest challenges came in the formation of New Harmony Presbytery in northeast South Carolina "in what was an Old South territory where you might expect racism still to be a difficulty." But according to John Lyles, who served his last pastorate there, it became "a very happy and harmonious Presbytery" (55-16).

When Evans came to that presbytery in 1988 to provide executive leadership, he wisely approached it as if he were going "to bring about a union presbytery after union." It was a presbytery where one-fourth of its churches and one-sixth of its members were African American, ninety percent of them from the Northern Church, coming from the northern half of Atlantic Presbytery and the eastern sixth of Fairfield-McClelland Presbytery. On top of this, the new presbytery included the former PCUS presbyteries of Pee Dee and Harmony, both of which had voted against reunion and, according to Evans, in their former life "didn't like each other, didn't trust each other, didn't know each other, didn't do things the same way, so that when our Presbytery was born, the white majority was not on the same page" (56-14).

Evans was faced with a gathering of reluctant strangers who did not know each other. When they sat down at the table to get organized, they took the time to get acquainted. They were starting to make progress in getting to know each other when disaster struck in the form of Hurricane Hugo in the second year of that presbytery's life. Evans said this was "the best thing that happened" because people said: "We're going to work together. . . . Hugo was no respecter of whites or blacks." The beauty of it for Evans was that "it helped the white side of New Harmony Presbytery, that was very states' rights in its orientation, discover that there were churches in Ohio and Pennsylvania who became their partners in recovery . . . and suddenly we are part of a Presbyterian Church" (56-14).

John Lyles in retirement became a member of Charlotte Presbytery. When he first came and observed the floor debates and the discussions around the dinner table as he tried to get to know the people in the Presbytery, he sensed that "there just wasn't that full, at that time, sense of acceptance and mutual trust." There was a different climate here than he had experienced when a member of New Harmony Presbytery in South Carolina, but over time "it has improved" (55-16).

Robert J. Rea, Jr., executive presbyter of Providence Presbytery (PC(USA)) in South Carolina, observed that even as the 1990s were coming to a close, "those large presbyteries they created particularly in North Carolina, New Hope and Coastal Carolina . . . [were] still seeking [their new] identity." There was a heavy turnover in synod executive staff and "those are the areas that probably could have benefited from the former union presbyteries' consultation with them on how do you go about restructuring your presbyteries." He said "there was very little help from General Assembly for that sort of thing. . . . I don't think that South Carolina or North Carolina would have really wanted New

York/Atlanta to come in and tell them how to do it. But they probably would have appreciated colleagues who had already gone through the reorganization, helping them with some practical issues" (47-18).

The remaining part of the PCUS in the Mid-Atlantic states and in the heart of central Appalachia in the mountains of West Virginia had at once both possibly the easiest and most difficult transitions of any of the synod realignments. The former Greenbrier Presbytery (PCUS) in West Virginia basically was included in the existing Synod of the Trinity (UPCUSA). Although in the years immediately before reunion there was some interest in forming a union presbytery there, the long programmatic cooperative association and the sociological demographic profiles made this inclusion a natural decision.

Closer to the eastern seaboard it was another story. After a long tortuous journey, the PCUS Synods of North Carolina and Virginias [without West Virginia] finally joined with the UPCUSA Synod of the Piedmont to form the Synod of Mid-Atlantic. It was anything but an easy transition in attempting to mold at least four very diverse cultures into a functioning ecclesiastical synod with very large presbyteries. There were at least two distinctly different Northern Presbyterian cultures and two distinctly different Southern Presbyterian cultures in three sub-regions that impacted and impeded the development of the new synod for over a decade.

One UPCUSA subculture was centered in the three urban presbyteries—National Capital, Baltimore, and New Castle—in the northern sub-region of the Synod. H. Davis Yeuell, former executive of the PCUS Synod of the Virginias, observed that those three presbyteries continued some of the traditions of the Synod of the Chesapeake (UPCUSA), their predecessor synod. Yeuell remembered how the former UPCUSA Presbyteries of Washington City, Baltimore, and New Castle had "operated very well without a synod, though they met annually in the Synod of Chesapeake Meeting, and . . . circulated the leadership around that." The unique factor was that "all three of those presbyteries in the old Northern Church system were Administrative Units, which meant that they had access to the dollars in New York that didn't have to flow through the synod" (98-29).

The other UPCUSA subculture, which spread across all three sub-regions and was still in existence in 1988, was centered in the four all-black presbyteries—Cape Fear, Catawba, Yadkin, Southern Virginia—that once comprised the Catawba Synod (UPCUSA). The long years of support from the Board of National Missions and the Program Agency had created a formidable power base and a strong sense of identity among these African-American Presbyterians. The threatened loss of this base was the largest source of resistance to reunion in the

UPCUSA, not only from those in the region but in the denomination. Mac Hart recalled the seriousness of the situation from the days when he was general presbyter in Hanover Presbytery (PCUS) in Virginia. "The UP[CUSA] Presbytery was very small, felt vastly outnumbered by Hanover, had boundaries bigger than Hanover's boundaries, though not completely contiguous. . . . [It was] almost entirely Black, [and they] felt threatened by the notion of reunion or merger" (50-4).

One PCUS subculture was centered in the Commonwealth of Virginia, the central sub-region of the new synod. The old PCUS Synod of Virginia was essentially a rural synod, centered in the Valley of Virginia, with some urban areas in Norfolk and Richmond. This rural perspective was the dominant culture of this sub-region well into the formation of the new synod. The farmers in the Valley, though not in agribusiness, still set the dominant tone for stewardship and finances. Yeuell said, "[T]hey'll give but they are hesitant about pledging, because you don't know what your farm is going to produce" (98-29).

The other PCUS subculture was centered in North Carolina, the southern sub-region of the new synod. Yeuell said John Evans reminded him one time that "North Carolina has been a mill town Synod with certain growing cities in metropolitan areas," creating a very different cultural juxtaposition to the other two sub-regions (98-29). The old PCUS Synod of North Carolina had so persistently resisted regional synods that, when they came into existence in the PCUS in the early 1970s, North Carolina remained a strong state-line "regional" synod. Its attitude toward what a synod should be was no different this time around, so it resisted becoming a part of the new synod in the late 1980s as long as it could.

The clashes of these four subcultures continued for years with several organizational plans concocted to make the new synod work. Davis Yeuell said in this process the Synod had gone through about three interim executives. One plan tried to capitalize structurally and programmatically on the three sub-regions, especially in the area of Campus Ministry. In the last of the 1990s the Synod appointed the Synod Review Task Force, on which Yeuell served, to look at program and structure. One of the issues before the Task Force was the question raised as to whether to overture the Assembly to divide the Synod and let North Carolina go its way (98-28). This did not happen and North Carolina is still included, though much is yet to be accomplished. In Yeuell's opinion the "Synod of Mid-Atlantic has yet to overcome that early history" (98-27).

The world was not put right completely and the kingdom did not come fully, but countless insurmountable obstacles—threats, fears, reservations, and oppositions—did not prevail. Denominational reunion had been culminated on that beautiful and bright "Day" in Atlanta, Georgia, on June 10, 1983. Union Presbyteries in their original configurations were now history and, with the passing years, *de facto* no longer seemed to be an adequate description for presbyteries in the new denomination. The Movement, in trying to alleviate the tension accrued from living in two worlds, had threatened to sap the energy out of the ghosts of Stamford Bridge and Hastings; but in the final push to achieve denominational reunion and in its aftermath, the ghosts got a new lease on life.

Notes

1. *Minutes* of the One-Hundred-Eighty-Ninth General Assembly (UPCUSA), 1977, p. 215.

2. *Minutes* of the One-Hundred-Seventeenth General Assembly (PCUS), 1977, pp. 324–325.

3. *Minutes* of the One-Hundred-Nineteenth General Assembly (PCUS), 1979, p. 126.

4. "Presbyterians Defeat Union Synod Amendment," *The Open Letter*, vol. 11, no. 3 (March 1980), p. 4.

5. Ibid.

6. *Minutes* of the One-Hundred-Twentieth General Assembly (PCUS), Myrtle Beach, NC, 1980, p. 138.

7. "Report and Recommendations of the Task Force on Union Presbyteries," Minutes of Mackinac Presbytery, December 7, 1979, p. 6.

8. A series of letters in the spring of 1981 between Freundt and McAtee indicated the depth of the pain and emotions they experienced in this episode, as well as the "candor and disclosure" that they "sought to keep in our developing relationship" that began out of commitments made during the Belhaven Ethics Conference (1966). Letters in personal collection of William G. McAtee. During the course of the interview McAtee conducted with Freundt in November 1997, Freundt shared with McAtee a copy of an assignment he had done for his McCormick Seminary Doctor of Ministry conflict management course. It was mailed to the instructor, Hugh Halverstadt, at about the same time as the aforementioned exchange of letters. The focus was on the conflict generated between the two in their appearance before the PJC in the Mackinac matter. It included with an in-depth analysis of power dynamics exhibited in this episode between these two ecclesiastical officers. The interview exchange plus sharing of this paper added new insights into their long relationship and brought a sense of closure to the long-passed conflict. Mutual expressions of relief were shared, wishing "we could have talked this way years ago" (17-29).

9. Letter from R. Neal Dean, stated clerk of Middle Tennessee Presbytery to James E. Andrews, Stated Clerk, PCUS General Assembly, November 8, 1980, copy in personal collection of William G. McAtee.

10. Albert H. Freundt, Jr., "Does the Mackinac Presbytery Plan and Procedure Meet the Provisions of the P.C.U.S. Constitution?" Addendum submitted November 20, 1980, to the PCUS Permanent Judicial Commission, copy in personal collection of William G. McAtee.

11. William G. McAtee, "Addendum and Supplemental Brief to a Reference to the 121st General Assembly of the Presbyterian Church in the United States from the Synod of the Mid-South," submitted November 20, 1980, to the PCUS Permanent Judicial Commission, copy in personal collection of William G. McAtee.

12. *A Digest of the Acts and Proceedings of the General Assembly of the Presbyterian Church in the United States—1861–1965* (Atlanta: Office of the General Assembly, 1966), pp. 84–85.

13. "Will Renewal Be the Road to Reunion?" *The Open Letter*, vol. 11, no. 2 (February 1980), p. 4.

14. "The 'Mackinac Maneuver,' " *The Open Letter*, vol. 11, no. 3 (March 1980), p. 3.

15. *Minutes* of the Consultation on Union Presbyteries, March 11–13, 1981, p. 3.

16. *Minutes* of the One-Hundred-Twenty-First General Assembly (PCUS), Houston, TX, May 20–27, 1981, p. 201.

17. Ibid., p. 202.

18. McAtee, as a presenter before the PJC hearing the previous November, was not present for the hearing before the Standing Committee, because of his emergency departure. During the early part of the Assembly meeting, elder Quenton Keen, commissioner from Transylvania (Union) and member of First Presbyterian Church, Richmond, Kentucky, died of a massive heart attack. Elder Keen, on the morning of his death, had delivered the devotional at the opening of his Standing Committee. He was thrilled to be a commissioner to the General Assembly, since his father, an elder from the Buckhorn Presbyterian Church, had been a commissioner decades before to the USA General Assembly. McAtee helped make arrangements for the return of his wife and his remains to Kentucky and then drove their car back to Lexington.

19. Letter from A. M. Hart to Colleagues in the Mackinac Effort, June 1, 1981, p. 1, copy in personal collection of William G. McAtee.

20. Ibid., p. 1.

21. Ibid., pp. 1–2.

22. *Minutes* of the One-Hundred-Twenty-First General Assembly (PCUS), 1981, pp. 196–197.

23. Harry Sharp Hassall, *On Jordan's Stormy Banks I Stand: A Historical Commentary of the Life and Times of The Covenant Fellowship of Presbyterians, 1969–1989* (Dallas, TX: privately printed, 1989), p. 62. For the Covenant Fellowship of Presbyterians' Statement on Plan of Reunion including the thirteen points, see pp. 62–63.

24. Margaret Skutsch, "Goals and Goal Setting: A Delphi Approach" (Master's Thesis, Department of Industrial Engineering, Northwestern University, 1972), p. i.

25. Ibid., p. 15.

26. *The Plan for Reunion of the Presbyterian Church in the United States and The United Presbyterian Church in the United States of America*, final edition, second printing (Atlanta: Stated Clerk of the Presbyterian Church in the United States, 1981), "Articles of Agreement," 8.2, p. 22.

27. Ibid., 9.1, p. 23.

28. Ibid., 9.3, p. 23.

29. Ibid., 13.4, p. 29.

30. Ibid., 3.2, p. 16.

31. Rogers, *Presbyterian Creeds*, see pp. 14–15 for chart.

32. *The Plan for Reunion*, "Articles of Agreement," 7.1, p. 20.

33. Ibid., 7.5, p. 21.

34. Ibid., 7.6, p. 21.

35. *Five-Synod Boundaries Consultation Notebook*, copy in personal collection of William G. McAtee, pp. 1.1–1.2, 1.6.

Chapter 14
Place in American History

The PCUS experience with race as a matter of racial ideology and church polity after World War II was a prism for the rest of Southern society. As the only major denomination still bounded by its Civil War borders, and noted as well for its social power, the Presbyterian Church in the United States was an important part of Southern history and society. This peculiar conjunction makes this denominational experience in racial affairs a unique one in America's continuing struggle for racial justice. Although only part of the story, it represents a significant part as it chronicles how black and white people of a common religious commitment variously interpreted and practiced that religion in their own time and place.

—*Joel L. Alvis, Jr.*[1]

What role did the Union Presbytery Movement and the reunion of the denominations play in the healing of the scars created by the Civil War and racism, the residual effect of slavery? What was their place in American history? What impact did they have on society in general, or society on them? Did they make any contribution to the development of the new realities of North and South? It may have been somewhat ambitious to dare raise these primary questions for this study to address in any great depth. Some who read this work may be so far removed from the firsthand experience of reunion, much less union presbyteries, that they have not a clue as to how these questions could be valid for twenty-first-century reflection. The Civil War is even more ancient history to the modern and postmodern reader.

Change is occurring with laser speed in this postmodern world, so fast that the age-old processes of cultural validation and assimilation of new ideas into lasting values and behavior seem to be omitted or ignored in moments of serious reflection. Sense of time is so truncated that it is almost a nuisance in this fast-paced world to think in terms of 25-, 35-, 70- or 140-year spans of time. And yet that is what these questions are asking. What is at once startling and disarming is the realization that the span of time between when the author's great-grandfather was killed during the last siege of Vicksburg in 1863 and the author's birth in 1934 is the same span of time between his birth and the writing of this book—71 years. At this writing it has been not quite 25 years since reunion and 35 years since the first union presbytery was created. The realization of the far-reaching changes that occurred during these time spans may not mean much to the person whose majority of life is still in the future, but it is very profound for the person in the twilight years of life.

Ken McCall recalled one day when he was a seminary student at McCormick, one of his professors, Hulda Niebuhr, invited him to come over and visit with her brother, "Reiny" [Reinhold]. McCall said he was "not a soft person like she was, a little rough, but still quite interesting." One of the comments Reinhold Niebuhr made during the visit was something that stayed with McCall all of his life: "Most people have the capacity, with great effort, to change once in their lifetime, from the pattern that was ingrained in them when they grew up." He said, "Rarely will people ever change twice, but the great majority of people will live the life they learned when they were young, and they will carry that with them" (66-31).

If it is true that people rarely have the capacity to change twice or even once in their lifetime, what happened in the PCUS—in terms of the contribution that the Union Presbytery Movement and the reunion of the denominations made toward healing of the scars created by the Civil War and racism, the residual effect of slavery—was an extraordinary beginning and truly unique phenomenon. The key was that those deeply involved in working for union presbyteries were also working for social and racial justice, passions driving them toward denominational reunion. The two went hand in hand for them. It would be an understatement to say that these efforts took place in a cultural vacuum.

The times in which these organizational manifestations of church were created made what happened even more extraordinary. During the period bracketed between the end of World War II and "the Day" in Atlanta in June 1983, unbelievable social, political, and economic changes were generated across North America and in the world. Definitions of regional identities were turned topsy-turvy. Benchmarks for understanding denominational growth were set in this period, marks against which progress or decline would be measured well into the twenty-first century. Church membership and leadership pools, as well as religious attitudes of the twenty-first century, were birthed and fashioned by these formative bracket years between 1945 and 1983, an aberration in church history. It would be impossible within the scope of this study to document the full spectrum of social, political, and economic events and changes witnessed during these bracket years. A selective summary of these events and changes that took place between 1945 to 1983 is necessary to set the context for understanding what happened in the PCUS in terms of the contribution the Union Presbytery Movement and the reunion of the denominations made toward healing the scars created by the Civil War and racism, the residual effect of slavery, a determination very difficult for whites alone to judge.

Post–World War II America

Harry Truman became president of the United States with the death of Franklin D. Roosevelt at the close of World War II in 1945. The troops came home to cheering crowds in Times Square from a devastating war that rid the world of two tyrannies across the Atlantic and the Pacific Oceans. This generation had mounted an almost impossible undertaking, but they had prevailed and felt there was not anything they could not do as they returned home to build a new life.

African Americans, who had served their country honorably as part of that effort, came back to the same segregated society that they had left. Truman addressed a wide range of racially discriminating issues through the President's Committee on Equality of Treatment and Opportunity in the Armed Services. The background information gleaned from the committee's reports became material for Truman's 1948 campaign speeches and civil rights speeches, and the 1952 State of the Union address.[2] Although Truman did not remain in office long enough to see the thorny issues of racial discrimination and the need for equal employment practices, fair housing, and the like resolved, he did lay the foundation for many resolutions to come. He did take steps to integrate the military.

Dwight D. Eisenhower, the military commander turned politician, became president in the landslide election of 1952. The troops were eager to follow the lead of their former commander to create an unprecedented period of economic growth and development built on the technologies generated by the recent war's industries. One of those technological developments was the Univac I computer produced by Eckert & Mauchly and marketed by Remington Rand starting in 1952. It attracted attention by predicting the Eisenhower landslide election "even before the polls closed in California; statistical sampling techniques related to results from previous elections were used." Television commentators were skeptical and did not declare victory until the actual results were announced, quite unlike some future experiences. This feat of prediction was not simply attributed to the power of the computer, but was possible because of new political analytical techniques as well as skillfully produced and tested program models.[3]

Congress rewarded GIs with legislative bills that provided the funding for education and other amenities of life that had been so scarce during the War. The industrial expansion provided new income that overshadowed anything reminiscent of the Great Depression of the 1930s. New cars were available in bright colors rather than simply prewar blacks, subdued greens, blues or maroons. Gasoline was cheap and city and urban housing was cramped. All across the country, GI starter-home subdivisions cropped up like spring mushrooms after a heavy rain. And those homes needed to be filled with all sorts of new "labor-saving" devices. The advent of room air-conditioners changed the South and made it receptive to new industrial migrations from the North.

The old industrial belt of the North had not yet begun to rust, but there were hints in the Sun Belt of things to come. Pre-World War II efforts like the Balance Agriculture with Industry (BAWI) program touted by Governor Hugh White of Mississippi during his first term (1936–1940) had laid the groundwork for the wartime economy that would end the Great Depression and still be prominent in the postwar years. Ingalls Shipbuilding had established its shipyard in Pascagoula, Mississippi [home of future U.S. Senator Trent Lott], on December 6, 1938, under Governor White's BAWI program.[4] Ingalls was positioned for the great demands for wartime ships created three years later by the bombing of Pearl Harbor.

The Eisenhower years introduced new seismic shifts in location of industries across America. There were lingering effects of the war economy on industry in the South. Governor White rekindled interest in the BAWI program during his second term (1952–1956)[5] by tempting garment and other industries to relocate in his state because of the non-union and cheaper labor environment. This was the pattern of economic development exhibited during this time across the South. The textile mills in the Carolinas were making similar pitches to the New England industries. Other industries looked favorably toward the South for new economic opportunities and the industrialization of the South launched into high gear. Although the rest of the country also experienced phenomenal growth in these postwar years, for the purposes of this work, the focus is on the industrialization of the South.

An Industrial Prototype

Over a long span of time beginning in the early 1950s, one company served as a microcosm of what other industries experienced in the industrialization of the South. Its lifetime of advertising campaigns touted slogans like: "Progress is Our Most Important Product," "We Bring Good Things to Life," "Live Better Electrically," "Imagination at Work." All caught the spirit of the times in which these "progress" ad campaigns were launched in juxtaposition with cultural and racial dissonance. That company was General Electric, "with 2004 revenues expected to approach $3.5 billion."[6]

GE had a long history, beginning when Thomas Edison attended the Centennial Exposition in Philadelphia in 1876 (ironically the same time and place kudzu was introduced into this country!). Here he got new ideas for dynamo and electrical devices to explore in his laboratory. By 1890 he organized his companies into the Edison

General Electric Company that would merge in 1892 with the Thomson-Houston Company, a major competitor in the electrical business, to form the General Electric Company. Thomas-Houston earlier had merged with other companies consolidating patents and technologies and creating a dominant force in the industry. One of those other companies included a shoe manufacturer from Lynn, Massachusetts, led by Charles A. Coffin, who brought his managerial expertise to GE. Over the years GE manufactured lighting, transportation, industrial products, power transmissions, heating and cooking devices, and medical equipment. As early as 1917 it began to make the first airplane engine "booster" for the U.S. Government in World War I. Other government contracts followed during World War II, and even later included those for GE Aircraft Engines Division in 1987.[7]

GE purchased property in south Louisville, Kentucky, in 1951, and began to construct GE Appliance Park. "Bricks, mortar and steel went into the construction, but the true foundation wasn't laid until later in 1953 when employees started to work and began producing their first appliances at the Park."[8] This state-of-the-art plant began "to produce washers and dryers, dishwashers and disposers, refrigerators and freezers and electric ranges and ovens" to fill up those GE tract-housing developments across the country.[9] GE made history in 1954 when it purchased the very first commercial Univac I computer to automate the manufacturing planning and control functions at its new production facilities. The Louisville Appliance Park became a showplace plant and also utilized the Univac I "to process payroll, general ledger, accounts receivable and payable and other accounting functions."[10]

GE's headquarters and plant in Schenectady, New York, and the new plant in Louisville were corporately linked in many ways. Both Louisville and Schenectady were in the same Eastern time zone that made coordination of management more compatible, following "the principal standard" that time zones are for the "convenience of commerce."[11] One wonders, though this is unconfirmed, if GE's Large Steam Turbine Department at the Schenectady Plant had had any government contracts with the Jeffersonville Boat and Machine Co., across the Ohio River in Jeffersonville, Indiana, that produced LST landing craft for the U.S. Government during the Second World War. This experience with a satisfactory work force and other community contacts might have influenced the choice of Louisville as the site for Appliance Park.

Managerial and technical personnel were transferred to Louisville from Schenectady to direct the construction of the Park and get it up and running.[12] Resident company employees welcomed newcomers and gave them pointers regarding realtors, churches, schools, clubs, shopping areas, medical and other services—making their inclusion in the community as seamless a transition as possible.

It is personally known to the author that management personnel came to Louisville and settled in many parts of northeast Louisville, in the Brownsboro Road area. Calvin Presbyterian Church, a new church development of the Northern Presbyterian Church on Rudy Lane in Windy Hills, became the new home church for many Presbyterian GE transfers from Schenectady and other GE locations. Its flamboyant pastor was Arie D. Bestebreurtje, a former Dutch resistance fighter during World War II in his homeland, the Netherlands. Bestebreurtje, who displayed a fragment of a German Messerschmitt fighter plane wing on his study wall at the church, attracted many new young parishioners who had recently served in the armed forces. Two Southern Presbyterian Churches, Buechel and Okolona, bracketed Appliance Park to the north and the south, providing a Presbyterian presence in neighborhoods where the labor force at the Park resided.

GE had the reputation of being a "good employer and a good corporate citizen." Loyalty to company, church, and community were hallmarks of GE employees, who gave much back to the community in volunteer time and talent as well as making contributions to charitable organizations. GE's impact on the community was significant. "During the six years it took to build the Park, thousands of construction workers had regular employment earning top dollar." From the beginning, GE's local and state taxes helped pay for essential community services.[13] During the time Appliance Park was under construction, building of the Henry Watterson Expressway was begun.[14] It was the first major circumference highway in Louisville. Eventually as it expanded, exits were strategically placed at Brownsboro and Shelbyville Roads in northeast Louisville and at Bardstown, Newburg, and Poplar Level Roads in south Louisville, providing convenient access to and from Appliance Park for managers and commuting laborers alike.

Other Replications

This industrial microcosm was replicated across the Sun Belt during this time and in succeeding years when rural populations, both black and white, migrated to urban and suburban centers. GE's move was not limited to Louisville but it went to Waynesboro, Virginia, and other places. NASA created entirely new industries in Texas, Alabama, and Florida. These drew a conglomerate of subsidiary aerospace industries. The plans for the construction of the Tombigbee Waterway were brought out of mothballs in order to facilitate the transshipment of launch rockets from Huntsville to Cape Canaveral through Tennessee, Mississippi, and Alabama. Other transportation industries began to burgeon on land, air, and sea. FedEx and UPS changed the way goods were delivered. CNN and TBS in Atlanta symbolized the dawn of new ways of disseminating information via cable television. Petrochemical empires, furniture plants, communications systems, banking and investment institutions, service industries—you name it—sprung up around metropolitan areas and regional communities, only scratching the surface of the economic expansion story in the New South.

Corporate transfers of company personnel were a way of life, now a form of internal migration that had some characteristics in common with what all migrants faced in other generations. Now "franchise living"—one mold fits all, no matter where—initially may have been an expectation but not a norm, a way of expecting that institutions and life would be the same no matter where one was located. Simple loyalty to one's group, as a strong norm for guiding membership decisions, was taken for granted. But it soon became evident that this was not the case. Some came seeking voter registration cards only to find that familiar party labels with assumed core values and political alignments no longer fit the definitions in the new locale. Some were denied access to the voting process altogether. Democrats or Republicans here could be very different from what they had been in a previous location. Social fabric and mores for inclusion often clashed as new met old; each other's cultures were not understood or fully appreciated. Sometimes these collisions were invisible or opaque, leaving deep scars.

This social and cultural dissonance was especially true in some cases when it came time for the corporate transferees to find a new church home in the South. In some locations there was only one kind of Presbyterian church for Northern Presbyterians to attend—the Southern brand—that many times had very different norms from what they had been accustomed to. In other locations like Louisville, Presbyterians transferred in had a choice of either Northern or Southern Presbyterian churches. David Stitt remembered that "people moving into the Houston area did not know the difference at all. And they would be much surprised to find out it was a different branch of the Presbyterian Church from the one they knew before they came there." He noted that when Gulf Oil moved some 300 Presbyterian families to Houston from Pennsylvania, "many people that moved there were old United Presbyterians [UPNAs], neither North nor South, but the psalm singers" (52-7).

It was a different situation for Robert L. Thompson in Florida. He found that "loyalty to separate denominations was particularly high among the clergy because they were trained in schools that had all that fraternity type stuff, you know, kissin' cousins." He said it was true among some "laypeople who were active in the presbytery or the synod on one side or another. But to the average person who was in the Church, they didn't care. . . . ..They wanted a church that served their needs." It got even more complicated because "it wasn't just two kinds of Presbyterians because it was a great mixing of people of different denominational and religious backgrounds" (68-11).

Thompson noted that following World War II where there had been a lot of the mixing and blending on the battlefield as buddies in the war, "you weren't worrying about what [was] the religion of that guy beside you." He felt that all that mixing made a difference in the postwar years when "trying to explain the differences and make them sound sensible just didn't make sense at all" (68-11). The GIs' experience with religion had been very interdenominational under military chaplains and it gave them a different perspective from what they had known before the war, removing barriers between denominations. Many had had battlefield conversions and pursued new calls to ministry by attending seminary after they returned.

Thompson held that it got even more complicated to explain in the late 1970s and early 1980s when they began new union church developments and work on deliberate strategies to bring about the union presbyteries. People were not only coming from different Presbyterian traditions, but also from different or even nondenominational backgrounds. Thompson said we were "not only addressing the scandal of trying to explain our denominations, defend them in this culture, [but] we began to see, because we were relating then as a union presbytery, . . . we related denominationally to two synods and two general assemblies" (68-12).

The dynamics of relocation took many different twists and turns, sometimes presenting little or unusual challenges at best, with regard to denominational choices. Washington, DC, was a different type of "company town." Ed White said that for years "people came from all over the country, North and South, most of them didn't pay any attention to the distinction between Northern and Southern, so they would join the nearest Presbyterian Church where they moved. And so, there were a lot of Northern Presbyterians in Southern congregations and vice versa. And so, a lot of the regionalism had already melted at the congregational level" (86-3).

After reunion other variations of the corporate relocation trauma and its impact on the church were played out. For some, denominational differences were a non-issue; for others it was everything. When Whirlpool Corporation moved from Pennsylvania into Danville in Boyle County, Kentucky, four clerks of session from four separate Presbyterian congregations in Pennsylvania were transferred and became members of the one Presbyterian church in town, a previously union congregation, and changed its dynamics. It gave new meaning to the words "We can't do it the way we always have!" The

Presbyterian Church (U.S.A.) experienced this trauma in a dramatic way when it decided to move its corporate headquarters to Louisville/Jeffersonville from New York and Atlanta, spearheaded by a coalition of civic leaders, persons from Louisville Presbytery and Louisville Seminary. But that story came later.

Judicial Decisions and Injustices

The first judicial mega-bombshell to rock the sociological and political landscape in the bracket years (1945–1983) came with what was simply referred to in the South as *The* Supreme Court Decision. At its heart were unresolved issues of the Civil War and racism. Though the high court rendered many decisions, it was clear to those who lived during those times that *The* Decision was *Brown v. Board of Education*, which, in May 1954, outlawed not only segregation in the public schools but all separate-but-equal services or accommodations sanctioned by the states.

The Decision reversed fifty-eight years of legal segregation that had been established by the Supreme Court's decision in the *Plessy v. Ferguson* case in 1896, a case that prohibited blacks and whites from riding in the same railroad cars in Louisiana. The *Plessy* decision was not unanimous. Justice John Marshall Harlan, born in Boyle County, Kentucky, was a remarkable man who "alone among the justices of his era was comfortable socializing with Hispanics, Negroes, and Chinese." Justice Oliver Wendell Holmes, his contemporary, referred to Harlan as the last "tobacco chomping justice," who also "drank bourbon, played golf, loved baseball, and wore colorful clothing not often associated with Supreme Court Justices." Harlan strongly opposed Plessy's "separate but equal" doctrine with memorable words: "Our Constitution is color blind and neither knows nor tolerates classes among citizens." This no doubt may have been the seminal evidence of Harlan's allotted once in a lifetime change of heart; in pre-Civil war days he had been a slaveholder.[15]

The lasting legacy of Harlan's dissent in *Plessy* stemmed from his passionate declaration that the thirteenth and fourteenth Amendments outlawed any "badges of slavery and servitude." He further reasoned that "any action by the states on account of race, color or previous *condition* of servitude was prohibited." This became the basis for the Brown decision in 1954.[16]

Harlan in 1906 was involved with forestalling the first attempted lynching of Ed Johnson in Chattanooga, Tennessee, by persuading the Supreme Court to stay the execution until it could hear arguments in the case. This was an almost unheard of victory in which "state's rights" usually carried the day. Harlan, along with Justice Holmes, took the lead in pressing for a federal response to this lynching of the accused, claiming that, "Whether guilty or innocent, he had a right to a fair trial."[17]

Johnson had been convicted of "assaulting Miss Nevada Taylor of St. Elmo on the night of January 23." The *Chattanooga Times* reported on March 20, 1906, that on the previous night Johnson "was resting calmly in his cell happy over an official order from the United States supreme court which gave him an indefinite time to live." Within an hour a mob entered the jail and, uninterrupted for two hours, broke into his cell, pulled him out and proceeded to march their victim to the nearby County Bridge where he was shot fifty times, when "any one of the shots was sufficient to produce death." The headlines read, "GOD BLESS YOU ALL—I AM INNOCENT." The article declared these were "Ed Johnson's Last Words Before Being Shot to Death By Mob Like a Dog."[18]

Lynchings were not a thing of the past. According to records in the Tuskegee University archives, between 1882 and 1968 there were a total of 4,743 (3,446 blacks; 1,297 non-blacks) lynchings reported in the United States. Many were public spectacles in which the victims were hanged before a jeering mob, wanting to avenge a crime or right a wrong in a humiliating or dehumanizing fashion. Reported lynchings were not limited to any race or religion or state. Only Massachusetts, Rhode Island, New Hampshire, and Vermont reported no lynchings. States with the highest number of reported lynchings were Mississippi, Georgia, Texas, Louisiana, and Alabama.[19] Lynchings are still deeply embedded in the black psyche.

In the summer of 1955, at the height of the Presbyterian Church's membership "glory days" and two years before Sputnik launched the space race between the Soviet Union and the United States, this hateful legacy was again acted out when Emmett Till, a young African American from Chicago, visited relatives in Money, Mississippi. He was dumped in the Tallahatchie River with a bullet hole in his head and a 75-pound cotton-gin fan around his neck for allegedly uttering remarks to a white woman that her relatives found offensive. Justice was yet to be meted out in 2005 in this half-century-old cold case.

Clarence Page, in a syndicated column in the *Lexington (KY) Herald Leader* on the Till case, wrote that the *Jackson (MS) Clarion-Ledger* reported in February 2005 that U.S. Attorney Jim Greenlee of Oxford, Mississippi, had "asked the Justice Department to take a new look at the case." Page recalled how "under J. Edgar Hoover, the FBI turned a blind eye to such civil rights violations, leaving them to the states." Page reminded his readers that later revelations showed that "Hoover wiretapped and harassed black activists like Martin Luther King Jr. and the Black Panthers." He concluded, "Justice delayed does not have to be totally denied."[20] The *Lexington Herald-Leader* noted, in its June 2, 2005, edition in an obscure fourteen-line summary, that federal investigators had exhumed the body of Emmett Till "in hopes of finding clues to his slaying."[21] It appeared that the FBI was reopening the case.

Boycotts and School Desegregation

In the fall of 1955 in Montgomery, Alabama, fifteen-year-old Claudette Colvin boarded a city bus and refused to give up her seat to a white passenger. She was arrested. Later in the fall, Mary Louise Smith, an eighteen-year-old black student, was arrested for failing to give up her seat on the bus. Anger among the black citizens of Montgomery heated up until it reached a flash point on the evening of December 1, 1955, when Rosa Parks, a seamstress and former NAACP secretary, got on the Cleveland Avenue bus in downtown Montgomery and remained seated in the front of the bus after the driver asked the blacks to move to the back. She was immediately arrested and placed in the Montgomery jail.[22]

Within a week the Montgomery Improvement Association (MIA) and the Montgomery Bus Boycott were organized under the leadership of E. D. Nixon, former chair of the NAACP of Alabama, Martin Luther King, Jr., Ralph Abernathy and others. The boycott demanded guaranteed polite treatment of blacks by the drivers, the abolishment of segregation and establishment of a first-come seat policy, and the employment of black bus drivers. Participation in the boycott by the black community was nearly 100 percent, as people walked, used cabs, car-pooled. Some even rode mules to work.[23]

The Boycott was based on the theological principles of nonviolent resistance that King had formulated from what he had learned from the Christian doctrine of love, the Christian ideals applied to modern society as taught by Walter Rauschenbusch, and nonviolent methods practiced by Mahatma Gandhi. These principles would guide King's involvement in the civil rights movement that was only beginning to emerge.[24]

The struggle to achieve the goals of the Boycott proceeded for months, growing stronger through the unrelenting persistence of the blacks. Opposition by whites[25] began to mount through a variety of tactics, such as increased harassment by the police, the swift cancellation of insurance policies, and suits against the leaders of the movement citing that car pools were a "public nuisance" and an illegal "private enterprise." The leadership of the Boycott decided to challenge the segregated busing laws of Montgomery as being in opposition to the Fourteenth Amendment. Finally, King received a simple message, "the motion to affirm is granted and the judgment is affirmed," meaning that segregation on the buses was illegal. The Boycott was over on December 20, 1956, more than a year after it began.[26]

Though the Montgomery Bus Boycott was important in raising to visibility the cause of civil rights, it did not have the media appeal that would equal the desegregation of Little Rock High School in 1957, a time when most white teenagers were listening to Buddy Holly's "Peggy Sue" or watching Elvis Presley gyrate in "Jailhouse Rock." Senate majority leader Lyndon B. Johnson, then senator from Texas, pushed through the U.S. Senate a tepid civil rights bill, inoffensive to Southern senators reluctant to give up the status quo, that "barely changed anything but was more a symbol of hope that the law could be used to change Southern society." No civil rights legislation had passed Congress before this one since the Civil War, dubbed by the *New York Times* as "incomparably the most significant domestic action of any Congress this century."[27]

The power of television brought into focus for millions of people the crippling effects of segregation in the South. They were mesmerized before their TV sets by the sight of the authority of the federal government dramatically displayed by Eisenhower's combat-clad 101st Airborne Division paratroopers facing off against Orville Faubus's Arkansas National Guard troopers.[28]

Two months earlier, Eisenhower had said he would not send the paratroopers to enforce the law out of the belief that such an approach would be counterproductive; but the situation had reached the point where he had no other choice. This course of action, in the face of escalating violence and lawlessness, was needed to protect the lives of the nine black students as they entered Little Rock High and to restore law and order to the community. It was the first time since the Civil War and Reconstruction that federal troops had been deployed to the South for the purpose of reducing racial conflict. The confrontation between the federal and state forces was deescalated when the National Guard was ordered by a federal court to leave. They were subsequently federalized.[29]

At the close of the 1950s, Eisenhower's fears were realized in part. He had prevailed in assuring the admission of the nine students to Little Rock High, but during the following school year (1958–1959), Faubus "closed all the schools in Little Rock rather than accept desegregation." Central High reopened on a desegregated basis in 1960.[30]

Presbyterian Church growth was in its "Glory Days" during these years; strong boards and agencies guided its corporate life, relational networks were at their peak providing denominational leadership, one major reunion failed and another succeeded.

Camelot, Protests, and Violence

The 1960s began with a momentary reprieve from the turbulence that erupted in wake of *The* Supreme Court Decision of the last decade, though the new tactic of lunch counter sit-ins was introduced as a new form of protest. John F. Kennedy defeated Richard M. Nixon for the presidency and the era of youthful Camelot was ushered in with high hopes. The reprieve was short lived, for armed conflict began to take on new forms. The new president was soon faced in 1961 with the failed Bay of Pigs invasion in Cuba, an operation that was part of his inheritance from the previous administration. The Soviets put a man in space early in the year; the president promised to put a man on the moon by the end of the decade; Kennedy later witnessed the first American in space in May.

But before May of 1961 was over, Kennedy was plunged into the civil disorder created in response to the Freedom Riders, who were challenging the Jim Crow laws governing interstate public transportation, by riding buses, trains, and planes headed for the Deep South. On May 5, on such a bus, black and white Riders set out from Washington, DC, for New Orleans, Louisiana, riding seated together on the bus, eating together at segregated lunch counters and ignoring White Only restroom signs. They faced little resistance until they got to Rock Hill, South Carolina, where they received the first of many beatings from angry mobs.[31]

On Mother's Day, May 14, 1961, a few miles outside Anniston, Alabama, their bus was firebombed. The Freedom Riders exited the exploding bus into the hands of waiting vigilantes, only to be saved from being lynched by an undercover agent on board "as he fired his gun in the air." The driver, who was opposed to the whole venture, "fled in glee."[32]

A replacement bus was reluctantly dispatched to continue delivering the Riders to their destination by way of Jackson, Mississippi. President Kennedy, fearful of what might be in store for the Riders once they crossed over into Mississippi, sent his brother Robert, the Attorney General, to cut a deal with Mississippi officials to make sure no violence would occur. The deal was, that the Mississippi National Guard would guarantee their safe passage across the state, with the understanding that they would be arrested upon arrival in Jackson. The Riders chose to stay in jail rather than appeal their arrest. Due to the overcrowded conditions in the Jackson jails, many men and women were transferred to Parchman Farm, the state penitentiary, where the situation deteriorated rapidly. The Riders survived the harsh treatment there by singing freedom songs. Though "scattered hunger strikes weakened many of the Freedom Riders physically" their morale was not weakened.[33]

The outside world in August witnessed the building of the Berlin Wall. Kennedy in November dispatched 16,000 "advisors" to Vietnam, another extension of his presidential inheritance. John Glenn's orbit of the earth in February of 1962 gave a positive terrestrial spin to the spirits of the American people, but conflict came much too quickly, dampening those spirits. The international Cuban Missile Crisis of October was averted by Kennedy at the last minute, but the domestic crises at Ole Miss, surrounding the entrance of James Meredith as a student, was not. Once again the president of the United States had to federalize a state's National Guard at the eleventh hour to prevent the destruction of life and property at a place where the fall's excitement, in a world being rudely awakened to the devastating cruelties of racism, had been the anticipation of next weekend's football game. Law and order prevailed but at a high price.[34]

Medgar Evers, who had applied for admission to the University of Mississippi (Ole Miss) soon after The Supreme Court decision but was denied, began organizing boycotts of gas stations that did not allow blacks to use their facilities. He also organized chapters of the NAACP in Mississippi Delta towns. Evers and his wife moved from Mound Bayou to Jackson, Mississippi, where they set up the NAACP office for the state. As state field secretary, Evers had finally gotten federal help when Meredith was entering Ole Miss. On June 12, 1963, Evers was gunned down in the driveway of his home by a single sniper. Thirty-one years later, Byron De La Beckwith was convicted of his murder.[35] On the following day, the author along with other ministers and elders committed to the cause of racial justice, were embroiled with other ministers and elders across town in Jackson where the Synod of Mississippi (PCUS) had been meeting, trying to arrive at some appropriate response to the tragedy. The best that could be achieved at the moment was a tepid resolution deploring what had happened. For some it was too little, too late; for others it was simply too much.

The day before Evers was gunned down, Governor George Wallace went to the University of Alabama to fulfill a campaign pledge "to stand in the schoolhouse door to block integration of Alabama pubic schools." In a mini–political drama he stood in a doorway blocking the entrance of two black students, Vivian Malone and James Hood, who were attempting to register. Federalized Alabama National Guard units had been deployed to the university campus by President Kennedy. When Wallace completed his prepared statement and proclamation, he stepped aside and allowed the students to proceed.[36]

On September 15, 1963, Denise McNair, Addie Mae Collins, Cynthia Wesley, and Carol Robertson entered the all-black Sixteenth Street Baptist Church in Birmingham to attend Sunday school. While their

Dreams, Where Have You Gone?

class was being taught, a powerful bomb exploded in the basement, snuffing out their young lives. Thirty-four years later, in 1997, the filmmaker Spike Lee produced a feature-length documentary, "Four Little Girls," based on what became known as "the Birmingham Bombing." In July of the same year the FBI announced that it was "reopening the bombing case based on 'new information.' "[37]

Assassinations, Civil Disorder, and Conventions

Then came November and Dallas. The Texas School Book Depository overlooking Dealey Plaza in downtown Dallas became the Ford's Theatre of 1963, and Lee Harvey Oswald became its John Wilkes Booth. The nation immediately came to a stunned standstill and plunged into deepened grief over President Kennedy's assassination. The glittering dreams of a modern Camelot were snuffed out with this vibrant life. But not all were brokenhearted; school children, having been molded by parental vitriolic diatribes against the young president, cheered the news in some parts of the South. Making sense of the insensible was almost impossible; conspiracy theories abounded. The long season of mourning began; for some, resolution and closure were elusive for decades.

The shaken nation greeted 1964 with the ratification of the Twenty-fourth Amendment to the Constitution on January 23, outlawing the poll tax, one of the last vestiges of discrimination in the voting process. The invasion of the Beatles soon followed. Andrew Goodman, Michael Schwerner, and James Chaney, civil rights workers from "up East," vanished in the June night, their bodies not to be unearthed from the dam of a small lake near Philadelphia, Mississippi, until August. On that very weekend, civil rights workers along with chaplains recruited by the National Council of Churches were trained in Oxford, Ohio, to converge on Mississippi, to conduct "Freedom Schools" in what was called "the long hot summer." In the heat of July, President Johnson pushed the Civil Rights Act through Congress, after which he reportedly said, "I just delivered the South to the Republicans." In a twisted turn of events, Johnson, on another front, signed the Gulf of Tonkin Resolution in August enabling him to escalate U.S. involvement in Vietnam. November gifted Johnson, in his bid for election to the presidency in his own right, with a landslide victory over Barry Goldwater.

Rival factions in the Nation of Islam, led by Louis Farrakhan on one side and Malcolm X on the other, were locked in a divisive ideological power struggle that finally led to X's assassination on February 21, 1965. This was a prelude to more violence. Grainy film footage of protest marchers being attacked at the Edmund Pettus Bridge in Selma on March 7 by Alabama guardsmen and police with tear gas, dogs, bullwhips, and nightsticks seared the corporate memory of the nation with the Selma to Montgomery protest march on "Bloody Sunday." Two days later, state troopers stopped the marchers a second time, but no violence occurred. Two weeks later on March 21, a third attempt to get the four-day march on its way from Selma was successful under the protection of Federal Troops.[38]

President Johnson in 1965, while faced with the situation in Vietnam growing out of control, continued to press for his "Great Society." One centerpiece of that dream was the passage of the Voting Rights Bill. Other concerns were that social injustice, unemployment, poverty, and hunger would be eradicated. Though legislation to those ends was enacted, the translation into reality was not that easy. As summer heated up, so did the riots in the Watts section of Los Angeles in the wake of growing racial tensions.

James Meredith, in June 1966, following time as a student at Ole Miss, set out on his "walk against fear" from Memphis to Jackson down the main north-south highway through the State of Mississippi. Before he got very far he was wounded from the bullet of a sniper along the roadway. What began as a somewhat peaceful march now turned into a *cause celebre.* Stokely Carmichael (he later changed his name to Kwame Ture) with the Student Nonviolent Coordinating Committee (SNCC), along with other civil rights leaders, vowed to continue the walk. When the walk reached Greenwood, Carmichael was arrested and his anger reached a fevered pitch. He blurted out the demand for "Black Power." It was not a phrase original to him. Adam Clayton Powell had used it in a speech at Howard University in May, but it was a term that would be associated with Carmichael forever. "It electrified young blacks, frightened many whites, commandeered the headlines."[39]

The injection of "Black Power" into the struggle for justice and freedom divided the black community. Roy Wilkins of the NAACP denounced it as "reverse racism." The Congress of Racial Equality (CORE) endorsed it; King's Southern Christian Leadership Conference (SCLC) did not. It was in essence a rejection of King's dream of integration and cultural assimilation, shattering a seemingly united black front into individual self-interest groups. It rebuffed nonviolence in favor of violence as a legitimate strategy to achieve one's goals.

Carmichael's rhetoric became more shrill in 1967 and chants of "Burn, Baby, Burn" stoked the fires of civil disturbance that raged in Detroit and Newark, from where terrifying images flickered across TV screens. The Poor People's March descended on Washington as a witness to the failure of the Great Society to alleviate poverty and unemployment. The Tet Offensive ushered in 1968, with disturbing scenes of disarrayed U.S. Armed Forces displayed on evening news broadcasts. Anti-war demonstrators numbering 300,000 surged into Central Park, also adding to civil disruption and sending President Johnson a powerful message of dissent regarding U.S. policies in Vietnam. The cumulative effect of this, along with other events and policy setbacks, led Johnson eventually to announce on March 31, 1968, that he would not seek reelection later that year.

James Earl Ray added the Lorraine Motel in Memphis to the list of historic assassination sites on April 4, 1968, with the crack of a high-powered rifle that struck down Martin Luther King, Jr., the Dreamer of the Dream. It was as if the gates of hell were flung wide open. Riots broke out in Memphis, New York, Boston, Chicago, Detroit, and other places across the land.

Robert Kennedy broke the news about King to a crowd of two thousand people gathered to hear him speak in Indianapolis; they had not heard. Through their cries of anguish he reminded them that King "dedicated his life to love and to justice for his fellow human beings, and he died because of that effort." He affirmed his belief that "the vast majority of white people and the vast majority of black people in this country want to live together, want to improve the quality of our life, and want justice for all human beings who abide in our land." He closed with an invocation: "Let us dedicate ourselves to that, and say a prayer for our country and for our people."[40]

Time was running out for RFK, but he was still running; running for the presidency of the United States, that grand pulpit from which to lead the country in improving the quality of life and justice for all. The majority party was still the Democratic Party in 1968; the shift had not yet been made to a Republican majority, though the Nixon Southern strategy was about to be launched. "[V]oting Democrat was still a habit for a nation whose youngest voters were born only a few years after the passing of Franklin Roosevelt."[41]

Robert Kennedy entered the ballroom of the Ambassador Hotel in Los Angeles late in the evening of June 4 to claim his winning of the prized California primary over Senator Eugene McCarthy. The crowd was ecstatic. Kennedy thanked a list of his faithful supporters and dwelt on the divisions the country had faced in the past few years. "We are a great country, an unselfish country and a compassionate country." His intention was to build on those beliefs to overcome the country's divisions in the coming campaign. He concluded his remarks with: "So my thanks to all of you, and it's on to Chicago, and let's win there."[42] He took only a few steps toward that destination. As he left the podium, he was guided through the kitchen to avoid the crowded ballroom. Sirhan Sirhan, in one more act of violence, made that nondescript place another historic assassination site.

The 1968 Republican Convention in Miami Beach on August 5–8, which nominated Richard M. Nixon as its candidate for president, was locked down tight to shield it from angry protesters and demonstrators. A riot broke out in a nearby black neighborhood; four persons died and several hundred were injured. It was a Sunday school picnic compared to what erupted at the Democratic Convention in Chicago, during August 22–29, that nominated Hubert Humphrey as its candidate. Nixon defeated Humphrey for the presidency on November 5, 1968.

The 1960s mercifully ended in 1969 in a drug-induced psychedelic haze with a massive love-in at Woodstock's "Festival of Life" in upstate New York awash in mud and ear-splitting sounds of musical hard rock protests. Armstrong and Aldrin, fulfilling Kennedy's promise, serenely walked on the moon. The Presbyterian Churches had introduced their new "Faith and Life Curriculum" and "Covenant Life Curriculum" during the 1960s. They also began to see their youth—the "Church of the Future"—going out the back door as the institution underwent restructures and the Union Presbytery Movement got into high gear.

Vietnam, Watergate, and Iran Hostages

During the previous decade of the 1960s the United States crossed the most volatile political, social, and cultural watershed the country had ever faced, yet there was still unfinished business to be done in the new decade. The fruits of Alfred C. Kinsey's 1948 and 1953 studies on sexual behavior in the human male and female, along with the development of "The Pill," unleashed an unprecedented sexual revolution in the 1960s—first heterosexual, then later homosexual, the likes of which transformed society as never before. The women's liberation movement and the environmental movement were building momentum and beginning to take an influential place alongside the civil rights movement and the peace movement in shaping the social agenda. The drug counterculture tuned out conventional wisdom and violently attacked irrelevant and oppressive institutions; flower children blossomed, not trusting anyone over thirty. Suspicions about the assassinations of John, Martin, and Robert hung over the country like a pall.

The first half of 1970 saw the Chicago Eight (later Seven) found not guilty of indictments growing out of their involvement in the 1968 Democratic Convention. The Vietnam War, a war that had already brought down one presidency, was rapidly deteriorating; four students were killed at Kent State University in Ohio during a Vietnam protest; the Mai Lai massacre was perpetrated against civilians in Vietnam; the invasion of Cambodia followed; the Gulf of Tonkin Resolution was repealed by June.

The following year, in June 1971, the *New York Times* began to publish the Pentagon Papers—a secret Defense Department study of U.S. involvement in Vietnam. Nixon was now fully immersed in Vietnam and struggled with domestic issues, all a buildup to the presidential campaign of 1972. On June 17, the five burglars, who had broken into the Democratic National Committee headquarters located in a building whose name would ever be linked with the scandal that brought downfall to the Nixon presidency, were arrested. The country did not yet believe what it read in the paper about the White House involvement. The mounting volume of evidence implicating the White House's involvement notwithstanding, and because of his success in other areas, such as his triumphal establishment of diplomatic ties with China, Nixon won his bid for reelection by a landslide over his Democratic opponent, George McGovern, on November 7, 1972.

In a long series of almost comic but deadly serious ploys throughout 1972–1973, an anonymous tipster who became known for decades only as Deep Throat until he revealed his own identity in the summer of 2005, fed two *Washington Post* reporters, Bob Woodward and Carl Bernstein, with enough clues for the White House scandal to be exposed. The final straw came during the Senate Watergate Committee hearings with the news that all conversations in the Oval Office were taped and officials were forced by a Supreme Court ruling to release the tapes to the prosecutors. On August 9, 1974, President Nixon resigned his office.[43]

Deep distrust of historic American institutions, both inside and outside of government, had been building in the heart and psyche of the nation for over a decade. Though the revelations of Woodward and Bernstein had given the institution of print media a momentary boost, Watergate itself dragged institutional respect to the depths and cynicism abounded. Nixon's successor, Gerald Ford, tried to stem the tide, but in an act that received mixed reviews, he pardoned President Nixon on September 8, 1974.[44] Ford did preside over the conclusion of U.S. involvement in Vietnam. On April 30, 1975, the last American personnel flew out of Saigon from the roof of the U.S. Embassy. Saigon became Ho Chi Minh City. Normalization of diplomatic relations between the two countries would not be reestablished for years. The nation in the twenty-first century still has some healing to do over Vietnam.

Jimmy Carter was elected president in November of 1976, and as he strolled down Pennsylvania Avenue with Rosalynn on inauguration day, January 20, 1977, his intention was to signal a more peaceful and open presidency. On his watch he signed the Panama Canal Treaty, the Salt II Agreement with the Soviets, the Camp David Accords between Egypt and Israel. Andrew Young resigned as Ambassador to the United

Nations. The American Embassy in Tehran was overrun in November of 1979, and the Soviets invaded Afghanistan in December. The reality of new international crises hung in the air. In April of 1980 Carter made the decision to attempt the ill-fated hostage rescue mission in Iran. Its failure and the inability to gain the timely release of the hostages doomed his attempt at a second presidential term.[45]

Ronald Reagan defeated Carter in the presidential election on November 4. While a lame-duck president, Carter by the end of the year had signed the Alaska Land Bill, and the Superfund Bill to clean up toxic waste dumps, and warned the Soviets against military intervention in Poland. Shortly after the first of January 1981, the final terms were negotiated for the release of the American hostages in Iran. Ronald Reagan was inaugurated at noon on January 20. Twenty minutes later in Tehran, the hostages were released. The next day Reagan dispatched Carter to welcome the hostages home when they touched down in Germany.[46]

Reagan, the first conservative president in over fifty years and known as the "Great Communicator," began his presidency in his charismatic way on an upbeat note in the face of double-digit inflation and high interest rates. His economic vision for the country was termed "Reaganomics," a retooling of a theory called "supply side economics." In 1982 the country was hit with a severe recession with high unemployment. During the course of his two-term presidency, his policies would reverse these trends, but at a cost of a record annual deficit and a ballooning national debt. He was determined to reduce the federal government's responsibility for solving social problems, lift restrictions on business, and pass historic tax cuts. He was deeply committed to rearming a strong military and curtailing the threat of communism, being especially supportive of the Strategic Defense Initiative Program, popularly known as "Star Wars." In 1983 he coined the name "evil empire" for the Soviet Union.[47] Presbyterians marched in Atlanta in June.

Presbyterians for Social and Racial Justice

Oftentimes symbols say volumes when one is trying to comprehend the importance of great sweeps of cultural, social, political, and economic changes and movements that brought them into being. What symbolic images might capture the significance of the formative bracket years of 1945 and 1983? The opening bracket might best be depicted by Alfred Eisenstaedt's famous photograph for *Life* magazine of a sailor kissing a nurse at the V-J Day celebration in Times Square on August 14, 1945, the end of World War II.[48] It symbolized the sheer joy and relief at being delivered from the horrors of war while at the same time teetering on unabashed hopes for the future. The closing bracket might be an imaginary 1983 animated video sequence of a "Star Wars" rocket streaking through space to intercept an incoming hostile missile targeting the U.S. Capitol building. It would symbolize a defensive stance attempting to pacify the country's fears against the threats of the Cold War.

Between these two symbolic brackets, the industrialization of the South was juxtaposed with desegregation, protests, violence, assassinations, civil disorder, political upheaval, war, and an economic roller coaster. This was the context in which Presbyterians attempted to make a contribution toward healing of the scars created by the Civil War and racism, the residual effect of slavery. Parallel chronologies of events in society in general and in the Presbyterian Church in particular are both revealing and instructive about the close proximity and dynamic interaction between the two. The symbolic image of the Presbyterian Church (U.S.A.) might be an aerial photo of Presbyterians marching on "the Day" from the World Congress Center to City Hall in Atlanta on June 10, 1983.

And what did that symbolize? It was a witness to the Unity of the Church in the act of reuniting parts of a church that was ripped asunder by the fury of the Civil War, another tangible evidence of attempts to put that episode in American history to rest. This was not the final act of removing the scars of that conflict on American institutions, but it was a symbol and a significant step in that direction. The Union Presbytery Movement had played a pivotal role in it. It also was a witness to Presbyterian attempts to eradicate the damning reality of racism, the residual effect of slavery. Clarity on this reality may be a bit more elusive.

The operative word in that assessment is "attempts." Though great strides have been made, there is a long way to go before "eradication" of racism in the church and in the world will become the descriptive word. Nevertheless, to understand the contribution of Presbyterians during these bracket years, it must be recognized that those deeply involved in working for union presbyteries and denominational reunion were also deeply involved in working for social and racial justice. For them, the two went hand in hand. The influence exerted by the Presbyterian Church in the realm of social and racial justice was both corporate and individual.

It would be impossible within the scope of this study to document the full range of corporate and individual contributions Presbyterians North and South have made toward the cause of social and racial justice or to pay tribute to the scores of individuals involved. A full accounting of the corporate contributions in the field of social justice concerns and public policy made by the UPCUSA, though they are myriad, are beyond the scope of this study and their absence from it should not discount their lasting significance. However, a selective summary of these contributions made in the PCUS is necessary to illustrate what happened to that end. The purpose of illustrating the corporate contribution made in the PCUS is to show how concerns for social justice and public policies were achieved in a very difficult social climate and location while at the same time trying to clear the way for union presbyteries and achieve denominational reunion.

Presbyterian Corporate Contributions

In the tradition of the prophet, Jeremiah, and the reformer, John Calvin, Presbyterians believed that the proper response to God's grace freely given them was to "seek the welfare of the city" (Jer. 29:7). Presbyterian corporate contributions to that end in the PCUS were illustrated in many different ways. The General Assembly (PCUS), exercising moral persuasion, issued study papers prepared for it by various permanent committees or councils to give guidance to the church on a variety of subjects. The Permanent Committee on Christian Relations (PCCR), its successor, the Council on Church and Society (CCS), and the Permanent Theological Committee (PTC) were very active in this educational effort.

A sample of such study papers issued in the critical years of 1965–1970 included "The Civil Rights Movement in Light of Christian Teaching: Demonstrations and Civil Disobedience" (PCCR–1965); "Theological Basis for Christian Social Action," "Capital Punishment," "Policy on Vietnam" (PTC–1966); "God's Work in Our Rapidly Changing World" (CCS–1967); "Toward an Understanding of Racial Disorders," "The Church and Its Use of Economic Power," "Equal Opportunity in Housing" (CCS–1968); "Hunger," "Justice, Law and Order" (CCS–1969); "Christian Responsibility in World Economic Development," "Vietnam," "Abortion" (CCS–1970). The Assembly in 1970 also received a report that "A Message to the Presbyterian Church, U.S. concerning the Black Manifesto from the Moderator of the General Assembly and the Council on Church and Society," signed by R. Matthew Lynn, Moderator, and Wayne P. Todd, chair of CCS, had been distributed to the Church.[49]

In addition to issuing study papers, the PCUS Assembly passed resolutions advising various public officials of its position on certain matters and encouraging them to take these positions into consideration in their decision-making process. For example, in 1969, William S. McLean, chair of the Standing Committee on Church and Society (PCUS), presented to the Assembly resolutions on "Selective Conscientious Objection" to participation in a particular war and

"Alternative to Combative Service" pointing out that the Selective Service system had failed to provide such an alternative, although the Universal Military Training and Service Act stipulated such a provision. The copies of the adopted resolutions were sent to the president of the United States, the Secretary of Defense, the president of the Senate, and the Speaker of the House of Representatives asking them to rectify the situation.[50] A "Resolution on Nuclear Disarmament" was also adopted and sent to these same national elected officials.[51]

The PCUS Assembly also exercised review and control over its boards and agencies and lower governing bodies and their agencies. In 1967 the Assembly adopted a position paper, "Repenting of Discrimination in Our Institutional Life," in which it called on all bodies under its review and control to submit an annual audit on progress made in compliance in their respective areas. The Assembly also in its budgeting process had leverage in exercising efforts at social and racial justice. The Board of Church Extension (PCUS) and the Board of Christian Education (PCUS), as they were responding to a request for funds from the National Council of Churches, asked the Council on Church and Society to conduct a special review of the Mississippi Delta Ministry (DM), before they made their budgetary decisions. The special review committee was positive about what it found regarding the DM, found no reason not to commend it for support, but noted "with shame for ourselves and our denomination that the Presbyterian Church, U.S. has been conspicuous in the paucity of its support for the DM."[52]

Southern Presbyterians loved Montreat Conferences. In the middle of August 1968, the Board of National Missions and the Board of Christian Education cosponsored a conference there with the theme: "New Days! New Ways?" The conference, which convened immediately prior to the Democratic Convention in Chicago, was radically different from past conferences and reflected the time of social upheaval. Andrew Young was the keynote speaker. All sorts of resource people were brought in to bring a dose of reality to the proceedings.

A group of African Americans, a street gang known as the "Five Black Cats," were brought from an experimental ministry in inner-city Houston at the recommendation of William J. Fogleman, executive presbyter of Brazos Presbytery (PCUS). They were housed in Assembly Inn and caused quite a stir in this old staid hotel by eating in the dining room barefooted in their military fatigues. Thomas L. Jones, one of the codirectors of the conference, said "they were really nice guys" who kept coming to him throughout the conference for guidance on what to do in this strange environment (85-8).

The Sunday evening Communion service, planned by Jones and Frank Brooks, Director of the Office of Music and Worship in the Board of Christian Education (PCUS), was punctuated with multimedia rapid-fire images of poverty and other expressions of injustice in the world, "a compelling documentary on behalf of the poor." An image of the wounded head of a Vietnamese with head bandaged in a filthy rag provided the backdrop to the singing of verses from "All Hail the Power of Jesus' Name."[53]

John F. Anderson preached the sermon in front of a banner on which the words, "For the Church in Political Action," were emblazoned. He, wearing "informal attire," challenged the congregation dressed in "sport or athletic shirts, slacks, occasionally sneakers . . . to be politically active in a constructive and Christian way. . . . Set your mind on God's Kingdom and His justice first." Anderson said that the Preamble to the U.S. Constitution is "still a radically new idea." He admonished his hearers: "Do not say that government and politics are not the Church's business unless you are prepared to say that government and politics are not God's business." On understanding what kind of justice is meant when the term is invoked, he said, "Don't talk to me about law and order when there is price-fixing at General Electric." One observer complained that, "like the rest of the conference," he found little emphasis in the sermon on "the Gospel or the Church's mission according to the Great Commission."[54]

"We Shall Overcome," the theme song of the "freedom" movement, was sung as the offering was received. The highlight of the service came when, in joyful procession led by the celebrants holding the elements of the Lord's Supper high overhead, congregants "filed forward to the tables, singing, swaying and clapping in dance rhythm: 'Be swift my soul, to answer Him; be jubilant, my feet! Our God is marching on.' " The Howard Hanger Trio broke into a jazzed-up version of "The Battle Hymn of the Republic," as much of an anathema to some Southerners as "Dixie" was to some Northerners. It took more than an hour for the participants to follow the banners they had made for the occasion to receive the sacrament.[55]

Not all in the crowd were jubilant. Some people left the auditorium before and during "communion"; a few remained seated and silent; "evangelical, conservative, and even concerned-type Presbyterians obediently shuffled along to the tables, ashamed to be non-conformists." One retired missionary, with tears in his eyes, was reported as having kept repeating, "My sister, my own sister went down there!" It was a day that would be remembered for a long time. For some it would be a moment of pure joy; for others, a time of shock and dismay. One young minister was heard asking the rhetorical question: "Do you suppose the place [Montreat] will ever be the same again?"[56] For the twenty-first-century reader, the account of this event may rightly seem a bit quaint and leave a less than enthusiastic feeling about the PCUS in 1968. But for those who participated in fomenting change in those days, it was radical beyond one's imagination, and Montreat and the PCUS became a different place.

Years later, in the 1980s, when Tom Jones was pastor of Chevy Chase Presbyterian Church in urban Washington, DC, he teamed up with the editor of *Christianity in Crisis* and conducted seminars for twelve pastors in the summer, where he exposed "people to how Washington works and theologized about it." On one occasion, they invited Congressman Mickey Leland, representative of the 18th District of Texas, the primarily black and Hispanic district where he had grown up. Leland, a social activist since college, and Freshman Majority Whip in his first term, soon became a spokesperson for hungry and homeless persons on the world stage. Speaker Thomas P. "Tip" O'Neill named Leland chairman of the House Select Committee on Hunger. He became the architect for the USAID Leland Initiative, an African Global Information Infrastructure Project in twenty-one partner countries in Africa.[57] On this occasion in the Jones seminar Leland spent the entire hour and a half talking about the 1968 Montreat National Missions–Christian Education Conference and what it meant to him. He said he remembered it as if it were yesterday: "It changed my life." It sent him in new directions of advocacy and action to help poor people. He was one of the "Five Black Cats" (85-8). Shortly after the seminar, Leland died on August 7, 1989, in a plane crash while on a fact-finding mission to "an isolated refugee camp, Fugnido, in Ethiopia, which sheltered thousands of unaccompanied children fleeing the civil conflict in neighboring Sudan."[58]

Individual Presbyterians' Contributions

The corporate acts of the PCUS were not the only contributing acts in pursuit of social and racial justice that made a difference in the world at large. There were the quiet and not so quiet, the pastoral and the prophetic acts of individuals that also made their contribution. It could be a disservice to those countless individual Presbyterians, North and South, who made a difference, to think that mentioning a few would do justice to their efforts. Examples have been sprinkled all through the story to this point. But now a brief litany of a few is given to honor the many.

Parham Rufus Shaw, elder at the College Hill Presbyterian Church (then PCUS, now PCA) outside Oxford, Mississippi, in the early 1950s was responsible for filling the pulpit during vacancies. At the elder's request, his son Sid recruited a college chaplain from Ole Miss as supply preacher one Sunday. Another member, a high-ranking administrator at the university,[59] got wind of it and adamantly suggested the chaplain be "uninvited" because he had played ping-pong with a black man. His son recalled years later that his father, being an open-minded person, responded to the "uninvitation" by saying, "I believe we need to hear this chaplain," and they did. The chaplain was Will D. Campbell, who years later called himself a "bootleg preacher" of Baptist persuasion.[60]

Tom Jones, Harry Simrall, Ed Sanders, and John Reeves Crumpton, elders at First Presbyterian Church, Starkville, Mississippi, refused in the early 1960s to back down from their "open door" convictions when the session came under unbelievable pressure and reversed its policy of seating Negro worshipers with the elders in a special section of the sanctuary. They stood by their pastor, Robert H. Walkup, who came under fire for his prophetic stance against racism, his opposition to the segregationist Governor, and his support of the National Council of Churches. He chaired the Synod Commission investigating the Mac Hart Case. In later years he commented about that judicial proceeding: "I saw more 'Christian' hate than I knew existed this side of hell. My soul sickened and my mind fuzzed over."[61] Walkup's life was once mysteriously threatened. One day he discovered an unlit gas space heater in his office; he was an avid pipe smoker at the time.

William F. Winter, longtime elder in Fondren Presbyterian Church, Jackson, Mississippi, and governor of the state, continued to champion the cause of racial justice after he left the governorship in 1984. With the zeal of his youth for change, he helped form the Institute for Racial Reconciliation that bears his name at the University of Mississippi. He declared in a seminar for Southern state legislators in November 2004 that "the problem of race, despite all the progress that we have made, remains the thorniest, trickiest and most difficult barrier that we have to confront to achieve a truly successful and united region." His assessment was that "Most white folks think that we have come a lot further in race relations than most black people do." In 2004 on the 40th anniversary of the murders of the three civil rights workers in Neshoba County, Mississippi, the Institute, in response to a request from black and white residents, helped organize a local coalition that openly shared their feelings and concerns about the unresolved tragedy. The coalition, which included Choctaw Indians (who had long lived separately in the county), issued a public call for justice in the still-open murder case that eventually led to the trial and conviction of one of the aging conspirators.[62]

Ken McCall, while growing up, was part of the "Call to United Christian Youth Action" of the National Council of Churches Youth Department along with Andrew Young (66-5). When McCall served a UPCUSA church in Cicero, Illinois, in the early 1960s, he developed a community organization, an industrial ministry to all the local industries. While Martin Luther King, Jr., was marching on the south side of Chicago in the mid-1960s, McCall said, "[W]e had a small march into Cicero of 200 people, and we had 3,000 National Guard with live ammunition, machine guns pointed, to allow these 200 people to walk through. And I vividly remember walking the streets, trying to be sure that if people had any weapons, we could try to get them away from them" (66-6).

Ed White's in-laws were the Lafars, who back then were THE pillars of the First Presbyterian Church in Gastonia, North Carolina, and owners of a string of cotton mills that Liston Pope wrote about in his book *Mill Hands and Preachers*. Other relatives of his wife lived in Rock Hill, South Carolina. The first time White and his wife had gone to visit them after they married they got "this incredible red carpet treatment." However, White had been briefed ahead of time on three subjects not to be discussed: labor unions, race, and the reunion of the Northern and Southern Presbyterian churches. But later, in the early 1960s, White accompanied seven black Protestant ministers, seven white Protestant ministers, and two rabbis on one of the freedom rides down the East Coast testing interstate facilities. His wife's kinfolk in North and South Carolina "virtually disowned" White for about five years "until 1965 [1966] when I was down in Chicago and Martin Luther King came north to march for open housing in Cicero, Illinois, and it became evident for the first time that the racial crisis was not a southern phenomen[on], it was a national phenomen[on]." White said his Carolina relatives because of this "somehow relaxed and we rebuilt the relationships so they came to my installation when I was installed as a Presbytery Executive [National Capitol Union]" (86-30).

Will Kennedy went to Montgomery, Alabama, on a Sunday in the mid-1960s to try and integrate Trinity Presbyterian Church, where his father-in-law, Albert Grady Harris, had served as interim pastor. One of Billy Graham's associates was preaching there that day. Kennedy, along with a black deacon of a Southern Presbyterian Church in town and the deacon's twelve-year-old son, when met by two elders, declared that they were there to worship. The elders responded, "We can't let you in because we've determined that you're sociological agitators" and, by the way, "where are you from?" One of the elders recognized Kennedy and asked, "Haven't I played tennis with you at Montreat?" The other elder asked, "Didn't you write a curriculum book?" The answer to both questions was yes. In good southern fashion for a while they played "Do you know?" In the end, when asked again about admittance to worship, the elders said, "No we can't let you in to worship," so they left. Kennedy's later reflection was, "it was such an interesting mixture of the advantages and pain of this little denomination and its interrelationships of people" (53-10).

Kennedy and George Chauncey, from the Board of Christian Education, with José Williams, Ralph Abernathy, Walter Reuther, and Andy Young, supported the black women hospital workers' strike over low salaries in the Mother's Day march in Charleston, South Carolina, in 1969. Kennedy later learned that the father of one of his Union seminary students, a sheriff in South Carolina serving in the National Guard, was one of the ones with rifles on the roof overlooking the march. The next day Kennedy and Chauncey had breakfast with several local Presbyterian pastors, many longtime friends, who "were mad as hell" over what this was doing to them locally. Over grits and a southern menu they struggled with the implications for the Southern Church of not being involved; some agreeing the Church should be involved, and others saying "you don't understand the witness of the Church" (53-11).

Rachael Henderlite and Betty L. Blanton were pioneers who had a revolutionary effect on the PCUS. Henderlite, a biblical scholar and a prolific writer, was the first woman ordained as a minister of the Word and Sacrament in the PCUS. She was ordained by Hanover Presbytery on May 12, 1965, and became a professor at Austin Seminary. Blanton, a consummate social activist, was the second woman ordained as a minister of the Word and Sacrament in the PCUS. She was ordained on April 4, 1967, and served as associate pastor at Hunter Presbyterian Church, Lexington, Kentucky, where Mort McMillan was pastor. Both these outstanding women went through the doors opened for them by their male clergy cohorts blazing the way for countless women in the PCUS.

Church and Society

It is impossible to measure scientifically the direct impact Presbyterians have had on society through their corporate and individual witness of faithfulness to the gospel in pursuit of social and racial justice. This especially applies in attempts to determine the role union presbyteries and denominational reunion played in healing scars created by the Civil War and racism, the residual effect of slavery. The Union Presbytery Movement and denominational reunion were conceived and birthed in those dynamic bracket years between 1945 and 1983, when the industrialization of the South was juxtaposed with desegregation, protests, violence, assassinations, civil disorder, political upheaval, war, and an economic roller coaster. This was the context in which Presbyterians, who neither fought in the Civil War nor owned slaves but were heirs of that dark legacy, sought in their own time to exert influence in the realm of social and racial justice as a matter of faithful witness, both corporately and individually.

Which was the nursemaid that nurtured the other—the church or the society? Viscerally one can feel a very influential two-way relationship between the two when the story is told. A measure for documenting influence is in assessing the evolving status of the corporate and individual memory of a society. Several components exist in the concept "story," one of which is its sacramental nature. A definition of a sacramental act or symbol is "that which propels new meaning forward into some future memory." The sacramental acts or symbols of the Union Presbytery Movement and denominational reunion reshaped the corporate memory of both church and society. The new meaning these acts gave to church and society made the memories of both take on new perspectives about God's intention for people relating to one another.

Changes in the boxes and structures on Presbyterian organizational charts made as a result of the Union Presbytery Movement, and then denominational reunion, began to free the PCUS and the UPCUSA from their Civil War borders and their Civil War mentality. But these were not what secured the place of the Union Presbytery Movement or denominational reunion in American history. Presbyterian corporate and individual sacramental acts were of utmost significance, demonstrating a new way of being church in the world, embedding that reality into future corporate and individual memories, and enhancing the possibility for new attitudes and behaviors in new generations to come. More time must elapse before the lasting impact of these sacramental acts is known. Maybe this is the best one can do at this moment in determining the rightful place of the Union Presbytery Movement and denominational reunion in American history. But where were the ghosts of Stamford Bridge and Hastings in all of this?

Notes

1. Alvis, *Religion and Race*, pp. 144–145.

2. Harry S Truman Papers, Staff Member and Office Files, Philleo Nash Files, Truman Presidential Museum & Library. [Available online, http://www.trumanlibrary.org/hstpaper/nashhst.htm.]

3. Burton Grad, "The First Commercial Univac I Installation" (Burton Grad, 1997), p. 1. [Available online, http://www.softwarehistory.org/history/Grad1.html.]

4. Sean Farrell, "Not Just Farms Anymore: The Effects of World War II on Mississippi's Economy," Mississippi History Now: An online publication of the Mississippi Historical Society. [Available online, http://mshistory.k12.ms.us/features/feature19/wwii_ms.html.]

5. The author, along with future writer and editor Willie Morris, attended Mississippi Boys State, held at Belhaven College, Jackson, Mississippi, in the summer of 1951. During this simulated state government event, the Boys State-ers were marched to the new football stadium in Jackson to hear the six or seven gubernatorial candidates, including Governor Hugh White, deliver typical Mississippi political stump speeches of the times in which they tried to outdo each other on their segregationist views. Later the author joined his fellow Key Club members from Brookhaven High School who were invited to build a float for Governor White's second inaugural parade in early 1952. The float was a thing of beauty—accented with formally attired southern belles, flowing angel hair and plaster-of-paris faux fountains, and tons of magnolia leaves on the trailer skirts and reconstructed trees. Governor White's home church was Columbia Presbyterian Church, where the author served after the Governor's death, when several of the family were still members there.

6. "Company Information." [Available online, http://www.ge.com/en/company/companyinfo/index.htm.]

7. "A History of GE." [Available online, http://www.ge.com/en/company/companyinfo/at_a_glance/history_story.htm.]

8. "GE to Celebrate 50th Anniversary of Operation of Louisville in 2003." [Available online, http://www.geappliances.com/pressroom/comm/articles/50th.htm.]

9. Grad, "The First Commercial Univac I Installation," p. 1.

10. Ibid.

11. "History of Standard Time in the U.S." [Available online, http://www.aa.usno.navy.mil/faq/docs/us_tzones.html.] It is part of Kentucky lore, though unsubstantiated, that the rationale for Louisville being in the Eastern Time zone during the Second World War was so that construction of boats under government contract at the Jeffersonville Boat & Machine Co. could be more easily coordinated with the Navy Department in Washington, DC.

12. Grad, "The First Commercial Univac I Installation," p. 2.

13. "GE to Celebrate 50th Anniversary of Operation of Louisville in 2003."

Dreams, Where Have You Gone?

14. The expressway was named in honor of Henry Watterson (1840–1921), influential nineteenth century editor of *The Courier-Journal* in Louisville. Watterson, an ardent supporter of the Confederacy and a Democrat, once was invited sometime prior to the 1872 election as a weekend guest of President Ulysses S. Grant at Long Branch, New Jersey. Watterson responded to the invitation through John Russell Young, his friend from boyhood, "I don't dare to do so. I know that I shall fall in love with General Grant. We have a rough presidential election ahead of us. If I go down to the seashore and go in swimming and play penny-ante with General Grant I shall not be able to do my duty as a Democrat." In later years Watterson and Grant "became good friends." [excerpts *from Henry Watterson, Marse Henry: An Autobiography* (New York: George H. Doran Co., 1919), vol. 1, pp. 222–223. Printed in a selection of examples of Southern admiration for Ulysses S. Grant, from nineteenth century civilian or ex-Confederate Southern sources. [Available online, http://www.mscomm.com/ulysses/page172.html.]

15. "Justice John Marshall Harlan." [Available online, http://www.law.umkc.edu/faculty/projects/ftrials/shipp/harlan.html.]

16. Paul L. Whalen, "Kentucky's ties to 'Brown,' " *Lexington (KY) Herald-Leader*, May 16, 2004, p. F6.

17. "Justice John Marshall Harlan."

18. "GOD BLESS YOU ALL—I AM INNOCENT," article, *Chattanooga (TN) Times*, March 20, 1906. [Available online, http://www.law.umkc.edu/faculty/projects/ftrials/shipp/newsgodbless.html.]

19. Alvis Thomas-Lester, writer for the *Washington Post*, "Lynching era was 'the American holocaust,' " *Lexington (KY) Herald-Leader*, June 13, 2005, pp. A1, A10.

20. Clarence Page, "Resolutions still needed in 1955 Till Case," *Lexington (KY) Herald-Leader*, May 16, 2004, p. F5.

21. "50-year-old Crime," *Lexington (KY) Herald-Leader*, June 2, 2005, p. A3.

22. "What Was the Montgomery Bus Boycott?" p. 1. [Available online, http://www.home.att.net/-reniqua/what.html.]

23. Ibid.

24. "Theology of the Movement." [Available online, http://www.home.att.net/reniqua/theology.html.]

25. "White and Opposition Reaction," samples of what was written by the opposition. [Available online, http://www.home.att.net/reniqua/whiteandopposition.html.]

26. "What Was the Montgomery Bus Boycott?" p. 2.

27. "Little Rock, Arkansas—1957," p. 1. [Available online, http://www.historylearning site.co.uk/little_rock.htm.]

28. Ibid.

29. Ibid., p. 2.

30. Ibid., p. 3.

31. "A Brief History of the Freedom Riders," p. 2. [Available online, http://www.freedomridersfoundation.org/brief.history.html.]

32. Ibid.

33. Ibid., p. 3.

34. Late on the Sunday afternoon when the confrontation at Ole Miss was building between federal and state authorities, the author, then pastor of the First Presbyterian Church, Amory, was visiting with a nonmember friend, Tommy Morgan, who was struggling with whether to permit his daughter to return, in the face of impending danger, to Ole Miss where she was a student, after a weekend at home. The author advised, "Tommy, you can't deny her the opportunity to be part of history." He relented and she returned. Later it was discovered that the federalized national guard entered the campus around midnight just in the nick of time to prevent the insurgents from burning down the dormitory where she had gone upon her arrival.

35. "Medger Evers." [Available online, http://www2.nemcc.edu/mspeople/medger_evers.htm.] Note: "Medger" is spelled this way in the title and http address.

36. "Governor George Wallace's School House Door Speech," p. 1. [Available online, http://www.archives.state.al.us/govs_list/schooldoor.html.]

37. Monica Moorehead, "The FBI & the Birmingham church bombing," From the July 24, 1997, issue of *Workers World* newspaper, p. 1. [Available online, http://www.4littlegirls.com/97news.htm.]

38. Dwain C. Epps, a student at San Francisco Seminary, led a contingent of students who served in the mobile kitchen that fed the some 300 marchers. He remained in Alabama during the summer of 1964 dispersing funds collected at the Seminary to local blacks who had suffered economic hardships as a direct or indirect result of the march. Epps had served with the author as summer intern at Columbia Presbyterian Church in 1964. Prior to that, while stationed at Kessler Air Force Base in Gulfport, Mississippi, he had been active in Westminster Presbyterian Church as lay assistant to Frank A. Brooks, pastor. Epps later had a distinguished career on the staff of the World Council of Churches.

39. Paula Span (Washington Post staff writer), "The Undying Revolutionary: As Stokely Carmichael, He fought for Black Power. Now Kwame Ture's Fighting For His Life," *Washington Post*, April 8, 1998, p. DO1. [Available online, http://www.interchange.org/kuameture/washingtonpoststory.html.]

40. C. David Heymann, *RFK: A Candid Biography of Robert F. Kennedy* (New York: Dutton, 1998), pp. 461–462.

41. Ibid., p. 495.

42. Ibid., p. 496.

43. "Deep Throat: The story that helped bring down a presidency," *Lexington (KY) Herald-Leader*, Sunday, June 5, 2005, p. A3. On Tuesday, May 31, 2005, W. Mark Felt, former No. 2 man at the FBI, publicly revealed that he was Deep Throat.

44. "The Watergate scandal," *Lexington (KY) Herald-Leader*, Wednesday, June 1, 2005, p. A6.

45. "Chronology of Jimmy Carter's Presidency." [Available online, http://www.jimmycarterlibrary.org/documents/jec/chron.phtml.]

46. Ibid.

47. "The Reagan Presidency." [Available online, http://www.reagan.utexas.edu/archives/reference/pressketch.html.]

48. "LIFE, V-J Day Kiss 50 Years Later." [Available online, http://www.life.com/Life/specialkiss01.html.]

49. Copy in Wayne P. Todd Collection, Presbyterian Historical Society

50. *Minutes* of the One-Hundred-Ninth General Assembly (PCUS), 1969, pp. 105–106.

51. Ibid., pp. 101–102.

52. *Minutes* of the One-Hundred-Seventh General Assembly (PCUS), 1967, p. 186.

53. "Sunday Evening Service," *The Southern [Presbyterian] Journal*, Special Reprint from the issue of August 21, 1968, p. 7.

54. Ibid.

55. Ibid., p. 8. One of the banners in the procession was particularly controversial and was mentioned in this article. A student at Montreat-Anderson College and also a summer employee of the Montreat Conference center began making the banner in a workshop of the National Ministries/Christian Education conference. When school administrators and his summer employer got wind of the subject of his banner, the young man was threatened with the loss of his scholarship and job if he finished making the banner, which read, "SOCK IT TO 'EM JESUS." William Neal McAtee, five-year old son of the author, completed the unfinished banner with splashes of wildly colorful paint. Ann Laird Jones, daughter of Thomas L. Jones, co-director of the conference, carried the banner in the Communion procession. At this writing, Ann Jones is associate pastor at First Presbyterian Church, PC(USA), Greenville, Mississippi; Neal McAtee is a deacon in Second Presbyterian Church (EPC), Memphis, Tennessee; and the banner is in the Historical Society Archives, Montreat, NC.

56. Ibid., p. 9.

57. "Biography of Mickey Leland." [Available online, http://www.usaid.gov/leland/newbio.htm.]

58. Ibid.

59. The author, a senior in college in the academic year 1955–1956, was also a pulpit supply at the College Hill Church. One Sunday, after extolling the virtues of *Brown v. Board of Education* in a sermon, felt the scathing ire of the same university administrator on the way out of church. The person, a Delta planter, had been a political appointee of Governor Bilbo in the aftermath of his failed purge of the university in an attempt to move the university from Oxford to Jackson in 1936.

60. Will D. Campbell, *Soul among Lions: Musings of a Bootleg Preacher* (Louisville, KY: Westminster John Knox Press, 1999).

61. Letter from Robert H. Walkup to Margo Reitz Cochrane, his former Director of Christian Education at Starkville, November 3, 1964, copy in the personal collection of William G. McAtee.

62. David S. Broder, "Winter Still Seeks Racial Justice," *The Commercial Appeal*, Memphis, TN, January 16, 2005.

Chapter 15
Threats to the Dream

What is to be learned from this experience [the Union Presbytery Movement] about how we can be redeemed from our prejudices—to be free in the Gospel? Is there anything here to learn about that? I don't know. I don't know. I'd like to think there is because that's the freest experience in the Gospel I ever had in this Church.

—Lewis L. Wilkins (21-39)

This retrospective on the long history leading up to, during, and following that brief time when union presbyteries and COUP existed and had such a profound impact on their two parent denominations has provided a lens through which to look for timely learning perspectives for today and tomorrow. The historical context of Church and Society in the twenty-first century is radically different from their historical context of the 1960s and 1970s. However, the issues facing the church a generation ago were not all that different from a twenty-first-century perspective when the issues have to do with our need to "be redeemed from our prejudices." Certainly the foundations of the gospel remain sure.

Can anything be learned from the unique experiences of the Union Presbytery Movement, whose nature and style ran counter to the dominant organizational cultures of both of the denominations of which it was a part, and, as it has turned out, counter to the culture of the PC(USA)? Do the traits that made the Movement—the most unique phenomenon in the experience of North American Presbyterianism—have something to say to the PC(USA) as it struggles to redefine its identity, now and in the future, in terms by which its prejudices are redeemed?

In particular in the Union Presbytery Movement, for all its positive contributions to North American Presbyterianism, several problematic dynamics cohabited with it that still persist in a more virulent manner in the twenty-first century. These dynamics threatened to negate much of what was achieved during "a long run for a short slide," as Louis Weeks put it. They threatened the Dream and set in motion patterns of behavior that transferred from the time of the Movement over into reunion and landed the church on a path to polarity. In both the Movement and later after reunion, people experienced being treated as stereotypes and caricatures; differences were both real and imagined; close majority votes shaped their destinies; special interest groups developed and created fissions in the body politic; decision-making crossed the line into destructive win-lose mentalities; theological

---

reflection that produced clear directions for the life of the church appeared anemic; and yet a brief flirtation with a new polity and consensus-building ignited memorable excitement. These threatening dynamics warrant closer examination to see how they can be put in check by the application of learnings from the experience of the Union Presbytery Movement.

Stereotypes and Caricatures

The two worlds between which the union presbyteries flourished were in many ways very different worlds. Some have described these differences in the form of stereotypes or caricatures. One of the great contributions made by union presbyteries was helping get both worlds beyond stereotypes and caricatures, which may have been more exaggerated in certain regions and paid less attention to in others. For instance, the Southwest was not caught up in the North/South thing the way those from the Deep South were, because there was "not so much blood on the ground, in our own personal history and family histories and organizational histories," according to Linda B. Team (27-5).

West Texas was more affected by the historic struggles with Mexico. The Alamo and other Texas battle sites were more prominent in defining their folklore than Gettysburg and Vicksburg. East Texas was more attuned to the conflicts stemming from the Civil War. Ecclesiastical stereotypes existed in a lot of places in Texas. E. L. Coon, who served for many years on staff of Texas presbyteries, recalled that one often heard the remark, "Now, PCUS, you all are just a little, old, southern, regional denomination, and the UP church is a national church across the whole nation. . . . a kind of an elitist, condescending sort of an attitude, so that there was really bad blood" between some presbyteries for a long time (30-6).

Other stereotypes expressed in the two Presbyterian Churches were things like "All Yankees are ultra-liberals and all Southerners are ultra-conservatives." In some cases there was evidence of this stereotypical behavior, but for the most part the truth in these stereotypes and caricatures was symbolic, tinged with latent or not so latent prejudice. They only became threats to be overcome; though stereotypical, their impact was profound. But when deep personal relationships were formed, it was like one elder said to Philip Bembower, "You know, you Yankees don't have horns like we thought you would have, horns and a tail" (43-17).

Caricatures were not always directed at others; some were self-inflicted. Throughout the years, some Southern Presbyterians tended to be influenced by images drawn from Civil War battles to describe "ecclesiastical engagements" of which they were a part. Terms like,

"Beauregard circled behind the armies and showed them who was best," sprinkled their conversations. Many a time in after-hour gatherings, some combatants jokingly compared the leadership of the Southern Presbyterian Church, themselves included, as an "uninterrupted line of Confederate Generals," the likes of which existed nowhere else in the annals of military history. Winning was not the real issue, it was the sheer joy of the engagement that mattered most. For some this caricature was a way of life, but for others, life was more than a caricature. They realized that these old Civil War caricatures fostered misconceptions of reality leading to destructive outcomes that needed to be put to rest.

Some Kentuckians referred to one very contentious and pivotal synod consultation that eventually shaped the formation of the Synod of the Mid-South (PCUS) as "The Battle of Montgomery Bell." It so happened that the meeting was held at Montgomery Bell State Park in Tennessee, named after a bachelor who came to middle Tennessee in the early 1800s to set up his iron furnace on the Cumberland River; he was from Lexington, Kentucky, where it was said he was one who had "aided the Lexington [First] Presbyterian Church by subscriptions to pastors' salary and to the building fund and in numerous other ways."[1]

This consultation was an attempt to unravel the conflict over putting Mississippi, Alabama, Tennessee, and Kentucky together in a new regional synod. In the beginning it had the feel of a reunion of Confederate generals going full bore at each other. At one point all the Kentucky representatives stood up and withdrew from the fray to another part of the building. Those remaining were mystified and perplexed at this maneuver. What appeared to be an orchestrated strategy was nothing other than a spontaneous expression of the Kentucky freewheeling, problem-solving, trusting style. No consensus was present at first, but as various viewpoints and options were explored, a consensus emerged from the representatives of the three very different Kentucky presbyteries. The Kentuckians returned to the total group and made a constructive suggestion that changed the tone and direction of the consultation. Plans for the new synod were set in motion, resulting in a unique four-state regional middle governing body—the Synod of the Mid-South (PCUS). Relationships developed in this new climate laid the groundwork for growing appreciation and eventual support for denominational reunion that might not have occurred without it.

The three smaller Kentucky union presbyteries, though viewed by some as "those Southerners," also played a noncaricature swing-vote role in many "engagements" between the larger presbyteries in Michigan and Ohio as the Synod of the Covenant (UPCUSA) was being formed and later as it continued to function. George Morgan, executive of the Synod of the Covenant (UPCUSA), recalled: "Kentucky was always regarded as a different part of the world. There was a real appreciation for Kentucky in the Synod because it became a balance to what had been a very rigid Michigan style of Church structure and programming. . . . It was a little bit of a relief for Ohio Presbyteries and churches because they were a little uncomfortable in the Michigan style." Morgan was "not sure that the Michigan style was intentional, but was a result of a series of executive styles that had eventually kind of congealed." According to Morgan, Detroit Presbytery as an administrative unit was the "dog that wagged several tails . . . the other Presbyteries besides Detroit in Michigan." Whatever Detroit wanted, the Synod of Michigan did (67-7).

In Ohio it was a much different operation. "The synod and the presbyteries pretty well hummed in a partnership that was not controlled by any presbytery. The synod didn't control the presbyteries; the presbyteries didn't control the synod. It was much more of a partnership" (67-8). Into the clash between the Michigan style and the Ohio style came the Kentucky freewheeling, problem-solving, trusting style in which its view of the synod's primary function was to support its presbyteries. In its own way, the Kentucky style, far out of proportion to its size and number, became the mediating influence in the clash of the two giants of Michigan and Ohio. When reunion came and the synods were realigned, Morgan remembered "the sorrow and the grief that the presbyteries in Michigan and Ohio felt when they were separated from the presbyteries in Kentucky. And that was a very genuine grief" (67-15).

One area where personal caricatures did circulate was among women in both denominations. Some Northern women might say: "Well, Southern women, you know, aren't direct, and you can't deal with them up front because they can't talk straight about anything," implying that you couldn't trust their manipulative communications (27-4). Some Southern women might say: "Northern women can't be trusted because they are uppity, don't know their place, and are not nurturing enough," implying that they are too ambitious and aggressive. A few may have been swayed by these caricatures, but holding these views served no good purpose.

Neither caricature was descriptive of Carol E. Davies, a member of a PCUS congregation in Independence, Missouri. She was deeply involved in the church at the local, presbytery, synod, and national levels. She participated in many of the COUP events. Her experience at the local level taught her that union or reunion was "not as hard locally because women wanted to work together and did." She felt it was harder at the national level "because of the point at which the structures had moved, where the PCUS was with women being incorporated into the program of the whole Church" (49-7). In the UPCUSA the United Presbyterian Women (UPW) organization maintained a highly independent profile at the time.

The Synod of Missouri (UPCUSA) elected Davies, especially because she was from a PCUS Church background, to serve on the National Executive Committee for UPW when the reunion discussions were taking place. At the time there were many misconceptions in the UP Church about the women's organizations in the PCUS and vice versa. One UP misconception about the PCUS was that it didn't have any women's organizations; another was they just didn't understand that the women in the PCUS still locally had circles that met as a group. In reality there was a strong Women of the Church (WOC) organization at all levels in the PCUS, though it was not the same kind of organization as in the United Presbyterian Church. Davies's role on the UPW National Executive Committee was to clear up these misconceptions about the PCUS. "That's why I was elected," to help UPW women to understand that, though the organizations might be different locally, regionally, and nationally, PCUS women also contributed to mission work. It was just done in a different way; women pretty much had control of what they had given, even in the PCUS Church (49-7).

Many union presbyteries made sure there were "crossover elections" where persons from one former denomination were elected to serve in positions across the board in the other former denomination to dispel previous misconceptions about each other. Union Presbyteries and COUP made some significant progress at eliminating relating with each other as stereotypes or caricatures and established deep, lasting relations. They realized that old Civil War caricatures, stereotypes about ultraliberals and ultraconservatives, and stereotypes about women fostered misconceptions of reality leading to destructive outcomes that needed to be put to rest. However, with the coming of reunion, some folk who had not had this common experience of the union presbyteries and COUP, or those who lapsed into old patterns, never tended to build the personal relations, never moved beyond treating others stereotypically or as caricatures as the structures of the new denomination were being formed. Learnings from the union presbyteries about eradicating stereotypes and caricatures are sorely needed in the PC(USA) in the twenty-first century.

Real and Imagined Differences

Some shorthand attempts at describing differences in the cultures and styles come closer to the truth than others. Words often used for the

Southern culture include "family-county seat-ranch, agrarian-grassroots, bottom up-local option." Words often used for the Northern culture are "industrial-corporate, urban-treetop, top down-national." But these were not universally or exclusively limited to Southern or Northern culture. They may be perceived as style descriptions that may or may not have reflected reality.

James E. Andrews recalled that when the vote on reunion came before the United Presbyterian Church [UPCUSA] Assembly in Hartford (1982), "there appeared to be "a 'grieve-in' over the viewpoint that the vote for reunion represented a slap in the face to women and rejection of women's rights and so forth. We had a parade of people going to microphones saying, 'I am in pain tonight.' You sort of wanted to go around and give everybody tranquilizers." Andrews did observe that a number of women commissioners out of PCUS experiences brought another perspective to the debate. Sensing that some were making assumptions based on their fear that women's concerns were not taken seriously by the PCUS, they testified quite to the contrary, pointing to the fact that reunion "will eventually, given a certain span of time, be beneficial to both parts." That seemed to ease the pain. Andrews's contention was that familiarity between persons would go a long way to overcome the discrepancies created by caricatures of each other (02-12).

Andrews, out of his experience in both denominations, was well aware of the commitment of each to empowerment of women for full participation in the life of the church. He also perceived that one of the characteristics common to the two ecclesiastical systems was that women achieved what they concentrated on achieving. Awareness of this was not universal. Some United Presbyterian women perceived that women were not broadly represented on the national staff in the Southern Church; some PCUS women did not see women broadly represented in the elected positions of the Northern Church (02-12).

To determine the truth of the matter, Joyce Tucker, an OGA staff person in the PCUS, along with Andrews, went to the *Minutes* of the two Assemblies and looked at total numbers. What they found was that United Presbyterian women concentrated on filling staff positions as the goal of empowerment and women occupied roughly 25 percent of all staff positions. They did not focus as much on getting women elected to voting positions in the structures, though some were there (02-13).

In the PCUS, women concentrated on the policy of getting women to serve in elected positions as a way of achieving empowerment, because that is where the power was focused in that denomination, not in staff, though some were there, too. Tucker and Andrews found in the PCUS that more than 25 percent of all voting members on boards, agencies, and commissions were women. When the staff numbers were combined with the elected position numbers in the UPCUSA and elected position numbers were combined with the staff numbers in the PCUS, the total number of women involved was close to 28 percent of all positions in each denomination. Women in the two ecclesiastical systems achieved what they concentrated on achieving during that time, but they had different targets in mind (02-13).

Flynn V. Long, Jr., did an in-depth investigation, originally in the South, but eventually expanded to the whole country, into the identity of Presbyterians. The product of this study became his famous five-hour lecture titled "The Great Speckled Bird." From what he discovered in his study of church politics in order to get union presbyteries passed and to enhance the cause of reunion, he set out to help "the church come to terms with itself as a politically diverse group and understanding that that political diversity is not really a reason for division but is the basis for constructive conversation." Long felt: "Altogether too often, I think naively, we have thought that it's 'them' and 'us'; the ones who are for 'us' and ones who are against 'us' " (24-2).

Long also said, "[S]ometimes it's put, the liberals and the conservatives, or the social gospelers and the fundamentalists; all kinds of labels like that are used . . . , oftentimes without any justification but simply because of a stereotype that a person who's from a certain place or has voted a certain way . . . [was] good or bad people" (24-3). Long warned that in understanding Presbyterianism this way, the church, "if it's not really careful, . . . will fall into the stereotypical idea of dividing because Presbyterians not only come from a number of different places in terms of their catholicity, but they . . . meet at meetings and they vote. And when they vote, that frequently creates a sense of division in [the church] that may or may not be a real dividing line" (24-3).

The difficulty in treating each other as stereotypical opposites is that too often what is imagined becomes real. Many differences did exist between the Southern and Northern Churches; many times they were more imagined than real. Nonetheless, the Union Presbytery Movement was instrumental in sorting out the two by focusing first on what was actually held in common and then seeing how appreciating and utilizing real differences contributed to the welfare of the whole, rather than detracting from it.

Close Majority Votes

Close majority votes have played key roles when important decisions have been made in various settings throughout secular and ecclesial history. One-vote margins can prove to be a threat to the body's health and well-being or it can be nothing more than a decision that produced no adverse effect. One-vote margins of victory can be won, whether the prescribed requirement for winning is a simple, two-thirds, or three-fourths majority. The only difference between these three requisites is that portion of the deciding body or group deemed sufficient for an affirmative or negative decision.

Ordinarily, the size of the majority indicates the level of importance of the issue involved and the level of tolerance required for a satisfactory outcome. In some instances it is considered very important to have as many people or groups as possible declare in favor of, or against, a particular issue; the larger the majority, the closer to a unanimous decision and greater the comfort with it. In other instances, a smaller margin suffices. In any majority—simple, two-thirds, or three-fourths—the absolute minimum margin for winning or losing is by one. Simply saying, "This vote was won by a majority" is a relative statement that does not always tell the whole story about the degree of importance or the level of support.

Close votes have been decisive in Presbyterian history in North America, some healthy, some adverse. This is not an unusual occurrence with a polity that is based on the principle that "majority prevails but minorities have rights." One ecclesial example cited in this work of a shining testament to the old polity of majority rule at its best was the vote in 1967 PCUS General Assembly for Moderator where on the second ballot Marshall C. Dendy was elected Moderator by a vote of 226 to 225 over P. D. Miller. This election was important, but the close vote was not divisive. Miller's resolution of thanks at the close of the Assembly saluting the way in which Dendy had moderated the meeting of the Assembly, a genuine gesture of civility of a bygone era affirmed by the rising vote of appreciation, was truly an expression of the fundamental role that relations played in the life of the PCUS.

Other close votes were not always greeted with such magnanimous affirmations. The effects of a win-lose mentality, a divisive testament to the old polity of majority rule at its worst, may often accompany close votes. In close votes relating to critical constitutional issues of polity or confessional issues of doctrine and theology, emotions can run high and ill feelings can poison relations between combatants. Winners sometimes experience only a sense of gaining a Pyrrhic victory at great cost, tantamount to defeat. Losers, fueled by a sense of "we wuz robbed," feel victorious anyway and do not consider the matter closed.

One close majority vote that caused an unintended adverse effect was the vote in the PCUS on the union presbyteries and synods amendments. The Northern Church prerequisite for advice and consent for organic union was by two-thirds of its presbyteries. The Southern Church required advice and consent by three-fourths of its presbyteries in cases of organic union. It was not clear in the PCUS whether the union presbyteries and synods amendments fell under the organic union provision or was a matter of amending the *Book of Church Order*, requiring a simple majority vote.

The proponents' interpretation was that the union presbyteries and synods amendments fell under the simple majority rule of the amending of the *Book* provision; the opponents' interpretation was that the union presbyteries and synods amendments fell under the three-fourths rule of the organic union provision. The three-fourths rule was a serious obstacle to overcome, and challenging this interpretation was politically motivated. Political decisions juggling majority prerequisites come down to "what votes can we get and still prevail." Such a decision is motivated, not by having as many people or groups as possible declare in favor of a particular issue, but by knowing how few are needed to declare and still gain passage of the measure.[2]

Advocates for union presbyteries and union synods felt almost certain at the time that the motion to send down the amendments to presbyteries on the three-fourths rule would pass in this Assembly. They were concerned that if the amendments ever got sent down on that basis and failed, it would be ten years or more before an effort to create union presbyteries could be mounted again. However, their political strategy of requiring only advice and consent of a majority of the presbyteries with regard to the union presbyteries and synods amendments prevailed in the PCUS Assembly (1968) without too much rancor. Opponents felt they had a good chance of defeating them in the presbyteries.

Advice-and-consent close votes taken in the PCUS presbyteries in the late fall of 1968 and early winter of 1969 on the union presbytery amendment provided classic examples of the profound impact of one-vote margins. The union presbyteries amendment was defeated initially by a vote of 39–38 by the presbyteries, failing to gain a simple majority by one vote. Winners in the overall vote of the presbyteries that defeated the amendment by one vote felt they had won it "fair and square."

Those in favor of the union presbytery amendment, who lost by one vote, would not rest but focused on certain presbyteries where the legitimate parliamentary procedure for "reconsideration of the vote" might reverse the outcome in their favor. Mobile and Northeast Texas Presbyteries reversed their vote from no to yes on the union presbytery amendment. The deep feelings of the winners and losers of the first vote were now reversed by this new vote.

It may be debated as to whether the outcome of the union presbytery amendment vote in the PCUS was a shining example of the old polity of majority rule at its best or a divisive testament to the old polity of majority rule at its worst. This decision posed a threat to the

Dream and had a far-reaching impact on all the ecclesiastical battles from that time on, through denominational reunion to the polarization of the first decade of the twenty-first century. Opposing combatants in future ecclesial battles could no doubt trace their rationales, if not direct their personal affilial lineage, to one side or the other of this watershed decision.

One of the greatest ironies is that out of this old polity decision that permitted the formation of union presbyteries came a new polity based on the belief that win-win consensus building creates a more desirable form of decision-making for the church, a polity demonstrated throughout the life of COUP and the union presbyteries.

Special Interest Syndrome

The vote on the union presbyteries and synods amendments passed the PCUS General Assembly (1968) by a fairly narrow vote, not an overwhelming vote, but it was significant enough to where there was a very clear majority to send them down under the simple majority rule. The destructive polarization of the church had not begun to sprout in the fissions of the PCUS at the Mobile Assembly (1969) in that poignant moment when after the final vote Walter Johnson and Jack Williamson, the two floor managers of sorts for the opposing "liberal" and "conservative" forces respectively, hugged each other.

But there were other early signs of dis-ease, almost undetectable, cultivated in the less fertile soil of the old polity of win-lose, that would grow over the following decades into an infestation of emotional and political weeds threatening Will Kennedy's accommodating image of the "oddity of family Church." The full bloom of this threat would not flower until well into the twenty-first century. This infestation might best be called the "special interest syndrome," a condition that threatened the Dream of diversity and of inclusion in the gradation of interrelated governing bodies, dreamed at reunion, from being fully realized.

Gathering in groups is a natural human sociological function. Groups may form around kinship, heritage, place of origin, common cause, special issue, self-interest, or the like. Forming groups is not inherently "good" or "bad." Qualifications of membership, rituals of initiation, litanies of value, codes of conduct, symbols of identity, legacies of passage and all sorts of other identifying behaviors in between persist to differentiate a group from other groups. Varying degrees of mutual respect may exist between groups, emblematic of sensitivity to each other's uniqueness and differences.

However, in modern society in general a line of demarcation stands within "groupness" that distinguishes between when it is being functional and when it is dysfunctional. That line is not always easily discernable and there are many expressions of it. Dysfunctionality may occur when a particular group in the diversity spectrum develops such a strong sense of its own self-identity that it considers itself to be "THE primary group," not just one of the many diverse groups of the whole. These groups tend to become ingrown and spring up largely at the edges of the spectrum of society. Their rhetoric of special interest can become extremely vocal, consume more corporate airtime and drive away those who disagree, leaving little room for constructive conversation. Dividing walls mount up in a protective culture of silence with few openings, inviting interchange between the edges and those that have been driven away.

The destructive dysfunctional nature of the "special interest syndrome" may best be seen in the way these siloic special interest groups deal with inclusion. A group's sense of identity may be so strong that it feels that the "not-like-us" persons need not be included or may even be explicitly excluded. "They" would not appreciate or support "our" special self-interest, and may actually be a threat to it. So we have to set "ourselves" over against "them." The intensity with which this "over-against-ness" occurs may be in direct proportion to the degree to which the particular group had previously been or felt excluded from the whole. "They/we" may experience a deep sense of alienation from some loss of identity. Grasping for shreds of self-esteem and self-preservation, a prejudicial, almost self-righteous stance against "not-like-us" persons or groups may be taken.

Sometimes, in very extreme situations, one-up/one-down attitudes may dominate: "I am going to rise up, by putting you down." Roles with their attendant prejudices are reversed and the oppressed becomes the oppressor; a sense of entitlement supersedes a sense of service as motivation for action or inaction. Diversity becomes an end in itself with little interest or concern expressed for true inclusion. Diversity, whether espoused from the perspective of the "right" or the "left" or even from the "center," without the practice of welcoming inclusiveness, becomes destructive, no matter what its group's identifying classification.

Engendered by the divisive context of America and the world, the peace, unity and purity of the PC(USA), and possibly its very existence, are threatened by the vocal polar edges of this creeping "special interest syndrome" in the twenty-first century. For a brief period during its lifetime, the Union Presbytery Movement neutralized the early stages of the "special interest syndrome" through its open stance toward diversity and its sense of creative welcome to it. By embracing a similar stance, the less vocal majority in the reunited church has a great opportunity to stave off advanced stages of dysfunctional destruction festering from this syndrome over the ensuing decades by breaking free from its shackles.

Win-Lose Mentality

Overlooked in the turn of events in the same advice-and-consent voting period in the PCUS presbyteries, in the late fall of 1968 and early winter of 1969, was the fact that the Plan of Union with the Reformed Church in America received the requisite three-fourths majority by a slim margin and the union synods amendment was defeated by a vote of 40–37. Neither of these close votes generated the antagonistic steam that the close vote on the union presbyteries amendment did. What made the difference between these examples of close votes that created great animosity and divisiveness and those that did not? Part of the answer lay in the level of importance of the issue. But also part of the answer may lie in understanding the corrosive nature of a "win-lose mentality."

A basic assumption of human individual and corporate life is that there will be differences of opinion that range all the way from the insignificant to differences of ultimate significance; some will prevail; others will not. Individuals, groups, organizations, and institutions must make a range of decisions every day of their existence, decisions in which there will be winners and losers. These decisions are informed by a variety of considerations: values held and goals pursued, clarity of self-identity, clues from the environment and context, the degree of freedom and authority to act, the commitment and resources to make something happen, and the like.

Just as with the "special interest syndrome," a line of demarcation does exist within "decisions" that distinguishes between when they are functional and when dysfunctional. That line is not always easily discernable, and there are many expressions of it. The dysfunctionality of the "win-lose mentality" thrives best in a closed system where battle lines are drawn between "we/they" warring camps. People sometimes migrate to these camps because they feel there is something to gain personally from such an affiliation that they would not otherwise obtain. It is not so much a matter of coalescing in order to find the best solution to a real problem or to discover a lasting resolution to an issue, or to make a decision about a problem or issue, as it is to establish the "rightness" position "about" the problem or issue and to do battle over that position, defending it at any cost.

Anne Wilson Schaef and Diane Fassel, in *The Addictive Organization*, offer a view of organizations that does not usually appear in the literature on organizations, but that can be instructive in understanding the dysfunctionality of the "win-lose mentality." They maintain that addictive organizations display similar characteristics to those that individual addicts display in their lives.[3]

When "win-lose mentality" infects organizations, making them dysfunctional, Schaef and Fassel's understanding of addictive organizations, as closed systems[4] provides a hint of what is taking place. In particular, self-centeredness creates the "for" or "against" dichotomy on which "win-lose mentality" thrives. The writers further develop this concept in what they call the process of dualism. Schaef and Fassel maintain that dualistic thinking reduces a very complex world to two simple choices "with the underlying assumption that if we can decide which end of the dualism is right, we will be right and justified" and everybody who does not agree with us is wrong. This assumption gives practitioners the illusion of control to do what one pleases because "we know we are right." Such dualistic thinking leads into a false sense of security, because there are only two alternatives from which to choose, but at the risk of reducing the possibility of considering more effective options. The net result is that combatants in this dualism are perpetually stuck in a place with narrow horizons and little room to maneuver.[5] Charles Stanford summarized it this way: "There is not anything that I see in them that says let's all get together. I see them saying we are the righteous ones and the rest of you are not" (07-24).

The ramification of the "win-lose mentality" for the two combatant sides is to win at any cost; winning is everything. The winning and losing never ends; a return match is a foregone conclusion; the battle is always joined *seriatim*. The true character of this posture is seen when the opposition is personally discounted, disdained, devalued, demonized, and in extreme cases, destroyed. One has only to look at the long Scottish heritage of American Presbyterianism to see this. The culture wars in their extremities abroad in society in general during the late twentieth and early twenty-first centuries over gender, abortion, sexual orientation, same-sex marriage, racial ethnic identity, affirmative action, and the like give a vivid picture of the dysfunctionality of the "win-lose mentality" that exhibits addictive characteristics.

The full truth about what really took place in the structures of the PC(USA) since reunion that caused the Dream to be partially unrealized, and what contributed to the church's inability to form a new identity reflective of the Dream, has not been completely determined. However, without question it can be argued that the Presbyterian Church (U.S.A.), at times exhibiting the characteristics of an addictive organization, still has an identity crisis, and the Dream of unity is threatened and could be shattered by the grip of the "win-lose mentality." The corrosive nature of the "win-lose mentality" of the close vote that created union presbyteries in 1969 has had an enduring effect, since its inception, on the reunited church's ability to create a new identity.

However, it is reasonable to conclude that the Union Presbytery Movement, when its focus was on the union presbyteries themselves and the consultations, had the clearly defined identity of a healthy, open system, whose characteristics were, point by point, the antithesis of the characteristics of an addictive organization. "Win-win" was its primary mentality. When it became engaged in the effort to achieve denominational reunion, its unique identity became somewhat diminished as it got entangled in a "win-lose" posture of that campaign. This fact, however, should not preclude the creative experiences of the Movement in providing a "win-win" model for restoring the Dream and finding a new identity for the PC(USA) in the twenty-first century.

Residue from the Civil War

Part of the Dream conceived by the PC(USA) was to make a contribution to bringing closure to the Civil War and racism, the residual effect of slavery. Determining the long-term winners and losers in the Civil War seems not to be too complicated at first blush. The North won and the South lost. For winners, it was the restoration of the union; for losers, it was "the Lost Cause." Of even more critical importance than simply determining winners and losers of that decades-old conflict is the degree to which racism has been repudiated over time. Though more complex to determine, the psychological and emotional, as well as the economic and social, winners and losers may give clues as to the degree to which this repudiation has or has not happened. This cannot be lightly passed over or ignored. A closer look must be taken at various "residues from the Civil War" in the twenty-first century as indicators to determine if they remain a threat to the repudiation called for by the Dream.

One of the deadly contributions of slavery was the breakup of the nuclear family. The nuclear family, for the sons and daughters of slavery, was not a winner in that conflict, for it was not restored with the official cessation of hostilities achieved at Appomattox. The residue of that legacy still exists in the poverty cycles of the twenty-first century. The myriad of social ills and the denial of a wide range of opportunities due to that loss are at the heart of efforts at reparation to redress those ills and losses. Losses from the breakup of the nuclear family have not been regained.

Over the last half of the twentieth century, hard-won gains in education, public transportation, and public services are fraught with vestiges of losses that appear to be one step forward and two steps back in progress gained for African Americans, Native Americans, and other ethnic minorities. White flight to private academies from public schools have left many public schools as segregated as before *Brown v. Board of Education*, though improved in quality of education. Public transportation in many locations is designed to meet the needs of the low-income segment of the population; routes are carefully laid out to take the people to where they work, often at minimum wage, and there is a spectrum of social and public services they need to survive. The government—local, state, and national—has become their caretaker through income, food, medical, and housing supplements, subsidies, tax breaks, and the like. This development is indicative of a widening gap between the haves and the have-nots and the emergence of a new economic class system that dictates the political configurations and directions of society. This new class system is defined, not exclusively along racial lines, but with affluence as the line of demarcation.

Other residue from the Civil War is somewhat to be seen in NASCAR nation on whose oval arenas win-lose battles are fought weekly in high-powered racing cars with the ferocity of the Pickett's charge at Gettysburg. Their beloved Winston Cup Series label fell victim to anti-tobacco sentiment. Many of them are descendants of independent-spirited Scotch-Irish warriors who, in effect, refused to surrender at Appomattox. James Webb, in *Born Fighting*, historically described their culture as "a culture of isolation, hard luck, and infinite stubbornness that has always shunned formal education and mistrusted—even hated—any form of aristocracy."[6] He went on to say that these particular Scotch-Irish "had nothing in common with either the English aristocracy in Virginia or the New England WASP settlements."[7]

NASCAR nation was caricatured on TV in the late 1970s and early 1980s by the freewheeling, hard-driving, fun-loving "Dukes of Hazzard." Airborne images of "General Lee," the 1969 Dodge Charger, symbolized clean-living young fellows with a strong sense of family on the way to help out friends and neighbors in distress. TV's twenty-first-century reality version of this "residue" is Jeff Foxworthy's "Blue Collar Comedy Tour" profanely bashing all politically correct comers. But stereotypes and caricatures do not do justice to Scotch-Irish descendants.

Webb significantly observed: "In the age of political correctness and ultraethnic sensitivities, it has become delicate, to say the least, to celebrate many of this culture's hard-won accomplishments." Their story and ethnic origins have "been lost to common identification."[8] Yet these blue-collar workers, historically the major backbone of the American workforce in all regions of the country, are virtually absent from "every major debate where ethnicity plays a role."[9]

Tex Sample, in *Ministry in an Oral Culture: Living with Will Rogers, Uncle Remus, & Minnie Pearl*, maintains that the culture of these Scotch-Irish [a subset of the group now called Anglo-European whites], along with Native Americans, African Americans, Hispanics, and Asian Americans, is best described as "traditional orality" or a "culture of oral tradition."[10] Although most can read and write, their understanding of life is reached through relationships and experiences, and that understanding is then passed on to others through proverbs, sayings, stories, and tales.[11] Those who think in abstract concepts and rational dissertations, and consider themselves to be "literate," may not appreciate the oral culture and may overtly discount persons who comprise it.

Cultures still clash in the twenty-first century, for not all cultures tolerate each other. Though there are occasional cross-burnings and parades by the hooded KKK and reopenings of 1960s murder cases, "residue" battles are enacted in policy and court decision cases. Sometimes when displaying proud symbols of one person's heritage becomes an offensive reminder to another's sensibilities of previous great pain and humiliation, the community determines if the display must be removed for the common good. In June of 2005 it was reported that a federal judge ruled in a West Virginia case that "a high school dress code that banned items bearing the 'Rebel Flag' is overly broad and violates students' rights to free speech." The judge, however, did warn that, "if they use the Confederate battle flag as a symbol to violate the rights of others, 'the very ban struck down today might be entirely appropriate.' " For some the flag symbolized hate and racism; for others it was a way of honoring Southern history.[12]

On Memorial Day 2005, Missouri's Republican governor, Matt Blunt, ordered the one-day flying of the Confederate flag at a Confederate memorial service along with singing of *Dixie* and laying of roses at a Confederate monument. A previous Democratic governor, Bob Holden, had ordered the flag's removal from historic sites. Representatives of the NAACP said, "They had no problem with the memorial service, just with Blunt's decision to fly the Confederate flag."[13]

This version of the cultural wars continues over the contemporary residue from the Civil War. The struggle could be activated with the sight of any Confederate or Union monument in any town or place; it could be stirred up with the request that a picture of Jefferson Davis be removed from an office at a Kentucky university. Time does not permit us to probe the deeper issues here. However, one wonders if this is a remnant of the boiling resentment some white Southerners had against Reconstruction; a kind of backlash against an alien authority; a role reversal that, when Reconstruction was abolished in 1876, the "solid" South, meaning a "solid white" South, came back to power and relegated the recently deposed authorities and supporters to second-class citizenship with a vengeance. One also has to wonder if the civil rights movement of the 1960s and what it achieved in the last quarter of the twentieth century has been perceived as a second Reconstruction by some, generating a second backlash fueling new "residue" conflicts in the early twenty-first century. It is all about power and freedom.

Dreams, Where Have You Gone?

One final residue from the Civil War ironically comes from the side of the victor before the cause was actually won or lost. It is rooted in the rarely explored history of slavery in New England, the gradual post-Revolutionary emancipation of the enslaved there, and the subsequent role of the ideological construct of "race" as a conceptual substitute for slavery in public discourse. Joanne Pope Melish, an associate professor of history at the University of Kentucky, spent fifteen years researching and reconstructing this story only to discover that its elusiveness was largely intentional from the beginning. She found that the systematic erasure of the experience of slavery in New England from its historical memory and the gradual emancipation over many decades created the illusion of the absence of people of color in the region.[14] This discovery "displaced a more complex reality in which economic, political, and social relations were structured by 'race,' which itself had emerged from a still earlier set of relations structured by slavery."[15]

Melish reasoned that the construction of the concept of "race" grew out of the assumption on the part of New England whites that "emancipated slaves, likely to be dependent and disorderly, would constitute a problem requiring firm management in the new republic." Free people of color, being different, would suddenly "leave whites vulnerable to radical and unwelcome alterations in their social entitlements." To protect themselves from these unwelcome alterations, New England whites took the next step of assuming racial superiority over these newly freed slaves. These whites believed by a strange twist of logic that abolitionist rhetoric promised that, by ending "the sin of slavery and the troublesome presence of slaves," the result would be the "eventual absence of people of color themselves." New England whites used all sorts of flimsy tactics to make this assumption become a reality, including everything from "representing people of color as dangerous strangers . . . conducting official roundups . . . vandalizing black neighborhoods . . . and rais[ing] funds to ship them to Africa."[16]

The fabrication of New England as being historically free allowed white New Englanders, who wanted little to do personally with people of color, to assume "claims to a superior moral identity," the antithesis of an enslaved South. "Triumphant whiteness and debased blackness were complementary productions of the 'racializing' process" in New England.[17] Such a perspective should not be a blanket indictment of all New Englanders, but on many occasions this fervor of moral superiority found its way into Northern perceptions of the South across the subsequent decades. This moral superiority was later matched at times by that of Southerners when, having fought on behalf of the cause of civil rights at home, they perceived the North's blindness to its own history of slavery and racism hypocritical. Such behavior did not absent itself from the edges of the reunion discussion.

During the Union Presbytery Movement, in its bridge-building activities, and later in the subsequent days of denominational reunion, certain benign neglect was evident in silent sub-currents of moral superiority and literate disdain for persons of the "Residue from the Civil War." The most notable omission was the absence of any meaningful discussion regarding the North's blindness to its own history of slavery and racism. Evident in the reunion experience at times was a subtle racial arrogance on the part of some Northerners in their disdain for their "racially sinful" Southern brothers and sisters. Some Southerners were not reticent to express their disdain for some Northerners because of their racial arrogance. These omissions and subtleties were more the exception than the rule. Guilt, that Reformed theological commodity staple, was either in an abundant oversupply or almost totally absent.

Residue from the Civil War in the twenty-first century indicates that racism has not been completely repudiated in the years subsequent to the end of that conflict, though great strides have been made. Describing illustrations of the residue conjures up deep-seated, worrisome emotions from all different perspectives that one might prefer to keep buttoned up in the recesses of one's being. But racism is a worrisome reality in the twenty-first century seen in the breakup of nuclear families, poverty cycles, education, public transportation, public services, loss of common ethnic identification, inflammatory symbols of prejudice, and expressions of moral superiority. What is more troubling, however, is that contemporary subtle racial sub-currents, some not so subtle, still bubble in the twenty-first century beneath the surface of the PC(USA) and need silence-breaking, out-in-the-open, serious attention. The call to the PC(USA) is still to find common ground in being engaged within itself and beyond in the repudiation of this threatening blight of racism on our soul.

Theological Anemia

As has been pointed out, one among many of the traits of the Scottish heritage was the foundational role theology played in creating its legacy, though sometimes it got lost in the heat of battle. Theology and religious beliefs were often cast in terms of either absolute certainty or flexibility. For some the free exchange of ideas, the freedom to express one's opinions, meant nothing. Flexibility, tolerance, and rational restraint were everything for others. The battle between these two poles was manifest in the great theological controversies of the nineteenth and twentieth centuries, and it continued into the twenty-first century, posing a threat to the Dream.

Somehow theology fell short of its foundational promise in many ways as union presbyteries and denominational reunion became realities. Seeking the unity of the church was a motivational cornerstone of the Union Presbytery Movement and the eventual establishment of the PC(USA), but resolving the long-standing conflicts between the theological dichotomies of absolute certainty and flexibility got lost in the heat of the organizational and structural battles where the motivation of "practical necessity" took precedece over theology. Maybe "resolving" was too ambitious an expectation; "seriously addressing" may be a more accurate expectation.

Attention to theological foundations was being given at the same time that the constitutional changes were being made to permit union presbyteries, though not necessarily for the reason of enhancing that process *per se*. The UPCUSA was involved with passage and ratification of the Confession of 1967 and the new *Book of Confessions*. The time-honored precedent for the creation of creeds and confessions in times of great historical upheaval was certainly the case with C-67. Its primary focus was on reconciliation: God's work of reconciliation, the ministry of reconciliation, and the fulfillment of reconciliation in human life and environment. This confession addressed the contemporary problems of racial discrimination (civil rights), peace among nations (Vietnam), enslaving poverty in a world of abundance (Euro–Third World), and relations between men and women (sexism).[18]

As early as 1962, the PCUS began trying to get a "contemporary educational interpretation" of the Westminster Confession. The PCUS General Assembly did approve "A Brief Statement of Belief" but did not send it through the confessional amendment process to the presbyteries. In 1969 at the Mobile Assembly a committee was named to develop a confessional statement couched in contemporary language that would augment Westminster in the life of the PCUS. The result was "A Declaration of Faith," which passed the PCUS Assembly (1976) in the amendment process but failed to get the majority required in the presbyteries.

By the time the reunion decision rolled around, both assemblies had been so immersed in practical considerations of restructure and reorganization that there seemed to be little appetite for a major theological and doctrinal restatement of faith or even a serious theological discussion on which to form the shape of the new church. Not everyone was oblivious to the theological anemia of the reunion debates. As has been noted, the likes of Dr. McDowell Richards and Doug Harper had unsuccessfully tried to get a new *Book of Confessions* as part of *The Plan for Reunion* leading up to 1983, but had to settle for "A Brief Statement of Faith" and a theological point made in chapter II the *Book of Order*, "The Church and Its Confessions."

Harry Hassall was convinced in 1983 that, in resolving the split with the Northern Church, it was necessary to go back to the Old School/New School split of 1837 and deal with unresolved theological issues growing out of that division. He felt in the reunion discussions of the 1980s "that the Southern Church, having had 95 percent of its history connected to the Old School, was being sort of propagandized to join a church from which we had not split" (65-9). It made no sense to him for a Northern Church and a Southern Church to survive, but it made a lot of sense for a conservative Church to survive "what I considered was at that time a takeover from a liberal Church" (65-10). Needless to say, the theological discussion did not revert to 1837 in the reunion debates.

Al Freundt was struck by the paucity of theological reflection at the time. He noted: "All sorts of theological perspectives were bantered about in the reunion debates. Some of the ministers, theologians, thought the issues were theological. But if you took everything that they said was a theological issue and added up those, to my mind, you can't turn a hundred rabbits into a horse [laughter]. It was a quantitative thing instead of a qualitative thing, but prominent in the debates, at least in our area, were about church property and what about the race questions" (17-21). It is ironic that those who initially opposed reunion were the very ones that insisted that theology was a critical ingredient in the reunion process.

Theology was not seriously addressed in the reunion of 1983 through any formal confessional process. Maybe it was not the fullness of time in 1983 for confession-making; the markings of a historical watershed were there on the surface, but the life-giving wells of common experience had not had time to form a new community to the degree needed for creating an authentic confession. Maybe the euphoria surrounding "the Day" in Atlanta on June 10, 1983, dulled Presbyterian sensibilities to the coming chaos of the culture wars of the next decades.

Fullness of Time

Perhaps life had not reached the traumatic and threatening magnitude in 1983 that historically warranted a confessional statement to guide the church through the turmoil. But that is exactly the kind of atmosphere in which all the historical creeds, confessions, and catechisms of the PC(USA) had been fostered. Creeds, confessions, catechisms, doctrinal statements, hymns, poetic expressions, and the like are nothing more than recorded generalized statements and revelatory reflections about deep spiritual encounters in concrete experiences of life. Too often the great theological battles in church history have been over the wording of one generalization as compared to another, becoming nothing more than cheap attempts to discount the persons who drew the generalizations by discrediting their experiences and the beliefs they held. Too often these theological conflicts have been void of any deep spiritual encounters between the combatants in common concrete experiences that might genuinely have produced new meaning for all involved. This was the case in the reunion discussions.

Maybe the time is ripe in the middle of the first decade of the twenty-first century to make a serious attempt to create a new confessional statement growing out of the chaos of the times. Events surrounding and following September 11, 2001, certainly have reached the traumatic and threatening magnitude that would warrant a new authoritative confessional statement to guide the Church through the turmoil. One question internal to the PC(USA) is whether the intensity generated by the special version of the nightmare of polarization—the theological dichotomies of absolute certainty and flexibility—is too great for a statement of theological unity to emerge.

The theological pluralism in the PC(USA) in the twenty-first century has gone far beyond the classic "spirituality of the church" positions on the right, "social activism" positions on the left, and "wobbly anything-goes" positions in the center. Heretofore, there was a modicum of mutual respect with a rapprochement of "agreeing to disagree." Ratcheting up a litany of stringent pro and con positions on single cultural-war issues magnifies the distance between the extreme poles of the right and left. Heated exchanges, getting precipitously close to personal destruction of the opposition, characterize the quality of relationships. Fading benign tolerance replaces a sense of mutual respect as the center withdraws from any engagement of meaningful relationships into an uncomfortable truce with the far right and the left. The church loses a clear identity and a common vision as a result of this pluralistic dysfunction.

Much has been written about the demise of mainline denominations' identity and strength. Robert Bacher and Kenneth Inskeep, in *Chasing Down a Rumor: The Death of Mainline Denominations*, have a very different perspective on the conventional wisdom of that rumor. They express a very strong belief in mainline denominations, not only in their role in American society, but in their resilience as an institution. They believe that "mainline denominations serve as caretakers of a wonderfully important American expression of the Christian faith and . . . if they are weak or lost, American society and the universal church will be the worse for it." The unique value of mainline denominations is seen in their concern for the "American community" and their "traditions that have always taken the world into account." Bacher and Inskeep want to give mainline denominations every chance for their restoration, if they have faded. They are confident that this is possible under certain conditions.[19]

Confidence in their resilience is based on the premise that "mainline denominations will get better if they do things that fulfill their mission purposes within the framework of their long and well established and clearly articulated identities." These writers contend that members of mainline denominations have not been excited or motivated "in a mission that reaches out and is at the same time distinctively" faithful to the traditions of the particular denomination of which they are members.[20] They believe that each denomination, as it thinks about the future, must ask itself the question: "What does the tradition tell us about the core of a [our] mainline religious identity and how can it be used to make the world a better place in the here and now?"[21] The answer to the first part of that question for the PC(USA) is that "A theology that is relative to the world about it is the core of Presbyterian tradition and identity." Getting a clear definition and consensus on the meaning of that answer is essential to the cure of the church's theological anemia in the turmoil of the twenty-first century.

In 1992, writers in *The Re-Forming Tradition* rightly pointed out the predicament that pluralism poses "as a political platform and theological principle." The plethora of voices and values in a pluralistic world make the possibility of penning common statements or finding common cause extremely problematic, creating "agonizing questions about what American Presbyterians should or could say together and what they would do cooperatively as witnesses to Jesus Christ." Seeing "no quick or easy solution to this predicament," the writers warned against the divisive temptation of "retreating into insulated special-interest enclaves of like-minded Presbyterians" or "ignoring the disaffiliation of Presbyterians with different viewpoints."[22] What was true in 1992 is certainly true in 2005, but these warnings are not being heeded.

To avoid this temptation, the writers advised that the starting point in facing theological pluralism is "by making theology the central focus of conversation whenever and wherever Presbyterians gather in congregations and governing bodies so that sincere differences in perspective can be recognized and evaluated openly in a spirit of shared searching for God's word today." They were not overly optimistic that this would "ensure consensus." But the cure for theological anemia is to begin the struggle for theological consensus, so "at the very least it will place the difficult questions of Christian discipleship at the center of Presbyterians' common life, thereby fulfilling the church's most important function."[23] Whether or not the PC(USA) has the will to fulfill this function in 2006 and beyond may be problematic, but there are signs that it just might happen.

The Movement—A Summary Look

Gather a group of people together who had been active participants in the Union Presbytery Movement and ask them what they thought was the most significant contribution it made to the life of the church, and they would invariably say "It was about building relationships" both in the union presbyteries themselves and in the consultations they created for mutual support. It was about building trust and building bridges across great divides that had lingered for years. This was done in many ways. Attention was paid to different heritages and styles; importance was given to each other's cultures. This did not happen overnight but, because of corporate and geographic proximity to each other, these differences were overcome, respect for each other grew and new dreams about what the church could become were dreamed. In many cases it was soon discovered that differences did not matter because, in fact, many perceived differences did not exist in reality.

The motivation for this new life was drawn out of the twin wells of theology and the everyday demands of life. Combined in common commitment was a deep theological conviction and desire that the "Church Be One," with the practical necessity to display a consistent and coherent witness to that end. Long years of cooperative work, cemented by a cooperative spirit, developed a credible witness to the fact that threats could be overcome and such a union could work. Structures could be transformed by a steadfast belief that God is the Redeemer of history; living out respect for differences within it could enhance the integrity of the church and a sense of common mission could be fashioned.

In consultation, solutions for common problems were found in the Movement by consensus building, making sense of the challenge of living in and between two worlds. The old polity based on "majority prevails but minorities have rights" was predicated on the fact that, going into a decision on the front end, the expectation was that in the outcome some will win and some will lose, creating something with which not all can live. At times it had the capacity to lapse into a "win-lose mentality" and become extremely dysfunctional. The new polity based on consensus building was predicated on the fact that, going into the decision on the front end, the expectation was that the outcome would be something with which all have decided they can live. Basically, functional consensus-building created the possibility of the widest ownership of a decision by the greatest number of people across the diversity spectrum.

The Union Presbytery Movement proved that consensus building was an effective way of decision-making, especially in small groups where building lasting relationships so critical to it was a reality. The

---

question arose as to whether it would be realistic to expect consensus building to function effectively in a larger body or in complex systems like the General Assembly and the governing bodies of the church. The question never had a chance to be answered during the lifetime of the Movement, but it has since been answered in the affirmative.

The Uniting Church in Australia in 2000 found a way to get beyond win-lose mentality in the polity for its new denomination. It fashioned a polity that began with the premise of discerning the Spirit in community building as the basis for its union. In the process it made time for building, maintaining, and constantly rebuilding community. In its *Manual for Meetings*, the reason given for meeting together was "to build community: to welcome each other, share something of ourselves and start to develop trust as we worship and celebrate together." It went on to declare further its purpose, "to be informed: let's learn as we explore ideas and concepts together, and are enthused by the challenge of shared knowledge; to develop new paths: let's listen, struggle, devise and refine together; to share a cup of tea: let's drink together!"[24]

Getting to the "business of the Church" came later in order of significance. Of course decisions had to be made, and the Uniting Church of Australia crafted a process built on the assumption that decisions could and should be made by consensus. However, it recognized that there may be a few times, after all avenues for consensus have been exhausted without resolution, when the body must decide to put the question to a majority vote as the last resort.[25] Consensus building kept the decision-making process in proper perspective, and it forestalled setting the twin traps of the "special interest syndrome" and the "win-lose mentality." Though it was not spelled out in such elaborate detail, COUP basically governed its life on the new polity based on consensus building, a process worthy of consideration by the PC(USA) in the twenty-first century.

Now What?

Does what is said here about the Union Presbytery Movement sound almost too idyllic to be true? The Movement and union presbyteries had their bumps and curves in the road. They were not perfect and all their dreams were not realized. But something special took place. When asked in the research project years later, "Would you do it over knowing what you know now," all interviewees gave a spontaneous and resounding, "YES, at the drop of a hat!" But the Movement was a temporary state, the need for which would one day end. The larger vision was that one day the two denominational worlds of which they were a part would become one in reunion.

The response to the question "Would you do it over knowing what you know now" might be very different if the question were asked about denominational reunion. Generally with the coming of reunion, a deep loss of identity was experienced and the relational nature of the church was radically disrupted. Institutional loyalties were disintegrating in the culture at large, affecting loyalties within the church. Continual restructuring of denominational agencies and the advent of regional synods added to the relational disconnect. The old relational networks that had been the pipeline for developing ecclesial leaders—camps and conferences, campus ministries, colleges, seminaries—no longer functioned as effectively as in the past.

Part of the difference between the "do it over" response to the Union Presbytery Movement and any response to denominational reunion is that they were by nature two distinct phenomena, though interrelated; part is that they existed in two different seasons of history. The conduct of their lives was perceived differently. William P. Thompson, years later, reflecting on his perception of the consultations and union presbyteries, said, "My impression is that the consultations that took place around the idea of union presbyteries were conducted in a much more civil manner than some of the things that are happening today" (01-16).

Lewis Wilkins observed that the Union Presbytery Movement engaged in problem-solving conversations that went beyond the repetitive, cyclical, destructive, non-conversations that developed later in the reunited church. He concluded that the "Union Presbytery conversation happened at the end of a period in which the church normally engaged in that kind of conversation, and it was sort of the last gasp of an old style . . . and [that] the new, post-television, postmodern, post–ideologically fractured and pulverized sound bite conversation, that we had ever since then, was really the new style of political discourse. And there's not any way to get beyond divisive, confrontational sound bites" (21–38). He said another "way of framing it would say, the union presbyteries experience was a kind of last gasp of real Presbyterianism of the old sort. And, when it died, that's the end of the dog's tail" (21–39).

Could the threats to the Dream, mounted in the seasons of history in which the Movement took place and denominational reunion came into being, be nothing more than the uncivil and deadly frolicking about of the ghosts of Stamford Bridge and Hastings in all of this? Much has happened in the intervening years since those seasons of history, especially since 9/11, to indicate that the world has now changed irrevocably. The world of the twenty-first century has migrated to the very vocal extreme right and left margins of culture, leaving a

---

bewildered silent mass in the middle to tend its wounds. All across this cultural landscape, many have taken refuge in prejudiced silos of self-interest from which to attack the "other."

More than enough evidence exists in the twenty-first century to declare that the "special interest syndrome" abounds and the "win-lose mentality" is the *modus operandi* of choice. The noise of the cultural wars still rings in one's ears temptingly, sending out the call to battle stations. Overshadowed by all this, however, is the most important call of all: The unfinished business of healing the broken and reconciling the divided still beckons the PC(USA) to faithful witness. For a viable future, the dividing walls of these silos of self-interest with their culture of silence must be actively and audibly breached, not for the mere joy of the engagement, but because life must be redeemed and lived beyond the grasp of the "special interest syndrome" and the "win-lose mentality," ending the nightmare of polarization. Learnings from the Union Presbytery Movement provide constructive clues for meeting all threats to the Dream, so *all* persons may have the *freest experience of the gospel* that Wilkins celebrated.

But Dreams, where have you gone?

Notes

1. Rev. Robert Stuart Sanders, D.D., *Annals of the First Presbyterian Church, Lexington, Kentucky: 1784–1959* [with continuation by Elizabeth G. Leggett], 1959–1984 (Lexington, KY: privately printed, 1984), pp. 13–14.

2. Such was the situation in 2005 in the battle over the nomination of federal judges by the president of the United States and the "advice and consent" by the Senate. One side advocated the use of the filibuster, requiring a larger majority of 60 senators, while the other side advocated for a simple majority of 51 senators. In either case, the margin of the winning or losing side could be by a vote of one. This strategy was clearly a win-lose political struggle over "what votes can we get and still prevail." It was not a matter of intending that either vote be an indicator of the broadest base of support that could be garnered for a particular candidate.

3. Anne Wilson Schaef and Diane Fassel, *The Addictive Organization* (New York: HarperCollins Publishers, 1988; paperback ed. 1990), p. 5.

4. For Schaef and Fassel's full treatment of the addictive organization as an addictive closed system with its general characteristics, see pp. 61–68.

5. Ibid., pp. 72–73.

6. Webb, *Born Fighting*, p. 12.

7. Ibid., p. 15.

8. Ibid., p. 17.

9. Ibid., p. 13.

10. Tex Sample, *Ministry in an Oral Culture: Living with Will Rogers, Uncle Remus, and Minnie Pearl* (Louisville, KY: Westminster/John Knox Press, 1994), pp. 6–7. The author, who was in the third grade, first met Sample when he was in the second grade in Brookhaven Elementary School!

11. Ibid.

12. "Ban on Rebel flag items is overruled," *Lexington (KY) Herald-Leader*, June 2, 2005, p. B3.

13. "400 at Confederate Service," *Lexington (KY) Herald-Leader*, June 6, 2005, p. A9.

14. Joanne Pope Melish, *Disowning Slavery: Gradual Emancipation and "Race" in New England, 1780–1860* (Ithaca, NY: Cornell University Press, 1998), p. xiv.

15. Ibid., p. xv.

16. Ibid., p. 2.

17. Ibid., p. 3.

18. The Constitution of the Presbyterian Church (U.S.A.), Part I, *Book of Confessions*, pp. 252–262.

19. Robert Bacher and Kenneth Inskeep, *Chasing Down a Rumor: The Death of Mainline Denominations* (Minneapolis: Augsburg, 2005), p. 10.

20. Ibid., p. 18.

21. Ibid., p. 19.

22. Coalter, Mulder, and Weeks, eds., *The Re-Forming Tradition*, p. 142.

23. Ibid., pp. 142–143.

24. The Uniting Church of Australia, *A Manual for Meetings*, rev. ed. (Collingswood, Australia: Uniting Education, 2001), p. 11.

25. Ibid., "Consensus Procedures—Flow Chart," p. 28.

Chapter 16
Dreams, Where Have You Gone?

Now, the Union Presbytery Movement in its very dissolving, tried to say, "We are one Church, and we are not going to remain a faction that is divisive in this Church. We're all one now." And it's not "we," the old guys that are still in charge that had the experience that brought us there, and try to keep being Moses for the whole Church. You know, we want to be partners and help everyone, and this is now the norm. So, that is a way of looking positively at the Union Presbytery Movement going out of existence, which still is driven by a vision and an idealism of what the Church is. And [chuckling] it may say something about the longevity of the groups because, where our churches are today, we're back in the first-century Church of Corinth [in which some] follow Cephas and some Paul and some Christ. And we don't talk to each other very well.
—*Thomas M. Johnston (79-18)*

The Dream hoped for in reunion was to strengthen and create a new Presbyterian identity based on the church's shared heritage, shared theology, and shared vision of relationships to the community and the world. The Dream also was that, as the Presbyterian identity was strengthened in this marriage, the legacy of racism would be addressed by becoming more diverse and inclusive as a new church. The Dream was to bring closure to one of the ravages of the Civil War and be an antioxidant to the still venomous residue of racism stemming from the institution of slavery. The Dream was to begin a new way for Presbyterians to *be church*. That was the Dream.

Realized Dreams
The Dream for the new, reunited church has been fulfilled in many ways. Especially fundamental to the commitments made by the church in ratifying the *Plan for Reunion* were the principles of diversity, inclusiveness, and working for justice in the church and in the world. These were a continuation of commitments already practiced by the two former denominations. The leadership of the church lived out these commitments. Women and racial ethnic persons assumed roles as General Assembly moderators and commissioners and filled high-level administrative positions in the national headquarters. Three women became presidents of theological seminaries.

Committees on Representation at all governing body levels called for in *The Plan for Reunion* over time changed the face of the structures of the church. Fulfilling their mandate by challenging the conscience of the church, they assured the fair representation of women and racial ethnic membership throughout the system. Racial ethnic caucuses were consulted in determining the priorities for assisting racial ethnic churches and ministries, developing denominational strategy for racial church development, and finding ways to assure the funding and operational needs of schools and other institutions that historically have served black Americans and other racial ethnic groups.[1]

Two official advocacy groups, the Advocacy Committee for Racial Ethnic Concerns (ACREC) and the Advocacy Committee for Women's Concerns (ACWC) are functioning well into the twenty-first century, serving the church on behalf of their special interests.[2] Also the Advisory Committee on Social Witness Policy (ACSWP) is following in the tradition of respective units in the former denominations by preparing study and position papers to guide the Assembly in setting policies in a full range of justice issues. The Gay-Lesbian issue came to prominence after denominational reunion took place, and it continues to dominate the diversity and inclusiveness discussion as well as the theological agenda of the church. The group now named "More Light Presbyterians," formerly "Presbyterians for Gay and Lesbian Concerns," has led the advocacy for these issues with the organizational manifestation advanced by the More Light Church Movement.

A radical change has taken place in the increased number of racial ethnic persons and women in the ranks of ordained clergy, although some congregations appear reluctant to extend them calls. Women clergy candidates and theological students are becoming the rising majority. Of the total of 2,730 candidates and inquirers in 2004, 1,371 (50.2 percent) were women. In 2004 there were 55 women in head-of-staff positions of congregations of 500 or more members, an increase of 29.1 percent since 1990. In 2004 there were 488 (1.8 percent) racial ethnic candidates, an increase of 29.9 percent since 1990.[3] Racial ethnic members comprised 7.6 percent of the total membership of the PC(USA) in 2003.[4] The 210th General Assembly in 1998 adopted the ongoing Racial Ethnic Church Growth Strategy, which had a comprehensive range of program objectives including racial ethnic congregational growth, pastoral leadership recruitment and anti-racism training. Special attention was given to the new wave of racial ethnic immigrants to this country from Asia and Africa.[5]

Seminaries have taken the lead in raising awareness in the areas of inclusive language, gender issues, sexual conduct, and anti-racism or cultural proficiency training. Constructive theology, liberation theology, feminist theology, and African American theology, along with a buffet of complementary studies in these areas, provided new and contemporary avenues for theological formulation and reflection on critical issues of the times.

The most visible, tangible symbol of the Dream was the selection and location of the new national headquarters, although achieving a sense of unity there has been a work in progress over the years. Consolidation of the national program agentry and the Office of the General Assembly was achieved by making the decision to locate the national headquarters at 100 Witherspoon Street in Louisville, Kentucky. The location of The Presbyterian Foundation across the Ohio River in Jeffersonville, Indiana, was determined to a large degree by tax laws in the Commonwealth of Kentucky adverse to its operation. The Board of Pensions remained in Philadelphia, Pennsylvania.

The last-minute pitch to the PC(USA) General Assembly (1987) in Biloxi by leaders like John M. Mulder and Grayson L. Tucker, Jr., of Louisville Seminary, Charles L. Stanford of Louisville Presbytery, Louisville Mayor Jerry E. Abramson, and other church and civic leaders swayed the decision in favor of Louisville, over close rival Kansas City and Kansas City Presbytery. Some win-lose hard feeling lingered for a while between the two former union presbyteries over the location decision. Space to be renovated in the old Belknap Hardware warehouse to house the headquarters was made available by David A. Jones, a Louisville Presbyterian. This location for the new Presbyterian headquarters, together with the location of Humana, Inc., a health-care organization, began the cultural and economic revival of the riverfront and East Main area of Louisville.

The Dream has been fulfilled to a degree at middle governing body and local levels of the church in various ways, too numerous to mention here. It is obvious that union presbyteries had the least problem with reunion, for they had been living the Dream. Carol Davies felt there was a valuable "sense of personally knowing people that were struggling with this together from both denominations" in the union presbytery experience. She also suspected that people "outside of that geographical area that were struggling, had a harder time with reunion" (49-18). Non-overlapping areas of the former denominations may still be trying to figure out what the big deal was about reunion, and their life may not have changed that much.

Unrealized Dreams

The closest the Dream might have come to being realized was in that special moment when Presbyterians marched on "the Day" from the World Congress Center to City Hall in Atlanta on June 10, 1983. It was a fleeting, serendipitous moment of pure "being" with little thought of the "doing" that was yet to come. Nothing has happened since to equal it. Even with the parade of examples just given of the Dream realized, an even more impressive list might be garnered to prove otherwise— dreams unrealized. At the top of the list of unrealized dreams would be unresolved style and cultural issues, both reflected in the structural life of the church. These unresolved issues translate into a corporate identity yet to be discovered.

Jill Hudson, reflecting on the progress made in creating a reunited church that she continues to support for "ethical and theological reasons that we should be one Church," was very realistic in assessing what it is still taking to make that happen. She said, "I think it has been extraordinarily difficult, and I think that I will not live to see the day when we truly do have a new Church because . . . from my experience in family systems work, and systems in general, it's going to take a long time to reshape a new system. And twenty years is a drop in the bucket." She went on to describe how style issues and cultural issues have not yet been resolved and "are still going to be hammered out . . . . even though the people who may be doing the hammering may not have, in their memory range, the experience of union presbyteries or life prior to reunion" (90-21).

When the final gavels fell in the two General Assemblies in Atlanta on the afternoon of June 10, 1983, more took place in that act than the signal to leave the hall and join the throng marching to City Hall. A much more profound reality was marked by that signal—the loss of identity of two very strong and proud North American Presbyterian denominations. These previous identities were not formed overnight, and their replacement identity in the Presbyterian Church (U.S.A.) would not be either. Before the new Assembly was barely up and walking, the beginning division, over the motion to add four advisory members from the evangelical wing of the church to the General Assembly Council (GAC) was probably the first real effort in defining the new identity by the Assembly itself.

The Consultation on Union Presbyteries (COUP) spent a great deal of time at its last meeting in March 1983 reflecting on what could be expected as a result of reunion. It recognized that there would be deep hurts caused by this loss of identity; that every change needed to be perceived as a loss; that plenty of time needed to be spent on the healing process. COUP anticipated that the progressive stages of the grief process could be expected in varying degrees in certain areas of the church. The deepest hurt could possibly come among those who were on the losing side of the reunion vote: PCUS presbyteries in the Southeast who lost by close votes; members of the UPCUSA in the Southeast, both black and white, who felt overwhelmed; and persons in the UPCUSA and PCUS who perceived that too many concessions were made.[6]

Others felt like losers even though they supported reunion: Church educators in both groups; institutions whose constituencies had shifted; women in both groups with concerns about how various aspects of the *Plan* affected them; people on the PCUS side who lost their sense of "family"; those shocked in the PCUS who had to look at issues in a national context; those shocked in the UPCUSA who had to consider the Southeast as a strong area of the country; those in both groups who were uncertain where to go for information; some ministers who were shocked by new provisions for equal representation in committee structures; and the major part of the UPCUSA in non-overlapping territories who did not realize what they had gained and were surprised at what they had lost. One very crucial group that needed special care so as not to repeat the trauma created by reorganization in both former denominations was the national staff. They were faced with the uncertainty of moves, job shifts, office relocation, and the possibility that their work might be terminated.[7]

All these were indicators of loss of identity. They had to be taken seriously and addressed specifically in a pastoral, even therapeutic manner, though one wonders how thorough was the attention given. Sadly, these expectations that COUP had so carefully laid out related to coping with grief and loss were never really met and the PC(USA) remains in grief. It would be too easy to blame all the losses in general on the simple fact of reunion itself. Finding a common enemy can be a unifying factor in a negative way.

COUP's Dreams

COUP, approaching the need for healing from its own long productive experience, felt that reunion was an organic process in which things grow together stronger and healthier, not a mechanical process in which things are stuck together. The real objective was creating a new community, taking considerable time, energy, and intentionality. The theological basis for this new community had similarities to Dietrich Bonhoeffer's *sanctorum communio* (communion of saints) that he described in his dissertation of the same name to the Theological Faculty in Berlin in 1927.[8]

Bonhoeffer wrote that the communion of saints was founded on the "spiritual unity of the church . . . a primal synthesis willed by God." When persons found themselves in conflict [Jew-Greek, Northerner-Southerner] "as a result of the completely different nature of their psychological structure, sensibility and outlook . . . unity was established by the divine will." He felt that the greater the conflict, the greater the potential for "objective unity." To Bonhoeffer, the New Testament did not proclaim "one theology and one rite, one opinion upon all things both public and private." More appropriately it was, as Ephesians 4:4–6 RSV puts it, "one body and one Spirit, . . . one Lord, one faith, one baptism, one God and Father of us all," yet allowing for a collective of persons. This collective was not monolithic in nature. It exhibited "varieties of gifts, but the same Spirit; . . . varieties of service, but the same Lord; . . . varieties of working, it is the same God who inspires them all in everyone" (1 Cor. 12:4–6 RSV).[9]

The community was made up of a great many individuals who brought a variety of gifts to share. Bonhoeffer made a clear distinction between "oneness in the spirit" and the "unity of the spirit," and the two are not identical. The former tended to imply a collection of single-minded individuals in a blob of groupthink. The latter established a community of persons holding a consensus of due respect for diverse individuals where "spiritual unity, community of spirit and multiplicity of spirits necessarily and factually belong together." The communion of saints became a collective person whose unity was established by God and not the organizing efforts of the humans involved.[10]

This theological perspective was explicitly and implicitly the basis on which COUP formed as a new community of faith. COUP's dream of community took seriously the Presbyterian system of governance, whose organizational manifestation was divided into four governing bodies in gradation, each having clearly defined spheres of mission and functions, yet being interrelated with all the others as a part of the whole. Each partner brought different gifts and perspectives to the whole that made the community stronger. The dream understood that these parts were connected as partners in many different ways, based on mutual respect.

Each partner's mission was to be planned "in light of" and "in consultation with" all the other partners as the basis on which leadership and resources would be deployed across the system. COUP's annual gatherings came close to being the one forum where this dream of a new consultative community was most nearly expressed. The formal gradation of governing bodies never quite functioned in this sense as COUP did during its lifetime. COUP never intended to supplant the four governing bodies as THE new community, but saw itself simply as a new consultative part of the Presbyterian system that conducted "new polity–style" conversations horizontally across it. With reunion, whatever conversations took place between governing bodies reverted primarily to "old polity–style" vertical communications between them.

In its more functional perspective with regard to denominational reunion, the feeling was expressed in the COUP discussions that transition periods were seldom too long and often too short, becoming disastrous usually because some "special pleader" got the upper hand, seeking to get on with the structure. COUP felt that "readiness or ripeness" was consistent with its organic process and that rushing into structure before the "right time" could actually damage community.[11] Some may have been too overwhelmed and stunned by the increased numbers and size of the new organization, demanding massive modifications in previous styles and procedures to be even aware of the dynamics of community building. For them the priority was to "fix the structure."

Others got caught up in settling the "staff situation" because "staff distress" had become too great, inadvertently regressing the healing process. COUP recognized the importance of staff, but many also cautioned against making staff the most important agenda in the reunion process, a caution that still goes unheeded, echoing into the twenty-first century. Though staff do provide a modicum of continuity, hearing national staff say at the time that "unity was more important to them than their current jobs" usually went a long way to clear the air as concerns arose when it seemed staff were becoming the most important agenda. However, many in COUP were still "very apprehensive that the 'dead hand' of the past (read: New York and Atlanta) [would] clutch the new situation and that this golden opportunity to do a 'new thing' [would] be smothered in 'special interests, gate-keeping, and security motivated by keeping of old ways and old people.' " COUP saw things differently and dreamed of creating "a new framework, new categories/concepts of thought for a New Church."[12] This had been their experience for fourteen years, and the dream of a new way realized in their situations was their hope for the future.

COUP had been involved long enough in living in two worlds to discover that cooperation between the two national organizations maybe tended "persistently to be in innocuous areas or less crucial areas," even though the laundry list of cooperation was long and valuable. What some in COUP perceived was that where there was "money, funding, real estate, institutional property, goals, and heavy tradition involved, cooperation is low and/or perfunctory." COUP concluded: "It is in these 'more central' matters [from an institutional point of view] where more difficulty can be anticipated." Nevertheless, those areas where cooperation was already happening provided the best beginning point for a smooth transition from the old to the new.[13]

Despite unresolved issues related to those who had experienced losses in the reunion vote, structures, staff, and areas reticent to cooperation, COUP remained committed to the belief that "plenty of goodwill, trust and open dialogue will make it [reunion] happen right; it needs to meld slowly enough so that all the appropriate publics can be appropriately involved." Those publics included the four governing bodies of the church whose interrelatedness was changing from old patterns built on parent-child models to strong peer relations built on adult-adult models. The older model was "no longer helpful and cannot work because of change in both Church and Society."[14]

Central to COUP's understanding of the organic nature of a healthy reuniting process was finding a common mission. Deep theological underpinning, in addition to the challenges of the world context, was essential in the formulation of this common mission. COUP knew that strong relationships were absolutely essential in establishing broad ownership of the common mission. It also had learned that strong relationships are built when shoulders are put side by side in some common endeavor, enabling a spirit of unity to begin to flourish. COUP was committed to getting the new denomination to approve a new Confession of Faith as part of its healthy reuniting process.[15] Some had wanted this to happen before reunion even took place but that was not to be. Brief statements of faith and organizational mission statements would have to do initially. But again COUP's dream of an organic healthy process that finds a common mission in community still eludes the PC(USA) in the twenty-first century.

COUP began as an instrument for mutual support and celebration, sharing of information, and cooperative problem-solving among the union presbyteries. In retrospect, it would have been strengthened had serious theological reflection been a more central part of its agenda. However, its success in these activities, and the advancement of the Union Presbytery Movement, rapidly established COUP as an annual event, an ongoing process, with growing influence in the life of American Presbyterianism. These achievements brought the union presbyteries toward a point in their life together where, for the sake of both their own faithfulness and their responsible participation in the PCUS and the UPCUSA, they needed "to devote a major portion of an annual meeting agenda to reflection (1) on the role of COUP in the historical development of American Presbyterianism, (2) on the theological definition of this kind of consultative/council process as a legitimate new feature in the working polity of our denominations, and (3) on the future administrative and ecclesiastical relationships which will enable us to continue in responsibility toward this new thing into which God is leading us."[16] Unfortunately that attention was never really devoted to reflection on these items in great detail and they remained on the unfinished agenda of COUP at the time it went out of existence.

COUP had accomplished its twofold purposes: to serve as an instrument for mutual support and celebration, sharing of information, and cooperative problem-solving among the union presbyteries, and to work for the reunion of the denominations. But some of its members were haunted with the questions: Was COUP dissolved too soon? Could it have done more to fulfill its dreams? Could it have had a more lasting impact on shaping the reunited church if it had continued to exist for a little while longer? Some felt there was no logical rationale for COUP's continuing existence; union presbyteries no longer existed. Others felt differently about its affecting change in the new denomination.

Bill Peterson summed it up this way: "I think maybe if we had stuck together for another two years, maybe three, there might have been enough drive to keep that change going, that it would have made a difference in how things shaped up for national offices." He went on to say, "[W]e were not much of a force with all the organizing commissions of the new denomination. So some of the things that we developed and worked on that worked so well for us, got lost in the process" (36-22). COUP was dissolved and the dreams it dreamed for the reunited church in large measure went unrealized.

Y'all Come and Rocking Chair Gatherings

COUP was not the only gathering giving serious consideration to having influence on shaping the new, reunited church. In the spring of 1982, before the passage of reunion was even certain, a group of thirty persons from the PCUS's "y'all come-cousin network," who had played key roles in the reunion effort, were invited to come to Camp Maranatha in North Alabama Presbytery to spend three days "informally" reflecting on the past experience of the PCUS and dreaming strategies for the 1980s. Time was given to fellowship, worship, and discussion of the issues, certainly not without political ramifications. This "informal" gathering at Maranatha may have been the kind of thing Bob Stevenson was referring to when he said the UPCUSA may not have been ready for this kind of caucusing.

Wayne Todd prepared a study paper on "Strategic Implications for the 1980s from the Last 25 Years." From his handwritten notes of his introduction, Todd described "Who we are" at this meeting. He acknowledged that some would say we are the "Presbyterian mafia," successor to the "Texas Mafia." Others would call us "the liberals in the PCUS. I would say we're the only true 'conservatives' in the PCUS because we have been those in our generation who have 'conserved' the Calvinistic principle of 'always reforming' the Church." He went on to say: "I believe we have been agents of the Holy Spirit in confronting racism, sexism, nationalism, provincialism, denominationalism, and various other 'isms' in the PCUS and in our society." He concluded by saying: "We have certainly confronted the neo-gnosticism of an inherited and long-established 'spirituality of the church' movement which has characterized the PCUS since shortly after the Civil War."[17]

In the paper, Todd summarized the dramatic changes in polity, program, and organizational structure in the PCUS. He gave a theological analysis of the nature of change and an understanding of the agents and opponents of it. He included a summary of the sources and forces of change at work recently in the PCUS. He concluded with a description of the changing of the guard—the people, polity and politics—in which he dealt with the personal element in PCUS leadership; the covenant community and the "clan" or "cousin system"; when prophets become managers; advocacy in relation to inclusiveness, pluralism, and consensus-building; the System—its nature and use in Reformed theology; and our failure to incorporate our learnings and the reversion to "pre-change" attitudes and styles.[18]

Lewis Wilkins prepared a second study paper titled, "Polity Issues for the 1980s—A Personal Presbyterian View." In this paper he summarized the assumptions underlying Presbyterian and Reformed polity; the issues underlying Reformed catholicity and American voluntarism; the stresses of being a "bridge Church"; test cases of these assumptions and concepts in the 1980s—Presbyterian reunion, COCU, and other union initiatives. He concluded with reflections on the essentiality of "oversight" in the church; the scale of the system; leadership legitimacy and the ethics of power; and finally the question: "Is the Presbyterian Church reformable?"[19]

Smaller groups worked on the issues chosen by the whole group and developed proposed strategies for them to consider, some "go" and others "no-go," depending on the outcome of the reunion vote. The object was to find the most effective ways to get the group's views before the General Mission Board (PCUS) if reunion fails, or the General Assembly Council if it passes. The larger problem was how to communicate these concerns so that they become incorporated in the total life of the church. Getting presbyteries to become more theological reflection settings and less program and administrative settings was critical to incorporating these concerns into their life and mission. Presbytery executives were seen as key to making this happen. One small group worked on connecting the long list of existing networks or building new ones as a way of getting the right people in the right positions and in touch with each other. Consideration was given to how this Maranatha gathering fit in with the networks. The consensus was that it should be maintained on a "y'all [certain 'y'alls'] come" basis, gathering around the edges of other existing formal meetings. It was essential to cultivate and include younger persons so that there would be a lasting effect on the future.[20]

One of the immediate outcomes of Maranatha was to have another similar informal gathering of about 10 to 12 persons from each denomination "who could function in that kind of informal setting."

People from each denomination generated a list of key General Assembly, synod, and presbytery elected and staff persons to be invited.[21] The gathering, known simply as "The Rocking Chair," met in Louisville, Kentucky, October 3–5, 1982. It was scheduled at the same time a Higher Education Consultation was being held in Louisville across town so there was considerable 'in-and-out-ness' on the part of some participants.[22]

The meeting included worship, an exploration of the informal, nondeciding, dialogical "rocking chair" style of meetings, and a lengthy discussion of the concerns about the emerging new church that individuals brought to the event. The 32-item laundry list of concerns generated reaffirmed the main issues that had punctuated the reunion conversation over the years, such as building trust, keeping lines of communication open, allaying fears that some have about reunion, creating a new agenda for a new church, exhibiting strong leadership that stands for something, advocating for the marginalized in society, maintaining a prophetic-social edge; modeling true partnership, bringing creative energy to focus from our two traditions; moving ahead in mission instead of reorganizing for ten years, and keeping the momentum of joint work going if reunion fails. The meeting closed with a lengthy discussion of the vision of what the participants would like the new Church to be, and what to bring in and what to keep out.[23]

Life and Mission Statement

Participants in COUP regarding the start-up activities of the new denomination made several miscellaneous, yet very significant comments. One such piece of advice was: "Don't get so caught up in the mechanics of reorganization that mission emphases and programs get obscured and lost." COUP saw the heart and spirit of reunion dependent more upon people and their evolving relationships to one another than upon particular ecclesiastical and administrative structures. For COUP, structure should evolve not as a primary end in itself but rather as a means to be a worshiping and serving community. Some encouraging signs were evident to members of COUP that some attention was already being given to maintaining mission while new structure was developed.[24]

COUP suggested that regional consultations be held to generate data for new mission directions, with representatives then participating in a national consultation. It felt that the new GAC should develop the process to accomplish this. One of the responses the Administrative Implications of Reunion Task Force of COUP got when it did a survey of COUP members regarding the urgent need of a mission consultation was: "Spend 2 million to do it or don't do it."[25]

One of the first orders of business of the 195th General Assembly (1983) was to affirm "the value of holding a major mission consultation" and instructed the General Assembly Council to explore with the agencies ways and means to accomplish the objective within the next two years." The Council established a process that included a year of consultations involving the entire church and appointed a Mission Design Committee to oversee it. A series of churchwide consultations named "Today Into Tomorrow" were held that generated data from which the mission of the reunited church would be formulated and become the basis for creating a structure for fulfilling that mission.[26] It was a classic "form follows function" strategy.

Once the findings of the churchwide consultations were compiled, the "Life and Mission Event" was held at the Presbyterian Mo-Ranch Assembly, in Hunt, Texas, on February 12–17, 1985. A core of seventy-one participants came from sessions, presbyteries, synods, General Assembly agencies, racial ethnic caucuses, the General Assembly Council, and the Mission Consultation Planning Team. In addition to these were sixteen ecumenical representatives from international partner churches, five theological reflectors, and a team of four writers to assist the participants. Bill Peterson, who served as a process consultant to the event, later commented, "that was a widely diverse group. There were some very, very, nearly fundamentalist people in there, and some very, very liberal, left-wing folk; it was a good meeting of the minds" (36-23).

"The Life and Mission Statement" that came out of the event had two functions: "(1) To provide a means by which the reunited church, in all its parts, might speak about and reflect upon a common vision of its life and work. (2) To provide a commonly agreed upon foundation for structuring the life of the Presbyterian Church (U.S.A.)." This document was created from the findings of the churchwide consultations and was informed by "careful reflection of Scripture, *The Book of Confessions*, the *Book of Order*, and participants' interaction with one another."[27]

The Statement was structured around four Parts. Part I: Who We Are—a people of God, living between faith affirmation and daily reality; a North American institution, but part of one Church of Jesus Christ. Part II: Who We Are Called to Be—the body of Christ, a new creation, a servant church. Part III: What We Are Called to Do—be open to the renewal by God, to prepare for servanthood and to demonstrate the new creation. Part IV: How We Live and Work Together—being the body of Christ requires a certain way of living together and requires a certain way of working together.[28]

The Statement concluded with a declaration: "We are one part of the body of Christ: a community of mutual interdependence in which diversity contributes to wholeness. We are called to live according to the model of the suffering servant: poured out on behalf of all people. We are becoming a new creation by the power of God's grace: to proclaim the good news of Christ and to manifest the justice of God."[29]

Peterson felt that the document "was a rather significant statement. And there was a lot of union presbytery involvement in the writing of that statement, not deliberately, but folk who had come out of that experience [were participants]. . . . So some of the same impetus we had in union presbyteries was present at that Mo-Ranch Consultation" (36-32).

Old Patterns in New Structures

The time period immediately following the organizing Assembly in 1983 was very critical in setting the climate for the new structures of the reunited denomination. Article 5 of *The Plan for Reunion* indicated that the authority for the management of the new structure was vested in the General Assembly Council and clearly specified that its composition would consist of twenty-four members from the GAMC (UPCUSA) and twenty-one members from the GAMB (PCUS) and three members from the Committee on Assembly Operations (PCUS).[30] The total group was to reflect the organizational and representative demographics of both former denominations. Half were to be ministers and half laypersons.[31]

Article 5 of *The Plan for Reunion* also provided for the transitional work of the General Assembly Council and other agencies. Even though this article stipulated that the GAMC (UPCUSA) would cease to exist immediately after the adjournment of the 1983 Assembly, its Program Agency, Support Agency, and Vocation Agency along with the GAMB (PCUS), "consisting of the members remaining after the election of the General Assembly Council," would "continue to administer the programs, previously conducted by each of them, for five years unless earlier terminated by action of the General Assembly."[32] Article 5 stipulated that for five years the GAC would elect its own moderator and vice-moderator and designate its own staff, subject to confirmation by the General Assembly.[33] These provisions may have generated the unintended consequences of locking in place powerful dynamics and personalities that created certain inertia precluding the possibility of significant change.

Many roadblocks to creating something that was basically new as a denominational structure continued to cause detours in the formation of a new identity. Lost identities of former denominations played a major role in this. Classic organizational behavior at the formation of any new group almost guaranteed that there would be control issues in the new structure. A power struggle erupted over the number of top elected and administrative positions filled from each of the former denominations. Some felt that the number of former PCUS persons serving as Division heads in the new structure was disproportionate to the size of that former denomination. Other strong leaders were "very clear that we're not going to create anything new . . . and greatly different from the old UP bureaucratic system" (36-22). The debate about a careful balancing act on the top positions focused attention on structures and staffing.

Old patterns began to be entrenched in the reunited church during those first two years of its existence before the "Life and Mission Statement" was created. COUP's dream of a long transition of building trust and relationships in which mission would determine structure and staff went unrealized. The identity being established was not one depicting newfound unity based on a common mission, although a genuine effort to be faithful to its intended purpose was made by those responsible for implementing the "Life and Mission Statement" in the new structure. But the horse was out of the barn before the gate was shut. The new church got so caught up in the mechanics of reorganization that the new missional foundations laid out in the "Life and Mission Statement" on which structure and staff were to be determined got obscured and lost. A case could be made that in those early years the new church had not lived together long enough to build strong trusting relations from whom a common mission could emerge to determine structure and staffing.

Nightmare of Polarization

Something happened after the "Life and Mission Statement" was adopted by the General Assembly in 1985. Bill Peterson later, from his perspective over the years, concluded: "[T]hat statement in a sense really just was always ignored as it got anything beyond the theoretical and the visioning, so that it didn't come out in terms of organization. It didn't come out in terms of trying to describe why things existed or what we were trying to do and be" (36-23). Others have confirmed this perception. As so often happens, win-lose mentality can commingle with good and honorable intentions.

The elusive new identity was reflected in a series of reorganizations and restructurings in the following years. The self-absorption in these internal endeavors seemed only a minor distraction compared to the massive upheaval that was brewing in the external world. The church, as so often was the case in other periods of history, got swept up in the American and world social history in which homeostatic equilibrium between corporate and individual interests in society was dramatically thrown out of kilter. The spirit of the "me-generation" that spilled over from the late 1960s and 1970s, along with the special interest revolutions, created a climate of dis-ease, imbalance, and separatism. It became every person or every group for himself or herself or itself, yet ironically corporate power stealthily grew in domination. Every dream has a potentially unintended corollary nightmare; the corollary to the dream of unity was the extreme nightmare of polarization.

The Dream at reunion had high hopes for the place of diversity and inclusiveness in the new church. Everybody was not only welcomed at the table, but also was expected to bring their gifts as a contribution to the welfare of the whole. However, over the years this part of the Dream became susceptible to the "special interest syndrome" that prohibited the Dream from being fully realized. Diversity became an end in itself and little interest or concern was shown for inclusiveness or welcome across the board. Creeping "special interest syndrome" was one of the pivotal factors in the formation of the nightmare of polarization.

Ed White, thinking about what he had learned from his experience about diversity and inclusiveness, said: "I think I have learned to appreciate how you cannot simply have inclusiveness but [must] make inclusiveness work for you as a positive value. It'll only work for you if you are able somehow to honor and use the diversity in a positive way rather than to tolerate it as something that is necessary in order to be inclusive" (86-30).

John M. Coffin, reflecting on what this homeostatic imbalance produced within the church over the years, said, "We're disconnected. Congregations care less and less about what the presbytery is; and presbyteries are fightin' to figure out what they ought to be; and synods, heaven knows, they don't know what they're in. The same deal for the General Assembly, they are afraid of getting into a congregation; . . . the Assembly is fumbling all over itself trying to recreate 1950s or something; . . . and everybody is pretty uptight about moving anything now, because when you get threatened, of course, what you do is, you ridge it up" (03-25).

It seemed as though the grassroots' distrusted of the treetops and the treetops had disdain for the grassroots. This is but one of the many examples of polarization within the church. Coffin wished that "somehow we could find that same kind of freedom and creativity and . . . that same kind of spirit, which was a terrific openness to let's sit down and talk about it; if we could somehow find some of that same kind of spirit that you guys had back in those days [in the Union Presbytery Movement] to talk about where we would like to be and how to fix it and how to do it," things might be different now (03-25).

In many ways the Presbyterian Church reflected the mood of the country in the waning decades of the twentieth century and had its own versions of the special interest groups. Diversity was touted as a value, but interchange between the camps was subtle and in many cases superficial. The culture of silence at times erupted into a culture of criticism. Yet there was some evidence of a genuine response to competent leadership on those rare occasions when it rose above sectarian interests for the common good.

Clues for Unity

Interviews conducted in the Union Presbytery Movement Research Project indicated that union presbyteries and the Consultation on Union Presbyteries were fundamentally an open and healthy system, one of the things that made this Movement a unique phenomenon in American Presbyterianism. That openness was based on the theological belief in Jesus' prayer that the "church be one" was not some hollow theoretical concept, but was a reality that could be acted out in the flesh-and-blood body of a faithful community of humans transformed by the power of the Holy Spirit. Out of that openness it was free enough to exist as a movement and not become an institution. As a witness to that commitment, the Movement ceased to exist by its own volition when its purposes were achieved. Specific learnings from the Union Presbytery Movement provide valuable clues in working toward unity in the present situation in the Presbyterian Church (U.S.A.) and in any future union efforts, Reformed or ecumenical.

The first clue from the union presbytery experience is: *The quality of the identity of an organization is determined to a large degree by the quality of relations—trust, mutual respect, good faith actions—built by those involved.* Building quality and lasting relations that creates a "community of saints" takes time and attention, especially in the face of the urgency of the task or threat at hand. The complexity, size, and scope of an organization offer no excuse to discount the absolute importance of quality relationships as a key indicator of a healthy organization.

The second clue is: *The extent of diversity as a positive social quality is dependent on the manner in which true welcome is practiced across the entire spectrum of the Church.* Diversity can only be a positive quality if in espousing inclusiveness it is learned how genuinely to abandon the "special interest syndrome" and to welcome and include "strangers within our gates." Diversity must be more than a collection of silos of self-interest; diversity must encourage breaking down relational barriers between silos; diversity must establish patterns of communication that are not mere mechanical transfers of data between silos, but true conveyors of mutual understanding and respect.

The third clue is: *Then the mission of the organization—and subsequently structures, deployment of leadership, and resources—is shaped as an outgrowth of the first two clues, working for the common good of the whole and the context in which it is found.* Depending on the narrow confines of one corner of the world, one view of reality—be it treetop or grassroots—to define the mission for the whole is not acceptable. Long years of cooperative efforts between disparate parties can provide the proving ground for discerning and determining the formation of mutual mission from which structures, deployment of leadership and resources can then rightly evolve, reflecting both treetop and grassroots perspectives in balance.

The fourth clue is: *The win-lose nature of our old polity creates a dynamic that is counterproductive to achieving the first three clues.* New polity that rejects the "win-lose mentality" and relies more on consensus building needs to become more operative in the life of the church, rather than functioning purely on "majority rule with minority having rights"—the wider the margins, the better.

The fifth clue is: *Basically it all is a theological matter.* In the final analysis, the church is not just a human institution subject to self-destruction. The church is God incarnate in the body with Christ as head. That defines who we are and whose we are corporately and individually, forever being formed and transformed by the workings of the Holy Spirit. This is the theological underpinning upon which all other clues—*relations, diversity, inclusiveness, mission, polity*—must be built. Ignore this realization at one's peril; the stakes are too high. Lay hold of this foundational reality and a new way of being church can be recouped.

Glimmers of Hope

Every dream can turn into a nightmare when unrealized, and for the Presbyterian Church (U.S.A.), the Dream's nightmare is polarization, evidencing a loss or lack of identity. This is but a reflection of the polarization in twenty-first-century American society and the world at large. The clashes of the 1960s may some day in retrospect seem like a Sunday school picnic compared to the convulsions of the first quarter of the twenty-first century. History may one day conclude that these two decades were as devastating to America as the rupture caused by the Civil War.[34]

Faced with this nightmare, the 213th General Assembly (2001) created the Theological Task Force on Peace, Unity, and Purity of the Church (TTF) "to lead the Presbyterian Church (U.S.A.) in spiritual discernment of our Christian identity in and for the 21st century."[35] During the three years that followed the creation of the twenty-member task force, it met on eight occasions lasting from two to four days each. The membership of the task force reflected the demographic and theological diversity of the church and was led by co-chairs Gary W. Demarest and Jean S. (Jenny) Stoner. What transpired with the task force was an expanded version somewhat reminiscent of the "Life and Mission Statement" process of twenty years earlier.

A covenant was drafted through which all members of the task force were committed to pray for each other and for their work; to seek to be guided by their study of Scripture together; to worship together and celebrate the Lord's Supper; to speak the truth with love; to listen to each other, respecting differing views in a spirit of openness and vulnerability; to work as a community of believers under the guidance of the Holy Spirit with all that entails—respecting confidences, being faithful in relationships and trusting each other's motivations and dedication. Their commitment was to model a "respectful, loving process of discernment and dialogue, seeking to reach consensus whenever possible, ever mindful of our responsibilities to all the members of our beloved Church." The work was conducted in good faith within the open-meeting policy of the General Assembly. All members of the press and other observers were invited to participate in worship experiences with the task force.[36]

In preparation for the task force's final report to the 217th General Assembly (2006) it engaged in extensive study of the social and religious context in which the church has existed; Christology; principles of biblical interpretation; biblical and theological perspectives on human sexuality; Reformed understandings of the church; the theology of ordination; Presbyterian history and Reformed traditions of church order, with special emphasis on Presbyterian confessionalism, the development of the Constitution and principles of Presbyterian polity; the denomination's recent history and other historical periods; and on the diversity of racial and ethnic decision-making traditions in the church.[37]

The TTF participated in many consultations, focus groups, workshops, meetings with various Presbyterian organizations, and individual interviews. Members of the task force visited at least forty synods and presbyteries to share "effective experiences of building relationships across lines of division." Professionally analyzed data on the range and diversity of Presbyterians' convictions about critical issues were gathered and studied. A series of resources was provided to be used in congregations, governing bodies, and other groups as they work for the peace, unity, and purity of the church. Two videos were produced: the first one focused on how to go about a process of building a community of trust through worship, Bible study and prayer; and the second one focused on Christology, one of the themes assigned to the task force.[38]

The task force generated four preliminary affirmations about the peace, unity, and purity of the church. First, "The only way forward, as

the reformers long ago insisted, is the way that leads through grace";
second, "The church's peace flows from the work of Jesus Christ";
third, "Unity with one another is not an optional feature of life in
Christ"; and fourth, "The quest for purity is a call to self-examination,
repentance, and mutual accountability in love."[39]

The final report of the task force was scheduled to be available in
the fall of 2005 for study by the church in preparation for the General
Assembly in June of 2006. In preparation for that report the task force
responded to many expressions of concerns about the final results of
their work. It committed itself to hold any "process" or "instrument" it
should "discover or devise" to a clear set of criteria: faithfulness to the
gospel of Jesus Christ; theological grounding; clarity about the
relationship of the Presbyterian Church (U.S.A.) and the larger Church
of Jesus Christ; and continuity with Presbyterian tradition.[40]

The task force was keenly aware that no measures it proposed will
serve "unless the whole church fervently wants to find different and
better ways to express its identity as Christ's body in and for the world
in the twenty-first century."[41] Through the encouragement and example
of the task force, persons and groups began to break out of the silos of
self-interest, breaking down the walls of hostility that divide, and
reaching out to each other. *The Presbyterian Outlook*, in its issue of
May 30, 2005, ran a series of articles captioned "Common Ground"
reporting on how groups, made up of participants from all across the
spectrum of opinion were meeting in local congregations, presbyteries,
and seminaries to face their differences. Some came together in
anticipation of the task force's report; others came together on their
own out of deep concern over the direction the debate was taking.[42]

One can only hope this was the "ferment that begins with the
involvement of people at the middle governing body level" that Jack
McLaney said made the Union Presbytery Movement so effective in
multiplying its effectiveness in dealing with other structures in the
denomination (06-28). Certainly as these efforts expand, the report of
the TTF will have a better chance not to suffer the being-shelved fate
of the "Life and Mission Statement" of the 1980s.

The Theological Task Force on Peace, Unity, and Purity of the
Church was not the only task force at work during this period of time.
The General Assembly Council (GAC) was involved in a "strategic
visioning process, which led to the 2005–2006 Mission Work Plan—a
comprehensive statement of the Council's priorities, goals and
objectives." The motivation for this effort, according to John Detterick,
executive director of the GAC, was to underscore its understanding of
"the essential connectedness we must share with the governing bodies
to be most effective in the larger mission of the PC(USA)." To that end

the GAC in 2004 established a Governance Task Force to "evaluate, develop and propose a structure of the GAC that will strengthen connectedness with presbyteries and synods." Another GAC task force was working on program review and evaluation.[43]

At the same time a Mission Funding Task Force had been "charged through the 2005–2006 Mission Work Plan with developing and proposing a conceptual framework for a new mission-funding system for the PC(USA)." This task force gathered data from "a wide range of people, including staff at the Presbyterian Center and representatives of the PC (USA) middle bodies" to see what had been working, what had not been working, and what changes might be needed to make the mission funding system more effective.[44]

All the final recommendations of these task forces were scheduled to be presented to the 2006 General Assembly in Birmingham, a meeting that promised to be another historic watershed in the life the PC(USA), similar in import to the prior ecclesial watersheds of 1969 and 1983. Of all the task force reports to be presented, the report of the Theological Task Force on Peace, Unity, and Purity of the Church was expected to be the most critical in helping the church find a new identity that will bring unity to its life and mission.

Over the past generation there have been numerous restructures and realignments, new staffing patterns, and mission-funding strategies that were essentially subsidiary to the identity and mission of the church. The success or failure of these subsidiary activities played an important role, but in themselves were not the critical factors in defining the church's identity and mission. Theological underpinning, or the lack thereof, was the critical factor. As this new historic watershed approached in the search of a new identity and mission, one hoped the theological underpinning would not be short-circuited by the already high investments in these subsidiary activities, reminiscent of the theological anemia and the debacle of the "Life and Mission Statement" at reunion in the 1980s.

The Presbyterian Church (U.S.A.) in the first decade of the twenty-first century is very diverse and has not fully found its abiding strength in its diversity. Some of its constituents have a strong preference for a traditional Presbyterian legacy regaled with mournful squeals of bagpipes; some constituents for whom the scars of racism have not been healed find this traditional legacy offensive and search for their own meaningful expressions; other recent immigrant newcomers or new non-Presbyterian communicants to the PC(USA) are bewildered when they try to fathom the importance of the fact that there used to be two or more American Presbyterian denominations; still other young postmodern members born after 1983 could care less that somewhere over three decades ago something existed called a union presbytery. These constituents live in a severely divided and prejudiced land surrounded by countless millions for whom the fact that a Presbyterian Church exists at all is a totally alien thought; these constituents live in a violent and troubled world where a growing of number of hate-filled zealots want nothing more than the total annihilation of America and all its Christian churches.

How this diverse Presbyterian Church (U.S.A.) as a whole creatively and positively comes to terms with the polarization that threatens its very existence, thereby forming a new identity for itself in this watershed moment of history, may also in some small way give a glimmer of hope, not only for the church itself, but for the country and the world. The country and the world need the church to dream a new Dream, to model an alternative, redemptive, and reconciling way of prevailing in the mortal battle with the nightmare of polarization that engulfs us.

Some murmuring of discontent with this polarized existence and longing for such a new Dream come from those caught in the middle between the extreme warring factions of the right and left ideological margins both in the church and in society. The degree to which theirs will become the prevailing wind of opinion remains yet to be seen. A great deal depends on whether the discontented fall prey to, or avoid, the historical dysfunctional flaws of the "special interest syndrome" and a "win-lose mentality" in their quest for a new Dream.

The new Dream is essentially the same as the 1983 Dream: The new way of being church that is diverse and inclusive is formed on a shared heritage, a shared theology, and a shared vision of relationships to the community and the world. The challenge before the "communion of saints" is now to live its way into this new identity for the twenty-first century.

Stamford Bridge and Hastings Revisited

The fall of 1066 was a watershed in English and Western history, the divide between the medieval world and the premodern world. Two distinct cultures of civil order began to develop in the aftermath of Hastings that would have enormous future implications for the island kingdoms and the New World beyond that lasted for 900 years until the Empire, which had sprung from it, began to disintegrate in the 1960s. Little did those winners and losers, who did battle on that gloomy September afternoon, realize the full import of what had taken place. How could they know that Stamford Bridge was the last battle fought with medieval warfare tactics and Hastings was the first premodern one? Only a long look back over the centuries would make possible such a realization. How could they know the extent to which those two distinct cultures of civil order would do perpetual battle over the years? One, the highly structured treetop, national view of reality, would collide constantly on a global scale over that long period of history (1066–1966) with the other one, the highly relational, tribal, grassroots view of reality, with someone winning, and someone losing.

This clash was being acted out globally in 1968, the year that Mark Kurlansky called "The Year that Rocked the World." The British, faced with serious financial and economic crises, were in the throes of decolonizing their top-down Empire under immense grassroots pressure from the colonies. The "American Colonies" were experiencing the same internal upheaval and conflict. The French put pressure on the British once more [remember William the Conqueror!] as Charles de Gaulle, in the twilight of his illustrious career, exacerbated their decolonization process "by endorsing Quebecois separatism from the town balcony in Montreal while on a state visit to Canada." He also threatened the survival of the European Common Market by three times blocking British entry into the group.[45]

The European Common Market had its own crises from the lack of momentum of its member countries to support it adequately and their failure to move forward with its development. Nonetheless, The Common Market was faced with "the fact that on July 1, 1968, customs between member countries would cease." Almost to add insult to injury, Jean-Jacques Servan-Schreiber, publisher of the "slightly left-of-center" weekly news magazine, *L'Express*, wrote a bestseller aimed at the establishment. *The American Challenge*, the English version of *Le Defi Americain*, held that "in the next thirty years the United States would become so dominant that Europe would be little more than a colony."[46]

Anti–Vietnam War protests found their way to the British shores in 1968 and matters worsened in Northern Ireland. But the most serious issue faced in Britain that year was racism. The parliamentary election was infected with "a virulent strain of what the American civil rights movement called white backlash set off by the Labour government's proposed Commonwealth Immigration Bill." With the decolonization of the Empire, there was rising fear that "brown and black people" from the former colonies would flock to Britain seeking jobs. One member of Parliament, Enoch Powell, campaigned on the slogan, "Keep Britain White."[47]

The story had come full circle; the historical threads of the island kingdoms and the New World intertwined over this 900-year period, culminating in the chaos of the 1960s. The upper hand in the battle with the dysfunctional flaws of win-lose was yet to be gained. But another watershed had been reached in a remote corner of that history.

Somewhat analogous to what happened at the Battle of Stamford Bridge and the Battle of Hastings, happened at the 1969 PCUS General Assembly (Mobile) and in the subsequent PCUS vote on denominational reunion in 1982–1983. The Mobile Assembly watershed marked the passing of a generation of tall-steeple pastors and strong heads of boards and agencies who had long given stable, traditional leadership to the church. The Young Turk generation replaced them with dreams of radical social change, reunion, and new ways of being church, only to be replaced themselves at the close of the twentieth century with a new postmodern generation. No doubt these passing generations did not realize the full import of what was taking place on those days of April 24-29, 1969, in Mobile.

The jubilation of the victory at the Mobile Assembly on behalf of union presbyteries, leading to the subsequent victory fourteen years later for denominational reunion, had a poignant quality to it like the victories at Stamford Bridge and Hastings. There were winners and losers. This Mobile Assembly was the watershed moment that marked the passing of a demographic generation of Presbyterian political operatives and the rise of new operatives that in turn would give way to the battle camps of the early twenty-first century. The victory for union presbyteries and the subsequent victory for denominational reunion were the last major "Battles of the White Guys" in North American Presbyterian history.

Ironically, the victors in that great win-lose campaign made it so, because they stipulated that the new demographics of the church must be diverse and inclusive. By doing this, these victors delivered to the PC(USA) the possibility that the Dream might yet be realized in the present and future generations and thus opened the field of engagement. But the win-lose flaws of Stamford Bridge and Hastings still haunt the PC(USA) and threaten the "peace, unity, and purity of the church" as it faces a new historic watershed moment in 2006.

An analogy may be drawn from the computer, as used for word-processing. Four settings are available on computers to align the margins, three of which are: align left, align center, and align right. Adverse conditions are created for the margins when each selection is made, if one's goal is to orient the text to a preferred and defined point of reference. When the left button is selected, all the characters are oriented to the left margin as point of reference and the right margin is irregularly defined. When the right button is selected, all the characters are oriented to the right margin as point of reference and the left margin is irregularly defined. When the center button is selected, the point of reference is in the center and the margins of the right and left are irregularly defined. The fourth button is simply labeled, "justify," a strikingly Calvinistic term! Select this button and space is created for all the characters between the left and right margins; all are included, even welcomed, in the text with the widest possible points of reference. The text may look a little bit unusual and different from other orientations, but breathing spaces are scattered across the line to make room for all comers; no character is left out; all can relate to new marginal points of reference and everything in between! Sounds like good news and a dream come true!

Stories have beginnings and endings. Between "Once upon a time" and "The End," strange and wonderful, painful and joyful things transpire among the casts of characters involved. Dreams are dreamed; some are fulfilled and others go unfulfilled. Some characters live to tell the story; others do not. Some heed its lessons and dream new dreams; others discount it as being irrelevant. This story, the story of the Union Presbytery Movement, from at least one perspective, has now been told. So be it.

The End

But stories have new beginnings because there are old endings; so let the new dreams and the new story begin . . . !

Notes

1   *The Plan for Reunion*, "Articles of Agreement," 8.3, p. 22.

2. Ibid., 5.6, p. 19. "Until such times as the design for work of the General Assembly is completed and these functions are ensured, the existing structures of these bodies shall be maintained."

3. "Snapshot of PC(USA) Leadership Trends," Statistics supplied by the Office of Research Services and Leadership and Vocation, National Ministries Division, PC(USA), May 2005.

4. "Table 14: Race/Ethnicity and Gender of PC(USA) . . . ," Statistics supplied by the Office of Research Services, 2003.

5. "Program Objectives," Racial Ethnic Ministries. Available online, [http://www.pcusa.org/racialethnic/objectives.htm.]

6. *Minutes* of Consultation on Union Presbyteries, March 12–14, 1983, "Hurts and Healing," notes from various discussion groups of COUP.

7. Ibid.

8. Dietrich Bonhoeffer, *The Communion of Saints: A Dogmatic Inquiry into the Sociology of the Church* (New York: Harper & Row, 1960).

9. Ibid., p. 137.

10. Ibid., p. 138.

11. *Minutes* of Consultation on Union Presbyteries, March 12–14, 1983, "Major Learnings from the Union Presbytery Experience which may be Applicable to Denominational Reunion."

12. Ibid.

13. Ibid.

14. Ibid.

15. *Minutes* of Consultation on Union Presbyteries, March 12–14, 1983, "Hurts and Healing,"

16. *Report* of Consultation on Union Presbyteries, February 20–22, 1979.

17. Wayne P. Todd, "Strategic Implications for the 1980s from the Last 25 Years," in Wayne P. Todd File, Presbyterian Historical Society

18. Ibid.

19. Lewis L. Wilkins, "Polity Issues for the 1980s—A Personal Presbyterian View," in Wayne P. Todd File, Presbyterian Historical Society

20. Ibid.

21. Letter from A. M. Hart to Wayne P. Todd, dated August 4, 1982, in Wayne P. Todd File, Presbyterian Historical Society, it was noted in the letter that the UPCUSA "list includes Bill McAtee and Bob Frere."

22. *Meeting Notes*, "The Rocking Chair," Louisville, Kentucky, October 2–5, 1982, in Wayne P. Todd File, Presbyterian Historical Society

23. Ibid.

24. *Minutes* of Consultation on Union Presbyteries, March 12–14, 1983, "Miscellaneous Comments and Issues," notes from various discussion groups of COUP.

25. Ibid., "A.I.R. Questions to C.O.U.P./J.C.U.P."

26. *Minutes* of the One-Hundred-Ninety-Seventh General Assembly(1983) of the PC(USA), Part I, Journal, p. 240.

27. Ibid.

28. Ibid., pp. 240–248.

29. Ibid., p. 248.

30. The author was to have been a member of the new GAC by virtue of being chair of the PCUS Committee on Assembly Operations. The Personnel Committee of Transylvania Presbytery advised against this nomination, because the author had only been serving as executive presbyter for a little more than two years and the committee felt his service was needed more in the Presbytery.

31. *The Plan for Reunion*, "Articles of Agreement," 5.2, p. 18.

32. Ibid., 5.4, p. 18.

33. Ibid., 5.3, p. 18.

34. See Strauss and Howe, *The Fourth Turning: An American Prophecy* (1997), chapter 10, "A Fourth Turning Prophecy," for a detailed description of the

dramatic transition that they expected to happen around 2005 between the unraveling third turning, Cultural Wars (1984–2005?) and the fourth turning, Millennial Crises (2005?–2026?) in their schema of understanding history.

35. *Preliminary Report*, Theological Task Force on Peace, Unity, and Purity of the Church, to the 216th General Assembly (PCUSA), 2004, p. 3.

36. Ibid., p. 15.

37. Ibid., p. 3.

38. Ibid., p. 4.

39. Ibid., pp. 5–7.

40. Ibid., pp. 8–9.

41. Ibid, p. 9.

42. *Presbyterian Outlook*, vol. 187, no. 20, (May 30, 2005).

43. *NEWS*, Presbyterian News Service, Office of Communication, Release #05171, March 31, 2005. Available online, http://www.pocusa.org/pcnews/2005/05171.htm.]

44. *NEWS*, Presbyterian News Service, Office of Communication, Release #05173, March 31, 2005. Available online, [http://www.pocusa.org/pcnews/2005/05173.htm.]

45. Mark Kurlansky, *1968: The Year That Rocked the World* (New York: Random House, trade paperback 2004), pp. 210, 371.

46. Ibid., p. 211.

47. Ibid., p. 154.

Epilogue

I Learn that the Yankey army have falen back to Corinth. that is a great relieaf to me & I aprehind no danger from that sorce for the present. three weeks ago I expected that our portion of the state would be in the hands of the enemy before this but thank God it is otherwise & I hope that by a deturmend resistance on our part will drive the enemy to turms of peace. Peace. Peace. how my heart yearn for it.
    —Wm. G. Fatheree, Camp Blake, Mississippi, December 24, 1862[1]

The journey in telling this story began for me over eight years ago, that is, the telling of it, not the living of it; that has a much earlier genesis. I never dreamed that the timing of the eventual publication of this work would so closely coincide with the presentation of the final report of the Theological Task Force on Peace, Unity, and Purity of the Church to the 217th General Assembly (2006) meeting in Birmingham, Alabama. Could this be another watershed in American Presbyterian history in Alabama?

I never planned it this way. The manuscript for this work was essentially completed before the first draft of the final report of the Theological Task Force became available. Maybe this is simply the way of providence; only time will tell. My fervent prayer is that this work will make some contribution to the conversation in which the church is presently feverishly engaged, and thus, be part of the healing process so sorely needed in our beloved denomination. In the words of my great-grandfather William Fatheree, "Peace. Peace. how my heart yearn for it." He did not live to see peace, nor did he make it home. Will we?

I remember a number of years ago one spring flying at 35,000 feet on a Delta Airlines flight from Dallas to Atlanta. I looked out the window to the north as we crossed over the Mississippi River into Mississippi near Greenville. It was an unusually clear day and I could see almost all the way to the lobby of the Peabody Hotel in Memphis, where folklore says the Mississippi Delta begins. My eyes followed Highway 82 east to Leland and then north up old Highway 61 to a dot of a village, Shaw, where I was born in the middle of the Depression. I was born at home in the manse on Bayou Street overlooking Porters Bayou. My daddy was the Presbyterian preacher in town. Names of other Delta places scrolled through my mind as I looked down— Arcola, Hushpukena, Midnight, Pantha Burn, Meltonia, Benoit, Rosedale, Skene, Lambert, and Marks.

The farmers that day were spring-plowing the Delta from one end to the other. I was overwhelmed for the first time by the grand alluvial patterns—raw siennas, yellow ochres, burnt umbers, sepias, paynes grays, lamp blacks—painted on this primordial tapestry over aeons by the residue of flowing rivers from far and near, North and South. The Platte, the Arkansas, the Missouri, the Illinois, the Ohio, the Tennessee, the Kentucky, the Cumberland, and many more; closer at hand the Coldwater, the Tallahatchie, the Yacona, the Skuna, the Yalabusa, the Sunflower, the Yazoo, Steel Bayou, and Deer Creek.

These patterns had been etched into the earth by the annual fury of swirling waters yet untamed by the Corp of Engineers' snaking levees of the 1920s or later mammoth aquatic redoubts of Arkabutula, Sardis, Enid, and Grenada. These patterns were never seen with such grandeur a century ago, but were gradually discovered as ancient thick growth was ripped from the earth's surface by rivers of sweat rolling from the toiling backs of enslaved and impoverished human beings.

I knew that somewhere below me to the south, Chickasaw Bayou spilled into the Yazoo close to where it commingled with the mighty Mississippi at the southern terminus of the Delta. Here on a cold dank day in December of 1862 one of my great-grandfathers had penned his lament for peace. Even farther south ran the Bayou Pierre, where as a teenager I had waded neck-deep, hand-grabbing for catfish; the Bogue Chitto, in whose river bottom I had hunted; and the Homochitto, where I had set trotlines at its mouth as it emptied into the broad Mississippi.

As the plowed ground gave way to patches of green loblolly pines to the east, I could see the Big Black, the Yokanochany, and the Noxubee—all looking for meandering ways to find the Gulf. It was along the canebrakes of Senasha Creek, a Big Black tributary, that another great-grandfather, William McAtee I, cleared hardwoods from the river bottoms and the virgin pine from bordering red clay hills to plant cotton. He gave land nearby for the small cemetery where three generations of William McAtees, their wives, and other family members now rest.

Farther upstream, at the headwaters of Bolatusha Creek on sandstone hills was a family named Meek with a young redheaded daughter. Her name was Sarah and her daddy was the Methodist Bishop of Alabama-Mississippi and missionary to the Choctaw Indians, who by now had been removed and traveled their trail of tears west across the Mississippi to Oklahoma. She became the bride of William I and bore his children.

Continuing this brief flyover I saw on to the east the Tombigbee on whose banks was Amory, the location of my first parish, where our first son, William Neal, was born to Millye and me. To the south was the Pearl, on whose banks was Columbia, location of my second parish, where our second son, Walter Bunn, was born. From here in the heat of 1966 we packed up and left Mississippi for the last time, an emotionally laden thing for a fourth generation Mississippian to do.

In the time as brief as it took to tell about my flight that day, my entire life seemed to flash before my mind. Water, with both its life-giving and life-threatening qualities, seemed to be the thread that tied it all together. As the plane crossed over into Alabama, I thought about the first time I temporarily lived outside this place of childhood and youth. I journeyed north on the Illinois Central's twin rivers of steel aboard the "City of New Orleans" to college at Southwestern at Memphis on the Chickasaw bluffs of the Mississippi. Later my journey took me on farther north to Louisville Seminary on the banks of the Ohio. I followed the well-beaten ecclesiastical path candidates for the ministry had traveled for years that went from Mississippi parishes to Southwestern to Louisville and back.

This path, which I labeled "the Connection," went back and forth between Kentucky, Tennessee, and Mississippi, following long-established commercial patterns along the rivers and Indian trails and was later enhanced by the twin rivers of steel plied by the iron horse. While at Louisville Seminary, I discovered that there was a northern version of "the Connection" across the river. People of the southern version of "the Connection" traveled north from the land of the magnolia; people of the northern version of "the Connection" traveled south from the land of the birch, meeting on the border in Louisville to create new relations.

It was here in the late 1950s where I first began to catch the vision about the Unity of the Church and the need to heal the denominational breaches that had divided Presbyterians, the latest being caused by the Civil War and the existence of slavery. It was here that I learned in a very personal way that racial prejudice and separation can be reconciled through building lasting relationships. It was here that my wife Millye and I first "socialized" and shared a meal with seminary classmate Irvin Moxley and his wife, Rubee. Irv was one of the first African American students at Louisville Seminary. This was an extraordinary experience of breaking down the dividing walls for all of us and the bond between us has remained strong through the years.

As the plane droned on to Atlanta, I drifted off to sleep thinking about parts of the rest of my life still tied to that place of my birth, the land of living waters, many of which have been alluded to in this book.

Bringing this book to its conclusion has been difficult because I wanted desperately to do justice to the larger story being told. Also I wanted my own experience in the story and my perception of its relevance for today and tomorrow to be fairly portrayed in proper proportion to the telling of the whole. The heart of the story is about relations—broken and reconciled—between God and us, and between us and us. Numerous illustrations of brokenness and reconciliation punctuate the story, with not just one necessarily taking precedence over others.

Recently I was acutely reminded once more of my life's journey from its unsolicited advantaged point of birth when I stood inside a reassembled slave pen on my first visit to the National Underground Railroad Freedom Center in Cincinnati, Ohio. When I saw a map of the old slave-trade route on the wall outside the pen, I was overwhelmed by the realization that hundreds of slaves were herded on foot from the original site of the pen on a farm within the bounds of Transylvania Presbytery down through Kentucky and Tennessee to connect with the Natchez Trace running on through Mississippi, passing near my ancestral home. This realization led me from my perspective to recognize anew that progress has been made in healing the scars created by the Civil War and racism, the residual effect of slavery, but that we still have a long way to go. As I stood in the Center listening to others' comments, I was reminded that one must also hear from slavery's descendants to gain their perspectives before conclusions are drawn about the healing.

My heritage and life are not subject to revisionist history nor are anyone else's, for that matter. I have long since come to believe that to deny or judge another's experience is a great sin against the Holy Spirit. This is neither to condone our experiences nor condemn them. To honor each other's experience simply creates a level starting point to begin to reconcile the hurts of the past, whatever the source of brokenness, and a place from which to build new future relationships of goodwill and mutual respect.

Mississippians have at times been circuitous in discovering points of reference and long-toothed in establishing relevant relations. To some this excursion along waterways of my childhood, youth, and adulthood may be no exception. What is the point of all of this and what does it mean?

One does not approach two words like "alluvial" or "primordial" lightly or use them in a single sentence on a regular basis. It is better to let them loll around like summer bream in the deep shadows of the mind. For to bring them to surface in the light of day for more precise definition runs the risk that they may become ordinary. For years I have been held in some mystical spell by these two words, a tug back to some time and place long ago, some unseen life-giving source, some elusive point of reference, some magnetic attraction always out there, something akin to trying to figure out one's relation with a mentor or a friend or family.

Some early mornings are slow and I fill the time by reading the dictionary. Beside the word "alluvial" in our 1959 College Edition of *Webster's New World Dictionary* I found: "adj. [L. *alluvius*] 1. of or found in alluvium. 2. made up of alluvium." Clear as mud! On to "alluvium": ". . . [L., neut. of *alluvius*; see ALLUVION], sand, clay, etc. deposited by flowing water, especially along a river bed." Now to "alluvion": "[. . . L. *alluvio*, an overflowing, *alluere* . . . to wash], 1. the washing of water against a shore or bank. 2. a flood. 3. alluvium. 4. in *law*, an increase in land, as by alluvium."[2]

I felt the magnetic pull increase, and turned to "primordial": [. . . L. *primus*, first + *ordiri*, to begin], 1. first in time; existing at or from the beginning; primitive; primeval. 2. Underived; fundamental; original . . ."[3]

How do "alluvial" and "primordial" describe the relation with those dear to us? For those of us brought together from "the Connection" [the Mississippi version], it is not just the fact that the route we have traveled to get there was by imaginary rivers and forgotten rails. It is not just another Mississippian's romanticized recounting of attachment to land and place, or kith and kin, or even the literally life-giving and life-threatening properties of water. There is something more underived and fundamental or original than that, something not limited to our experience.

Our experiences were made tenuous by swirling waters and silting sandbars. Our lives grew intertwined and were enriched by the alluvium of relations. We were tossed about by strong currents but remained agile enough to ride them out; letting go here, reaching out and holding on to each other there, and somehow finding a moment's footing even while feeling it beginning to shift out from under us again, sweeping us away toward the unfamiliar and the new.

An underived primordial power was working its Divine will in and through these special relations, blessing us and holding us firm. In them we received the local application of some eternal alluvial washing. In the joy and mystery of this washing and the fluidity of life, we were empowered to act justly, love constantly, and be humble in relation with each other and our God.

A person from the Northern version of "the Connection" in New Hampshire might find solace and stability in the very legitimate imagery of stern and stolid terms like "granite" or "bedrock" verities, impervious to the constant pounding of the rainstorms of life. We all yearn from time to time for these underpinning images and desperately need to have them in our lives to give us certainty. But growing up in the Southern version of "the Connection," I did not experience these "granite" or "bedrock" verities in an abstract way. For me they came concretely through the fluidity of relations. Different perspectives on abstract verities and concrete relations were not necessarily mutually exclusive in either the Northern or Southern versions of "the Connection"; they merely seemed to be treated with different emphases.

How does one fully understand all this? One does not; one only basks in the warmth of it. How does one adequately compensate another for adding to the mix, be it abstract or concrete, and making such a relation so rich and lasting? One does not; one merely utters a simple "Thank you!"

Through the years I have stood around funeral homes hearing people utter such laments as "There was so much I wanted to tell (the deceased) but never got around to it." Or, "If I had another chance, I'd say . . ." I decided a while back not to let that happen to me with some special folk in my life. I have written to several of those people, my seniors, expressing my appreciation to them for the special things they meant to me. I wanted to be sure they knew how I felt "before it was too late." Now that I am rapidly becoming "senior," many of those I need to thank are my "juniors" as well as the others. So, my friends encountered along the way in this story who helped make it happen, be you from the Southern or Northern version of "the Connection," count this work as my letter of appreciation to you. Here is a simple "Thank you!"

Funerals in dysfunctional families can be extremely traumatic, dicey, and sometimes downright entertaining in a perverse way. Such laments as "There was so much I wanted to tell (the deceased) but never got around to it," or "If I had another chance, I'd say . . ," take on new meaning, especially when fueled by anger or resentment or guilt. Unreconciled feelings from broken relations and dividing walls clutter the visitation. Revisiting the part of the church's story told in this book may dredge up painful un-reconciled memories. To those who felt excluded from the story I have told, or have been wounded by its legacy, or have been offended by what I put in or left out, or even have taken exception to my perception of how it happened, I deeply regret that being the case. Here is a simple "I am sorry!"

Some would have us believe that it is time to gather for the wake for our beloved Presbyterian Church (U.S.A.), to stand around and exchange quiet pleasantries about what once was and what might have been had we not fallen into dis-union. To let this denomination be torn asunder, weakened to the point of death by falling into an avoidable trap of a "win-lose mentality," would constitute a travesty of faith in the providence of God and would become the latest great tragedy in American Presbyterianism! I, for one, do not believe it is time to summon the undertaker and will not settle for that view of the future.

I, for one, also do not want to endure once again, for myself or with the church, the pain inflicted by fractured relationships induced by the PCA split in 1973. I have a greater vision for the present and the future. Just as funerals are a very important part of the privileges of being a pastor, so are weddings. I have a vision of walking into a grand banquet room and observing a series of wedding receptions over time.

In my vision, at the first reception in this grand banquet room, a magnificent table was properly set with the finest linens, silverware, crystal punch bowls and cups, surrounded with little dishes of mixed nuts and mints. In the middle was a three-tiered wedding cake with a miniature couple perched lovingly on top. The wedding party and invited guests gathered around the happy couple as the wedding cake was cut and toasts were offered on their behalf. The air was abuzz with excitement and the sounds of festive celebration. They all danced the night away in sheer ecstasy to the sounds of a six-piece band. A feeling of serene joy and peace settled on the scene as a blessed benediction.

The second reception I walked into had all the elements as described in the first one, with only a slight change. In addition to the main table with the three-tiered cake were two smaller tables off to the side, each holding a different kind of cake. The main body of the wedding party was gathered around the large table, but a small group of people gathered around each of the smaller tables talking quietly to each other. When I asked someone what this was about, the person replied, "One table is the groom's table for him and his special friends, and the other is the bride's table for her and her special friends." Few noticed that a slight edge had been taken off the joy of the whole occasion and most of the people danced the night away to the music of a string quartet.

The third reception I walked into had most of the elements as described in the first two, with a few changes. In addition to the main table with a two-tiered cake and the two smaller tables off to the side, were two more new tables, each holding a different kind of cake. Many of the main body of the wedding party were gathered around the large table, but more people gathered around each of the four smaller tables talking intently to each other. When I asked someone what this was about, the person replied, "One of the new tables is the bridesmaids' table for them and their special friends and the other is the groomsmen's table for them and their special friends." Some guests noticed that something was different about the reception but could not put their finger on it; a few danced for a while in different parts of the banquet room to the disjointed beat of a three-piece combo.

The fourth reception I walked into had some of the elements as described in the first three, but with even more changes. The smaller main table with a single-layered cake was now sitting to one side. The four smaller tables along with two more new tables, each holding larger kinds of cake, were arranged in the middle of the banquet hall. Hardly any of the main body of the wedding party was gathered around the main table, for most people gathered around each of the six smaller tables talking intently to each other in a loud and boisterous manner unaware of what was going on around them. When I asked someone what this was about, the person replied, "One of the new tables is the flower girl's table for her and her little friends and the other is the ring bearer's table for him and his little friends." The climate in the ballroom was very different and discordant now. It was obvious that people in the dwindling wedding party were more interested in their own small group than in celebrating with the bride and groom. In fact, several people were seen pulling out a moveable divider partition in order to cordon off their small group's table from the rest of the wedding party in the banquet room. The piano somberly played to an empty dance floor. Peace and joy were gone.

Finally, someone walked over to the uncut single-layered cake, looked around the banquet room, and exclaimed, "What has gone wrong? How did this happen? Remember what a celebration the first wedding reception was? Oh, to have one table again!"

God, the Transformer Host, uses radical and scandalous means to reconcile the unreconciled and fulfill the promise: a simple invitation to a wedding and reception. John in the book of Revelation declared he had heard that the time had come for the wedding of the Lamb and his bride, who had prepared herself for it. The union of Christ as groom and church as bride was a familiar image in Scripture. John was further inspired to write: "Happy are those who have been invited to the wedding feast of the Lamb" (Rev. 19:9). Who have been invited? Luke said: "People will come from east and west, from north and south, and will eat in the kingdom of God" (Luke 13:29). Who are these people? Paul implied they are Jews and Gentiles, slaves and free, men and women. "You are all one in Christ Jesus" (Gal. 3:28 RSV). *All* means everyone is invited to the table without reservation.

When this Jesus, God-with-us, set his face toward Jerusalem, he engaged in a radical act. It was not so much the ultimate conclusive act of submitting to the crucifixion and subsequent resurrection that was so radical, though this submission certainly was that. It also was the culmination of his life and teachings that was so radical. He demonstrated public affirmation of his radical purpose when he rode into Jerusalem, not astride a mighty warhorse as conquering hero, but humbly on a common donkey; when he wept for the city for killing the prophets; when he pled for the stones and people to cry out for peace. His whole ministry flew in the face of the conventional wisdom of worldly bean counters, libel defenders, and risk managers, this Prince of Peace.

In this humble public demonstration, Jesus affirmed his radical call to ministry:

- Be servant of all, for all are invited to the table; welcome the outcast; forbid not the children nor cause them to stumble; the last shall be first; bless the poor.
- Cure the sick, comfort the sorrowing, raise the dead, cleanse the lepers, cast out demons; bless the mourners.
- Sell what you have and give it generously away in secret; you cannot serve God and riches; bless the meek.
- Defend the defenseless, the widows and orphans; feed the hungry; forgive seventy times seven; bless the merciful.
- Love your enemies; turn the other cheek; pray in secret for those who persecute you and say all manner of evil against you for my sake; bless the peacemakers.
- Seek the security only God can give; worry not about your life, what you will eat or drink, or your body, what you will wear; strive first for God's kingdom; bless the righteous.
- Take up your cross and follow me; those who find their life will lose it, those who lose their life—even family and friends—for my sake will find it; bless the pure in heart. (Based on Matt. 5:3–10)

The church as institution may falter and be divided at the hands of dysfunctional human beings, but the hands of an everlasting God unite the church as the body of Christ. Human institutions can divide and disintegrate in watershed moments, or they can be united and transformed into the body of Christ by *el Espiritu Santo* [the Holy Spirit] when least expected. Some, when faced with such transforming moments, may stubbornly not want to be changed. I believe we are at such a watershed moment in the life of the Presbyterian Church (U.S.A.). Will the church be dysfunctionally divided or will it become *one* as God intended? At this writing the answer is not clear.

The promise of peace, purity, and unity has been here all along, but we have savored our bickering too much to lay hold of the power of that promise. We have enjoyed too much strategizing the attacks and counterattacks from our "special interest syndrome" to stop the warring madness. The win-lose dysfunctional flaws of our heritage drive us to believe: "We" can't stop now, because "they" are doing this and "we" must counter with that . . . or "they" will win and "we" will lose. The

---

feast is disrupted; we are divided and retreat to our own separate tables. It does not have to be that way, but where will it all end? Oh, to have one table again!

The promise is about stopping old things and having funerals, yes; but it is more about starting new relations and having weddings, not about divisions and deathly war. We are in no position in our present condition to declare victory in our own doings. But what if some one person would start the ball rolling by saying, "no more warring madness"? What would happen if that someone would simply accept the Transformer Host's invitation to table and "declare peace, live to see it, make it home, welcome all comers to the feast, and dance the night away"?

"Peace. Peace. My heart yearns for it."

"Behold, I make all things new!" (Rev. 21:5, RSV)

Notes

1. Letter from Wm G. Fatheree to his "dear wife," M. E. Fatheree, from Camp Blake, Mississippi, dated December 24, 1862, in the possession of author's family. In Fatheree's letter to his wife, among other domestic concerns he mentioned that their young baby daughter, Emma, "must not Let her teeath make her sick if she can help it!" Emma grew up to become the author's paternal grandmother, wife of William McAtee II.

2. *Webster's New World Dictionary*, College Edition, 1959, s. v. alluvial, alluvium, alluvion.

3. Ibid., s. v. primordial.

Appendix A: List of Union Presbyteries and Consultations

A. Union Presbyteries by Organizing Dates

1970
Missouri (Union)*	3/12/70
John Calvin (Union)*	4/11/70
Western Kentucky (Union)*	7/1/70
Ozark (Union) [dissolved in 1974 to form Arkansas (Union)]	11/24/70

1971
Central Texas (Union) [dissolved in less than a year]	1/1/71
Kansas City (Union)*	1/1/71
Louisville (Union)*	1/1/71
Transylvania (Union)*	1/1/71

1972
National Capital (Union)*	1/6/72
Palo Duro (Union)*	1/6/72

1974
Arkansas (Union)*	1/1/74

1979
Grace (Union)	1/1/79

1980
Indian Nations [first not to include "Union" in official name]	1/16/80
Tres Rios (Union)	6/24/80
New Covenant (Union)	7/1/80
Mission (Union)	10/15/80

1982
Southwest Florida (Union)	1/1/82
Eastern Oklahoma (Union)	7/13/82

1983
North Alabama (Union)	1/1/83
St. Augustine**	1/1/83

* Referred to as "the Nine Original Union Presbyteries" by 1974.
** Had not denominational reunion passed, it would have become a union presbytery.

B. Union Presbyteries by Geographic Location and PCUS/UPCUSA Organizing Synods

Alabama
North Alabama (Union)   Mid-South (PCUS)/South (UPCUSA)

Arkansas
Ozark (Union)   Arkansas-Oklahoma (PCUS)/
                                         Oklahoma-Arkansas (UPCUSA)
Arkansas (Union)   Red River (PCUS)/Sun (UPCUSA)

District of Columbia
National Capital (Union)   Virginia (PCUS)/Chesapeake (UPCUSA)

Florida
Southwest Florida (Union)   Florida (PCUS)/South (UPCUSA)
St. Augustine   Florida (PCUS)/South (UPCUSA)

Kentucky
Western Kentucky (Union)   Kentucky (PCUS)/Kentucky (UPCUSA)
Louisville (Union)   Kentucky (PCUS)/Kentucky (UPCUSA)
Transylvania (Union)   Kentucky (PCUS)/Kentucky (UPCUSA)

Missouri
Missouri (Union)   Missouri (PCUS)/Missouri (UPCUSA)
John Calvin (Union)   Missouri (PCUS)/Missouri (UPCUSA)
Kansas City (Union)   Missouri (PCUS)/Missouri (UPCUSA)

Oklahoma
Indian Nations   Red River (PCUS)/Sun (UPCUSA)
Eastern Oklahoma (Union)   Red River (PCUS)/Sun (UPCUSA)

Texas
Central Texas (Union)   Texas (PCUS)/Texas (UPCUSA)
Palo Duro (Union)   Red River (PCUS)/Sun (UPCUSA)
Grace (Union)   Red River (PCUS)/Sun (UPCUSA)
Tres Rios (Union)   Red River (PCUS)/Sun (UPCUSA)
New Covenant (Union)   Red River (PCUS)/Sun (UPCUSA)
Mission (Union)   Red River (PCUS)/Sun (UPCUSA)

C. Union Presbyteries by Geographic Location and Predecessor Presbyteries

[Note: Occasionally a church or churches were included in a new presbytery from presbyteries other than the predecessors mentioned below.]

Alabama

North Alabama (Union)
North Alabama (PCUS)
Huntsville (UPCUSA)

Arkansas

Ozark (Union)
Washburn (PCUS)
Arkansas (UPCUSA)

Arkansas (Union)
Ozark (Union)
East Arkansas (PCUS)
Part of Ouachita (PCUS)

District of Columbia

National Capital (Union)
Potomac (PCUS)
Washington City (UPCUSA)

Florida

Southwest Florida (Union)
Westminster (PCUS)
West Florida (UPCUSA)

St. Augustine
Suwannee (PCUS)
Northeast Florida (UPCUSA)

Kentucky

Western Kentucky (Union)
Muhlenberg (PCUS)
Western Kentucky (UPCUSA)

Louisville (Union)
Louisville (PCUS)
Louisville [Transylvania] (UPCUSA)

Transylvania (Union)
Guerrant-Transylvania (PCUS)
Ebenezer-Transylvania (UPCUSA)

Missouri

Missouri (Union)	Missouri (PCUS)
	Kirk (UPCUSA)
John Calvin (Union)	John Calvin (PCUS)
	Carthage-Ozark (UPCUSA)
Kansas City (Union)	Lafayette (PCUS)
	Kansas City (UPCUSA)

Oklahoma

Indian Nations	Oklahoma (PCUS)
	Washita (UPCUSA)
Eastern Oklahoma (Union)	Part of Washita (PCUS)
	Part of Oklahoma (PCUS)
	Eastern Oklahoma (UPCUSA)

Texas

Central Texas (Union)	Central Texas (PCUS)
	Brazos (UPCUSA)
Palo Duro (Union)	Part of Central Texas (Union)
	Southwest (PCUS)
	Plains (UPCUSA)
Grace (Union)	Covenant (PCUS)
	Trinity (UPCUSA)
Tres Rios (Union)	Tres Rios (PCUS)
	Tres Rios (UPCUSA)
	Union Churches from Central Texas (Union)
New Covenant (Union)	Brazos (PCUS)
	Gulf Coast (UPCUSA)
Mission (Union)	Del Salvador (PCUS)
	Alamo (UPCUSA)

D. Consultations on Union Presbyteries

Pre-COUP Consultations

General Assembly Councils' Consultation, St. Louis, MO, January 6, 1971

Joint Committee on Union's Consultation on Women's Concerns, September 27–29, 1973

Synods of Covenant/Mid-South/Kentucky Presbyteries Consultation, Louisville, KY, at Louisville Seminary, December 5–6, 1973

COUP Consultations

1. Louisville, KY, at The Vineyard, May 5–7, 1975
2. Louisville, KY, at The Vineyard, March 1–3, 1976
3. Overland Park, KS, at the Breech Training Academy, February 7–9, 1977
4. Washington, D.C., at the National 4–H Center, February 21–23, 1978
5. Dallas, TX, at The Executive Inn, February 20–22, 1979
6. Fort Mitchell, KY, at the Drawbridge Motor Inn, March 5–7, 1980
7. Wichita, KS, at the Holiday Inn Plaza, March 11–13, 1981
8. Washington, D.C., at the National 4-H Center, February 1–3, 1982
9. San Antonio, TX, at the Menger Hotel, March 12–14, 1983

Appendix B: List of Interviews

No.	Name	Location	Date	Pages
01.	William P. Thompson	La Grange, IL	07-03-97	20
02.	James E. Andrews	Louisville Seminary	08-07-97	33
03.	John M. Coffin	Louisville Seminary	08–07–97	32
04.	David E. Rule	Stanton, KY	08-28-97	23
05.	T. Morton McMillan	Nashville, TN	09-29-97	30
06.	John A. McLaney	Nashville, TN	09-29-97	33
07.	Charles L. Stanford	Caruthersville, MO	10-07-97	33
08.	J. Allen Oakley	Caruthersville, MO	10-07-97	25
09.	Dorothy G. Barnard	St. Louis, MO	10-08-97	32
10.	Richard Huey	St. Louis, MO	10-08-97	13
11.	Kenneth R. Locke	Jefferson City, MO	10-08-97	26
12.	Cecil Culverhouse	Fulton, MO	10-09-97	22
13.	John L. Williams	Kansas City, KS	10-10-97	41
14.	Ronald L. Patton	Fairway, KS	10-10-97	37
15.	Thomas H. Cavicchia	Springfield, MO	10-13-97	27
16.	Robert F. Stevenson	Springfield, MO	10-13-97	24
17.	Albert H. Freundt, Jr.	Jackson, MS	11-11-97	36
18.	John A. Kirstein	Jackson, MS	11-11-97	19
19.	James M. Collie	Albuquerque, NM	11-12-97	25
20.	Paul D. Young	Sante Fe, NM	11-13-97	31
21.	Lewis L. Wilkins, Carolyn Taylor, Murray W. Travis	Lubbock, TX	11-14-97	41
22.	Charles J. Hollingsworth, Lewis L. Wilkins	Midland, TX	11-17-97	17
23.	Flynn V. Long	Big Spring, TX	11-17-97	34
24.	Flynn V. Long, J. Allan Guthrie, Lewis L. Wilkins	Big Spring, TX	11-17-97	16
25.	L. Robert Frere	San Antonio, TX	11-18-97	37
26.	James Baskin	San Antonio, TX	11-18-97	13
27.	Linda B. Team	Austin, TX	11-19-97	22
28.	John R. Hendrick	Austin, TX	11-19-97	15
29.	C. Ellis Nelson	Austin, TX	11-19-97	19
30.	E. L. Coon	Houston, TX	11-20-97	15
31.	H. Richard Siciliano	Houston, TX	11-20-97	18
32.	Charles M. Hanna, Jr.	Lexington, KY	12-03-97	37
33.	No Interview			
34.	Henry C. Barnett	Fort Thomas, KY	12-09-97	17

Dreams, Where Have You Gone?

35.	David B. Lowry	Cincinnati, OH	12-09-97	26
36.	H. William Peterson	Louisville, KY	12-11-97	34
37.	Thomas A. Spragens	Danville, KY	12-16-97	18
38.	Theodore A. Jaeger	Danville, KY	12-16-97	15
39.	James H. Rucker, Sr.	Maysville, KY	12-17-97	21
40.	J. Harold Jackson	Louisville, KY	01-20-98	30
41.	John W. Frazer	Danville, KY	08-11-98	30
42.	Fred S. Malott	Frankfort, KY	08-11-98	33
43.	Wm. Philip Bembower	Knoxville, TN	08-19-98	28
44.	Edwin W. Albright, Jr.	Atlanta, GA	09-10-98	17
45.	George B. Telford, Jr.	Atlanta, GA	09-10-98	10
46.	M. Anderson Sale	Lynchburg, VA	09-11-98	36
47.	Robert J. Rea, Jr.	Rock Hill, SC	09-11-98	32
48.	Tom M. Castlen	Commack, NY	01-27-99	33
49.	Carol E. Davies	Louisville, KY	03-18-99	25
50.	A. M. Hart	Hendersonville, NC	03-22-99	28
51.	William S. McLean	Black Mountain, NC	03-23-99	13
52.	David L. Stitt,			
	Robert R. Collins	Black Mountain, NC	03-23-99	19
53.	William B. Kennedy	Black Mountain, NC	03-23-99	35
54.	J. Randolph Taylor	Black Mountain, NC	03-24-99	26
55.	John S. Lyles	Davidson, NC	03-25-99	21
56.	John B. Evans	Davidson, NC	03-25-99	27
57.	M. Douglas Harper	Ft. Worth, TX	06-23-99	31
58.	Roy T. Sherrod	Ft. Worth, TX	06-23-99	17
59.	William M. Gould	Ft. Worth, TX	06-23-99	13
60.	Beth Wells	Ft. Worth, TX	06-24-99	22
61.	William G. Henning, Jr.	Ft. Worth, TX	06-24-99	14
62.	Robert E. Adcock	Ft. Worth, TX	06-24-99	21
63.	Charles F. Kriner	Ft. Worth, TX	06-24-99	13
64.	Robert P. Douglass	Ft. Worth, TX	06-25-99	21
65.	Harry S. Hassall	Brentwood, TN	08-25-99	38
66.	Kenneth L. McCall	Manistique, MI	09-04-99	42
67.	George P. Morgan	Palm Harbor, FL	11-15-99	24
68.	Robert L. Thompson	St. Petersburg. FL	11-15-99	30
69.	Robert E. Veley	Port Charlotte, FL	11-16-99	17
70.	William M. Clark	Port Charlotte, FL	11-16-99	14
71.	Lacy R. Harwell	St. Petersburg, FL	11-17-99	34
72.	Donald L. Harris	Orlando, FL	11-18-99	21
73.	Dennis M. Salmon	Orlando, FL	11-18-99	21
74.	Graham Gordon	Lexington, KY	06-24-00	15
75.	Robert C. Worley	Manistique, MI	07-20-00	17
76.	John M. Reagan	Southern Pines, NC	09-02-00	36

77.	J. Richard Hershberger	Oklahoma City, OK		
		(phone)	10-23-00	22
78.	Kenneth G. McCullough	Yukon, OK (phone)	10-28-00	9
79.	Thomas M. Johnston	Camp Hill, PA (phone)	11-02-00	25
80.	Murdoch M. Calhoun	Austin, TX (phone)	11-03-00	11
81.	John H. Swan	Jackson Hole, WY		
		(phone)	11-08-00	14
82.	Wayne P. Todd	Salem, SC (phone)	11-10-00	30
83.	J. F. Austin	Edmond, OK (phone)	11-10-00	12
84.	Estha F. Nowlin	Tulsa, OK (phone)	11-21-00	11
85.	Thomas L. Jones	Washington, DC	11-28-00	32
86.	Edward A. White	Washington, DC	11-29-00	37
87.	James W. Hartman	Cincinnati, OH (phone)	11-30-00	11
88.	Marilee Story	Tulsa, OK (phone)	11-30-00	14
89.	Barbara Campbell Davis	Rocky Mount, NC		
		(phone)	12-05-00	20
90.	Jill M. Hudson	Indianapolis, IN (phone)	12-18-00	25
91.	Cecil M. Jividen	Black Mountain, NC		
		(phone)	06-09-03	29
92.	Sandra S. Jividen	Black Mountain, NC		
		(phone)	06-19-03	31
93.	William G. McAtee	Lexington, KY	12-10-02	39

(Last part of Interview 93 was recorded on Tape 94)

94.	William G. McAtee	Lexington, KY	12-20-02	25
95.	William G. McAtee	Lexington, KY	01-06-03	24
96.	William G. McAtee	Lexington, KY	02-14-03	19
97.	William H. McLean	Mobile, AL (phone)	06-08-03	19
98.	H. Davis Yeuell	Richmond, VA (phone)	08-20-03	46
99.	Howard L. Bost	Lexington, KY	10-31-03	36

Appendix C: Demographic Data

A. Elders/Ministers—Ordination: Listed by Denomination and Gender

	Elders	Ministers	Subtotal
PCUS			
Male	3	51	54
Female	6	0	6
Subtotals	9	51	60
USA			
Male	1	19	20
Female	0	0	0
Subtotals	1	19	20
UPCUSA			
Male	2	10	12
Female	3	1	4
Subtotals	5	11	16
Union Presbytery			
Male	0	0	0
Female	1	0	1
Subtotals	1	0	1
UPNA			
Male	0	1	1
Female	0	0	0
Subtotals	0	1	1
TOTAL	**16**	**82**	**98**

Elders		Ministers	
Male	6	Male	81
Female	10	Female	1
Total	**16**	**Total**	**82**

B. Birth Years

1910–1919	10	The G.I. Generation—Hero
1910–1		(Born 1901–1924)
1912–2		**22**
1916–1		
1917–2		
1918–4		
1920–1929	49	
1921–4		
1922–2		
1923–4		
1924–2		
1925–5		The Silent Generation—Artist
1926–6		(Born 1925–1942)
1927–4		**72**
1928–6		
1929–16		
1930–1939	29	
1930–3		
1931–5		
1932–3		
1933–3		
1934–6		
1936–5		
1937–1		
1938–1		
1939–2		
1940–1949	10	
1940–3		
1941–2		
1942–1		
1946–1		The Boom Generation
Prophet		
1947–1		(Born 1943–1960)
1948–2		**4**
TOTAL		**98**

Dreams, Where Have You Gone?

C. Birthplace

Alabama	4	Iowa	1	North Carolina	6
Arizona	1	Kansas	3	Ohio	5
Arkansas	1	Kentucky	7	Oklahoma	3
California	1	Louisiana	4	Pennsylvania	4
China	1	Massachusetts	1	South Africa	1
Connecticut	1	Michigan	1	South Carolina	4
Florida	3	Mississippi	4	Tennessee	3
Georgia	3	Missouri	5	Texas	18
Illinois	1	New Jersey	2	Virginia	1
Indiana	2	New York	1	West Virginia	6

TOTAL   **98**

D. College Attended

Amherst	1	Presbyterian College	1
API (Auburn)	1	Princeton University	1
Ashland College	1	SE State Teachers (OK)	1
Austin College	6	Southern Methodist	1
Birmingham Southern	1	Southwestern at Memphis	8
Bloomfield College	1	Texas Christian University	1
Campbellsville College	1	Texas Southern	1
Carroll College	1	Texas Tech	1
Centre College	5	Trinity College/University	3
Davidson College	10	Tusculum College	1
Duquesne College	1	University of Alabama	1
Eastern Kentucky	1	University of Cincinnati	1
Erskine College	1	University of Colorado	1
Howard University	1	University of Connecticut	1
Indiana State	1	University of Houston	1
King College	3	University of Indiana	1
Lafayette College	1	University of Kentucky	1
Louisiana State	1	University of Missouri	1
Marshall College	2	University of North Carolina	1
Maryville College	3	University of Tennessee	1
McPherson College	1	University of Texas	5
Mercer University	1	University of the South	1
Miami University	1	Washington and Jefferson College	1
Mississippi Southern	1	Washington University	1
Mississippi State	1	Wesleyan College (CN)	1
Muskingum College	2	West Texas University	1
Naval Academy	1	Westminster College	2
NW Missouri State	1	Wheaton College	1
Notre Dame	1	Wichita State	1
Oklahoma State	1	Wofford College	1

TOTAL   98

E. Seminary Attended (BD or MDiv)

Ministers

Austin Seminary	11
Colgate Rochester Divinity School	1
Columbia Seminary	9
Louisville Seminary	18
McCormick Seminary	9
Pittsburgh Seminary	1
Princeton Seminary	9
Union Seminary (NY)	1
Union Seminary (VA)	19
Western Seminary	2
Yale Divinity School	2

TOTAL   82

Elders

PSCE (Masters in CE)	1

TOTAL   1

F. Service to the Church by Positions Filled
(*Note:* Individual interviewees filled more than one position.)

1. Congregation	**98**
Pastor (served at least one pastorate)	76
Associate Pastor	1
Minister of Education	1
Elders (at least once)	16
Clerk of Session	2
Director of Education	2
2. Presbytery (non-union)	**77**
Moderator	10
PC(USA)	3
UPC	6
USA	1
Stated Clerk	13
PCUS	6
PC(USA)	1
UPCUSA	3
USA	3
Council/ Committee Member	6
Joint	2
PCUS	2
UPCUSA	2
Moderator PW (PCUS)	1
Moderator UPW (UPCUSA)	1
Executive/General Presbyter	32
PCUS	11
PCUSA	10
UPCUSA	11
Associate EP/GP	8
PCUS	5
PC(USA)	2
UPCUSA	1
Other Staff	5
PCUS	4
UPCUSA	1
Administrative Assistant	1

3. Presbytery (union)   40

Moderator	4
Vice-Moderator	1
Stated Clerk	7
Associate Stated Clerk	1
Council/Committee Member	3
Moderator of Presbyterian Women	1
Executive/General Presbyter	16
Co-Executive	2
Associate EP/GP	4
Other Staff	1

4. Synod   68

Moderator	16
"Joint"	2
PCUS	10
UPCUSA	3
USA	1
Vice-Moderator	1
USA	1
Stated Clerk	7
"Joint"	1
PCUS	3
PC(USA)	1
UPCUSA	1
USA	1
Council/Committee Member	10
"Joint" CE (PCUS)	1
CE	3
Westminster Fellowship	1
Institutions	1
UPCUSA	4
Moderator UPW (UPCUSA)	2
Joint Women's Council	1
Executive	8
"Joint"	1
PCUS	4
PC(USA)	2
UPCUSA	1
Associate Ex.	7
PCUS	1
UPCUSA	6

Regional Communicator (PCUS)	2
Other Staff	9
PCUS	4
UPCUSA	5
Campus Ministry	5

5. General Assembly (PCUS) **51**

Moderator	2
Stated Clerk	2
Associate Stated Clerk	2
Commissioner (3 to 1969 Assembly)	6
Elected Positions	12
GAMB	4
GEB	2
Annuities and Relief	1
Christian Education	1
Com. on Assembly Operations	1
Hunger Program	1
TRAV	1
Women's Work Board	1
Staff Positions	27
GEB	3
GAMB	4
Christian Education	9
CE Regional Directors	5
Church Extension	1
National Ministries	2
World Missions	1
Overseas Missionary	2

6. General Assembly (UPCUSA) **20**

Moderator	1
Stated Clerk	1
Associate Stated Clerk	1
Commissioner (2 to 1983 Assembly)	4
Elected Positions	6
GAMC	1
CAS	1
Support Agency	1
National Missions	1
Program Agency	1
National UPW	1

Staff Positions	7
GAMC	1
Christian Education	2
CE Regional Directors	3
Criminal Justice	1

7. General Assembly (PCUSA) — 18

Moderator	1
Vice-Moderator	1
Stated Clerk	1
Co-Stated Clerk	2
Commissioner	1
Elected Positions	8
GAC	5
Office of GA	1
GA Boundaries Committee	2
Staff Positions	4

8. Union/Reunion-Related Committees — 37

Committee of Eight	6
GA Committee on Cooperation/Union (PCUS)	1
Joint Committee on Reunion (1 Co-Chair)	5
Joint Committee/TF on Union Presby. (3 Committee Moderators)	9
BO/Brief Statement Com.	1
Synod/Presbytery Reunion Com.	14
Presbytery Boundaries Com.	1

9. Institutions — 24

Colleges	9
Trustee	2
President	1
Professor	1
Assoc. Professor	2
Instructor	1
Adm. Staff	2
Seminaries	11
President	2
Vice-Pres.	2
Dean	1
Professor	5
Adjunct Faculty	1

Montreat	2
Ex. Director	1
Program Director	1
Mo-Ranch (President)	1
Southwest Career Dev. Ctr. (Director)	1

10. Ecumenical Bodies — 11

COCU	4
Delegate	1
Program Unit	2
GA Committee	1
Local/Regional Staff	2
United Ministries in Higher Ed (Elected Position)	1
WARC (Staff)	2
World Council of Churches	2
Assembly Delegate	1
Staff	1

11. Other — 1

COFOP	
Executive Secretary	1

TOTAL POSITIONS FILLED: **445**

Bibliography

Books

Alvis, Joel L., Jr. *Religion and Race: Southern Presbyterians, 1946–1983*. Tuscaloosa: University of Alabama Press, 1944.

Bacher, Robert, and Kenneth Inskeep. *Chasing Down a Rumor: The Death of Mainline Denominations*. Minneapolis: Augsburg Books, 2005.

Bonhoeffer, Dietrich. *The Communion of Saints: A Dogmatic Inquiry into the Sociology of the Church*. New York: Harper & Row, Publishers, 1960.

Book of Church Order of The Presbyterian Church in the United States. Richmond, VA: Whittet & Shepperson, Printers, 1908.

Book of Church Order of The Presbyterian Church in the United States. Rev. ed. Richmond, VA: Presbyterian Committee of Publication, 1925.

Book of Church Order of The Presbyterian Church in the United States. Rev. ed. Richmond, VA: Board of Christian Education, May 1961.

Campbell, Will D. *Soul among Lions: Musings of a Bootleg Preacher*. Louisville, KY: Westminster/John Knox Press, 1999.

Clinton, William Jefferson. *My Life*. New York: Alfred A. Knopf, 2004.

Constitution of the Presbyterian Church (U.S.A.), Part I, *Book of Confessions*. Louisville, KY: Office of the General Assembly, 1999.

Constitution of the United Presbyterian Church in the United States of America, Part II, *Book of Order*. Philadelphia: Office of the General Assembly, 1967.

Coalter, Milton J., John M. Mulder, and Louis B. Weeks, eds. *The Organizational Revolution: Presbyterians and American Denominationalism*. Louisville, KY: Westminster/John Knox Press, 1992.

—. *The Re-Forming Tradition: Presbyterians and Mainstream Protestantism*. Louisville, KY: Westminster/John Knox Press, 1992.

Dabbs, James McBride. *Haunted by God*. Richmond, VA: John Knox Press,1972.

Digest of the Acts and Proceedings of the General Assembly of the Presbyterian Church in the United States 1861–1965. Atlanta: Office of the General Assembly, 1966.

Dowey, Edward A., Jr. *A Commentary on the Confession of 1967 and an Introduction to the Book of Confessions*. Philadelphia: Westminster Press, 1968.

Doyle, William. *An American Insurrection: The Battle of Oxford, Mississippi, 1962*. New York: Doubleday, 2001.

Green, James Benjamin. *A Harmony of the Westminster Presbyterian Standards*. Richmond, VA: John Knox Press, 1951.

Guidelines of the Presbytery of Transylvania (Union). The Preface. April 1971.

Haskins, Jim. *I Have a Dream: The Life and Words of Martin Luther King, Jr.* Brookfield, CN: The Millbrook Press, 1992.

Hassall, Harry Sharp. *On Jordan's Stormy Banks I Stand: A Historical Commentary of the Life and Times of The Covenant Fellowship of Presbyterians, 1969–1989.* Dallas, TX: privately printed, 1989.

Herman, Arthur. *How the Scots Invented the Modern World.* New York: Crown Publishers, 2001; Three Rivers Press, 2001.

Heymann, C. David. *RFK: A Candid Biography of Robert F. Kennedy.* New York: Dutton, 1998.

Kurlansky, Mark. *1968: The Year That Rocked the World.* New York: Random House, trade paperback, 2004.

Leyburn, James G. *The Scotch-Irish: A Social History.* Chapel Hill: University of North Carolina Press, 1962.

Loetscher, Lefferts A. *A Brief History of the Presbyterians,* 4th ed. Philadelphia: Westminster Press, 1978, 1983.

—. *The Broadening Church.* Philadelphia: University of Pennsylvania Press, 1954.

MacLean, Fitzroy. *Scotland: A Concise History.* New York: Thames & Hudson, 1983. Rev. ed., 1993.

Melish, Joanne Pope. *Disowning Slavery: Gradual Emancipation and "Race" in New England, 1780–1860.* Ithaca, NY: Cornell University Press, 1998.

Ministerial Directory of the Presbyterian Church, U.S., 1861–1951. E. C. Scott, Stated Clerk.

Ministerial Directory of the Presbyterian Church, U.S., 1861–1967. James A. Millard, Jr., Stated Clerk.

Ministerial Directory of the Presbyterian Church, U.S., 1975. James E. Andrews, Stated Clerk.

Ministerial Directory of the Presbyterian Church, U.S., 1983. James E. Andrews, Stated Clerk.

Morrill, John, ed. *The Oxford Illustrated History of Tudor and Stuart Britain.* New York: Oxford University Press. 1997.

Murray, Andrew E. *Presbyterian and the Negro—A History.* Philadelphia: Presbyterian Historical Society, 1966.

Newton, Michael, and Judy Ann Newton. *Ku Klux Klan: An Encyclopedia.* New York: Garland Publishing, 1991.

Nutt, Rick. *Many Lamps, One Light.* Grand Rapids: Wm. B. Eerdmans Publishing Co., 2002.

Plan for Reunion of the Presbyterian Church in the United States and the United Presbyterian Church in the United States of America, The. Final edition (2nd printing). Atlanta: Stated Clerk of the Presbyterian Church in the United States, 1981.

Report on Regional Synod and Church Administration, Design for Mission. Philadelphia: Office of the General Assembly, UPCUSA, 1969.

Rogers, Jack. *Presbyterian Creeds: A Guide to The Book of Confessions.* Louisville, KY: Westminster/John Knox Press, 1985, 1991.

Sample, Tex. *Ministry in an Oral Culture: Living with Will Rogers, Uncle Remus, and Minnie Pearl.* Louisville, KY: Westminster/John Knox Press. 1994.

Sanders, Rev. Robert Stuart, D.D. *Annals of the First Presbyterian Church, Lexington, Kentucky: 1784–1959* [with continuation by Elizabeth G. Leggett], 1959–1984. Tallahassee, FL: Rose Printing Co., 1984.

Schaef, Anne Wilson, and Diane Fassel. *The Addictive Organization.* New York: HarperCollins Publishers, 1988; Harper & Row paperback ed., 1990.

Schama, Simon. *A History of Britain,* vol. II, *The Wars of the British,* 1603–1776. New York: Talk Miramax Books, Hyperion, 2001.

Skutsch, Margaret. "Goals and Goal Setting: A Delphi Approach." Master's thesis, Department of Industrial Engineering, Northwestern University, 1972.

Special Committee of the 201st General Assembly (1989). *All-Black Governing Bodies: The History and Contributions of All-Black Governing Bodies.* Louisville, KY: Office of the General Assembly, 1996.

Speck, W. A. *A Concise History of Britain, 1707–1975.* Cambridge: Cambridge University Press, 1993.

Strauss, William, and Neil Howe. *Generations: The History of America's Future, 1584–2069.* New York: William Morrow & Co., 1991.

—. *The Fourth Turning: An American Prophecy.* New York: Broadway Books, 1997.

Tetlow, Edwin. *The Enigma of Hastings.* New York: St. Martin's Press. 1974.

Thompson, Ernest Trice. *Presbyterians in the South.* Richmond: John Knox Press, 1963.

Uniting Church of Australia, The. *A Manual for Meetings.* Rev. ed. Collingswood, Australia: Uniting Education, 2001.

Telleen, Maurice. "The Mind-Set of Agrarianism . . . New and Old," in *The Essential Agrarian Reader,* ed. Norman Virzba. Lexington: University Press of Kentucky, 2003.

Vander Velde, Lewis G. *The Presbyterian Church and the Federal Union, 1861–1869.* Cambridge, MA: Harvard University Press, 1932.

Webb, James. *Born Fighting: How the Scots-Irish Shaped America.* New York: Broadway Books, 2004.

Webster's Collegiate Dictionary. Springfield, MA: G. & C. Merriam Co., Publishers, 1948.

Webster's New World Dictionary, College Edition. Cleveland, OH: World Publishing Co., 1958

Consultations

Five-Synod Boundaries Consultation Notebook. In personal collection of William G. McAtee.

Handbook for the Joint Consultation of Union Presbyteries and the Joint Committee/Task Force on Union Presbyteries (First edition). In personal collection of William G. McAtee.

Handbook of the Consultation on Union Presbyteries and the Joint Committee on Union Presbyteries (1980 Revision). In personal collection of William G. McAtee.

Notes—Consultation on Union Presbyteries. St. Louis, MO, January 8, 1971. In personal collection of William G. McAtee.

Realization of Togetherness: An Introduction to Union Presbyteries, A. Initially prepared in 1980 by David E. Rule, John A. McLaney, and Flynn V. Long, Jr., it provided a useful what-is and how-to-become manual for union presbyteries. In personal collection of William G. McAtee.

Report to the Committee of Eight. General Assemblies' Joint Special Committee/Task Force on Problems of Union Presbyteries, The Vineyard, Louisville, KY. November 17–18, 1975. In personal collection of William G. McAtee.

Report, Consultation on Union Presbyteries, The Vineyard, Louisville, KY, May 5–7, 1975. In personal collection of William G. McAtee.

Report [Minutes] of Joint Consultation of Union Presbyteries, The Vineyard, Louisville, KY. March 1–3, 1976. In personal collection of William G. McAtee.

Report of Consultation of Union Presbyteries, Breech Training Academy, Overland Park, KS, February 7–9, 1977. In personal collection of William G. McAtee.

Report of Consultation on Union Presbyteries, National 4-H Center, Washington, DC, February 21–23, 1978. In personal collection of William G. McAtee.

Report of Consultation on Union Presbyteries, The Executive Inn, Dallas, TX, February 20–22, 1979. In personal collection of William G. McAtee.

Report [Minutes] of Consultation on Union Presbyteries, Drawbridge Motor Inn, Ft. Mitchell, KY. March 5–7, 1980. In personal collection of William G. McAtee.

Report [Minutes] of Consultation on Union Presbyteries, Holiday Inn Plaza, Wichita, KS, March 11–13, 1981. In personal collection of William G. McAtee.

Report [Minutes] of Consultation on Union Presbyteries, National 4-H Center, Washington, DC, February 1–3, 1982. In personal collection of William G. McAtee.

Report [Minutes] of Consultation on Union Presbyteries, Menger Hotel, Alamo Plaza, San Antonio, TX. March 12–14, 1983, and List of Registrants. In personal collection of William G. McAtee.

Report, PCUS/UPCUSA Consultation (Synod of the Covenant–Synod of the Mid-South), Louisville Theological Seminary, Louisville, KY, December 6–7, 1973. In personal collection of William G. McAtee.

Report, Special Union Presbytery Consultation, "Interpreting One Mission," Thompson Center, St. Louis, MO. October 21–22, 1975. In personal collection of William G. McAtee.

Summary, A, The St. Louis Consultation, September 27–29, 1973. In personal collection of William G. McAtee.

Electronic Resources

"Amazing Story of Kudzu, The." Available online, [http://www.cptr.ua.edu/kudzu/].

"Biography of Mickey Leland." Available online, [http://www.usaid.gov/leland/newbio.html].

"Brief History of the Freedom Riders, A." Available online, [http://www.freedomridersfoundation.org/brief.history.html].

"Chronology of Jimmy Carter's Presidency." Available online, [http://www.jimmycarterlibrary.org/documents/jec/chron.html].

"Company Information." Available online, [http://www.ge.com/en/company/companyinfo/index.html].

Farrell, Sean. "Not Just Farms Anymore: The Effects of World War II on Mississippi's Economy." Mississippi History Now: An online publication of the Mississippi Historical Society. Available online, [http://mshistory.k12.ms.us/features/feature19/wwii_ms.html].

"GE to Celebrate 50th Anniversary of Operation of Louisville in 2003." Available online, [http://www.geappliances.com/pressroom/comm/articles/50th.html].

"GOD BLESS YOU ALL—I AM INNOCENT," article from *Chattanooga [TN] Times*, March 20, 1906. Available online, [http://www.law.umkc.edu/faculty/projects/ftrials/shipp/newsgodbless.html].

"Governor George Wallace's School House Door Speech." Available online, [http://www.archives.state.al.us/govs_list/schooldoor.html].

Grad, Burton. "The First Commercial Univac I Installation." 1997.

Available online, [http://www.softwarehistory.org/history/Grad1.html].

"Harry S Truman Papers." Staff Member and Office Files, Philleo Nash Files, Truman Presidential Museum and Library. Available online, [http://www.trumanlibrary.org/hstpaper/nashhst.htm].

"Henry Watterson" (1840–1921), influential nineteenth century editor of *The Courier-Journal* in Louisville. Available online, [http://www.mscomm.com/-ulysses/page172.html].

***

Bibliography

"History of GE, A." Available online,
[http://www.ge.com/en/company/companyinfo/at_a_glance/history_story.html].

History of the Presbyterian Lay Committee, The. Available online,
[http://www.laymen.org/].

"History of Standard Time in the U.S." Available online,
[http://www.aa.usno.navy.mil/faq/docs/us_tzones.html].

"Justice John Marshall Harlan." Available online,
[http://www.law.umkc.edu/faculty/projects/ftrials/shipp/harlan.html].

"LIFE, V-J Day Kiss 50 Years Later." Available online,
[http://www.life.com/Life/specialkiss01.html].

"Little Rock, Arkansas–1957." Available online,
[http://www.historylearningsite.co.uk/little_rock.html].

"Medger Evers." (*Note:* "Medger" is spelled this way in the title and http
address.) Available online,
[http://www2.nemcc.edu/mspeople/medger_evers.html].

Moorehead, Monica. "The FBI & the Birmingham Church Bombing." From the
July 24, 1997, issue of *Workers World* newspaper. Available online,
[http://www.4littlegirls.com/97news.html].

NEWS. Presbyterian News Service, Office of Communication. Release #05171,
March 31, 2005. Available online,
[http://www.pocusa.org/pcnews/2005/05171.html].

—, Release #05173, March 31, 2005. Available online,
[http://www.pocusa.org/pcnews/2005/05173.html].

"Program Objectives." Racial Ethnic Ministries. Available online,
[http://www.pcusa.org/racialethnic/objectives.html].

"Reagan Presidency, The." Available online,
[http://www.reagan.utexas.edu/archives/reference/pressketch.html].

Span, Paula (Washington Post staff writer), "The Undying Revolutionary: As
Stokely Carmichael, He Fought for Black Power. Now Kwame Ture's
Fighting For His Life." *Washington Post,* Wednesday, April 8, 1998. Available
online, [http://www.interchange.org/kuameture/washingtonpoststory.html].

"Theology of the Movement" [civil rights movement]. Available online,
[http://www.home.att.net/-reniqua/theology.html].

"What Was the Montgomery Bus Boycott?" Available online,
[http://www.home.att.net/-reniqua/what.html].

"White and Opposition Reaction." Available online,
[http://www.home.att.net/-reniqua/whiteandopposition.html].

Letters and E-mails

Bembower, Wm. Philip, chair of Joint Committee of Kentucky, to the two General Assembly Stated Clerks, identical letters of invitation. Copy of Millard's letter dated October 4, 1965, in the file of T. Morton McMillan, secretary of Joint Committee. Copy of McMillan file in personal collection of William G. McAtee.

—, chairman, to Kentucky Reunion Committee, November 15, 1965. Copy of memo in the file of T. Morton McMillan, secretary of Joint Committee. Copy of McMillan file in personal collection of William G. McAtee.

Burleigh, P. B., to William H. McAtee, dated March 13, 1957. In personal collection of William G. McAtee.

—, to William G. McAtee, dated March 4, 1971. In personal collection of William G. McAtee.

Cogswell, James A., chairperson, Friends of the Historical Foundation at Montreat, Inc., to "Friends," September 24, 2004.

Corbett, Gordon L., to J. Hoytt Boles, Dawson W. Tunnell, Robert J. Rodisch, James E. Spivey, and Eugene Carson Blake. Copy of Corbett's letter in the file of T. Morton McMillan, secretary of Joint Committee. Copy of McMillan file in personal collection of William G. McAtee.

Dahmann, Donald C., to William G. McAtee, e-mail dated February 10, 2005.

Dean, R. Neal, stated clerk of Middle Tennessee Presbytery, to James E. Andrews, Stated Clerk, PCUS General Assembly, letter dated November 8, 1980. File in personal collection of William G. McAtee.

Fatheree, Wm. G., to his "dear wife," M. E. Fatheree, from Camp Blake, Mississippi, dated December 24, 1862. In possession of author's family.

Galbraith, John P., general secretary, The Committee on Home Missions and Church Extension, The Orthodox Presbyterian Church, to P. B. Burleigh, dated November 10, 1955. In personal collection of William G. McAtee.

—, to P. B. Burleigh, dated November 18, 1955. In personal collection of William G. McAtee.

Hart, A. M., to Colleagues in the Mackinac Effort, letter dated June 1, 1981, p. 1. Copy in personal collection of William G. McAtee.

—, to Wayne P. Todd, dated August 4, 1982. In Wayne P. Todd File, Presbyterian Historical Society.

Johnson, Richard K., to Wayne P. Todd, July 14, 1969. In Wayne P. Todd File, Presbyterian Historical Society

Little, G. Dan, to synod and presbytery executives, to exempt staff at 475 Riverside Drive, New York, and to a number of selected individuals, letter dated February 12, 1982. In personal collection of William G. McAtee.

Locke, Kenneth R., to H. William Peterson, letter dated 4-20-78, with document. In H. William Peterson Collection, Presbyterian Historical Society.

—, letter of invitation to COUP meeting in Wichita, KS, dated February 27, 1981. In personal collection of William G. McAtee.

McAtee, William G., to Peggy Collins, Transylvania staff, Living Devotional Letter dated June 12, 1983. In personal collection of William G. McAtee.

—, to Lawrence W. McMaster, letter dated December 9, 1973. In personal collection of William G. McAtee.

—, to H. William Peterson, executive presbyter, Western Kentucky (Union), Living Devotional Letter dated June 15, 1983. In personal collection of William G. McAtee.

—, to Ruth Settle, Transylvania staff, Living Devotional Letter dated June 11, 1983. In personal collection of William G. McAtee.

—, to Anne Stipp, Transylvania staff, Living Devotional Letter dated June 13, 1983. In personal collection of William G. McAtee.

McMaster, Lawrence W., to William G. McAtee, letter dated December 26, 1973. In personal collection of William G. McAtee.

Salmon, John M., to William G. McAtee, e-mail dated 10/18/04. In personal collection of William G. McAtee.

Todd, Wayne P., to James A. Millard, Jr., Stated Clerk, June 8, 1970, letter with Complaint enclosed. In Wayne P. Todd File, Presbyterian Historical Society

Walkup, Robert H., to Margo Reitz Cochrane [Cooke], his former Director of Christian Education at Starkville, letter dated November 3, 1964. Copy in the personal collection of William G. McAtee.

Meeting Notes and Reports

Freundt, Albert H., Jr. "Does the Mackinac Presbytery Plan and Procedure Meet The Provisions of the P.C.U.S. Constitution?" Submitted November 20, 1980, to the PCUS Permanent Judicial Commission. Copy in personal collection of William G. McAtee.

McAtee, William G. "Addendum and Supplemental Brief to a Reference to the 121st General Assembly of the Presbyterian Church in the United States from the Synod of the Mid-South." Submitted November 20, 1980, to the PCUS Permanent Judicial Commission. Copy in personal collection of William G. McAtee.

Meeting Notes, "The Rocking Chair," Louisville, KY, October 2–5, 1982. In Wayne P. Todd File, Presbyterian Historical Society.

Minutes of the Reunion Committee [Kentucky], October 29, 1965. Copy of minutes in the file of T. Morton McMillan, secretary of Joint Committee. Copy of McMillan file in personal collection of William G. McAtee.

Minutes of the Reunion Committee [Kentucky], January 24, 1966. Copy of minutes in the file of T. Morton McMillan, secretary of Joint Committee; copy of McMillan file in personal collection of William G. McAtee.

Preliminary Report, Theological Task Force on Peace, Unity, and Purity of the Church to the Two-Hundred-Sixteenth General Assembly (PC(USA)), 2004.

Minutes of General Assemblies

Minutes of the One-Hundred-Sixth General Assembly (PCUS). Montreat, NC, April 21–26, 1966.

Minutes of the One-Hundred-Seventh General Assembly (PCUS), Bristol, TN, June 8–14, 1967.

Minutes of the One-Hundred-Eighth General Assembly (PCUS), Montreat, NC, June 6–11, 1968.

Minutes of the One-Hundred-Ninth General Assembly (PCUS), Mobile, AL, April 24–29, 1969.

Minutes of the One-Hundred-Eleventh General Assembly (PCUS), Massanetta Springs, VA, June 13–18, 1971.

Minutes of the One-Hundred-Twelfth General Assembly (PCUS), Montreat, NC, 11–16, 1972.

Minutes of the One-Hundred-Fourteenth General Assembly (PCUS), Louisville, KY, June 16–22, 1974.

Minutes of the One-Hundred-Seventeenth General Assembly (PCUS), Nashville, TN, June 18–24, 1977.

Minutes of the One-Hundred-Nineteenth General Assembly (PCUS), Kansas City, MO, May 22–30, 1979.

Minutes of the One-Hundred-Twentieth General Assembly (PCUS), Myrtle Beach, NC, 1980.

Minutes of the One-Hundred-Twenty-First General Assembly (PCUS), Houston, TX, May 20–27, 1981.

Minutes of the Sixty-Fourth General Assembly (PCUSA), San Antonio, TX, May 15–22, 1924.

Minutes of the One-Hundred-Seventy-Eighth General Assembly (UPCUSA), Boston, MA, May 18–25, 1966.

Minutes of the One-Hundred-Seventy-Ninth General Assembly (UPCUSA), Portland, OR, May 18–24, 1967.

Minutes of the One-Hundred-Eightieth General Assembly (UPCUSA), Minneapolis, MN, May 16–22, 1968.

Minutes of the One-Hundred-Eighty-Ninth General Assembly (UPCUSA). 1977.

Minutes of the One-Hundred-Ninety-Seventh General Assembly (PC(USA)), 1983, Part I.

Minutes of Synods

Minutes of the 117th Annual Session of the Synod of Arkansas (PCUS), May 21–22, 1968.

Minutes of the Synod of Alabama, 1969.

Minutes of the 137th Stated Meeting of the Synod of Missouri (PCUS), June 9, 1969.

Minutes of the One-Hundred-Sixty-Eighth Meeting of the Synod of Kentucky (PCUS), Louisville, KY, June 24–25, 1969.

Minutes of the Special Meeting of the Synod of the Chesapeake (UPCUSA), Meeting as a Delegated Synod, Catonsville, MD, May 1, 1971.

Minutes of Presbyteries

Minutes of the Twenty-Fifth Stated Meeting (Winter 1970) of John Calvin Presbytery (Southwest Presbytery), PCUS.

Minutes of the Initial Stated Meeting of Union Presbytery of the Ozarks, Clarksville, AR, November 24, 1970.

Minutes of the Stated Meeting of Union Presbytery of the Ozarks, Little Rock, AR, January 26, 1971.

Minutes of Transylvania Presbytery (Union), Report of the General Council, September 6, 1973.

Minutes of the Stated Meeting of Presbytery of Arkansas (Union), Little Rock, AR, January 15, 1974.

Minutes of Mackinac Presbytery, "Report and Recommendations of the Task Force on Union Presbyteries," December 7, 1979.

Minutes, Initial Meeting of Indian Nations Presbytery, January 16–17, 1980.

Minutes of Constituting Meeting of the Union Presbytery of Tres Rios, June 24, 1980.

Minutes, Constituting Meeting of the Union Presbytery of New Covenant, June 28, 1980.

Minutes of Southwest Florida Union Presbytery, January 3, 1982, Constituting Meeting Celebration.

Periodicals and Newspapers

—. "50-year-old Crime" (Emmett Till case). June 2, 2005.

—. "400 at Confederate Service." June 6, 2005.

Broder, David S., "Winter Still Seeks Racial Justice." *The Commercial Appeal* (Memphis, TN), January 16, 2005.

Concerned Presbyterian, The. "Majority of Presbyteries Vote 'No'—Union Amendments Defeated." No. 12 (April 1969).

General Assembly News (Richmond, VA). "Preacher Defends 'Late-Comers.' " June 30, 2004.

"Ban on Rebel Flag Items Is Overruled." *Lexington Herald–Leader*, June 2, 2005.

"Deep Throat: The Story that Helped Bring Down a Presidency." *Lexington Herald–Leader*, Sunday, June 5, 2005.

Lincoln County Advertiser. "Brookhaven Presbyterians Record Sentiment on Segregation Issue." November 28, 1957.

—. "Will Renewal Be the Road to Reunion?" Vol. 11, no. 2, February 1980.

—. "Presbyterians Defeat Union Synod Amendment." Vol. 11, no. 3, March 1980.

Open Letter, The. "The 'Mackinac Maneuver.'" Vol. 11, no. 3, March 1980.

Page, Clarence. "Resolutions Still Needed in 1955 Till Case." *Lexington Herald Leader,* May 16, 2004.

Presbyterian Outlook, The. Series of articles entitled "Common Ground." Vol. 187, No. 20. (May 30, 2005.)

—. "Presbytery Voting on 3 Major Union Proposals." April 9, 1969, and April 30, 1969.

Southern [Presbyterian] Journal, The. "Union Court Advocates Plan More Cooperation." April 9, 1969.

—. "Sunday Evening Service." Special reprint from the issue of August 21, 1968.

Thomas-Lester, Alvis (writer for *The Washington Post*). "Lynching era was 'the American Holocaust.'" *Lexington Herald Leader,* June 13, 2005.

—. "Watergate Scandal, The. June 1, 2005.

—. Whalen, Paul L. "Kentucky's ties to 'Brown.'" May 16, 2004.

Published and Unpublished Articles

Manuscripts Presented at Christian Ethics Conference, Belhaven College, Jackson, MS. May 30—June 1, 1966. In personal collection of William G. McAtee.

"Message to the Presbyterian Church, U.S., concerning the Black Manifesto, A." Copy in Wayne P. Todd Collection, Presbyterian Historical Society

McAtee, William G. "Rivers, Railroads and Relations" [A Tribute to Bob Walkup Before He Left Us]. Unpublished paper. In personal collection of William G. McAtee.

—. "*Circulating Funds in the Re-United Church? A Contribution to the Informal Discussion Concerning What the New Church Is to Become . . . .*" Unpublished paper, winter 1983, in personal collection of William G. McAtee.

Peterson, H. William. *And Then There Were ~~Ten, Eleven~~, Twelve! Anymore?— A Study of the Union Presbytery Movement—1970–1980.* Unpublished paper, 1979. In personal collection of William G. McAtee.

"Snapshot of PC(USA) Leadership Trends." Statistics supplied by the Office of Research Services and Leadership and Vocation, National Ministries Division, PC(USA), May 2005.

Stuart, Albert R. *Diminishing Distinctives: A Study of the Ingestion of the United Presbyterian Church of North America by the Presbyterian Church in the United States of America.* Rock Stream, NY: privately printed, 2000.

"Table 14: Race/Ethnicity and Gender of PC (USA) Members, Elders, Deacons,

Active Clergy, and Commissioned Lay Pastors." Statistics supplied by the Office of Research Services, 2003.

Todd, Wayne P. "Strategic Implications for the 1980s from the Last 25 Years." Copy in Wayne P. Todd File, Presbyterian Historical Society.

Wilkins, Lewis L. "Polity Issues for the 1980s—A Personal Presbyterian View." Copy in Wayne P. Todd File, Presbyterian Historical Society.

About the Author

The Rev. Dr. William G. McAtee is a fourth-generation Mississippian and Minister of the Word and Sacrament of the Presbyterian Church (U.S.A.), now honorably retired. In the late 1950s and 1960s he served two pastorates in Mississippi and later as staff on the national Board of Christian Education (PCUS). Beginning in 1971, McAtee served Transylvania Presbytery, an original Union Presbytery in Kentucky, for twenty-six years as associate executive and then as executive presbyter.

McAtee holds a bachelor of arts degree from Southwestern at Memphis, bachelor of divinity and master of theology degrees from Louisville Presbyterian Theological Seminary, and a doctor of ministry degree from McCormick Seminary. He has been involved in a wide range of elected and appointed positions throughout the church, including serving as chair of the Committee of Assembly Operations (PCUS) during the time that it was responsible for planning the reuniting General Assemblies in 1983.

McAtee has taught as adjunct faculty at Louisville, McCormick, and Lexington Theological Seminaries. He currently serves on the Board of Trustees of Louisville Presbyterian Theological Seminary. He has led numerous educational seminars and workshops on a variety of subjects for both lay people and clergy. From 1997 through 2002, McAtee served as an international volunteer in mission, leading experiential study seminars to Cuba for the PC(USA).

Bill married Millicent Bunn (Millye) in 1956. They have two sons, Neal and Walt. Neal, his wife Amy, and their children Abby, Maggie, and Will live in Memphis, Tennessee. Walt lives in Lexington, Kentucky. Millye and Bill have lived in Lexington since 1971 and are active in Second Presbyterian Church, Lexington.

Index

Index

Dreams, Where Have You Gone?

Index   427

Millard, James A., 107, 173

Miller, Belle (McMaster), 143

Miller, Florine "Killer," 218

Miller, John Reed, 78, 88

Miller, P. D., 134, 135, 179

Miller, P. D., Jr., 143

Mill Hands and Preachers (Pope), 319

"The Mind-Set of Agrarianism . . . New and Old" (Telleen), 93

Ministerial Directory of the Presbyterian Church, U.S., 2, 96

Ministry in an Oral Culture: Living with Will Rogers, Uncle Remus, & Minnie Pearl (Sample), 341

Mission Design Committee, 366

Mission (Union), 221–223

Mississippi Delta Ministry (DM), 315

Missouri Presbytery (PCUS), 190, 192, 199

Missouri Presbytery (UPCUSA), 190, 331

Missouri (Union), 190–191

Mobile Presbytery vote, 148–151

Moffett, Charles H. "Chuck," Jr., 238

Montgomery Bus Boycott, 303–304

Montgomery Improvement Association (MIA), 303

Montreat National Missions Christian Education Conference, 317

Moon, Richard M. "Dick," 3–4

More Light Church Movement, 356

More Light Presbyterians ("Presbyterians for Gay and Lesbian Concerns"), 356

Morgan, George P., 330

Mosley, Sara Bernice, 212

Mother's Day March, 320

Mount, C. Eric, Sr., 201

The Mountain Retreat Association Conference Center, 101

movements, x, 93–94

Moxley, Irvin S., 201, 383

Moxley, Rubee, 383

Muhlenberg Presbytery (PCUS), 193

Mulder, John M., 357

NAACP, 303, 306, 342

NASA, 298

NASCAR nation, 341

National and World Councils of Churches, 71

National Capital (Union), 202–204, 287

National Christian Councils of Japan, 100

National Council of Churches (NCC), 125

  Youth Department, 318

National Covenant, 24–25

National Executive Committee for UPW, 331

National Presbyterian Church. *See* Presbyterian Church in America (PCA)

Nation of Islam, 307

Native Americans

  culture of oral tradition, 341–342

  education of, 73, 340

  migration of, 39, 46, 48

  mission work, 214

  slavery, 60

Neal, Bob, 251

Neigh, Kenny, 178

Nelson, C. Ellis, 107

neo-orthodoxy, 66, 67

Nevin, Alfred, ix

New Albany Seminary, 105

New Castle Presbytery, 74, 287

New Covenant (Union), 218–221

"New Days! New Ways?", 315

New Harmony Presbytery, 285–286

New Light Presbytery of Hanover, 49, 59, 60, 63, 64

New Providence Presbyterian Church, 60

New York Times, 304, 311

Niebuhr, Hulda, 294

Niebuhr, Reinhold, 294

Nixon, E. D., 303

Nixon, Richard M., 305, 310, 311

North Alabama (Union), 228–231

Northeast Florida Presbytery (UPCUSA), 231, 232

North Alabama Presbytery (PCUS), 147, 148, 151–152, 228–231

Northern Church. See United Presbyterian Church in the United States of America (UPCUSA)

Northern Presbyterian Church, 298

Nova Scotia, 44

Nowlin, Estha F., 227–228, 282

Oaklands United Presbyterian Church of Laurel, Maryland, 255

Oakley, J. Allen, 199

Ohio Presbytery (OPC), 81

Oklahoma/Arkansas Presbytery (UPCUSA), 195

Oklahoma Presbyteries (PCUS), 213, 214, 226

Okolona Presbyterian Church, 298

Old Light, 49, 59

Old School/New School controversy, 62–65, 105–108, 272, 346

O'Neill, Thomas P. "Tip," 317

The Open Letter, 268, 274

oral history, defined, xviii

ordination, of Elders/Ministers

  by denomination, 399

  vows, 133–134, 243, 281

  of women, 89, 95, 233, 399

Origin of the Species (Darwin), 65

Orthodox Presbyterian Church (OPC), xvii, 66, 80–82

Ostenson, Robert J., 82

Oswald, Lee Harvey, 307

Ouachita Presbytery (PCUS), 133, 195–196, 206

  Part of Ouachita, 206

Dreams, Where Have You Gone?

Index

Index

United Brethren, 112

United Church of Christ (UCC), 112

United Ministries in Higher
Education (UMHE), 112

United Presbyterian Church,
Harrodsburg, Kentucky, 79

United Presbyterian Church in
North America (UPCNA or
UPNA), xvi, 60, 66

Lay Committee, 83

PCUSA union, 82–83

United Presbyterian Church in the
United States of America
(UPCUSA), x, xvi, 1

UPCNA/PCUSA union, 82–83

United Presbyterian Church of
Oregon, 59

United Presbyterian Women
(UPW), 113, 211, 227, 247,
256, 331

National Executive Committee
for, 331

Univac I computer, 295

Universal Military Training and
Service Act, 315

University of Alabama, 306

University of Glasgow, 30

University of Mississippi (Ole
Miss), 306, 308

Valley of Virginia, 288

Vander Velde, Lewis G., ix

Veley, Robert E., 224

Victoria, Queen, 33

Vietnam War, 9, 17, 131, 169, 310,
376

Villa Clara-Sancti Spiritus, 123

Vincell, Tom, 2

Virginia Company, 44

Virginia Presbytery (PCUS), 182,
184, 203

V-J Day celebration, 312

Voting Rights Bill, 308

Walkup, John, 98

Walkup, Robert H. "Bob," 96, 98,
318

Walkup, Robert Lee "Jake," 98

Wallace, George, 306

Walton, Howard, 228

Warfield, Benjamin, 65

War of Independence, 47

Washburn Presbytery (PCUS), 195

Washer, Sylvia, 227

Washington City Presbytery
(UPCUSA), 122, 202, 203, 287

Washington Post, 311

Washita Presbytery (UPCUSA),
213, 214, 215, 226

Watergate, 9, 310–312, 311

"We are a New Creation," 221

Weaver, Rebecca, 212

Webb, James, 95, 341

Webster's New World Dictionary,
College Edition, 385

Weedon, M. Ralph, 201

Weller, Jack E., 201

Wells, Beth, 211, 212, 249, 254

Wesley, Cynthia, 306–307

Western Kentucky Presbytery
(UPCUSA), 193–194

Western Kentucky (Union),
193–194

Western Progressive Democratic
Party, 106

Western Seminary, 83

West Florida Presbytery
(UPCUSA), 223, 225

Westlake Hills Church, Austin, 222

Westminster Assembly, 7, 24–26

Westminster Confession, 26, 49,
62–66, 76, 78, 79, 85, 345

Westminster Fellowship (First
Presbyterian Church,
Auburn), 96

Westminster Presbyterian Church,
Charlottesville, Virginia, 131

Westminster Presbyterian Church,
Piqua, Ohio, 3

Westminster Presbytery (PCUS),
223, 225

Westminster Standards, 7, 25, 26,
45, 59, 60

West Texas, 106, 108

Whirlpool Corporation, 300

White, Edward A., 203, 204, 300,
319, 369

White, Hugh, 296

White River Presbytery, 76

Whitledge, William, 238

Wilkins, Lewis L., 102–103, 158,
238, 327, 351–352, 364

Wilkins, Roy, 308

Wilkinson, D. Doug, 228

Williams, John, L., 229–231

Williams, José, 320

Williamson, Jack, 144, 145, 158, 336

William the Conquer, 22–23

Wilson, George, 256

win-lose mentality, 52, 53, 338–340

Winn, Albert C. "Al," 67, 274

Winter, William H., 318

Witherspoon, John, 61

Women of the Church (WOC),
112–113, 212, 227, 247, 256,
331

Women's Board of Home
Missions, 168

Woodstock, 310

Woodward, Bob, 311

Woodward, Leonard E., 79

Worcester, Massachusetts, 45

World Alliance of Reformed
Churches, 71, 407

World Congress Center, 2, 3, 4,
313, 357

World Council of Churches, 100,
123, 407

World War II, post, in America,
295–296

Worley, Robert C. "Bob," 109,
173, 205, 216

Wright, Jim, 106

Yadkin Presbytery, 73

y'all come-cousin network, 363

The Year that Rocked the World
(Kurlansky), 376

Yeuell, H. Davis, 287, 288

Young, Andrew, 3, 311–312, 315,
318, 320

Young, Paul D., 205–206, 245

Young Turk generation, 9, 132, 377